P9-CAU-891

Halsbury's Laws of Canada

First Edition

Halsbury's Laws of Canada, First Edition
Condominiums; Constitutional Law—Division of Powers

December 2011

Library and Archives Canada Cataloguing in Publication

Halsbury's laws of Canada. — 1st ed.

Contents: [v. 64]. Condominiums. Constitutional law:
division of powers.
ISBN 978-0-433-46569-0 (v. 64)

1. Law—Canada. I. Title: Laws of Canada.

KE180.H34 2006 348.71 C2008-900720-4
KF154.H34 2006

Published by LexisNexis Canada, a member of the LexisNexis Group
LexisNexis Canada Inc.
123 Commerce Valley Dr. E., Suite 700
Markham, Ontario
L3T 7W8

Customer Service
Telephone: (905) 479-2665 • Fax: (905) 479-2826
Toll-Free Phone: 1-800-668-6481 • Toll-Free Fax: 1-800-461-3275
Email: customerservice@lexisnexis.ca
Web Site: www.lexisnexis.ca

Printed and bound in Canada.

LexisNexis Editorial

Halsbury's Laws of Canada
First Edition

Condominiums

Contributed by

Marko Djurdjevac
LL.B.

Contributing Editors

Shirley Margolis
B.A., J.D.

Wendy Litner
H.B.A., LL.B.

Constitutional Law – Division of Powers

Contributed by

Martin William Mason
B.A., M.A., LL.B.

Guy Régimbald
LL.B., B.C.L. (Oxon.)

Contributing Editor

Charlene Quincey
B.A., J.D.

About the Contributors

Condominiums

Marko Djurdjevac, LL.B., is a partner in the Condominium Practice Group of Miller Thomson LLP in Toronto. He has extensive experience in all aspects of condominium law and has represented and advised numerous condominium corporations and unit owners in various matters, including: the interpretation of condominium documents and contracts; enforcement proceedings (including mediation and arbitration); shared facilities/reciprocal agreement issues; and statutory rights and remedies applicable to condominiums.

Constitutional Law – Division of Powers

The late Martin William Mason, B.A., M.A., LL.B., was a senior partner at Gowling Lafleur Henderson LLP, where he practised in the Ottawa office for 26 years. He practised in the areas of administrative law, constitutional law and civil litigation and appeared before such courts as the Ontario Court of Appeal, the Federal Court of Appeal and the Supreme Court of Canada. He also worked in the area of aboriginal law and wrote on the subject of First Nations governance. He was involved with the development of legislation through his work with the Constitutional Law section of the Canadian Bar Association and appearances before Senate Committees. He served as a co-chair of the Federal Court Bench and Bar Committee and taught constitutional law at the University of Ottawa for 13 years. Prior to entering the legal profession, Martin taught political science at Carleton University and the University of Saskatchewan.

Guy Régimbald, LL.B., B.C.L. (Oxon.), is an Ottawa-based associate in the Advocacy Department of Gowling Lafleur Henderson LLP. He practises mainly in the areas of constitutional law, administrative law and government relations. He has appeared as Counsel in such courts as the Supreme Court of Canada and the Ontario Court of Appeal. He clerked for The Honourable Mr. Justice Marshall Rothstein and The Honourable Mr. Justice John C. Major of the Supreme Court of Canada, as well as for The Honourable Mr. Justice Marc Noël at the Federal Court of Appeal. He received his B.C.L. first class honours (Master's in Law) from the University of Oxford. He earned his LL.B. from the University of Ottawa, and is a member of the Law Society of Upper Canada as well as the Barreau du Québec. He is the author of *Canadian Administrative Law* and *Halsbury's Laws of Canada – Administrative Law*, and he is co-author of *Standards of Review of Federal Administrative Tribunals.*

General Table of Contents

Page

An Overview of Halsbury's Laws of Canada........................ 11

Table of Cases

Condominiums.. 25
Constitutional Law – Division of Powers.................... 37

Table of Statutes and Statutory Instruments

Condominiums.. 57
Constitutional Law – Division of Powers.................... 83

Condominiums

Ambit of Title, Statement of Currency,
Related Titles.. 91
Table of Contents
I. Introduction 103
II. Creation of Condominiums......................... 111
III. General Management by the Condominium
Corporation 161
IV. The Board of Directors.............................. 187
V. Transfer of Control and Sale and Lease of
Units 201
VI. Unit Owners 217
VII. Common Expenses, Repair and
Maintenance and Changes to the
Condominium.. 227
VIII. Compliance, Enforcement, Remedies and
Dispute Resolution 249
IX. Amalgamation and Termination of
Condominiums 315

Constitutional Law – Division of Powers

Ambit of Title, Statement of Currency,
Related Titles.. 331
Table of Contents
I. Sources of Constitutional Law and
Institutions... 343

Page

II. Constitutional Conventions and the Unwritten Principles of the Constitution...... 359
III. Courts, Independence of Judiciary and Judicial Review 401
IV. Constitutional Interpretation: Pith and Substance, Double Aspect, Paramountcy and Interjurisdictional Immunity 425
V. Peace, Order and Good Government........... 443
VI. Criminal Law – Federal and Provincial Jurisdiction 449
VII. The Regulation of Trade and Commerce 463
VIII. The Raising of Revenue, the Spending Power and Federal Authority in Relation to Financial Matters 469
IX. Works and Undertakings, Communications and Transportation and Labour Relations ... 501
X. Property and Civil Rights and Provincial Authority in Relation to Local and Private Matters.. 515
XI. The Environment and Natural Resources..... 525

Index

Condominiums.. 541
Constitutional Law – Division of Powers.................... 553

Selected Secondary Sources

Condominiums.. 571
Constitutional Law – Division of Powers.................... 573

Glossary

Condominiums.. 575
Constitutional Law – Division of Powers.................... 633

An Overview of Halsbury's Laws of Canada

I. Introduction

II. The Component Parts

III. How to Use Halsbury's Laws of Canada

1. Main Work
   (1) Commentary Volumes
      (a) Title Structure and Layout
         (i) Generally
         (ii) Paragraph Structure
         (iii) Numbering Scheme
         (iv) Dealing with Multiple Jurisdictions
      (b) Volume Layout
   (2) Consolidated Volumes
      (a) General
2. Updating Materials

I. Introduction

Since the publication of *Halsbury's Laws of England* in 1907, under the eponymous auspices of Britain's renowned Lord Chancellor, *Halsbury's Laws* has been synonymous with legal excellence. Today, more than 100 years later, *Halsbury's Laws* continues to be the world's best known and most relied upon legal reference, with counterparts in various common law jurisdictions, such as Australia, New Zealand, India, Singapore, Malaysia and Hong Kong.

Halsbury's Laws of Canada incorporates the best aspects of *Halsbury's* around the world and delivers it to Canadian lawyers in an accessible and contemporary format. Publication of the first edition of *Halsbury's Laws of Canada* began in 2006 and it will comprise, upon its completion, at least 57 volumes of commentary divided into more than 100 alphabetically-ordered subject titles. These titles vary in size from 50 pages to 1,000 pages, and are authored by leading academics, practitioners and jurists.

Statutory material and case law are drawn together within a narrative text to give a clear exposition on every aspect of the current law of Canada, making it the essential first point of reference for every legal professional.

II. The Component Parts

At completion, *Halsbury's Laws of Canada* will comprise:

Main Work:

Commentary Volumes (as published)
Consolidated Volumes:
Companion: Guide and Consolidated Index
Consolidated Table of Cases
Consolidated Table of Statutes and Statutory Instruments

Updating Materials:

Cumulative Supplement

III. How to Use Halsbury's Laws of Canada

1. Main Work

(1) Commentary Volumes

(a) Title Structure and Layout

(i) Generally

The main work consists of commentary volumes containing one or more subject titles arranged alphabetically. The designations used for these titles are intended to reflect current legal practice. A regularly updated list of titles in *Halsbury's Laws of Canada* may be found in the Cumulative Supplement. The cover and spine of every volume clearly shows the titles that it contains.

Each subject title is, as far as possible at the time of publication, a complete statement of Canadian law pertaining to that particular area. The date to which the law in each title is current is provided in the Statement of Currency located in the preliminary pages towards the front of the volume.

Sources are not usually quoted verbatim, but the statutory material is generally canvassed in full and details are given of cases, reports, classic textbooks, etc., should the user need to make direct references to these. The footnotes also contain any qualifications, exceptions, ancillary matters, and, where helpful, comment on areas of uncertainty.

(ii) Paragraph Structure

Within each title, the text is arranged in numbered paragraphs, with footnotes which refer the reader to all the authorities from which the statements in the text are derived. Two different kinds of paragraph will be found throughout the commentary:

Major paragraphs are identified with:

1) a title identifier – a three-character acronym beginning with "H" (for Halsbury's) that identifies the subject title, situated between inverted triangles.

2) a paragraph number – begins at 1 and runs consecutively until the end of the title; and

3) a descriptive heading.

For example:

> **▼HMH-94▼ Pertinent legislation.** Advance directives and substitute decision-makers are mandated by the *Health Care Directives and Substitute Health Care Decision Makers Act.*[1] The legislation addresses certain matters that include: persons who may make directives and when the directive is in effect; the effect and requirements of the directive; revocation of the directive; and the form of the directive.

Major paragraphs will generally be organized under a larger subheading, and are analogous to sub-subheadings in that they represent a significant sub-topic. A "major paragraph" will generally consist of more than one typeset paragraph.

Minor paragraphs are those paragraphs which are located under the major paragraphs noted above. Minor paragraphs will generally contain a descriptive heading, but this will not always be the case.

For example:

> **Procedure and punishment.** The offence of flight is a hybrid offence. The maximum sentence when prosecuted by indictment is five years imprisonment.[2] However, where the flight results in bodily harm to or the death of another person by dangerous operation of a motor vehicle, the offence is indictable and the maximum sentence is 14 years imprisonment where bodily harm was caused, and life imprisonment where death was caused.[3]
>
> A discretionary driving prohibition order may be granted upon a finding of guilt.[4] Where this offence is committed by means of a motor vehicle, vessel or aircraft and alcohol is involved, evidence that the accused's blood alcohol level exceeded .160 at the time when the offence was committed is deemed to be an aggravating factor on sentencing.[5]
>
> **Double jeopardy.** Under the *Kienapple* principle, a charge of failing to stop his vehicle for police was stayed conditionally upon the accused's conviction for dangerous driving.[6]

Specific cross-references to other paragraphs within the same title are given where appropriate, and users are directed to other titles in *Halsbury's Laws of Canada* where related information is treated in full.

(iii) Numbering Scheme

Each title adheres to the following numbering scheme and organizational nomenclature for headings and subheadings:

I. Chapter

1. Section

(1) Subsection

(a) Paragraph

(i) Subparagraph

A. Clause

(iv) Dealing with Multiple Jurisdictions

In order to make *Halsbury's Laws of Canada* a truly national publication, each title integrates relevant federal and provincial law into the commentary, and deals with all Canadian jurisdictions.

Some subjects are almost exclusively federal, others exclusively provincial, and some will fall under both jurisdictions. However, *Halsbury's Laws of Canada* strives to deal with every jurisdiction in a balanced manner. If there is a legislative provision dealing with a particular issue in every province, then each province will be mentioned, either in the body of the paragraph or in a footnoted reference. If a point is exclusive to one or more jurisdictions, but not to all, that fact will be clearly highlighted.

The following are some examples of how general situations with respect to multiple jurisdictions are dealt with in the commentary:

1. **Where a general statement of law applies to every jurisdiction and will be based on common case law principles, such as a Supreme Court of Canada decision or a consensus of appellate cases in various provinces, or on a common statutory provision, such as a similar provincial rule of civil procedure, or common employment standards legislation:**

> **▼HEM-26▼ No automatic exclusion from "employee" status.** Canadian courts and tribunals have not treated the fact that a worker is part-time or casual as *ipso facto* excluding him or her from the definition of "employee". Regarding part-time workers, merely completing less hours of work than a full-time employee does not make any difference to the worker's legal status.[1] After all, it is not uncommon for persons to work less than the regular hours but still be economically dependent on their employers, nor is there any other policy reason for excluding part-timers from the statutory and common law "floor of rights".
>
> ***Note***
>
> 1. *E.g.*, *Canada Safeway Ltd. v. Saskatchewan*, [1993] S.J. No. 678, 94 C.L.L.C. para. 14,021 (Sask. Q.B.).

2. **Where a general statement of law based on case law principles or a statutory provision will apply to one or more juris-**

dictions, but there is a lacuna with respect to it in other jurisdictions:

▼**HAP-151**▼ **Length of extension.** A custodian may extend the time limit required to respond to a request under certain circumstances in Ontario, Alberta or Saskatchewan. In Ontario and Saskatchewan, a custodian may extend the time period for a maximum of an additional 30 days;[1] in Alberta, the custodian may extend the time period for up to 30 days, but can also apply to the Commissioner for permission to have a longer period of time to respond to the requester.[2] The Manitoba Act does not provide an extension of time to respond to a request, unless the request is transferred to another custodian wherein the new custodian has a maximum of 30 days in which to respond.[3]

3. **Where a general statement of law based on case law or legislative principles will apply to some jurisdictions, but will be contradicted in other jurisdictions by case law or legislation:**

(c) Discretionary Exemptions

▼**HAP-15**▼ **Government relations.** In most jurisdictions, the head of a public body may refuse to disclose information if the disclosure could reasonably be expected to prejudice the conduct of international affairs or intergovernmental relations, or reveal information received in confidence from another government (including aboriginal government) or an international organization of states.[1] Some jurisdictions require the prescribed official to consent to the disclosure.[2] In Ontario, the head of the public body requires the permission of the Executive Council before disclosing the record.[3] The exemption does not apply to relevant records that have been in existence for more than 15 years.[4]

Federal. The head of a federal institution may refuse to disclose any record that may prejudice or damage the relationship between the federal government and the government of any province.[5]

Manitoba. The head of a public body may refuse to disclose information if disclosure could reasonably be expected to harm relations between the provincial government or a government agency and any of the following or their agencies: the Government of Canada; the government of another province or territory of Canada; a local public body; the government of a foreign country, or of a state, province or territory of a foreign country; an organization representing one or more governments; or an international organization of states.[6] If a local public body receives the request, the head of the local public body is only permitted to disclose the information with the consent of a prescribed body, of the head of the department of the provincial government or of the government agency affected.[7]

Saskatchewan. The head of a public body may refuse to give access to a record, the release of which could reasonably be expected to prejudice, interfere with or adversely affect: relations between the Government of Saskatchewan and another government; or the defence or security of Canada or of any foreign state allied or associated with Canada.[8]

4. **Where there is a significant variation between jurisdictions (usually because of unique statutory requirements), each jurisdiction (or similar groups of jurisdictions, if the law is essentially the same) will be given a separate subheading:**

2. Relevant Legislation

(1) General
(2) British Columbia
(3) Alberta
(4) Saskatchewan
(5) Manitoba
(6) Ontario
(7) Québec
(8) Newfoundland and Labrador
(9) New Brunswick
(10) Nova Scotia
(11) Prince Edward Island
(12) Northwest Territories
(13) Yukon

A discussion by jurisdiction will generally be presented in alphabetical order, and the following designated abbreviations are used in the footnotes:

Canada	CAN
Alberta	AB
British Columbia	BC
Manitoba	MB
New Brunswick	NB
Newfoundland and Labrador	NL
Nova Scotia	NS
Ontario	ON
Prince Edward Island	PE
Québec	QC
Saskatchewan	SK
Northwest Territories	NT
Nunavut	NU
Yukon	YT

(b) Volume Layout

Every commentary volume contains the following features:

Tables of Contents

1. A general table of contents to the level of Chapter headings
2. A detailed table of contents to the level of clause headings
3. Detailed sectional contents set out within the commentary for each chapter and section

Ambit of Title

Providing a brief discussion of the scope and content of each title.

Statement of Currency

Providing the date to which the law in each title is current.

List of Related Titles

Setting out titles which should be referred to for related and complementary information, or a more detailed discussion of particular topics.

References and Abbreviations

An alphabetical listing of special references and abbreviations used in the volume, with an explanation of their meaning.

Table of Cases

Listing all cases found in the title alphabetically, with full citations given. References are to paragraph number.

Table of Statutes

An alphabetical listing of all statutes cited in the title, with references given to individual sections, Schedules and their component parts. References are to paragraph number.

Table of Statutory Instruments

An alphabetical consolidation of all statutory instruments, regulations, Orders in Council and related instruments cited in the title. References are to paragraph number.

Where appropriate, other tables may also appear, such as:

Table of Treaties and Conventions
Table of Non-statutory Materials

Index

Every text volume is indexed, with each title treated separately. References are to paragraph number.

Selected Secondary Sources

Setting out selected texts, articles, and other secondary sources pertaining to the subject that the reader may find to be relevant and helpful.

Glossary of Definitions

Identifying words and phrases defined in legislation relevant to the subject matter of the title, and providing the text of the definition for easy reference.

Example:

"Agreement"	CBA	35(1)	has the same meaning as	*in this section...* *in the Canada-United States Free Trade Agreement Implementation Act.*
"alcoholic beverage"	CBARR CBATBR	2 2	means	*in respect of a commercial message...* *an alcoholic beverage the sale of which is regulated by the law of the province in which the commercial message is broadcast;*
"AM station"	CBABDR	1	means	*a station that broadcasts in the AM frequency band of 525 to 1 705 kHz. It does not include a carrier current undertaking or a transmitter that only rebroadcasts the radiocommunications of another station.*

Example – *Halsbury's Laws of Canada* general layout:

II. Jurisdiction

1. The Bases of Judicial Jurisdiction

(1) Introduction ....
(2) The Principles of Order and Fairness ....
(3) Jurisdiction Based on Consent.............
(4) Jurisdiction Based on Presence, Residence or Domicile........................
(5) Jurisdiction over Plaintiffs in Class Proceedings...
(6) Jurisdiction over Matters with a Real and Substantial Connection to the Forum ....
(7) Admiralty Jurisdiction In Rem and In Personam ....

2. Declining Jurisdiction

(1) Stays Granted on Grounds of Forum Non Conveniens ....
(2) Forum Selection Clauses ....
(3) Antisuit Injunctions: Restraining Foreign Proceedings ....

....

Sectional tables of contents - Detailed and multi-layered sectional contents are strategically located throughout each title to provide for powerful navigation and a quick overall appreciation of the principles discussed in each section

Generous use of headings and subheadings lets users move easily through a title

(4) Jurisdiction Based on Presence, Residence or Domicile

(a) Individuals

(i) Generally

Bolded descriptors at the beginning of paragraphs allow the reader to quickly scan the contents and zero in on the information of interest

▼HCL-8▼Presence or residence in the territory. The presence of the defendant in the territory of the forum has been held at common law to be an independently sufficient basis for jurisdiction.[1] It is sometimes called "jurisdiction as of right".[2] Jurisdiction based on the defendant's presence in the territory is exercised through personal service of the originating process and, if not challenged, may result in a default judgment that is binding on the defendant even if the defendant leaves the territory of the forum immediately upon being served. The provincial rules for service generally provide for service at the residence of defendants temporarily absent from the jurisdiction.[3]

Extracting the context and key points is easy with a style that is structured to provide greater **contextual flow**

Temporary presence. Jurisdiction may be exercised on the basis of a defendant's presence or residence even where there is little connection between the matter and the forum.[4] It is doubtful whether exercising jurisdiction solely on the basis of a defendant's temporary presence, particularly where the visit is for reasons unrelated to the dispute, meets the requirements of the principles of order and fairness.[5] In any event, even if the court is not prepared to regard itself as incapable of deciding the case,[6] it is likely to hold that it *should* not decide the case because there is some other forum that is clearly more appropriate.[7] Where defendants have been induced by fraud or physically forced to enter the territory for the purpose of serving them with the originating process, the service may be set aside as an abuse of process.[8]

Assets in the territory. Apart from actions on foreign judgments,[9] jurisdiction has been declined where it is based solely on the presence of the defendant's assets in the territory of the forum,[10] particularly where the property is unrelated to the dispute and there is no other substantial connection between the matter and the forum.[11]

National scope and jurisdiction specific commentary provides a complete and integrated analysis

Alberta, Manitoba and New Brunswick. The courts apply local law to matrimonial disputes and confine their exercise of jurisdiction to spouses with substantial ties to the province. In Manitoba and Alberta, the provincial legislation applies to all spouses wherever married, if their last common habitual residence was in the province, or in the absence of a common habitual residence, if both were habitually resident in Manitoba at the time of their marriage.[12]

Québec. In the absence of any special provision, Québec courts have jurisdiction when the defendant is domiciled in Québec. This is the traditional rule *actor sequitur forum rei.*[13]

Notes

1. *Morguard Investments Ltd. v. De Savoye*, [1990] S.C.J. No. 88, [1990] 3 S.C.R. 1077 (S.C.C.); *Northern Sales Co. v. Government Trading Corp. of Iran*, [1991] B.C.J. No. 3088, 81 D.L.R. (4th) 316 at 321 (B.C.C.A.); *Cook v. Parcel, Mauro, Hultin & Spaanstra*, [1996] B.C.J. No. 1552, 136 D.L.R. (4th) 414 (B.C.S.C.), affd [1997] B.C.J. No. 428, 143 D.L.R. (4th) 213 (B.C.C.A.), leave to appeal refused (1997), 147 D.L.R. (4th) viii (S.C.C.) (neither the defendant nor the action had a real and substantial connection with the province); *Tortel Communication Inc. v. Suntel Inc.*, [1994] M.J. No. 631, 120 D.L.R. (4th) 100 (Man. C.A.) (plaintiff's action had no real and substantial connection with Manitoba); *Janke v. Budd Canada Inc.*, [1994] M.J. No. 336, 94 Man. R. (2d) 251 (Man. Q.B.), affd [1994] M.J. No. 744, 100 Man. R. (2d) 316 (Man. C.A.) (no real and substantial connection between defendant or the action and the province); *Olde v. Capital Publishing Ltd. Partnership*, [1996] O.J. No. 3215 (Ont. Gen. Div.) (court had no real and substantial connection with subject-matter of litigation).

References strategically consolidated at the end of each major paragraph grouping facilitates easy access to the supporting information

2. It is called jurisdiction as of right because the right to serve the defendant with process is unqualified. *E.g.*, (AB) Alberta Rules of Court, Alta. Reg. 97/98, R. 15; (SK) Rules of the Court of Queen's Bench, Sask. Reg. 102/84, R. 18; (ON) Rules of Civil Procedure, O. Reg. 153/98, Rr. 14 and 16.02. Jurisdiction as of right is derived from the historic capacity of the sovereign to arrest and detain the defendant until the dispute is resolved: *McDonald v. Mabee*, 243 U.S. 90 at 91 *per* Holmes J. (1917) ("the foundation of jurisdiction is physical power").
3. *E.g.* Rule 16.03 of (ON) Rules of Civil Procedure, O. Reg. 153/98.
4. *Kvaerner U.S. Inc. v. Amec E & C Services Ltd.*, [2004] B.C.J. No. 959, 2004 BCSC 635 (B.C.S.C.).
5. *Beals v. Saldanha*, [2003] S.C.J. No. 77, 234 D.L.R. (4th) 1 (S.C.C.).

6. *Edwards v. Bell*, [2003] B.C.J. No. 2467 (B.C.S.C.).
7. *Camco Int'l (Canada) Ltd. v. Porodo*, [1997] A.J. No. 1120, 211 A.R. 71 (Alta. Q.B.).
8. *Lewis v. Wiley*, [1923] O.J. No. 170, 53 O.L.R. 608 at 609 (Ont. S.C.). Note that a non-resident defendant who was compelled to come to Alberta to defend a lawsuit was granted an order of immunity from service in another lawsuit, on the basis...

---

(2) Consolidated Volumes

(a) General

Text volumes will, at the appropriate time, be accompanied by several volumes of consolidated material, which bring together all references from the individual tables and indexes published in the main commentary volumes. Consolidated volumes will include:

Consolidated Table of Cases

An alphabetical listing of all cases referred to in all published commentary volumes of *Halsbury's Laws of Canada.* The consolidated Table of Cases makes it possible to locate every reference to a particular case within the commentary volumes.

Consolidated Table of Statutes and Statutory Instruments

An alphabetical listing of all statutes, regulations, statutory instruments, and Orders in Council referred to in all published commentary volumes of *Halsbury's Laws of Canada.* The consolidated Table of Statutes and Statutory Instruments provides every reference within all published commentary volumes to a particular statute or statutory instrument, and to each specific section of that statute or instrument that has been referred to.

Consolidated Index

Combines all the information from individual title indexes in the commentary volumes, arranged alphabetically according to subject-matter. The consolidated index makes it possible to locate where a particular subject is discussed without knowing within which title it falls, and to find every reference to that subject within the commentary volumes.

Because each paragraph in *Halsbury's Laws of Canada* has a unique paragraph identifier, it is easy to identify each specific consolidated reference. Each consolidated volume will include a full list of title acronyms to assist users in locating the particular title.

Example:

excise tax : HAP-232, HAP-233, HIT-147, HTX-145, HTX-167, HTX-198

2. Updating Materials

Halsbury's Laws of Canada is updated:

1) by the periodic reissue of specific volumes for which continued updating has become impractical because of the sheer number of changes to the law; and

2) by publication of the Cumulative Supplement.

Periodic Reissue Program

When changes to the law render a specific title significantly out-of-date, that title will be replaced by a new, fully revised and updated version. When this occurs, the previous title which has been replaced may be discarded.

Cumulative Supplement

To maintain the currency of *Halsbury's Laws of Canada*, each title is updated on an annual basis following that title's publication. The Cumulative Supplement sets out those annual developments in the law that pertain to the titles referenced herein, providing a two-step process for keeping current with relevant legal changes. First, users should reference the original published title for a comprehensive narrative of the law up to the date referenced in that title's Statement of Currency. Second, users should refer to the Cumulative Supplement for those legislative and case law developments affecting that title that have taken place in the year subsequent to that title's original publication. Because titles are updated on an annual basis, titles will not appear in the Cumulative Supplement before the first anniversary of their original publication. Releases of the Cumulative Supplement are issued four times per year, with each Release enumerating developments to the titles and consolidating them with previous Releases. Each new Release of the Cumulative Supplement replaces earlier versions, and the earlier versions should be discarded.

The order of the material in the Cumulative Supplement corresponds to the title and paragraph order of the original published *Halsbury's Laws of Canada* volume, with titles set out alphabetically.

Table of Cases — Condominiums

Para.

215 Glenridge Ave. Ltd. Partnership v. Waddington, [2005] O.J. No. 665 (Ont. S.C.J.) HCD-105

500 Glencairn v. Farkas, [1994] O.J. No. 138, 36 R.P.R. (2d) 270 (Ont. Gen. Div.) HCD-87

934859 Alberta Inc. v. Condominium Corp. No. 0312180, [2007] A.J. No. 1233 (Alta.Q.B.) HCD-2, HCD-86, HCD-111

1240233 Ontario Inc. v. York Region Condominium Corp. No. 852, [2009] O.J. No. 1 (Ont. S.C.J.) HCD-95

1420041 Ontario Inc. v. 1 King West Inc., [2010] O.J. No. 5613 (Ont. Div. Ct.) HCD-32

2475813 Nova Scotia Ltd. v. Rodgers, [2001] N.S.J. No. 21 (N.S.C.A.) HCD-1, HCD-4, HCD-5, HCD-121

Abdool v. Somerset Place, [1992] O.J. No. 2115, 10 O.R. (3d) 120 (Ont. C.A.), leave to appeal to S.C.C. refused [1992] S.C.C.A. No. 575 (S.C.C.) HCD-3, HCD-87, HCD-90

Aiken v. Dockside Village Inc., [1993] O.J. No. 369 (Ont. Gen. Div.) HCD-87

Aita v. Silverstone Towers Ltd., [1978] O.J. No. 3362, 19 O.R. (2d) 681 (Ont. C.A.) HCD-95

Ally v. Harding Addison Properties Ltd., [1990] O.J. No. 2213, 1 O.R. (3d) 167 (Ont. Gen. Div.) HCD-95

Apartments International Inc. v. Metropolitan Toronto Condominium Corp. No. 1170, [2002] O.J. No. 3821 (S.C.J.) HCD-26, HCD-104

Armstrong v. London Life Insurance Co., [1999] O.J. No. 3507 (Ont. S.C.J.), affd [2001] O.J. No. 2080 (Ont. C.A.) HCD-95

Atkinson v. TWS Developments Inc., [2005] O.J. No. 2300, 32 R.P.R. (4th) 38 (Ont. S.C.J.) HCD-87

Aviawest Resort Club v. Strata Plan LMS1863, [2005] B.C.J. No. 2748 (B.C.S.C.) HCD-109

AW-NMV Ventures Ltd. v. Strata Plan LMS 2856, [2004] B.C.J. No. 1004 (B.C.S.C.) HCD-84

Baer v. Condominium Plan 9123697, [2000] A.J. No. 534 (Alta. Q.B.) HCD-77

Bare Land Condominium Plan 8820814 v. Birchwood Village Greens Ltd., [1998] A.J. No. 1300 (Alta. Q.B.) HCD-93

Basmadjian v. York Condominium Corp. No. 52, [1981] O.J. No. 2973, 32 O.R. (2d) 523, 32 O.R. (2d) 523 (H.C.J.) HCD-2

BCE Inc. v. 1976 Debentureholders, [2008] S.C.J. No. 37, [2008] 3 S.C.R. 560 (S.C.C.) HCD-43, HCD-110

Belcourt v. 860619 Alberta Ltd., [2005] A.J. No. 1276 (Alta. Prov. Ct.) HCD-87

Para.

Benner v. HLS York Developments Ltd., [1985] O.J. No. 2647, 52 O.R. (2d) 243 (Ont. H.C.J) HCD-90, HCD-94

Bilorosek v. Vaitkus, [2004] O.J. No. 5072 (Ont. Sm. Cl. Ct.) HCD-95

Blair v. Consolidated Enfield Corp., [1993] S.C.C.A. No. 514 (S.C.C.) HCD-67

Blue-Red Holding Ltd. v. Strata Plan VR 857, [1994] B.C.J. No. 2293, 42 R.P.R. (3d) 421 (B.C.S.C.) HCD-110, HCD-111

Boland v. Allianz Insurance Co. of Canada, [2006] O.J. No. 2002 (Ont. S.C.J.) HCD-45

Bond v. Strata Plan VR2538, [1996] B.C.J. No. 2137 (B.C.S.C.) HCD-103

Bondy v. P.C. Cove Builders Inc., [1991] O.J. No. 2185, 22 R.P.R. (2d) 217 (Ont. Gen. Div.) HCD-87

Borthwick v. St. James Square Associates Inc. [1989] O.J. No. 172 (Ont. H.C.J.), additional reasons at [1989] O.J. No. 279 (Ont. H.C.J.) HCD-95

Boschetti v. Sanzo, [2003] O.J. No. 5227 (Ont. S.C.J.), affd [2006] O.J. No. 3318 (Ont. C.A.) HCD-95

Brooker v. Silver, [2006] O.J. No. 5553 (Ont. S.C.J.), revd on other grounds 2007 CarswellOnt 7790 (Ont. Div. Ct.) HCD-87

Buchar v. Birchwood Village Greens Ltd., 1997 CarswellAlta 292 (Alta. Q.B.) HCD-87

Bugar v. 928028 Alberta Ltd., [2006] A.J. No. 1254 (Alta. Prov. Ct.) HCD-87

Buskell v. Linden Real Estate Services Inc. [2003] M.J. No. 328 (M.B.Q.B.) HCD-77

Buyanovsky v. Townsgate 1 Ltd., [1993] O.J. No. 518, 30 R.P.R. (2d) 269 (Ont. Gen. Div.), additional reasons at (1993), 30 R.P.R. (2d) 269n (Ont. Gen. Div.) HCD-87

Campbell v. Metropolitan Toronto Condominium Corporation No. 694, [2002] O.J. No. 3879 (O.N.C.A.) HCD-67

Camrost York Development Corp. v. Metropolitan Condominium Corporation No. 989 (unreported) 1996, Lane J. (Ont. Div. Ct.) HCD-69

Carleton Condominium Corp. No. 32 v. Camdev Corp., [1999] O.J. No. 3448 (Ont. C.A.) HCD-91

Carleton Condominium Corp. No. 279 v. Rochon, [1987] O.J. No. 417 (Ont. C.A.) HCD-1, HCD-3, HCD-86

Carleton Condominium Corp. No. 291 v. Weeks, [2003] O.J. No. 1204 (Ont. S.C.J.) HCD-106, HCD-114

Carleton Condominium Corp. No. 347 v. Trendsetter Developments Ltd. et al., [1992] O.J. No. 1767 (Ont. C.A.) HCD-5, HCD-95

Carleton Condominium Corp. No. 555 v. Lagacé, [2004] O.J. No. 1480 (Ont. S.C.J.) HCD-86

Ceolaro v. York Humber Ltd., [1994] O.J. No. 604 (Ont. Gen. Div.) HCD-5

Chapman v. HLS York Development Ltd., [1988] O.J. No. 722, 64 O.R. (2d) 498 (Ont. H.C.J) HCD-90

Para.

Chawla v. Hayter Street Development Inc., [1994] O.J. 1908, 41 R.P.R. (2d) 94 (Ont. Gen. Div.), affd [1997] O.J. No. 1997, 10 R.P.R. (3d) 33 (Ont. C.A.) HCD-95

Cheung v. Greens at Tam O'Shanter Inc., [1993] O.J. No. 821, 31 R.P.R. (2d) 52 (Ont. C.A.) HCD-87

Chiang v. Yang, [1999] B.C.J. No. 966 (B.C. Prov. Ct.) HCD-103

Chow v. Strata Plan LMS 1277, [2006] B.C.J. No. 430 (B.C.S.C.) HCD-111

Christie Corp. v. Lawrence [1995] O.J. No. 4532 (Ont. Gen. Div), affd [1997] O.J. No. 3776, 35 O.R. (3d) 412 (Ont. C.A.) HCD-87

Chung v. 741501 Ontario Ltd., [1996] O.J. No. 3731 (Ont. C.A.) HCD-95

Ciddio v. York Region Condominium Corp. No. 730, [2002] O.J. No. 553 (Ont. S.C.J.) HCD-1, HCD-86

Citifinancial Mortgage Corp. v. Simcoe Condominium Corp. No. 27, [2005] O.J. No. 2755 (Ont. S.C.J.), additional reasons at 2005 CarswellOnt 4649 (Ont. S.C.J.) HCD-95

Condominium Corp. No. 0111505 v. Anders, [2005] A.J. No. 653 (Q.B.) HCD-41

Condominium Corp. No. 8110264 v. Farkas, [2009] A.J. No. 911 (Alta. Q.B.) HCD-86

Condominium Plan 7722911 v. Marnel, [2008] A.J. No. 305 (Alta. Q.B.) HCD-31, HCD-86, HCD-111

Condominium Plan 832 1384 v. McDonald, [1998] A.J. No. 885 (Alta. Q.B.) HCD-95

Condominium Plan N. 86-S-36901 v. Remai Construction (1981) Inc., [1991] S.J. No. 410 (Sask. C.A.) HCD-5, HCD-87, HCD-90, HCD-91

Condominium Plan No. 0020701 v. Investplan Properties Inc., [2006] A.J. No. 368 (Alta. Q.B.) HCD-2, HCD-32, HCD-93

Condominium Plan No. 0020701 v. Investplan Properties Inc., [2007] A.J. No. 1478 (Alta. Q.B.) HCD-93

Condominium Plan No. 022 1347 v. N.Y., [2003] A.J. No. 1227 (Alta.Q.B.) HCD-1, HCD-86, HCD-112

Condominium Plan No. 8111679 v. Elekes, [2003] A.J. No. 329 (Alta. Q.B.) HCD-111

Condominium Plan No. 822 2630 v. Danray Alberta Ltd., Danny Taran, [2007] A.J. No. 32 (Alta. C.A.) HCD-81

Condominium Plan No. 932 2887 v. Redweik, [1994] A.J. No. 1020 (Alta. Q.B.) HCD-86

Condominium Plan No. 9422336 v. Canada, [2004] T.C.J. No. 304 (T.C.C.) HCD-30

Condominium Plan No. 9524710 (c.o.b. West Edmonton Commerce Park) v. Webb (c.o.b. Blue Bay Massage), [1999] A.J. No. 10 (Alta. Q.B.) HCD-1

Condominium Plan No. 982 2595 v. Fantasy Homes Ltd., [2007] A.J. No. 50 (Alta. Q.B.) HCD-93

Condominium Plan No. 982 2595 v. Fantasy Homes Ltd., [2008] A.J. No. 1057 (Alta. Q.B.) HCD-93

Para.

Condominium Plan No. 982-2595 v. Fantasy Homes Ltd., [2006] A.J. No. 495 (Alta.Q.B.) HCD-2, HCD-93, HCD-110, HCD-111

Condominium Plan Number 752-1207 v. Terrace Corp. (Construction), [1983] A.J. No. 773 (C.A.) HCD-32

Corchis v. Essex Condominium Corp. No. 28, [2003] O.J. No. 3364 (C.A.) HCD-32

Coupal v. Strata Plan LMS 2503, [2004] B.C.J. No. 2276, B.C.L.R. (4th) 238 (B.C.C.A.) HCD-111

Dazol Developments Ltd. v. York Condominium Corp No. 329, [1979] O.J. No. 4149, 24 O.R. (2d) 46 (Ont. H.C.J.) HCD-94

Deluce Holdings Inc. v. Air Canada, [1992] O.J. No. 2382, 98 D.L.R. (4th) 509 (Ont. Gen. Div.) HCD-111

Desjardins v. Winnipeg Cond. Corp. No. 75, [1990] M.J. No. 523 (Man. Q.B.) HCD-86

Di Cecco v. 733725 Ontario Inc., [1990] O.J. No. 2559 (Ont. Gen Div.), affd [1991] O.J. No. 3126 (Ont. C.A.) HCD-95

Diligenti v. RWMD Operations Kelowna Ltd., [1976] B.J. No. 38, 1 B.C.L.R. 36 (B.C.S.C.) HCD-110

Dimitrov v. Summit Square Strata Corp., [2006] B.C.J. No. 1532 (S.C.) HCD-39

Dinicola v. Huang & Danczkay Properties, [1996] O.J. No. 1733, 29 O.R. (3d) 161 (Ont. Gen. Div.), affd [1998] O.J. No. 2570, 40 O.R. (3d) 252 (Ont. C.A.) HCD-88

Drummond v. Strata Plan NW2654, [2004] B.C.J. No. 2280 (S.C.) HCD-24

Dunn v. Condominium Plan No. 89PA14638, [2003] S.J. No. 76 (Sask. Q.B.) HCD-86

Durham Condominium Corporation No. 63 v. On-Cite Solutions Ltd., [2010] O.J. No. 5214, 2010 ONSC 6342 (Ont. S.C.J.) HCD-95

East Gate Estates Essex Condominium Corp. No. 2 v. Kimmerly, [2003] O.J. No. 582 (Ont. S.C.J.) HCD-86

Eberts v. Carleton Condominium Corp. No. 396, [2000] O.J. No. 3773 (Ont.C.A.) HCD-5

Eglinton Place Inc. v. Ontario (Ministry of Consumer & Corporate Relations), [2000] O.J. No. 498, 47 O.R. (3d) 344 (Ont. S.C.J.) HCD-69

Elkishawi v. Metro Toronto Condominium Corp. No. 1130, [2004] O.J. No. 6264 (Ont. Sm. Cl. Ct.) HCD-95

Ernest & Twins Venture (PP) Ltd. v. Strata Plan LMS 3259, [2004] B.C.J. No. 2455 (B.C.C.A.) HCD-111

Essex Condominium Corp. No. 5 v. Rose-Ville Community Center Assn., [2007] O.J. No. 2067 (Ont. S.C.J.) HCD-95

Essex Condominium Corp. No. 89 v. Glengarda Residences [2010] O.J. No. 822, 2010 ONCA 167 (Ont. C.A.) HCD-90

Esteem Investments Ltd. v. Strata Plan No. VR 1513, [1988] B.C.J. No. 1956 (B.C.C.A.) HCD-110, HCD-111

Para.

Eva Osvath v. Carleton Condominium Corp. No. 237 (Small Claims Court, January 11, 2005) HCD-112

Extra Gift Exchange Inc. v. Chung, [2006] B.C.J. No. 697 (B.C.S.C.) HCD-45

Extra Gift Exchange Inc. v. Ernest & Twins Ventures (PP) Ltd., [2007] B.C.J. No. 636 (B.C.S.C.) HCD-37

Ferguson v. Imax Systems Corp., [1983] O.J. No. 3156, 43 O.R. (2d) 128 (Ont. C.A.) HCD-110

Fisher v. Metropolitan Toronto Condominium Corp. No. 596, [2004] O.J. No. 5758 (S.C.J.) HCD-38, HCD-95

Foster v. MFD Warehouse Restorations Ltd., [2008] S.J. No. 122 (Sask. C.A.) HCD-87, HCD-90

Gentis v. Strata Plan VR 368, [2003] B.C.J. No. 140 (B.C.S.C.) HCD-110

Goetz v. Whitehall Development Corp., [1978] O.J. No. 3277, 19 O.R. (2d) 33 (Ont. C.A.) HCD-95

Goldex Mines Ltd. v. Revill, [1974] O.J. No. 2245, 7 O.R. (2d) 216 (Ont. C.A.) HCD-110

Gore Plaza Inc. v. Bains, [2007] O.J. No. 5023 (Ont. S.C.J.) HCD-87

Grinberg v. Law Development Group (Thornhill) Ltd. [1996] O.J. No. 1722, 2 R.P.R. (3d) 209 (Ont. Gen. Div.) HCD-87, HCD-90, HCD-95

Gyulay v. Kenderry Corp., [1998] O.J. No. 5328, 24 R.P.R. (3d) 84 (Ont. Gen. Div.) HCD-95

Harding v. Wyldewyn Village Inc., [1994] O.J. No. 578, 38 R.P.R. (2d) 268 (Ont. Gen. Div.) HCD-95

Harding Addison Properties Ltd. v. Campbell, [1992] O.J. No. 2732, 28 R.P.R. (2d) 284 (Ont. C.A.) HCD-95

Hatch v. Quadra Plex Development Corp., [2002] B.C.J. No. 2708 (Prov. Ct.) HCD-32

Hidden Harbour Estates, Inc. v. Norman, 309 So.2d 180 (Fla. 4th DCA 1975) HCD-1, HCD-38

Ho v. Camrost York Development Corp., [1994] O.J. No. 592 (Ont. Gen. Div.), affd [1996] O.J. No. 950 (Ont. C.A.) HCD-87

Holmes v. Jastek Master Builder 2004 Inc., [2008] S.J. No. 590 (Sask. Q.B.) HCD-90, HCD-91

Holmes v. Jastek Master Builder 2004 Inc., [2009] S.J. No. 680 (Sask. Q.B.) HCD-90, HCD-91

Israel v. Townsgate 1 Ltd., [1994] O.J. No. 3187 (Ont. Gen. Div.) HCD-90

Italiano v. Toronto Standard Condominium Corp. No. 1507, [2008] O.J. No. 2642 (Ont. S.C.J.) HCD-71, HCD-103

Jankowski v. 990088 Ontario Inc., [1998] O.J. No. 2764 (Ont. Gen. Div.), affd [2000] O.J. No. 444 (Ont. C.A.) HCD-112

Para.

Jaremko v. Shipp Corp. [1995] O.J. No. 2015, 47 R.P.R. (2d) 229 (Ont. Gen. Div.), affd [1996] O.J. No. 2155 (Ont. C.A.) HCD-90

Jasinski v. Trinchini, [1994] O.J. No. 576, 37 R.P.R. (2d) 240 (Ont. Gen. Div.) HCD-95

John Campbell Law Corp. v. Strata Plan 1350, [2001] B.C.J. No. 2037 (B.C.S.C.) HCD-77

Justein v. 3900 Yonge St. Ltd., [1983] O.J. No. 1177, 29 R.P.R. 80 (Ont. H.C.J.) HCD-95

Kelly v. Reardon, [2004] N.J. No. 30 (Nfld. Prov. Ct.) HCD-32

Keyes v. Metropolitan Toronto Condominium Corp. No. 876, [1990] O.J. No. 1006, 73 O.R. (2d) 568 (Ont. H.C.J.) HCD-67, HCD-92

Kierdorf v. Reemark East Hamptons Ltd., [1992] O.J. No. 1902, 26 R.P.R. (2d) 16 (Ont. Gen. Div.) HCD-95

Kornfeld v. Intrawest Corp., [2005] B.C.J. No. 230 (B.C.S.C.) HCD-96

Kornfeld v. Intrawest Corp., [2005] B.C.J. No. 1824 (B.C.S.C.) HCD-96

Kovats v. M.F. Property Management Ltd., [2009] O.J. No. 1972 (Ont. S.C.J.) HCD-114

Kozourek v. Carlyle Residence (III) Inc., [1996] O.J. No. 1467 (Ont. Gen. Div.), affd [1998] O.J. No. 4175 (Ont. C.A.) HCD-87, HCD-95

Kratz v. Parkside Hill Ltd., [1995] O.J. No. 2890, 48 R.P.R. (2d) 98 (Ont. C.A.) HCD-95

Lahrkamp v. Metropolitan Toronto Condominium Corp. No. 932, unreported (2010) (Ont. Sm. Cl. Ct.) HCD-95

Laidis v. MTCC No. 727, [2005] O.J. No. 726 (Ont. S.C.J.) HCD-39

Lamarche v. Mastercraft Development Corp., [1995] O.J. No. 620 (Ont. Gen. Div.) .. HCD-90

Landmark of Thornhill Ltd. v. Jacobson, [1995] O.J. No. 2819, 47 R.P.R. (2d) 211 (Ont. C.A.) HCD-87

Landmark of Thornhill Ltd v. Maleki-Yazdi, [1995] O.J. No. 759. 45 R.P.R. (2d) 280 (Ont. Gen. Div.), affd [1998] O.J. No. 2300 (Ont. C.A.) HCD-95

Landmark of Thornhill Ltd. v. Sobhi, [1995] O.J. No. 1733 (Ont. C.A.), leave to appeal to S.C.C. refused [1995] S.C.A.A. No. 404, 94 O.A.C. 320n (S.C.C.) HCD-90

Lexington on the Green Inc. v. Toronto Standard Condominium Corp. No. 1930, [2010] O.J. No. 4853 (Ont.C.A.) HCD-3, HCD-89

Lightner v. Condominium Plan No. 772 3097, [2009] A.J. No. 9 (Alta. Q.B.) HCD-95

Little v. Condominium Plan No. 82S15667, [2006] S.J. No. 307 (Sask. C.A.) HCD-95

Little v. Metropolitan Toronto Condominium Corp. No. 590, [2006] O.J. No. 3294 (Ont. S.C.J.) HCD-81

Lougheed & Co. v. Calgary (City), [2003] A.J. No. 945 (Alta. C.A.) HCD-30

Lyon v. Apex Lifestyle Communities Inc., [2006] A.J. No. 1331 (Alta. Master) HCD-87

Mancuso v. York Condominium Corp. No. 216, [2008] O.J. No. 1737 (Ont. Sup. Ct.) HCD-69

Para.

Mason v. Intercity Properties Ltd., [1987] O.J. No. 448, 59 O.R. (2d) 631 (Ont. C.A.) HCD-111

Maverick Equities Inc. v. Condominium Plan No. 942 2336, [2008] A.J. No. 616 (Alta. C.A.) HCD-24, HCD-26, HCD-84, HCD-112

McKay v. Waterloo North Condominium Corp. No. 23, [1992] O.J. No. 2435 (Ont. Gen. Div.) HCD-36, HCD-37, HCD-38, HCD-95

McKinstry v. York Condominium Corp. No. 472, [2003] O.J. No. 5006 (Ont. S.C.J.) HCD-110, HCD-114

Metro Toronto Condominium Corp. No. 545 v. Stein, [2006] O.J. No. 2473 (Ont. C.A.) HCD-114

Metropolitan Toronto Condominium Corp. 551 v. Adam, [2006] O.J. No. 4836 (Ont. S.C.J.) HCD-39, HCD-111

Metropolitan Toronto Condominium Corp. No. 539 v. Chapters Inc., [1999] O.J. No. 2806 (Ont. S.C.J.) HCD-32

Metropolitan Toronto Condominium Corp. No. 601 v. Hadbavny, [2001] O.J. No. 4176 (Ont. S.C.J.) HCD-86, HCD-105

Metropolitan Toronto Condominium Corp. No. 650 v. Klein, [1988] O.J. No. 581 (Ont. Dist. Ct.) HCD-26

Metropolitan Toronto Condominium Corp. No. 706 v. Quinto, [1990] O.J. No. 2981 (Ont. Dist. Ct.), affd [1991] O.J. No. 2776 (Ont. C.A.) HCD-104

Metropolitan Toronto Condominium Corp. No. 776 v. Gifford, [1989] O.J. No. 1691 (Ont. Dist. Ct.) HCD-86, HCD-105

Metropolitan Toronto Condominium Corp. No. 850 v. Oikle, [1994] O.J. No. 3055 (Ont. Gen. Div.) HCD-104

Metropolitan Toronto Condominium Corp. No. 932 v. Lahrkamp, [2008] O.J. No. 3885 (S.C.J.), vard [2009] O.J. No. 1785 (C.A.) HCD-37, HCD-38, HCD-40, HCD-95, HCD-103

Metropolitan Toronto Condominium Corp. No. 949 v. Staib, [2005] O.J. No. 5131 (Ont. C.A.) HCD-86, HCD-105

Metropolitan Toronto Condominium Corp. No. 985 v. Vanduzer, [2010] O.J. No. 571 (Ont. S.C.J.) HCD-43

Metropolitan Toronto Condominium Corp. No. 1021 v. Metropolitan Toronto Condominium Corp. No. 1008, [2006] O.J. No. 479 (Ont. C.A.) HCD-89

Metropolitan Toronto Condominium Corp. No. 1170 v. Zeidan, [2001] O.J. No. 2785 (Ont. S.C.J.) HCD-104

Metropolitan Toronto Condominium Corp. No. 1250 v. Mastercraft Group Inc. [2007] O.J. No. 603 (Ont. S.C.J.), vard [2009] O.J. No. 3104 (Ont. C.A.) HCD-91, HCD-94

Metropolitan Toronto Condominium Corp. No. 545 v. Stein (2005), 53 C.L.R. (3d) 155 .... HCD-77

Para.

Metropolitan Toronto Condominium Corp. No. 747 v. Korolekh, [2010] O.J. No. 3491 (Ont. S.C.J.) HCD-106

Metropolitan Toronto Condominium Corp. No. 1272 v. Beach Development (Phase II) Corp. [2010] O.J. No. 5025 (Ont. S.C.J.) HCD-5, HCD-89

Metropolitan Toronto Condominium Corp. No. 1385 v. Skyline Executive Properties Inc., [2005] O.J. No. 1604 (Ont. C.A.) HCD-112

Middlesex Condominium Corp. No. 87 v. 600 Talbot Street London Ltd., [1998] O.J. No. 450 (Ont.C.A.) HCD-2, HCD-85, HCD-90

Miehm v. Doering, [2001] O.J. No. 5187 (Ont. S.C.J.), additional reasons at [2002] O.J. No. 3752 (Ont. S.C.J.) HCD-89, HCD-95

Milgram v. York Humber Ltd., [1992] O.J. No. 283, 22 R.P.R. (2d) 102 (Ont. Gen. Div.) HCD-87

Morris v. Cam-Nest Developments Ltd., [1988] O.J. No. 720, 64 O.R. (2d) 475 (Ont. H.C.J.) HCD-95

MTCC No. 1250 v. Mastercraft Group, [2006] O.J. No. 3600 (Ont. S.C.J.) HCD-91

Murkute v. Owners Condominium Plan 8210034, [2006] A.J. No. 1335 (Alta. C.A.) HCD-32

Muskoka Condominium Corp. No. 39 v. Kreutzweiser, [2010] O.J. No. 1720 (Ont. S.C.J.) HCD-1, HCD-43, HCD-86, HCD-105

National Trust Co. v. Grey Condominium Corp. No. 36, [1995] O.J. No. 2079 (Gen. Div.) HCD-5, HCD-36

Newman v. Law Development Group (Georgetown) Ltd., [1996] O.J. No. 393 (Ont. Gen. Div.) HCD-95

Niagara North Condominium Corp. No. 46 v. Chassie, [1999] O.J. No. 1201 (Ont. Ct. Gen. Div.) HCD-86, HCD-105

Niedermeier v. York Condominium Corporation No. 50, [2006] O.J. No. 2612 (Ont. S.C.J.) HCD-111

Nipissing Condominium Corp. No. 4 v. Simard, [2009] O.J. No. 4430 (Ont. C.A.) ... HCD-114

Oldaker v. Strata Plan VR 1008 [2007] B.C.J. No. 991 (B.C.S.C.) HCD-109

Oldaker v. Strata Plan VR 1008 [2008] B.C.J. No. 493 (B.C.S.C.) HCD-77, HCD-111

Oldaker v. Strata Plan VR 1008, [2009] B.C.J. No. 1061 (B.C.S.C.) HCD-77, HCD-111

Ormond v. Richmond Square Development Corp., [2003] O.J. No. 668, 8 R.P.R. (4th) 234 (Ont. S.C.J.) HCD-3, HCD-87

Orr v. Metropolitan Toronto Condominium Corp.n No. 1056, [2011] O.J. No. 3898 (Ont. S.C.J.) HCD-86, HCD-102, HCD-111

Ottawa-Carleton Standard Condominium Corp. No. 650 v. Claridge Homes Corp., [2009] O.J. No. 2139 (Ont. S.C.J.) HCD-91

Peel Condominium Corp. No. 33 v. Johnson, [2005] O.J. No. 2875 (Ont. S.C.J.) HCD-114

Para.

Peel Condominium Corp. No. 199 v. Sanrose Construction (Dixie) Ltd. [1989] O.J. No. 766, 68 O.R. (2d) 513 (Ont. H.C.J.), affd [1992] O.J. No. 3223, 10 O.R. (3d) 640 (Ont. C.A.) HCD-95

Peel Condominium Corp. No. 505 v. Cam-Valley Homes Ltd. [2001] O.J. No. 714 (Ont. C.A.) HCD-3, HCD-5, HCD-90

Peel Condominium Corp. No. 283 v. Genik, [2007] O.J. No. 2544 (Ont. S.C.J.) HCD-84, HCD-114

Peel Condominium Corp. No. 338 v. Young, [1997] O.J. No. 1478 (Ont. Gen. Div.) HCD-112

Peel Condominium Corp. No. 449 v. Hogg, [1997] O.J. No. 623 (Ont. Gen. Div.) HCD-112

Pelletier v. Couture, [2003] J.Q. No 3355, J.E. 2003-1056 (Qué Sup. Ct.) HCD-103

Point of View Marketing & Management Inc. v. Condominium Corp. No. 0111661, [2003] A.J. No. 1371 (Alta. Q.B.) HCD-111

Re Jermyn Street Turkish Baths Ltd., [1971] 3 All E.R. 184 (C.A.) HCD-111

Regehr v. Camrose Crown Care Corp., [2006] A.J. No. 466 (Alta. Q.B.) HCD-88

Reid v. Strata Plan LMS 2503, [2003] B.C.J. No. 417 (B.C.S.C.) HCD-110

Remo Valente Real Estate (1990) Ltd v. Portofino Riverside Tower Inc., [2008] O.J. No. 1887 (Ont. S.C.J.), additional reasons to [2007] O.J. No. 3271 (Ont. S.C.J.) HCD-95

Richardson v. Strata Plan LMS2435 [2005] B.C.J. No. 948 (BCSC) HCD-77

Rogers Cable Communications Inc. v. Carleton Condominium Corp. No. 53, [2005] O.J. No. 921 (Ont S.C.J.) HCD-3, HCD-42

Rogers Cove Ltd. v. Sloot, [1991] O.J. No. 1937, 19 R.P.R. (2d) 154 (Ont. Gen. Div.) HCD-87

Rohoman v. York Condominium Corp. No. 141, [2000] O.J. No. 2356 (S.C.J.) HCD-36, HCD-38, HCD-95

Rohoman v. York Condominium Corp. No. 141, [2001] O.J. No. 4927 (Ont. S.C.) HCD-67

Rossi v. York Condominium Corp. No. 123, [1989] O.J. No. 1424 (Ont. H.C.J.), affd [1991] O.J. No. 3174 (Ont. C.A.) HCD-89

Russ-Cad Management Ltd. Bayview 400 Industrial Developments Inc., [1992] O.J. No. 695, 24 R.P.R. (2d) 6 (Ont. Gen. Div.) HCD-95

Rylands v. Fletcher (1868), L.R. 3 H.L. 330 ..... HCD-77

Sabine v. Excelsior Loft Enterprises Corp., [1994] A.J. No. 384, 39 R.P.R. (2d) 86 (Alta. Master) HCD-87

Sauve v. McKeage, [2006] B.C.J. No. 1144 (B.C.S.C.) HCD-112

Sauve v. Paglione, [2006] O.J. No. 3523 (S.C.J.) HCD-39

Para.

Scanlon v. Castlepoint Development Corp., [1992] O.J. No. 2692, 11 O.R. (3d) 744 (Ont. C.A.) HCD-95

Scaroni v. Rosepol Holdings Ltd., [1995] O.J. No. 3212, 48 R.P.R. (2d) 276 (Ont. Gen. Div) HCD-87, HCD-95

Schaper-Kotter v. Strata Plan 148, [2006] B.C.J. No. 924 (B.C.S.C.) HCD-86, HCD-111

Scotwick Realty Services Inc. v. Condominium Plan No. 7510479, [2003] A.J. No. 831 (Alta. Q.B.) HCD-81

Shaw Cablesystems Ltd. v. Concord Pacific Group Inc., [2007] B.C.J. No. 2529 (B.C.S.C.), affd [2008] B.C.J. No. 1014 (B.C.C.A.) HCD-1, HCD-4, HCD-12

Shoihet v. 110 Bloor West Development Corp., [1984] O.J. No. 411, 32 R.P.R. 179 (Ont. H.C.J.) HCD-95

Simcoe Condominium Corp. No. 78 v. Simcoe Condominium Corp. Nos. 50, 52, 53, 56, 59, 63 and 64, [2006] O.J. No. 605 (Ont. S.C.J.) HCD-89

Singer v. Reemark Sterling I Ltd., [1992] O.J. No. 1083 (Ont. Gen. Div.), affd [1997] O.J. No. 653 (Ont. C.A.) HCD-95

Skyline Executive Properties Inc. v. Metropolitan Toronto Condominium Corp. No. 1280, [2001] O.J. No. 3512 (Ont. S.C.J.) HCD-104

Skyline Executive Properties Inc. v. Metropolitan Toronto Condominium Corp. No. 1385, [2002] O.J. No. 5117 (S.C.J.) HCD-26, HCD-104

Skyrise Developments Ltd v. Aldrovandi, [1997] O.J. No. 393 (Ont. Gen. Div.), affd [1999] O.J. No. 983 (Ont. C.A.) HCD-87, HCD-90

Smithers v. York Condominium Corp. No. 60, [2003] O.J. No. 851 (Ont. Div. Ct.)..... HCD-45

Sokoloff v. 5 Rosehill Avenue Development Inc., [1998] O.J. No. 4911, 21 R.P.R. (3d) 176 (Ont. Gen. Div.) HCD-95

Stafford v. Frontenac Condominium Corp. No. 11, [1994] O.J. No. 2072 (Ont. Gen. Div.) HCD-95

Strata Plan LMS 888 v. Coquitlam (City), [2003] B.C.J. No. 1422 (S.C.) HCD-32

Strata Plan LMS 1537 v. Alvarez, [2003] B.C.J. No. 1610, 17 B.C.L.R. (4th) 63 (B.C.S.C.) HCD-111

Strata Plan LMS 1564 v. Lark Odyssey Project Ltd. (c.o.b. Lark Group), [2008] B.C.J. No. 2407 (B.C.C.A.) HCD-96

Strata Plan LMS 2940 v. Quick as a Wink Courier Service Ltd., [2007] B.C.J. No. 1448 (S.C.) HCD-32

Strata Plan NW87 v. Karamanian, [1989] B.C.J. No. 629 (B.C.S.C.) HCD-103

Strata Plan VIS 4534 v. Seedtree Water Utility Co., [2006] B.C.J. No. 82 (S.C.) HCD-32

Strata Plan VR19 v. Collins, [2004] B.C.J. No. 2757 (B.C.S.C.) HCD-112

Strata Plan VR 1280 v. Oberto Oberti Architecture, [2003] B.C.J. No. 129 (S.C.) HCD-32

Strata Plan VR2654 v. Mason, [2004] B.C.J. No. 106 .... HCD-81

Summerside v. Le Turnberry, [2003] J.Q. no. 2285 (QCCS) HCD-77

Para.

Summerville Condominium Corporation v. Dynamic Physiotherapy, [2003] N.J. No. 332 (N.L.S.C.) HCD-86, HCD-112

Syndicat des copropriétaires Copropriété du Square St-David I c. Chevalier, [2005] J.Q. no 9815 (Qué C.S.) HCD-86

Syndicat Northcrest v. Amselem, [2004] S.C.J. No. 56 (S.C.C.) HCD-84

Taychuk v. Strata Plan LMS744, [2002] B.C.J. No. 2653 (BCSC) HCD-77

Terry v. Strata Plan LMS 2153, [2006] B.C.J. No. 1404 (B.C.S.C.) HCD-111

Toronto Standard Condominium Corp. No. 1443 v. Cecutti, [2003] O.J. No. 4144 (Ont. S.C.J.) and [2003] O.J. No. 4145 (Ont. S.C.J.) HCD-106

Towne Meadow Development Corp v. Chong, [1993] O.J. No. 693, 30 R.P.R. (2d) 228 (Ont. Gen Div.) HCD-87

Village Condominium Inc. v. Breitenback, 251 So.2d 585 (1971) HCD-1

Waterloo North Condominium Corp. No. 168 v. Webb, [2011] O.J. No. 2195 (Ont. S.C.J.) HCD-106

Weir v. Strata Plan NW 17, [2010] B.C.J. No. 1057 (B.C.S.C.) HCD-86, HCD-102

Wellington Condominium Corp. No. 61 v. Marilyn Drive Holdings Ltd., [1998] O.J. No. 448 (Ont. C.A.) HCD-90

Wentworth Condominium No. 12 v. Wentworth Condominium No. 59, [2007] O.J. No. 2741 .... HCD-74

Wilfert v. Ward, [2004] B.C.J. No. 423 (B.C.S.C.) HCD-81

Winfair Holdings (Lagoon City) v. Simcoe Condominium Corp. No. 46, [1998] O.J. No. 5022 (Ont. C.A.) HCD-3

Wong v. Reemark Sterling II Ltd., [1992] O.J. No. 2105, 26 R.P.R. (2d) 93 (Ont. Gen. Div.) HCD-95

Wright v. Strata Plan No. 205, [1996] B.C.J. No. 381 (B.C.S.C.), affd [1998] B.C.J. No. 105 (B.C.C.A.) HCD-77

Yanos v. Darkeff, [2008] O.J. No. 5559 (Ont. Sm. Cl. Ct.) HCD-95

York Condominium Corp. No. 42 v. Miller, unreported decision of Justice M.R.R. German, released January 5, 1988 .... HCD-112

York Condominium Corp. No. 42 v. Hashmi, [2007] O.J. No. 2085 (S.C.J.) HCD-33

York Condominium Corp. No. 59 v. York Condominium Corp. No. 87, [1983] O.J. No. 3088 (Ont. C.A.) HCD-71, HCD-85, HCD-102

York Condominium Corp. No. 60 v. Brown, [2001] O.J. No. 5951 (S.C.J.) HCD-36, HCD-38, HCD-95

York Condominium Corp. No. 98 v. Jeffers, [2008] O.J. 2646 (Ont. Div. Ct.) HCD-112

York Condominium Corp. No. 128 v. McKenzie, [1996] O.J. No. 2878 (Ont. Gen. Div.) HCD-61

Para.

York Condominium Corp No. 162 v. Noldan Investment Ltd. (1977) 1 R.P.R. 236 (Ont. H.C.) HCD-89, HCD-94

York Condominium Corp. No. 166 v. Nunez, [1990] O.J. No. 649 (Ont. Dist. Ct.) HCD-103

York Condominium Corp. No. 167 v. Newrey Holdings Ltd. [1981] O.J. No. 2965, 32 O.R. (2d) 458 (Ont. C.A.), leave to appeal to S.C.C. refused [1981] 1 S.C.R. xi, 32 O.R. (2d) 458n (S.C.C.) HCD-89

York Condominium Corp. No. 206 v. Almeida & Almeida Landscaping Co., [1992] O.J. No. 1073 (Ont. Gen. Div.) HCD-61

York Condominium Corp. No. 219 v. Naumovich., unreported decision of Justice D.J. Taliano, released January 3, 1985 .... HCD-112

York Condominium Corp. No. 382 v. Dvorchik, [1997] O.J. No. 378 (C.A.) HCD-26, HCD-43, HCD-86, HCD-105

York Condominium Corp. No. 435 v. Starburst Investments Ltd., [1984] O.J. No. 3481 (Ont. Co. Ct.) HCD-94

York Condominium Corp. No. 482 v. Christansen, [2003] O.J. No. 343 (S.C.J.) HCD-2, HCD-69, HCD-71

York Region Condominium Corp. No. 622 v. Pisman, [2001] O.J. No. 2913 (Ont. S.C.J.), affd [2002] O.J. No. 105 (Ont. C.A.) HCD-103

York Region Condominium Corp. No. 771 v. Year Full Investments (Canada) Inc, [1993] O.J. No. 769 (C.A.) HCD-69, HCD-71, HCD-72

York Region Condominium Corp. No. 889 v. York Region Condominium Corp. No. 878, [2008] O.J. No. 1743 (Ont. S.C.J.) HCD-89

York Region Condominium Corp. No. 921 v. ATOP Communications Inc., [2003] O.J. No. 5255 (S.C.J.) HCD-14, HCD-89

Table of Cases — Constitutional Law — Division of Powers

Para.

620 Connaught Ltd. v. Canada (Attorney General), [2008] 1 S.C.J. No. 7, [2008] 1 S.C.R. 131 (S.C.C.) HCL-15, HCL-137, HCL-140, HCL-141, HCL-150, HCL-151, HCL-153, HCL-156

2747-3174 Québec Inc. v. Quebec (Régie des permis d'alcool), [1996] S.C.J. No. 112, [1996] 3 S.C.R. 919 (S.C.C.) HCL-63, HCL-64

114957 Canada Ltée (Spraytech, Société d'arrosage) v. Hudson (Town), [2001] S.C.J. No. 42, [2001] 2 S.C.R. 241 (S.C.C.). HCL-101

A. (L.L.) v. B (A.), [1995] S.C.J. No. 102, [1995] 4 S.C.R. 536 (S.C.C.). HCL-48

Abbott v. St. John (City), [1908] S.C.J. No. 44, 40 S.C.R. 597 (S.C.C.) HCL-148

Abdelrazik c. Canada (Ministre des Affaires étrangéres), [2009] F.C.J. No. 656, [2010] 1 R.C.F. 267. (C.F.) HCL-11

Agence Maritime v. Canada (Labour Relations Board), [1969] A.C.S. no 105, [1969] S.C.R. 851 (S.C.C.). HCL-185

Air Canada v. British Columbia, [1989] S.C.J. No. 44, [1989] 1 S.C.R. 1161 (S.C.C.). HCL-144

Air Canada v. Ontario (Liquor Control Board), [1997] S.C.J. No. 66, 148 D.L.R. (4th) 193 (S.C.C.). HCL-184

Alberta (Attorney General) v. Canada (Alta. Bill of Rights), [1947] A.C. 503 (P.C.) HCL-106

Alberta (Attorney General) v. Canada (Attorney General), [1938] J.C.J. No. 3, [1939] A.C. 117 (P.C.) HCL-153

Alberta (Attorney General) v. Canada (Attorney General), [1947] J.C.J. No. 5, [1947] A.C. 503 (P.C.) HCL-163

Alberta (Attorney General) v. Putnam, [1981] S.C.J. No. 85, [1981] 2 S.C.R. 267 (S.C.C.) HCL-122

Alberta (Provincial Treasurer) v. Kerr, [1933] J.C.J. No. 2, [1933] A.C. 710 (P.C.) HCL-144, HCL-147, HCL-149

Alberta (Treasury Branches) v. Canada (Minister of National Revenue), [1996] S.C.J. No. 45, [s1][1996] 1 S.C.R. 963 (S.C.C.) HCL-168

Alberta Government Telephones v. Canada (Canadian Radio-television and Telecommunications Commission), [1989] S.C.J. No. 84, [1989] 2 S.C.R. 225 (S.C.C.). HCL-179

Allard Contractors Ltd. v. Coquitlam (District), [1993] S.C.J. No. 126, [1993] 4 S.C.R. 371 (S.C.C.) HCL-15, HCL-142, HCL-143, HCL-145, HCL-150, HCL-152, HCL-157

Para.

Alworth Estate v. British Columbia (Minister of Finance), [1977] S.C.J. No. 52, [1978] 1 S.C.R. 447 (S.C.C.) HCL-144

Amendment of Canadian Constitution (Re), [1982] S.C.J. No. 101, [1982] 2 S.C.R. 793 (S.C.C.) HCL-19, HCL-21, HCL-22, HCL-23, HCL-28, HCL-33

Application under s. 83.28 of the Criminal Code (Re), [2004] S.C.J. No. 40, [2004] 2 S.C.R. 248 (S.C.C.) HCL-28, HCL-41, HCL-62

Atlantic Smoke Shops Ltd. v. Conlon, [1943] S.C.J. No. 1, [1943] A.C. 550 (P.C.) HCL-144

Attorney-General for British Columbia v. Canadian Pacific Railway Co., [1927] A.C. 934 (P.C.) HCL-142

Attorney-General for Manitoba v. Attorney-General for Canada, [1925] A.C. 561 (P.C.) HCL-142

Attorney-General for Ontario v. Reciprocal Insurers, [1924] A.C. 328 (P.C.) HCL-91

Augustine's School Bus Inc. v. Asher, [1999] F.C.J. No. 1926, 179 F.T.R. 266 (F.C.T.D.) HCL-183

Auton (Guardian ad litem of) v. British Columbia (Attorney General), [2004] S.C.J. No. 71, [2004] 3 S.C.R. 657 (S.C.C.) HCL-162

Babcock v. Canada (Attorney General), [2002] S.C.J. No. 58, [2002] 3 S.C.R. 3 (S.C.C.) HCL-27, HCL-28, HCL-29, HCL-32

Bank of Montreal v. Hall, [1990] S.C.J. No. 9, [1990] 1 S.C.R. 121 (S.C.C.) HCL-99, HCL-101, HCL-163, HCL-164, HCL-165

Bank of Toronto v. Lambe (1887), L.R. 12 App. Cas. 575 (P.C.) HCL-97, HCL-142, HCL-143, HCL-145, HCL-148,

Beauregard v. Canada, [1986] S.C.J. No. 50, [1986] 2 S.C.R. 56 (S.C.C.) HCL-26, HCL-28, HCL-37, HCL-41, HCL-62, HCL-64, HCL-67

Bell v. Prince Edward Island (Attorney General), [1973] S.C.J. No. 131, [1975] 1 S.C.R. 25 (S.C.C.) HCL-183

Bell Canada v. Canadian Telephone Employees Assn., [1998] F.C.J. No. 313, [1998] 3 F.C. 244 (F.C.T.D.) HCL-63

Bell Canada v. Canadian Telephone Employees Assn., [2003] S.C.J. No. 36, [2003] 1 S.C.R. 884 (S.C.C.) HCL-63

Bell Canada v. Québec (Commission de la santé et de la sécurité du travail du Québec), [1988] S.C.J. No. 41, [1988] 1 S.C.R. 749 (S.C.C.) HCL-96, HCL-104

Bell ExpressVu Limited Partnership v. Rex, [2002] S.C.J. No. 43, [2002] 2 S.C.R. 559 (S.C.C.) HCL-40

Bisaillon v. Keable, [1983] S.C.J. No. 65, [1983] 2 S.C.R. 60 (S.C.C.) HCL-121

Para.

Black v. Canada (Prime Minister), [2001] O.J. No. 1853, 54 O.R. (3d) 215 (Ont. C.A.) HCL-8, HCL-10

Bradley and the Queen (Re), [1975] O.J. No. 2374, (1975) 9 O.R. (2d) 161 (Ont. C.A.) HCL-123

British Columbia v. Imperial Tobacco Canada Ltd., [2005] S.C.J. No. 50, [2005] 2 S.C.R. 473 (S.C.C.). .... HCL-27, HCL-28[s2], HCL-41, HCL-62

British Columbia (Attorney General) v. Canada (Attorney General), [1923] J.C.J. No. 5, [1924] A.C. 222 (P.C.). HCL-136, HCL-138

British Columbia (Attorney General) v. Canada Trust Co., [1980] S.C.J. No. 86, [1980] 2 S.C.R. 466 (S.C.C.) HCL-149

British Columbia (Attorney General) v. Christie, [2007] S.C.J. No. 21, [2007] 1 S.C.R. 873 (S.C.C.) HCL-33

British Columbia (Attorney General) v. Esquimalt and Nanaimo Railway Co., [1949] J.C.J. No. 2, [1950] A.C. 87 (P.C.) HCL-142, HCL-146

British Columbia (Attorney General) v. Lafarge Canada Inc., [2007] S.C.J. No. 23, [2007] 2 S.C.R. 86 (S.C.C.) HCL-105

British Columbia (Attorney General) v. McDonald Murphy Lumber Co., [1930] J.C.J. No. 1, [1930] A.C. 357 (P.C.) HCL-136

British Columbia (Attorney General) v. Smith, [1967] S.C.J. No. 64, [1967] S.C.R. 702 (S.C.C.). HCL-128

British Columbia Electric Railway Co. v. Canadian National Railway Co., [1931] S.C.J. No. 76, [1932] S.C.R. 161 (S.C.C.) HCL-173, HCL-183

British Columbia v. Imperial Tobacco Canada Ltd., [2005] S.C.J. No. 50, [2005] 2 S.C.R. 473 (S.C.C.). HCL-33, HCL-36, HCL-97

Burland v. The King; Alleyn Sharples v. Barthe, [1921] J.C.J. No. 5, [1922] 1 A.C. 215 (P.C.) HCL-144, HCL-149

C.F.R.B. and Attorney-General for Canada (Re), [1973] O.J. No. 2098, [1973] 3 O.R. 819 (Ont. C.A.) HCL-178

Cairns Construction Ltd. v. Saskatchewan, [1960] S.C.J. No. 35, [1960] S.C.R. 619 (S.C.C.) HCL-142, HCL-143, HCL-144

Calgary and Edmonton Land Co. v. Alberta (Attorney-General), [1911] S.C.J. No. 36, 45 S.C.R. 170 (S.C.C.) HCL-139

Campbell-Bennett Ltd. v. Comstock Midwestern Ltd., [1954] S.C.J. No. 14, [1954] S.C.R. 207 (S.C.C.) HCL-183

Canada (Attorney General) v. Canadian National Transportation Ltd., [1983] S.C.J. No. 73, [1983] 2 S.C.R. 206 (S.C.C.) HCL-123, HCL-134

Canada (Attorney General) v. JTI-Macdonald Corp., [2007] S.C.J. No. 30, [2007] 2 S.C.R. 610 (S.C.C.) HCL-115, HCL-117

Para.

Canada (Attorney General) v. Law Society of British Columbia, [1982] S.C.J. No. 70, [1982] 2 S.C.R. 307 (S.C.C.)....HCL-83, HCL-84, HCL-101

Canada (Attorney General) v. Ontario (Attorney General), [1894] S.C.J. No. 54, 23 S.C.R. 458 (S.C.C.)....HCL-8

Canada (Attorney General) v. Ontario (Attorney General), [1937] J.C.J. No. 6, [1937] A.C. 355 (P.C.)....HCL-153

Canada (Attorney General) v. P.E.I. (Legislative Assembly), [2003] P.E.I.J. No. 7 (P.E.I. S.C. (T.D.))....HCL-49

Canada (Attorney General) v. PHS Community Services Society, [2011] S.C.J. No. 44, 2011 S.C.C. 44 (S.C.C.)....HCL-4, HCL-97, HCL-102, HCL-103, HCL-104, HCL-115, HCL-118

Canada (Attorney General) v. Quebec (Attorneys General), [1946] J.C.J. No. 11, [1947] A.C. 33 (P.C.)....HCL-163

Canada (Attorney General) v. St. Hubert Base Teachers' Assn., [1989] S.C.J. No. 57, [1983] 1 S.C.R. 498 (S.C.C.)....HCL-184

Canada (Attorney General) v. Toronto (City), [1893] S.C.J. No. 47, 23 S.C.R. 514 (S.C.C.)....HCL-138

Canada (Attorney-General) of Canada v. British Columbia (Registrar of Titles, Vancouver), [1934] B.C.J. No. 101 [1934] 4 D.L.R. 764 (B.C.C.A.)....HCL-138

Canada (Aud. General) v. Canada (Min. of Energy, Mines & Resources), [1989] S.C.J. No. 80, [1989] 2 S.C.R. 49 (S.C.C.)....HCL-28, HCL-29, HCL-30

Canada (House of Commons) v. Vaid, [2005] S.C.J. No. 28, [2005] 1 S.C.R. 667 (S.C.C.)....HCL-13, HCL-28, HCL-49, HCL-50, HCL-54, HCL-55, HCL-56, HCL-57

Canada (Human Rights Commission) v. Canada Liberty Net, [1998] S.C.J. No. 31, [1998] 1 S.C.R. 626 (S.C.C.)....HCL-80, HCL-82

Canada (Labour Relations Board) v. Paul L'Anglais Inc., [1983] S.C.J. No. 31, [1983] 1 S.C.R. 147 (S.C.C.)....HCL-84

Canada (Labour Relations Board) v. Yellowknife (City), [1977] S.C.J. No. 25, [1977] 2 S.C.R. 729 (S.C.C.)....HCL-185

Canada (Prime Minister) v. Khadr, [2010] S.C.J. No. 3, [2010] 1 S.C.R. 44 (S.C.C.)....HCL-8, HCL-10

Canada (Solicitor General) v. Ontario (Royal Commission of Inquiry into the Confidentiality of Health Records), [1981] S.C.J. No. 95, [1981] 2 S.C.R. 494 (S.C.C.)....HCL-48

Canada v. Independent Order of Foresters, [1940] J.C.J. No. 3, [1940] A.C. 513....HCL-171

Canada v. Industrial Acceptance Corp., [1953] S.C.J. No. 47, [1953] 2 S.C.R. 273 (S.C.C.)....HCL-118

Canada v. National Fish Co., [1931] Ex. C.R. 75 (Ex. Ct.)....HCL-141

Canada v. Shearwater Co., [1934] S.C.J. No. 8, [1934] S.C.R. 197 (S.C.C.)....HCL-136

Para.

Canada v. Solosky, [1979] S.C.J. No. 130, [1980] 1 S.C.R. 821 (S.C.C.) HCL-48

Canadian Assn. of Broadcasters v. Canada, [2008] F.C.J. No. 672, [2009] 1 F.C.R. 3 (Fed. C.A.), leave to appeal to S.C.C. granted [2008] S.C.C.A. No. 423 (S.C.C.), appeal discontinued. HCL-152, HCL-154

Canadian Broadcasting Corp. v. Quebec (Police Commission), [1979] S.C.J. No. 60, [1979] 2 S.R.C. 618 (S.C.C.). HCL-77

Canadian Generic Pharmaceutical Assn. v. Canada (Minister of Health), [2010] F.C.J. No. 1582, 2010 FCA 334 (F.C.A.), leave to appeal dismissed [2011] S.C.C.A. No. 54 (S.C.C.) HCL-118

Canadian Industrial Gas & Oil Ltd. v. Saskatchewan, [1977] S.C.J. No. 124, [1978] 2 S.C.R. 545 (S.C.C.) HCL-146, HCL-207

Canadian Labour Code (Re), [1986] F.C.J. No. 756, [1987] 2 F.C. 30 (Fed. C.A.). HCL-175

Canadian Pacific Air Lines Ltd. v. British Columbia, [1989] S.C.J. No. 43, [1989] 1 S.C.R. 1133 (S.C.C.) HCL-144

Canadian Pacific Ltd. v. Matsqui Indian Band, [1995] S.C.J. No. 1, [1995] 1 S.C.R. 3 (S.C.C.) HCL-63, HCL-64

Canadian Pacific Railway Co. v. British Columbia (Attorney General), [1949] J.C.J. No. 1, [1950] A.C. 122 (P.C.)..............................HCL-175, HCL-185

Canadian Pacific Railway Co. v. Saskatchewan (Attorney General), [1952] S.C.J. No. 21, [1952] 2 S.C.R. 231 (S.C.C.)........................HCL-143, HCL-146

Canadian Pioneer Management Ltd. v. Saskatchewan (Labour Relations Board), [1979] S.C.J. No. 15, [1980] 1 S.C.R. 433 (S.C.C.)...........................HCL-163, HCL-165, HCL-166, HCL-167

Canadian Western Bank v. Alberta, [2007] S.C.J. No. 22, [2007] 2 S.C.R. 3 (S.C.C.)... HCL-39, HCL-88, HCL-89, HCL-91, HCL-96, HCL-97, HCL-99, HCL-101, HCL-102, HCL-103, HCL-105, HCL-163, HCL-165, HCL-166

Cannet Freight Cartage Ltd. (Re), [1975] F.C.J. No. 113, [1976] 1 F.C. 174 (Fed. C.A.) affd [1990] S.C.J. No. 136, [1990] 3 S.C.R. 1112 (S.C.C.). HCL-173

Capital Cities Communications v. C.R.T.C., [1977] S.C.J. No. 119, [1978] 2 S.C.R. 141 (S.C.C.). HCL-178, HCL-180

Carnation Co. v. Quebec (Agricultural Marketing Board), [1968] S.C.J. No. 11, [1968] S.C.R. 238 (S.C.C.). HCL-133, HCL-196

Central Canada Potash Co. v. Saskatcewan, [1978] S.C.J. No. 72, [1979] 1 S.C.R. 42 (S.C.C.)..HCL-207

Chaoulli v. Québec (Attorney General), [2005] S.C.J. No. 33, [2005] 1 S.C.R. 791 (S.C.C.)...HCL-1, HCL-162

Charkaoui v. Canada (Citizenship and Immigration), [2007] S.C.J. No. 9, 2007 SCC 9, [2007] 1 S.C.R. 350 (S.C.C.)...HCL-33

Para.

Chatterjee v. Ontario (Attorney General), [2009] S.C.J. No. 19, [2009] 1 S.C.R. 624 (S.C.C.)....... HCL-199

Citizens Insurance Company of Canada v. Parsons (1881), 7 App. Cas. 96 (H.L.)....... HCL-108, HCL-129, HCL-130, HCL-190, HCL-195

Comeau's Sea Foods Ltd. v. Canada (Minister of Fisheries and Oceans), [1997] S.C.J. No. 5, [1997] 1 S.C.R. 12 (S.C.C.)....... HCL-219

Committee for Justice and Liberty v. Canada (National Energy Board), [1976] S.C.J. No. 118, [1978] 1 S.C.R. 369 (S.C.C.)....... HCL-67

Confédération des syndicats nationaux v. Canada (Attorney General), [2008] S.C.J. No. 69, [2008] 3 S.C.R. 511 (S.C.C.)....... HCL-137, HCL-141, HCL-150, HCL-151, HCL-154

Consolidated Fastfrate Inc. v. Western Canada Council of Teamsters, [2009] S.C.J. No. 53, [2009] 3 S.C.R. 407, 2009 SCC 53 (S.C.C.)....... HCL-173, HCL-183, HCL-185, HCL-186, HCL-187, HCL-188, HCL-189, HCL-190

Cooper v. Canada (Canadian Human Rights Commission), [1996] S.C.J. No. 115, [1996] 3 S.C.R. 854 (S.C.C.)....... HCL-37, HCL-41, HCL-47, HCL-62

Copello v. Canada (Minister of Foreign Affairs), [2001] F.C.J. No. 1835, [2002] 3 F.C. 24 (F.C.), affd [2003] F.C.J. No. 1056, 308 N.R. 175 (F.C.A.)....... HCL-11

Cotton v. The King, [1913] J.C.J. No. 3, [1914] A.C. 176 (P.C.)....... HCL-142, HCL-149

Crevier v. Québec (Attorney General), [1981] S.C.J. No. 80, [1981] 2 S.C.R 220 (S.C.C.)....... HCL-71

Croft v. Dunphy, [1932] J.C.J. No. 4, [1933] A.C. 156 (P.C.)....... HCL-136

Deloitte Haskins & Sells Ltd. v. Alberta (Workers' Compensation Board), [1985] S.C.J. No. 35, [1985] 1 S.C.R. 785 (S.C.C.)....... HCL-169

Derrickson v. Derrickson, [1986] S.C.J. No. 16, [1986] 1 S.C.R. 285 (S.C.C.)....... HCL-105

Descôteaux v. Mierzwinski, [1982] S.C.J. No. 43, [1982] 1 S.C.R. (S.C.C.)....... HCL-48

Di Iorio v. Montreal (City) Common Jail, [1976] S.C.J. No. 113, [1978] 1 S.C.R. 152 (S.C.C.)....... HCL-121, HCL-122

Dion v. Hudson Bay Co., [1917] 51 Que. S.C. 413 (Que. S.C.)....... HCL-192

Dominion of Canada v. Levis (City), [1919] A.C. 505 (P.C.)....... HCL-150

Doucet-Boudreau v. Nova Scotia (Minister of Education), [2003] S.C.J. No. 63, [2003] 3 S.C.R. 3 (S.C.C.)....... HCL-47

Douglas/Kwantlen Faculty Assn. v. Douglas College, [1990] S.C.J. No. 124, [1990] 3 S.C.R. 570 (S.C.C.)....... HCL-47

Duke of Newcastle v. Morris (1870), L.R. 4 H.L. 661 (H.L.)....... HCL-57

Dunsmuir v. New Brunswick, [2008] S.C.J. No. 9, [2008] 1 S.C.R. 190 (S.C.C.)....... HCL-71

Para.

Early Recovered Resources Inc. v. British Columbia, [2005] F.C.J. No. 1234, 276 F.T.R. 267 (F.C.).. HCL-216

Edwards v. Canada (Attorney General), [1930] A.C. 124 (Can. P.C.)......................... HCL-14

Eldridge v. British Columbia (Attorney General), [1997] S.C.J. No. 86, [1997] 3 S.C.R. 624 (S.C.C.)... HCL-35, HCL-162

Ell v. Alberta, [2003] S.C.J. No. 35, [2003] 1 S.C.R. 857 (S.C.C.),............................ HCL-28, HCL-41, HCL-62

Erie Beach Co. v. Ontario (Attorney General), [1929] J.C.J. No. 3, [1930] A.C. 161 (P.C.)... HCL-144, HCL-147

Eurig Estate (Re), [1998] S.C.J. No. 72, [1998] 2 S.C.R. 565 (S.C.C.)........................ HCL-28, HCL-46, HCL-137, HCL-140, HCL-141, HCL-152, HCL-154

Farrah v. Quebec (Attorney General), [1978] S.C.J. No. 24, [1978] 2 S.C.R. 638 (S.C.C.).. HCL-79

Federal Business Development Bank v. Quebec (Commission de la santé et de la sécurité du travail du Quèbec), [1988] S.C.J. No. 44, [1988] 1 S.C.R. 1061 (S.C.C.)... HCL-168, HCL-169

Fédération des producteurs de volailles du Québec v. Pelland, [2005] S.C.J. No. 19, [2005] 1 S.C.R. 292 (S.C.C.).. HCL-196

Fédération Franco-Ténoise v. Canada, [2001] F.C.J. No. 1093, [2001] 3 F.C. 641 (Fed. C.A.).. HCL-136

Fédération Franco-Ténoise v. Canada (Attorney General), [2008] N.W.T.J. No. 45, 440 A.R. 56 (N.W.T.C.A.), supp. reasons [2008] N.W.T.J. No. 48, [2009] 12 W.W.R. 376 (N.W.T.C.A.), leave to appeal to S.C.C. refused [2008] S.C.C.A. No. 432, [2008] C.S.C.R. no 432 (S.C.C.)................................. HCL-136

Ferguson Bus Lines Ltd. v. Amalgamated Transit Union, Local 1374, [1990] F.C.J. No. 274, [1990] 2 F.C. 586 (Fed. C.A.)... HCL-183

Fielding v. Thomas, [1896] A.C. 600 (P.C.)... HCL-57

Figueroa v. Canada (Attorney General), [2003] S.C.J. No. 37, [2003] 1 S.C.R. 912 (S.C.C.)... HCL-28, HCL-37

Firestone Tire and Rubber Co. of Canada v. Canada (Commissioner of Income Tax), [1942] S.C.J. No. 40, [1942] S.C.R. 476 (S.C.C.)........................... HCL-144

Forbes v. Manitoba (Attorney General), [1936] J.C.J. No. 1, [1937] A.C. 260 (P.C.).. HCL-148

Four B. Manufacturing Ltd. v. United Garment Workers of America, [1979] S.C.J. No. 138, [1980] 1 S.C.R. 1031 (S.C.C.) HCL-185

Fraser v. Canada (Public Service Staff Relations Board), [1985] S.C.J. No. 71, [1985] 2 S.C.R. 455 (S.C.C.) HCL-45, HCL-47

Friends of the Oldman River Society v. Canada (Minister of Transport), [1992] S.C.J. No. 1, [1992] 1 S.C.R. 3 (S.C.C.).. HCL-200, HCL-201, HCL-203

Para.

Fulton v. Alberta (Energy Resources Conservation Board), [1981] S.C.J. No. 16, [1981] 1 S.C.R. 153 (S.C.C.).. HCL-183, HCL-214

Gagliano v. Canada, [2005] F.C.J. No. 683, 253 D.L.R. (4th) 701 (F.C.)...... HCL-50, HCL-51

General Motors of Canada Ltd. v. City National Leasing Ltd., [1989] S.C.J. No. 28, [1989] 1 S.C.R. 641 (S.C.C.). HCL-97, HCL-98, HCL-135, HCL-153

Global Securities Corp. v. British Columbia (Securities Commission), [2000] S.C.J. No. 5, [2000] 1 S.C.R. 494 (S.C.C.)................................. HCL-88, HCL-89, HCL-90, HCL-92, HCL-97

Goodis v. Ontario (Ministry of Correctional Services), [2006] S.C.J. No. 31, [2006] 2 S.C.R. 32 (S.C.C.).. HCL-48

Halifax (City) v. Fairbanks Estate, [1927] J.C.J. No. 1, [1928] A.C. 117 (P.C.).. HCL-146

Halifax (City) v. Halifax Harbour Commissioners, [1934] S.C.J. No. 70, [1935] S.C.R. 215 (S.C.C.) HCL-139

Hunt v. T&N plc, [1993] S.C.J. No. 125, [1993] 4 S.C.R. 289 (S.C.C.). HCL-28, HCL-58

Husky Oil Operations Ltd. v. Canada (Minister of National Revenue), [1995] S.C.J. No. 77, [1995] 3 S.C.R. 453 (S.C.C.).. HCL-168, HCL-169, HCL-170

Idziak v. Canada (Minister of Justice), [1992] S.C.J. No. 97, [1992] 3 S.C.R. 631 (S.C.C.).. HCL-67

Income Tax Act, 1932 and Proctor and Gamble Co. (Re), [1937] S.C.J. No. 70, [1938] 2 D.L.R. 597 (Sask. K.B.). HCL-144

International Harvester Co. of Canada v. Saskatchewan (Provincial Tax Commission), [1948] J.C.J. No. 2, [1949] A.C. 36 (P.C.)..................................... HCL-144

International Woodworkers of America, Local 2-69 v. Consolidated-Bathurst Packaging Ltd., [1990] S.C.J. No. 20, [1990] 1 S.C.R. 282 (S.C.C.)....................... HCL-63

Interprovincial Co-operatives Ltd. v. Dryden Chemicals Ltd., [1975] S.C.J. No. 42, [1976] 1 S.C.R. 477 (S.C.C.). HCL-201

J.R. Théberge Ltée v. R., [1970] Ex. C.R. 649 (Ex. Ct.) HCL-8

Johannesson v. West St. Paul (Rural Mun.), [1951] S.C.J. No. 50, [1952] 1 S.C.R 292 (S.C.C.). HCL-108, HCL-184

John Deere Plow Co. v. Wharton, [1915] A.C. 330 (P.C.).. HCL-129

Jones v. New Brunswick (A.G.), [1974] S.C.J. No. 91, [1975] 2 S.C.R. 182 (S.C.C.). HCL-108

Jorgenson v. Canada (Attorney General), [1971] S.C.J. No. 64, [1971] S.C.R. 725 (S.C.C.). HCL-176

Jorgenson v. North Vancouver Magistrates and North Vancouver (City), [1959] B.C.J. No. 80, 28 W.W.R. 265 (B.C.C.A.).. HCL-184

Para.

Katz v. Vancouver Stock Exchange, [1996] S.C.J. No. 95, [1996] 3 S.C.R. 405 (S.C.C.) HCL-63

Kerr v. Alberta (Superintendent of Income Tax), [1942] S.C.J. No. 36, [1942] S.C.R. 435 (S.C.C.) HCL-144, HCL-148

Khadr v. Canada (Attorney General), [2006] F.C.J. No. 888, [2007] 2 F.C.R. 218 (F.C.) HCL-10, HCL-11

Khadr v. Canada (Prime Minister), [2009] F.C.J. No. 462, [2010] 1 F.C.R. 34 (F.C.) HCL-10

Kirkbi AG v. Ritvik Holdings Inc., [2005] S.C.J. No. 66, [2005] 3 S.C.R. 302 (S.C.C.). HCL-98, HCL-130, HCL-134, HCL-135

Kitkala Band v. British Columbia (Minister of Small Business, Tourism and Culture), [2002] S.C.J. No. 33, [2002] 2 S.C.R. 146 (S.C.C.) HCL-88, HCL-89, HCL-90, HCL-91, HCL-98

Klein v. Bell, [1955] S.C.J. No. 19, [1955] S.C.R. 309 (S.C.C.) HCL-121

L'Union St-Jacques de Montréal v. Belisle (1874), L.R. 6 P.C. 31 .... HCL-192

Labatt Brewing Co. v. Canada, [1979] S.C.J. No. 134, [1980] 1 S.C.R. 914 (S.C.C.). HCL-132

Labour Relations Board of Saskatchewan v. John East Iron Works, Ltd., [1949] A.C. 134 (P.C.) HCL-74, HCL-76, HCL-79

Lalonde v. Ontario (Commission de restructuration des services de santé), [2001] O.J. No. 4767, 56 O.R. (3d) 505 (Ont. C.A.). HCL-28, HCL-42

Lambe v. Manuel, [1902] J.C.J. No. 1, [1903] A.C. 68 (P.C.) HCL-144

Larue v. Royal Bank of Canada, [1928] J.C.J. No. 1, [1928] A.C. 187 (P.C.), affg [1269] S.C.J. No. 4 [1926] S.C.R. 218 (S.C.C.). ....

Lavallee, Rackel & Heintz v. Canada (Attorney General); White, Ottenheimer & Baker v. Canada (Attorney General); R. v. Fink, [2002] S.C.J. No. 61, [2002] 3 S.C.R. 209 (S.C.C.). HCL-28, HCL-48

Law Society of British Columbia v. Mangat, [2001] S.C.J. No. 66, [2001] 3 S.C.R. 113 (S.C.C.). HCL-99, HCL-100

Lawson v. Interior Tree Fruit and Vegetables Committee of Direction, [1931] S.C.J. No. 84, [1931] S.C.R. 357 (S.C.C.) HCL-157

Letter Carriers' Union of Canada v. Canadian Union of Postal Workers, [1973] S.C.J. No. 140, [1975] 1 S.C.R. 178 (S.C.C.). HCL-175, HCL-185

Local Prohibition case (Attorney-General for Ontario v. Attorney-General for the Dominion), [1896] A.C. 348 (H.L.). HCL-109

Lovelace v. Ontario, [2000] S.C.J. No. 36, [2000] 1 S.C.R. 950 (S.C.C.). HCL-162

Luscar Collieries Ltd. v. McDonald, [1927] J.C.J. No. 4, [1927] A.C. 925 (P.C.). HCL-175, HCL-183

Para.

Lymburn v. Mayland, [1932] A.C. 318 (P.C.) HCL-97

M & D Farm Ltd. v. Manitoba Agricultural Credit Corp., [1999] S.C.J. No. 4, [1999] 2 S.C.R. 961 (S.C.C.). HCL-99

MacDonald v. Vapor Canada, [1976] S.C.J. No. 60, [1977] 2 S.C.R. 134 (S.C.C.) HCL-106

Mackin v. New Brunswick (Minister of Finance); Rice v. New Brunswick, [2002] S.C.J. No. 13, [2002] 1 S.C.R. 405 (S.C.C.) .... HCL-28, HCL-41, HCL-62, HCL-64, HCL-65 , HCL-66

MacMillan Bloedel Ltd. v. Simpson, [1995] S.C.J. No. 101, [1995] 4 S.C.R. 725 (S.C.C.). HCL-60, HCL-61, HCL-79

Manitoba (Attorney General) v. Burns Foods Ltd., [1973] S.C.J. No. 51, [1975] 1 S.C.R. 494 (S.C.C.). HCL-133

Manitoba (Attorney General) v. Manitoba Egg and Poultry Association, [1971] S.C.J. No. 63, [1971] S.C.R. 689 (S.C.C.) HCL-133, HCL-196

Manitoba (Treasurer) v. Bennett Estate, [1937] S.C.J. No. 5, [1937] S.C.R. 138 (S.C.C.) HCL-144

Manitoba v. Air Canada, [1980] S.C.J. No. 69, [1980] 2 S.C.R. 303 (S.C.C.) HCL-144

Massey-Ferguson Industries Ltd. v. Government of Saskatchewan, [1981] S.C.J. No. 90, [1981] 2 S.C.R. 413 (S.C.C.) HCL-76

McEvoy v. New Brunswick (Attorney General), [1983] S.C.J. No. 51, [1983] 1 S.C.R. 704 (S.C.C.). HCL-79, HCL-120

Merchants' Bank of Canada v. Smith, [1884] S.C.J. No. 1, 8 S.C.R. 512 (S.C.C.) HCL-163

MiningWatch Canada v. Canada (Fisheries and Oceans), [2010] S.C.J. No. 2, [2010] 1 S.C.R. 6 (S.C.C.). HCL-203

Mississauga (City) v. Greater Toronto Airports Authority, [2000] O.J. No. 4086, 50 O.R. (3d) 641 (Ont. C.A.). HCL-184

Mississauga (City) v. Peel (Regional Municipality), [1979] S.C.J. No. 46, [1979] 2 S.C.R. 244 (S.C.C.). HCL-79

Molson v. Lambe, [1888] S.C.J. No. 13, 15 S.C.R. 253 (S.C.C.) HCL-157

Montreal (City) v. Canada (Attorney General), [1922] J.C.J. No. 2, [1923] A.C. 136 (P.C.) HCL-139

Montréal (City) v. Montreal Port Authority, [2010] S.C.J. No. 4, [2010] 1 S.C.R. 427 (S.C.C.). HCL-139

Montreal (City) v. Montreal Street Railway, [1912] J.C.J. No. 1, [1912] A.C. 333 (P.C.) HCL-173, HCL-183

Moore v. Johnson, [1982] S.C.J. No. 113, [1982] 1 S.C.R. 155 at 122 (S.C.C.). HCL-219

Morguard Investments Ltd. v. De Savoye, [1990] S.C.J. No. 135, [1990] 3 S.C.R. 1077 (S.C.C.). HCL-28, HCL-58

Para.

Multiple Access Ltd. v. McCutcheon, [1982] S.C.J. No. 66, [1982] 2 S.C.R. 161 (S.C.C.). HCL-99, HCL-100

National Energy Board (Re), [1987] F.C.J. No. 1060, [1988] 2 F.C. 196 (Fed. C.A.) HCL-173, HCL-175, HCL-183

New Brunswick (Electric Power Commission) v. Maritime Electric Co., [1985] S.C.J. No. 93, [1985] 2 F.C. 13 (Fed. C.A.), leave to appeal refused [1985] S.C.C.A. No. 314, [1985] S.CR. ix (S.C.C.). HCL-82

New Brunswick Broadcasting Co. v. Nova Scotia (Speaker of the House of Assembly), [1993] S.C.J. No. 2. [1993] 1 S.C.R. 319 (S.C.C.) HCL-2, HCL-13, HCL-25, HCL-28, HCL-47, HCL-49, HCL-51, HCL-52, HCL-53, HCL-57

Newfoundland and Labrador (Workplace Health, Safety and Compensation Commission) v. Ryan Estate, [2011] N.J. No. 207, 2011 NLCA 42 (Nfld. C.A.) HCL-102, HCL-103, HCL-182

Newfoundland Telephone Co. v. Newfoundland (Board of Commissioners of Public Utilities), [1992] S.C.J. No. 21, [1992] 1 S.C.R. 623 (S.C.C.) HCL-67

Nickel Rim Mines Ltd. v. Attorney-General for Ontario, [1965] O.J. No. 1177, [1966] 1 O.R. 345 (Ont. C.A.), affd [1967] S.C.J. No. 17, [1967] S.C.R. 270 (S.C.C.). HCL-148

Northern Telecom Ltd. v. Communications Workers of Canada, [1979] S.C.J. No. 98, [1980] 1 S.C.R. 115 (S.C.C.). HCL-186

Nova Scotia (Board of Censors) v. McNeil, [1978] S.C.J. No. 25, [1978] 2 S.C.R. 622 (S.C.C.) HCL-87, HCL-106, HCL-192, HCL-197, HCL-181, HCL-191, HCL-199

O.P.S.E.U. v. Ontario (Attorney General), [1987] S.C.J. No. 48, [1987] 2 S.C.R. 2 at 57 (S.C.C.) HCL-25, HCL-27, HCL-28, HCL-37, HCL-45

O'Brien v. Allen, [1900] S.C.J. No. 22, 30 S.C.R. 340 (S.C.C.). HCL-183

O'Grady v. Sparling, [1960] S.C.J. No. 48, [1960] S.C.R. 804 (S.C.C.) HCL-96, HCL-198

O'Hara v. B.C., [1987] S.C.J. No. 69, [1987] 2 S.C.R. 591 (S.C.C.). HCL-122

Ocean Port Hotel Ltd. v. British Columbia (General Manager, Liquor Control and Licensing Branch), [2001] S.C.J. No. 17, [2001] 2 S.C.R. 781 (S.C.C.). HCL-63

Ontario v. Canada (Board of Transport Commissioners), [1967] S.C.J. No. 82, [1968] S.C.R. 118 (S.C.C.) HCL-183

Ontario v. Williams Estate, [1942] J.C.J. No. 3, [1942] A.C. 541 (P.C.). HCL-147

Ontario (Attorney General) v. Canada (Attorney General), [1912] A.C. 571 (P.C.) HCL-28, HCL-29

Ontario (Attorney General) v. Canada Temperance Federation, [1946] A.C. 193 (H.L.) HCL-109

Ontario (Attorney General) v. Pembina Exploration Canada Ltd., [1989] S.C.J. No. 9, [1989] 1 S.C.R. 206 (S.C.C.). HCL-59

Para.

Ontario (Attorney General) v. Policy Holders of Wentworth Ins. Co., [1969] S.C.J. No. 49, [1969] S.C.R. 779 (S.C.C.) HCL-168

Ontario (Attorney General) v. Winner, [1954] J.C.J. No. 1, [1954] A.C. 541 (P.C.) HCL-174, HCL-183

Ontario (Attorney General) v. Woodruff, [1908] J.C.J. No. 4, [1908] A.C. 508 (P.C.) HCL-144

Ontario (Attorney-General) v. Reciprocal Insurers, [1924] J.C.J. No. 1, [1924] A.C. 328 (P.C.) HCL-157

Ontario English Catholic Teachers' Assn. v. Ontario (Attorney General), [2001] S.C.J. No. 14, [2001] 1 S.C.R. 470 (S.C.C.) HCL-46, HCL-28, HCL-141

Ontario Home Builders' Association v. York Region Board of Education, [1996] S.C.J. No. 80, [1996] 2 S.C.R. 929 (S.C.C.) HCL-141, HCL-142, HCL-146, HCL-150, HCL-153, HCL-154

Ontario Hydro v. Ontario (Labour Relations Board), [1993] S.C.J. No. 99, [1993] 3 S.C.R. 327 (S.C.C.) HCL-159, HCL-176, HCL-185, HCL-207, HCL-212

Ontario Liquor License Case (Re), [1896] J.C.J. No. 1, [1896] A.C. 348 (P.C.) HCL-191, HCL-193

Operation Dismantle Inc. v. Canada, [1983] F.C.J. No. 1095, [1983] 1 F.C. 745 (F.C.A.), affd [1985] S.C.J. No. 22, [1985] 1 S.C.R. 441 (S.C.C.) HCL-10, HCL-12, HCL-34

Ordon Estate v. Grail, [1988] S.C.J. No. 84, [1998] 3 S.C.R. 437 (S.C.C.) HCL-82, HCL-105, HCL-182

Osborne v. Canada (Treasury Board), [1991] S.C.J. No. 45, [1991] 2 S.C.R. 69 (S.C.C.) HCL-28, HCL-45

Ottawa-Carleton Regional Transit Commission and Amalgamated Transit Union, Local 279 (Re), [1983] O.J. No. 3281, 44 O.R. (2d) 560 (Ont. C.A.) HCL-174, HCL-183

Paul v. British Columbia, [2003] S.C.J. No. 34, [2003] 2 S.C.R. 585 (S.C.C.) HCL-215

Peel (Regional Municipalit)y v. MacKenzie, [1982] S.C.J. No. 58, [1982] 2 S.C.R. 9 (S.C.C.) HCL-106

Phillips v. Sault St. Marie (City), [1954] S.C.J. No. 27, [1954] S.C.R. 404 (S.C.C.) HCL-139

Pigeon v. Recorder's Court, [1890] S.C.J. No. 19, 17 S.C.R. 495 (S.C.C.) HCL-157

Port Enterprises Ltd. v. Newfoundland (Minister of Fisheries and Aquaculture), [2006] N.J. No. 171, 269 D.L.R. (4th) 613 (N.L.C.A.), leave to appeal to S.C.C. refused [2006] S.C.C.N. No. 357 (S.C.C.) HCL-220

Prince Edward Island (Secretary) v. Egan, [1941] S.C.J. No. 20, [1941] S.C.R. 396 (S.C.C.) HCL-183, HCL-192, HCL-198

Proprietary Articles Trade Association v. Canada (Attorney General), [1931] J.C.J. No. 1, [1931] A.C. 310 (P.C.) HCL-136

Para.

Provincial Court Judges' Assn. of New Brunswick v. New Brunswick (Minister of Justice); Ontario Judges' Assn. v. Ontario (Management Board); Bodner v. Alberta; Conférence des juges du Québec v. Quebec (Attorney General); Minc v. Quebec (Attorney General), [2005] S.C.J. No. 47, [2005] 2 S.C.R. 286 (S.C.C.), reconsideration denied [2005] S.C.J. No. 60, [2005] 3 S.C.R. 41 (S.C.C.) HCL-28, HCL-41 HCL-62

Provincial Treasurer of Alberta v. Kerr, [1933] A.C. 710 (P.C.) HCL-144

Quebec (Attorney General) v. Canada (Attorney General), [1978] S.C.J. No. 84, [1979] 1 S.C.R. 218 (S.C.C.) HCL-122

Québec (Attorney General) v. Canada, [2011] S.C.J. No. 11, 412 N.R. 115 (S.C.C.). HCL-115

Quebec (Attorney General) v. Canadian Owners and Pilots Assn., [2010] S.C.J. No. 39, [2010] 2 S.C.R. 536 (S.C.C.). HCL-99, HCL-103, HCL-184

Quebec (Attorney General) v. Lacombe, [2010] S.C.J. No. 38, [2010] 2 S.C.R. 453 (S.C.C.) HCL-89 HCL-97 HCL-184

Québec (Commission du Salaire Minimum) v. Bell Telephone Co. of Canada, [1966] S.C.J. No. 51, [1966] S.C.R. 767 (S.C.C.) HCL-102 HCL-153

Quebec (Minimum Wage Commission) v. Construction Montcalm Inc., [1978] S.C.J. No. 110, [1979] 1 S.C.R. 754 (S.C.C.) HCL-185

Quebec (Public Service Board) v. Canada (Attorney General), [1977] S.C.J. No. 120, [1978] 2 S.C.R. 191 (S.C.C.). HCL-180

Quebec Fisheries (Re), [1920] J.C.J. No. 4, [1921] 1 A.C. 413 (P.C.). HCL-218

Quebec Railway, Light and Power Co. v. Beauport, [1944] S.C.J. No. 47, [1945] S.C.R. 16 (S.C.C.). HCL-176

R. v. Bain, [1992] S.C.J. No. 3, [1992] 1 S.C.R. 91 (S.C.C.) HCL-67

R. v. Boggs, [1981] S.C.J. No. 6., [1981] 1 S.C.R. 49 (S.C.C.). HCL-113

R. v. Boucher, [1950] S.C.J. No. 41, [1951] S.C.R. 265 (S.C.C.). HCL-28

R. v. Breault, [2001] N.B.J. No. 64, 198 D.L.R. (4th) 669 (N.B.C.A.). HCL-220

R. v. Campbell, [1999] S.C.J. No. 16, [1999] 1 S.C.R. 565 (S.C.C.). HCL-33, HCL-48

R. v. Chamney, [1973] S.C.J. No. 154, [1975] 2 S.C.R. 151 (S.C.C.). HCL-176

R. v. Crown Zellerbach Canada Ltd., [1988] S.C.J. No. 23, [1988] 1 S.C.R. 401 (S.C.C.). HCL-109, HCL-202

R. v. Dick, [1985] S.C.J. No. 62, [1985] 2 S.C.R. 309 (S.C.C.) HCL-105

R. v. Dominion Stores Ltd., [1979] S.C.J. No. 131, [1980] 1 S.C.R. 844 (S.C.C.). HCL-131

R. v. Dunba, [1982] S.C.J. No. 581, 68 C.C.C. (2d) 13 at 43-45 (Ont. C.A.) HCL-48

R. v. Fowler, [1980] S.C.J. No. 58, [1980] 2 S.C.R. 213 (S.C.C.) HCL-216, HCL-219

R. v. Généreux, [1992] S.C.J. No. 10, [1992] 1 S.C.R. 259 (S.C.C.) HCL-63, HCL-64, HCL-70

Para.

R. v. Goodyear Tire and Rubber Co., [1956] S.C.J. No. 8, [1956] S.C.R. 303 (S.C.C.) HCL-127

R. v. Gruenke, [1991] S.C.J. No. 80, [1991] 3 S.C.R. 263 (S.C.C.) HCL-48

R. v. Hauser, [1979] S.C.J. No. 18, [1979] 1 S.C.R. 984 (S.C.C.) HCL-108, HCL-118, HCL-123

R. v. Hydro Québec, [1997] S.C.J. No. 76, [1997] 3 S.C.R. 213 (S.C.C.). HCL-88, HCL-89, HCL-116, HCL-203, HCL-204

R. v. Lippé, [1991] S.C.J. No. 128, [1991] 2 S.C.R. 114 (S.C.C.). HCL-63

R. v. Malmo-Levine, [2003] S.C.J. No. 79, [2003] 3 S.C.R. 571 (S.C.C.) HCL-111, HCL-113, HCL-114, HCL-118

R. v. Mercure, [1988] S.C.J. No. 11, [1988] 1 S.C.R. 234 (S.C.C.) HCL-28, HCL-29, HCL-36

R. v. Morgentaler, [1993] S.C.J. No. 95, [1993] 3 S.C.R. 463 (S.C.C.) HCL-88, HCL-89, HCL-90, HCL-91, HCL-92, HCL-125 HCL-153, HCL-197

R. v. National Post, [2010] S.C.J. No. 16, [2010] 1 S.C.R. 477 (S.C.C.). HCL-48

R. v. Nichol, [2007] N.J. No. 357, 270 Nfld. & P.E.I.R. 74 (Nfld. C.A.) HCL-219

R. v. Northwest Falling Contractors Ltd., [1980] S.C.J. No. 68, [1980] 2 S.C.R. 292 (S.C.C.). HCL-217, HCL-219

R. v. Power, [1994] S.C.J. No. 29, [1994] 1 S.C.R. 601 (S.C.C.). HCL-47

R. v. Seaboyer; R. v. Gayme, [1991] S.C.J. No. 62, [1991] 2 S.C.R. 577 (S.C.C.) HCL-48

R. v. Smith, [1960] S.C.J. No. 47, [1960] S.C.R. 776 (S.C.C.). HCL-96, HCL-100

R. v. St. Jean, [1986] Y.J. No. 76, 2 Y.R. 116 (Y.T.S.C.). HCL-136

R. v. Valente, [1985] S.C.J. No. 77, [1985] 2 S.C.R. 673 (S.C.C.) HCL-28, HCL-41, HCL-62, HCL-65, HCL-66, HCL-67, HCL-68, HCL-69

R. v. Westendorp, [1983] S.C.J. No. 6, [1983] 1 S.C.R. 43 (S.C.C.) HCL-125, HCL-197, HCL-199

R. v. Wetmore (County Court Judge), [1983] S.C.J. No. 74, [1983] 2 S.C.R. 284 (S.C.C.). HCL-115, HCL-118, HCL-123

R. v. Zelensky, [1978] S.C.J. No. 48, [1978] 2 S.C.R. 940 (S.C.C.). HCL-124, HCL-189

R.J.R. MacDonald v. Canada (Attorney General), [1995] S.C.J. No. 18, [1995] 3 S.C.R. 199 (S.C.C.) HCL-115, HCL-117

R.W.D.S.U. v. Dolphin Delivery Ltd., [1986] S.C.J. No. 75, [1986] 2 S.C.R. 573 (S.C.C.) HCL-28

Rattenbury v. British Columbia (Land Settlement Board), [1928] S.C.J. No. 77, [1929] S.C.R. 52 (S.C.C.) HCL-146

Para.

Ref. re Amendment of Constitution of Canada, [1981] S.C.J. No. 58, [1981] 1 S.C.R. 753 (S.C.C.) HCL-25, HCL-28, HCL-37, HCL-38

Reference re Amendments to the Residential Tenancies Act (N.S.), [1996] S.C.J. No. 13, [1996] 1 S.C.R. 186 (S.C.C.) HCL-60, HCL-61, HCL-76, HCL-77

Reference re Assisted Human Reproduction Act, [2010] S.C.J. No. 61, [2010] 3 S.C.R. 457, 2010 SCC 61 (S.C.C.) HCL-115

Reference re Canada Assistance Plan (B.C.), [1991] S.C.J. No. 60, [1991] 2 S.C.R. 525 (S.C.C.) HCL-28, HCL-29, HCL-31, HCL-162

Reference re Family Relations Act (B.C.), [1982] S.C.J. No. 112, [1982] 1 S.C.R. 62 (S.C.C.) HCL-76, HCL-77

Reference re Quebec Sales Tax, [1994] S.C.J. No. 56, [1994] 2 S.C.R. 715 (S.C.C.) HCL-142, HCL-143

Reference re Remuneration of Judges of the Provincial Court of Prince Edward Island; Reference re Independence and Impartiality of Judges of the Provincial Court of Prince Edward Island, [1997] S.C.J. No. 75, [1997] 3 S.C.R. 3 (S.C.C.) HCL-26, HCL-28, HCL-31, HCL-33, HCL-37, HCL-41, HCL-47, HCL-62, HCL-67, HCL-68, HCL-69

Reference re Secession of Quebec, [1998] S.C.J. No. 61, [1998] 2 S.C.R. 217 (S.C.C.). HCL-1, HCL-24, HCL-26, HCL-27, HCL-28, HCL-33, HCL-37, HCL-38, HCL-39, HCL-40, HCL-43, HCL-44, HCL-47

Reference re: Adoption Act, [1938] S.C.J. No. 21, [1938] S.C.R. 398 (S.C.C.) HCL-73, HCL-74, HCL-76, HCL-77

Reference re: Agricultural Products Marketing Act, 1970 (Canada), [1978] S.C.J. No. 58, [1978] 2 S.C.R. 1198 (S.C.C.) HCL-106, HCL-137, HCL-140, HCL-153, HCL-196

Reference re: Alberta Legislation, [1938] S.C.J. No. 2, [1938] S.C.R. 100 (S.C.C.). HCL-28, HCL-163

Reference re: Anti Inflation Act, [1976] S.C.J. No. 12, [1976] 2 S.C.R. 373 (S.C.C.). HCL-110, HCL-185

Reference re: British North America Act, 1867, s. 108 (Can.), [1898] J.C.J. No. 1, [1898] A.C. 700 (P.C.) HCL-218, HCL-136

Reference re: Dairy Industry Act (Canada) s. 5(a), [1948] S.C.J. No. 42, [1949] S.C.R. 1 (S.C.C.). HCL-92, HCL-113

Reference re: Employment and Social Insurance Act, [1936] S.C.J. No. 30, [1936] S.C.R. 427 (S.C.C.). HCL-144, HCL-161

Reference re: Farm Products Marketing Act (Ontario), [1957] S.C.J. No. 11, [1957] S.C.R. 198 (S.C.C.). HCL-132, HCL-150, HCL-157, HCL-191

Para.

Reference re: Firearms Act (Can.), [2000] S.C.J. No. 31, [2000] 1 S.C.R. 783 (S.C.C.). HCL-87, HCL-91, HCL-93, HCL-119

Reference re: Goods and Services Tax, [1992] S.C.J. No. 62, [1992] 2 S.C.R. 445 (S.C.C.). HCL-153

Reference re: Insurance Act, [1931] J.C.J. No. 3, [1932] A.C. 41 (P.C.) HCL-153

Reference re: Legislative Jurisdiction over Hours of Labour, [1925] S.C.J. No. 24, [1925] S.C.R. 505, 510 (S.C.C.) HCL-185

Reference re: Liquor License Act s. 51, ss. 2, [1897] J.C.J. No. 1, [1897] A.C. 231 (P.C.) HCL-142, HCL-143, HCL-148, HCL-157

Reference re: Liquor License Act of 1877 (Ont.), [1883] J.C.J. No. 2, 9 App. Cas. 117 (P.C.) HCL-28 HCL-29, HCL-96, HCL-136, HCL-141, HCL-194

Reference re: Manitoba Language Rights, [1985] S.C.J. No. 36, [1985] 1 S.C.R. 721 (S.C.C.). HCL-33

Reference re: Minimum Wage Act (Sask.), [1948] S.C.J. No. 166, [1948] S.C.R. 248 (S.C.C.) HCL-185

Reference re: Ownership of Off Shore Mineral Rights (British Columbia), [1967] S.C.J. No. 70, [1967] S.C.R. 792 (S.C.C.). HCL-108, HCL-213

Reference re: Ownership of the Bed of the Strait of Georgia and related areas, [1984] S.C.J. No. 21, [1984] 1 S.C.R. 388 (S.C.C.). HCL-213

Reference re: Proposed Federal Tax on exported Natural Gas, [1982] S.C.J. No. 52, [1982] 1 S.C.R. 1004 (S.C.C.). HCL-138, HCL-153, HCL-209

Reference re: Residential Tenancies Act, 1979 (Ontario), [1981] S.C.J. No. 57, [1981] 1 S.C.R. 714 (S.C.C.). HCL-47, HCL-74, HCL-75, HCL-76, HCL-78, HCL-79

Reference re: Seabed and subsoil of the continental shelf offshore Newfoundland, [1984] S.C.J. No. 7, [1984] 1 S.C.R. 86 (S.C.C.). HCL-213

Reference re: Upper Churchill Water Rights Reversion Act 1980, [1984] S.C.J. No. 16, [1984] 1 S.C.R. 297 (S.C.C.) HCL-92, HCL-214

Reference re: Vehicles Act, 1957 (Sask.), s. 92(4), [1958] S.C.J. No. 47, [1958] S.C.R. 608 (S.C.C.) HCL-183

Reference re: Wartime Leasehold Regulations, P.C. 9029, [1950] S.C.J. No. 1, [1950] S.C.R. 124 (S.C.C.). HCL-110

Reference re: Young Offenders Act (P.E.I.), [1990] S.C.J. No. 60, 1991 1 S.C.R. 252. .... HCL-60, HCL-120

Regina Industries Ltd. v. Regina (City), [1947] S.C.J. No. 16, [1947] S.C.R. 345 (S.C.C.) HCL-139

Regulation and Control of Aeronautics in Canada (Re), [1931] J.C.J. No. 4, [1932] A.C. 54 (P.C.). HCL-108, HCL-184

Para.

Regulation and Control of Radio Communication in Canada (Re), [1932] J.C.J. No. 1, [1932] A.C. 304 .... HCL-178

Renvoi re: Juridiction de la Cour de Magistrat (Loi Concernant) (Québec), 55 D.L.R. (2d) 701, [1965] S.C.R. 772 (S.C.C.) HCL-76, HCL-77

Rio Hotel Ltd. v. New Brunswick (Liquor Licensing Board), [1987] S.C.J. No. 46, [1987] 2 S.C.R. 59 (S.C.C.) HCL-96, HCL-192, HCL-199

RJR MacDonald Inc. v. Canada (Attorney General), [1995] S.C.J. No. 68, [1995] 3 S.C.R. 199 (S.C.C.) HCL-47

Roberts v. Canada, [1989] S.C.J. No. 16, [1989] 1 S.C.R. 322 at 331 (S.C.C.) HCL-82

Rogers (Re), [1909] 7 E.L.R. 212 (P.E.I. C.A) HCL-192

Roncarelli v. Duplessis, [1959] S.C.J. No. 1, [1959] S.C.R. 121 (S.C.C.) HCL-33

Ross River Dena Council Band v. Canada, [2002] S.C.J. No. 54, [2002] 2 S.C.R. 816 (S.C.C.) HCL-8, HCL-183, HCL-198

Rothmans, Benson & Hedges Inc. v. Saskatchewan, [2005] S.C.J. No. 1, [2005] 1 S.C.R. 188 (S.C.C.) HCL-99, HCL-100

Ruffo v. Conseil de la magistrature, [1995] S.C.J. No. 100, [1995] 4 S.C.R. 267 (S.C.C.) HCL-67

Russell v. The Queen (1882), 7 App. Cas. 829 (P.C.) HCL-108

Samson Indian Nation and Band v. Canada, [2004] F.C.J. No. 1238, [2004] 1 F.C.R. 556 (F.C.) HCL-53

Saskatchewan Power Corp. v. TransCanada Pipelines, [1978] S.C.J. No. 87, [1979] 1 S.C.R. 297 (S.C.C.) HCL-183

Saumur v. Quebec (City), [1953] S.C.J. No. 49, [1953] 2 S.C.R. 299 (S.C.C.) HCL-28, HCL-88

Schneider v. British Columbia, [1982] S.C.J. No. 64, [1982] 2 S.C.R. 112 (S.C.C.) HCL-118, HCL-193, HCL-115

Scowby v. Glendinning, [1986] S.C.J. No. 57, [1986] 2 S.C.R. 226 (S.C.C.) HCL-111

Segal v. Montreal (City), [1931] S.C.J. No. 19, [1931] S.C.R. 460 (S.C.C.) HCL-157

Séminaire de Chicoutimi v. Quebec (Attorney General), [1972] S.C.J. No. 99, [1973] S.C.R. 681 (S.C.C.) HCL-77

Shannon v. Lower Mainland Dairy Products Board, [1938] A.C. 708 (P.C.) HCL-15, HCL-150, HCL-157, HCL-196

Siemens v. Manitoba (Attorney General), [2002] S.C.J. No. 69, [2003] 1 S.C.R. 6 (S.C.C.) HCL-87, HCL-192

Simpsons-Sears Ltd. v. New Brunswick (Secretary), [1978] S.C.J. No. 44, [1978] 2 S.C.R. 869 (S.C.C.) HCL-142

Slaight Communications Inc. v. Davidson, [1989] S.C.J. No. 45, [1989] 1 S.C.R. (S.C.C.) HCL-34, HCL-35

Para.

Smith v. Canada (Attorney General), [2009] F.C.J. No. 234, [2010] 1 F.C.R. 3 (F.C.), supp. reasons [2009] F.C.J. No. 522, 348 F.T.R. 290 (F.C.)....... HCL-10, HCL-11

Smith v. Jones, [1999] S.C.J. No. 15, [1999] 1 S.C.R. 455 (S.C.C.)............................. HCL-48

Smith v. Vermillion Hills (Rural Council), [1916] 2 A.C. 569 (P.C.).......................... HCL-139

Solosky v. The Queen, [1979] S.C.J. No. 130, [1980] 1 S.C.R. 821 (S.C.C.)............... HCL-48

Southern Alberta Land Co. v. McLean (Rural Municipality), [1916] S.C.J. No. 20, 53 S.C.R. 151 (S.C.C.)... HCL-139

Spooner Oils Ltd. v. Turner Valley Gas Conservation, [1933] S.C.J. No. 54, [1933] S.C.R. 629 (S.C.C.)... HCL-206

Switzman v. Elbling, [1957] S.C.J. No. 13, [1957] S.C.R. 285 (S.C.C.)....................... HCL-28

Téléphone Guèvremont Inc. v. Quebec (Régie des télécommunications), [1994] S.C.J. No. 31, [1994] 1 S.C.R. 878 (S.C.C.)... HCL-179

Telezone Inc. v. Canada (Attorney General), [2004] O.J. No. 5, 69 O.R. (3d) 161 (Ont. C.A.)... HCL-53

Tennant v. Union Bank of Canada, [1893] J.C.J. No. 1, [1894] A.C. 31 (P.C.).......... HCL-163

Tétrault-Gadoury v. Canada (Employment & Immigration Commission), [1991] S.C.J. No. 41, [1991] 2 S.C.R. 22 (S.C.C.).. HCL-83

Texada Mines Ltd. v. British Columbia (Attorney General), [1960] S.C.J. No. 43, [1960] S.C.R. 713 (S.C.C.).. HCL-146, HCL-153

The King v. Lovitt, [1911] J.C.J. No. 2, [1912] A.C. 212 (P.C.)................................ HCL-144

Theodore v. Duncan, [1919] A.C. 696 (Aus. P.C.)... HCL-8

Tomell Investments Ltd. v. East Marstock Lands Ltd., [1977] S.C.J. No. 91, [1978] 1 S.C.R. 974 (S.C.C.).. HCL-171

Tomko v. Nova Scotia (Labour Relations Board), [1975] S.C.J. No. 111, [1977] 1 S.C.R. 112 (S.C.C.)... HCL-74, HCL-79

Toronto (City) v. Bell Telephone Co. of Canada, [1904] J.C.J. No. 2, [1905] A.C. 52 .... HCL-174, HCL-179

Toronto Electric Commissioners v. Snider, [1925] A.C. 396 (P.C.).......... HCL-110, HCL-131

TransCanada Pipelines Ltd. v. Ontario (Ministry of Community Safety and Correctional Services), [2007] O.J. No. 3014 (Ont. S.C.J.)................................. HCL-183

Union Colliery Co. v. Bryden, [1899] A.C. 580 (P.C.).. HCL-95

Union des employés de service, local 298 v. Bibeault, [1988] S.C.J. No. 101, [1988] 2 S.C.R. 1048 (S.C.C.)... HCL-71

United Transportation Union v. Central Western Railway Corp., [1990] S.C.J. No. 136, [1990] 3 S.C.R. 1112 (S.C.C.)... HCL-173, HCL-175, HCL-183

Vadeboncoeur v. Three Rivers (City), [1885] S.C.J. No. 6, 11 S.C.R. 25 (S.C.C.).. HCL-157

Valente v. The Queen, [1985] S.C.J. No. 77, [1985] 2 S.C.R. 673 (S.C.C.)................ HCL-41

Para.

Valin v. Langlois, [1879] S.C.J. No. 2, 3. S.C.R. 1 (S.C.C.) HCL-59

Vancouver Island Peace Society v. Canada, [1993] F.C.J. No. 601, [1994] 1 F.C. 102 (F.C.T.D.), affd [1995] F.C.J. No. 70, 179 N.R. 106 (F.C.A.) HCL-10

Villeneuve v. Northwest Territories (Legislative Assembly), [2008] N.W.T.J. No. 40, [2008] 10 W.W.R. 704 (N.W.T.S.C.) HCL-49, HCL-54

Vriend v. Alberta, [1988] S.C.J. No. 29, [1998] 1 S.C.R. 493 (S.C.C.) HCL-1, HCL-28, HCL-42, HCL-44

Ward v. Canada (Attorney General), [2002] S.C.J. No. 21, [2002] 1 S.C.R. 569 (S.C.C.) HCL-93, HCL-219, HCL-220

Westbank First Nation v. British Columbia Hydro and Power Authority, [1999] S.C.J. No. 38, [1999] 3 S.C.R. 134 (S.C.C.) HCL-137, HCL-138, HCL-139, HCL-139, HCL-140, HCL-150, HCL-151, HCL-153, HCL-154, HCL-156

Westcoast Energy v. Canada (National Energy Board), [1998] S.C.J. No. 27, [1998] 1 S.C.R. 322 (S.C.C.) HCL-159, HCL-175

Whitbread v. Walley, [1990] S.C.J. No. 138, [1990] 3 S.C.R. 1273 (S.C.C.) HCL-182

Winnipeg (City) v. Canadian Pacific Railway Co., [2003] M.J. No. 303, [2003] 11 W.W.R. 729 (Man. Prov. Ct.) HCL-183

Workmen's Compensation Board v. Canadian Pacific Railway Co., [1920] A.C. 184 (P.C.) HCL-97

Yeomans v. Sobeys Stores Ltd., [1989] S.C.J. No. 113, [1989] 1 S.C.R. 238 (S.C.C.) HCL-61, HCL-77

YMHA Jewish Community Centre of Winnipeg Inc. v. Brown, [1989] S.C.J. No. 57, [1989] 1 S.C.R. 1532 (S.C.C.) HCL-161, HCL-185

Zinck's Bus Co. v. Canada, [1998] F.C.J. No. 1093, 152 F.T.R. 279 (F.C.) HCL-183

Table of Statutes — Condominiums

Para.

B

Business Corporations Act, R.S.A. 2000, c. B-9, s. 242 .... HCD-110

Business Corporations Act, S.B.C. 2002, c. 57, s. 227 .... HCD-110

C

Canada Business Corporations Act, R.S.C. 1985, c. C-44, s. 241 .... HCD-110

Civil Code of Québec, S.Q. 1991, c. 64.. HCD-36
arts. 1038-1040............................ HCD-14
art. 1039 ....HCD-14, HCD-29
arts. 1041, 1052, 1053, 1055 .... HCD-17
art. 1042 .... HCD-10
arts. 1043, 1047 .... HCD-9
arts. 1043-1045............................... HCD-9
art. 1046 .... HCD-10
art. 1047 .... HCD-9
art. 1050 .... HCD-30
arts. 1054, 1084 .... HCD-24
arts. 1056, 1058 .... HCD-20
arts. 1059-1062............................. HCD-14
art. 1066 .... HCD-31
arts. 1068, 1096-1100................... HCD-23
art. 1070 .... HCD-36
art. 1076 ....HCD-29, HCD-64
art. 1077 .... HCD-32
art. 1078 .... HCD-32
art. 1081 .... HCD-32
art. 1084 ....HCD-41, HCD-45
art. 1085 .... HCD-40
art. 1086 .... HCD-41
art. 1087 .... HCD-62
art. 1088 .... HCD-62
art. 1089 .... HCD-62
art. 1090-1093 .... HCD-64
art. 1094 .... HCD-66
art. 1095 .... HCD-67
art. 1096 and 1097......................... HCD-68
arts. 1098, 1099, 1101, 1102 .... HCD-68
art. 1108 .... HCD-120
art. 1109 .... HCD-124

Condominium Act 1998, S.O. 1998, c. 19.. HCD-53
ss. 1, 94(1)-(7).............................. HCD-81

Para.

s. 1(1).................HCD-6, HCD-9, HCD-10, HCD-11, HCD-13
ss. 1(1), 6(1)....................... HCD-6, HCD-8
ss. 1(1), 8 .... HCD-14
ss. 1(1), 11(1)-(2)........................... HCD-10
ss. 1(1), 94(7), 97(7) HCD-69
ss. 1(1), 138(1)-(2)........................... HCD-7
ss. 1(1), 155 .... HCD-7
s. 1(2).. HCD-9
s. 2(1).. HCD-14
ss. 2(1), 164(1)................................ HCD-9
s. 2(3).. HCD-14
s. 3 .... HCD-15
ss. 4(2), 4(3)................................. HCD-58
s. 5(1).. HCD-14
s. 5(2).. HCD-28
s. 5(3).. HCD-14
s. 6(2).. HCD-7
s. 7(1).. HCD-17
s. 7(2).. HCD-17
s. 7(2)(f).. HCD-9
s. 7(3).. HCD-17
s. 7(4).. HCD-20
s. 8(1).. HCD-21
s. 10 .... HCD-9
s. 11(3).. HCD-10
s. 11(4).. HCD-10
s. 11(5).. HCD-10
s. 12(1).. HCD-12
s. 12(2).. HCD-12
s. 13 .... HCD-13
s. 14(1).. HCD-13
s. 14(2).. HCD-13
ss. 15(1)-(2) HCD-30
ss. 15(3)-(4) HCD-30
s. 16(1).. HCD-28
ss. 16(1)-(2) HCD-28
s. 17(1).. HCD-29
s. 17(2).. HCD-29
s. 17(3)...........HCD-29, HCD-59, HCD-86
ss. 17.1, 18(1.1) HCD-29
s. 18(1).. HCD-29
s. 18(2).. HCD-29
s. 19 .... HCD-31
s. 21(1).. HCD-10
ss. 21(1), 56(1)(d), (e), (f), (h), (o), 57, 160........................ HCD-24
ss. 22(5)-(8) HCD-12
ss. 23(1), 23(5)............................. HCD-32
s. 23(2).. HCD-32

Para.

Condominium Act 1998, S.O. 1998, c. 19 — *cont'd*
s. 23(4) HCD-32
s. 23(6) HCD-32
ss. 24, 25 .... HCD-123
s. 26 .... HCD-32
s. 27(1) HCD-40
ss. 27(2)-(3), 42(4) HCD-41
s. 28(1) HCD-41
s. 29(1)(a) HCD-41
s. 29(1)(b) HCD-41
s. 29(1)(c) HCD-41
s. 29(2) HCD-41
s. 30 .... HCD-41
ss. 31(1)-(2) HCD-41
s. 32(1) HCD-42
s. 32(2) HCD-42
ss. 33(1), 51(8) HCD-41
ss. 34(1)-(2) HCD-42
s. 34(4) HCD-42
s. 35(1) HCD-42
ss. 35(2)-(3) HCD-42
s. 35(5) HCD-42
ss. 36(1)-(2) HCD-40
s. 37(1) HCD-43
s. 37(2) HCD-43
s. 37(3) HCD-43
s. 38(1) HCD-45
s. 38(2) HCD-45
s. 39 .... HCD-45
s. 40(1) HCD-44
s. 40(2) HCD-44
ss. 40(3)-(5) HCD-44
s. 40(6) HCD-44
ss. 40(7)-(8) HCD-44
s. 41 .... HCD-44
s. 42(1) HCD-46
s. 42(2) HCD-46
s. 42(3) HCD-46
s. 42(6) HCD-46
s. 43(1) HCD-48, HCD-92
s. 43(3) HCD-48
ss. 43(4), (5), (7) HCD-48, HCD-92
s. 43(6) HCD-48
ss. 43(8)-(9) HCD-92
ss. 43(9)(a)-(b) HCD-92
ss. 43(9)(c)-(d) HCD-92
s. 44(1) HCD-91
ss. 44(2)-(3), (5)-(6), (8)-(9), 153(1)-(2) HCD-91
s. 44(4) HCD-91
s. 45(1) HCD-61

Para.

ss. 45(2), (3) HCD-61
ss. 45(2), (4) HCD-61
ss. 45, 48(4), 51(1), 51(2) HCD-64
s. 46(1) HCD-62
s. 46(2) HCD-62
s. 46(3) HCD-62
s. 46(4) HCD-62
s. 47 .... HCD-31
ss. 47(1), (3), (6), (7), (8), (11), s. 54(11) HCD-62
s. 47(10) HCD-62, HCD-63
s. 48(1) HCD-65
s. 49 .... HCD-66
s. 49(3) HCD-64
s. 50(1) HCD-62
s. 51(3) HCD-64
ss. 52(1), (3) HCD-67
s. 53 .... HCD-68
s. 55(1) HCD-36
ss. 55(1), 115(9) HCD-36
s. 55(3) HCD-37, HCD-38
s. 55(4) HCD-38
s. 55(6) HCD-37
s. 55(8) HCD-39, HCD-95
ss. 55(9)-(10) HCD-95
s. 55(10) HCD-39
s. 56(1) HCD-24, HCD-25, HCD-45, HCD-70
ss. 56(1)(e), 56(3) HCD-33
s. 56(1)(g) HCD-69, HCD-71
s. 56(2) HCD-45
ss. 56(6)-(7) HCD-24
s. 56(8) HCD-24
ss. 56(9)-(10) HCD-25
s. 57.5 .... HCD-71
s. 58(1)(a) HCD-26
ss. 58(1)(b), 58(2) HCD-26
s. 58(4) HCD-26
s. 58(5) HCD-26
s. 58(6) HCD-26
s. 58(7) HCD-26
s. 58(10) HCD-26
s. 59(1) HCD-27
s. 59(2) HCD-27
s. 59(3) HCD-27
s. 59(5) HCD-27
s. 59(6) HCD-27
s. 59(7) HCD-27
ss. 59(8)-(9) HCD-27
ss. 69(1), (2) HCD-61
s. 72(1) HCD-49
s. 72(3), (4), (5), (6) HCD-50

Para.

Condominium Act 1998, S.O. 1998, c. 19 — *cont'd*

s. 73(1) ... HCD-87
s. 73(2) ... HCD-87
s. 74(1), (4) ... HCD-52
ss. 74(2), 180(2) ... HCD-52
s. 74(3) ... HCD-52
s. 74(5) ... HCD-87
s. 74(6) ... HCD-87
s. 74(8) ... HCD-87
s. 74(9) ... HCD-87
ss. 74(9)-(10) ... HCD-87
s. 75(1) ... HCD-94
s. 75(2) ... HCD-94
s. 75(3) ... HCD-94
s. 75(4) ... HCD-94
s. 75(5) ... HCD-94
s. 75(6) ... HCD-94
s. 76(1) ... HCD-34
s. 76(2) ... HCD-34
s. 76(3) ... HCD-53
s. 76(4) ... HCD-34, HCD-53
s. 76(5) ... HCD-34, HCD-53
s. 76(6) ... HCD-34, HCD-53, HCD-95
s. 77 ... HCD-35
ss. 78(1), (2) ... HCD-54
s. 78(3) ... HCD-95
s. 79(1) ... HCD-54
s. 79(2) ... HCD-88
s. 79(3) ... HCD-88
s. 79(4) ... HCD-88
s. 79(5) ... HCD-88
s. 80 ... HCD-55
ss. 81(1)-(7) ... HCD-56
s. 82 ... HCD-57
s. 83(1) ... HCD-58
s. 83(2) ... HCD-58
s. 84(1) ... HCD-69
s. 84(3) ... HCD-72
s. 85(1) ... HCD-97
s. 85(2) ... HCD-97
s. 85(3) ... HCD-97
ss. 85(4)-(5) ... HCD-97
s. 85(6) ... HCD-97
s. 85(7) ... HCD-97
s. 86(1) ... HCD-97
s. 86(1)(a) ... HCD-97
ss. 86(1)(b)-(c) ... HCD-97
ss. 86(3)-(4) ... HCD-97
s. 86(5) ... HCD-97
s. 86(6) ... HCD-97
s. 87(1) ... HCD-99

Para.

ss. 87(1)-(4) ... HCD-99
s. 87(6) ... HCD-99
ss. 88(1)(a), (b), (e) ... HCD-100
ss. 88(1)(c)-(d) ... HCD-100
s. 88(2) ... HCD-35, HCD-100
s. 89(1) ... HCD-74
s. 89(2) ... HCD-74
ss. 89(2)-(5) ... HCD-74
ss. 90(1), (2) ... HCD-76
ss. 90(1), 91(b) ... HCD-76
ss. 90(1), 94(8)-(10) ... HCD-81
s. 90(2) ... HCD-73, HCD-75
s. 91 ... HCD-74
s. 91(c) ... HCD-74, HCD-76
ss. 92(1)-(4) ... HCD-78
s. 92(4) ... HCD-71
ss. 93(1)-(2) ... HCD-33
ss. 93(1)-(4), 95(1) ... HCD-81
ss. 93(5)-(7) ... HCD-81
s. 93(7) ... HCD-33
s. 94(4) ... HCD-81
s. 95(2) ... HCD-81
s. 95(3) ... HCD-29, HCD-81
ss. 96(1)-(2) ... HCD-91
ss. 96(1)-(3) ... HCD-82
s. 96(3) ... HCD-91
s. 97(1) ... HCD-73, HCD-75
ss. 97(1)-(6) ... HCD-83
s. 97(7) ... HCD-83
ss. 98(1), (3), (4), (5) ... HCD-84
s. 98(2) ... HCD-84
s. 98(4) ... HCD-71
s. 99 ... HCD-77
s. 105(1) ... HCD-69
ss. 105(2), (3) ... HCD-71
s. 107(2) ... HCD-23
ss. 107(5)-(6) ... HCD-23
s. 107(7) ... HCD-23
s. 108 ... HCD-28
s. 109(1) ... HCD-23
s. 109(2) ... HCD-23
s. 109(3) ... HCD-23
s. 109(4) ... HCD-23
s. 110(1) ... HCD-23
s. 110(2) ... HCD-23
s. 110(3) ... HCD-23
s. 110(4) ... HCD-23
s. 111(1) ... HCD-89
ss. 111(2), 154(2) ... HCD-89
ss. 112(1)-(3) ... HCD-89
s. 112(4) ... HCD-89
s. 112(5) ... HCD-89, HCD-96

Para.

Condominium Act 1998, S.O. 1998, c. 19 — *cont'd*
s. 113 .... HCD-110
ss. 113(1)-(2) HCD-89
s. 113(3) HCD-89
s. 114 .... HCD-89
s. 115(1) HCD-33
s. 115(2) HCD-33
ss. 115(6)-(8) HCD-33
s. 116 .... HCD-101
s. 117 .... HCD-77, HCD-106
s. 118 .... HCD-31
s. 119(1) HCD-59
ss. 119(1), (4)-(5) HCD-86
ss. 119(2) HCD-59
ss. 119(2), (4) HCD-86
s. 119(3) HCD-59
s. 119(4) HCD-59
s. 119(5) HCD-59
s. 120 .... HCD-116
s. 120(3) HCD-62
ss. 121 .... HCD-117
ss. 121(1)(e), 121(3) HCD-41
s. 121(1)(g) HCD-29
ss. 121(1)(g)-(i) HCD-32
s. 122(1) HCD-119
s. 122(2) HCD-119
ss. 123(1)-(10) HCD-120
s. 123(2) HCD-120
ss. 123(2)-(4), (7), (10) HCD-74
ss. 124(1), (2) HCD-121
ss. 124(3) HCD-121
ss. 124(4), (5), 125, 126(2), (3) HCD-124
s. 124(5) HCD-121
s. 125 .... HCD-121
ss. 125(1)-(2) HCD-114
s. 125(4) HCD-114
s. 125(7) HCD-71
ss. 126(1)-(3) HCD-123
ss. 127(1), (2), 42 .... HCD-124
s. 127(2) HCD-124
s. 128 .... HCD-122
s. 129 .... HCD-124
s. 130(1) HCD-107
s. 130(2) HCD-107
s. 130(3) HCD-107
s. 130(4) HCD-107
s. 130(5) HCD-107
ss. 131(1)-(2) HCD-109
s. 131(3) HCD-109
s. 131(4) HCD-109, HCD-114
s. 132(1)(a) HCD-114

Para.

s. 132(1)(b) HCD-114
s. 132(2) HCD-114
s. 132(3) HCD-114
s. 133(2) HCD-90
s. 134 .... HCD-98
s. 134(1) HCD-86, HCD-93
s. 134(2) HCD-86, HCD-114
ss. 134(3)-(4) HCD-86
s. 134(4) HCD-104
s. 134(5) HCD-71, HCD-112
s. 135 .... HCD-110
s. 136 .... HCD-85
s. 137(1) HCD-93, HCD-115
s. 137(2) HCD-93, HCD-115
s. 138(3) HCD-15, HCD-115
s. 139(1) HCD-15
s. 139(2) HCD-15
s. 139(3) HCD-10
ss. 139(3) and (4) HCD-15
s. 139(4) HCD-10
s. 139(5) HCD-97
ss. 139(6)-(7) HCD-97
s. 140 .... HCD-17
s. 141 .... HCD-21
s. 143 .... HCD-50
ss. 144 (1), (2) HCD-80
ss. 145(1)-(2) HCD-7
s. 145(3) HCD-7, HCD-10
ss. 146(3), 146(8)-(9), 149(1) HCD-15
s. 146(4) HCD-17
ss. 146(7), 158(4) HCD-23
s. 147(1), (5) HCD-50
s. 149(2) HCD-96
ss. 149(3)-(4) HCD-96
s. 149(5) HCD-96
s. 150(1) HCD-90
s. 150(2) HCD-90, HCD-96
ss. 152(1), (2) HCD-48, HCD-92
ss. 152(2), (4)-(5) HCD-96
ss. 152(4)-(5) HCD-92
s. 152(5) HCD-92
s. 152(6) HCD-48
s. 153(1) HCD-96
s. 153(4) HCD-81
s. 154(1) HCD-89, HCD-96
ss. 154(1)-(4) HCD-96
s. 154(2) HCD-96
s. 154(3) HCD-96
ss. 154(3)-(4) HCD-89
s. 154(4) HCD-96
s. 154(5) HCD-96
ss. 154(5)-(6) HCD-89

Para.

Condominium Act 1998, S.O. 1998, c. 19 — *cont'd*
s. 154(6) HCD-96
s. 155(3) HCD-15
s. 155(4) HCD-79
s. 156(1)(d) HCD-79
s. 157(1) HCD-21
s. 157(2) HCD-21
s. 158(1) HCD-15
s. 159(1) HCD-10
s. 160 .... HCD-79
s. 161 .... HCD-50
ss. 162(1)-(4) HCD-79
ss. 162(4), (6) HCD-71
ss. 162(5), (6) HCD-79
ss. 163(1)-(4) HCD-79
s. 165(1) HCD-11
s. 165(2) HCD-11
ss. 165(3)-(4) HCD-11
ss. 166(1)-(2) HCD-18
s. 166(3) HCD-18
ss. 166(4), 167(3) HCD-23
s. 167(2) HCD-16, HCD-22
ss. 168(1)-(2) HCD-11
ss. 168(3)-(4) HCD-114
s. 169 .... HCD-51
ss. 171(1)-(3) HCD-69
s. 172 .... HCD-125
ss. 173, 174 .... HCD-125
s. 174(8)-(9) HCD-23
s. 175 .... HCD-125
s. 175(2) HCD-124
s. 180(1) HCD-54, HCD-57

Condominium Act, 2009, S.N.L. 2009, c. C-29.1
ss. 2, 49(2), (6), (7), 63(3) HCD-81
ss. 2, 49(3)-(5) HCD-81
ss. 2(1), 16(3) HCD-10
s. 2(1)(b) HCD-9
s. 2(1)(bb) HCD-9
ss. 2(1)(cc), 79(1)-(2) HCD-7
s. 2(1)(e) HCD-9
ss. 2(1)(f), 68(1)-(2) HCD-7
ss. 2(1)(g), 52(2) HCD-69
ss. 2(1)(i), 91(1) HCD-7
s. 2(1)(p) HCD-13
ss. 2(1)(t)(i), 2(1)(bb), 16(2) HCD-10
s. 2(1)(t)(ii) HCD-10
s. 2(1)(v) HCD-9
s. 2(2) HCD-9
s. 6(2) HCD-23

Para.

s. 7 .... HCD-15
ss. 7(2)-(3) HCD-28
s. 8(1) HCD-9
s. 8(2) HCD-14
s. 8(4) HCD-14
s. 9(1) HCD-10, HCD-17
s. 9(1)(h) HCD-9
ss. 9(2), 27(8) HCD-20
ss. 10(1), 12(1), 18(3) HCD-23
ss. 10(2), 12(2) HCD-23
ss. 10(3), 12(3) HCD-23
ss. 10(5), 12(5) HCD-23
s. 11 .... HCD-14
s. 11(1) HCD-21
ss. 13(1), 13(3) HCD-13
s. 13(2) HCD-13
s. 13(4) HCD-13
s. 14(1) HCD-13
s. 16(1) HCD-9
s. 16(4) HCD-10
s. 16(5) HCD-10
s. 16(6) HCD-10
s. 17(1) HCD-14
s. 17(2) HCD-28
s. 18(1) HCD-29
s. 18(3)(a) HCD-29
s. 18(3)(b) HCD-33
s. 18(3)(h) HCD-70
s. 18(6) HCD-40
s. 18(7) HCD-14
s. 19(1)(a) HCD-29
s. 19(1)(b) HCD-74
ss. 19(1)(b), 55(1) HCD-76
ss. 19(1)(b), 85(1)-(6) HCD-79
s. 19(1)(c) HCD-29, HCD-86
s. 19(2) HCD-31
s. 19(3) HCD-31
ss. 14(2)-(3) HCD-13
ss. 18(3)-(4) HCD-12
ss. 20(1), (2) HCD-62
s. 21 .... HCD-65
s. 21(1) HCD-64
ss. 21(2), (3) HCD-64
s. 21(4) HCD-67
ss. 22, 23(2) HCD-36
s. 22(1) HCD-48
s. 23(1) HCD-36, HCD-37
s. 23(4) HCD-37
s. 24 .... HCD-29
s. 25 .... HCD-32
s. 26(1) HCD-32
s. 26(2) HCD-32

Para.

Condominium Act, 2009, S.N.L. 2009, c. C-29.1 — *cont'd*
s. 27(1) HCD-41
s. 27(2) HCD-46
s. 27(4) HCD-41
s. 27(5) HCD-42
s. 27(8) HCD-45
ss. 27(8), 35(1) HCD-24, HCD-25
s. 28(1)(a) HCD-41
s. 28(1)(b) HCD-41
s. 28.1(2) HCD-125
ss. 28.2(1)-(5), (7) HCD-125
ss. 28.2(6), (8), (9) HCD-125
s. 30(1) HCD-41
s. 31 ....HCD-43
s. 32(1) HCD-43
s. 32(2) HCD-43
s. 33 ....HCD-45
s. 34(1) HCD-44
ss. 34(2), (4)-(6) HCD-44
s. 34(3) HCD-44
s. 34(7) HCD-44
s. 34(8) HCD-44
s. 35(1) HCD-24
ss. 35(1)(d), (g)-(i), 83 ....HCD-24
s. 35(2) HCD-25
ss. 35(3)-(4) HCD-25
s. 36(1) HCD-101
ss. 36(1)-(2) HCD-26
s. 36(2) HCD-101
s. 36(3) HCD-26
s. 36(4) HCD-26
s. 37(3) HCD-61
s. 39(8) HCD-61
s. 40(1) HCD-49
ss. 40(2), (3) HCD-53
s. 40(4) HCD-121
ss. 40(5), (6) HCD-121
ss. 41, 44 ....HCD-50
s. 42(1) HCD-34
s. 42(2) HCD-34
s. 42(3) HCD-34, HCD-53
s. 42(4) HCD-34, HCD-53, HCD-95
s. 43(1) HCD-87
s. 43(2) HCD-87
s. 43(3) HCD-87
s. 45(1) HCD-94
s. 45(2) HCD-94
s. 45(3) HCD-94
s. 45(4) HCD-94
s. 45(5) HCD-94
s. 45(6) HCD-94

Para.

s. 45(7) HCD-94
s. 46(1) HCD-30
s. 47(1) HCD-12
s. 47(1)(a) HCD-12
s. 48(a) HCD-33
ss. 48(a), 44(3) HCD-69
s. 48(d)(i) HCD-98
s. 48(d)(i)(ii) HCD-102
s. 48(d)(iii) HCD-112
s. 49(1) HCD-33
ss. 49(1), (10) HCD-81
ss. 49(2), (8), (9) HCD-81
ss. 49(3), (5) HCD-81
s. 49(8) HCD-33
s. 49(11) HCD-29, HCD-81
s. 49(12) HCD-72
s. 50 ....HCD-81
s. 51(1) HCD-97
ss. 51(1), (3) HCD-97
s. 51(2) HCD-97
s. 51(4) HCD-100
s. 51(5) HCD-97
s. 51(6) HCD-97
s. 52(1) HCD-83
s. 52(2) HCD-83
s. 53 ....HCD-59, HCD-86
s. 54(1) HCD-73, HCD-74
ss. 54(1), 35(1)(g) HCD-74
ss. 54(2)-(5) HCD-74
s. 55(1) HCD-76
s. 55(2) HCD-75
s. 55(3) HCD-106
ss. 58(2), (3) HCD-71
ss. 59, 63(3), 62(2)-(5) HCD-124
s. 60(1) HCD-123
ss. 60(2), (3), 61(5)-(13) HCD-124
s. 61(1) HCD-121
ss. 61(2), (3) HCD-121
s. 62 ....HCD-120
s. 62(1) HCD-120
ss. 62(1), (2) HCD-74
s. 62(6) HCD-74
s. 63(1) HCD-119
s. 63(2) HCD-119
s. 64(1) HCD-113
ss. 64(3)-(4) HCD-113
s. 64(4) HCD-113
s. 64(6) HCD-85
ss. 65, 66 ....HCD-116
ss. 65, 66(7) HCD-119
ss. 65, 67 ....HCD-81, HCD-117
ss. 67(1)(f), (4) HCD-41

Para.

Condominium Act, 2009, S.N.L. 2009, c. C-29.1 — *cont'd*
s. 67(1)(g) HCD-29
ss. 67(1)(g)-(h) HCD-32
s. 68(3) HCD-15
s. 69(1) HCD-15
s. 69(2) HCD-15
s. 69(3) HCD-10
s. 69(4) HCD-10
s. 69(5) HCD-97
ss. 69(6)-(7) HCD-97
s. 70 .... HCD-17
s. 71 .... HCD-21
s. 72 .... HCD-50
ss. 73(1), (2) HCD-80
ss. 74(1)-(2) HCD-7
s. 74(3) HCD-15
s. 75 .... HCD-50
ss. 75-77 .... HCD-15
s. 76 .... HCD-17
s. 77(4) HCD-17
s. 77(8) HCD-17
s. 78 .... HCD-48
s. 79(3) HCD-15
s. 81(1) HCD-21
s. 81(2) HCD-21
s. 82(1) HCD-10
s. 87 .... HCD-13
s. 90 .... HCD-115
s. 90(c) HCD-93

The Condominium Act, C.C.S.M. c. C170
s. 1 .... HCD-6, HCD-7, HCD-8, HCD-9, HCD-10, HCD-13
ss. 1, 6 .... HCD-14
s. 2(2) HCD-9
s. 3 .... HCD-2
s. 4(2) HCD-14
s. 4(3) HCD-14, HCD-15
s. 4(3)(a) HCD-28
ss. 4(4), 5(3.1)-(3.2), 5.1-5.16 .... HCD-15
s. 5(1) HCD-17
s. 5(2)(a) HCD-19
s. 5(2)(b) HCD-19
s. 5(2)(c) HCD-19
s. 5(2)(d) HCD-19
ss. 5(2.2)-(2.3) HCD-19
ss. 5(3)-(5.1) HCD-20
ss. 5(6), 6(3) HCD-23
ss. 5(7), 6(4) HCD-23
s. 5(3)(b) HCD-9

Para.

s. 5(3.1) HCD-17
s. 5(8) HCD-17
ss. 5.2-5.6 .... HCD-17
s. 5.11(4)(d) HCD-96
s. 5.11(4)(e) HCD-96
ss. 6(1), (2) HCD-21
s. 7(1) HCD-9
s. 7(2) HCD-10
s. 7(3) HCD-106
s. 7(4) HCD-31
s. 8(1) HCD-49
s. 8(1.1) HCD-49, HCD-50
s. 8(2) HCD-10
s. 8(3) HCD-101
s. 8(4) HCD-10
s. 8(5) HCD-10
ss. 8(6)-(7) HCD-13
s. 8(9) HCD-13
s. 8(10) HCD-13
s. 8(11) HCD-30
s. 8(12) HCD-32
s. 9(1) HCD-12
s. 9(2) HCD-12
s. 9(3) HCD-12
s. 10(1) HCD-28
ss. 10(1)-(2) HCD-14
s. 10(2) HCD-29
s. 10(3) HCD-14
s. 10(4) HCD-29
s. 10(5) HCD-29
s. 10(7) HCD-36, HCD-37
s. 10(8) HCD-28
s. 10(9) HCD-29
s. 10(10) HCD-28, HCD-32
s. 10(11) HCD-32
s. 10(12) HCD-124
s. 11(1) HCD-40, HCD-41, HCD-45
s. 11(2) HCD-40, HCD-42, HCD-43
s. 11(3) HCD-43
s. 11(4) HCD-46
s. 11(5) HCD-48
s. 12(1) HCD-24, HCD-25
ss. 12(1.1)-(1.4) HCD-62
ss. 12(1.1)-(1.5), (6) HCD-25
s. 12(1.5) HCD-62
s. 12(2) HCD-24
s. 12(3) HCD-25
s. 12(4) HCD-24
s. 12(5) HCD-26
s. 13(1) HCD-29, HCD-86
s. 13(1.1) HCD-29, HCD-86
ss. 13(2)-(3) HCD-86

Para.

The Condominium Act, C.C.S.M. c. C170 — *cont'd*
s. 13.1(1) HCD-104
s. 13.1(7) HCD-113
s. 14(1)(a)....................................HCD-33
s. 14(1)(d)(i)................................HCD-98
ss. 14(1)(d)(ii)-(iii)......................HCD-102
s. 14(1)(e)....................................HCD-97
s. 14(1)(f) HCD-97
s. 14(1.1) HCD-97
s. 14(2) HCD-97
s. 14(4) HCD-97
s. 15(1) HCD-64
s. 15(2) HCD-65
s. 15(3) HCD-67
ss. 16(1), (1.1)-(1.6), (3), (4) HCD-83
ss. 16(1), 22(1)-(2) HCD-119
s. 16(2) HCD-83
ss. 16(3)-(4)................................HCD-113
s. 17(1) HCD-77
s. 18(1) HCD-73, HCD-74
s. 18(2) HCD-74
s. 18(2), 19(1), (2), 20(1), (2)......HCD-74
s. 18(3) HCD-76
s. 18(5)(a)....................................HCD-74
s. 18(6) HCD-78
ss. 19, 20 ....HCD-120
s. 19(1) HCD-74, HCD-120
ss. 19(1), (2), 20(1), (2) HCD-74
s. 20(3) HCD-124
s. 21(1) HCD-121
ss. 21(2)-(4)................................HCD-121
s. 21(5) HCD-124
s. 21(6) HCD-121
s. 21(7) HCD-113
ss. 21(7), (8) HCD-121
s. 22(3) HCD-124
s. 23 ....HCD-122
s. 24 ....HCD-112
s. 24(1) HCD-86
s. 24(2) HCD-86, HCD-109
s. 24(3) HCD-109
s. 24(4) HCD-85
ss. 25(1), (3) HCD-113
ss. 26(1), 27(2) HCD-33
s. 26(2) HCD-29
s. 27(1) HCD-33
s. 29(2) HCD-33

Condominium Act, R.S.N.S. 1989, c. 85 ....HCD-50
s. 2..HCD-2

Para.

s. 3(1)(c) HCD-9
s. 3(1)(f)..HCD-9
s. 3(1)(j)..HCD-7
ss. 3(1)(n), 12...............................HCD-14
s. 3(1)(o)..HCD-13
s. 3(1)(s) HCD-9
s. 3(1)(x)..HCD-9
s. 3(2)..HCD-9
s. 6(1)..HCD-9
s. 6(2)..HCD-14
ss. 6(3A), 23(2A)-(2B) HCD-25
s. 6(4)..HCD-28
s. 6(5)..HCD-14
s. 7(1)(a) HCD-28
s. 8(2)..............................HCD-7, HCD-15
ss. 7, 9-10, 12C HCD-15
ss. 11(1)-(2) HCD-17
s. 11(2)(b) HCD-9
ss. 11(3), 11(3A)...........................HCD-20
ss. 11(3B), 12(3)...........................HCD-23
ss. 11(3C)-(3D).............................HCD-23
ss. 11(4) HCD-23
s. 11(4A)..HCD-23
s. 12(1)..HCD-21
s. 13(1)..HCD-14
s. 13(2)..HCD-28
s. 13(3)..HCD-14
s. 14(1)..HCD-29
s. 14(2)..HCD-10
s. 14(3)(a) HCD-29
s. 14(3)(b) HCD-33
ss. 14(3)-(4) HCD-12
ss. 14A(1), (2)...............................HCD-62
s. 15(1)..........................HCD-40, HCD-41
ss. 15(1A), (1B) HCD-46
s. 15(2)..HCD-41
s. 15(3)..HCD-42
s. 15(4)..HCD-42
ss. 15(5), 15C.................................HCD-43
s. 15A(1)(a) HCD-41
s. 15A(1)(b) HCD-41
s. 15B(1) HCD-41
s. 15D(1)..HCD-43
s. 15D(2)..HCD-43
s. 15E HCD-45
s. 15F(1) HCD-44
ss. 15F(2), 15F(4)-(6) HCD-44
s. 15F(3) HCD-44
s. 15F(7) HCD-44
s. 15F(8) HCD-44
s. 16 ....HCD-40
s. 17 ....HCD-48

Para.

Condominium Act, R.S.N.S. 1989, c. 85 — *cont'd*
s. 18(1) HCD-36, HCD-37
s. 18(1A) HCD-36
s. 18(1D) HCD-37
s. 18(2) HCD-29, HCD-86
s. 19(2) HCD-29
s. 20(1) HCD-32
s. 20(2) HCD-32
s. 21 .... HCD-32
s. 23(1) HCD-24, HCD-25
s. 23(2) HCD-24
s. 23(3) HCD-25
ss. 23(3)-(4) HCD-25
s. 23(5) HCD-24
ss. 24(1)-(2) HCD-26
s. 24(3) HCD-26
s. 27(1) HCD-9
s. 27(2) HCD-10
s. 27(3) HCD-106
s. 27(4) HCD-31
ss. 28(1)-(2) HCD-10
ss. 28(3) HCD-10
s. 28(4) HCD-101
s. 28(5) HCD-10
s. 28(6) HCD-10
ss. 28(7)-(8) HCD-13
s. 28(9) HCD-13
s. 28(10) HCD-13
s. 28(11) HCD-30
s. 28(12) HCD-32
s. 29(1) HCD-12
s. 29(2) HCD-12
s. 29(3) HCD-12
ss. 29A, B HCD-116
s. 29B(3) HCD-53
s. 29C HCD-117
s. 29C(1)(g) HCD-29
ss. 29C(1)(g)-(h) HCD-32
s. 30(3) HCD-86
s. 31(1)(a) HCD-33
s. 31(1A) HCD-33
s. 31(1H) HCD-33
s. 31(1)(e)(i) HCD-98
ss. 31(1)(e)(ii)-(iii) HCD-102
s. 31(4) HCD-29
s. 31(6) HCD-97
s. 31(7) HCD-97
s. 31(7A) HCD-97
s. 31(7B) HCD-97
s. 31(8) HCD-99, HCD-100
s. 31(9) HCD-97

Para.

s. 31(10) HCD-97
s. 32(1) HCD-83
s. 32(2) HCD-83,
s. 33(2) HCD-113
s. 33(2)(d)-(e) HCD-113
s. 34(1) HCD-77
s. 35(1) HCD-73
s. 36(1) HCD-120
ss. 36(1)-(5) HCD-120
s. 37 .... HCD-64
s. 37(3) HCD-67
s. 38(2)(a) HCD-109
ss. 38(2)(c) HCD-112
s. 38(3) HCD-109
s. 38(4) HCD-85
s. 39 .... HCD-123
s. 40(5) HCD-113
s. 41(1) HCD-119
s. 41(2) HCD-119
s. 43 .... HCD-122
s. 44A HCD-86

Condominium Act, R.S.N.W.T. 1988, c. C-15
s. 1(1) HCD-7, HCD-9, HCD-10, HCD-13
ss. 1(1), 6 .... HCD-14
ss. 1(1), 7(2) HCD-10
ss. 1(1), 8(1)-(2) HCD-10
ss. 1(1), 8(6) HCD-6, HCD-8
s. 2(2) HCD-9
s. 3 .... HCD-2
ss. 5(3)-(4), 6(6)-(7) HCD-23
ss. 5(5), 6(8) HCD-23
ss. 5(6), 6(9) HCD-23
ss. 5(7)-(10), 6(10)-(13), 17(6)-(10) HCD-110
s. 4(1) HCD-14
s. 4(2) HCD-14, HCD-15
s. 5(1) HCD-17
s. 5(10) HCD-23
s. 5(2) HCD-20
s. 5(2)(b) HCD-9
s. 5(7) HCD-23
s. 5(8) HCD-23
s. 6(2) HCD-21
ss. 6(3)-(4) HCD-21
ss. 6.2(1)-(6) HCD-116
s. 6.2(7) HCD-117
s. 6.2(7)(c) HCD-29
ss. 6.2(7)(c)-(f) HCD-32
s. 6.2(7)(h) HCD-41
s. 6.3(1) HCD-54

Para.

Condominium Act, R.S.N.W.T. 1988, c. C-15 — *cont'd*
ss. 6.3(3), (4) HCD-56
ss. 6.3(5), (6) HCD-57
s. 6.4(1) HCD-49, HCD-50
s. 6.4(2) HCD-87
ss. 6.4(2)-(3) HCD-87
s. 6.4(4) HCD-87
s. 6.4(5) HCD-87
s. 6.5(1) HCD-52
s. 6.5(2),(4) HCD-52
s. 6.5(3) HCD-52
s. 6.5(6) HCD-87
s. 6.6(a) HCD-19
s. 6.6(b) HCD-19
s. 6.6(c) HCD-19
s. 6.6(d) HCD-19
s. 7(1) HCD-9
s. 7(3) HCD-106
s. 7(4) HCD-31
s. 8(3) HCD-101
s. 8(4) HCD-10
s. 8(5) HCD-10
s. 8(6) HCD-16
s. 8.1(1) HCD-11
s. 8.1(2) HCD-11
ss. 8.1(3)-(4) HCD-11
ss. 9(1)-(2) HCD-13
s. 9(3) HCD-13
s. 9(4) HCD-13
s. 10 .... HCD-32
s. 11(1) HCD-12
s. 11(2) HCD-12
s. 11(4) HCD-12
s. 12(1) HCD-28
ss. 12(1)-(2) HCD-14
s. 12(2) HCD-29
s. 12(3) HCD-14
s. 12(4) HCD-29
s. 12(5) HCD-29
s. 12(7) HCD-36, HCD-37
ss. 12(7), 19.17(2) HCD-37
s. 12(8) HCD-28
ss. 12.1(1), (2) HCD-48
ss. 12.2(2), (3)(a) HCD-89
ss. 12.2(3)(b) HCD-89
s. 12.2(4) HCD-89
s. 13 .... HCD-29
s. 13.1(1) HCD-10
ss. 13.1, 17.1 .... HCD-24
s. 14(1) HCD-28, HCD-32
s. 14(2) HCD-32

Para.

ss. 15, 25(3) HCD-124
s. 16(1) HCD-40, HCD-41, HCD-45
s. 16(2) HCD-40, HCD-42, HCD-43
s. 16(3) HCD-43
s. 16(4)(a) HCD-44
ss. 16(4)(b)-(c), (5) HCD-44
ss. 16(6) HCD-44
s. 16.1 .... HCD-46
ss. 16.2(1), (2), (3) HCD-61
s. 16.2(2) HCD-62
s. 16.2(3) HCD-61
s. 17(2) HCD-24, HCD-25
ss. 17(3), (5) HCD-25
ss. 17(3), (6), (8), (10) HCD-25
s. 17(11) HCD-24
s. 17(12) HCD-24
s. 17(13) HCD-26
ss. 17.2(5), 19.16 .... HCD-112
ss. 17.2(7), 30(4) HCD-85
s. 18(1) HCD-29, HCD-86
ss. 18(2)-(3) HCD-86
ss. 19, 19.1(1) HCD-58
s. 19.1(2) HCD-58
s. 19.2 .... HCD-59, HCD-86
ss. 19.3(1), (2) HCD-60
ss. 19.4(1)(a) HCD-60
ss. 19.5(1), 19.8(1) HCD-104, HCD-106
s. 19.7(1) HCD-99
ss. 19.7(1)-(2) HCD-99
s. 19.7(2) HCD-99
ss. 19.7(3)(a), (c), (d) HCD-99
s. 19.7(3)(b) HCD-99
ss. 19.8(1)(a) HCD-60
ss. 19.8(1)(a)-(b) HCD-99
ss. 19.8(1)(c)-(d) HCD-99
s. 19.9(1)(a) HCD-33
ss. 19.9(1)(a)-(c) HCD-69
s. 19.9(1)(d)(i) HCD-98
ss. 19.9(1)(d)(ii)-(iii) HCD-102
s. 19.9(1)(e) HCD-69
s. 19.9(1)(f) HCD-97
ss. 19.9(1)(f), 19.15, 19.16 .... HCD-97
s. 19.9(1)(g) HCD-97
s. 19.9(2) HCD-72
s. 19.9(3) HCD-97
ss. 19.10(1)-(2) HCD-33
ss. 19.10(1)-(4) HCD-81
s. 19.10(4) HCD-29, HCD-81
ss. 19.11(10)-(11), (13)-(15) HCD-81
ss. 19.11(2)-(9),
ss. 19.11(12)-(15) HCD-81
ss. 19.11(5), (6) HCD-81

Para.

Condominium Act, R.S.N.W.T. 1988, c. C-15 — *cont'd*
ss. 19.12(1), (2) HCD-81
ss. 19.13(1)-(3), 19.14(2), 19.15(1)-(3) HCD-81
s. 19.14(1) HCD-33
s. 19.14(2) HCD-33
s. 19.17(1) HCD-34, HCD-53
ss. 19.17(1), (4) HCD-53
s. 19.17(2) HCD-53
s. 19.17(3) HCD-34, HCD-53, HCD-95
s. 19.17(4) HCD-34
s. 19.17(5) HCD-35
s. 20(1) HCD-64
s. 20(3) HCD-65
s. 20(4) HCD-67
s. 20(5) HCD-66
s. 20(6) HCD-67
ss. 21(1), (3) HCD-83
s. 21(2) HCD-83
ss. 21(3)-(4) HCD-113
ss. 23(1), (5) HCD-76
ss. 23(2), (5) HCD-76
s. 23(3) HCD-74
s. 23(4) HCD-73, HCD-74
s. 23(5) HCD-74
ss. 23(6) HCD-79
ss. 23(7), (8) HCD-78
ss. 24, 25 .... HCD-120
s. 24(1) HCD-120
ss. 24(1), (2) HCD-74
ss. 25(3), 26(5)-(7), s. 28(3) HCD-124
s. 26(1) HCD-121
ss. 26(2)-(4) HCD-121
ss. 26(7), 27 .... HCD-124
s. 27(1) HCD-113
s. 28(1) HCD-119
s. 28(2) HCD-119
s. 28.1(1) HCD-74, HCD-83
s. 29 .... HCD-122
s. 30(1) HCD-86, HCD-93
s. 30(2) HCD-86, HCD-109
s. 30(3) HCD-109

Condominium Act, R.S.N.W.T. (Nu.) 1988, c. C-15
s. 1(1) HCD-10, HCD-13, HCD-6, HCD-7, HCD-8, HCD-9
ss. 1(1), 6 .... HCD-14
ss. 1(1), 8(1)-(2) HCD-10
s. 2(2) HCD-9
s. 3 .... HCD-2

Para.

s. 4(1) HCD-14
s. 4(2) HCD-14, HCD-15
s. 5(1) HCD-17, HCD-20
s. 5(2)(b) HCD-9
ss. 5(3), 6(6) HCD-23
ss. 5(4), 6(7) HCD-23
s. 6(2) HCD-21
ss. 6(3)-(4) HCD-21
s. 7(1) HCD-9
s. 7(2) HCD-10
s. 7(3) HCD-106
s. 7(4) HCD-31
s. 8(3) HCD-101
s. 8(4) HCD-10
s. 8(5) HCD-10
ss. 9(1)-(2) HCD-13
s. 9(3) HCD-13
s. 9(4) HCD-13
s. 10 .... HCD-32
s. 11(1) HCD-12
s. 11(2) HCD-12
s. 11(4) HCD-12
s. 12(1) HCD-28
ss. 12(1)-(2) HCD-14
s. 12(2) HCD-29
s. 12(3) HCD-14
s. 12(4) HCD-29
s. 12(5) HCD-29
s. 12(7) HCD-36, HCD-37
s. 12(8) HCD-28
s. 13 .... HCD-29
s. 14(1) HCD-28, HCD-32
s. 14(2) HCD-32
s. 15 .... HCD-124
s. 16(1) HCD-40, HCD-41, HCD-45
s. 16(2) HCD-40, HCD-42, HCD-43
s. 16(3) HCD-43
s. 17(1) HCD-24, HCD-25
s. 17(2) HCD-24
s. 17(3) HCD-25
s. 17(4) HCD-24
s. 17(5) HCD-26
s. 18(1) HCD-29, HCD-86
ss. 18(2)-(3) HCD-86
s. 19(1)(a) HCD-33
s. 19(1)(d) HCD-112
s. 19(1)(d)(i) HCD-98
s. 19(1)(d)(ii)-(iii) HCD-102
s. 19(1)(e) HCD-97
s. 19(1)(f) HCD-97
s. 19(3) HCD-97
s. 20(1) HCD-64

Para.

Condominium Act, R.S.N.W.T. (Nu.) 1988, c. C-15 — *cont'd*
s. 20(2) HCD-65
s. 20(3) HCD-67
ss. 21(3)-(4) HCD-113
s. 22(1) HCD-77
s. 23(4) HCD-73
s. 24(1) HCD-120
ss. 25(3), 26(5)-(6), 28(3) HCD-124
ss. 26(7), 27 .... HCD-124
s. 27(1) HCD-113
s. 28(1) HCD-119
s. 28(2) HCD-119
s. 29 .... HCD-122
s. 30(1) HCD-86
s. 30(2) HCD-86, HCD-109
s. 30(3) HCD-109
s. 30(4) HCD-85

Condominium Act, R.S.O. 1990, c. C-26, s. 24 .... HCD-32

Condominium Act, R.S.P.E.I. 1988, c. C-16
s. 1(1)(b) HCD-9
s. 1(1)(e) HCD-9
s. 1(1)(h) HCD-7
ss. 1(1)(k), 4 .... HCD-14
s. 1(1)(l) HCD-13
s. 1(1)(o) HCD-9
s. 1(1)(s) HCD-9
s. 1(1)(t) HCD-7, HCD-10
s. 1(2) HCD-9
s. 2(1) HCD-9
s. 2(2) HCD-14
s. 2(3) HCD-14
s. 3(1) HCD-17
s. 3(1)(g) HCD-9
s. 3(2) HCD-20
ss. 3(3) HCD-23
s. 3(4) HCD-23
s. 3(5) HCD-28
s. 3(6) HCD-23
s. 4(1) HCD-21
s. 5 .... HCD-15
s. 6(1) HCD-9
s. 6(2) HCD-10
s. 6(3) HCD-106
s. 6(4) HCD-31
ss. 7(1)-(2) HCD-10
s. 7(3) HCD-10
s. 7(5) HCD-10
s. 7(6) HCD-10

Para.

ss. 7(7)-(8) HCD-13
s. 7(9) HCD-13
s. 7(10) HCD-13
s. 7(11) HCD-32
s. 8(1) HCD-12
s. 8(2) HCD-12
s. 9(1) HCD-10
s. 9(1), 13(1)(i) HCD-24
s. 10(1) HCD-14
s. 10(2) HCD-28
s. 10(3) HCD-29
s. 10(4) HCD-40, HCD-41
s. 10(5) HCD-41
s. 10(6) HCD-42
s. 10(7) HCD-41
s. 10(8) HCD-42
s. 10(9) HCD-43
s. 10(10) HCD-40, HCD-41, HCD-42, HCD-43, HCD-45
s. 10(11) HCD-36, HCD-37
s. 10(12) HCD-29, HCD-86
s. 10(15) HCD-29
s. 10(16) HCD-29
s. 10(17) HCD-32
s. 10(18) HCD-32
s. 10(19) HCD-124
s. 11(1) HCD-61
s. 11(3) HCD-62
s. 11(4) HCD-62
s. 11(7) HCD-64
s. 12(1) HCD-46
s. 11(2) HCD-61
ss. 11(5), (6) HCD-62
s. 13(1) HCD-24, HCD-25
s. 13(1)(i) HCD-33
s. 13(2) HCD-24
s. 13(3) HCD-25
ss. 14(1)-(2) HCD-26
s. 14(3) HCD-26
ss. 15(1)-(2) HCD-86
s. 15(3) HCD-86
s. 16(4) HCD-97
s. 16(5) HCD-97
s. 16(6) HCD-97
s. 16(7) HCD-97
s. 16(8) HCD-97
s. 16(9) HCD-97
ss. 17(1), (4), (5) HCD-83
s. 17(3) HCD-83
s. 17(5) HCD-113
s. 18(1) HCD-77
s. 19 .... HCD-89

Para.

Condominium Act, R.S.P.E.I. 1988, c. C-16
— *cont'd*
s. 20(2) HCD-107
s. 20(3) HCD-107
s. 20(4) HCD-33
s. 21(1) HCD-73
ss. 22, 23........ HCD-120
s. 22(1) HCD-120
ss. 23(3), 24(3), 25(3)........ HCD-124
s. 24(1) HCD-121
s. 24(2) HCD-121
s. 24(5) HCD-113
s. 25(1) HCD-119
s. 25(2) HCD-119
s. 26........ HCD-122
s. 27(2) HCD-30
ss. 27(2)(a)-(b)........ HCD-30
ss. 27(2)(c)-(e)........ HCD-30
ss. 27(3)(a)-(b)........ HCD-30
s. 28........ HCD-65
s. 29(1) HCD-86
s. 29(2) HCD-86
s. 29(3) HCD-86, HCD-104
s. 29(4) HCD-85
s. 30(2) HCD-88
s. 30(3) HCD-88
s. 30(4) HCD-88
s. 35........ HCD-115

Condominium Act, R.S.Y. 2002, c. 36
s. 1 ....HCD-6, HCD-7, HCD-8, HCD-9, HCD-10, HCD-13, HCD-69
ss. 1, 6........ HCD-14
ss. 1, 7(2)........ HCD-10
ss. 1, 8(1)-(2)........ HCD-10
ss. 1, 21(7)-(9)........ HCD-124
s. 2(2) HCD-9
s. 3........ HCD-2
s. 4........ HCD-15
s. 4(1) HCD-14
s. 4(2) HCD-14
s. 4(2)(a)........ HCD-28
s. 5(1) HCD-17
ss. 5(2), 18(5) HCD-20
s. 5(2)(b)........ HCD-9
ss. 5(3), 6(4)-(5) HCD-23
ss. 5(4), 6(6) HCD-23
s. 6(1) HCD-21
ss. 6(2)-(3)........ HCD-21
s. 7(1) HCD-9
s. 7(3) HCD-106
s. 7(4) HCD-31

Para.

s. 8(3)........ HCD-101
s. 8(4)........ HCD-10
s. 8(5)........ HCD-10
ss. 8(6)-(7) HCD-13
s. 8(8)........ HCD-13
s. 8(9)........ HCD-13
s. 8(10)........ HCD-30
s. 8(11)........ HCD-32
s. 9(1)........ HCD-12
s. 9(2)........ HCD-12
s. 9(4)........ HCD-12
s. 10(1)........ HCD-28
ss. 10(1)-(2) HCD-14
s. 10(2)........ HCD-29
s. 10(3)........ HCD-14
s. 10(4)........ HCD-29
s. 10(5)........ HCD-29
s. 10(7)........ HCD-36, HCD-37
s. 10(8)........ HCD-28
s. 10(9)........ HCD-29
s. 10(10)........ HCD-33
s. 10(11)........ HCD-28, HCD-32
s. 10(12)........ HCD-32
s. 10(13)........ HCD-124
s. 11(1)........HCD-40, HCD-41, HCD-45
s. 11(2)........HCD-40, HCD-42, HCD-43
s. 11(3)........ HCD-43
s. 12(1)........ HCD-24, HCD-25
s. 12(2)........ HCD-24
s. 12(3)........ HCD-25
s. 12(4)........ HCD-24
s. 12(5)........ HCD-26
s. 13(1)........ HCD-29, HCD-86
ss. 13(2)-(3) HCD-86
s. 14(1)(a) HCD-33
ss. 14(1)(a), (b), (g)........ HCD-69
s. 14(1)(d)(i)........ HCD-98
ss. 14(1)(d)(ii)-(iii)........ HCD-102
s. 14(1)(e) HCD-97
s. 14(1)(f)........ HCD-97
s. 14(1)(g) HCD-53
s. 14(2)........ HCD-72
s. 14(3)........ HCD-97
s. 15(1)........ HCD-64
s. 15(2)........ HCD-65
s. 15(3)........ HCD-67
ss. 16(1), (3)........ HCD-83
s. 16(2)........ HCD-83
ss. 16(3)-(4) HCD-113
s. 17(1)........ HCD-77
ss. 18(1), (5)........ HCD-76
s. 18(3)........ HCD-74

Para.

Condominium Act, R.S.Y. 2002, c. 36 — *cont'd*
s. 18(4) ... HCD-73, HCD-74, HCD-75
s. 18(5) ... HCD-74
s. 18(6) ... HCD-79
ss. 18(7), (8) ... HCD-78
ss. 19, 20 ... HCD-120
s. 19(1) ... HCD-120
ss. 19(1), (2) ... HCD-74
s. 20 ... HCD-124
s. 21(1) ... HCD-121
ss. 21(2)-(4) ... HCD-121
ss. 21(5), (6), 22(3) ... HCD-124
s. 21(8) ... HCD-113
s. 22(1) ... HCD-119
s. 22(2) ... HCD-119
s. 23 ... HCD-122
ss. 23(1), (3)-(5) ... HCD-123
s. 24(1) ... HCD-86
s. 24(2) ... HCD-86, HCD-109
s. 24(2)(a) ... HCD-109
s. 24(2)(b) ... HCD-112
s. 24(3) ... HCD-109
s. 24(4) ... HCD-85

The Condominium Property Act, 1993, S.S. 1993, c. C-26.1 ... HCD-61, HCD-62, HCD-74, HCD-76, HCD-81, HCD-83, HCD-84
ss. 2(1), 6(1) ... HCD-10
ss. 2(1), 55(1)(b), 55(3)-(6) ... HCD-81
ss. 2(1)(b), 2(1)(r), 2(1)(z.1), 2(1)(bb) ... HCD-10
s. 2(1)(bb) ... HCD-9
ss. 2(1)(c), 2(1)(bb)(ii) ... HCD-7, HCD-10
s. 2(1)(e) ... HCD-9
s. 2(1)(h) ... HCD-9
ss. 2(1)(j) ... HCD-14
s. 2(1)(k) ... HCD-7
s. 4(2) ... HCD-9
s. 5.1 ... HCD-14, HCD-15
s. 5.2 ... HCD-15, HCD-17
s. 5.2(3) ... HCD-95
s. 5.2(4) ... HCD-95
s. 6(3) ... HCD-10
s. 7(2) ... HCD-32
ss. 9-10(1) ... HCD-21
s. 9(3) ... HCD-21
s. 10(1)(b) ... HCD-21
s. 10(5) ... HCD-21
s. 12(1) ... HCD-48
s. 12(2) ... HCD-48

Para.

ss. 13(6)-(8) ... HCD-93
s. 14 ... HCD-23
s. 14(4) ... HCD-23
s. 14(5) ... HCD-23
s. 14(8) ... HCD-23
s. 14(12) ... HCD-23
s. 15 ... HCD-116
ss. 15(5.1), 15(6), (7) ... HCD-117
s. 15(6) ... HCD-29
ss. 15(6)(c)-(e) ... HCD-32
s. 15(7) ... HCD-41
ss. 16-19, 23 ... HCD-15
s. 16(2) ... HCD-7, HCD-15
s. 20(1) ... HCD-96
ss. 20(2)-(3) ... HCD-96
s. 21(7) ... HCD-15
s. 23(1) ... HCD-62
s. 24 ... HCD-90
s. 24(b) ... HCD-91
s. 26(1)(g) ... HCD-49
ss. 26(1)(g), 28 ... HCD-50
s. 26(2) ... HCD-87
ss. 26(2)-(3) ... HCD-87
s. 26(4) ... HCD-87
s. 26(5) ... HCD-87
s. 27 ... HCD-87
s. 28(a)(iii) ... HCD-49
ss. 29(2), (3)(a) ... HCD-89
s. 29(3)(b) ... HCD-89
s. 29(4) ... HCD-89
s. 30 ... HCD-12
s. 31(1) ... HCD-12
s. 31(2) ... HCD-12
s. 32 ... HCD-12
s. 33 ... HCD-12
ss. 34(1)-(1.1) ... HCD-28
s. 34(3) ... HCD-14
s. 34(4) ... HCD-32
s. 34(5) ... HCD-29
s. 34(5.1)(a) ... HCD-33
s. 34(6) ... HCD-14
s. 35(1) ... HCD-29, HCD-86
s. 35(2) ... HCD-76
ss. 35(2)(a), (b) ... HCD-74
s. 35(2)(c) ... HCD-35
s. 36(1) ... HCD-31
s. 36(2) ... HCD-31
s. 36.11(2) ... HCD-31
s. 37(2) ... HCD-43
ss. 37.11(3)-(4) ... HCD-31
s. 38(1) ... HCD-46
ss. 39, 65(4.1), 51.5 ... HCD-61

Para.

The Condominium Property Act, 1993, S.S. 1993, c. C-26.1 — *cont'd*
s. 39(1) HCD-40
s. 39(2) HCD-36, HCD-43
ss. 39(2), 44(4) HCD-37
s. 39(2)(g) HCD-37
ss. 40(1), (2) HCD-61
s. 41(1) HCD-64
s. 41(2), (4)-(7), (12), 47(1)(d), (j), (k), (l), (m.1) HCD-24
s. 41(3) HCD-68
s. 41(4) HCD-68
s. 41(8) HCD-66
ss. 41(9)-(12) HCD-66
ss. 41.1(1) HCD-67
s. 42(1) HCD-65
s. 43(1) HCD-64, HCD-67
ss. 44(1), 47(1) HCD-24
s. 44(2) HCD-24
s. 44(3), 45 .... HCD-24
ss. 44.1, 47(1)(m.1), 47.1 .... HCD-24
s. 46(2) HCD-25
s. 46(3) HCD-25
s. 47(1) HCD-10, HCD-33, HCD-45
s. 47(1)(i) HCD-71
s. 47(2) HCD-24
ss. 47.1(4)-(10), 104(2) HCD-25
s. 48(1)(a) HCD-44
ss. 48(1)(b)-(c), 48(2) HCD-44
s. 48(2) HCD-44
ss. 49-50, 53 .... HCD-44
s. 51 .... HCD-81
ss. 51-52 .... HCD-44
ss. 54(1), 55(1), 56(1), 57(1) HCD-69
ss. 55(1)(a), 55(2) HCD-33
ss. 55(1)(b), 55(3) HCD-33
ss. 55(2), 65(1.2), 101(3) HCD-69
ss. 56(1)(b), 58(1), (2), 59(1)-(3), 60(1), (2) HCD-81
ss. 57(2), 58(4) HCD-98
ss. 58.1(1)-(10), 58.2(1), (2) HCD-81
s. 60(1) HCD-33
s. 60(2) HCD-33
s. 61(1) HCD-29
ss. 61(1), 61(3) HCD-81
s. 61(2) HCD-33
s. 63(1) HCD-97
ss. 63(1), (2), (4) HCD-97
s. 63(2)(b) HCD-97
s. 63(3) HCD-97
s. 63.1(1) HCD-97
s. 63.1(2) HCD-97

Para.

ss. 63.1(3)-(4) HCD-97
s. 63.1(5) HCD-97
s. 63.1(6) HCD-97
ss. 63.2(1)(a), (b), (e) HCD-100
ss. 63.2(1)(c)-(d) HCD-100
ss. 63.2(2) HCD-100
s. 64(1) HCD-34, HCD-53
s. 65 .... HCD-77
ss. 65(1.3), (1.4) HCD-71
s. 65.2(2) HCD-35
ss. 70-71.1 .... HCD-29
s. 70(1) HCD-10
ss. 70(1), (2) HCD-121
ss. 70(3)-(5), 70.1, 71(1), (2), 88(2)-(4), 88.1, 89 .... HCD-121
ss. 70(5), 88(1) HCD-121
s. 71(3) HCD-124
s. 72(1) HCD-9
s. 72(2) HCD-74, HCD-76
s. 73(1) HCD-12
s. 73(2) HCD-12
s. 74(1) HCD-12
s. 74(2) HCD-12
ss. 75, 78(1) HCD-58
s. 76 .... HCD-59
ss. 77(1), (2) HCD-60
s. 78(2) HCD-58
s. 79(a) HCD-60
ss. 80(1), 82(1) HCD-104, HCD-106
s. 81(1) HCD-99
ss. 81(1)-(1.1) HCD-99
s. 81(1.1) HCD-99
ss. 81(2)-(3) HCD-99
s. 81(3)(c) HCD-99
s. 82(1) HCD-99
s. 82(1)(a) HCD-60
ss. 83, 2(1)(aa) HCD-119
ss. 84, 90(1), (2) HCD-122
ss. 85, 87 .... HCD-124
ss. 92(1)-(2) HCD-30
s. 92(3) HCD-30
ss. 97(3)-(4) HCD-30
s. 98 .... HCD-102, HCD-112
ss. 99(1), (3) HCD-86
s. 99(6) HCD-85
ss. 100(1), (3) HCD-113
ss. 101(3)-(5) HCD-109
ss. 101(6) HCD-109
s. 101(1) HCD-109
s. 101(2) HCD-109
s. 102(1) HCD-102
s. 102(2) HCD-102

Para.

The Condominium Property Act, 1993, S.S. 1993, c. C-26.1 — *cont'd*
s. 102(3) HCD-102
s. 103 .... HCD-31
s. 104(1) HCD-28
ss. 105(1)-(2) HCD-28
s. 106 .... HCD-37
s. 111(1) HCD-115
s. 111(2) HCD-115
ss. 111(3)-(4) HCD-115
s. 111.1 .... HCD-115

Condominium Property Act, R.S.A. 2000, c. C-22 ..... HCD-50, HCD-53, HCD-81, HCD-116, HCD-117
Apps. 1-2 .... HCD-24
App. 1, ss. 1(1)(x), 35, App. 2, s. 32(2) HCD-25
App. 1, s. 2(a), App. 2, s. 1(a) HCD-31
App. 1, s. 2(e) HCD-101
App. 1, s. 2(2)(b) and Appendix 2, ss. 1(b), (c) HCD-74
App. 1, s. 3(b), App. 2, s. 3(b) HCD-33
App. 1, ss. 4(1)-(2) HCD-41
App. 1, s. 4(3) HCD-41
App. 1, s. 5(2)(b) HCD-41
App. 1, s. 6 .... HCD-41
App. 1, s. 7(1) HCD-61
App. 1, ss. 7(1)-(3) HCD-41
App. 1, s. 8, App. 2, s. 5 .... HCD-41
App. 1, s. 9 .... HCD-41
App. 1, s. 10 .... HCD-42
App. 1, ss. 11(1)-(3) HCD-40
App. 1, ss. 12(1), 13, 16(1), 18 .... HCD-42
App. 1, s. 12(2) HCD-42
App. 1, s. 14(1) HCD-28
App. 1, s. 14(1)(a) HCD-28
App. 1, ss. 14(1)-(2) HCD-28
App. 1, s. 16, s. 19 .... HCD-61
App. 1, ss. 16(2)-(3), App. 2, ss. 10(b)-(c) HCD-40
App. 1, s. 17, App. 2, s. 11 .... HCD-36, HCD-43
App. 1, s. 18 .... HCD-61
App. 1, ss. 21(1)-(3) HCD-62
App. 1, s. 26(2) HCD-64
App. 1, ss. 31(1), (2) HCD-64
App. 1, s. 34 .... HCD-74
App. 1, s. 36(2)(a), App. 2, s. 1(d) HCD-101
App. 1, ss. 36(2)(a), (b), (d), App. 2, Sch. A, ss. 1(d)-(e), App. 2, Sch. B, s. 1(b) HCD-103

Para.

App. 1, ss. 36(2)(b), (g), App. 2, Sch. A, s. 1(e) HCD-106
App. 1, s. 36(2)(e), App. 2, s. 1(c) HCD-105
App. 1, By-laws, s. 2(b)(ii) HCD-69, HCD-71
App. 2, s. 11 .... HCD-37
App. 2, s. 18, s. 19 .... HCD-62
App. 2, Sch. A, s. 31 .... HCD-28
App. 2, Sch. B, s. 1(a) HCD-106
ss. 1(1), 6(2) HCD-10
ss. 1(1)(b), 1(y)(ii), 1(w)(ii) HCD-7, HCD-10
s. 1(1)(d) HCD-9
s. 1(1)(f) HCD-9
ss. 1(1)(g), 8 .... HCD-14
s. 1(1)(h) HCD-7
ss. 1(1)(m), 1(1)(s), 1(1)(w), 1(1)(y) HCD-10
s. 1(1)(s)(ii) HCD-6, HCD-8
ss. 1(s)(ii), 4(4)-4(5) HCD-9
ss. 1(1)(x), 61(4), 38(1)-(3), Appendix 1, ss. 1(1)-(4), s. 3(f), Appendix 2, s. 3(e) HCD-83
s. 1(1)(y) HCD-9
ss. 2, 3, 49 .... HCD-124
ss. 2, 25(1) HCD-14
s. 4 .... HCD-14, HCD-15
s. 6(3) HCD-10
s. 7 .... HCD-32
ss. 8(1), 10(1) HCD-21
s. 10(1)(b)(ii) HCD-21
s. 11 .... HCD-54
s. 12(1) HCD-49
s. 12(3) HCD-87
ss. 12(3)-(4) HCD-87
s. 12(5) HCD-87
s. 13 .... HCD-50, HCD-87
s. 13(a) HCD-49
ss. 14(1)-(15), 16 .... HCD-56
ss. 14(6), (7) HCD-57
s. 14(13) HCD-93
ss. 14(13)-(14) HCD-109
s. 14(14) HCD-93
ss. 17(2), (3)(a) HCD-89
s. 17(3) HCD-89
s. 17(3)(b) HCD-89
s. 18 .... HCD-23
s. 19 .... HCD-7, HCD-15
ss. 20(1), (2) HCD-62
s. 22 .... HCD-12
s. 23(1) HCD-12

Para.

Condominium Property Act, R.S.A. 2000, c. C-22 — *cont'd*
s. 23(2) HCD-12
s. 24(1) HCD-12
s. 24(2) HCD-12
s. 24(5) HCD-12
s. 25(1) HCD-28
ss. 25(1)-(2) HCD-14
s. 25(3) HCD-32
s. 25(5) HCD-14
s. 26(1) HCD-64
ss. 26(2), (3) HCD-65
s. 26(4), Appendix 1, s. 29 .... HCD-67
s. 26(5), Appendix 1, s. 30 .... HCD-66
s. 27 .... HCD-64
s. 27(1) HCD-67
s. 28(2) HCD-43
s. 28(3)(a) HCD-44
ss. 28(3)(b)-(c), 28(4) HCD-44
s. 28(4) HCD-44
s. 28(5) HCD-35
s. 28(7) HCD-40
s. 28(9) HCD-43
s. 28(10), App. 1, ss. 5(1)-(2)(a), App. 2, s. 4 .... HCD-41
s. 29(1) HCD-46
ss. 30(1), (2) HCD-61
s. 30(3), (3), Appendix 1, s. 17, Appendix 2, s. 11 .... HCD-61
s. 31 .... HCD-42, HCD-62
s. 32(1) HCD-24
s. 32(2) HCD-86
ss. 32(2), 32(6), 33-34 .... HCD-24
s. 32(3) HCD-25
s. 32(4) HCD-25
s. 32(4)(b) HCD-25
s. 32(5) HCD-24
s. 32(7) HCD-24
s. 33, Appendix 1, s. 2(b)(i), s. 2(c), s. 34, Appendix 2, ss. 1(b), (c), (d) HCD-76
s. 33, Appendix 1, s. 34 .... HCD-76
s. 33, Appendix 1, s. 1(1), s. 2(e) HCD-84
s. 35 .... HCD-24, HCD-62
ss. 35(1), (4) HCD-86
s. 35(2) HCD-86
s. 35(6) HCD-86
ss. 36(1), (3), (4), (5) HCD-86
ss. 36(3)(d), (5), 67(2) HCD-112
ss. 36(7), 80(2) HCD-85
s. 37(1) HCD-29, HCD-86

Para.

s. 37(2) HCD-29
s. 37(2) and Appendix 2, Schedule A, ss. 2(b), (d) HCD-74
s. 37(2), s. 34, Appendix 1, ss. 2(b), (c), (d) HCD-76
s. 37(3) HCD-29
s. 38(1) HCD-33, HCD-81
s. 38(2) HCD-81
s. 38(3) HCD-29, HCD-81
s. 39(1) HCD-33, HCD-69
ss. 39(1)(d), 39(2) HCD-98, HCD-102
ss. 39(3), 41 .... HCD-100
s. 39(4) HCD-99
s. 39(5) HCD-99
s. 39(7) HCD-97
ss. 39(7)-(8), 41, 42 .... HCD-97
s. 39(9) HCD-97
ss. 39(9), (12) HCD-97
s. 39(11) HCD-97
s. 43(1) HCD-33
ss. 43(2)-(3) HCD-33
s. 44 .... HCD-34, HCD-37
s. 46(1) HCD-48
s. 46(2) HCD-48
s. 47 .... HCD-77
s. 47(1), 39(1)(c) HCD-70
s. 49 .... HCD-29
s. 49(1) HCD-10
ss. 49(1)-(3), s. 1(1)(x) HCD-121
ss. 49(4)-(6) HCD-121
s. 50(1) HCD-9
s. 51 .... HCD-12
s. 52(1) HCD-12
s. 52(3) HCD-12
s. 52(7) HCD-12
s. 53(2) HCD-59, HCD-86
ss. 53(2)-(3) HCD-106
s. 53(3) HCD-74, HCD-102
ss. 53(3), (4) HCD-60
ss. 53(3)-(7) HCD-74, HCD-76
ss. 53(4)-(7) HCD-102
s. 53(6) HCD-58
ss. 53(7)(a) HCD-60
ss. 54(1), 55(1), (4) HCD-104
ss. 53(1), (5) HCD-58
s. 56(1) HCD-104
s. 56(4) HCD-104
s. 58(1) HCD-109
s. 58(2) HCD-109
ss. 58(3)-(5) HCD-109
s. 58(6) HCD-109
s. 59(1) HCD-102

Para.

Condominium Property Act, R.S.A. 2000, c. C-22 — *cont'd*
s. 59(2) HCD-102
s. 59(3) HCD-102
ss. 60, 1(1)(x) HCD-119
ss. 61, 64(1), (2) HCD-122
s. 62(1) HCD-124
s. 63 .... HCD-124
ss. 63(1), (2) HCD-121
ss. 63(3)-(6) HCD-121
s. 65, App. 1, s. 2(b)(ii), App. 2, s. 1(b) HCD-30
s. 67(1)(a)(i) HCD-86
s. 67(1)(b) HCD-86
s. 67(2)(a) HCD-108
ss. 67(2)-(3) HCD-86
ss. 67-68 .... HCD-110
ss. 69(1)-(2) HCD-113
s. 70 .... HCD-31
s. 71(1) HCD-28
ss. 73(1)-(2) HCD-28
s. 74 .... HCD-34, HCD-37
s. 79(1) HCD-115
ss. 79(2)-(3) HCD-115
s. 80(3) HCD-88

Condominium Property Act, S.N.B. 2009, c. C-16.05
s. 1(1) HCD-7, HCD-9, HCD-10, HCD-13
s. 1(2) HCD-9
s. 4(c) HCD-7, HCD-10
s. 5(1) HCD-14
s. 6(2)(i) HCD-9
ss. 6(3)-(4) HCD-20
s. 7 .... HCD-14
s. 9 .... HCD-15
s. 9(1)(a) HCD-28
ss. 10(1)-(2) HCD-14
s. 10(2) HCD-14
s. 11 .... HCD-17
s. 12(1) HCD-7
s. 12(2) HCD-15
s. 13 .... HCD-116
s. 14 .... HCD-117
ss. 14(1), (3), (4) HCD-83
ss. 14(1)(g), 14(3) HCD-41
s. 14(1)(h) HCD-29
ss. 14(1)(h)-(i) HCD-32
s. 14(2) HCD-83
s. 15(1) HCD-9
s. 15(2) HCD-10

Para.

s. 15(3) HCD-106
s. 15(4) HCD-31
s. 15(5) HCD-31
ss. 16(1)-(2) HCD-10
s. 16(3) HCD-10
s. 16(4) HCD-101
s. 16(5) HCD-10
s. 16(6) HCD-10
s. 16(7) HCD-30
ss. 17(1)-(2) HCD-13
s. 17(3) HCD-13
s. 17(4) HCD-13
s. 18(1) HCD-12
s. 18(2) HCD-12
s. 18(3) HCD-12
s. 19(1) HCD-29
s. 19(2) HCD-14
s. 19(4) HCD-29, HCD-86
s. 19(6) HCD-32
s. 19(7) HCD-33
s. 19(7)(a) HCD-29
ss. 19(7)-(8) HCD-12
s. 20 .... HCD-29
s. 21(1) HCD-36
s. 21(3) HCD-37
s. 21(4) HCD-37
ss. 23(1)-(2) HCD-86
s. 23(3) HCD-86
s. 24(1) HCD-32
s. 24(2) HCD-32
s. 25(1) HCD-64, HCD-65
s. 26 .... HCD-62
s. 27(1) HCD-40, HCD-41
s. 27(3) HCD-42
s. 27(4) HCD-41
ss. 27(8)-(10) HCD-41
s. 27(11) HCD-42
s. 27(13) HCD-41
ss. 28(1)-(2) HCD-40
ss. 29(1) HCD-41
ss. 29(1)-(2) HCD-41
s. 29(3) HCD-43
s. 30(1) HCD-43
s. 30(2) HCD-43
s. 30(3) HCD-45
s. 31(1) HCD-44
ss. 31(2)-(5) HCD-44
s. 31(6) HCD-44
ss. 31(7)-(8) HCD-44
ss. 32(2)-(3) HCD-24
s. 32(3) HCD-25
s. 32(5) HCD-24

Para.

Condominium Property Act, S.N.B. 2009, c. C-16.05 — *cont'd*
s. 32(6) HCD-24
s. 32(7) HCD-25
s. 32(12) HCD-24
ss. 33(1)-(2) HCD-26
s. 33(3) HCD-26
s. 37(1) HCD-33
s. 37(5)(a) HCD-98
ss. 37(5)(b)-(c) HCD-102
s. 38(2), 42(1) HCD-33
s. 38(3) HCD-33
s. 38(6) HCD-29
ss. 43(1), 44(1) HCD-23
ss. 43(2), 44(2) HCD-23
ss. 43(4), 44(4) HCD-23
ss. 43(8), 44(8) HCD-23
s. 46(1) HCD-97
s. 46(2) HCD-97
s. 46(4) HCD-97
ss. 46(5)-(6) HCD-97
s. 46(7) HCD-97
ss. 46(8)-(9) HCD-97
s. 46(10) HCD-97
ss. 46(13)-(14) HCD-97
s. 46(14) HCD-97
s. 47(6) HCD-113
s. 48(1) HCD-73
s. 48(2) HCD-74
ss. 48(2), 49 .... HCD-74
s. 48(3) HCD-76
s. 48(6) HCD-78
s. 49 .... HCD-74
s. 50(1) HCD-77
s. 51(1) HCD-50
s. 52(2) HCD-49
s. 53 .... HCD-58
s. 53(4) HCD-59
s. 53(5) HCD-59
s. 53(6) HCD-113
s. 54 .... HCD-119
ss. 59(1)-(2) HCD-113
ss. 59(3)-(4) HCD-113
s. 60(1) HCD-86
s. 60(2) HCD-86, HCD-109
ss. 60(3)-(4) HCD-109
s. 60(4) HCD-112
s. 60(5) HCD-85

E

Energy Consumer Protection Act, R.S.O. 2010, c. 8, ss. 33(1)-(3) HCD-71

Para.

P

Personal Information Protection and Electronic Documents Act, S.C. 2000, c. 5 .... HCD-38

R

Residential Tenancies Act, S.A. 2004, c. R-17.1, s. 57 .... HCD-58, HCD-59, HCD-74, HCD-76

S

Strata Property Act, S.B.C. 1998, c. 43 .... HCD-69
Part 6 .... HCD-81
Part 8 .... HCD-58
Part 9 .... HCD-77
ss. 1, 2 .... HCD-14
s. 1(1) HCD-7, HCD-9, HCD-10
ss. 1(1), 73 .... HCD-9
s. 2 .... HCD-14
s. 2(1)(b) HCD-28
s. 3 .... HCD-29
s. 5(1) HCD-47
s. 5(2) HCD-47
s. 6 .... HCD-47
ss. 6, 31 .... HCD-43
ss. 7-8 .... HCD-47
s. 9 .... HCD-47
s. 10 .... HCD-47
ss. 12-15 .... HCD-47
ss. 12(1), (4)-(5), 92(b) HCD-33
s. 16 .... HCD-46
ss. 23, 35 .... HCD-36
s. 25 .... HCD-41, HCD-61
s. 25, Schedule of Standard Bylaws, s. 10 .... HCD-41
s. 26 .... HCD-40
s. 28(1) HCD-41
s. 29(1) HCD-41
s. 30(1) HCD-43
s. 32(c) HCD-44
s. 32(d) HCD-44
s. 34 .... HCD-45
s. 36(1) HCD-37
s. 36(3) HCD-37
s. 36(4) HCD-37
s. 37 .... HCD-89
s. 39(1) HCD-89
ss. 39(1)-(2) HCD-89
s. 40 .... HCD-61
ss. 40-52 .... HCD-42

Para.

Strata Property Act, S.B.C. 1998, c. 43 — *cont'd*
s. 42 .... HCD-62
ss. 42, 43 .... HCD-61
s. 43 .... HCD-62
ss. 45, 47 .... HCD-62
s. 46 .... HCD-62
s. 48 .... HCD-62
s. 48(1) HCD-42
ss. 53-58 .... HCD-41
ss. 53, 54 .... HCD-64
s. 54 .... HCD-65
s. 56 .... HCD-67
s. 58 .... HCD-67
s. 59(1) HCD-34
s. 59(3) HCD-34
s. 59(5) HCD-34
s. 59(6) HCD-95
s. 62(3) HCD-28
s. 64 .... HCD-28
s. 66 .... HCD-10
s. 67 .... HCD-30
s. 69(1) HCD-12
s. 69(2) HCD-12
s. 69(3)(a) HCD-12
s. 69(3)(e) HCD-12
ss. 70, 257-266 .... HCD-23
s. 71 .... HCD-83
s. 72 .... HCD-74
s. 72(1) HCD-73, HCD-74, HCD-76
s. 72(2) HCD-74
ss. 72(2), (3) HCD-76
s. 77 .... HCD-31
ss. 78-80, 82 .... HCD-29
ss. 78(1), 79(a), 80(2)(a), 82(3) HCD-29
s. 92 .... HCD-81
s. 92(a) HCD-33
s. 95(2)(a) HCD-33
s. 95(2)(b) HCD-33
s. 95(3) HCD-33
ss. 99, 109 .... HCD-81
s. 111(1) HCD-33
s. 112(2) HCD-97
ss. 114-115 .... HCD-56
s. 116(1) HCD-97
ss. 116(1)-(2) HCD-97
ss. 116(1), 118 .... HCD-97
s. 116(5) HCD-97
s. 116(6) HCD-97
s. 117 .... HCD-98
s. 119(2) HCD-24
s. 120 .... HCD-24, HCD-39

Para.

ss. 121(1)-(2) HCD-24
s. 123(1) HCD-105
ss. 125(1), (3)-(6) HCD-26
ss. 125(2), 129 .... HCD-26
s. 127 .... HCD-25
s. 128(1) HCD-25
s. 128(2) HCD-25
ss. 133, 135(1)(b) HCD-112
s. 146 .... HCD-59
s. 163 .... HCD-32
ss. 163(1)-(2) HCD-32
s. 164(1) HCD-110
ss. 165, 173 .... HCD-85, HCD-86
s. 166(1) HCD-32
s. 169(1) HCD-38
ss. 171(1)-(2) HCD-32
s. 172(1) HCD-32
ss. 174(1)-(2) HCD-109
s. 174(3) HCD-109
ss. 174(3)-(5) HCD-109
s. 174(6) HCD-109
s. 177 .... HCD-113
ss. 187-188 .... HCD-113
ss. 191-193 .... HCD-10
ss. 194-198 .... HCD-10
s. 199 .... HCD-6, HCD-8
s. 200 .... HCD-9
s. 201 .... HCD-16
ss. 202-203 .... HCD-16
ss. 221-222, 224-225, 244(1)(h)(i), (iii) HCD-17
ss. 223, 226-230 .... HCD-15
ss. 231-232, 235 .... HCD-17
ss. 233-234 .... HCD-17
s. 235(3) HCD-96
s. 235(6) HCD-96
s. 240 .... HCD-14
s. 243 .... HCD-15
s. 244 .... HCD-21
s. 244(1)(h)(ii)-(iii) HCD-17
ss. 244-245 .... HCD-17
ss. 247-248 .... HCD-20
ss. 249-252 .... HCD-15
ss. 257-266 .... HCD-23
ss. 269-270 .... HCD-116
s. 271 .... HCD-32, HCD-117
s. 271(b) HCD-29
s. 290 .... HCD-115
s. 291(1) HCD-14

Para.

Strata Property Act, S.B.C. 1998, c. 43, Schedule of Standard Bylaws HCD-24
s. 3 .... HCD-101
ss. 3(1)(a)-(c)............................... HCD-103
s. 3(1)(a), (d) HCD-106
s. 3(2) HCD-106
s. 3(3) HCD-105
s. 3(4) HCD-105
ss. 5(1), 6(1) HCD-101

Para.

s. 5(2).. HCD-101
ss. 9(1)-(2) HCD-41
s. 11 .... HCD-41
s. 12(1).. HCD-42
ss. 13(1)-(4) HCD-40
ss. 14, 17-18.................................. HCD-42
s. 16(1).. HCD-42
s. 20 .... HCD-40
s. 22(1).. HCD-43
s. 29(1)... HCD-113

Table of Statutory Instruments — Condominiums

Para.

C

Condominium Property Regulation, Alta. Reg. 168/2000
s. 1(2) HCD-56
s. 2 .... HCD-15
ss. 13-18 .... HCD-121
ss. 16(1), (2) HCD-124
ss. 21(1), 28 .... HCD-83
ss. 21(1)-(2), 22, 23(1)-(3), 24(2), 25, 26(1), (2), 30, s. 55 .... HCD-81
ss. 21(1), (4)-(7), 24(1)-(3), 25, 26(1), (2), 29(1), (2), 30, 31(1), (2), 55 .... HCD-81
s. 21(1)(d), 27(1)-(3) HCD-81
ss. 25, 28, 55 .... HCD-81
ss. 26(2), 29, 31(2) HCD-53
s. 29(1) HCD-61
s. 30 .... HCD-81
ss. 35, 43 .... HCD-50
ss. 35-36, 38-42 .... HCD-15
s. 36(5) HCD-90, HCD-96
ss. 36(7)-(8) HCD-96
s. 37 .... HCD-88, HCD-96
s. 44 .... HCD-46
ss. 46-51 .... HCD-116
s. 47(2), s. 51(3), (4), ss. 52-56 .... HCD-117
ss. 52(1)-(2), 54 .... HCD-41
s. 56 .... HCD-32
s. 56(a) HCD-29
ss. 63-69 .... HCD-95
s. 71(1) HCD-23
s. 71(2) HCD-23
s. 71(3) HCD-23
s. 71(5) HCD-23
Sch. 2 .... HCD-33

Condominium Property Regulations, 2001, R.R.S. c. C-26.1, Reg. 2
ss. 8, 17-25 .... HCD-15
s. 10 .... HCD-87
s. 11 .... HCD-61
ss. 11, 51.1-51.7 .... HCD-81
s. 11(c) HCD-81
ss. 17-21, 26-30, 38 .... HCD-15
s. 19(3) HCD-62
ss. 22(1)-(4) HCD-62
s. 27 .... HCD-64
s. 30 .... HCD-66
ss. 30, 36 .... HCD-116
s. 33 .... HCD-60

Para.

s. 41.5(1) HCD-28
ss. 41.6-41.7 .... HCD-28
s. 41.8 .... HCD-117
s. 44, 44.1, Condominium Bylaws, ss. 1(1)-(4), s. 4(f) HCD-83
s. 44, s. 44.1, Interpretation, Condominium Bylaws, ss. 1(1)-(4), s. 2(f) HCD-84
s. 47, s. 48 .... HCD-69
s. 47, ss. 48-51 .... HCD-81
s. 51.2 .... HCD-81
s. 53 .... HCD-53
ss. 61, 62 .... HCD-121
ss. 63, 64 86(1), 88, 88.1 .... HCD-124
App., Part II, Condominium Bylaws, s. 2(d) HCD-76
App., Part II, Condominium Bylaws, s. 4(b) HCD-33
App., Part II, Condominium Bylaws, s. 10 .... HCD-41
App., Part II, Condominium Bylaws, s. 11 .... HCD-42
App., Part II, Condominium Bylaws, s. 13(2) HCD-42
App., Part II, Condominium Bylaws, s. 15 .... HCD-28
App., Part II, Condominium Bylaws, s. 17(1) HCD-43
App., Part II, Condominium Bylaws, s. 17(4) HCD-43
App., Part II, Condominium Bylaws, s. 2(a) HCD-30, HCD-31
App., Part II, Condominium Bylaws, s. 3(a) HCD-29
App., Part II, Condominium Bylaws, ss. 5(1)-(2) HCD-41
App., Part II, Condominium Bylaws, s. 5(3) HCD-41
App., Part II, Condominium Bylaws, s. 6(1) HCD-41
App., Part II, Condominium Bylaws, s. 6(2) HCD-41
App., Part II, Condominium Bylaws, s. 6(3)(a) HCD-41
App., Part II, Condominium Bylaws, s. 6(3)(b) HCD-41
App., Part II, Condominium Bylaws, s. 6(3)(c) HCD-41
App., Part II, Condominium Bylaws, s. 7 .... HCD-41

Para.

Condominium Property Regulations, 2001, R.R.S. c. C-26.1, Reg. 2 — *cont'd*
App., Part II, Condominium Bylaws, ss. 8(1)-(3) ... HCD-41
App., Part II, Condominium Bylaws, s. 9 ... HCD-41
App., Part II, Condominium Bylaws, ss. 12(1)-(4), 17(2)-(3) ... HCD-40
App., Part II, Condominium Bylaws, ss. 13(1), 14(1), 17(1)(a)-(b), 19 ... HCD-42
App., Part II, Condominium Bylaws, ss. 18(a)-(b) ... HCD-40
App., Part II, Condominium Bylaws, s. 2(f) ... HCD-101
App., Part II, Condominium Bylaws, s. 33(b) ... HCD-104, HCD-106
App., Part II, Condominium Bylaws, s. 33(c) ... HCD-99
App., Part II, Condominium Bylaws, s. 34(2)(a) ... HCD-101
App., Part II, Condominium Bylaws, ss. 34(2)(a), (b), (d) ... HCD-103
App., Part II, Condominium Bylaws, ss. 34(2)(b), (e) ... HCD-106
App., Part II, Condominium Bylaws ... HCD-24
App., Part II, Condominium Bylaws, s. 1(4) ... HCD-24
App., Part II, Condominium Bylaws, ss. 48-50.1 ... HCD-25
App., Part II, Condominium Bylaws, s. 2(a) ... HCD-74
App., Part II, Condominium Bylaws, s. 2(b) ... HCD-74
App., Part II, Condominium Bylaws, s. 8 ... HCD-61
App., Part II, Condominium Bylaws, ss. 17(1), (2) ... HCD-61
App., Part II, Condominium Bylaws, s. 21 ... HCD-62

Condominium Regulations, N.S. Reg. 60/71
s. 54AA ... HCD-116
s. 75(2) ... HCD-50

Condominium Regulations, N.W.T. Reg. 098-2008
s. 1, ss. 7(1)- (3), ss. 8-11(2) ... HCD-81
ss. 2, 3 ... HCD-116
s. 4 ... HCD-50
s. 4(a) ... HCD-49
s. 12 ... HCD-33
s. 14 ... HCD-34

D

Description and Registration Regulation, O. Reg. 49/01
s. 2(1)(b) ... HCD-9
s. 4 ... HCD-121
ss. 4, 18, 28, 42 ... HCD-116
s. 4(2) ... HCD-21
s. 19(1) ... HCD-21
s. 22 ... HCD-15
s. 27(3) ... HCD-28
s. 27(6) ... HCD-117
ss. 28(1)(g), 28(3)(h), 28(7), 31(2), 32, 33 ... HCD-15
ss. 28(2), 28(5) ... HCD-16
s. 34 ... HCD-119
ss. 34, 47(2)-(5) ... HCD-120
ss. 34, 49(1) ... HCD-123
ss. 34, 50 ... HCD-122
s. 38(1) ... HCD-25
ss. 40(1), 40(2) ... HCD-58
ss. 44(2), 47(4)-(6), 48(1), (3), (4), 50 ... HCD-125
ss. 49(1)-(2) ... HCD-125
ss. 47(1), (3), (4), (5) ... HCD-119
s. 48 ... HCD-121
s. 51 ... HCD-124

G

General Regulation, N.B. Reg. 2009-169
s. 4(1) ... HCD-17
s. 4(2) ... HCD-15
ss. 5, 6 ... HCD-116
s. 7 ... HCD-17
s. 8(1) ... HCD-17
ss. 8(2)-(5) ... HCD-17
s. 11(1) ... HCD-28

General Regulation, O. Reg. 48/01
s. 2 ... HCD-14
s. 5 ... HCD-17
ss. 7, 34-37 ... HCD-116
s. 12 ... HCD-91
s. 13 ... HCD-67
s. 14 ... HCD-25
s. 17 ... HCD-50
s. 18 ... HCD-53
s. 18(2) ... HCD-34
s. 19(1) ... HCD-55
ss. 19(2), (3) ... HCD-57

Para.

General Regulation, O. Reg. 48/01 — *cont'd*
s. 20, s. 39 .... HCD-56
s. 23 .... HCD-58
ss. 25(1), (2) HCD-84
s. 26 .... HCD-74, HCD-119, HCD-120
s. 27-32 .... HCD-81
s. 31(2) HCD-81
ss. 33(1)-(3), ss. 38(1)-(6) HCD-81
s. 38 .... HCD-81, HCD-117
ss. 39, 39.1 .... HCD-15
s. 40 .... HCD-17
s. 44 .... HCD-64
ss. 48, 51 .... HCD-15
s. 49 .... HCD-17
s. 51 .... HCD-10
s. 52 .... HCD-17
s. 53(3) HCD-21
s. 55 .... HCD-50
s. 56 .... HCD-17
s. 56(1)(a) HCD-15
s. 59 .... HCD-16
s. 60 .... HCD-18
ss. 62(2), 62(4) HCD-125
Form 3 .... HCD-53

General Regulations, P.E.I. Reg. EC10/78,
s. 4(1)(e) HCD-28

S

Strata Property Regulation, B.C. Reg. 43/2000
s. 4.4 .... HCD-34
s. 17.11(1) and (2) HCD-81
s. 43 .... HCD-89
s. 64 .... HCD-81

Table of Statutes — Constitutional Law — Division of Powers

Para.

A

Act of Settlement 1700 (U.K.), 12 & 13 Will. III, c. 2..........HCL-6, HCL-41, HCL-62

Administration of Justice Act, R.S.O. 1990, c. A.6....................................HCL-140

Aeronautics Act, R.S.C. 1985, c. A-2...HCL-184

Alberta Act (U.K.), 4 & 5 Edw. VII, c. 3...............................HCL-5, HCL-25

Atomic Energy Control Act, R.S.C. 1985, c. A-16......................................HCL-214

B

Bank Act, S.C. 1991, c. 46 ....HCL-167

Bankruptcy and Insolvency Act, R.S.C. 1985, c. B-3.....HCL-169, HCL-168, HCL-170

Bill of Rights 1688 (U.K.), 1 Will. & Mar. sess. 2, c. 2 ....HCL-6, HCL-37
- art. 4 ....HCL-137
- art. 9 ....HCL-51, HCL-49

British North America Act, 1867 (U.K.), 30 & 31 Vict., c. 3...........................HCL-3
- s. 92(16) HCL-118

British North America Act, 1871 (U.K.), 34 & 35 Vict., c. 28
- s. 91 ....HCL-110
- s. 91(1)(a)....................................HCL-108
- s. 92..HCL-110

British North America Act, 1949 (U.K.), 12, 13 & 14 Geo. VI, c. 22.............HCL-38

Building Code Act, 1992, S.O. 1992, c. 23..HCL-184

C

Canada (Ontario Boundary) Act, 1889 (U.K.), 52 & 53 Vict., c. 28.........HCL-5

Para.

Canada Act 1982 (U.K.), 1982, c. 11 .... HCL-5, HCL-6

Canada Evidence Act, R.S.C. 1985, c. C-5 .... HCL-121

Canada Temperance Act, 1878, R.S.C. 1927, c. 196 ....HCL-108

Canadian Bill of Rights, S.C. 1960, c. 44 .... HCL-7

Canadian Charter of Rights and Freedoms, Part I of the *Constitution Act, 1982*, being Schedule B to the *Canada Act 1982* (U.K.), 1982, c. 11 .... HCL-1, HCL-4, HCL-10, HCL-25, HCL-28, HCL-30, HCL-32, HCL-40, HCL-44, HCL-57, HCL-84
- s. 4(1) HCL-15
- s. 5 .... HCL-15
- s. 7 .... HCL-48, HCL-62
- s. 11(d) HCL-41, HCL-62, HCL-64, HCL-65, HCL-66, HCL-67, HCL-68, HCL-69, HCL-70, HCL-117
- s. 15 .... HCL-42
- s. 35 .... HCL-4
- s. 40 .... HCL-4
- s. 41 .... HCL-4
- s. 42 .... HCL-4
- s. 43 .... HCL-4
- s. 44 .... HCL-4
- s. 52 .... HCL-1
- s. 52(1) HCL-4

Colonial Laws Validity Act 1865 (U.K.), 28 & 29 Vict., c. 63 .... HCL-6

Combines Investigation Act, R.S.C. 1927, c. 26.......................................HCL-127

Constitution Act (No. 1), 1975, R.S.C. 1985, App. II, No. 41........................... HCL-5

Constitution Act (No. 2), 1975, R.S.C. 1985, App. II, No. 42........................... HCL-5

Para.

Constitution Act, 1867 (U.K.), 30 & 31 Vict., c. 3 ....HCL-3, HCL-4, HCL-5, HCL-6, HCL-15, HCL-16, HCL-24, HCL-25, HCL-26, HCL-29, HCL-30, HCL-32, HCL-37, HCL-38, HCL-41, HCL-47, HCL-53, HCL-55, HCL-58, HCL-84, HCL-107, HCL-108, HCL-120, HCL-136, HCL-141, HCL-148, HCL-177, HCL-200, HCL-203, HCL-205, HCL-214
- preamble....HCL-6, HCL-13, HCL-28, HCL-29, HCL-33, HCL-53
- s. 8 ....HCL-8
- s. 9....HCL-6, HCL-8
- s. 12....HCL-6, HCL-8
- s. 17....HCL-13, HCL-16
- s. 18....HCL-13, HCL-49, HLC-50, HCL-51, HCL-53
- s. 19(1A) HCL-160
- s. 21....HCL-14
- s. 22....HCL-14
- s. 23....HCL-14
- s. 24....HCL-14
- s. 26 ....HCL-14
- s. 28....HCL-14
- s. 29....HCL-14
- s. 37....HCL-15
- s. 38....HCL-15
- s. 47(1) HCL-14, HCL-15
- s. 50....HCL-15
- s. 51....HCL-15
- s. 51(a) HCL-15
- s. 52....HCL-15
- s. 52(2) HCL-6
- s. 53....HCL-14, HCL-46, HCL-136, HCL-137, HCL-140, HCL-141
- s. 53(a) HCL-15
- s. 55....HCL-14
- s. 90....HCL-140, HCL-141
- s. 91....HCL-32, HCL-38, HCL-86, HCL-88, HCL-94, HCL-95, HCL-97, HCL-102, HCL-107, HCL-108, HCL-120, HCL-122, HCL-131, HCL-181, HCL-191, HCL-193, HCL-202, HCL-218, HCL-219
- s. 91(1A) HCL-207, HCL-216, HCL-217
- s. 91(2) HCL-129, HCL-130, HCL-195, HCL-196, HCL-210
- s. 91(3) HCL-136, HCL-138, HCL-140, HCL-160, HCL-200, HCL-209
- s. 91(7) HCL-122

Para.

- s. 91(10) HCL-172, HCL-177, HCL-182
- s. 91(12) HCL-200, HCL-217, HCL-219
- s. 91(15) HCL-163
- s. 91(16) HCL-163
- s. 91(19) HCL-171
- s. 91(21) HCL-168, HCL-169
- s. 91(24) HCL-200
- s. 91(27)... HCL-111, HCL-112, HCL- 115, HCL-121, HCL-123, HCL-126
- s. 91(28) HCL-112, HCL-126
- s. 91(29) HCL-172, HCL-186
- s. 92 .... HCL-32, HCL-38, HCL-86, HCL-88, HCL-94, HCL-95, HCL-97, HCL-102, HCL-107, HCL-108, HCL-129, HCL-204, HCL-218
- s. 92(1)(a) HCL-178
- s. 92(2) HCL-136, HCL-140, HCL-142, HCL-143, HCL-144, HCL-146, HCL-158, HCL-200, HCL-207
- s. 92(4)....HCL-59
- s. 92(5)...... HCL-192, HCL-200, HCL-205, HCL-207, HCL-215, HCL-217
- s. 92(6)....HCL-112, HCL-126
- s. 92(8) HCL-122
- s. 92(9) HCL-136, HCL-138, HCL-157, HCL-158
- s. 92(10) HCL-172, HCL-183, HCL-200, HCL-205, HCL-207, HCL-211, HCL-216
- s. 92(10)(a) ... HCL-173, HCL-182, HCL-183, HCL-184, HCL-187, HCL-188, HCL-208
- s. 92(10)(c) HCL-176, HCL-183, HCL-185, HCL-210, HCL-214
- s. 92(10)(g) HCL-182
- s. 92(13) HCL-129, HCL-130, HCL-131, HCL-158, HCL-189, HCL-190, HCL-191, HCL-192, HCL-194, HCL-195, HCL-196, HCL-197, HCL-200, HCL-205, HCL-207, HCL-215, HCL-219
- s. 92(14) HCL-59, HCL-61, HCL-73, HCL-112, HCL-120, HCL-122, HCL-123, HCL-126, HCL-197
- s. 92(15).... HCL-112, HCL-125, HCL-126, HCL-167, HCL-197
- s. 92(16) ... HCL-115, HCL-129, HCL-131, HCL-158, HCL-181, HCL-190, HCL-191, HCL-192, HCL-193, HCL-194, HCL-197, HCL-199, HCL-207
- s. 92(27) HCL-59, HCL-197

Para.

Constitution Act, 1867 (U.K.), 30 & 31 Vict., c. 3 — *cont'd*
s. 92A HCL-86, HCL-205, HCL-207, HCL-210, HCL-215
s. 92A(1) HCL-210
s. 92A(4) HCL-136, HCL-159, HCL-207
s. 92A(5) HCL-159
s. 93 ....HCL-86
s. 94 ....HCL-86
s. 94A HCL-86
s. 95 ....HCL-86
s. 96 ....HCL-41, HCL-60, HCL-61, HCL-62, HCL-64, HCL-71, HCL-72, HCL-73, HCL-74, HCL-75, HCL-76, HCL-77, HCL-79, HCL-120
s. 97 ....HCL-41, HCL-61, HCL-62, HCL-64, HCL-71, HCL-72, HCL-73
s. 98 ....HCL-41, HCL-61, HCL-62, HCL-64, HCL-71, HCL-72, HCL-73
s. 99 ....HCL-41, HCL-61, HCL-62, HCL-64, HCL-65, HCL-69, HCL-71, HCL-72, HCL-73
s. 100 ....HCL-41, HCL-60, HCL-61, HCL-62, HCL-64, HCL-71, HCL-72, HCL-73
s. 101 ....HCL-61, HCL-71, HCL-72, HCL-80, HCL-81, HCL-83, HCL-85, HCL-86, HCL-120
s. 102 ....HCL-160
s. 106 ....HCL-160
s. 109 ....HCL-205
s. 125 ....HCL-136, HCL-138, HCL-139, HCL-140, HCL-151, HCL-155, HCL-209
s. 126 ....HCL-162
s. 129 ....HCL-123
s. 132 ....HCL-86

Constitution Act, 1871 (U.K.) 34 & 35, c. 28..........HCL-5, HCL-25
s. 2 ....HCL-86
s. 3 ....HCL-86
s. 4 ....HCL-86

Constitution Act, 1886 (U.K.), 49 & 50 Vict., c. 35..........HCL-5

Constitution Act, 1907 (U.K.) 7 Edw. VII, c. 11..........HCL-5

Constitution Act, 1915 (U.K.), 5 & 6 Geo. V, c. 45..........HCL-5

Para.

Constitution Act, 1930 (U.K.), 20 & 21 Geo. V, c. 26 ....HCL-5, HCL-25

Constitution Act, 1940 (U.K.) 3 & 4 Geo. VI, c. 36 ....HCL-5

Constitution Act, 1960 (U.K.), 9 Eliz. II, c. 2 ....HCL-5

Constitution Act, 1964 (U.K.), 12 & 13 Eliz. II, c. 73 ....HCL-5

Constitution Act, 1965, R.S.C. 1985, App. II, No. 39 ....HCL-5

Constitution Act, 1967 being Schedule B to the *Canada Act 1982* (U.K.), 1982, c. 11, s. 15 ....HCL-24

Constitution Act, 1974, R.S.C. 1985, App. II, No. 40 ....HCL-5

Constitution Act, 1982, being Schedule B to the *Canada Act 1982* (U.K.), 1982, c. 11 ....HCL-2, HCL-3, HCL-4, HCL-5, HCL-16, HCL-25, HCL-32
preamble HCL-28, HCL-33
s. 35 ....HCL-42
s. 41(a) HCL-6
s. 41(c) HCL-7
s. 41(d) HCL-7
s. 43 ....HCL-7
s. 52 ....HCL-1, HCL-30
s. 52(1) HCL-1, HCL-4, HCL-32, CL-43
s. 52(2) HCL-4, HCL-5, HCL-25
s. 52(2)(b) HCL-5
s. 52(2)(c) HCL-5
s. 55 ....HCL-17
s. 58 ....HCL-20

Constitution Act, 1985 (Representation) S.C. 1968, c. 8 ....HCL-5

Constitution Act, 1999 (Nunavut), S.C. 1998, c. 15, Part II HCL-5

Controlled Drugs and Substances Act, S.C. 1996, c. 19 ....HCL-118

Para.

Criminal Code, R.S.C. 1985, c. C-46 .... HCL-119, HCL-120, HCL-121, HCL-123, HCL-124, HCL-125, HCL-127, HCL-183, HCL-197, HCL-198
s. 672.54 .... HCL-127
s. 743.1(1) HCL-112

F

Federal Courts Act, R.S.C. 1985, c. F-7 .... HCL-82

Firearms Act, S.C. 1995, c. 39 .... HCL-119

Fisheries Act, R.S.C. 1985, c. F-14 .... HCL-219

Food and Drugs Act, R.S.C. 1985, c. F-27 .... HCL-118, HCL-123

H

Heroin Treatment Act, S.B.C. 1978, c. 24 .... HCL-118

I

Interest Act, R.S.C. 1970, c. I-18 .... HCL-171

Interpretation Act, R.S.C. 1985, c. I-21, s. 42(1) HCL-31

J

Juvenile Delinquents Act, R.S.C. 1952, c. 160 .... HCL-128

M

Manitoba Act, 1870, 33 Vict., c. 3 ..... HCL-5, HCL-25

N

Narcotic Control Act, R.S.C. 1985, c. N-1 .... HCL-108, HCL-123

National Defence Act, R.S.C. 1985, c. N-5 .... HCL-70

Newfoundland Act (U.K.), 12 & 13 Geo. VI, c. 22 .... HCL-5

Para.

Newfoundland Act, 1949 (U.K.), 212 & 213 Geo. VI, c. 22, reprinted in R.S.C. 1985, App. II, No. 32 .... HCL-25

O

Ocean Dumping Control Act, S.C. 1974-75-76, c. 55 .... HCL-202
s. 4(1) HCL-202

Official Languages Act , R.S.C. 1985, c. 31 (4th Supp.) HCL-7, HCL-108

P

Parliament of Canada Act, 1875 (U.K.), 38 & 39 Vict., c. 38 .... HCL-5

Parliament of Canada Act, R.S.C. 1985, c. P-1 .... HCL-51, HCL-55
s. 4 .... HCL-49, HCL-51, HCL-55

R

Retails Sales Tax Act, R.S.M. 1970, c. R150 .... HCL-144

S

Saskatchewan Act (U.K.) 4 & 5 Edw. VII, c. 42 .... HCL-5

Statute of Westminster, 1931 (U.K), 22 Geo. V, c. 4 .... HCL-5, HCL-6, HCL-18, HCL-25
s. 2 .... HCL-86
s. 3 .... HCL-86

Supreme Court Act, R.S.C. 1985, c. S-26 .... HCL-7

T

Tobacco Products Control Act, S.C. 1998, c. 20 .... HCL-117

Y

Young Offenders Act, R.S.C. 1985, c. Y-1 .... HCL-128

Youth Criminal Justice Act, S.C. 2002, c. 1 .... HCL-128

Table of Statutory Instruments — Constitutional Law — Division of Powers

Para.

A

Adjacent Territories Order, R.S.C. 1985, App. II, No. 14 .... HCL-5

Air Regulations HCL-184

B

British Columbia Terms of Union, R.S.C. 1985, App. II, No. 10 .... HCL-5

Building Code, O. Reg. 350/06 .... HCL-184

C

Constitution Amendement Proclamation, 1983, S.I./84-102 .... HCL-5

Constitution Amendment, 1987 (Newfoundland Act), S.I./88-11 .... HCL-5

Constitution Amendment, 1993 (New Brunswick), S.I./93-54 .... HCL-5

Constitution Amendment, 1993 (Prince Edward Island) S.I./94-50 .... HCL-5

Constitution Amendment, 1997 (Newfoundland Act), S.I./97-55 .... HCL-5

Constitution Amendment, 1997 (Quebec), S.I./97-141 .... HCL-5

Constitution Amendment, 1998 (Newfoundland Act), S.I./98-25 .... HCL-5

Constitution Amendment, 2001 (Newfoundland and Labrador), S.I./ 2002-117 .... HCL-5

P

Prince Edward Island Terms of Union, R.S.C. 1985, App. II, No. 12 ..... HCL-5

R

Rupert's Land and North-Western Territory Order, R.S.C. 1985, App. II, No. 9 .... HCL-5

Halsbury's
Laws of Canada
First Edition

Condominiums

Contributed by

Marko Djurdjevac
LL.B.

Contributing Editors

Shirley Margolis
B.A., J.D.

Wendy Litner
H.B.A., LL.B.

Ambit of Title

The title **Condominiums** examines the legislation and cases which govern condominium law issues in every jurisdiction in Canada. Topics covered include: creation of general, freehold and leasehold condominiums; management by the condominium corporation and board of directors; sale and lease of condominium units; common expenses, repair and maintenance of condominium units and common expenses; compliance, enforcement, remedies and dispute resolution; and amalgamation and termination of condominiums.

Statement of Currency

The law stated in this title is in general that in force on October 1, 2011. However, at the time of publication, the Office of the Legislature in Newfoundland and Labrador announced that the *Condominium Act, 2009*, S.N.L. 2009, c. C.29.1 will come into force on December 1, 2011. Subsequent developments may be located by referring to this volume's Annual Cumulative Supplement.

Related Titles

Please refer to the following titles (when published) for related and complementary information:

Business Corporations
Landlord and Tenant
Mortgages
Planning and Zoning
Real Property

References and Abbreviations

AB	Alberta
BC	British Columbia
CAN	Canada
MB	Manitoba
NB	New Brunswick
NL	Newfoundland and Labrador
NS	Nova Scotia
NT	Northwest Territories
NU	Nunavut
ON	Ontario
PE	Prince Edward Island
QC	Québec
SK	Saskatchewan
YT	Yukon

Table of Contents — Condominiums

Page

Table of Cases 25

Table of Statutes 57

Table of Statutory Instruments 79

Ambit of Title, Statement of Currency, Related Titles 91

References and Abbreviations 93

I. Introduction

1. The Nature of Condominiums 103

2. The Nature of Condominium Legislation 105

3. The Balance between Consumer Protection and Commercial Realities 107

4. The Role of the Common Law 107

5. Fiduciary Duties in Condominiums 108

II. Creation of Condominiums

1. Types of Condominium Properties

(1) General 112
(2) Freehold Condominiums 112
(3) Leasehold Condominiums 114

2. Types of Property Interests in a Condominium Property

(1) Ownership Interests
(a) General 115

Page

(b) Freehold Condominiums 119
(c) Leasehold Condominiums 123
(2) Other Interests
(a) Easements 123
(b) Encumbrances 127

3. Registration

(1) General 129
(2) Freehold Condominium Corporations 131
(3) Leasehold Condominium Corporations 135

4. Declaration and Description or Plan

(1) Declaration
(a) Required Contents
(i) Freehold Condominiums 136
(ii) Leasehold Condominiums 139
(iii) Property Containing Occupied Rental Units 140
(b) Permitted Contents 141
(2) Description or Plan
(a) Freehold Condominiums 143
(b) Leasehold Condominiums 146
(3) Amendments 146

5. By-Laws and Rules

(1) By-Laws
(a) Subject Matter of By-Laws 150
(b) Procedure for Making, Amending and Repealing By-Laws 153
(2) Rules 155
(3) Joint By-Laws and Rules 158

III. General Management by the Condominium Corporation

1. Introductory Matters 161

2. Objects and Duties 163

Page

3. **Assessment and Taxation** 166
4. **Entry by Corporation and Others** 168
5. **Action By or Against Corporation** 169
6. **Corporation's Money** 172
7. **Information**
   (1) With a Fee 175
   (2) Without a Fee 178
8. **Records**
   (1) Duty to Maintain Records 179
   (2) Access to Records
       (a) General 181
       (b) Restrictions on Access 183
       (c) Failure to Provide Access 184

IV. The Board of Directors

1. **General Duty** 187
2. **Number, Term, Election, Qualification and Removal** 188
3. **Conduct of Business** 192
4. **Standard of Care** 194
5. **Disclosure of Interest** 196
6. **Financial Matters** 198

Page

V. Transfer of Control and Sale and Lease of Units

1. Transfer of Control by Owner/Declarant

(1) First Board of Directors or Council 201
(2) The Owner-Developer and the Corporation 203
(3) Election of New Board of Directors and Turn-over of Records and Other Items 204

2. Sale of Units

(1) Disclosure Requirements for Condominium Corporation
(a) Disclosure Statement
(i) Freehold Condominium Corporation 207
(ii) Leasehold Condominium Corporation 209
(b) Material Changes to Disclosure Statements 209
(2) Access to Information and Records Regarding the Corporation 209
(3) Implied Covenants and Conditions and Statutory Duties 211
(4) Interim Occupancy 212
(5) Money Held in Trust... 213
(6) Interest 213

3. Lease of Units

(1) Notification by Owner... 214
(2) Deemed Covenants or Conditions 215
(3) Deposits 216

VI. Unit Owners

1. Meetings

(1) Types of Meetings 217
(2) Procedure for Calling Meetings........................... 219

Page

2. Voting

(1) General 222
(2) Persons Entitled to Vote
  (a) Owner 222
  (b) Mortgagee 223
(3) Loss of Right to Vote 224
(4) Method of Voting 224
(5) Number of Votes Required 225

VII. Common Expenses, Repair and Maintenance and Changes to the Condominium

1. Common Expenses

(1) Contribution of Owners 228
(2) Special Levies, Assessments and User Fees 230
(3) Additions to Common Expenses 230
(4) No Avoidance of Common Expenses 232

2. Repair and Maintenance

(1) Repair After Damages
  (a) General 233
  (b) Condominium Property 233
(2) Maintenance
  (a) General 236
  (b) Condominium Property 236
(3) Common Law Application of Statutory Duty 238
(4) Work Done for Owner 240
(5) Vacant Land Condominium Corporation 240
(6) Common Elements Condominium Corporation 241
(7) Reserve Fund 241
(8) Warranties 245

3. Changes to the Condominium Property, Assets and Services

(1) Changes Made by Corporation 245
(2) Changes Made by Owners 246

Page

VIII. Compliance, Enforcement, Remedies and Dispute Resolution

1. **Introduction** 250

2. **Compliance with the Act, Declaration, By-Laws and Rules** 251

3. **Purchase and Sale of Units and Development of the Condominium Property**

   (1) Rescission of Agreement of Purchase and Sale by Purchaser 257
   (2) Termination of Agreement of Purchase and Sale by Developer 260
   (3) Termination of Other Types of Agreements 261
   (4) Damages for Developer's Statement or Information 264
   (5) Warranties and Performance Audit Related to Construction of the Condominium Property 266
   (6) Remedies Related to Developer's Turn-Over Obligations 267
   (7) Remedies Related to Money Held in Trust 268
   (8) Obligations Related to First-Year Deficit 270
   (9) Remedies for Other Obligations 271
   (10) Obligations and Remedies Related to Phased Development 274

4. **Non-Payment of Common Expenses or Other Contributions by Owners**

   (1) Statutory Lien 278
   (2) Court Proceedings 283
   (3) Payment of Arrears by Tenant 284
   (4) Mortgagee's Rights 285

5. **Occupation and Use of Units and Common Elements**

   (1) Use of Common Elements and Changes to Units and Common Elements 287

Page

(2) Repair and Maintenance 288
(3) Noise, Nuisance and Harassment 290
(4) Tenants and Occupants 291
(5) Pets 293
(6) Dangerous Activities 295

6. Court-Appointed Officers

(1) Appointment of Inspector 297
(2) Appointment of Investigator 298
(3) Appointment of Administrator 298

7. Oppression Remedy

(1) Statutory Basis 300
(2) Application of Oppression Remedy 302

8. Costs and Indemnification 304

9. Alternative Dispute Resolution

(1) Optional Alternative Dispute Resolution 306
(2) Mandatory Alternative Dispute Resolution 309

10. Offences 312

IX. Amalgamation and Termination of Condominiums

1. Amalgamation

(1) Requirements for Amalgamation 315
(2) Effect of Amalgamation 316

2. Termination or Winding Up of Condominium or Strata Corporation

(1) Termination
(a) With Consent 318
(b) Upon Substantial Damage 319
(c) By Sale 320
(d) By the Court 322

Page

(2) Expropriation 323
(3) Effect of Termination or Expropriation 324
(4) Leasehold Condominium Corporations 326

Index 541

Selected Secondary Sources 571

Glossary of Defined Terms in Condominium Legislation 575

I. Introduction

1. The Nature of Condominiums HCD-1
2. The Nature of Condominium Legislation HCD-2
3. The Balance between Consumer Protection and Commercial Realities HCD-3
4. The Role of the Common Law HCD-4
5. Fiduciary Duties in Condominiums HCD-5

---

1. The Nature of Condominiums

▼HCD-1▼ Meaning. The term "condominium" is a reference to a unique system of real property ownership and administration. Typically, the condominium property is comprised of units and common elements or common property. The units are individually owned and the common property is owned by all the unit owners collectively. A condominium corporation is created for the purposes of administering the condominium property as a whole.[1]

Unique system of individual and shared ownership. Although the condominium concept of individual and shared ownership of property is relatively new, this system combines many previously developed legal relationships. It resembles living in small communities in the past "with all the benefits and the potential problems that go with living in close collaboration with former strangers", as observed by the British Columbia Supreme Court[2] It has also been described as a little democratic sub-society which necessitates more restrictions with respect to the use of the condominium property when compared to the ownership of real property outside the condominium system.[3]

Balancing individual and collective interests. Owners in a condominium have many of the same rights associated with sole ownership of real property; however, some of those rights are subordinated to the will of the majority in light of the co-ownership of property.[4] The law will not permit individual owners to disrupt the integrity of the common scheme of a condominium.[5] For a condominium to be successful and promote the health, happiness, and peace of mind of the majority of the unit owners, there must be an equitable balance between the independence of the individual owners and the interdependence of all of them in a co-operative community.[6] The common features of all condominiums are the need for this balance and the possibility of tension between individual and collective interests.[7] In exchange for the advantages gained through common ownership, a certain degree of control over what can be done with the common property is given up, the details of which are set out in the condominium documents, *i.e.*, the declaration or plan and the by-laws and rules. It is both the right and the obligation of unit owners to see that these governing documents are obeyed.[8]

Judicial approach to determination of rights. The courts will be very cautious to find absolute rights in individual owners that cannot be modified by the considered view of the majority of owners, and controlled by judicial supervision where appropriate.[9] The effective joint ownership and management of a condominium requires that differences of opinion about what is in the best interests of the owners must be resolved, and decisions must be made, in a timely fashion.[10]

Notes

1. A.H. Oosterhoff & W.B. Rayner, *Anger and Honsberger Law of Real Property*, vol. 2 (Aurora, Ont.: Canada Law Book, 1985); and Alvin B. Rosenberg, *Condominium in Canada* (Toronto, Ont.: Canada Law Book, 1969).
2. *Shaw Cablesystems Ltd. v. Concord Pacific Group Inc.*, [2007] B.C.J. No. 2529 at para. 10, 2007 BCSC 1711 (B.C.S.C.), affd [2008] B.C.J. No. 1014, 2008 BCCA 234 (B.C.C.A.).
3. *Hidden Harbour Estates, Inc. v. Norman*, 309 So.2d 180 (Fla. 4th DCA 1975).
4. Robert J. Owens *et al.*, eds., *Corpus Juris Secundum* (1996), Estates 195, Vol. 31, at 260.
5. *Condominium Plan No. 9524710 (c.o.b. West Edmonton Commerce Park) v. Webb (c.o.b. Blue Bay Massage)*, [1999] A.J. No. 10, 1999 ABQB 7 (Alta. Q.B.) where Murray J. adopted the reasoning of the District Court of Appeal of Florida in *Village Condominium Inc. v. Breitenback*, 251 So.2d 585 (1971). See also *Condominium Plan No. 022 1347 v. N.Y.*, [2003] A.J. No. 1227, 2003 ABQB 790 (Alta. Q.B.) and *Ciddio v. York Region Condominium Corp. No. 730,* [2002] O.J. No. 553 (Ont. S.C.J.).
6. A.H. Oosterhoff & W.B. Rayner, *Anger and Honsberger Law of Real Property*, vol. 2 (Aurora, Ont.: Canada Law Book, 1985); *Hidden Harbour Estates, Inc. v. Norman*, 309 So.2d 180 (Fla. 4th DCA 1975).
7. A.H. Oosterhoff & W.B. Rayner, *Anger and Honsberger Law of Real Property*, vol. 2 (Aurora, Ont.: Canada Law Book, 1985)
8. *Carleton Condominium Corp. No. 279 v. Rochon*, [1987] O.J. No. 417, 59 O.R. (2d) 545 (Ont. C.A.); *Muskoka Condominium Corp. No. 39 v. Kreutzweiser*, [2010] O.J. No. 1720, 2010 ONSC 2463 (Ont. S.C.J.).
9. *Shaw Cablesystems Ltd. v. Concord Pacific Group Inc.*, [2007] B.C.J. No. 2529 at para. 10, 2007 BCSC 1711 (B.C.S.C.), affd [2008] B.C.J. No. 1014, 2008 BCCA 234 (B.C.C.A.).

10. *2475813 Nova Scotia Ltd. v. Rodgers,* [2001] N.S.J. No. 21, 2001 NSCA 12 (N.S.C.A.).

---

2. The Nature of Condominium Legislation

▼HCD-2▼ Legislative framework. Each province and territory in Canada has one primary statute, as well as regulations under that statute, governing condominiums. In some jurisdictions a provision of the statute itself codifies its object or purpose as the facilitation of the division of property into parts that are to be owned individually, and parts that are to be owned in common, and to provide for the use and management of such properties and to expedite dealings with such properties. These provisions also provide that the statute shall be construed in a manner to give the greatest effect to these objects.[1]

Object and purpose of legislation. In other jurisdictions the purpose and objects of the condominium legislation has been elucidated in the common law, as follows. The condominium statute permits the creation of a unique scheme for the ownership of land. It provides some guidelines and rules related to their development along with an element of consumer protection. It provides for a mechanism to manage and administer a complex joint ownership structure having regard to the need for responsible and efficient management of the common elements created by the structure. It includes the ability of a majority to control the administration and management of the property which permits infringement upon property rights otherwise enjoyed by a fee simple owner of real property.[2] The condominium statute creates a way of holding an interest in residential land unlike anything at common law, but with individual features that are familiar, such as mortgages, priorities, tenancies, liens, attachment of rents, *etc.* Peculiar to the condominium are such features as common expenses and the power of a condominium corporation to make rules affecting an individual's private residence. As such, a principal object of the Act is to achieve fairness among the parties — owners, their tenants, their mortgagees, and the condominium corporation itself — in raising the money to keep the common enterprise solvent. Hence the Act provides for owners to contribute to the fund for common expenses in their proportionate share as determined by the governing documents. The common expenses fund is the central financial mechanism of the condominium corporation and the duty of contributing to it is the central mechanism to achieve financial fairness among the owners.[3] It has also been found that condominium legislation is remedial and should not be rigidly or narrowly construed to the extent that it confers rights on the condominium corporation.[4]

Nature of condominium corporation. The condominium corporation is unlike any other corporation and is entirely a creature of the condominium statute. As such, it is the statutory manager of the common property which belongs to the individual owners and not the corporation. The powers of the corporation and its relationship with unit owners are governed by the respective condominium statute of each province and territory.[5]

Nomenclature. The terms "corporation", "condominium corporation", "strata corporation" in British Columbia and "syndicate" in Québec refer to the corporations created under the respective condominium or strata legislation of each Canadian province and territory. The terms "condominium", "condominium property" and "strata plan" in British Columbia refer to the property, namely the land and buildings on the land, governed by the respective condominium or strata legislation of each Canadian province and territory.

Notes

1. (MB) *Condominium Act,* C.C.S.M. c. C170, s. 3

   (NS) *Condominium Act*, R.S.N.S. 1989, c. 85, s. 2

   (NT) *Condominium Act*, R.S.N.W.T. 1988, c. C-15, s. 3

   (NU) *Condominium Act*, R.S.N.W.T. (Nu.) 1988, c. C-15, s. 3

   (YT) *Condominium Act*, R.S.Y. 2002, c. 36, s. 3.

2. *Condominium Plan No. 982-2595 v. Fantasy Homes Ltd.*, [2006] A.J. No. 495, 2006 ABQB 325 (Alta. Q.B.); *934859 Alberta Inc. v. Condominium Corp. No. 0312180*, [2007] A.J. No. 1233, 2007 ABQB 640 (Alta. Q.B.).

3. *York Condominium Corp. No. 482 v. Christiansen*, [2003] O.J. No. 343, 64 O.R. (3d) 65 (Ont. S.C.J.).

4. *Middlesex Condominium Corp. No. 87 v. 600 Talbot Street London Ltd.*, [1998] O.J. No. 450, 37 O.R. (3d) 22 (Ont. C.A.).

5. *Condominium Plan No. 0020701 v. Investplan Properties Inc.*, [2006] A.J. No. 368, 2006 ABQB 224 (Alta. Q.B.); See also *Basmadjian v. York Condominium Corp. No. 52*, [1981] O.J. No. 2973, 32 O.R. (2d) 523 (Ont. H.C.J.).

3. The Balance between Consumer Protection and Commercial Realities

▼HCD-3▼ Interpretation and application of condominium legislation. The condominium statute has been categorized by the courts as "consumer protection legislation".[1] As such, the "indoor management rule" has no application to condominium corporations, for example.[2] However, the interpretation and application of the condominium legislation must always reflect a proper balance between consumer protection and the commercial realities of the condominium industry.[3] Accordingly, in addition to consumer protection, an important purpose of the condominium statute is to provide predictability and sufficient certainty to those involved in condominium projects, including developers and unit purchasers, to enable them to make informed decisions about their investments. The statute provides a regime for the creation of condominium projects, the sale of units and the management of condominium corporations. That regime must have sufficient certainty so as not to discourage development, or prospective purchasers from acquiring units in a development.[4]

Notes

1. *Ormond v. Richmond Square Development Corp.*, [2003] O.J. No. 668, [2003] O.T.C. 106 (Ont. S.C.J.); *Rogers Cable Communications Inc. v. Carleton Condominium Corp. No. 53*, [2005] O.J. No. 921, 137 A.C.W.S. (3d) 1031 (Ont. S.C.J.).
2. *Winfair Holdings (Lagoon City) v. Simcoe Condominium Corp. No. 46*, [1998] O.J. No. 5022, 115 O.A.C. 332 (Ont. C.A.); *Carleton Condominium Corp. No. 279 v. Rochon*, [1987] O.J. No. 417, 59 O.R. (2d) 545 (Ont. C.A.); and *Rogers Cable Communications Inc. v. Carleton Condominium Corp. No. 53*, [2005] O.J. No. 921, 137 A.C.W.S. (3d) 1031 (Ont. S.C.J.).
3. *Abdool v. Somerset Place Developments of Georgetown Ltd.*, [1992] O.J. No. 2115, 10 O.R. (3d) 120 (Ont. C.A.); *Peel Condominium Corp. No. 505 v. Cam-Valley Homes Ltd.*, [2001] O.J. No. 714, 73 O.R. (3d) 1 (Ont. C.A.).
4. *Lexington on the Green Inc. v. Toronto Standard Condominium Corp. No. 1930*, [2010] O.J. No. 4853, 2010 ONCA 751 (Ont. C.A.).

---

4. The Role of the Common Law

▼HCD-4▼ Combination of legal principles. Condominium legislation has also been found to reflect the combination of several legal concepts and to incorporate, by reference, principles drawn from several different areas of law. The law relating to individual ownership of real property is central because the owners of the individual units are entitled to exclusive ownership and use of their respective units, subject to certain limitations and restrictions. The law relating to joint ownership is significant because the owners are tenants in common with respect to the common property. The law relating to easements and covenants is relevant because the unit owners have rights to compliance by the others with the governing documents of the condominium and certain easements are, by statute, appurtenant to each unit. The law relating to corporations is also of importance because the condominium is administered by the condominium corporation in which the unit holders are in a position analogous to shareholders.[1] The condominium statute regulates the legal aspects of condominium ownership against an extensive background of general legal principles which will frequently be relevant to the interpretation and application of the condominium legislation.[2]

Notes

1. *2475813 Nova Scotia Ltd. v. Rodgers*, [2001] N.S.J. No. 21, 2001 NSCA 12 (N.S.C.A.); *Shaw Cablesystems Ltd. v. Concord Pacific Group Inc.*, [2008] B.C.J. No. 1014, 2008 BCCA 234 (B.C.C.A).
2. Robert J. Owens *et al.*, eds., *Corpus Juris Secundum* (1996), Estates 195, Vol. 31, at 260.

---

5. Fiduciary Duties in Condominiums

▼HCD-5▼ Application of fiduciary law. A fundamental purpose of the law relating to fiduciaries is to reinforce the integrity of social institutions and enterprises, fiduciary principles must be applied in the context of condominium law in a manner which further strengthens the integrity of the socially valuable relationships upon which the condominium system is based. This raises two potentially conflicting considerations. Firstly, condominiums are created by a comprehensive statutory code; accordingly, the courts should be cautious about imposing rights and duties which are not expressly included in the statute.[1] Secondly, a residential condominium will often be the owner's home; therefore, the decisions of the corporation will intimately affect the everyday lives of the unit owners, as well as their financial security.[2] In determining whether fiduciary obligations arise in particular circumstances, it is important for courts to balance the business efficacy required for effective management of the collective interests with the security of individual ownership.[3]

Condominium developer as fiduciary. In some jurisdictions the developer of a condominium is seen as owing fiduciary duties to unit purchasers. Although the existence and extent of these duties will depend on several considerations, including the relevant legislation and the terms of the governing condominium documents, it has been found that developers have certain fiduciary obligations to protect the interests of all unit owners, present and prospective, as well as the interests of the condominium corporation.[4] However, the Ontario Court of Appeal has held that a prospective unit purchaser cannot be the fiduciary of the developer in, any accepted equitable sense, otherwise the developer would be unable to negotiate with the buyer at all. The developer does not hold the condominium property in trust for the unit purchaser; it holds the title to the units in trust for the prospective purchasers who have executed an agreement of purchase and sale to purchase a unit. The developer's good faith duty or obligation is to carry out the terms of the agreement and deliver the title and documents that the agreement of purchase and sale and the condominium statute requires. There is no overarching fiduciary duty arising out of the relationship of the developer as vendor and the prospective unit owner, as purchaser, in this regard. The suggestion that a prospective purchaser is entitled to repose some element of trust in the developer that it will deal with the purchaser's reasonable expectations in the disclosure documents introduces an element of paternalism that the Ontario Court of Appeal has found to be unjustified in such a relationship. As such, the protection of the consumer in Ontario rests solely with compliance by the developer with the disclosure provisions of the condominium statute, and the unit owner is not a fiduciary in any circumstance. The prospective purchaser is protected by the statutory requirement of full disclosure and not by the extension of fiduciary principles to the bargaining process. After executing an agreement of purchase and sale, the prospective purchasers are entitled to rely only on the good faith of the developer to carry out the agreement honestly.[5]

Notes

1. *Eberts v. Carleton Condominium Corp. No. 396*, [2000] O.J. No. 3773, 136 O.A.C. 317 (Ont. C.A.); *National Trust v. Grey Condominium Corp. No. 36*, [1995] O.J. No. 2079, 47 R.P.R. (2d) 60 (Ont. Gen. Div.); *Ceolaro v. York Humber Ltd.*, [1994] O.J. No. 604, 53 C.P.R. (3d) 276 (Ont. Gen. Div.); *2475813 Nova Scotia Ltd. v. Rodgers*, [2001] N.S.J. No. 21, 2001 NSCA 12 (N.S.C.A.).
2. *Carleton Condominium Corp. No. 347 v. Trendsetter Developments Ltd.*, [1992] O.J. No. 1767, 9 O.R. (3d) 481 (Ont. C.A.).
3. *2475813 Nova Scotia Ltd. v. Rodgers*, [2001] N.S.J. No. 21, 2001 NSCA 12 (N.S.C.A.).
4. *2475813 Nova Scotia Ltd. v. Rodgers,* [2001] N.S.J. No. 21, 2001 NSCA 12 (N.S.C.A.); *Condominium Plan N. 86-S-36901 v. Remai Construction (1981) Inc.*, [1991] S.J. No. 410, 84 D.L.R. (4th) 6 (Sask. C.A.); see also A.H. Oosterhoff &

W.B. Rayner, *Anger and Honsberger Law of Real Property*, vol. 2 (Aurora, Ont.: Canada Law Book, 1985).

5. *Peel Condominium Corp. No. 505 v. Cam-Valley Homes Ltd.*, [2001] O.J. No. 714, 53 O.R. (3d) 1 (Ont. C.A.). See also *Metropolitan Toronto Condominium Corp. No. 1272 v. Beach Development (Phase II) Corp.*, [2010] O.J. No. 5025, 2010 ONSC 609 (Ont. S.C.J.).

II. Creation of Condominiums

1. Types of Condominium Properties

(1) General HCD-6
(2) Freehold Condominiums HCD-7
(3) Leasehold Condominiums HCD-8

2. Types of Property Interests in a Condominium Property

(1) Ownership Interests HCD-9
(2) Other Interests HCD-12

3. Registration

(1) General HCD-14
(2) Freehold Condominium Corporations HCD-15
(3) Leasehold Condominium Corporations HCD-16

4. Declaration and Description or Plan

(1) Declaration HCD-17
(2) Description or Plan HCD-21
(3) Amendments HCD-23

5. By-Laws and Rules

(1) By-Laws HCD-24
(2) Rules HCD-26
(3) Joint By-Laws and Rules HCD-27

---

1. Types of Condominium Properties

(1) General HCD-6
(2) Freehold Condominiums HCD-7
(3) Leasehold Condominiums HCD-8

---

(1) General

▼HCD-6▼ Freehold and leasehold condominiums. Some jurisdictions permit only freehold condominiums, whereas others permit both freehold and leasehold condominiums. In a freehold condominium, all units and appurtenant common interests are held by the owners in fee simple.[1] In a leasehold condominium, all units and appurtenant common interests are subject to leasehold interests held by the owners.[2]

Freehold condominiums. All jurisdictions with condominium corporations permit standard condominiums. Some also provide for one or more of the following additional types of freehold condominiums: phased condominiums; vacant land or bare land condominiums; and common elements condominiums.

Leasehold condominiums. In the jurisdictions that permit leasehold condominiums, the legislation either specifically defines the condominiums[3] or clearly implies their existence through other definitions.[4]

Notes

1. (ON) *Condominium Act, 1998*, S.O. 1998, c. 19, s. 1(1).
2. (ON) *Condominium Act, 1998*, S.O. 1998, c. 19, s. 1(1).
3. (ON) *Condominium Act, 1998*, S.O. 1998, c. 19, ss. 1(1), 6(1); (NT) *Condominium Act*, R.S.N.W.T. 1988, c. C-15, ss. 1(1), 8(6).
4. (AB) *Condominium Property Act*, R.S.A. 2000, c. C-22, s. 1(1)(s)(ii)
   (BC) *Strata Property Act*, S.B.C. 1998, c. 43, s. 199
   (MB) *Condominium Act*, C.C.S.M. c. C170, s. 1
   (NU) *Condominium Act*, R.S.N.W.T. (Nu.) 1988, c. C-15, s. 1(1)
   (YT) *Condominium Act*, R.S.Y. 2002, c. 36, s. 1.

---

(2) Freehold Condominiums

▼HCD-7▼ Four types of freehold condominiums. There are four types of freehold condominiums provided for in provincial and territorial legislation: standard; phased; vacant land; and common elements.

Standard condominiums. All jurisdictions permit standard condominiums, but not all employ this terminology. Only Ontario defines the term “standard condominium corporation”, which refers to both the type of condominium property and the corporation. The Ontario legislation specifically includes standard condominiums as one of the four types of freehold condominiums permitted under the statute, and defines them as freehold condominiums that are not phased condominiums, vacant land condominiums, or common elements condominiums.[1] In other jurisdictions, there is no definition or explicit mention of "standard condominiums" or "standard condominium corporations".

Phased condominiums. Several jurisdictions provide for phased condominium properties. In Alberta and Newfoundland and Labrador, a building or land that is subject to a condominium plan or proposed condominium plan may be developed in phases and, in the process of carrying out the phased development, additional units and common elements may be created.[2] In British Columbia, a phased strata plan is defined as a strata plan deposited in successive phases under the relevant part of the Act.[3] In Manitoba, a phase is defined as the creation of units or common elements or both that are created by the registration of a declaration and plan for phased development, or by an amendment to a declaration to convert a unit into additional units or common elements or both.[4] In New Brunswick and Ontario, a phase is defined as the additional units and common elements created on the registration of an amendment to a declaration and description.[5] In New Brunswick and Nova Scotia, the acceptance for registration of a phase constitutes a subdivision of land and creates a lot as described in the phase description.[6] In Ontario, a developer who registers a declaration and description may create additional units or common elements in a condominium if several criteria are met:[7]

- the condominium is a freehold condominium that is not a vacant land condominium or common elements condominium
- the declaration indicates that it is a phased condominium
- the description contains a legal description of the land that will be the servient tenement and
- the board was elected at an owner meeting held when the developer did not own the majority of units

The Saskatchewan legislation does not refer to a phased condominium, but includes a provision referring to additional units or common elements.[8]

Vacant land condominiums. Several jurisdictions provide for vacant land condominiums. In Newfoundland and Labrador and Ontario, a vacant land condominium is defined as a condominium in which, at the time of registration, one or more units are not part of and do not include part of a building or structure and in which none of the units are located above or below any other unit.[9] Other jurisdictions provide for such a condominium by virtue of the definitions of "bare-land condominium property",[10] "bare land unit",[11] "bare land strata plan"[12] or "vacant land unit".[13]

Common elements condominiums. Newfoundland and Labrador and Ontario provide for a common elements condominium, which is defined as a condominium created by the registration of a declaration and description that create common elements but do not divide the land into units.[14]

Notes

1. (ON) *Condominium Act, 1998*, S.O. 1998, c. 19, s. 6(2).
2. (AB) *Condominium Property Act*, R.S.A. 2000, c. C-22, s. 19; (NL) *Condominium Act, 2009*, S.N.L. 2009, c. C-29.1, s. 74(1)-(2) (not yet in force).
3. (BC) *Strata Property Act*, S.B.C. 1998, c. 43, s. 1(1).
4. (MB) *Condominium Act*, C.C.S.M. c. C170, s. 1.
5. (NB) *Condominium Property Act*, S.N.B. 2009, c. C-16.05, s. 1(1); (ON) *Condominium Act, 1998*, S.O. 1998, c. 19, s. 145(3).
6. (NB) *Condominium Property Act*, S.N.B. 2009, c. C-16.05, s. 12(1); (NS) *Condominium Act*, R.S.N.S. 1989, c. 85, s. 8(2).
7. (ON) *Condominium Act, 1998*, S.O. 1998, c. 19, s. 145(1)-(2).
8. (SK) *Condominium Property Act, 1993*, S.S. 1993, c. C-26.1, s. 16(2).
9. (NL) *Condominium Act, 2009*, S.N.L. 2009, c. C-29.1, ss. 2(1)(cc), 79(1)-(2) (not yet in force); (ON) *Condominium Act, 1998*, S.O. 1998, c. 19, ss. 1(1), 155.
10. (NB) *Condominium Property Act*, S.N.B. 2009, c. C-16.05, s. 4(c).
11. (AB) *Condominium Property Act*, R.S.A. 2000, c. C-22, ss. 1(1)(b), (w)(ii), (y)(ii)

    (MB) *Condominium Act*, C.C.S.M. c. C170, s. 1

    (SK) *Condominium Property Act, 1993*, S.S. 1993, c. C-26.1, ss. 2(1)(c), 2(bb)(ii)

    (NT) *Condominium Act*, R.S.N.W.T. 1988, c. C-15, s. 1(1)

    (NU) *Condominium Act*, R.S.N.W.T. (Nu.) 1988, c. C-15, s. 1(1)

    (YT) *Condominium Act*, R.S.Y. 2002, c. 36, s. 1.
12. (BC) *Strata Property Act*, S.B.C. 1998, c. 43, s. 1(1).
13. (PE) *Condominium Act*, R.S.P.E.I. 1988, c. C-16, s. 1(1)(t).
14. (NL) *Condominium Act, 2009*, S.N.L. 2009, c. C-29.1, ss. 2(1)(f), 68(1)-(2) (not yet in force); (ON) *Condominium Act, 1998*, S.O. 1998, c. 19, ss. 1(1), 138(1)-(2).

---

(3) Leasehold Condominiums

▼HCD-8▼ Condominiums defined or implied. Alberta, British Columbia, Manitoba, Ontario, Northwest Territories, Nunavut and Yukon permit leasehold condominiums. In British Columbia, Ontario and

Northwest Territories, the legislation specifically defines these condominiums. In British Columbia, a "leasehold strata plan" is defined as a strata plan in which the land shown on the strata plan is subject to a ground lease.[1] In Ontario, condominiums consist of both freehold and leasehold condominiums, and a leasehold condominium is one in which all units and appurtenant common interests are subject to leasehold interests held by the owners.[2] In Northwest Territories, a "leasehold condominium" is defined as a condominium established by the holder of a leasehold estate, and the condominium is deemed to be the lessee liable for the obligations under the lease.[3] By contrast, in Alberta, Manitoba, Nunavut and Yukon, the legislation does not define leasehold condominiums, but clearly provides for these condominiums by specifically including in the definition of "owner" the owner of a leasehold estate in a unit.[4]

Notes

1. (BC) *Strata Property Act*, S.B.C. 1998, c. 43, s. 199.
2. (ON) *Condominium Act, 1998*, S.O. 1998, c. 19, ss. 1(1), 6(1).
3. (NT) *Condominium Act*, R.S.N.W.T. 1988, c. C-15, ss. 1(1), 8(6).
4. (AB) *Condominium Property Act*, R.S.A. 2000, c. C-22, s. 1(1)(s)(ii)
   (MB) *Condominium Act*, C.C.S.M. c. C170, s. 1
   (NU) *Condominium Act*, R.S.N.W.T. (Nu.) 1988, c. C-15, s. 1(1)
   (YT) *Condominium Act*, R.S.Y. 2002, c. 36, s. 1.

---

2. Types of Property Interests in a Condominium Property

(1) Ownership Interests
(a) General HCD-9
(b) Freehold Condominiums HCD-10
(c) Leasehold Condominiums HCD-11
(2) Other Interests
(a) Easements HCD-12
(b) Encumbrances HCD-13

---

(1) Ownership Interests

(a) General

▼HCD-9▼ Definitions. Several jurisdictions define the terms "property", "building", "unit" and "common elements". Property means the land, the buildings on the land, and interests appurtenant to the land described in the description or plan and includes all land and interests appurtenant to the land that are added to the common elements.[1] Building means a building included in a property.[2] Unit (or "strata lot" in British Columbia and "private portion" in Québec) means a part of the property designated as a unit by the description or plan and includes the space enclosed by its boundaries and all of the land, structures and fixtures within that space in accordance with the declaration and description or plan.[3] Common elements means all the property except the units.[4] Common elements may generally be used by all owners; however, portions of the common elements may be designated as exclusive use common elements, in which case they are used by the owners of one or more designated units and not by all owners.[5] Both units and common elements are real property.[6]

Condominium property. In New Brunswick, Newfoundland and Labrador, Nova Scotia, Prince Edward Island and Saskatchewan, the condominium property is comprised of only freehold land and interests appurtenant to the land.[7] In Alberta, British Columbia, Manitoba, Ontario, Northwest Territories, Nunavut and Yukon, the condominium property is comprised of leasehold land and interests appurtenant to the land as well as freehold land and interests appurtenant to the land.[8] The ownership of land includes ownership of space.[9]

Notes

1. (MB) *Condominium Act*, C.C.S.M. c. C170, s. 1

   (NB) *Condominium Property Act*, S.N.B. 2009, c. C-16.05, s. 1(1). A "property" is referred to as a "condominium property".

   (NL) *Condominium Act, 2009*, S.N.L. 2009, c. C-29.1, s. 2(1)(v) (not yet in force)

   (NS) *Condominium Act*, R.S.N.S. 1989, c. 85, s. 3(1)(s)

   (ON) *Condominium Act, 1998*, S.O. 1998, c. 19, s. 1(1)

   (PE) *Condominium Act,* R.S.P.E.I. 1988, c. C-16, s. 1(1)(o)

   (NT) *Condominium Act*, R.S.N.W.T. 1988, c. C-15, s. 1(1)

   (NU) *Condominium Act*, R.S.N.W.T. (Nu.) 1988, c. C-15, s. 1(1)

   (YT) *Condominium Act*, R.S.Y. 2002, c. 36, s. 1.

2. (AB) *Condominium Property Act*, R.S.A. 2000, c. C-22, s. 1(1)(d)

   (MB) *Condominium Act*, C.C.S.M. c. C170, s. 1

   (NB) *Condominium Property Act*, S.N.B. 2009, c. C-16.05, s. 1(1)

   (NL) *Condominium Act, 2009*, S.N.L. 2009, c. C-29.1, s. 2(1)(b) (not yet in force)

   (NS) *Condominium Act*, R.S.N.S. 1989, c. 85, s. 3(1)(c)

   (ON) *Condominium Act, 1998*, S.O. 1998, c. 19, s. 1(1)

   (PE) *Condominium Act,* R.S.P.E.I. 1988, c. C-16, s. 1(1)(b)

(SK) *Condominium Property Act, 1993*, S.S. 1993, c. C-26.1, s. 2(1)(e)

(NT) *Condominium Act*, R.S.N.W.T. 1988, c. C-15, s. 1(1)

(NU) *Condominium Act*, R.S.N.W.T. (Nu.) 1988, c. C-15, s. 1(1)

(YT) *Condominium Act*, R.S.Y. 2002, c. 36, s. 1.

3. (BC) *Strata Property Act*, S.B.C. 1998, c. 43, s. 1(1)

(MB) *Condominium Act*, C.C.S.M. c. C170, s. 1

(NB) *Condominium Property Act*, S.N.B. 2009, c. C-16.05, s. 1(1)

(NL) *Condominium Act, 2009*, S.N.L. 2009, c. C-29.1, s. 2(1)(bb) (not yet in force)

(NS) *Condominium Act*, R.S.N.S. 1989, c. 85, s. 3(1)(x)

(ON) *Condominium Act, 1998*, S.O. 1998, c. 19, s. 1(1)

(PE) *Condominium Act,* R.S.P.E.I. 1988, c. C-16, s. 1(1)(s)

(NT) *Condominium Act*, R.S.N.W.T. 1988, c. C-15, s. 1(1)

(NU) *Condominium Act*, R.S.N.W.T. (Nu.) 1988, c. C-15, s. 1(1)

(YT) *Condominium Act*, R.S.Y. 2002, c. 36, s. 1.

The Alberta and Saskatchewan statutes provide more detailed definitions of "unit": (AB) *Condominium Property Act*, R.S.A. 2000, c. C-22, s. 1(1)(y); (SK) *Condominium Property Act, 1993*, S.S. 1993, c. C-26.1, s. 2(1)(bb).

4. (MB) *Condominium Act*, C.C.S.M. c. C170, s. 1

(NB) *Condominium Property Act*, S.N.B. 2009, c. C-16.05, s. 1(1)

(NL) *Condominium Act, 2009*, S.N.L. 2009, c. C-29.1, s. 2(1)(e) (not yet in force)

(NS) *Condominium Act*, R.S.N.S. 1989, c. 85, s. 3(1)(f)

(ON) *Condominium Act, 1998*, S.O. 1998, c. 19, s. 1(1)

(PE) *Condominium Act,* R.S.P.E.I. 1988, c. C-16, s. 1(1)(e)

(NT) *Condominium Act*, R.S.N.W.T. 1988, c. C-15, s. 1(1)

(NU) *Condominium Act*, R.S.N.W.T. (Nu.) 1988, c. C-15, s. 1(1)

(YT) *Condominium Act*, R.S.Y. 2002, c. 36, s. 1.

The Alberta, British Columbia and Saskatchewan definitions of "common property" are similar to the definitions of "common element": (AB) *Condominium Property Act*, R.S.A. 2000, c. C-22, s. 1(1)(f); (BC) *Strata Property Act*, S.B.C. 1998, c. 43, s. 1(1); (SK) *Condominium Property Act, 1993*, S.S. 1993, c. C-26.1, s. 2(1)(h). In Québec, the legislation defines "common portions" and provides examples of presumed common portions: (QC) *Civil Code of Québec*, L.R.Q. c. C-1991, arts. 1043-1045.

5. (AB) *Condominium Property Act*, R.S.A. 2000, c. C-22, s. 50(1)

(BC) *Strata Property Act*, S.B.C. 1998, c. 43, ss. 1(1), 73, called "limited common property"

(MB) *Condominium Act*, C.C.S.M. c. C170, s. 5(3)(b)

(NB) *Condominium Property Act*, S.N.B. 2009, c. C-16.05, s. 6(2)(i)

(NL) *Condominium Act, 2009*, S.N.L. 2009, c. C-29.1, s. 9(1)(h) (not yet in force)

(NS) *Condominium Act*, R.S.N.S. 1989, c. 85, s. 11(2)(b)

(ON) *Condominium Act, 1998*, S.O. 1998, c. 19, s. 7(2)(f); (ON) Description and Registration Regulation, O. Reg. 49/01, s. 2(1)(b)

(PE) *Condominium Act,* R.S.P.E.I. 1988, c. C-16, s. 3(1)(g)

(QC) *Civil Code of Québec*, L.R.Q. c. C-1991, arts. 1043, 1047
(SK) *Condominium Property Act, 1993*, S.S. 1993, c. C-26.1, s. 72(1)
(NT) *Condominium Act*, R.S.N.W.T. 1988, c. C-15, s. 5(2)(b)
(NU) *Condominium Act*, R.S.N.W.T. (Nu.) 1988, c. C-15, s. 5(2)(b)
(YT) *Condominium Act*, R.S.Y. 2002, c. 36, s. 5(2)(b).

6. (MB) *Condominium Act*, C.C.S.M. c. C170, s. 7(1)
(NB) *Condominium Property Act*, S.N.B. 2009, c. C-16.05, s. 15(1)
(NL) *Condominium Act, 2009*, S.N.L. 2009, c. C-29.1, s. 16(1) (not yet in force)
(NS) *Condominium Act*, R.S.N.S. 1989, c. 85, s. 27(1)
(ON) *Condominium Act, 1998*, S.O. 1998, c. 19, s. 10
(PE) *Condominium Act,* R.S.P.E.I. 1988, c. C-16, s. 6(1)
(QC) *Civil Code of Québec*, L.R.Q. c. C-1991, art. 1047
(NT) *Condominium Act*, R.S.N.W.T. 1988, c. C-15, s. 7(1)
(NU) *Condominium Act*, R.S.N.W.T. (Nu.) 1988, c. C-15, s. 7(1)
(YT) *Condominium Act*, R.S.Y. 2002, c. 36, s. 7(1).

7. (NB) *Condominium Property Act*, S.N.B. 2009, c. C-16.05, s. 1(1)
(NL) *Condominium Act, 2009*, S.N.L. 2009, c. C-29.1, s. 8(1) (not yet in force)
(NS) *Condominium Act*, R.S.N.S. 1989, c. 85, s. 6(1)
(PE) *Condominium Act,* R.S.P.E.I. 1988, c. C-16, s. 2(1)
(SK) *Condominium Property Act, 1993*, S.S. 1993, c. C-26.1, s. 4(2).

8. (AB) *Condominium Property Act*, R.S.A. 2000, c. C-22, ss. 1(s)(ii), 4(4)-(5)
(BC) *Strata Property Act*, S.B.C. 1998, c. 43, s. 200
(MB) *Condominium Act*, C.C.S.M. c. C170, s. 1
(ON) *Condominium Act, 1998*, S.O. 1998, c. 19, ss. 2(1), 164(1)
(NT) *Condominium Act*, R.S.N.W.T. 1988, c. C-15, s. 1(1)
(NU) *Condominium Act*, R.S.N.W.T. (Nu.) 1988, c. C-15, s. 1(1)
(YT) *Condominium Act*, R.S.Y. 2002, c. 36, s. 1.

9. (MB) *Condominium Act*, C.C.S.M. c. C170, s. 2(2)
(NB) *Condominium Property Act*, S.N.B. 2009, c. C-16.05, s. 1(2)
(NL) *Condominium Act, 2009*, S.N.L. 2009, c. C-29.1, s. 2(2) (not yet in force)
(NS) *Condominium Act*, R.S.N.S. 1989, c. 85, s. 3(2)
(ON) *Condominium Act, 1998*, S.O. 1998, c. 19, s. 1(2)
(PE) *Condominium Act,* R.S.P.E.I. 1988, c. C-16, s. 1(2)
(NT) *Condominium Act*, R.S.N.W.T. 1988, c. C-15, s. 2(2)
(NU) *Condominium Act*, R.S.N.W.T. (Nu.) 1988, c. C-15, s. 2(2)
(YT) *Condominium Act*, R.S.Y. 2002, c. 36, s. 2(2).

(b) Freehold Condominiums

▼HCD-10▼ General ownership interests. The nature of ownership interests depends on the nature of the condominium.

Standard condominiums. An owner in a standard condominium has property interests in the unit and the common elements. Subject to the applicable statute, as well as the declaration or plan and by-laws of each condominium, each owner is entitled to exclusive ownership and use of his or her unit.[1] Unit owners are also tenants in common of the common elements, and an undivided interest in the common elements is appurtenant to each unit.[2] The proportions of the common interests are specified in the condominium declaration.[3] The ownership of a unit cannot be separated from the ownership of the common interest, and any instrument dealing with a unit operates so as to deal with the common interest appurtenant to the unit, even if there is no express reference to the common interest in the instrument.[4] Except as provided by each jurisdiction's legislation, common elements cannot be partitioned or divided.[5] Condominiums may grant a lease or licence over the common elements,[6] but in some jurisdictions the granting of a lease or licence is not permitted with respect to a part of the common elements designated as exclusive use common elements.[7]

Phased condominiums. In British Columbia, a phased strata plan is defined as a strata plan deposited in successive phases under the relevant part of the Act.[8] In Manitoba, a phase is defined as the creation of units or common elements or both that are created by the registration of a declaration and plan for phased development, or by an amendment to a declaration to convert a unit into additional units or common elements or both.[9] In New Brunswick and Ontario, a phase is defined as the additional units and common elements created on the registration of an amendment to a declaration and description.[10] Ontario's regulations also provide that, for registering amendments to a declaration and description creating a phase, the phase must include at least one unit, and the units and common elements included in the phase cannot be part of an existing building on the condominium property.[11]

Vacant land condominiums. In general, the same provisions that apply to standard condominiums apply to vacant land condominiums. However, whereas some jurisdictions include buildings on the land, others specifically exclude them. In British Columbia, the Act does not specify whether buildings are included or excluded.[12] In Newfoundland and Labrador and

Ontario, the buildings and structures located on a unit or on the common elements of a vacant land condominium are real property and form part of the unit or common elements, whether or not the buildings and structures were constructed at the time of registration.[13] In Alberta, Manitoba, New Brunswick, Prince Edward Island, Saskatchewan, Northwest Territories, Nunavut and Yukon, the definitions of bare-land condominium property, bare land unit or vacant land unit specifically exclude buildings.[14]

Common elements condominiums. An owner in a common elements condominium owns a common interest in the common elements and a freehold interest in the parcel of land to which the common interest is attached (the parcel of tied land), as described in the declaration.[15] A common interest means the interest in the common elements appurtenant to an owner's parcel of tied land as described in the declaration.[16] If an owner's parcel of tied land is divided into two or more new parcels, the new parcel owners are joint owners of the common interest attached to the original parcel.[17] On the sale of a parcel of tied land or the enforcement of an encumbrance registered against the parcel, the owner's common interest is not terminated or severed from the parcel, but continues to be attached to the parcel.[18]

Sections and sectors. In British Columbia, an owner developer or strata corporation may create sections for the purpose of representing different interests within a strata corporation.[19] The British Columbia Act specifies the powers and duties of sections as well as expenses, administration, by-laws and rules and judgments relating to sections.[20] In Saskatchewan, a condominium may, by by-law, establish sectors within a condominium, may allocate units, common facilities and common property (common elements) to a sector, and may regulate the control, management, administration, use and enjoyment of the units, common property and common facilities within a sector.[21]

Notes

1. (AB) *Condominium Property Act*, R.S.A. 2000, c. C-22, s. 1(1)(m), (s), (w), (y)

   (MB) *Condominium Act*, C.C.S.M. c. C170, s. 7(2)

   (NB) *Condominium Property Act*, S.N.B. 2009, c. C-16.05, s. 15(2)

   (NL) *Condominium Act, 2009*, S.N.L. 2009, c. C-29.1, ss. 2(1)(t)(i), (bb), 16(2) (not yet in force)

   (NS) *Condominium Act*, R.S.N.S. 1989, c. 85, s. 27(2)

   (ON) *Condominium Act, 1998*, S.O. 1998, c. 19, ss. 1(1), 11(1)

   (PE) *Condominium Act,* R.S.P.E.I. 1988, c. C-16, s. 6(2)

(QC) *Civil Code of Québec*, L.R.Q. c. C-1991, art. 1042. The condominium unit is referred to as a "private portion"

(SK) *Condominium Property Act, 1993*, S.S. 1993, c. C-26.1, s. 2(1)(b), (r), (z.1), (bb)

(NT) *Condominium Act*, R.S.N.W.T. 1988, c. C-15, ss. 1(1), 7(2)

(NU) *Condominium Act*, R.S.N.W.T. (Nu.) 1988, c. C-15, s. 7(2)

(YT) *Condominium Act*, R.S.Y. 2002, c. 36, ss. 1, 7(2).

2. (AB) *Condominium Property Act*, R.S.A. 2000, c. C-22, ss. 1(1), 6(2)

(BC) *Strata Property Act*, S.B.C. 1998, c. 43, s. 66

(MB) *The Condominium Act*, C.C.S.M. c. C170, s. 8(2)

(NB) *Condominium Property Act*, S.N.B. 2009, c. C-16.05, s. 16(1)-(2)

(NL) *Condominium Act, 2009*, S.N.L. 2009, c. C-29.1, ss. 2(1), 16(3) (not yet in force)

(NS) *Condominium Act*, R.S.N.S. 1989, c. 85, s. 28(1)-(2)

(ON) *Condominium Act, 1998*, S.O. 1998, c. 19, ss. 1(1), 11(2)

(PE) *Condominium Act,* R.S.P.E.I. 1988, c. C-16, s. 7(1)-(2)

(QC) *Civil Code of Québec*, L.R.Q. c. C-1991, art. 1046

(SK) *Condominium Property Act, 1993*, S.S. 1993, c. C-26.1, ss. 2(1), 6(1)

(NT) *Condominium Act*, R.S.N.W.T. 1988, c. C-15, ss. 1(1), 8(1)-(2)

(NU) *Condominium Act*, R.S.N.W.T. (Nu.) 1988, c. C-15, ss. 1(1), 8(1)-(2)

(YT) *Condominium Act*, R.S.Y. 2002, c. 36, ss. 1, 8(1)-(2).

3. (NB) *Condominium Property Act*, S.N.B. 2009, c. C-16.05, s. 16(3)

(NL) *Condominium Act, 2009*, S.N.L. 2009, c. C-29.1, s. 16(4) (not yet in force)

(NS) *Condominium Act*, R.S.N.S. 1989, c. 85, s. 28(3)

(ON) *Condominium Act, 1998*, S.O. 1998, c. 19, s. 11(3)

(PE) *Condominium Act,* R.S.P.E.I. 1988, c. C-16, s. 7(3)

See also Section II.4. ("Declaration and Description or Plan").

4. (AB) *Condominium Property Act*, R.S.A. 2000, c. C-22, s. 6(3)

(MB) *Condominium Act*, C.C.S.M. c. C170, s. 8(4)

(NB) *Condominium Property Act*, S.N.B. 2009, c. C-16.05, s. 16(5)

(NL) *Condominium Act, 2009*, S.N.L. 2009, c. C-29.1, s. 16(5) (not yet in force)

(NS) *Condominium Act*, R.S.N.S. 1989, c. 85, s. 28(5)

(ON) *Condominium Act, 1998*, S.O. 1998, c. 19, s. 11(4)

(PE) *Condominium Act,* R.S.P.E.I. 1988, c. C-16, s. 7(5)

(SK) *Condominium Property Act, 1993*, S.S. 1993, c. C-26.1, s. 6(3)

(NT) *Condominium Act*, R.S.N.W.T. 1988, c. C-15, s. 8(4)

(NU) *Condominium Act*, R.S.N.W.T. (Nu.) 1988, c. C-15, s. 8(4)

(YT) *Condominium Act*, R.S.Y. 2002, c. 36, s. 8(4).

5. (AB) *Condominium Property Act*, R.S.A. 2000, c. C-22, s. 6(3)

(MB) *Condominium Act*, C.C.S.M. c. C170, s. 8(5)

(NB) *Condominium Property Act*, S.N.B. 2009, c. C-16.05, s. 16(6) (not yet in force)

(NL) *Condominium Act, 2009*, S.N.L. 2009, c. C-29.1, s. 16(6)
(NS) *Condominium Act*, R.S.N.S. 1989, c. 85, s. 28(6)
(ON) *Condominium Act, 1998*, S.O. 1998, c. 19, s. 11(5)
(PE) *Condominium Act,* R.S.P.E.I. 1988, c. C-16, s. 7(6)
(QC) *Civil Code of Québec*, L.R.Q. c. C-1991, art. 1046
(SK) *Condominium Property Act, 1993*, S.S. 1993, c. C-26.1, s. 6(3)
(NT) *Condominium Act*, R.S.N.W.T. 1988, c. C-15, s. 8(5)
(NU) *Condominium Act*, R.S.N.W.T. (Nu.) 1988, c. C-15, s. 8(5)
(YT) *Condominium Act*, R.S.Y. 2002, c. 36, s. 8(5).

6. (AB) *Condominium Property Act*, R.S.A. 2000, c. C-22, s. 49(1)
(NL) *Condominium Act, 2009*, S.N.L. 2009, c. C-29.1, s. 9(1) (not yet in force)
(NS) *Condominium Act*, R.S.N.S. 1989, c. 85, s. 14(2)
(ON) *Condominium Act, 1998*, S.O. 1998, c. 19, s. 21(1)
(PE) *Condominium Act,* R.S.P.E.I. 1988, c. C-16, s. 9(1)
(SK) *Condominium Property Act, 1993*, S.S. 1993, c. C-26.1, s. 70(1).
(NT) *Condominium Act*, R.S.N.W.T. 1988, c. C-15, s. 13.1(1)
7. (ON) *Condominium Act, 1998*, S.O. 1998, c. 19, s. 21(1)
(PE) *Condominium Act,* R.S.P.E.I. 1988, c. C-16, s. 9(1)
(NT) *Condominium Act*, R.S.N.W.T. 1988, c. C-15, s. 13.1(1).
8. (BC) *Strata Property Act*, S.B.C. 1998, c. 43, s. 1(1).
9. (MB) *Condominium Act*, C.C.S.M. c. C170, s. 1.
10. (NB) *Condominium Property Act*, S.N.B. 2009, c. C-16.05, s. 1(1); (ON) *Condominium Act, 1998*, S.O. 1998, c. 19, s. 145(3).
11. (ON) General Regulation, O. Reg. 48/01, s. 51.
12. (BC) *Strata Property Act*, S.B.C. 1998, c. 43, s. 1(1), definition of "bare land strata plan".
13. (NL) *Condominium Act, 2009*, S.N.L. 2009, c. C-29.1, s. 82(1) (not yet in force); (ON) *Condominium Act, 1998*, S.O. 1998, c. 19, s. 159(1).
14. (AB) *Condominium Property Act*, R.S.A. 2000, c. C-22, ss. 1(1)(b), 1(w)(ii), (y)(ii)
(MB) *Condominium Act*, C.C.S.M. c. C170, s. 1
(NB) *Condominium Property Act*, S.N.B. 2009, c. C-16.05, s. 4(c)
(PE) *Condominium Act*, R.S.P.E.I. 1988, c. C-16, s. 1(1)(t)
(SK) *Condominium Property Act, 1993*, S.S. 1993, c. C-26.1, s. 2(1)(c), (bb)(ii)
(NT) *Condominium Act*, R.S.N.W.T. 1988, c. C-15, s. 1(1)
(NU) *Condominium Act*, R.S.N.W.T. (Nu.) 1988, c. C-15, s. 1(1)
(YT) *Condominium Act*, R.S.Y. 2002, c. 36, s. 1.
15. (NL) *Condominium Act, 2009*, S.N.L. 2009, c. C-29.1, s. 2(1)(t)(ii) (not yet in force); (ON) *Condominium Act, 1998*, S.O. 1998, c. 19, s. 1(1).
16. (NL) *Condominium Act, 2009*, S.N.L. 2009, c. C-29.1, s. 2(1)(t)(ii) (not yet in force); (ON) *Condominium Act, 1998*, S.O. 1998, c. 19, s. 1(1).
17. (NL) *Condominium Act, 2009*, S.N.L. 2009, c. C-29.1, s. 69(3) (not yet in force); (ON) *Condominium Act, 1998*, S.O. 1998, c. 19, s. 139(3).

18. (NL) *Condominium Act, 2009*, S.N.L. 2009, c. C-29.1, s. 69(4) (not yet in force); (ON) *Condominium Act, 1998*, S.O. 1998, c. 19, s. 139(4).
19. (BC) *Strata Property Act*, S.B.C. 1998, c. 43, ss. 191-193.
20. (BC) *Strata Property Act*, S.B.C. 1998, c. 43, ss. 194-198.
21. (SK) *Condominium Property Act, 1993*, S.S. 1993, c. C-26.1, s. 47(1).

(c) Leasehold Condominiums

▼HCD-11▼ General ownership interests. In Ontario, an owner in a leasehold condominium owns a leasehold interest in a unit and its appurtenant common interest.[1] In Ontario and Northwest Territories, each leasehold interest in a unit and its appurtenant common interest is valid even if the lessor is the owner of the leasehold interest, in which case the legal title and the leasehold interest are deemed not to merge.[2] All leasehold interests in units and their appurtenant common interests are for the same term.[3] The unit owner may transfer, mortgage, lease or otherwise deal with the leasehold interest in the unit without the lessor's consent, but may not transfer less than the whole leasehold interest in the unit and its appurtenant common interest.[4] In Ontario only, the leasehold condominium must, on behalf of the owners, exercise all rights and perform all obligations of the owners respecting the leasehold estate in the property.[5]

Notes

1. (ON) *Condominium Act, 1998*, S.O. 1998, c. 19, s. 1(1).
2. (ON) *Condominium Act, 1998*, S.O. 1998, c. 19, s. 165(1); (NT) *Condominium Act*, R.S.N.W.T. 1988, c. C-15, s. 8.1(1).
3. (ON) *Condominium Act, 1998*, S.O. 1998, c. 19, s. 165(2); (NT) *Condominium Act*, R.S.N.W.T. 1988, c. C-15, s. 8.1(2).
4. (ON) *Condominium Act, 1998*, S.O. 1998, c. 19, s. 165(3)-(4); (NT) *Condominium Act*, R.S.N.W.T. 1988, c. C-15, s. 8.1(3)-(4).
5. (ON) *Condominium Act, 1998*, S.O. 1998, c. 19, s. 168(1)-(2).

---

(2) Other Interests

(a) Easements

▼HCD-12▼ Implied easements. Several jurisdictions provide for implied easements in favour of and against each unit owner. The legislative references to easements evince an intention to establish easements taking guidance from the common law.[1] All ancillary rights and obligations that are reasonably necessary to make the implied easements effective apply.[2] In Alberta, British Columbia and Saskatchewan, the legislation specifically provides for the right of a dominant tenement owner to enter a servient tenement and replace, renew or restore anything from which the dominant tenement is entitled to benefit.[3] In addition, in Alberta, British Columbia and Saskatchewan, easements or restrictions that are implied or created by the act or by the corporation's by-laws take effect and are enforceable without registration on title to the unit and common elements and without any express indication of the dominant and servient tenements.[4]

Easements in favour of unit owner. The following easements may be implied in favour of each unit owner as belonging to the unit:[5]

- an easement for the subjacent and lateral support of the unit by the common elements and by every other unit capable of affording support
- an easement for the shelter of the unit by the common elements and by every other unit capable of affording shelter and
- an easement for the passage or provision of water, sewerage, drainage, gas, electricity, garbage, artificially heated or cooled air and other services, including telephone, radio and television services, through or by means of any pipes, wires, cables or ducts existing in the parcel to the extent to which the pipes, wires, cables or ducts can be used in connection with the enjoyment of the unit

Easements against unit owner. The following easements may be implied against each unit owner:[6]

- an easement for the subjacent and lateral support of the common elements and of every other unit capable of enjoying support
- an easement to provide shelter to the common elements and to every other unit capable of enjoying shelter and
- an easement for the passage or provision of water, sewerage, drainage, gas, electricity, garbage, artificially heated or cooled air and other services, including telephone, radio and television services, through or by means of any pipes, wires, cables or ducts existing within the unit, as belonging to the common elements and to every other unit capable of enjoying those easements

Other easements. In Alberta and Saskatchewan, where an easement is implied, the owner of a utility service who provides service to the parcel or to any unit in the parcel is entitled to the benefit of any easement that is appropriate to the proper provision of that service, but not to the exclusion of the owner of any other utility service.[7] In Ontario, a corporation and any party that has entered into a telecommunications agreement with the corporation has a non-exclusive easement over the part of the condominium property designed to control, facilitate or provide telecommunications to, from or within the property if several criteria are met.[8]

Effect of owners' vote to accept easement. In New Brunswick, Newfoundland and Labrador and Nova Scotia, with the consent of a specified percentage of owners, a condominium may grant easements affecting the common elements, in which case the easements have the same effect as if they were granted by all owners to which the grants of easements relate.[9] In Alberta and Saskatchewan, a corporation may be directed by special resolution to accept on behalf of the owners a grant of easement benefitting the condominium property,[10] which may be registered against the titles issued under the condominium plan.[11] In addition, a corporation may be directed by special resolution to execute on behalf of the owners a grant of easement burdening the condominium property.[12] The corporation must execute the appropriate instrument to grant the easement where the board is satisfied that the resolution was approved by the requisite number of owner votes and that written consents to the release of interests were obtained from all persons with registered interests in the parcel.[13]

Notes

1. *Shaw Cablesystems Ltd. v. Concord Pacific Group Inc.*, [2008] B.C.J. No. 1014, 2008 BCCA 234 (B.C.C.A.).
2. (AB) *Condominium Property Act*, R.S.A. 2000, c. C-22, s. 24(2)
   (BC) *Strata Property Act*, S.B.C. 1998, c. 43, s. 69(3)(e)
   (MB) *Condominium Act*, C.C.S.M. c. C170, s. 9(3)
   (NB) *Condominium Property Act*, S.N.B. 2009, c. C-16.05, s. 18(3)
   (NL) *Condominium Act, 2009*, S.N.L. 2009, c. C-29.1, s. 47(1)(a) (not yet in force)
   (NS) *Condominium Act*, R.S.N.S. 1989, c. 85, s. 29(3)
   (SK) *Condominium Property Act, 1993*, S.S. 1993, c. C-26.1, s. 33
   (NT) *Condominium Act*, R.S.N.W.T. 1988, c. C-15, s. 11(4)
   (NU) *Condominium Act*, R.S.N.W.T. (Nu.) 1988, c. C-15, s. 11(4)
   (YT) *Condominium Act*, R.S.Y. 2002, c. 36, s. 9(4).
3. (AB) *Condominium Property Act*, R.S.A. 2000, c. C-22, s. 24(5)
   (BC) *Strata Property Act*, S.B.C. 1998, c. 43, s. 69(3)(e)
   (SK) *Condominium Property Act, 1993*, S.S. 1993, c. C-26.1, s. 33.
4. (AB) *Condominium Property Act*, R.S.A. 2000, c. C-22, s. 24(1)
   (BC) *Strata Property Act*, S.B.C. 1998, c. 43, s. 69(3)(a)

(SK) *Condominium Property Act, 1993*, S.S. 1993, c. C-26.1, s. 32.

5. (AB) *Condominium Property Act*, R.S.A. 2000, c. C-22, s. 22
   (BC) *Strata Property Act*, S.B.C. 1998, c. 43, s. 69(1)
   (MB) *Condominium Act*, C.C.S.M. c. C170, s. 9(1)
   (NB) *Condominium Property Act*, S.N.B. 2009, c. C-16.05, s. 18(1)
   (NL) *Condominium Act, 2009*, S.N.L. 2009, c. C-29.1, s. 47(1)(a) (not yet in force)
   (NS) *Condominium Act*, R.S.N.S. 1989, c. 85, s. 29(1)
   (ON) *Condominium Act, 1998*, S.O. 1998, c. 19, s. 12(1)
   (PE) *Condominium Act*, R.S.P.E.I. 1988, c. C-16, s. 8(1)
   (SK) *Condominium Property Act, 1993*, S.S. 1993, c. C-26.1, s. 30
   (NT) *Condominium Act*, R.S.N.W.T. 1988, c. C-15, s. 11(1)
   (NU) *Condominium Act*, R.S.N.W.T. (Nu.) 1988, c. C-15, s. 11(1)
   (YT) *Condominium Act*, R.S.Y. 2002, c. 36, s. 9(1).
6. (AB) *Condominium Property Act*, R.S.A. 2000, c. C-22, s. 23(1)
   (BC) *Strata Property Act*, S.B.C. 1998, c. 43, s. 69(2)
   (MB) *Condominium Act*, C.C.S.M. c. C170, s. 9(2)
   (NB) *Condominium Property Act*, S.N.B. 2009, c. C-16.05, s. 18(2)
   (NL) *Condominium Act, 2009*, S.N.L. 2009, c. C-29.1, s. 47(1) (not yet in force)
   (NS) *Condominium Act*, R.S.N.S. 1989, c. 85, s. 29(2)
   (ON) *Condominium Act, 1998*, S.O. 1998, c. 19, s. 12(2)
   (PE) *Condominium Act*, R.S.P.E.I. 1988, c. C-16, s. 8(2)
   (SK) *Condominium Property Act, 1993*, S.S. 1993, c. C-26.1, s. 31(1)
   (NT) *Condominium Act*, R.S.N.W.T. 1988, c. C-15, s. 11(2)
   (NU) *Condominium Act*, R.S.N.W.T. (Nu.) 1988, c. C-15, s. 11(2)
   (YT) *Condominium Act*, R.S.Y. 2002, c. 36, s. 9(2).
7. (AB) *Condominium Property Act*, R.S.A. 2000, c. C-22, s. 23(2); (SK) *Condominium Property Act, 1993*, S.S. 1993, c. C-26.1, s. 31(2).
8. (ON) *Condominium Act, 1998*, S.O. 1998, c. 19, s. 22(5)-(8).
9. (NB) *Condominium Property Act*, S.N.B. 2009, c. C-16.05, s. 19(7)-(8)
   (NL) *Condominium Act, 2009*, S.N.L. 2009, c. C-29.1, s. 18(3)-(4) (not yet in force)
   (NS) *Condominium Act*, R.S.N.S. 1989, c. 85, s. 14(3)-(4).
10. (AB) *Condominium Property Act*, R.S.A. 2000, c. C-22, s. 51; (SK) *Condominium Property Act, 1993*, S.S. 1993, c. C-26.1, s. 73(1).
11. (AB) *Condominium Property Act*, R.S.A. 2000, c. C-22, s. 52(7); (SK) *Condominium Property Act, 1993*, S.S. 1993, c. C-26.1, s. 73(2).
12. (AB) *Condominium Property Act*, R.S.A. 2000, c. C-22, s. 52(1); (SK) *Condominium Property Act, 1993*, S.S. 1993, c. C-26.1, s. 74(1).
13. (AB) *Condominium Property Act*, R.S.A. 2000, c. C-22, s. 52(3); (SK) *Condominium Property Act, 1993*, S.S. 1993, c. C-26.1, s. 74(2).

(b) Encumbrances

▼HCD-13▼ Effect of registration on encumbrance. An encumbrance is a claim that secures the payment of money or the performance of any other obligation, including a mortgage and a lien and, in some jurisdictions, a charge and an easement.[1] After the declaration and the description or plan are registered, an encumbrance against the common elements is no longer enforceable against the common elements, but is enforceable against all the units and their appurtenant common interests in the common elements.[2] Any unit and common interest may be discharged from an encumbrance by payment to the claimant of a portion of the sum claimed, as determined by the proportions specified in the declaration or plan for sharing the common expenses.[3] On demand and on payment of a portion of the encumbrance sufficient to discharge the encumbrance insofar as it affects a unit and its appurtenant common interest, the claimant must give the unit owner a discharge of the encumbrance insofar as it affects that unit and common interest.[4]

Provisions specific to Newfoundland and Labrador. Newfoundland and Labrador's statute contains provisions regarding notification to encumbrance-holders and agreements on prior encumbrances. With respect to notification, the owner must provide timely written notification to encumbrance-holders of the owner's intention to register a declaration and description, must send a copy of the declaration and description to the encumbrance-holders, and must file a certified copy of the notification with the registrar.[5] If an encumbrance-holder files a written notice of objection to the registration before registration is effected, the declaration and description cannot be accepted for registration until the objection is withdrawn.[6] Unless the encumbrance-holders provide written consent, the declaration and description cannot be registered until 30 days after notification.[7]

With respect to agreements on prior encumbrances, before registration, the owner and encumbrance-holder may enter into an agreement as to how the encumbrance is to be divided among the units and common elements or is otherwise to be dealt with.[8] The encumbrance-holder may register the agreement, in which case the encumbrance against the property is released and the encumbrances created by the agreement take effect.[9] After registration, no future encumbrance can be created or effective against the property while it remains subdivided into separate units with common elements.[10]

Notes

1. (MB) *Condominium Act*, C.C.S.M. c. C170, s. 1
   (NB) *Condominium Property Act*, S.N.B. 2009, c. C-16.05, s. 1(1)
   (NL) *Condominium Act, 2009*, S.N.L. 2009, c. C-29.1, s. 2(1)(p) (not yet in force)
   (NS) *Condominium Act*, R.S.N.S. 1989, c. 85, s. 3(1)(o)
   (ON) *Condominium Act, 1998*, S.O. 1998, c. 19, s. 1(1)
   (PE) *Condominium Act,* R.S.P.E.I. 1988, c. C-16, s. 1(1)(l)
   (NT) *Condominium Act*, R.S.N.W.T. 1988, c. C-15, s. 1(1)
   (NU) *Condominium Act*, R.S.N.W.T. (Nu.) 1988, c. C-15, s. 1(1)
   (YT) *Condominium Act*, R.S.Y. 2002, c. 36, s. 1.
2. (MB) *Condominium Act*, C.C.S.M. c. C170, s. 8(6)-(7)
   (NB) *Condominium Property Act*, S.N.B. 2009, c. C-16.05, s. 17(1)-(2)
   (NS) *Condominium Act*, R.S.N.S. 1989, c. 85, s. 28(7)-(8)
   (ON) *Condominium Act, 1998*, S.O. 1998, c. 19, s. 13
   (PE) *Condominium Act,* R.S.P.E.I. 1988, c. C-16, s. 7(7)-(8)
   (NT) *Condominium Act*, R.S.N.W.T. 1988, c. C-15, s. 9(1)-(2)
   (NU) *Condominium Act*, R.S.N.W.T. (Nu.) 1988, c. C-15, s. 9(1)-(2)
   (YT) *Condominium Act*, R.S.Y. 2002, c. 36, s. 8(6)-(7).
3. (MB) *Condominium Act*, C.C.S.M. c. C170, s. 8(9)
   (NB) *Condominium Property Act*, S.N.B. 2009, c. C-16.05, s. 17(3)
   (NS) *Condominium Act*, R.S.N.S. 1989, c. 85, s. 28(9)
   (ON) *Condominium Act, 1998*, S.O. 1998, c. 19, s. 14(1)
   (PE) *Condominium Act,* R.S.P.E.I. 1988, c. C-16, s. 7(9)
   (NT) *Condominium Act*, R.S.N.W.T. 1988, c. C-15, s. 9(3)
   (NU) *Condominium Act*, R.S.N.W.T. (Nu.) 1988, c. C-15, s. 9(3)
   (YT) *Condominium Act*, R.S.Y. 2002, c. 36, s. 8(8).
4. (MB) *Condominium Act*, C.C.S.M. c. C170, s. 8(10)
   (NB) *Condominium Property Act*, S.N.B. 2009, c. C-16.05, s. 17(4)
   (NS) *Condominium Act*, R.S.N.S. 1989, c. 85, s. 28(10)
   (ON) *Condominium Act, 1998*, S.O. 1998, c. 19, s. 14(2)
   (PE) *Condominium Act,* R.S.P.E.I. 1988, c. C-16, s. 7(10)
   (NT) *Condominium Act*, R.S.N.W.T. 1988, c. C-15, s. 9(4)
   (NU) *Condominium Act*, R.S.N.W.T. (Nu.) 1988, c. C-15, s. 9(4)
   (YT) *Condominium Act*, R.S.Y. 2002, c. 36, s. 8(9).
5. (NL) *Condominium Act, 2009*, S.N.L. 2009, c. C-29.1, s. 13(1), (3).
6. (NL) *Condominium Act, 2009*, S.N.L. 2009, c. C-29.1, s. 13(2) (not yet in force).
7. (NL) *Condominium Act, 2009*, S.N.L. 2009, c. C-29.1, s. 13(4) (not yet in force).
8. (NL) *Condominium Act, 2009*, S.N.L. 2009, c. C-29.1, s. 14(1) (not yet in force).
9. (NL) *Condominium Act, 2009*, S.N.L. 2009, c. C-29.1, s. 14(2)-(3) (not yet in force).
10. (NL) *Condominium Act, 2009*, S.N.L. 2009, c. C-29.1, s. 87 (not yet in force).

3. Registration

(1) General HCD-14
(2) Freehold Condominium Corporations................. HCD-15
(3) Leasehold Condominium Corporations............... HCD-16

---

(1) General

▼HCD-14▼ Effect of registration. A condominium declaration and description or plan may be registered by or on behalf of the owner in fee simple, or by the lessee, of the land described in the description or plan.[1] Upon registration of a declaration and description or plan, the condominium corporation is created and the land and the interest appurtenant to the land described in the description or plan are governed by the condominium or strata Act of each province or territory.[2] The corporation created on registration is a corporation without share capital whose members are the legally registered owners from time to time, and the owners share the assets of the corporation in the proportions set out in the declaration or plan.[3] Most jurisdictions provide that the other statutes of the jurisdiction related to incorporated entities do not apply to condominium corporations.[4]

Terminology. Whether the legislation requires a description or plan is a question of terminology, rather than substance; while some jurisdictions refer to descriptions,[5] others refer to plans.[6] In Alberta and Saskatchewan, the declaration and description or plan is a single document called a "condominium plan",[7] and in British Columbia the declaration and description or plan is a single document called a "strata plan".[8]

Notes

1. (AB) *Condominium Property Act*, R.S.A. 2000, c. C-22, s. 4
   (BC) *Strata Property Act*, S.B.C. 1998, c. 43, s. 240
   (MB) *Condominium Act*, C.C.S.M. c. C170, s. 4(2)
   (NB) *Condominium Property Act*, S.N.B. 2009, c. C-16.05, s. 5(1)
   (NL) *Condominium Act, 2009*, S.N.L. 2009, c. C-29.1, s. 8(2) (not yet in force)
   (NS) *Condominium Act*, R.S.N.S. 1989, c. 85, s. 6(2)
   (ON) *Condominium Act, 1998*, S.O. 1998, c. 19, s. 2(1)
   (PE) *Condominium Act,* R.S.P.E.I. 1988, c. C-16, s. 2(2)
   (QC) *Civil Code of Québec*, L.R.Q. c. C-1991, arts. 1038-1040
   (SK) *Condominium Property Act, 1993*, S.S. 1993, c. C-26.1, s. 5.1
   (NT) *Condominium Act*, R.S.N.W.T. 1988, c. C-15, s. 4(1)

(NU) *Condominium Act*, R.S.N.W.T. (Nu.) 1988, c. C-15, s. 4(1)
(YT) *Condominium Act*, R.S.Y. 2002, c. 36, s. 4(1).

2. (AB) *Condominium Property Act*, R.S.A. 2000, c. C-22, ss. 2, 25(1)
(BC) *Strata Property Act*, S.B.C. 1998, c. 43, s. 2
(MB) *Condominium Act*, C.C.S.M. c. C170, s. 4(3)
(NB) *Condominium Property Act*, S.N.B. 2009, c. C-16.05, s. 10(1)-(2)
(NL) *Condominium Act, 2009*, S.N.L. 2009, c. C-29.1, s. 8(4) (not yet in force)
(NS) *Condominium Act*, R.S.N.S. 1989, c. 85, s. 6(5)
(ON) *Condominium Act, 1998*, S.O. 1998, c. 19, s. 2(3)
(PE) *Condominium Act*, R.S.P.E.I. 1988, c. C-16, s. 2(3)
(QC) *Civil Code of Québec*, L.R.Q. c. C-1991, art. 1059-1062
(SK) *Condominium Property Act, 1993*, S.S. 1993, c. C-26.1, s. 5.1
(NT) *Condominium Act*, R.S.N.W.T. 1988, c. C-15, s. 4(2)
(NU) *Condominium Act*, R.S.N.W.T. (Nu.) 1988, c. C-15, s. 4(2)
(YT) *Condominium Act*, R.S.Y. 2002, c. 36, s. 4(2).

3. (AB) *Condominium Property Act*, R.S.A. 2000, c. C-22, s. 25(1)-(2)
(MB) *Condominium Act*, C.C.S.M. c. C170, s. 10(1)-(2)
(NB) *Condominium Property Act*, S.N.B. 2009, c. C-16.05, s. 10(2)
(NL) *Condominium Act, 2009*, S.N.L. 2009, c. C-29.1, s. 17(1) (not yet in force)
(NS) *Condominium Act*, R.S.N.S. 1989, c. 85, s. 13(1)
(ON) *Condominium Act, 1998*, S.O. 1998, c. 19, s. 5(1)
(PE) *Condominium Act*, R.S.P.E.I. 1988, c. C-16, s. 10(1)
(QC) *Civil Code of Québec*, L.R.Q. c. C-1991, art. 1039
(SK) *Condominium Property Act, 1993*, S.S. 1993, c. C-26.1, s. 34(3)
(NT) *Condominium Act*, R.S.N.W.T. 1988, c. C-15, s. 12(1)-(2)
(NU) *Condominium Act*, R.S.N.W.T. (Nu.) 1988, c. C-15, s. 12(1)-(2)
(YT) *Condominium Act*, R.S.Y. 2002, c. 36, s. 10(1)-(2).

4. (AB) *Condominium Property Act*, R.S.A. 2000, c. C-22, s. 25(5)
(BC) *Strata Property Act*, S.B.C. 1998, c. 43, s. 291(1)
(MB) *Condominium Act*, C.C.S.M. c. C170, s. 10(3)
(NB) *Condominium Property Act*, S.N.B. 2009, c. C-16.05, s. 19(2)
(NL) *Condominium Act, 2009*, S.N.L. 2009, c. C-29.1, s. 18(7) (not yet in force)
(NS) *Condominium Act*, R.S.N.S. 1989, c. 85, s. 13(3)
(ON) *Condominium Act, 1998*, S.O. 1998, c. 19, s. 5(3); (ON) General Regulation, O. Reg. 48/01, s. 2
(SK) *Condominium Property Act, 1993*, S.S. 1993, c. C-26.1, s. 34(6)
(NT) *Condominium Act*, R.S.N.W.T. 1988, c. C-15, s. 12(3)
(NU) *Condominium Act*, R.S.N.W.T. (Nu.) 1988, c. C-15, s. 12(3)
(YT) *Condominium Act*, R.S.Y. 2002, c. 36, s. 10(3).
See also *York Region Condominium Corp. No. 921 v. ATOP Communications Inc.*, [2003] O.J. No. 5255, [2003] O.T.C. 1116 (Ont. S.C.J.).

5. (NB) *Condominium Property Act*, S.N.B. 2009, c. C-16.05, s. 7

(NL) *Condominium Act, 2009*, S.N.L. 2009, c. C-29.1, s. 11 (not yet in force)
(NS) *Condominium Act*, R.S.N.S. 1989, c. 85, ss. 3(1)(n), 12
(ON) *Condominium Act, 1998*, S.O. 1998, c. 19, ss. 1(1), 8
(PE) *Condominium Act,* R.S.P.E.I. 1988, c. C-16, ss. 1(1)(k), 4.

6. (MB) *Condominium Act*, C.C.S.M. c. C170, ss. 1, 6
(NT) *Condominium Act*, R.S.N.W.T. 1988, c. C-15, ss. 1(1), 6
(NU) *Condominium Act*, R.S.N.W.T. (Nu.) 1988, c. C-15, ss. 1(1), 6
(YT) *Condominium Act*, R.S.Y. 2002, c. 36, ss. 1, 6.
7. (AB) *Condominium Property Act*, R.S.A. 2000, c. C-22, s. 1(1)(g), 8; (SK) *Condominium Property Act, 1993*, S.S. 1993, c. C-26.1, ss. 2(1)(j).
8. (BC) *Strata Property Act*, S.B.C. 1998, c. 43, ss. 1, 2.

---

(2) Freehold Condominium Corporations

▼HCD-15▼ General registration requirements. Unless otherwise noted, the registration requirements applicable to standard condominium corporations apply to other freehold condominium corporations and to leasehold condominium corporations.

Standard condominium corporations. Although jurisdictions vary in their precise requirements and terminology, in general, the prescribed land registrar must:[1]

- issue a certificate of title in the name of the corporation in the prescribed manner
- issue a separate certificate of title in the name of each owner for each unit described in the description or plan, which must set out the proportion of the common interest appurtenant to each unit
- keep a condominium corporation index in the prescribed manner and
- keep a condominium register in which declarations, plans, by-laws, notices of termination and other instruments respecting land must be registered

In Manitoba and Northwest Territories, where the property that is the subject of a declaration and plan contains rental units occupied by tenants on the date the declaration is submitted for registration, the declaration can only be registered if additional criteria regarding its content and accompanying statutory declarations are met.[2]

Phased condominium corporations. The Alberta regulations contain detailed provisions regarding the contents of phased development disclosure statements, the timing of registration for each phase, the registrar's issuance of certificates of title, amendments to condominium plans and the operation of phases.[3] The British Columbia statute contains detailed provisions regarding phased strata plans, including security for common facilities, contribution to expenses, effects of deposit, notification of deposit and the annual general meeting after deposit.[4] The Manitoba statute contains detailed provisions regarding phased development, including notices on title and declaration contents, and regarding phasing amendments, including consent requirements, amendment contents, notices, registration requirements and the effects of registration.[5] The statutes of New Brunswick, Newfoundland and Labrador and Nova Scotia are less detailed but provide that, when each subsequent phase is accepted for registration, the phase is consolidated into one lot with all previously accepted phases.[6] In Ontario, the developer must register an amendment to both the declaration and description to create a phase; all required facilities and services must be installed or provided, or the developer must provide a bond or other security in this regard; and the corporation must receive the required documents within the required timeframe.[7] In Saskatchewan, by registering an interest based on a developer's reservation, the developer reserves the right to construct additional units and common facilities on the parcel.[8]

Vacant land condominium corporations. In British Columbia, before a person applies to deposit a bare land strata plan, the person must obtain the approval of an approving officer, who must endorse the approval in accordance with the regulations.[9] In New Brunswick, a declaration and description for a bare-land condominium property must be accompanied by a letter from the relevant authority confirming that the property complies with zoning by-laws and regulations.[10] In Newfoundland and Labrador and Ontario, a declaration and description for a vacant land condominium cannot be registered unless the registration creates a condominium corporation that is not a common elements condominium corporation or a phased development condominium corporation.[11] In Ontario only, where there are buildings, structures, facilities and services to be included in common elements, all of those shown in the declaration and description must be completed, installed and provided, or the developer must provide a bond or other security in this regard.[12] In addition, a declaration cannot be registered unless none of the units are or include part of a building or structure, except if the building or structure is located entirely within the unit's boundaries.[13] In Saskatchewan, where an approved condominium plan purports to divide a parcel into bare land units, the application to issue titles pursuant to an approved condominium plan must be accompanied by an application to register an interest based on an endorsed declaration.[14]

Common elements condominium corporations. In Newfoundland and Labrador and Ontario, a declaration and description for a common elements condominium corporation cannot be registered unless the registration creates a condominium corporation that is not a phased development condominium corporation or a vacant land condominium corporation.[15] A declaration can only be registered if each of the owners of a common interest in the condominium:[16]

- also owns the freehold estate in a parcel of tied land that is not included in the land described in the description and that meets other requirements and
- has signed a certificate stating consent to the registration of the declaration and notice

Once the declaration and description are registered, the common interest attaches to the owner's parcel of tied land, and the developer must register a notice and certificate against each owner's parcel of tied land.[17] Ontario's regulations contain additional provisions regarding the place of registration, capacity to convey parcels under the *Planning Act*, and the land registrar's recording duties where the records of the property are and are not automated and where an amendment purports to add parcels of tied land to the property.[18]

Notes

1. (AB) *Condominium Property Act*, R.S.A. 2000, c. C-22, s. 4; (AB) Condominium Property Regulation, Alta. Reg. 168/2000, s. 2

   (BC) *Strata Property Act*, S.B.C. 1998, c. 43, ss. 249-252

   (MB) *Condominium Act*, C.C.S.M. c. C170, s. 4(3)

   (NB) *Condominium Property Act*, S.N.B. 2009, c. C-16.05, s. 9

   (NL) *Condominium Act, 2009*, S.N.L. 2009, c. C-29.1, s. 7 (not yet in force)

   (NS) *Condominium Act*, R.S.N.S. 1989, c. 85, ss. 7, 9-10, 12C

   (ON) *Condominium Act, 1998*, S.O. 1998, c. 19, s. 3

   (PE) *Condominium Act,* R.S.P.E.I. 1988, c. C-16, s. 5

   (SK) *Condominium Property Act, 1993*, S.S. 1993, c. C-26.1, s. 5.1

   (NT) *Condominium Act*, R.S.N.W.T. 1988, c. C-15, s. 4(2)

   (NU) *Condominium Act*, R.S.N.W.T. (Nu.) 1988, c. C-15, s. 4(2)

   (YT) *Condominium Act*, R.S.Y. 2002, c. 36, s. 4.

2. See Section II.4. ("Declaration and Description or Plan").
3. (AB) *Condominium Property Act*, R.S.A. 2000, c. C-22, s. 19; (AB) Condominium Property Regulation, Alta. Reg. 168/2000, ss. 35-36, 38-42.
4. (BC) *Strata Property Act*, S.B.C. 1998, c. 43, ss. 223, 226-230.
5. (MB) *Condominium Act*, C.C.S.M. c. C170, ss. 4(4), 5(3.1)-5(3.2), 5.1-5.16.
6. (NB) *Condominium Property Act*, S.N.B. 2009, c. C-16.05, s. 12(2)

   (NL) *Condominium Act, 2009*, S.N.L. 2009, c. C-29.1, s. 74(3) (not yet in force)

   (NS) *Condominium Act*, R.S.N.S. 1989, c. 85, s. 8(2).

   Newfoundland and Labrador's statute contains additional provisions regarding the contents of and amendments to disclosure statements and descriptions: (NL) *Condominium Act, 2009*, S.N.L. 2009, c. C-29.1, ss. 75-77 (not yet in force).
7. (ON) *Condominium Act, 1998*, S.O. 1998, c. 19, ss. 146(3), (8)-(9), 149(1). Ontario's regulations also contain provisions regarding amendments to declarations and descriptions, the place of registration and procedures for registering amendments: (ON) General Regulation, O. Reg. 48/01, ss. 48, 51; (ON) Description and Registration Regulation, O. Reg. 49/01, s. 22.
8. (SK) *Condominium Property Act, 1993*, S.S. 1993, c. C-26.1, s. 16(2). There are also several requirements regarding developers' reservations: (SK) *Condominium Property Act, 1993*, S.S. 1993, c. C-26.1, ss. 16-19; 23; (SK) Condominium Property Regulations, 2001, R.R.S., c. C-26.1, Reg. 2, ss. 17-21, 26-30, 38.
9. (BC) *Strata Property Act*, S.B.C. 1998, c. 43, s. 243.
10. (NB) General Regulation, N.B. Reg. 2009-169, s. 4(2).
11. (NL) *Condominium Act, 2009*, S.N.L. 2009, c. C-29.1, s. 79(3) (not yet in force); (ON) *Condominium Act, 1998*, S.O. 1998, c. 19, s. 155(3).
12. (ON) *Condominium Act, 1998*, S.O. 1998, c. 19, s. 158(1).
13. (ON) General Regulation, O. Reg. 48/01, s. 56(1)(a).
14. (SK) *Condominium Property Act, 1993*, S.S. 1993, c. C-26.1, s. 5.2. There are also provisions regarding compliance with (SK) *Planning and Development Act, 2007*, S.S. 2007, c. P-13.2 and developers' obligations with respect to assignments, certificates and security: (SK) *Condominium Property Act, 1993*, S.S. 1993, c. C-26.1, s. 21(7); (SK) Condominium Property Regulations, 2001, R.R.S., c. C-26.1, Reg. 2, ss. 8, 17-25.
15. (NL) *Condominium Act, 2009*, S.N.L. 2009, c. C-29.1, s. 68(3) (not yet in force); (ON) *Condominium Act, 1998*, S.O. 1998, c. 19, s. 138(3).
16. (NL) *Condominium Act, 2009*, S.N.L. 2009, c. C-29.1, s. 69(1) (not yet in force); (ON) *Condominium Act, 1998*, S.O. 1998, c. 19, s. 139(1).
17. (NL) *Condominium Act, 2009*, S.N.L. 2009, c. C-29.1, s. 69(2) (not yet in force)

    (ON) *Condominium Act, 1998*, S.O. 1998, c. 19, s. 139(2). See also ss. 139(3) and (4), which provide that if an owner's parcel is divided into new parcels, the new parcel owners are joint owners of the original parcel's common interest and that, on the sale of a parcel or the enforcement of an encumbrance registered against a parcel, the owner's common interest continues to be attached to the parcel.
18. (ON) General Regulation, O. Reg. 48/01, ss. 39, 39.1; (ON) Description and Registration Regulation, O. Reg. 49/01, ss. 28(1)(g), 28(3)(h), 28(7), 31(2), 32, 33; (ON) *Planning Act*, R.S.O. 1990, c. P.13.

(3) Leasehold Condominium Corporations

▼HCD-16▼ General registration requirements. Alberta, Manitoba, Northwest Territories, Nunavut and Yukon do not provide additional registration requirements for leasehold condominium corporations.[1]

Specific registration requirements. In British Columbia, the registrar may not accept a leasehold strata plan for deposit unless the title to the land is registered in the name of a leasehold landlord, the person applying is the registered lessee under the ground lease, the unexpired term of the ground lease is at least 50 years after the date of the application, all the land subject to the ground lease is shown on the plan, and the plan is signed by the leasehold landlord.[2] There are also provisions concerning requirements for the registrar and the effect of deposit.[3] In Ontario, a description for a leasehold condominium corporation may not be registered unless the buildings and improvements to the property form part of the property.[4] There are also detailed requirements concerning the nature of the leasehold interest required for registration of the declaration and description and the land registrar's recording duties where property records are not automated.[5]

Notes

1. However, Northwest Territories' legislation provides that, in the case of a leasehold condominium, the registration operates as a subdivision of the property against all persons except the lessor and those whose land interest derives from the lessor's: (NT) *Condominium Act*, R.S.N.W.T. 1988, c. C-15, s. 8(6).
2. (BC) *Strata Property Act*, S.B.C. 1998, c. 43, s. 201.
3. (BC) *Strata Property Act*, S.B.C. 1998, c. 43, ss. 202-203.
4. (ON) *Condominium Act, 1998*, S.O. 1998, c. 19, s. 167(2).
5. (ON) General Regulation, O. Reg. 48/01, s. 59; (ON) Description and Registration Regulation, O. Reg. 49/01, ss. 28(2), 28(5).

---

4. Declaration and Description or Plan

(1) Declaration
(a) Required Contents
(i) Freehold Condominiums HCD-17
(ii) Leasehold Condominiums HCD-18
(iii) Property Containing Occupied Rental Units HCD-19
(b) Permitted Contents HCD-20

(2) Description or Plan
(a) Freehold Condominiums HCD-21
(b) Leasehold Condominiums HCD-22
(3) Amendments HCD-23

---

(1) Declaration

(a) Required Contents

(i) Freehold Condominiums

▼HCD-17▼ General requirements. Unless otherwise noted, the requirements for declaration contents applicable to standard condominiums apply to other freehold condominiums and to leasehold condominiums.

Standard condominiums. A declaration can only be accepted for registration if the developer has executed it in the manner prescribed by the act under which it is to be registered.[1] Although jurisdictions vary in their precise requirements and terminology, in general, a declaration must contain:[2]

- a legal description of the land that is the subject of the declaration
- a statement of intention that the land or the leasehold interest therein and interests appurtenant to the land described in the description or plan are to be governed by the respective Act of each province and territory
- the consent of all holders of registered encumbrances against the land or interests appurtenant to the land described in the description or plan or interests or estates in the land in respect of which caveats have been filed[3]
- a statement indicating whether the property to which the declaration relates contains rental units occupied by tenants on the date the declaration is submitted for registration
- a statement of the proportions, expressed in percentages, allocated to the units in which the owners are to contribute to the common expenses and to share in the common interests
- a statement of the proportions, expressed in percentages, allocated to the units in which the owners are to have voting rights[4]

- an address for service for the condominium[5] and
- where the units are delineated in the condominium plan, a description of the manner of determining values in the event the property ceases to be governed by the Act[6]

Phased condominiums. In British Columbia, phased strata plans must meet additional requirements regarding approvals by approving officers,[7] amendments to declarations[8] and elections to proceed and not to proceed with a phase.[9] In Manitoba, New Brunswick, Newfoundland and Labrador and Ontario, declarations for phased condominiums must meet several additional requirements regarding declaration contents[10] and amendments to declarations required to create a phase.[11] In New Brunswick, Newfoundland and Labrador and Ontario, an amendment to a declaration required to create a phase must include:[12]

- the consent of every person with a registered mortgage against the land included in the phase or interests appurtenant to the land, as the land and interests are described in the amendment to the description required to create the phase
- a statement of the proportions, expressed in percentages, of the common interests appurtenant to the units in the condominium after the creation of the phase
- a statement of the proportions, expressed in percentages, allocated to the units in the condominium in which the owners are to contribute to the common expenses after the creation of the phase and
- a specification of all parts of the common elements contained in the phase that are to be exclusive use common elements

Vacant land condominiums. In British Columbia, a bare strata plan must be approved by the relevant approving officer.[13] In New Brunswick, a declaration for a bare-land condominium property must include the following additional information:[14]

- the services and amenities available to the units
- a statement of responsibility for connection costs of utilities for the units
- restrictions on structures that may be placed on the units
- the structures completed on registration that are to be maintained by the condominium
- a statement of responsibility for the maintenance and repair of common element structures erected after registration and

- a statement that the preliminary plans for the construction of a unit must be approved by the condominium

In Ontario, a declaration for a vacant land condominium must contain certain schedules and a statement that the registration of the declaration and description will create a vacant land condominium. In addition, the declaration can only be registered if none of the units are part of a building or structure and none include part of a building or structure, except if a building or structure is located entirely within the boundaries of the unit.[15]

Common elements condominiums. In Newfoundland and Labrador and Ontario, declarations for common elements condominiums must contain:[16]

- a statement that the common elements are intended for the owners' use and enjoyment
- a legal description of the parcels of land and
- all other material required by the regulations

Notes

1. (ON) *Condominium Act, 1998*, S.O. 1998, c. 19, s. 7(1).
2. (BC) *Strata Property Act*, S.B.C. 1998, c. 43, ss. 244-245
   (MB) *Condominium Act*, C.C.S.M. c. C170, s. 5(1)
   (NB) *Condominium Property Act*, S.N.B. 2009, c. C-16.05, s. 11
   (NL) *Condominium Act, 2009*, S.N.L. 2009, c. C-29.1, s. 9(1) (not yet in force)
   (NS) *Condominium Act*, R.S.N.S. 1989, c. 85, s. 11(1)-(2)
   (ON) *Condominium Act, 1998*, S.O. 1998, c. 19, s. 7(2); (ON) General Regulation, O. Reg. 48/01, s. 5
   (PE) *Condominium Act,* R.S.P.E.I. 1988, c. C-16, s. 3(1)
   (QC) *Civil Code of Québec*, L.R.Q. c. C-1991, arts. 1041, 1052, 1053, 1055
   (SK) *Condominium Property Act, 1993*, S.S. 1993, c. C-26.1, s. 5.2
   (NT) *Condominium Act*, R.S.N.W.T. 1988, c. C-15, s. 5(1)
   (NU) *Condominium Act*, R.S.N.W.T. (Nu.) 1988, c. C-15, s. 5(1)
   (YT) *Condominium Act*, R.S.Y. 2002, c. 36, s. 5(1).
3. In Ontario, a person whose consent is required cannot withhold consent by reason only of the developer's failure to enter into a specified number of agreements of purchase and sale for the sale of proposed units: (ON) *Condominium Act, 1998*, S.O. 1998, c. 19, s. 7(3). In Manitoba, a party may apply to court for an order dispensing with the required consent where the consent is unreasonably withheld or the encumbrance, interest or estate of any person whose consent is required would not be diminished or adversely affected by the registration of the declaration and plan: (MB) *Condominium Act*, C.C.S.M. c. C170, s. 5(8).
4. See Section VI.2. ("Voting").

5. See Section III.1. ("Introductory Matters") regarding service on condominium corporations.
6. See Section IX.2. ("Termination of Condominium or Corporation").
7. (BC) *Strata Property Act*, S.B.C. 1998, c. 43, ss. 221-222, 224-225, 244(1)(h)(i), (iii).
8. (BC) *Strata Property Act*, S.B.C. 1998, c. 43, ss. 233-234.
9. (BC) *Strata Property Act*, S.B.C. 1998, c. 43, ss. 231-232, 235.
10. (MB) *Condominium Act*, C.C.S.M. c. C170, s. 5(3.1)
    (NB) General Regulation, N.B. Reg. 2009-169, s. 7
    (NL) *Condominium Act, 2009*, S.N.L. 2009, c. C-29.1, s. 76 (not yet in force)
    (ON) General Regulation, O. Reg. 48/01, s. 49.
11. (MB) *Condominium Act*, C.C.S.M. c. C170, ss. 5.2-5.6
    (NB) General Regulation, N.B. Reg. 2009-169, s. 8(2)-(5)
    (NL) *Condominium Act, 2009*, S.N.L. 2009, c. C-29.1, s. 77(4) (not yet in force)
    (ON) General Regulation, O. Reg. 48/01, s. 52.
12. (NB) General Regulation, N.B. Reg. 2009-169, s. 8(1)
    (NL) *Condominium Act, 2009*, S.N.L. 2009, c. C-29.1, s. 77(8) (not yet in force)
    (ON) *Condominium Act, 1998*, S.O. 1998, c. 19, s. 146(4).
13. (BC) *Strata Property Act*, S.B.C. 1998, c. 43, s. 244(1)(h)(ii)-(iii).
14. (NB) General Regulation, N.B. Reg. 2009-169, s. 4(1).
15. (ON) General Regulation, O. Reg. 48/01, s. 56.
16. (NL) *Condominium Act, 2009*, S.N.L. 2009, c. C-29.1, s. 70 (not yet in force)
    (ON) *Condominium Act, 1998*, S.O. 1998, c. 19, s. 140. See also (ON) General Regulation, O. Reg. 48/01, s. 40 for further Ontario requirements.

(ii) Leasehold Condominiums

▼HCD-18▼ Additional Ontario requirements. In Ontario, in addition to the general requirements for declarations, a declaration for a leasehold condominium must be executed by the lessor and must contain:[1]

- a statement of the term of the owners' leasehold interests
- a schedule of the amount of rent for the property payable by the corporation on behalf of the owners to the lessor, the times at which it is payable and a formula to determine the amount and times
- a schedule of all provisions of the leasehold interests affecting the property and owners and
- all other material required by the regulations[2]

In addition, in Ontario, provisions of the leasehold interests in the property are not binding on the property or owners unless the declaration sets them out and states that they are binding.[3]

Notes

1. (ON) *Condominium Act, 1998*, S.O. 1998, c. 19, s. 166(1)-(2).
2. See also (ON) General Regulation, O. Reg. 48/01, s. 60 for further Ontario requirements.
3. (ON) *Condominium Act, 1998*, S.O. 1998, c. 19, s. 166(3).

(iii) Property Containing Occupied Rental Units

▼HCD-19▼ Contents of declaration and accompanying statutory declarations. In Manitoba and Northwest Territories, where the property that is the subject of a declaration and plan contains rental units occupied by tenants on the date the declaration is submitted for registration, the declaration can only be registered if additional criteria are met regarding its contents and the contents of two accompanying statutory declarations.

Contents of declaration. The declaration must contain a statement that each tenant in occupancy under a tenancy agreement on the date of registration and in occupancy on the date an option is given has been or will be given an option, exercisable within the prescribed time after receipt of the option, to purchase as a unit the rental unit that is the subject of the tenancy agreement at a price not exceeding the price at which the unit will be offered to the public and on terms that are not less favourable.[1] The declaration must also contain a statement that the rights and duties of each tenant in occupancy under a tenancy agreement of any kind on registration are continued in accordance with the landlord and tenant legislation of each jurisdiction.[2]

Contents of accompanying statutory declarations. The registered condominium declaration must be accompanied by two statutory declarations. The first statutory declaration must state that:[3]

- each tenant in occupancy received written notice from the developer of the developer's intention to file a declaration
- in the case of tenants in occupancy for a prescribed period of time, the notice was given in the prescribed time before the con-

dominium declaration was submitted for registration and at the time the tenant agreed to occupy the rental unit and

- notice of the registration will be given to each tenant who enters into occupancy after the condominium declaration is registered at the time the tenant agrees to occupy the rental unit

The second statutory declaration must state that each tenant in occupancy on the date of registration has been offered an agreement providing that:[4]

- despite any provision to the contrary in the landlord and tenant legislation, the tenant may continue to occupy the rental unit for a prescribed period of time after the registration
- where a landlord gives notice of an increase in rent to the tenant, the notice must be given in accordance with and the rent increase must be subject to the landlord and tenant legislation
- the tenancy may not be terminated by the landlord except in accordance with the landlord and tenant legislation and
- the agreement is binding on the heirs, successors and assigns of the landlord, but is not assignable by the tenant[5]

Notes

1. (MB) *Condominium Act*, C.C.S.M. c. C170, s. 5(2)(b); (NT) *Condominium Act*, R.S.N.W.T. 1988, c. C-15, s. 6.6(b).
2. (MB) *Condominium Act*, C.C.S.M. c. C170, s. 5(2)(c); (NT) *Condominium Act*, R.S.N.W.T. 1988, c. C-15, s. 6.6(c).
3. (MB) *Condominium Act*, C.C.S.M. c. C170, s. 5(2)(a); (NT) *Condominium Act*, R.S.N.W.T. 1988, c. C-15, s. 6.6(a).
4. (MB) *Condominium Act*, C.C.S.M. c. C170, s. 5(2)(d); (NT) *Condominium Act*, R.S.N.W.T. 1988, c. C-15, s. 6.6(d).
5. In Manitoba, this agreement must be served on each tenant in the prescribed manner. Where a tenant objects to the term of occupancy offered in the agreement, the tenant must notify the landlord within the prescribed time, failing which the tenant is deemed to have accepted the agreement and its contents. If a tenant notifies the landlord of an objection to the term of occupancy and the landlord and tenant cannot resolve the dispute, the landlord or tenant may refer the dispute for determination in accordance with the landlord and tenant legislation: (MB) *Condominium Act*, C.C.S.M. c. C170, ss. 5(2.2)-(2.3).

(b) Permitted Contents

▼HCD-20▼ Permitted specifications and provisions. In addition to the required contents of a declaration, a declaration may contain additional permitted contents. Although jurisdictions vary in the permitted contents of a declaration, in general, a declaration may contain the following specifications and provisions:[1]

- a specification of common expenses
- a specification of any parts of the common elements reserved for the exclusive use and/or possession of one or more owners
- provisions respecting the occupation and use of the units and common elements
- provisions restricting gifts, leases and sales of the units and common interests
- subject to the regulations or by-laws, a specification of the number, qualification, nomination, election, term of office, compensation and removal of board members and the meetings, quorum, functions and officers of the board
- a specification of the corporation's duties consistent with its objects
- provisions regulating the assessment and collection of contributions towards the common expenses
- provisions respecting the priority of a lien for common expense arrears
- a specification of the majority required to make substantial changes to the common elements and assets of the corporation
- a specification of any provision requiring the corporation to purchase the units and common interests of any owners who dissented after a substantial addition, alteration and/or improvement to the common elements or after a substantial change to the corporation's assets
- a specification of the obligations to repair and maintain the units and common elements
- a specification of the percentage of substantial damage to the buildings and the majority required to authorize repairs in lieu of termination of the corporation[2]
- a specification of the majority required for a sale of the property or a part of the common elements[3]
- a specification of the majority required for the termination of the corporation[4] and
- any other matters required by the regulations

Notes

1. (BC) *Strata Property Act*, S.B.C. 1998, c. 43, ss. 247-248

(MB) *Condominium Act*, C.C.S.M. c. C170, ss. 5(3)-(5.1)

(NB) *Condominium Property Act*, S.N.B. 2009, c. C-16.05, ss. 6(3)-(4)

(NL) *Condominium Act, 2009*, S.N.L. 2009, c. C-29.1, ss. 9(2), 27(8) (not yet in force)

(NS) *Condominium Act*, R.S.N.S. 1989, c. 85, s. 11(3), (3A)

(ON) *Condominium Act, 1998*, S.O. 1998, c. 19, s. 7(4)

(PE) *Condominium Act,* R.S.P.E.I. 1988, c. C-16, s. 3(2)

(QC) *Civil Code of Québec*, L.R.Q. c. C-1991, arts. 1056, 1058

(NT) *Condominium Act*, R.S.N.W.T. 1988, c. C-15, s. 5(2)

(NU) *Condominium Act*, R.S.N.W.T. (Nu.) 1988, c. C-15, s. 5(1)

(YT) *Condominium Act*, R.S.Y. 2002, c. 36, ss. 5(2), 18(5).

2. See Section IX.2. ("Termination of Condominium or Corporation").
3. See Section IX.2. ("Termination of Condominium or Corporation").
4. See Section IX.2. ("Termination of Condominium or Corporation").

---

(2) Description or Plan

(a) Freehold Condominiums

▼HCD-21▼ General requirements. Unless otherwise noted, the requirements for the contents of descriptions or plans applicable to standard condominiums apply to other freehold condominiums and to leasehold condominiums.

Standard condominiums. Although jurisdictions vary in their precise requirements and terminology, in general, a description or plan must:[1]

- show the external surface boundaries of the land and the location of any buildings in relation to the boundaries
- contain a statement of any particulars necessary to identify the title to the land
- show the boundaries, shape, dimensions and approximate location of each unit in relation to the other units, buildings and monuments
- illustrate the common elements
- be signed by the developer
- contain any additional contents prescribed in the regulations and
- be accompanied by a certificate of an architect, engineer and/or licensed land surveyor stating that all buildings have been constructed in accordance with the structural plans and that the dia-

grams of the units are substantially accurate and substantially in accordance with the structural plans

In Alberta and Saskatchewan, every description or plan must also be accompanied by a certificate of the clerk of the local authority stating that the proposed division of the buildings or land, as shown in the description or plan, has been approved by the local authority or designated official.[2]

Phased condominiums. In Ontario, in addition to the general requirements, which apply with respect to each phase, an amendment to a description required to create a phase must contain:[3]

- a description of all easements and similar interests to which the land included in the phase is subject
- the perimeter plan of survey of the land included in the phase
- separate sheets of the plans of survey designating the units included in the phase
- any exclusive use portions survey for the land included in the phase and
- any architectural plans and structural plans of the buildings included in the phase

Vacant land condominiums. In Newfoundland and Labrador and Ontario, the general requirements for descriptions do not apply to vacant land condominiums.[4] Instead, the descriptions must contain:[5]

- a plan showing the perimeter of the horizontal surface of the land, the perimeter of the buildings and structures on the common elements and the boundaries of each unit
- architectural and structural plans of the buildings and structures included in the common elements
- an architect's certificate that all buildings have been constructed in accordance with the architectural plans and, if there are structural plans, an engineer's certificate that all buildings have been constructed in accordance with the structural plans
- a description of all interests appurtenant to the land that are included in the property and
- all other material required by the regulations

In Saskatchewan, where the land is to be divided into bare land (vacant land) units, the condominium plan must show the boundaries of each unit by reference to boundaries governed by monuments and must show the approximate area of each unit.[6] In Northwest Territories, Nunavut and Yukon, the requirement that a plan delineate the perimeter of the buildings in relation to the perimeter of the surface of the land does not apply to plans of a bare land unit, and the horizontal boundaries of a bare land unit must be established by monuments.[7]

Common elements condominiums. In Newfoundland and Labrador and Ontario, the general requirements regarding specifications of unit boundaries by reference to buildings or other monuments and regarding certificates of architects and licensed land surveyors do not apply to common elements condominiums.[8] In Ontario only, the perimeter plan of survey for a common elements condominium must show the perimeter of the structures on the common elements.[9]

Notes

1. (AB) *Condominium Property Act*, R.S.A. 2000, c. C-22, ss. 8(1), 10(1)
   (BC) *Strata Property Act*, S.B.C. 1998, c. 43, s. 244
   (MB) *Condominium Act*, C.C.S.M. c. C170, s. 6(1), (2)
   (NL) *Condominium Act, 2009*, S.N.L. 2009, c. C-29.1, s. 11(1) (not yet in force)
   (NS) *Condominium Act*, R.S.N.S. 1989, c. 85, s. 12(1)
   (ON) *Condominium Act, 1998*, S.O. 1998, c. 19, s. 8(1)
   (PE) *Condominium Act*, R.S.P.E.I. 1988, c. C-16, s. 4(1)
   (SK) *Condominium Property Act, 1993*, S.S. 1993, c. C-26.1, ss. 9-10(1)
   (NT) *Condominium Act*, R.S.N.W.T. 1988, c. C-15, s. 6(2)
   (NU) *Condominium Act*, R.S.N.W.T. (Nu.) 1988, c. C-15, s. 6(2)
   (YT) *Condominium Act*, R.S.Y. 2002, c. 36, s. 6(1).
2. (AB) *Condominium Property Act*, R.S.A. 2000, c. C-22, s. 10(1)(b)(ii)
   (SK) *Condominium Property Act, 1993*, S.S. 1993, c. C-26.1, s. 10(1)(b). In Saskatchewan, the local authority must direct the issue of the certificate if it is satisfied that separate occupation of the proposed units will not contravene any development control or zoning by-law and that any consent or approval required under a zoning by-law or interim development control by-law has been given in relation to the separate occupation of the proposed units: (SK) *Condominium Property Act, 1993*, S.S. 1993, c. C-26.1, s. 10(5).
3. (ON) General Regulation, O. Reg. 48/01, s. 53(3); (ON) Description and Registration Regulation, O. Reg. 49/01, s. 19(1).
4. (NL) *Condominium Act, 2009*, S.N.L. 2009, c. C-29.1, s. 81(2) (not yet in force); (ON) *Condominium Act, 1998*, S.O. 1998, c. 19, s. 157(2).
5. (NL) *Condominium Act, 2009*, S.N.L. 2009, c. C-29.1, s. 81(1) (not yet in force); (ON) *Condominium Act, 1998*, S.O. 1998, c. 19, s. 157(1).
6. (SK) *Condominium Property Act, 1993*, S.S. 1993, c. C-26.1, s. 9(3).
7. (NT) *Condominium Act*, R.S.N.W.T. 1988, c. C-15, s. 6(3)-(4)
   (NU) *Condominium Act*, R.S.N.W.T. (Nu.) 1988, c. C-15, s. 6(3)-(4)

(YT) *Condominium Act*, R.S.Y. 2002, c. 36, s. 6(2)-(3).

8. (NL) *Condominium Act, 2009*, S.N.L. 2009, c. C-29.1, s. 71 (not yet in force); (ON) *Condominium Act, 1998*, S.O. 1998, c. 19, s. 141.
9. (ON) Description and Registration Regulation, O. Reg. 49/01, s. 4(2).

(b) Leasehold Condominiums

▼HCD-22▼ General requirements. The requirements for the contents of descriptions or plans applicable to standard condominiums apply to leasehold condominiums. In Ontario, a description for a leasehold condominium cannot be registered unless the buildings and improvements to the property form part of the property.[1]

Note

1. (ON) *Condominium Act, 1998*, S.O. 1998, c. 19, s. 167(2).

---

(3) Amendments

▼HCD-23▼ Three means of amendments. Provincial and territorial legislation may provide three possible means of amending a declaration and description or plan: (1) owner consent; (2) court order; and (3) land titles.

Amendment through owner consent. In general, a corporation may amend a declaration, description or plan only if:[1]

- the board of directions has approved the proposed amendment by resolution
- the board of directors has held a meeting of owners and the requisite number of owners has approved the amendment, depending on the nature of the amendment and
- the corporation has sent a notice of the proposed amendment to all mortgagees whose names appear in the record maintained by the corporation

In British Columbia, the requirements for amendment differ depending on the nature of the amendment.[2] In several jurisdictions, the corporation must register a copy of the amendment, which must include a certificate in the prescribed form made by authorized officers stating that the amendment complies with the requirements of the act and regulations.[3]

The amendment takes effect only on registration of a copy of the amendment.[4]

Amendment by court order. A corporation or an owner may apply for a court order to amend a declaration, description or plan.[5] Applicants must provide notice of the application to the corporation and to every owner and mortgagee who is listed in the record maintained by the corporation.[6] The court may make an order to amend the declaration, description or plan if it is satisfied that the amendment is necessary or desirable to correct an error or inconsistency that appears in the declaration, description or plan or that arises from carrying out the intent and purpose of the declaration, description or plan.[7] The amendment is ineffective until a certified copy of the court order has been registered on title.[8]

Amendment through land titles. A corporation or an interested person may apply to the local land titles authority for an order to amend a declaration, description or plan to correct an error or inconsistency that is apparent on the face of the declaration, description or plan.[9] The applicant must provide notice of the application in the form and manner directed by the land titles authority to the corporation and to every owner and mortgagee listed in the record of the corporation whose interest would be affected by the amendment.[10] The land titles authority must make an order to amend the declaration, description or plan if it is satisfied that the amendment would correct an error or inconsistency apparent on the face of the declaration, description or plan.[11] The amendment is ineffective until a certified copy of the order of the land titles authority has been registered on title.[12]

Leasehold condominiums. In Ontario, an amendment to a declaration or description that affects leasehold interests in property is ineffective unless the lessor has consented in writing to the amendment.[13] With respect to a declaration, if leasehold interests are renewed subject to provisions different from those that applied before the renewal, the declaration is deemed to be amended to contain the provisions that apply upon the renewal; in addition, the corporation must register a copy of the provisions as an amendment to the declaration, and the general requirements for amendments to declarations do not apply.[14]

Notes

1. (AB) *Condominium Property Act*, R.S.A. 2000, c. C-22, s. 18; (AB) Condominium Property Regulation, Alta. Reg. 168/2000, s. 71(1)

   (BC) *Strata Property Act*, S.B.C. 1998, c. 43, ss. 70, 257-266

(MB) *Condominium Act*, C.C.S.M. c. C170, ss. 5(6), 6(3)

(NB) *Condominium Property Act*, S.N.B. 2009, c. C-16.05, ss. 43(1), 44(1)

(NL) *Condominium Act, 2009*, S.N.L. 2009, c. C-29.1, ss. 10(1), 12(1), 18(3) (not yet in force)

(NS) *Condominium Act*, R.S.N.S. 1989, c. 85, ss. 11(3B), 12(3)

(ON) *Condominium Act, 1998*, S.O. 1998, c. 19, s. 107(2). Amendments to declarations and descriptions of phased condominiums and vacant land condominiums need not meet these requirements if they meet the more specific requirements for amendments applicable to these condominiums: (ON) *Condominium Act, 1998*, S.O. 1998, c. 19, ss. 146(7), 158(4).

(PE) *Condominium Act,* R.S.P.E.I. 1988, c. C-16, ss. 3(3)

(QC) *Civil Code of Québec*, L.R.Q., c. C-1991, arts. 1068, 1096-1100

(SK) *Condominium Property Act, 1993*, S.S. 1993, c. C-26.1, s. 14

(NT) *Condominium Act*, R.S.N.W.T. 1988, c. C-15, ss. 5(3)-(4), 6(6)-(7)

(NU) *Condominium Act*, R.S.N.W.T. (Nu.) 1988, c. C-15, s. 5(3), 6(6)

(YT) *Condominium Act*, R.S.Y. 2002, c. 36, ss. 5(3), 6(4)-(5).

2. (BC) *Strata Property Act*, S.B.C. 1998, c. 43, ss. 257-266.

3. (MB) *Condominium Act*, C.C.S.M. c. C170, ss. 5(7), 6(4)

(NB) *Condominium Property Act*, S.N.B. 2009, c. C-16.05, ss. 43(4), 44(4)

(NL) *Condominium Act, 2009*, S.N.L. 2009, c. C-29.1, ss. 10(2), 12(2) (not yet in force)

(NS) *Condominium Act*, R.S.N.S. 1989, c. 85, s. 11(4)

(ON) *Condominium Act, 1998*, S.O. 1998, c. 19, s. 107(5)-(6)

(PE) *Condominium Act,* R.S.P.E.I. 1988, c. C-16, s. 3(4)

(NT) *Condominium Act*, R.S.N.W.T. 1988, c. C-15, ss. 5(5), 6(8)

(NU) *Condominium Act*, R.S.N.W.T. (Nu.) 1988, c. C-15, s. 5(4), 6(7)

(YT) *Condominium Act*, R.S.Y. 2002, c. 36, ss. 5(4), 6(6).

4. (MB) *Condominium Act*, C.C.S.M. c. C170, ss. 5(7), 6(4)

(NB) *Condominium Property Act*, S.N.B. 2009, c. C-16.05, ss. 43(8), 44(8)

(NS) *Condominium Act*, R.S.N.S. 1989, c. 85, s. 11(4A)

(ON) *Condominium Act, 1998*, S.O. 1998, c. 19, s. 107(7)

(PE) *Condominium Act,* R.S.P.E.I. 1988, c. C-16, s. 3(4)

(NT) *Condominium Act*, R.S.N.W.T. 1988, c. C-15, ss. 5(6), 6(9)

(NU) *Condominium Act*, R.S.N.W.T. (Nu.) 1988, c. C-15, s. 5(4), 6(7).

5. (AB) Condominium Property Regulation, Alta. Reg. 168/2000, s. 71(2)

(NL) *Condominium Act, 2009*, S.N.L. 2009, c. C-29.1, s. 6(2) (not yet in force)

(ON) *Condominium Act, 1998*, S.O. 1998, c. 19, s. 109(1)

(PE) *Condominium Act,* R.S.P.E.I. 1988, c. C-16, s. 3(6)

(SK) *Condominium Property Act, 1993*, S.S. 1993, c. C-26.1, s. 14(4)

(NT) *Condominium Act*, R.S.N.W.T. 1988, c. C-15, s. 5(7).

6. (AB) Condominium Property Regulation, Alta. Reg. 168/2000, s. 71(3)

(ON) *Condominium Act, 1998*, S.O. 1998, c. 19, s. 109(2)

(PE) *Condominium Act,* R.S.P.E.I. 1988, c. C-16, s. 3(6)

(SK) *Condominium Property Act, 1993*, S.S. 1993, c. C-26.1, s. 14(5)

(NT) *Condominium Act*, R.S.N.W.T. 1988, c. C-15, s. 5(8).

7. (AB) Condominium Property Regulation, Alta. Reg. 168/2000, s. 71(5)

   (ON) *Condominium Act, 1998*, S.O. 1998, c. 19, s. 109(3)

   (PE) *Condominium Act,* R.S.P.E.I. 1988, c. C-16, s. 3(6)

   (SK) *Condominium Property Act, 1993*, S.S. 1993, c. C-26.1, s. 14(8)

   (NT) *Condominium Act*, R.S.N.W.T. 1988, c. C-15, s. 5(10).

8. (ON) *Condominium Act, 1998*, S.O. 1998, c. 19, s. 109(4)

   (PE) *Condominium Act,* R.S.P.E.I. 1988, c. C-16, s. 3(6)

   (SK) *Condominium Property Act, 1993*, S.S. 1993, c. C-26.1, s. 14(4).

9. (NB) *Condominium Property Act*, S.N.B. 2009, c. C-16.05, ss. 43(2), 44(2)

   (NL) *Condominium Act, 2009*, S.N.L. 2009, c. C-29.1, ss. 10(3), 12(3) (not yet in force)

   (NS) *Condominium Act*, R.S.N.S. 1989, c. 85, s. 11(3C)-(3D)

   (ON) *Condominium Act, 1998*, S.O. 1998, c. 19, s. 110(1)

   (SK) *Condominium Property Act, 1993*, S.S. 1993, c. C-26.1, s. 14(12).

10. (NB) *Condominium Property Act*, S.N.B. 2009, c. C-16.05, ss. 43(4), 44(4)

    (NS) *Condominium Act*, R.S.N.S. 1989, c. 85, s. 11(4)

    (ON) *Condominium Act, 1998*, S.O. 1998, c. 19, s. 110(2).

11. (ON) *Condominium Act, 1998*, S.O. 1998, c. 19, s. 110(3).

12. (NB) *Condominium Property Act*, S.N.B. 2009, c. C-16.05, ss. 43(8), 44(8)

    (NL) *Condominium Act, 2009*, S.N.L. 2009, c. C-29.1, ss. 10(5), 12(5) (not yet in force)

    (NS) *Condominium Act*, R.S.N.S. 1989, c. 85, s. 11(4A)

    (ON) *Condominium Act, 1998*, S.O. 1998, c. 19, s. 110(4).

13. (ON) *Condominium Act, 1998*, S.O. 1998, c. 19, ss. 166(4), 167(3).

14. (ON) *Condominium Act, 1998*, S.O. 1998, c. 19, s. 174(8)-(9).

---

5. By-Laws and Rules

(1) By-Laws
  (a) Subject Matter of By-Laws HCD-24
  (b) Procedure for Making, Amending and Repealing By-Laws HCD-25
(2) Rules HCD-26
(3) Joint By-Laws and Rules HCD-27

---

(1) By-Laws

(a) Subject Matter of By-Laws

▼HCD-24▼ General permissible subject matter of by-laws. In most jurisdictions, with the approval of a specified percentage of members, a corporation may make or amend by-laws with respect to the following:[1]

- the management of the property
- the use of units or any of them for the purpose of preventing unreasonable interference with the use and enjoyment of the common elements and other units
- the use of the common elements
- the maintenance of the units and common elements
- the use and management of the corporation's assets
- the board
- the duties of the corporation consistent with its objects
- the assessment and collection of contributions towards the common expenses and
- the general conduct of the corporation's affairs

Additional permissible subject matter of by-laws. Depending on the jurisdiction, a corporation may make by-laws with respect to one or more of the following:[2]

- the voting rights of corporation's members, namely the unit owners or those entitled to vote on their behalf
- the manner of conducting a vote
- the use of the reserve or contingency fund
- insurance coverage
- objection to assessments
- the procedure for mediation between the corporation and owners
- the establishment of standard units to determine responsibilities for repairing and insuring improvements to units
- the borrowing of money to carry out the corporation's objects and duties
- agents, officers and employees
- the establishment of exclusive use portions of the common elements

- the minimum maintenance requirements for a unit or a building or structure located on a unit
- the lease of the common elements, the grant or transfer of an easement or licence through the common elements, or the release of an easement that is part of the common elements
- the establishment of sectors
- the standards for the occupancy of units for residential purposes and
- the sanctions on owners, tenants and invitees for non-compliance with the Act, declaration, by-laws or rules

Prohibition on subject matter of by-laws. In several jurisdictions, a by-law or amendment or repeal of a by-law may not prohibit or restrict the devolution of a unit or any transfer, lease, mortgage or other dealing with a unit and may not destroy or modify any easement implied or created under the act.[3]

Reasonableness and consistency of by-laws. By-laws must be reasonable and consistent with the act and declaration and, in the case of a leasehold corporation, the lease.[4] In some jurisdictions, if a provision in a by-law or proposed by-law is inconsistent with the Act or regulations, the Act and regulations prevail and the by-law or proposed by-law is deemed to be amended accordingly.[5]

By-laws requiring board consent and providing age restrictions. Since a corporation's day-to-day operation is too complex and varied to enable setting down in the by-laws detailed rules covering every possible contingency, by-laws can provide that certain circumstances require board consent.[6] A by-law prohibiting persons of a certain age from residing in a unit may be a legitimate and justifiable restriction and may not contravene human rights legislation where the restriction relates to owners', and not tenants', rights of occupancy.[7]

By-laws in Alberta, British Columbia and Saskatchewan. In Alberta, British Columbia and Saskatchewan, the legislation itself sets out by-laws and provides that, on the registration or issuance of titles for a condominium plan or strata plan, the corporation's by-laws are the by-laws set out in the legislation, that those by-laws remain in force until they are repealed or replaced, and that those by-laws bind the corporation and unit owners.[8] The by-laws of Alberta, British Columbia and Saskatchewan address numerous subjects, including powers of owners, powers and duties of the corporation, powers and duties of the board or council, election of the board, board or council meetings, officers, majority vote and quorum of the board, written resolutions, seal and signing authority of the corporation, procedure for annual and general meetings, voting, enforcement of by-laws and rules, tenants, occupants and visitors, restrictions in use, voluntary dispute resolution, marketing activities and sectors.[9] In Saskatchewan, a corporation may also make by-laws with respect to sectors.[10]

Notes

1. (AB) *Condominium Property Act*, R.S.A. 2000, c. C-22, s. 32(1)

   (BC) *Strata Property Act*, S.B.C. 1998, c. 43, s. 119(2)

   (MB) *Condominium Act*, C.C.S.M. c. C170, s. 12(1)

   (NB) *Condominium Property Act*, S.N.B. 2009, c. C-16.05, s. 32(2)-(3), although the condominium is required, rather than permitted, to make by-laws respecting the listed subjects

   (NL) *Condominium Act, 2009*, S.N.L. 2009, c. C-29.1, ss. 27(8), 35(1) (not yet in force)

   (NS) *Condominium Act*, R.S.N.S. 1989, c. 85, s. 23(1)

   (ON) *Condominium Act, 1998*, S.O. 1998, c. 19, s. 56(1)

   (PE) *Condominium Act,* R.S.P.E.I. 1988, c. C-16, s. 13(1)

   (QC) *Civil Code of Québec*, L.R.Q. c. C-1991, arts. 1054, 1084

   (SK) *Condominium Property Act, 1993*, S.S. 1993, c. C-26.1, ss. 44(1), 47(1)

   (NT) *Condominium Act*, R.S.N.W.T. 1988, c. C-15, s. 17(2)

   (NU) *Condominium Act*, R.S.N.W.T. (Nu.) 1988, c. C-15, s. 17(1)

   (YT) *Condominium Act*, R.S.Y. 2002, c. 36, s. 12(1).

2. (AB) *Condominium Property Act*, R.S.A. 2000, c. C-22, s. 35

   (BC) *Strata Property Act*, S.B.C. 1998, c. 43, s. 121(1)-(2)

   (NL) *Condominium Act, 2009*, S.N.L. 2009, c. C-29.1, ss. 35(1)(d), (g)-(i), 83 (not yet in force)

   (ON) *Condominium Act, 1998*, S.O. 1998, c. 19, ss. 21(1), 56(1)(d), (e), (f), (h), (o), 57, 160

   (PE) *Condominium Act,* R.S.P.E.I. 1988, c. C-16, s. 9(1), 13(1)(i)

   (SK) *Condominium Property Act, 1993*, S.S. 1993, c. C-26.1, s. 41(2), (4)-(7), (12), 47(1)(d), (j), (k), (l), (m.1)

   (NT) *Condominium Act*, R.S.N.W.T. 1988, c. C-15, ss. 13.1, 17.1.

3. (AB) *Condominium Property Act*, R.S.A. 2000, c. C-22, s. 32(5)

   (MB) *Condominium Act*, C.C.S.M. c. C170, s. 12(4)

   (NB) *Condominium Property Act*, S.N.B. 2009, c. C-16.05, s. 32(12)

   (NS) *Condominium Act*, R.S.N.S. 1989, c. 85, s. 23(5)

   (SK) *Condominium Property Act, 1993*, S.S. 1993, c. C-26.1, s. 44(2)

   (NT) *Condominium Act*, R.S.N.W.T. 1988, c. C-15, s. 17(11)

   (NU) *Condominium Act*, R.S.N.W.T. (Nu.) 1988, c. C-15, s. 17(4)

(YT) *Condominium Act*, R.S.Y. 2002, c. 36, s. 12(4).

4. (MB) *Condominium Act*, C.C.S.M. c. C170, s. 12(2)
   (NB) *Condominium Property Act*, S.N.B. 2009, c. C-16.05, s. 32(5)
   (NL) *Condominium Act, 2009*, S.N.L. 2009, c. C-29.1, s. 35(1) (not yet in force)
   (NS) *Condominium Act*, R.S.N.S. 1989, c. 85, s. 23(2)
   (ON) *Condominium Act, 1998*, S.O. 1998, c. 19, s. 56(6)-(7)
   (PE) *Condominium Act,* R.S.P.E.I. 1988, c. C-16, s. 13(2)
   (NT) *Condominium Act*, R.S.N.W.T. 1988, c. C-15, s. 17(12)
   (NU) *Condominium Act*, R.S.N.W.T. (Nu.) 1988, c. C-15, s. 17(2)
   (YT) *Condominium Act*, R.S.Y. 2002, c. 36, s. 12(2).
5. (AB) *Condominium Property Act*, R.S.A. 2000, c. C-22, s. 32(7)
   (NB) *Condominium Property Act*, S.N.B. 2009, c. C-16.05, s. 32(6)
   (ON) *Condominium Act, 1998*, S.O. 1998, c. 19, s. 56(8)
   (SK) *Condominium Property Act, 1993*, S.S. 1993, c. C-26.1, s. 47(2); (SK) Condominium Property Regulations, 2001, R.R.S. c. C-26.1, Reg. 2, Bylaws, s. 1(4).
6. *Maverick Equities Inc. v. Condominium Plan No. 942 2336*, [2008] A.J. No. 616, 2008 ABCA 221 (Alta. C.A.).
7. *Drummond v. Strata Plan NW2654*, [2004] B.C.J. No. 2280, 2004 BCSC 1405 (B.C.S.C.).
8. (AB) *Condominium Property Act*, R.S.A. 2000, c. C-22, ss. 32(2), (6), 33-34
   (BC) *Strata Property Act*, S.B.C. 1998, c. 43, s. 120
   (SK) *Condominium Property Act, 1993*, S.S. 1993, c. C-26.1, s. 44(3), 45.
9. (AB) *Condominium Property Act*, R.S.A. 2000, c. C-22, Apps. 1-2
   (BC) *Strata Property Act*, S.B.C. 1998, c. 43, Schedule of Standard Bylaws.
   (SK) Condominium Property Regulations, 2001, R.R.S. c. C-26.1, Reg. 2, Bylaws.
10. (SK) *Condominium Property Act, 1993*, S.S. 1993, c. C-26.1, ss. 44.1, 47(1)(m.1), 47.1.

(b) Procedure for Making, Amending and Repealing By-Laws

▼HCD-25▼ General procedure. By-laws may be made on a vote or resolution of a specified percentage of voting rights.[1] When a by-law is made, amended or repealed, the corporation must register a copy of the by-law, amendment or repeal together with a certificate. Until the copy and certificate are registered, the by-law is ineffective.[2] In most jurisdictions, the certificate must be executed by the corporation and must certify that the by-law, amendment or repeal was made in accordance with the Act, declaration and by-laws.[3]

Specific procedures regarding registration. In Alberta, the registrar must make a memorandum of the by-law's filing on the condominium plan.[4] In Newfoundland and Labrador, the certificate must be signed by a specified percentage of the corporation's members, must state that the persons signing concur with the by-laws as filed and must specify the corporation's members.[5] In Ontario, the copy of the by-law must be registered in the appropriate land titles division or registry division, the owners of a majority of the units must vote in favour of confirming it, and the certificate must have the prescribed form and statements.[6] In Northwest Territories, the certificate must be under seal and must state that notice of the by-law instrument has been or will be given to each unit owner and registered encumbrance holder within the required timeframe and that the corporation has not been served with a notice of objection or has been served with a notice of objection but certain other requirements have been met.[7]

Other specific procedures. In Alberta and Manitoba, the corporation's vote with respect to the making or amending of by-laws must occur at a meeting of members convened for that purpose, and there are specific requirements regarding the notice of meeting and provision of a copy of the by-laws to each owner.[8] In British Columbia, the procedure for amending by-laws depends on whether the strata plan is a bare strata plan and on whether the strata lots in the strata plan are all residential, all non-residential or partly residential and partly nonresidential.[9] In Nova Scotia, proposed by-laws must be submitted together with the declaration and description, and the Governor in Council may prescribe a standard set of by-laws for a corporation or corporation class that are the by-laws where no by-laws are made and in effect.[10] In Saskatchewan, there are specific and more onerous requirements for by-laws relating to sectors as well as specific requirements regarding schemes of apportionment for owners' contributions to the general common expenses fund or reserve fund.[11]

Notes

1. (AB) *Condominium Property Act*, R.S.A. 2000, c. C-22, s. 32(3)

   (BC) *Strata Property Act*, S.B.C. 1998, c. 43, s. 128(1)

   (MB) *Condominium Act*, C.C.S.M. c. C170, s. 12(1)

   (NB) *Condominium Property Act*, S.N.B. 2009, c. C-16.05, s. 32(3)

   (NL) *Condominium Act, 2009*, S.N.L. 2009, c. C-29.1, ss. 27(8), 35(1) (not yet in force)

   (NS) *Condominium Act*, R.S.N.S. 1989, c. 85, s. 23(1)

   (ON) *Condominium Act, 1998*, S.O. 1998, c. 19, s. 56(1)

   (PE) *Condominium Act*, R.S.P.E.I. 1988, c. C-16, s. 13(1)

   (SK) *Condominium Property Act, 1993*, S.S. 1993, c. C-26.1, s. 46(2)

   (NT) *Condominium Act*, R.S.N.W.T. 1988, c. C-15, s. 17(2)

(NU) *Condominium Act*, R.S.N.W.T. (Nu.) 1988, c. C-15, s. 17(1)
(YT) *Condominium Act*, R.S.Y. 2002, c. 36, s. 12(1).

2. (AB) *Condominium Property Act*, R.S.A. 2000, c. C-22, s. 32(4)
(BC) *Strata Property Act*, S.B.C. 1998, c. 43, s. 128(2)
(MB) *Condominium Act*, C.C.S.M. c. C170, s. 12(3)
(NB) *Condominium Property Act*, S.N.B. 2009, c. C-16.05, s. 32(7)
(NL) *Condominium Act, 2009*, S.N.L. 2009, c. C-29.1, s. 35(3)-(4) (not yet in force)
(NS) *Condominium Act*, R.S.N.S. 1989, c. 85, s. 23(3)-(4)
(ON) *Condominium Act, 1998*, S.O. 1998, c. 19, s. 56(9)-(10)
(PE) *Condominium Act*, R.S.P.E.I. 1988, c. C-16, s. 13(3)
(SK) *Condominium Property Act, 1993*, S.S. 1993, c. C-26.1, s. 46(3)
(NT) *Condominium Act*, R.S.N.W.T. 1988, c. C-15, s. 17(3), (5)
(NU) *Condominium Act*, R.S.N.W.T. (Nu.) 1988, c. C-15, s. 17(3)
(YT) *Condominium Act*, R.S.Y. 2002, c. 36, s. 12(3).

3. (MB) *Condominium Act*, C.C.S.M. c. C170, s. 12(3)
(NB) *Condominium Property Act*, S.N.B. 2009, c. C-16.05, s. 32(7)
(NS) *Condominium Act*, R.S.N.S. 1989, c. 85, s. 23(3)
(PE) *Condominium Act*, R.S.P.E.I. 1988, c. C-16, s. 13(3)
(NU) *Condominium Act*, R.S.N.W.T. (Nu.) 1988, c. C-15, s. 17(3)
(YT) *Condominium Act*, R.S.Y. 2002, c. 36, s. 12(3).

4. (AB) *Condominium Property Act*, R.S.A. 2000, c. C-22, s. 32(4)(b).
5. (NL) *Condominium Act, 2009*, S.N.L. 2009, c. C-29.1, s. 35(2) (not yet in force).
6. (ON) *Condominium Act, 1998*, S.O. 1998, c. 19, s. 56(9)-(10); (ON) General Regulation, O. Reg. 48/01, s. 14; (ON) Description and Registration Regulation, O. Reg. 49/01, s. 38(1).
7. (NT) *Condominium Act*, R.S.N.W.T. 1988, c. C-15, s. 17(3), (6), (8), (10).
8. (AB) *Condominium Property Act*, R.S.A. 2000, c. C-22, ss. 1(1)(x), App. 1, s. 35, App. 2, s. 32(2); (MB) *Condominium Act*, C.C.S.M. c. C170, s. 12(1.1)-(1.5), (6).
9. (BC) *Strata Property Act*, S.B.C. 1998, c. 43, s. 127.
10. (NS) *Condominium Act*, R.S.N.S. 1989, c. 85, ss. 6(3A), 23(2A)-(2B).
11. (SK) *Condominium Property Act, 1993*, S.S. 1993, c. C-26.1, ss. 47.1(4)-(10), 104(2); (SK) Condominium Property Regulations, 2001, R.R.S. c. C-26.1, Reg. 2, Bylaws, ss. 48-50.1.

---

(2) Rules

▼HCD-26▼ Rules for common elements. In several jurisdictions, the by-laws may provide for the owners making reasonable rules consistent with the Act, declaration and by-laws respecting the use of the common elements for the purpose of preventing unreasonable interference with the use and enjoyment of the units and the common elements.[1] The rules are enforced and complied with in the same manner as the by-laws.[2]

Specific additional provisions. In British Columbia, the strata corporation may make rules to govern the use, safety and condition of the common property and common assets; all rules must be set out in a written document that can be photocopied; the strata corporation must inform owners and tenants of new rules as soon as feasible; if a rule conflicts with a by-law, the by-law prevails; and a rule ceases to have effect at the first annual general meeting after it is made, unless the rule is ratified by a resolution passed by a majority vote at that annual general meeting or at a special general meeting held before the annual general meeting.[3] In Manitoba, a copy of a rule must be given to each owner in the specified manner and time.[4] In Newfoundland and Labrador, rules must be approved by 66% of the condominium members.[5] In Ontario, rules may be made to promote the safety, security or welfare of the owners and of the condominium property and assets of the corporation.[6] If a rule or proposed rule is inconsistent with the Act, the act prevails and the rule or proposed rule is amended accordingly.[7] In Ontario, a rule may be amended or repealed by the owners at a meeting of owners called for that purpose.[8] The corporation must give owners notice of the rule in the specified form whenever a rule is made, amended or repealed.[9] The rule is not effective until 30 days after the board has given notice if the board does not receive a meeting requisition within 30 days after notice was given and is not effective until after the owners approve it at a meeting of owners if the board receives a meeting requisition within 30 days after notice was given.[10]

Reasonableness of rules. Although courts have found some condominium rules unenforceable on the basis that they are unreasonable or inconsistent with the Act,[11] there is generally a high threshold for overturning condominium rules.[12] In making rules, a board of directors is not performing a judicial role, and no judicialization should be attributed to its function or process.[13] On an application to enforce the corporation's rules, a court should not substitute its own opinion about the propriety of a rule unless the rule is clearly unreasonable or contrary to the legislative scheme. Without such unreasonableness, deference should be paid to rules deemed appropriate by a board charged with responsibility for balancing the private and communal interests of unit owners.[14] There is nothing illegal or unlawful in a condominium taking steps to ensure compliance with rules; the directors have a legal duty under the act to enforce the corporation's rules.[15]

Rules that address obtaining board consent. Where a by-law states that certain circumstances require board consent, the board is entitled to considerable scope in exercising its discretion, and there is nothing objectionable to the board setting down rules as to how its discretion will be exercised in the normal course.[16] Writing down rules gives unit owners a clear idea of expectations, and having them approved by unit owners gives them added legitimacy.[17] Although the existence of rules does not fetter the board's discretion, the withholding of consent or the provision of consent on different terms might call for explanation.[18]

Notes

1. (MB) *Condominium Act*, C.C.S.M. c. C170, s. 12(5)
   (NB) *Condominium Property Act*, S.N.B. 2009, c. C-16.05, s. 33(1)-(2)
   (NL) *Condominium Act, 2009*, S.N.L. 2009, c. C-29.1, s. 36(1)-(2) (not yet in force)
   (NS) *Condominium Act*, R.S.N.S. 1989, c. 85, s. 24(1)-(2)
   (ON) *Condominium Act, 1998*, S.O. 1998, c. 19, s. 58(1)(b), (2)
   (PE) *Condominium Act*, R.S.P.E.I. 1988, c. C-16, s. 14(1)-(2)
   (NT) *Condominium Act*, R.S.N.W.T. 1988, c. C-15, s. 17(13)
   (NU) *Condominium Act*, R.S.N.W.T. (Nu.) 1988, c. C-15, s. 17(5)
   (YT) *Condominium Act*, R.S.Y. 2002, c. 36, s. 12(5).
2. (BC) *Strata Property Act*, S.B.C. 1998, c. 43, ss. 125(2), 129
   (MB) *Condominium Act*, C.C.S.M. c. C170, s. 12(5)
   (NB) *Condominium Property Act*, S.N.B. 2009, c. C-16.05, s. 33(3)
   (NL) *Condominium Act, 2009*, S.N.L. 2009, c. C-29.1, s. 36(3) (not yet in force)
   (NS) *Condominium Act*, R.S.N.S. 1989, c. 85, s. 24(3)
   (ON) *Condominium Act, 1998*, S.O. 1998, c. 19, s. 58(10)
   (PE) *Condominium Act*, R.S.P.E.I. 1988, c. C-16, s. 14(3)
   (NT) *Condominium Act*, R.S.N.W.T. 1988, c. C-15, s. 17(13)
   (NU) *Condominium Act*, R.S.N.W.T. (Nu.) 1988, c. C-15, s. 17(5)
   (YT) *Condominium Act*, R.S.Y. 2002, c. 36, s. 12(5).
3. (BC) *Strata Property Act*, S.B.C. 1998, c. 43, s. 125(1), (3)-(6).
4. (MB) *Condominium Act*, C.C.S.M. c. C170, s. 12(5).
5. (NL) *Condominium Act, 2009*, S.N.L. 2009, c. C-29.1, s. 36(4) (not yet in force).
6. (ON) *Condominium Act, 1998*, S.O. 1998, c. 19, s. 58(1)(a).
7. (ON) *Condominium Act, 1998*, S.O. 1998, c. 19, s. 58(4).
8. (ON) *Condominium Act, 1998*, S.O. 1998, c. 19, s. 58(5).
9. (ON) *Condominium Act, 1998*, S.O. 1998, c. 19, s. 58(6).
10. (ON) *Condominium Act, 1998*, S.O. 1998, c. 19, s. 58(7).
11. *Metropolitan Toronto Condominium Corp. No. 650 v. Klein*, [1988] O.J. No. 581, 49 R.P.R. 205 (Ont. Dist. Ct.).

12. *York Condominium Corp. No. 382 v. Dvorchik*, [1997] O.J. No. 378, 12 R.P.R. (3d) 148 (Ont. C.A.); *Skyline Executive Properties Inc. v. Metropolitan Toronto Condominium Corp. No. 1385*, [2002] O.J. No. 5117, 17 R.P.R. (4th) 152 (Ont. S.C.J.)
13. *York Condominium Corp. No. 382 v. Dvorchik*, [1997] O.J. No. 378, 12 R.P.R. (3d) 148 (Ont. C.A.)
14. *York Condominium Corp. No. 382 v. Dvorchik*, [1997] O.J. No. 378, 12 R.P.R. (3d) 148 (Ont. C.A.); *Skyline Executive Properties Inc. v. Metropolitan Toronto Condominium Corp. No. 1385*, [2002] O.J. No. 5117, 17 R.P.R. (4th) 152 (Ont. S.C.J.)
15. *Apartments International Inc. v. Metropolitan Toronto Condominium Corp. No. 1170*, [2002] O.J. No. 3821, [2002] O.T.C. 733 (Ont. S.C.J.).
16. *Maverick Equities Inc. v. Condominium Plan No. 942 2336*, [2008] A.J. No. 616, 2008 ABCA 221 (Alta. C.A.).
17. *Maverick Equities Inc. v. Condominium Plan No. 942 2336*, [2008] A.J. No. 616, 2008 ABCA 221 (Alta. C.A.).
18. *Maverick Equities Inc. v. Condominium Plan No. 942 2336*, [2008] A.J. No. 616, 2008 ABCA 221 (Alta. C.A.).

---

(3) Joint By-Laws and Rules

▼HCD-27▼ Law in Ontario. In Ontario, the boards of two or more condominiums may make, amend or repeal joint by-laws or rules governing the use and maintenance of shared facilities and services.[1] A joint by-law or rule is a by-law or rule of each corporation.[2]

Joint by-laws. In Ontario, a joint by-law becomes effective when the majority of unit owners vote in favour of confirming it and each corporation registers a copy of it.[3] The joint by-law remains effective until the majority of unit owners vote in favour of repealing it and each corporation registers a copy of the repealing by-law.[4]

Joint rules. In Ontario, a joint rule may be amended or repealed by the owners at a joint meeting of owners or at a meeting of owners of each corporation called for that purpose.[5] The corporation must give owners notice of the joint rule in the specified form whenever a joint rule is made, amended or repealed.[6] The joint rule is not effective until 30 days after the board has given notice if neither board receives a meeting requisition within 30 days after notice was given and is not effective until after the owners approve it at a joint meeting of owners or at a meeting of owners of each corporation if either board receives a meeting requisition within 30 days after notice was given.[7]

Notes

1. (ON) *Condominium Act, 1998*, S.O. 1998, c. 19, s. 59(1).
2. (ON) *Condominium Act, 1998*, S.O. 1998, c. 19, s. 59(2).
3. (ON) *Condominium Act, 1998*, S.O. 1998, c. 19, s. 59(3).
4. (ON) *Condominium Act, 1998*, S.O. 1998, c. 19, s. 59(5).
5. (ON) *Condominium Act, 1998*, S.O. 1998, c. 19, s. 59(6).
6. (ON) *Condominium Act, 1998*, S.O. 1998, c. 19, s. 59(7).
7. (ON) *Condominium Act, 1998*, S.O. 1998, c. 19, s. 59(8)-(9).

III. General Management by the Condominium Corporation

1. **Introductory Matters** HCD-28

2. **Objects and Duties** HCD-29

3. **Assessment and Taxation** HCD-30

4. **Entry by Corporation and Others** HCD-31

5. **Action By or Against Corporation** HCD-32

6. **Corporation's Money** HCD-33

7. **Information**

   (1) With a Fee HCD-34
   (2) Without a Fee HCD-35

8. **Records**

   (1) Duty to Maintain Records HCD-36
   (2) Access to Records HCD-37

---

1. Introductory Matters

▼HCD-28▼ Name, seal and service. The legislation of each province and territory sets out requirements regarding corporate names, corporate seals and service on corporations.

Corporate name. On registration, the land registrar must assign a name to the corporation in the prescribed manner.[1] In several jurisdictions, the name must include the district name of the land titles or registry district, the words "Condominium Corporation", the abbreviation "No." and the next available consecutive number in the condominium corporations index.[2]

Corporate seal. In some jurisdictions, the corporation must also have a seal.[3] In Alberta and Saskatchewan, the seal can only be used under the authority of a board resolution given prior to its use,[4] and, in Alberta, in the presence of board members.[5] In Ontario, the board must adopt a seal and may change the seal, and the corporation's name must appear on the seal.[6]

Service on corporations. In Alberta, British Columbia and Saskatchewan, a document may be served on a corporation by registered mail addressed to the corporation or by personal service on a board member.[7] In Nova Scotia, service upon a recognized agent in the province is deemed to be sufficient service upon the corporation.[8] In several jurisdictions, the board may change a corporation's address for service by registering a notice of change of address in the prescribed form.[9]

Notes

1. (AB) *Condominium Property Act*, R.S.A. 2000, c. C-22, s. 25(1)

   (BC) *Strata Property Act*, S.B.C. 1998, c. 43, s. 2(1)(b)

   (MB) *Condominium Act*, C.C.S.M. c. C170, s. 4(3)(a)

   (NB) *Condominium Property Act*, S.N.B. 2009, c. C-16.05, s. 9(1)(a)

   (NL) *Condominium Act, 2009*, S.N.L. 2009, c. C-29.1, s. 7(2)-(3) (not yet in force)

   (NS) *Condominium Act*, R.S.N.S. 1989, c. 85, s. 7(1)(a)

   (ON) *Condominium Act, 1998*, S.O. 1998, c. 19, s. 5(2)

   (PE) *Condominium Act,* R.S.P.E.I. 1988, c. C-16, s. 10(2)

   (SK) *The Condominium Property Act, 1993*, S.S. 1993, c. C-26.1, s. 34(1)-(1.1)

   (NT) *Condominium Act*, R.S.N.W.T. 1988, c. C-15, s. 12(1)

   (NU) *Condominium Act*, R.S.N.W.T. (Nu.) 1988, c. C-15, s. 12(1)

   (YT) *Condominium Act*, R.S.Y. 2002, c. 36, s. 4(2)(a).

2. (AB) *Condominium Property Act*, R.S.A. 2000, c. C-22, s. 25(1)

   (MB) *Condominium Act*, C.C.S.M. c. C170, s. 10(1)

   (NB) General Regulation, N.B. Reg. 2009-169, s. 11(1)

   (NL) *Condominium Act, 2009*, S.N.L. 2009, c. C-29.1, s. 17(2) (not yet in force). In Newfoundland and Labrador, the name need only end with the words "condominium corporation" and be approved by the registrar.

   (NS) *Condominium Act*, R.S.N.S. 1989, c. 85, s. 13(2)

   (ON) Description and Registration Regulation, O. Reg. 49/01, s. 27(3). In Ontario, the name must also include the type of corporation.

   (PE) General Regulations, P.E.I. Reg. EC10/78, s. 4(1)(e)

   (SK) Condominium Property Regulations, 2001, R.R.S. c. C-26.1, Reg. 2, s. 41.5(1). In Saskatchewan, there are several restrictions on the use of names: (SK) Condominium Property Regulations, 2001, R.R.S. c. C-26.1, Reg. 2, ss. 41.6-41.7

   (NT) *Condominium Act*, R.S.N.W.T. 1988, c. C-15, s. 12(1)

   (NU) *Condominium Act*, R.S.N.W.T. (Nu.) 1988, c. C-15, s. 12(1)

   (YT) *Condominium Act*, R.S.Y. 2002, c. 36, s. 10(1).

3. (AB) *Condominium Property Act*, R.S.A. 2000, c. C-22, App. 1, s. 14(1), App. 2, Sch. A, s. 31

   (MB) *Condominium Act*, C.C.S.M. c. C170, s. 10(10)

   (ON) *Condominium Act, 1998*, S.O. 1998, c. 19, s. 16(1)

   (SK) Condominium Property Regulations, 2001, R.R.S. c. C-26.1, Reg. 2, App., Part II, Bylaws, s. 15

   (NT) *Condominium Act*, R.S.N.W.T. 1988, c. C-15, s. 14(1)

   (NU) *Condominium Act*, R.S.N.W.T. (Nu.) 1988, c. C-15, s. 14(1)

   (YT) *Condominium Act*, R.S.Y. 2002, c. 36, s. 10(11).

4. (AB) *Condominium Property Act*, R.S.A. 2000, c. C-22, App. 1, s. 14(1)(a)

   (SK) Condominium Property Regulations, 2001, R.R.S. c. C-26.1, Reg. 2, App., Part II, Bylaws, s. 15.

5. (AB) *Condominium Property Act*, R.S.A. 2000, c. C-22, App. 1, s. 14(1)-(2).

6. (ON) *Condominium Act, 1998*, S.O. 1998, c. 19, s. 16(1)-(2).

7. (AB) *Condominium Property Act*, R.S.A. 2000, c. C-22, s. 71(1)

   (BC) *Strata Property Act*, S.B.C. 1998, c. 43, s. 64

   (SK) *Condominium Property Act, 1993*, S.S. 1993, c. C-26.1, s. 104(1).

8. (NS) *Condominium Act*, R.S.N.S. 1989, c. 85, s. 6(4).

9. (AB) *Condominium Property Act*, R.S.A. 2000, c. C-22, s. 73(1)-(2)

   (BC) *Strata Property Act*, S.B.C. 1998, c. 43, s. 62(3)

   (MB) *Condominium Act*, C.C.S.M. c. C170, s. 10(8)

   (ON) *Condominium Act, 1998*, S.O. 1998, c. 19, s. 108

   (PE) *Condominium Act*, R.S.P.E.I. 1988, c. C-16, s. 3(5)

   (SK) *Condominium Property Act, 1993*, S.S. 1993, c. C-26.1, s. 105(1)-(2)

   (NT) *Condominium Act*, R.S.N.W.T. 1988, c. C-15, s. 12(8)

   (NU) *Condominium Act*, R.S.N.W.T. (Nu.) 1988, c. C-15, s. 12(8)

   (YT) *Condominium Act*, R.S.Y. 2002, c. 36, s. 10(8).

---

2. Objects and Duties

▼HCD-29▼ General objects and duties. The objects of the corporation are to manage the property and any assets of the corporation.[1] The corporation has a duty to control, manage and administer the common elements and, in some jurisdictions, the assets of the corporation.[2] The corporation has a duty to effect compliance by the owners with the Act, declaration, by-laws and rules.[3] In Manitoba, this duty extends to compliance by tenants[4] and in Newfoundland and Labrador and Ontario, this duty extends to compliance by occupiers of units, lessees of common elements and agents and employees of the corporation.[5]

Specific objects and duties regarding assets. In several jurisdictions, a corporation may own, acquire, encumber and dispose of real and personal property for the use and enjoyment of the owners.[6] In New Brunswick, Newfoundland and Labrador and Nova Scotia, the corporation may do so only with a specific percentage of owner consent,[7] and in Alberta, British Columbia and Saskatchewan, the corporation may do so only on special resolution.[8] Some jurisdictions provide that the members of the corporation share the corporation's assets in the proportions provided in the declaration,[9] whereas others provide that the members share the assets in the same proportions as the proportions of their common interests in accordance with the Act, declaration and by-laws.[10] In several jurisdictions, the amount in a reserve fund is an asset of the corporation and cannot be distributed to owners unless the property ceases to be governed by the Act, meaning the corporation is terminated.[11] In several jurisdictions, amalgamated corporations possess all assets of the amalgamating corporations.[12] In Alberta and Saskatchewan, there are provisions regarding the transfer and lease of common property, which can only occur by special resolution in Alberta and by unanimous resolution in Saskatchewan.[13] In Ontario, the corporation's assets do not include any real property or interest in real property that the corporation does not own, and the corporation may not deal with such real property or interests unless the Act specifically confers that power on the corporation.[14]

Notes

1. (AB) *Condominium Property Act*, R.S.A. 2000, c. C-22, s. 37(2)
   (BC) *Strata Property Act*, S.B.C. 1998, c. 43, s. 3
   (MB) *Condominium Act*, C.C.S.M. c. C170, s. 10(4)
   (NB) *Condominium Property Act*, S.N.B. 2009, c. C-16.05, s. 19(1)
   (NL) *Condominium Act, 2009*, S.N.L. 2009, c. C-29.1, s. 18(1) (not yet in force)
   (NS) *Condominium Act*, R.S.N.S. 1989, c. 85, s. 14(1)
   (ON) *Condominium Act, 1998*, S.O. 1998, c. 19, s. 17(1)
   (PE) *Condominium Act*, R.S.P.E.I. 1988, c. C-16, s. 10(3)
   (QC) *Civil Code of Québec*, L.R.Q. c. C-1991, art. 1039
   (NT) *Condominium Act*, R.S.N.W.T. 1988, c. C-15, s. 12(4)
   (NU) *Condominium Act*, R.S.N.W.T. (Nu.) 1988, c. C-15, s. 12(4)
   (YT) *Condominium Act*, R.S.Y. 2002, c. 36, s. 10(4).
2. (AB) *Condominium Property Act*, R.S.A. 2000, c. C-22, s. 37(1)
   (BC) *Strata Property Act*, S.B.C. 1998, c. 43, s. 3
   (MB) *Condominium Act*, C.C.S.M. c. C170, s. 10(5)
   (NL) *Condominium Act, 2009*, S.N.L. 2009, c. C-29.1, s. 19(1)(a) (not yet in force)
   (ON) *Condominium Act, 1998*, S.O. 1998, c. 19, s. 17(2)

(QC) *Civil Code of Québec*, L.R.Q. c. C-1991, c. 64, art. 1039

(SK) *Condominium Property Act, 1993*, S.S. 1993, c. C-26.1, s. 35(1); (SK) Condominium Property Regulations, 2001, R.R.S. c. C-26.1, Reg. 2, App., Part II, By-laws, s. 3(a)

(NT) *Condominium Act*, R.S.N.W.T. 1988, c. C-15, s. 12(5)

(NU) *Condominium Act*, R.S.N.W.T. (Nu.) 1988, c. C-15, s. 12(5)

(YT) *Condominium Act*, R.S.Y. 2002, c. 36, s. 10(5).

3. (AB) *Condominium Property Act*, R.S.A. 2000, c. C-22, s. 37(1)

(MB) *Condominium Act*, C.C.S.M. c. C170, s. 13(1)

(NB) *Condominium Property Act*, S.N.B. 2009, c. C-16.05, s. 19(4)

(NL) *Condominium Act, 2009*, S.N.L. 2009, c. C-29.1, s. 19(1)(c) (not yet in force)

(NS) *Condominium Act*, R.S.N.S. 1989, c. 85, s. 18(2)

(ON) *Condominium Act, 1998*, S.O. 1998, c. 19, s. 17(3)

(PE) *Condominium Act,* R.S.P.E.I. 1988, c. C-16, s. 10(12)

(SK) *Condominium Property Act, 1993*, S.S. 1993, c. C-26.1, s. 35(1)

(NT) *Condominium Act*, R.S.N.W.T. 1988, c. C-15, s. 18(1)

(NU) *Condominium Act*, R.S.N.W.T. 1988 (Nu.), c. C-15, s. 18(1)

(YT) *Condominium Act*, R.S.Y. 2002, c. 36, s. 13(1).

4. (MB) *Condominium Act*, C.C.S.M. c. C170, s. 13(1.1).

5. (NL) *Condominium Act, 2009*, S.N.L. 2009, c. C-29.1, s. 19(1)(c) (not yet in force); (NL) *Condominium Act*, R.S.N.L. 1990, c. C-29; (ON) *Condominium Act, 1998*, S.O. 1998, c. 19, s. 17(3).

6. (BC) *Strata Property Act*, S.B.C. 1998, c. 43, ss. 78-80, 82

(MB) *Condominium Act*, C.C.S.M. c. C170, s. 10(9)

(ON) *Condominium Act, 1998*, S.O. 1998, c. 19, s. 18(1)

(PE) *Condominium Act,* R.S.P.E.I. 1988, c. C-16, s. 10(15)

(QC) *Civil Code of Québec*, L.R.Q. c. C-1991, art. 1076

(NT) *Condominium Act*, R.S.N.W.T. 1988, c. C-15, s. 13

(NU) *Condominium Act*, R.S.N.W.T. (Nu.) 1988, c. C-15, s. 13

(YT) *Condominium Act*, R.S.Y. 2002, c. 36, s. 10(9).

7. (NB) *Condominium Property Act*, S.N.B. 2009, c. C-16.05, s. 19(7)(a)

(NL) *Condominium Act, 2009*, S.N.L. 2009, c. C-29.1, s. 18(3)(a) (not yet in force)

(NS) *Condominium Act*, R.S.N.S. 1989, c. 85, s. 14(3)(a).

8. (AB) *Condominium Property Act*, R.S.A. 2000, c. C-22, s. 37(3)

(BC) *Strata Property Act*, S.B.C. 1998, c. 43, ss. 78(1), 79(a), 80(2)(a), 82(3)

(SK) *Condominium Property Act, 1993*, S.S. 1993, c. C-26.1, s. 34(5).

9. (MB) *Condominium Act*, C.C.S.M. c. C170, s. 10(2)

(NT) *Condominium Act*, R.S.N.W.T. 1988, c. C-15, s. 12(2)

(NU) *Condominium Act*, R.S.N.W.T. (Nu.) 1988, c. C-15, s. 12(2)

(YT) *Condominium Act*, R.S.Y. 2002, c. 36, s. 10(2).

10. (NB) *Condominium Property Act*, S.N.B. 2009, c. C-16.05, s. 20

(NL) *Condominium Act, 2009*, S.N.L. 2009, c. C-29.1, s. 24 (not yet in force)

(NS) *Condominium Act*, R.S.N.S. 1989, c. 85, s. 19(2)
(ON) *Condominium Act, 1998*, S.O. 1998, c. 19, s. 18(2)
(PE) *Condominium Act*, R.S.P.E.I. 1988, c. C-16, s. 10(16).

11. (AB) *Condominium Property Act*, R.S.A. 2000, c. C-22, s. 38(3)
(MB) *Condominium Act*, C.C.S.M. c. C170, s. 26(2)
(NB) *Condominium Property Act*, S.N.B. 2009, c. C-16.05, s. 38(6)
(NL) *Condominium Act, 2009*, S.N.L. 2009, c. C-29.1, s. 49(11) (not yet in force)
(NS) *Condominium Act*, R.S.N.S. 1989, c. 85, s. 31(4)
(ON) *Condominium Act, 1998*, S.O. 1998, c. 19, s. 95(3)
(SK) *Condominium Property Act, 1993*, S.S. 1993, c. C-26.1, s. 61(1)
(NT) *Condominium Act*, R.S.N.W.T. 1988, c. C-15, s. 19.10(4).

12. (AB) Condominium Property Regulation, Alta. Reg. 168/2000, s. 56(a)
(BC) *Strata Property Act*, S.B.C. 1998, c. 43, s. 271(b)
(NB) *Condominium Property Act*, S.N.B. 2009, c. C-16.05, s. 14(1)(h)
(NL) *Condominium Act, 2009*, S.N.L. 2009, c. C-29.1, s. 67(1)(g) (not yet in force)
(NS) *Condominium Act*, R.S.N.S. 1989, c. 85, s. 29C(1)(g)
(ON) *Condominium Act, 1998*, S.O. 1998, c. 19, s. 121(1)(g)
(SK) *Condominium Property Act, 1993*, S.S. 1993, c. C-26.1, s. 15(6)
(NT) *Condominium Act*, R.S.N.W.T. 1988, c. C-15, s. 6.2(7)(c).

13. (AB) *Condominium Property Act*, R.S.A. 2000, c. C-22, s. 49
(SK) *Condominium Property Act, 1993*, S.S. 1993, c. C-26.1, ss. 70-71.1.

14. (ON) *Condominium Act, 1998*, S.O. 1998, c. 19, ss. 17.1, 18(1.1).

---

3. Assessment and Taxation

▼HCD-30▼ Separate parcels of land. For the purpose of assessment and taxation by an assessing authority, each unit and common interest constitutes a separate parcel of land, and the common elements do not constitute a separate parcel of land.[1] The owner must pay all rates, taxes, charges and assessments payable in respect of the owner's unit.[2]

Requirements for assessing authority. In Prince Edward Island and Saskatchewan, within a specified time after registration of the declaration and description or plan or any amendments thereto, a corporation must provide the assessing authority with a certified copy of the declaration and description or plan.[3] For the purposes of any assessment or recovery of rates, charges or taxes respecting any property that is the subject of the declaration and description or plan, the particulars shown on the certified copy are conclusive proof of those particulars, and the assessing authority's production of what purports to be a certified copy is *prima facie* proof that it is the certified copy provided to the assessing authority.[4] Any other legislation authorizing or affecting an assessing authority's assessment or valuation of land or improvements or an assessing authority's imposition of rates, charges or taxes in respect of land and improvements authorized by the legislation apply with necessary changes to each unit and common interest.[5]

Exemption from goods and services tax. While residential condominium corporations are specifically exempt from goods and services tax under the *Excise Tax Act*, commercial condominium corporations are not exempt unless they exist solely for the purpose of acting as the agent of the unit owners and do not conduct commercial activity.[6]

Determining market value of condominium unit. The market value of each condominium unit cannot be determined by determining the market value of the entire building and pro-rating that value among the individual condominium units on the basis of unit factors. Instead, an appropriate method must be established for the market value of the fee simple interest in each condominium, which requires an assessment of each condominium unit to reflect the unique characteristics and physical condition of each unit.[7]

Notes

1. (BC) *Strata Property Act*, S.B.C. 1998, c. 43, s. 67

   (MB) *Condominium Act*, C.C.S.M. c. C170, s. 8(11)

   (NB) *Condominium Property Act*, S.N.B. 2009, c. C-16.05, s. 16(7)

   (NS) *Condominium Act*, R.S.N.S. 1989, c. 85, s. 28(11)

   (ON) *Condominium Act, 1998*, S.O. 1998, c. 19, s. 15(1)-(2), but see the exceptions regarding common elements in s. 15(3)-(4)

   (PE) *Condominium Act*, R.S.P.E.I. 1988, c. C-16, ss. 27(3)(a)-(b)

   (QC) *Civil Code of Québec*, L.R.Q. c. C-1991, art. 1050

   (YT) *Condominium Act*, R.S.Y. 2002, c. 36, s. 8(10).
2. (AB) *Condominium Property Act*, R.S.A. 2000, c. C-22, s. 65, App. 1, s. 2(b)(ii), App. 2, s. 1(b)

   (NL) *Condominium Act, 2009*, S.N.L. 2009, c. C-29.1, s. 46(1) (not yet in force)

   (SK) Condominium Property Regulations, 2001, R.R.S. c. C-26.1, Reg. 2, App., Part II, Bylaws, s. 2(a).
3. (PE) *Condominium Act*, R.S.P.E.I. 1988, c. C-16, s. 27(2); (SK) *Condominium Property Act, 1993*, S.S. 1993, c. C-26.1, s. 92(1)-(2).
4. (PE) *Condominium Act*, R.S.P.E.I. 1988, c. C-16, s. 27(2)(a)-(b); (SK) *Condominium Property Act, 1993*, S.S. 1993, c. C-26.1, s. 92(3).
5. (PE) *Condominium Act*, R.S.P.E.I. 1988, c. C-16, s. 27(2)(c)-(e); (SK) *Condominium Property Act, 1993*, S.S. 1993, c. C-26.1, s. 97(3)-(4).

6. *Condominium Plan No. 9422336 v. Canada*, [2004] T.C.J. No. 304, 2004 TCC 406 (Alta. T.C.C.); (CAN) *Excise Act*, R.S.C. 1985, c. E-14.
7. *Lougheed & Co. v. Calgary (City)*, [2003] A.J. No. 945, 2003 ABCA 232 (Alta. C.A.).

---

4. Entry by Corporation and Others

▼HCD-31▼ Entry by corporation. The corporation or any person authorized by the corporation may enter any unit at any reasonable time to perform the objects and duties of the corporation.[1] In some jurisdictions, the right of entry also applies to parts of the common elements of which an owner has exclusive use.[2] Where a unit owner engages in improper conduct and breaches a condominium by-law, the board is authorized to enter the unit to cause compliance with the by-law if the unit owner fails to do so himself or herself.[3] In several jurisdictions, notice is required to exercise the right of entry,[4] but in all jurisdictions except Ontario based on a strict reading of the legislation, the notice requirement does not apply in emergencies.[5]

Entry by others. In Alberta and Saskatchewan, where a local authority, public authority or authorized person has a statutory right to enter any part of a parcel, the authority or person may enter any other part of the parcel to the extent necessary or expedient for the exercise of the statutory powers related to the right.[6] In Ontario and Saskatchewan, a corporation, agent, employee or officer may not restrict reasonable access to the property by certain candidates for election or their authorized representatives for the purpose of canvassing or distributing election materials.[7]

Notes

1. (AB) *Condominium Property Act*, R.S.A. 2000, c. C-22, App. 1, s. 2(a), App. 2, s. 1(a)

   (BC) *Strata Property Act*, S.B.C. 1998, c. 43, s. 77

   (MB) *Condominium Act*, C.C.S.M. c. C170, s. 7(4)

   (NB) *Condominium Property Act*, S.N.B. 2009, c. C-16.05, s. 15(4)

   (NL) *Condominium Act, 2009*, S.N.L. 2009, c. C-29.1, s. 19(2) (not yet in force)

   (NS) *Condominium Act*, R.S.N.S. 1989, c. 85, s. 27(4)

   (ON) *Condominium Act, 1998*, S.O. 1998, c. 19, s. 19

   (PE) *Condominium Act*, R.S.P.E.I. 1988, c. C-16, s. 6(4)

   (QC) *Civil Code of Québec*, L.R.Q. c. C-1991, art. 1066

   (SK) *Condominium Property Act, 1993*, S.S. 1993, c. C-26.1, s. 36(1)

   (NT) *Condominium Act*, R.S.N.W.T. 1988, c. C-15, s. 7(4)

(NU) *Condominium Act*, R.S.N.W.T. (Nu.) 1988, c. C-15, s. 7(4)
(YT) *Condominium Act*, R.S.Y. 2002, c. 36, s. 7(4).

2. (BC) *Strata Property Act*, S.B.C. 1998, c. 43, s. 77
(NL) *Condominium Act, 2009*, S.N.L. 2009, c. C-29.1, s. 19(2) (not yet in force)
(ON) *Condominium Act, 1998*, S.O. 1998, c. 19, s. 19
(SK) *Condominium Property Act, 1993*, S.S. 1993, c. C-26.1, s. 36(1).

3. *Condominium Plan 7722911 v. Marnel*, [2008] A.J. No. 305, 2008 ABQB 195 (Alta. Q.B.).

4. (AB) *Condominium Property Act*, R.S.A. 2000, c. C-22, App. 1, s. 2(a), App. 2, s. 1(a)
(NB) *Condominium Property Act*, S.N.B. 2009, c. C-16.05, s. 15(4)
(NL) *Condominium Act, 2009*, S.N.L. 2009, c. C-29.1, s. 19(2) (not yet in force)
(ON) *Condominium Act, 1998*, S.O. 1998, c. 19, s. 19. See also s. 47, which sets out requirements for notice
(PE) *Condominium Act*, R.S.P.E.I. 1988, c. C-16, s. 6(4)
(SK) *Condominium Property Act, 1993*, S.S. 1993, c. C-26.1, s. 36(1).

5. (AB) *Condominium Property Act*, R.S.A. 2000, c. C-22, App. 1, s. 2(a), App. 2, s. 1(a)
(NB) *Condominium Property Act*, S.N.B. 2009, c. C-16.05, s. 15(5)
(NL) *Condominium Act, 2009*, S.N.L. 2009, c. C-29.1, s. 19(3) (not yet in force)
(PE) *Condominium Act*, R.S.P.E.I. 1988, c. C-16, s. 6(4). Subsection 6(4) provides additional exceptions to the notice requirement
(SK) *Condominium Property Act, 1993*, S.S. 1993, c. C-26.1, s. 36(2); (SK) Condominium Property Regulations, 2001, R.R.S. c. C-26.1, Reg. 2, App., Part II, Bylaws, s. 2(a).

6. (AB) *Condominium Property Act*, R.S.A. 2000, c. C-22, s. 70; (SK) *The Condominium Property Act, 1993*, S.S. 1993, c. C-26.1, s. 103.

7. (ON) *Condominium Act, 1998*, S.O. 1998, c. 19, s. 118; (SK) *Condominium Property Act, 1993*, S.S. 1993, c. C-26.1, s. 36.11(2). See also s. 37.11(3)-(4) for requirements candidates and their agents must meet prior to entry.

---

5. Action By or Against Corporation

▼HCD-32▼ Corporation may sue and be sued. A condominium corporation may sue and be sued and, in particular, may bring an action with respect to the common elements and may be sued in respect of any matter connected with the property for which the owners are jointly liable.[1] Only a condominium corporation may assert a claim relating to the common elements,[2] and individual unit owners cannot sue anyone apart from the condominium corporation in relation to common property.[3] A judgment for the payment of money against the corporation is also a judgment against each owner at the time the cause of action arose for a portion of the judgment determined by the proportions specified in the declaration for sharing the common expenses.[4] An application by a condominium corporation for certification of an action may be granted even though the corporation is not a member of the class.[5] In some jurisdictions, an owner may be discharged from the judgment by paying the claimant his or her portion of the judgment debt and costs, after which the judgment holder must give the owner a discharge.[6] In some jurisdictions, a judgment for the payment of money in favour of the corporation in an action with respect to the common elements is an asset of the corporation.[7] In Ontario, subject to certain exceptions, before commencing an action, a corporation must provide written notice of the general nature of the action to all persons whose names are in the corporation's record.[8]

British Columbia. In British Columbia, the strata corporation be sued.[9] The strata corporation may sue as a representative of all owners about any matter affecting the strata corporation if, before the corporation sues, the lawsuit is authorized by a resolution passed by a 75% vote at an annual or special general meeting.[10] The strata corporation may sue on behalf of one or more owners about matters affecting only their strata lots if, before beginning the suit, the lawsuit is authorized by the same resolution and all of the owners in question provide written consent.[11] If these requirements are not met, the lawsuit is a nullity.[12] Evidence of the special resolution and copies of the written consents are not privileged and must be disclosed.[13] The running of time for the two-year limitation period for bringing an action can be postponed where necessary for the strata corporation to have a reasonable period of time to obtain the 75% vote.[14] All strata owners are jointly liable to a judgment creditor of the corporation.[15]

Amalgamated corporations. In some jurisdictions, on registration of the declaration and description or plan for an amalgamated corporation, the amalgamated corporation possesses all the assets, rights and privileges and is subject to all the liabilities, contracts, agreements and debts of each amalgamating corporation; a conviction against, or ruling, order or judgment in favour of or against an amalgamating corporation may be enforced by or against the amalgamated corporation; and the amalgamated corporation is deemed to be the plaintiff or defendant in all civil actions commenced by or against an amalgamating corporation before the amalgamation becomes effective.[16]

Occupier's liability. For the purposes of determining liability resulting from breach of the duties of an occupier of land, the corporation is deemed to be the occupier of the common elements, and the owners are deemed not to be occupiers of the common elements.[17]

Notes

1. (AB) *Condominium Property Act*, R.S.A. 2000, c. C-22, s. 25(3)
   (MB) *Condominium Act*, C.C.S.M. c. C170, s. 10(10)
   (NB) *Condominium Property Act*, S.N.B. 2009, c. C-16.05, s. 19(6)
   (NL) *Condominium Act, 2009*, S.N.L. 2009, c. C-29.1, s. 25 (not yet in force)
   (NS) *Condominium Act*, R.S.N.S. 1989, c. 85, s. 21
   (ON) *Condominium Act, 1998*, S.O. 1998, c. 19, s. 23(1), (5)
   (PE) *Condominium Act*, R.S.P.E.I. 1988, c. C-16, s. 10(18)
   (QC) *Civil Code of Québec*, L.R.Q. c. C-1991, art. 1081
   (SK) *Condominium Property Act, 1993*, S.S. 1993, c. C-26.1, s. 34(4)
   (NT) *Condominium Act*, R.S.N.W.T. 1988, c. C-15, s. 14(1)
   (NU) *Condominium Act*, R.S.N.W.T. (Nu.) 1988, c. C-15, s. 14(1)
   (YT) *Condominium Act*, R.S.Y. 2002, c. 36, s. 10(11).
2. *1420041 Ontario Inc. v. 1 King West Inc.*, [2010] O.J. No. 5613, 2010 ONSC 6671 (Ont. Div. Ct.); *Kelly v. Reardon*, [2004] N.J. No. 30, 234 Nfld. & P.E.I.R. 358 (Nfld. Prov. Ct.). See also *Condominium Plan Number 752-1207 v. Terrace Corp. (Construction)*, [1983] A.J. No. 773, 146 D.L.R. (3d) 324 (Alta. C.A.).
3. *Hatch v. Quadra Plex Development Corp.*, [2002] B.C.J. No. 2708, 2002 BCPC 502 (B.C. Prov. Ct.); (BC) *Strata Property Act*, S.B.C. 1998, c. 43, s. 163(1)-(2).
4. (AB) *Condominium Property Act*, R.S.A. 2000, c. C-22, s. 7
   (MB) *Condominium Act*, C.C.S.M. c. C170, s. 10(11)
   (NB) *Condominium Property Act*, S.N.B. 2009, c. C-16.05, s. 24(1)
   (NL) *Condominium Act, 2009*, S.N.L. 2009, c. C-29.1, s. 26(1) (not yet in force)
   (NS) *Condominium Act*, R.S.N.S. 1989, c. 85, s. 20(1)
   (ON) *Condominium Act, 1998*, S.O. 1998, c. 19, s. 23(6)
   (PE) *Condominium Act*, R.S.P.E.I. 1988, c. C-16, s. 10(17)
   (QC) *Civil Code of Québec*, L.R.Q. c. C-1991, art. 1078
   (SK) *Condominium Property Act, 1993*, S.S. 1993, c. C-26.1, s. 7(2)
   (NT) *Condominium Act*, R.S.N.W.T. 1988, c. C-15, s. 14(2)
   (NU) *Condominium Act*, R.S.N.W.T. (Nu.) 1988, c. C-15, s. 14(2)
   (YT) *Condominium Act*, R.S.Y. 2002, c. 36, s. 10(12).
5. *Condominium Plan No. 0020701 v. Investplan Properties Inc.*, [2006] A.J. No. 368, 2006 ABQB 224 (Alta. Q.B.).
6. (NB) *Condominium Property Act*, S.N.B. 2009, c. C-16.05, s. 24(2)
   (NL) *Condominium Act, 2009*, S.N.L. 2009, c. C-29.1, s. 26(2) (not yet in force)
   (NS) *Condominium Act*, R.S.N.S. 1989, c. 85, s. 20(2).
7. (NB) *Condominium Property Act*, S.N.B. 2009, c. C-16.05, s. 24(2)
   (NS) *Condominium Act*, R.S.N.S. 1989, c. 85, s. 21
   (ON) *Condominium Act, 1998*, S.O. 1998, c. 19, s. 23(4)
   (PE) *Condominium Act*, R.S.P.E.I. 1988, c. C-16, s. 10(18).
8. (ON) *Condominium Act, 1998*, S.O. 1998, c. 19, s. 23(2). With respect to the previous notification requirement under s. 24 of the now-repealed (ON) *Condominium*

Act, R.S.O. 1990, c. C-26, *see Metropolitan Toronto Condominium Corp. No. 539 v. Chapters Inc.*, [1999] O.J. No. 2806, 102 O.T.C. 387 (Ont. S.C.J.) and *Corchis v. Essex Condominium Corp. No. 28*, [2003] O.J. No. 3364, 11 R.P.R. (4th) 194 (Ont. C.A.).

9. (BC) *Strata Property Act*, S.B.C. 1998, c. 43, s. 163.
10. (BC) *Strata Property Act*, S.B.C. 1998, c. 43, s. 171(1)-(2).
11. (BC) *Strata Property Act*, S.B.C. 1998, c. 43, s. 172(1).
12. *Strata Plan LMS 888 v. Coquitlam (City)*, [2003] B.C.J. No. 1422, 2003 BCSC 941 (B.C.S.C.).
13. *Strata Plan VR 1280 v. Oberto Oberti Architecture*, [2003] B.C.J. No. 129, 2003 BCSC 112 (B.C.S.C.).
14. *Strata Plan LMS 2940 v. Quick as a Wink Courier Service Ltd.*, [2007] B.C.J. No. 1448 (B.C.S.C.).
15. *Strata Plan VIS 4534 v. Seedtree Water Utility Co.*, [2006] B.C.J. No. 82, 2006 BCSC 73 (B.C.S.C.); (BC) *Strata Property Act*, S.B.C. 1998, c. 43, s. 166(1).
16. (AB) Condominium Property Regulation, Alta. Reg. 168/2000, s. 56

    (BC) *Strata Property Act*, S.B.C. 1998, c. 43, s. 271

    (NB) *Condominium Property Act*, S.N.B. 2009, c. C-16.05, s. 14(1)(h)-(i)

    (NL) *Condominium Act, 2009*, S.N.L. 2009, c. C-29.1, s. 67(1)(g)-(h) (not yet in force)

    (NS) *Condominium Act*, R.S.N.S. 1989, c. 85, s. 29C(1)(g)-(h)

    (ON) *Condominium Act, 1998*, S.O. 1998, c. 19, s. 121(1)(g)-(i)

    (SK) *Condominium Property Act, 1993*, S.S. 1993, c. C-26.1, s. 15(6)(c)-(e)

    (NT) *Condominium Act*, R.S.N.W.T. 1988, c. C-15, s. 6.2(7)(c)-(f).
17. (MB) *Condominium Act*, C.C.S.M. c. C170, s. 8(12)

    (NS) *Condominium Act*, R.S.N.S. 1989, c. 85, s. 28(12)

    (ON) *Condominium Act, 1998*, S.O. 1998, c. 19, s. 26

    (PE) *Condominium Act*, R.S.P.E.I. 1988, c. C-16, s. 7(11)

    (QC) *Civil Code of Québec*, L.R.Q. c. C-1991, art. 1077

    (NT) *Condominium Act*, R.S.N.W.T. 1988, c. C-15, s. 10

    (NU) *Condominium Act*, R.S.N.W.T. (Nu.) 1988, c. C-15, s. 10

    (YT) *Condominium Act*, R.S.Y. 2002, c. 36, s. 8(11).

    See also *Murkute v. Owners Condominium Plan 8210034*, [2006] A.J. No. 1335, 2006 ABCA 315 (Alta. C.A.), which upheld the finding that the condominium corporation was an occupier but did not breach the standard of care in a slip and fall action.

---

6. Corporation's Money

▼HCD-33▼ Accounts. Where a condominium corporation or person receives money paid to or for the benefit of the corporation, the money and all proceeds arising from the money must be held in trust for the corporation's performance of its duties and obligations.[1] The corporation must establish a fund for the payment of common expenses, into which the owners contribute in the proportions specified in the declaration.[2] The corporation must also establish a reserve fund account for major repair and replacement of the common elements and the corporation's assets.[3]

Investment. A jurisdiction's Act may specify that the corporation may invest money that is not immediately required by the corporation,[4] that the corporation must do so in accordance with the regulations,[5] and/or that monies in a reserve fund may be invested in specified securities.[6] Interest earned on an investment forms part of the fund.[7] In Ontario, the board may invest money in eligible securities if they are registered in the corporation's name and held in a specified segregated account, and the board must develop an investment plan for its reserve fund before investing any money in the fund.[8]

Borrowing. Depending on the jurisdiction, a corporation may borrow money without meeting additional requirements,[9] may do so if a by-law authorizes the borrowing,[10] or may do so with a specified percentage of owner consent.[11]

Notes

1. (AB) *Condominium Property Act*, R.S.A. 2000, c. C-22, s. 43(2)-(3)
   (MB) *Condominium Act*, C.C.S.M. c. C170, s. 27(1)
   (ON) *Condominium Act, 1998*, S.O. 1998, c. 19, s. 115(1)
   (PE) *Condominium Act*, R.S.P.E.I. 1988, c. C-16, s. 20(4)
   (SK) *Condominium Property Act*, 1993, S.S. 1993, c. C-26.1, s. 61(2).
2. (AB) *Condominium Property Act*, R.S.A. 2000, c. C-22, s. 39(1)
   (BC) *Strata Property Act*, S.B.C. 1998, c. 43, s. 92(a)
   (MB) *Condominium Act*, C.C.S.M. c. C170, s. 14(1)(a)
   (NB) *Condominium Property Act*, S.N.B. 2009, c. C-16.05, s. 37(1)
   (NL) *Condominium Act, 2009*, S.N.L. 2009, c. C-29.1, s. 48(a) (not yet in force)
   (NS) *Condominium Act*, R.S.N.S. 1989, c. 85, s. 31(1)(a)
   (ON) *Condominium Act, 1998*, S.O. 1998, c. 19, s. 115(2)
   (SK) *Condominium Property Act, 1993*, S.S. 1993, c. C-26.1, s. 55(1)(a), (2)
   (NT) *Condominium Act*, R.S.N.W.T. 1988, c. C-15, s. 19.9(1)(a)
   (NU) *Condominium Act*, R.S.N.W.T. (Nu.) 1988, c. C-15, s. 19(1)(a)
   (YT) *Condominium Act*, R.S.Y. 2002, c. 36, s. 14(1)(a).
3. (AB) *Condominium Property Act*, R.S.A. 2000, c. C-22, s. 38(1)
   (BC) *Strata Property Act*, S.B.C. 1998, c. 43, ss. 12(1), (4)-(5), 92(b)
   (MB) *Condominium Act*, C.C.S.M. c. C170, ss. 26(1), 27(2)

(NB) *Condominium Property Act*, S.N.B. 2009, c. C-16.05, ss. 38(2), 42(1)

(NL) *Condominium Act, 2009*, S.N.L. 2009, c. C-29.1, s. 49(1) (not yet in force)

(NS) *Condominium Act*, R.S.N.S. 1989, c. 85, s. 31(1A)

(ON) *Condominium Act, 1998*, S.O. 1998, c. 19, s. 93(1)-(2)

(SK) *Condominium Property Act, 1993*, S.S. 1993, c. C-26.1, s. 55(1)(b), (3)

(NT) *Condominium Act*, R.S.N.W.T. 1988, c. C-15, s. 19.10(1)-(2).

4. (AB) *Condominium Property Act*, R.S.A. 2000, c. C-22, s. 43(1)

(ON) *Condominium Act, 1998*, S.O. 1998, c. 19, s. 115(1)

(SK) *Condominium Property Act, 1993*, S.S. 1993, c. C-26.1, s. 60(1)

(NT) *Condominium Act*, R.S.N.W.T. 1988, c. C-15, s. 19.14(1).

5. (AB) *Condominium Property Act*, R.S.A. 2000, c. C-22, s. 43(1); (AB) Condominium Property Regulation, Alta. Reg. 168/2000, Sch. 2

(BC) *Strata Property Act*, S.B.C. 1998, c. 43, s. 95(2)(a)

(MB) *Condominium Act*, C.C.S.M. c. C170, s. 29(2)

(ON) *Condominium Act, 1998*, S.O. 1998, c. 19, s. 115(1)

(NT) *Condominium Act*, R.S.N.W.T. 1988, c. C-15, s. 19.14(1); (NT) Condominium Regulations, N.W.T. Reg. 098-2008, s. 12.

6. (BC) *Strata Property Act*, S.B.C. 1998, c. 43, s. 95(2)(b)

(NB) *Condominium Property Act*, S.N.B. 2009, c. C-16.05, s. 38(3)

(NL) *Condominium Act, 2009*, S.N.L. 2009, c. C-29.1, s. 49(8) (not yet in force)

(NS) *Condominium Act*, R.S.N.S. 1989, c. 85, s. 31(1H).

7. (BC) *Strata Property Act*, S.B.C. 1998, c. 43, s. 95(3)

(ON) *Condominium Act, 1998*, S.O. 1998, c. 19, s. 93(7)

(PE) *Condominium Act*, R.S.P.E.I. 1988, c. C-16, s. 13(1)(i)

(SK) *Condominium Property Act, 1993*, S.S. 1993, c. C-26.1, s. 60(2)

(NT) *Condominium Act*, R.S.N.W.T. 1988, c. C-15, s. 19.14(2).

8. (ON) *Condominium Act, 1998*, S.O. 1998, c. 19, s. 115(6)-(8).

9. (SK) *Condominium Property Act, 1993*, S.S. 1993, c. C-26.1, s. 34(5.1)(a); (YT) *Condominium Act*, R.S.Y. 2002, c. 36, s. 10(10).

10. (AB) *Condominium Property Act*, R.S.A. 2000, c. C-22, App. 1, s. 3(b), App. 2, s. 3(b)

(ON) *Condominium Act, 1998*, S.O. 1998, c. 19, s. 56(1)(e), (3); see also *York Condominium Corp. No. 42 v. Hashmi*, [2007] O.J. No. 2085, 2007 CarswellOnt 3309 (Ont. S.C.J.)

(SK) *Condominium Property Act, 1993*, S.S. 1993, c. C-26.1, s. 47(1); (SK) Condominium Property Regulations, 2001, R.R.S. c. C-26.1, Reg. 2, App., Part 2, Bylaws, s. 4(b).

11. (BC) *Strata Property Act*, S.B.C. 1998, c. 43, s. 111(1)

(NB) *Condominium Property Act*, S.N.B. 2009, c. C-16.05, s. 19(7)

(NL) *Condominium Act, 2009*, S.N.L. 2009, c. C-29.1, s. 18(3)(b) (not yet in force)

(NS) *Condominium Act*, R.S.N.S. 1989, c. 85, s. 14(3)(b).

7. Information

(1) With a Fee HCD-34
(2) Without a Fee HCD-35

---

(1) With a Fee

▼HCD-34▼ Information to be provided. In some jurisdictions, a condominium corporation must, on request and with a fee, provide a certificate containing specified information to specified individuals. Depending on the jurisdiction, the certificate must contain some or all of the following information:[1]

- the date on which the certificate was made
- a statement of the common expenses for the unit and any default in their payment
- a statement of any increase in the common expenses for the unit the board has declared since the date of the corporation's budget for the current fiscal year and the reason for the increase
- a statement of any assessments the board has levied against the unit since the date of the corporation's budget for the current fiscal year to increase the contribution to the reserve fund and the reason for the assessments
- a statement of the address for service of the corporation
- a statement of the names and address for service of the directors and officers of the corporation
- a statement of the name and address of the corporation's management company or manager
- a copy of management agreements, recreational agreements, lease agreements and exclusive use agreements
- a copy of the current declaration, by-laws and rules
- a copy of the certificate of registration of the corporation from the registry
- a statement as to whether the corporation's by-laws have been registered
- a statement as to whether the common property has been mortgaged or transferred
- a copy of all applications to amend the declaration for which the court has not made an order

- a statement of all outstanding judgments against the corporation and the status of all legal actions to which the corporation is a party
- a copy of the corporation's budget for the current fiscal year, the last annual audited financial statements and the auditor's report on the statements
- a list of all current agreements between the corporation and another corporation or unit owner
- a statement that the person requesting the certificate has certain rights
- a statement whether the parties have complied with specified current agreements with respect to the unit
- a statement with respect to the most recent reserve fund study and updates to it, the amount of the reserve fund at a specified time and any current plans to increase the reserve fund
- a statement of the additions, alterations or improvements to the common elements and changes in the corporation's assets and service that are substantial and that the board has proposed but has not implemented, together with a statement of their purpose
- a statement setting out any structural deficiencies of which the corporation has knowledge at the time of the request in any of the buildings included in the condominium plan, except those constructed on bare land units
- a copy of any minutes of proceedings of a general meeting of the corporation or board
- a statement of the number of units for which the corporation has received notice that the unit was leased during the fiscal year preceding the date of the status certificate
- in the case of a leasehold condominium, a statement as to whether the provisions of the lease are in good standing and have not been breached, whether the lessor has provided a notice of intention to renew or not to renew the leasehold estate, and whether the lessor has applied for a termination order
- a certificate or memorandum of insurance for each of the current insurance policies
- a statement of any amounts the act requires be added to the common expenses payable for the unit
- a statement whether the court has made an order appointing an inspector or administrator and
- all other material required by the regulations

Individuals entitled to information. In Alberta and Northwest Territories, an owner and the purchaser or mortgagee of a unit is entitled to the information, and in Northwest Territories any other person with the owner's consent is also entitled.[2] In British Columbia, an owner, purchaser or person authorized by the owner or purchaser is entitled.[3] In Newfoundland and Labrador, an owner is entitled.[4] In Ontario, any person is entitled, provided that the prescribed fee is paid to the corporation.[5] In Saskatchewan, an owner or a person authorized in writing by an owner is entitled.[6]

Effect of providing and not providing certificate. If a corporation provides the requested certificate, the certificate binds the corporation; in British Columbia, it binds the corporation as against a person who relied reasonably on it, and in Ontario it binds the corporation as against a purchaser or mortgagee of a unit who relies on the certificate.[7] If the corporation does not provide the certificate within the required time, the corporation is deemed to have given a certificate on the next day stating that:[8]

- there has been no default in the payment of common expenses for the unit
- the board has not declared any increase in the common expenses for the unit since the date of the corporation's budget for the current fiscal year and
- the board has not levied any assessments against the unit since the date of the corporation's budget for the current fiscal year to increase the contribution to the reserve fund

If a certificate omits material required information, it is deemed to include a statement that there is no such information.[9]

Amount of fee. In Alberta, Newfoundland and Labrador and the Northwest Territories, the corporation may charge a reasonable fee for providing the information.[10] In British Columbia, the corporation may charge $35 plus the cost of photocopying or other reproduction, up to $0.25 per page.[11] In Ontario, the corporation may charge the prescribed fee, which cannot exceed $100.[12]

Notes

1. (AB) *Condominium Property Act*, R.S.A. 2000, c. C-22, s. 44, although that section does not refer to a certificate

   (BC) *Strata Property Act*, S.B.C. 1998, c. 43, s. 59(3)

(NL) *Condominium Act, 2009*, S.N.L. 2009, c. C-29.1, s. 42(1) (not yet in force)

(ON) *Condominium Act, 1998*, S.O. 1998, c. 19, s. 76(1)

(SK) *Condominium Property Act, 1993*, S.S. 1993, c. C-26.1, s. 64(1)

(NT) *Condominium Act*, R.S.N.W.T. 1988, c. C-15, s. 19.17(1); *see also* Condominium Regulations, N.W.T. Reg. 098-2008, s. 14.

2. (AB) *Condominium Property Act*, R.S.A. 2000, c. C-22, s. 44; (NT) *Condominium Act*, R.S.N.W.T. 1988, c. C-15, s. 19.17(1).
3. (BC) *Strata Property Act*, S.B.C. 1998, c. 43, s. 59(1).
4. (NL) *Condominium Act, 2009*, S.N.L. 2009, c. C-29.1, s. 42(1) (not yet in force).
5. (ON) *Condominium Act, 1998*, S.O. 1998, c. 19, s. 76(1).
6. (SK) *Condominium Property Act, 1993*, S.S. 1993, c. C-26.1, s. 64(1).
7. (NL) *Condominium Act, 2009*, S.N.L. 2009, c. C-29.1, s. 42(4) (not yet in force)

   (ON) *Condominium Act, 1998*, S.O. 1998, c. 19, s. 76(6)

   (NT) *Condominium Act*, R.S.N.W.T. 1988, c. C-15, s. 19.17(3).
8. (BC) *Strata Property Act*, S.B.C. 1998, c. 43, s. 59(5); (ON) *Condominium Act, 1998*, S.O. 1998, c. 19, s. 76(5).
9. (NL) *Condominium Act, 2009*, S.N.L. 2009, c. C-29.1, s. 42(3) (not yet in force); (ON) *Condominium Act, 1998*, S.O. 1998, c. 19, s. 76(4).
10. (AB) *Condominium Property Act*, R.S.A. 2000, c. C-22, s. 74

    (NL) *Condominium Act, 2009*, S.N.L. 2009, c. C-29.1, s. 42(2) (not yet in force)

    (NT) *Condominium Act*, R.S.N.W.T. 1988, c. C-15, s. 19.17(4).
11. (BC) Strata Property Regulations, B.C. Reg. 43/2000, s. 4.4.
12. (ON) *Condominium Act, 1998*, S.O. 1998, c. 19, s. 76(2); (ON) General Regulation, O. Reg. 48/01, s. 18(2).

---

(2) Without a Fee

▼HCD-35▼ Information to be provided. In Alberta and Saskatchewan, a corporation must, without a fee, provide the names and addresses of board members; in Alberta, the corporation must do so at a specified time without a request, whereas in Saskatchewan, the corporation must do so on reasonable request.[1] In Ontario and Northwest Territories, on request and without a fee, a corporation must provide the names and address for service of the corporation's directors and officers, the person responsible for the management of the corporation's property and the person to whom the corporation has delegated responsibility for providing certificates containing the information for which it may charge a fee.[2] In Ontario and Saskatchewan, on request and without a fee, a corporation must provide the mortgagee of a unit with a written statement setting out the common expenses in respect of the unit and any defaults in their payment.[3]

Notes

1. (AB) *Condominium Property Act*, R.S.A. 2000, c. C-22, s. 28(5); (SK) *Condominium Property Act, 1993*, S.S. 1993, c. C-26.1, s. 35(2)(c).
2. (ON) *Condominium Act, 1998*, S.O. 1998, c. 19, s. 77; (NT) *Condominium Act*, R.S.N.W.T. 1988, c. C-15, s. 19.17(5).
3. (ON) *Condominium Act, 1998*, S.O. 1998, c. 19, s. 88(2); (SK) *The Condominium Property Act, 1993*, S.S. 1993, c. C-26.1, s. 65.2(2).

---

8. Records

(1) Duty to Maintain Records HCD-36
(2) Access to Records
(a) General HCD-37
(b) Restrictions on Access HCD-38
(c) Failure to Provide Access HCD-39

---

(1) Duty to Maintain Records

▼HCD-36▼ Records to be kept by corporation. The board of directors or strata council is authorized to make decisions on behalf of individual unit owners with respect to the common interests in the property. A condition of this authority is that the affairs of the corporation and its board of directors or strata council are an open book to the members of the corporation.[1] Since unit owners are personally liable for any monetary judgments against the corporation, they have a unique interest in the corporation's administration and management.[2] The statutory provisions relating to the corporation's duties to maintain records and provide owners with access to records have been given a broad and liberal interpretation.[3] Corporations must keep adequate or proper records relating to the corporation's affairs.[4] In several jurisdictions, the legislation specifies the documents that are records and that must be kept by the corporation, including:[5]

- minutes of annual and special general meetings
- minutes of meetings of the strata council or board of directors
- books of account showing money received and spent and the reason for the receipt or expenditure
- contracts to which the corporation is a party
- budgets and financial statements and
- the declaration, by-laws and rules

In Québec, in addition to records specified in the *Civil Code of Québec*,[6] the syndicate must keep all other documents relating to the condominium property and syndicate.[7]

Adequate records. Adequate records include more than the documents listed under the statutory definitions of records or otherwise specified in the legislation. To be considered adequate, records must be sufficient to allow the corporation to fulfill its obligations.[8] Since the corporation has a statutory duty to manage and control the property and any assets of the corporation on behalf of owners, a board of directors or strata council may not restrict the scope of the access rights of owners by by-law or resolution or adopt a narrower definition of records than that provided by the legislation, particularly since the legislature intended an open and inclusive definition of records.[9] However, in the absence of any specific statutory or by-law requirements, the corporation need not keep records in any particular form or level of detail.

Notes

1. *McKay v. Waterloo North Condominium Corp. No. 23*, [1992] O.J. No. 2435, 11 O.R. (3d) 341 (Ont. Gen. Div.); *Rohoman v. York Condominium Corp. No. 141*, [2000] O.J. No. 2356 (Ont. S.C.J.); *York Condominium Corp. No. 60 v. Brown*, [2001] O.J. No. 5851, 109 A.C.W.S. (3d) 166 (Ont. S.C.J.).
2. *McKay v. Waterloo North Condominium Corp. No. 23*, [1992] O.J. No. 2435, 11 O.R. (3d) 341 (Ont. Gen. Div.).
3. *Rohoman v. York Condominium Corp. No. 141*, [2000] O.J. No. 2356 (Ont. S.C.J.).
4. (AB) *Condominium Property Act*, R.S.A. 2000, c. C-22, App. 1, s. 17, App. 2, s. 11

   (MB) *Condominium Act*, C.C.S.M. c. C170, s. 10(7)

   (NB) *Condominium Property Act*, S.N.B. 2009, c. C-16.05, s. 21(1)

   (NL) *Condominium Act, 2009*, S.N.L. 2009, c. C-29.1, s. 23(1) (not yet in force)

   (NS) *Condominium Act*, R.S.N.S. 1989, c. 85, s. 18(1)

   (ON) *Condominium Act, 1998*, S.O. 1998, c. 19, s. 55(1)

   (PE) *Condominium Act*, R.S.P.E.I. 1988, c. C-16, s. 10(11)

   (SK) *Condominium Property Act*, 1993, S.S. 1993, c. C-26.1, s. 39(2)

   (NT) *Condominium Act*, R.S.N.W.T. 1988, c. C-15, s. 12(7)

   (NU) *Condominium Act*, R.S.N.W.T. (Nu.) 1988, c. C-15, s. 12(7)

   (YT) *Condominium Act*, R.S.Y. 2002, c. 36, s. 10(7).
5. (AB) *Condominium Property Act*, R.S.A. 2000, c. C-22, App. 1, s. 17, App. 2, s. 11

   (BC) *Strata Property Act*, S.B.C. 1998, c. 43, ss. 23, 35

   (NB) *Condominium Property Act*, S.N.B. 2009, c. C-16.05, s. 21(1)

   (NL) *Condominium Act, 2009*, S.N.L. 2009, c. C-29.1, ss. 22, 23(2) (not yet in force)

(NS) *Condominium Act*, R.S.N.S. 1989, c. 85, s. 18(1A)
(ON) *Condominium Act*, 1998, S.O. 1998, c. 19, ss. 55(1), 115(9)
(SK) *Condominium Property Act*, 1993, S.S. 1993, c. C-26.1, s. 39(2).

6. (QC) *Civil Code of Québec*, L.R.Q. c. C-1991.
7. (QC) *Civil Code of Québec*, L.R.Q. c. C-1991, art. 1070.
8. *McKay v. Waterloo North Condominium Corp. No. 23*, [1992] O.J. No. 2435, 11 O.R. (3d) 341 (Ont. Gen. Div.).
9. *McKay v. Waterloo North Condominium Corp. No. 23*, [1992] O.J. No. 2435, 11 O.R. (3d) 341 (Ont. Gen. Div.); *National Trust Co. v. Grey Condominium Corp. No. 36*, [1995] O.J. No. 2079, 47 R.P.R. (2d) 60 (Gen. Div.).

---

(2) Access to Records

(a) General

▼HCD-37▼ Entitlement to records. Upon receiving a request, which in some jurisdictions must be in writing, a condominium corporation must permit an owner, purchaser, mortgagee of a unit or duly authorized agent to examine the records of the corporation.[1] An individual is entitled to records only during the time he or she has standing as an owner or other permitted person.[2] In several jurisdictions, the corporation may charge a fee to those requesting a copy of records and may refuse to supply the copy of the record until the fee is paid.[3]

Production of records. In most jurisdictions, the corporation must provide access to records upon reasonable notice.[4] What constitutes reasonable notice depends on the individual circumstances of each case, but a period of 48 hours has been held not to be unreasonable.[5] In some jurisdictions, the legislation specifies the timing of delivery of certain documents.[6]

Timing of production. Most jurisdictions include a statutory requirement that the corporation provide access to records to those entitled at a reasonable time,[7] which includes the regular business hours of the corporation or regular office hours of the property manager.[8] There is no explicit requirement for a corporation to keep records at the property, although this may be preferable. For larger corporations, records may be too voluminous to be kept onsite, even if there is a management office. In such cases, it may be more practical and convenient to store records at the premises of the property manager acting as agent for the corporation and to arrange for the delivery of records when needed.[9]

Notes

1. (AB) *Condominium Property Act*, R.S.A. 2000, c. C-22, s. 44

   (BC) *Strata Property Act*, S.B.C. 1998, c. 43, s. 36(1)

   (MB) *Condominium Act*, C.C.S.M. c. C170, s. 10(7)

   (NB) *Condominium Property Act*, S.N.B. 2009, c. C-16.05, s. 21(3)

   (NL) *Condominium Act, 2009*, S.N.L. 2009, c. C-29.1, s. 23(4) (not yet in force)

   (NS) *Condominium Act*, R.S.N.S. 1989, c. 85, s. 18(1)

   (ON) *Condominium Act, 1998*, S.O. 1998, c. 19, s. 55(3)

   (PE) *Condominium Act,* R.S.P.E.I. 1988, c. C-16, s. 10(11)

   (SK) *Condominium Property Act, 1993*, S.S. 1993, c. C-26.1, ss. 39(2), 44(4)

   (NT) *Condominium Act*, R.S.N.W.T. 1988, c. C-15, ss. 12(7), 19.17(2)

   (NU) *Condominium Act*, R.S.N.W.T. (Nu.) 1988, c. C-15, s. 12(7)

   (YT) *Condominium Act*, R.S.Y. 2002, c. 36, s. 10(7).

2. *Extra Gift Exchange Inc. v. Ernest & Twins Ventures (PP) Ltd.*, [2007] B.C.J. No. 636, 2007 BCSC 426 (B.C.S.C.).

3. (AB) *Condominium Property Act*, R.S.A. 2000, c. C-22, s. 74

   (BC) *Strata Property Act*, S.B.C. 1998, c. 43, s. 36(4)

   (NB) *Condominium Property Act*, S.N.B. 2009, c. C-16.05, s. 21(4)

   (NL) *Condominium Act, 2009*, S.N.L. 2009, c. C-29.1, s. 23(4) (not yet in force)

   (NS) *Condominium Act*, R.S.N.S. 1989, c. 85, s. 18(1D)

   (ON) *Condominium Act, 1998*, S.O. 1998, c. 19, s. 55(6); *Metropolitan Toronto Condominium Corp. No. 932 v. Lahrkamp*, [2008] O.J. No. 3885 (Ont. S.C.J.), vard [2009] O.J. No. 1785, 2009 ONCA 362 (Ont. C.A.)

   (SK) *Condominium Property Act, 1993*, S.S. 1993, c. C-26.1, s. 106.

4. (MB) *The Condominium Act*, C.C.S.M. c. C170, s. 10(7)

   (NB) *Condominium Property Act*, S.N.B. 2009, c. C-16.05, s. 21(3)

   (NL) *Condominium Act, 2009*, S.N.L. 2009, c. C-29.1, s. 23(1) (not yet in force)

   (NS) *Condominium Act*, R.S.N.S. 1989, c. 85, s. 18(1)

   (ON) *Condominium Act, 1998*, S.O. 1998, c. 19, s. 55(3)

   (PE) *Condominium Act,* R.S.P.E.I. 1988, c. C-16, s. 10(11)

   (NT) *Condominium Act*, R.S.N.W.T. 1988, c. C-15, ss. 12(7), 19.17(2)

   (NU) *Condominium Act*, R.S.N.W.T. (Nu.) 1988, c. C-15, s. 12(7)

   (YT) *Condominium Act*, R.S.Y. 2002, c. 36, s. 10(7).

5. *McKay v. Waterloo North Condominium Corp. No. 23*, [1992] O.J. No. 2435, 11 O.R. (3d) 341 (Ont. Gen. Div.).

6. (AB) *Condominium Property Act*, R.S.A. 2000, c. C-22, s. 44; (BC) *Strata Property Act*, S.B.C. 1998, c. 43, s. 36(1).

7. (AB) *Condominium Property Act*, R.S.A. 2000, c. C-22, App. 2, s. 11

   (BC) *Strata Property Act*, S.B.C. 1998, c. 43, s. 36(3), specifying the time period

   (MB) *Condominium Act*, C.C.S.M. c. C170, s. 10(7)

   (NB) *Condominium Property Act*, S.N.B. 2009, c. C-16.05, s. 21(3)

   (NL) *Condominium Act, 2009*, S.N.L. 2009, c. C-29.1, s. 23(1) (not yet in force)

(NS) *Condominium Act*, R.S.N.S. 1989, c. 85, s. 18(1)
(ON) *Condominium Act, 1998*, S.O. 1998, c. 19, s. 55(3)
(PE) *Condominium Act,* R.S.P.E.I. 1988, c. C-16, s. 10(11)
(SK) *Condominium Property Act, 1993*, S.S. 1993, c. C-26.1, s. 39(2)(g)
(NT) *Condominium Act*, R.S.N.W.T. 1988, c. C-15, s. 12(7)
(NU) *Condominium Act*, R.S.N.W.T. (Nu.) 1988, c. C-15, s. 12(7)
(YT) *Condominium Act*, R.S.Y. 2002, c. 36, s. 10(7).

8. *McKay v. Waterloo North Condominium Corp. No. 23*, [1992] O.J. No. 2435, 11 O.R. (3d) 341 (Ont. Gen. Div.).
9. A.M. Loeb, *Condominium Law and Administration*, 2d ed. (looseleaf) (Toronto: Carswell, 1989) at 11-10.

(b) Restrictions on Access

▼HCD-38▼ Right to records versus information. Although a board of directors or strata council cannot make the right to access records subject to its approval, the entitlement is to the records themselves. Unit owners cannot engage in an investigative exercise by requiring further explanations and demanding responses from the directors or management.[1]

Harassment. The right to access the corporation's records is abused when unit owners engage in a "campaign by siege" against the directors or property management or in any other conduct that constitutes harassment. Such unit owners or their representatives may be subject to court orders restricting the manner in which any requests for records are made and the method by which such owners may access them.[2]

Records relating to litigation. Those entitled to access the corporation's records are not entitled to any documents relating to litigation involving the corporation, particularly with respect to any legal proceeding between a unit owner and the corporation.[3] The primary purpose of this restriction is to protect the corporation's solicitor and client privilege and/or litigation privilege. Such records are only producible in accordance with the rules of court pertaining to documentary discovery.[4]

Privacy. It is unclear whether the *Personal Information Protection and Electronic Documents Act*[5] applies to corporations,[6] especially since the corporation is a not-for-profit entity without share capital and is entirely a creature of its condominium or strata plan statute.[7] Although there may be instances where individual rights to privacy and confidentiality override the open and liberal access to the affairs of the board of directors and the corporation,[8] in other instances any right to privacy and confidentiality is clearly superseded by the statutory right to access records.[9]

Notes

1. *York Condominium Corp. No. 60 v. Brown*, [2001] O.J. No. 5851, 109 A.C.W.S. (3d) 166 (Ont. S.C.J.); *McKay v. Waterloo North Condominium Corp. No. 23*, [1992] O.J. No. 2435, 11 O.R. (3d) 341 (Ont. Gen. Div.).
2. *Metropolitan Toronto Condominium Corp. No. 932 v. Lahrkamp*, [2008] O.J. No. 3885 (S.C.J.), vard [2009] O.J. No. 1785, 2009 ONCA 362 (Ont. C.A.).
3. (BC) *Strata Property Act*, S.B.C. 1998, c. 43, s. 169(1); (ON) *Condominium Act, 1998*, S.O. 1998, c. 19, s. 55(3).
4. *Fisher v. Metropolitan Toronto Condominium Corp. No. 596*, [2004] O.J. No. 5758, 31 R.P.R. (4th) 273 (Ont. S.C.J.).
5. (CAN) S.C. 2000, c. 5.
6. See *Halsbury's Laws of Canada, Access to Information and Privacy.*
7. See Chapter II ("Creation of Condominiums").
8. (ON) *Condominium Act, 1998*, S.O. 1998, c. 19, s. 55(4); *McKay v. Waterloo North Condominium Corp. No. 23*, [1992] O.J. No. 2435, 11 O.R. (3d) 341 (Ont. Gen. Div.).
9. *Rohoman v. York Condominium Corp. No. 141*, [2000] O.J. No. 2356 (Ont. S.C.J.). It appears that the right to access the record of owners' names and their respective addresses for service generally trumps privacy rights, given the political environment inherent in the condominium/strata plan concept. The finding of the American court in *Hidden Harbour Estates, Inc. v. Norman*, 309 So.2d 180 (Fla. 4th DCA 1975) that condominium unit owners "comprise a little democratic subsociety" is pertinent in this regard.

(c) Failure to Provide Access

▼HCD-39▼ Defence against enforcement proceedings. An owner who is not provided with a copy of a requested by-law or rule of the corporation is entitled to a statutory defence against any claim of the corporation that the owner contravened the by-law or rule on the basis that the owner had no knowledge of the by-law or rule.[1] If a corporation is late in providing an owner with access to records to which he or she is entitled, courts will consider whether the delay was intentional or deliberate in deciding whether the corporation breached the statute.[2]

Penalty for non-compliance. In Ontario, the corporation is subject to a statutory penalty payable to a unit owner who, without reasonable excuse, has not been permitted to examine or obtain a copy of a requested record.[3]

However, the owner must seek this redress in the forum mandated by the legislation.[4]

Order for production of records. In Ontario, if an owner has not been permitted to examine or obtain a copy of a requested record without reasonable excuse, the corporation may be ordered to produce the record for examination.[5] However, it is unclear whether the corporation must produce the record to the owner or whether the corporation must produce the record for the court to allow for the determination of whether the statute has been breached. Before an order for production of the record is made, there must be a hearing on the merits by way of trial to determine whether the corporation had a reasonable or lawful excuse for withholding production.[6]

Notes

1. (BC) *Strata Property Act*, S.B.C. 1998, c. 43, s. 120; *Dimitrov v. Summit Square Strata Corp.*, [2006] B.C.J. No. 1532, 2006 BCSC 967 (B.C.S.C.).
2. *Laidis v. MTCC No. 727*, [2005] O.J. No. 726, 140 A.C.W.S. (3d) 1058 (Ont. S.C.J.).
3. (ON) *Condominium Act, 1998*, S.O. 1998, c. 19, s. 55(8).
4. *Metropolitan Toronto Condominium Corp. 551 v. Adam*, [2006] O.J. No. 4836, 153 A.C.W.S. (3d) 296 (Ont. S.C.J.).
5. (ON) *Condominium Act, 1998*, S.O. 1998, c. 19, s. 55(10).
6. *Sauve v. Paglione*, [2006] O.J. No. 3523 (Ont. S.C.J.).

IV. The Board of Directors

1. **General Duty** HCD-40

2. **Number, Term, Election, Qualification and Removal** HCD-41

3. **Conduct of Business** HCD-42

4. **Standard of Care** HCD-43

5. **Disclosure of Interest** HCD-44

6. **Financial Matters** HCD-45

---

1. General Duty

▼HCD-40▼ Duty to manage affairs of corporation. The corporation board of directors or strata council is responsible for managing the affairs of the corporation.[1] This duty includes the duty to ensure that the corporation's employees and directors are not being harassed in the course of their duties.[2] In some jurisdictions, the board must hold meetings, perform functions, elect officers, and carry out duties as provided in the declaration or by-laws.[3]

Delegation and officers. In some jurisdictions, the board or council may delegate its duty to manage the affairs of the corporation to agents or others.[4] In some jurisdictions, the corporation must have certain officers. In Alberta, British Columbia and Saskatchewan, the board must designate from its members a president, vice-president, secretary and treasurer, and these officers must fulfill the duties set out in the legislation.[5] In New Brunswick and Ontario, subject to the by-laws, the directors must elect a president from among themselves, must appoint or elect a secretary, and may appoint or elect vice-presidents or other officers.[6]

Notes

1. (AB) *Condominium Property Act*, R.S.A. 2000, c. C-22, s. 28(7)
   (BC) *Strata Property Act*, S.B.C. 1998, c. 43, s. 26
   (MB) *Condominium Act*, C.C.S.M. c. C170, s. 11(1)
   (NB) *Condominium Property Act*, S.N.B. 2009, c. C-16.05, s. 27(1)

(NL) *Condominium Act, 2009*, S.N.L. 2009, c. C-29.1, s. 18(6) (not yet in force)
(NS) *Condominium Act*, R.S.N.S. 1989, c. 85, s. 15(1)
(ON) *Condominium Act, 1998*, S.O. 1998, c. 19, s. 27(1)
(PE) *Condominium Act*, R.S.P.E.I. 1988, c. C-16, s. 10(4)
(SK) *Condominium Property Act, 1993*, S.S. 1993, c. C-26.1, s. 39(1)
(NT) *Condominium Act*, R.S.N.W.T. 1988, c. C-15, s. 16(1)
(NU) *Condominium Act*, R.S.N.W.T. (Nu.) 1988, c. C-15, s. 16(1)
(YT) *Condominium Act*, R.S.Y. 2002, c. 36, s. 11(1).

2. *Metropolitan Toronto Condominium Corp. No. 932 v. Lahrkamp*, [2008] O.J. No. 3885 (S.C.J.).

3. (MB) *Condominium Act*, C.C.S.M. c. C170, s. 11(2)
(PE) *Condominium Act*, R.S.P.E.I. 1988, c. C-16, s. 10(10)
(NT) *Condominium Act*, R.S.N.W.T. 1988, c. C-15, s. 16(2)
(NU) *Condominium Act*, R.S.N.W.T. (Nu.) 1988, c. C-15, s. 16(2)
(YT) *Condominium Act*, R.S.Y. 2002, c. 36, s. 11(2).

4. (AB) *Condominium Property Act*, R.S.A. 2000, c. C-22, App. 1, s. 16(2)-(3), App. 2, s. 10(b)-(c)
(BC) *Strata Property Act*, S.B.C. 1998, c. 43, Schedule of Standard Bylaws, s. 20
(NL) *Condominium Act, 2009*, S.N.L. 2009, c. C-29.1, s. 18(6) (not yet in force)
(NS) *Condominium Act*, R.S.N.S. 1989, c. 85, s. 16
(QC) *Civil Code of Québec*, L.R.Q. c. C-1991, art. 1085
(SK) Condominium Property Regulations, 2001, R.R.S. c. C-26.1, Reg. 2, App., Part II, Bylaws, ss. 18(a)-(b).

5. (AB) *Condominium Property Act*, R.S.A. 2000, c. C-22, App. 1, s. 11(1)-(3)
(BC) *Strata Property Act*, S.B.C. 1998, c. 43, Schedule of Standard Bylaws, s. 13(1)-(4)
(SK) Condominium Property Regulations, 2001, R.R.S. c. C-26.1, Reg. 2, App., Part II, Bylaws, ss. 12(1)-(4), 17(2)-(3).

6. (NB) *Condominium Property Act*, S.N.B. 2009, c. C-16.05, s. 28(1)-(2)
(ON) *Condominium Act, 1998*, S.O. 1998, c. 19, s. 36(1)-(2).

---

2. Number, Term, Election, Qualification and Removal

▼HCD-41▼ Provided by declaration or by-law or provided by act. In some jurisdictions, the Act specifies that the number, term, nomination, election, qualification, compensation and removal of the board of directors are provided for in the declaration or by-laws.[1] In other jurisdictions, the Act provides requirements regarding these matters and permits the declaration and by-laws to amend the requirements. The following describes the requirements regarding the number, term, election, qualification and removal of the board where these requirements are provided by the Act.

Number. In several jurisdictions, the board must consist of at least three persons or such greater number as the declaration or by-laws provide.[2] In Alberta, British Columbia and Saskatchewan, subject to certain exceptions, the board or council must consist of between three and seven persons.[3]

Term. In several jurisdictions, the term of board members is three years or such lesser period as the declaration or by-laws provide, but board members may continue to act until their successors are elected and may be re-elected.[4] In Alberta and Saskatchewan, the provisions regarding the term of board members are more complex.[5] In British Columbia, the term of council members ends at the end of the annual general meeting at which the new council is elected, but a council member is eligible for re-election.[6]

Election. In British Columbia, the eligible voters who are present in person or by proxy must elect the council.[7] In New Brunswick, Newfoundland and Labrador and Ontario, the owners must elect the board.[8] In Ontario, a person may not be elected as a director unless he or she consents.[9] In Alberta and Saskatchewan, at an election of board members, each person entitled to vote may vote for the same number of nominees as there are board vacancies.[10] In several jurisdictions, on the registration required for an amalgamated condominium, the directors of the amalgamating corporations are the first directors of the amalgamated corporation and hold office until the owners elect their successors at a meeting called and held by the first directors within the required period of time.[11]

Qualification. In several jurisdictions, directors must meet minimum age requirements.[12] In some jurisdictions, directors must also meet requirements regarding unit ownership,[13] solvency,[14] payment of contributions,[15] mental capacity[16] and the absence of convictions for certain offences.[17] Directors who initially meet qualification requirements cease to be directors if requirements of solvency, payment of contributions, mental capacity, absence of convictions for certain offences and presence at meetings cease to be met.[18]

Removal. In several jurisdictions, directors or council members may be removed from office by a specified percentage of votes cast in favour of removal at a meeting of owners.[19] In Alberta and Saskatchewan, a board member may be removed at a general meeting of owners, except where the board consists of less than three individuals.[20] Issues of removal are internal matters that should be resolved at owner meetings and do not merit court intervention.[21]

Notes

1. (BC) *Strata Property Act*, S.B.C. 1998, c. 43, s. 29(1) with respect to number

   (MB) *Condominium Act*, C.C.S.M. c. C170, s. 11(1)

   (PE) *Condominium Act,* R.S.P.E.I. 1988, c. C-16, s. 10(10)

   (QC) *Civil Code of Québec*, L.R.Q. c. C-1991, art. 1084

   (NT) *Condominium Act*, R.S.N.W.T. 1988, c. C-15, s. 16(1)

   (NU) *Condominium Act*, R.S.N.W.T. (Nu.) 1988, c. C-15, s. 16(1)

   (YT) *Condominium Act*, R.S.Y. 2002, c. 36, s. 11(1).

2. (NB) *Condominium Property Act*, S.N.B. 2009, c. C-16.05, s. 27(1)

   (NL) *Condominium Act, 2009*, S.N.L. 2009, c. C-29.1, s. 27(1) (not yet in force)

   (NS) *Condominium Act*, R.S.N.S. 1989, c. 85, s. 15(1)

   (ON) *Condominium Act, 1998*, S.O. 1998, c. 19, ss. 27(2)-(3), 42(4)

   (PE) *Condominium Act,* R.S.P.E.I. 1988, c. C-16, s. 10(4).

3. (AB) *Condominium Property Act*, R.S.A. 2000, c. C-22, App. 1, s. 4(1)-(2)

   (BC) *Strata Property Act*, S.B.C. 1998, c. 43, Schedule of Standard Bylaws, s. 9(1)-(2)

   (SK) Condominium Property Regulations, 2001, R.R.S. c. C-26.1, Reg. 2, App., Part II, Bylaws, ss. 5(1)-(2).

4. (NB) *Condominium Property Act*, S.N.B. 2009, c. C-16.05, s. 27(8)-(10)

   (NL) *Condominium Act, 2009*, S.N.L. 2009, c. C-29.1, s. 27(4) (not yet in force)

   (NS) *Condominium Act*, R.S.N.S. 1989, c. 85, s. 15(2)

   (ON) *Condominium Act, 1998*, S.O. 1998, c. 19, s. 31(1)-(2)

   (PE) *Condominium Act,* R.S.P.E.I. 1988, c. C-16, s. 10(5).

5. (AB) *Condominium Property Act*, R.S.A. 2000, c. C-22, App. 1, s. 7(1)-(3); (SK) Condominium Property Regulations, 2001, R.R.S. c. C-26.1, Reg. 2, App., Part II, Bylaws, s. 8(1)-(3).
6. (BC) *Strata Property Act*, S.B.C. 1998, c. 43, s. 25, Schedule of Standard Bylaws, s. 10.
7. (BC) *Strata Property Act*, S.B.C. 1998, c. 43, s. 25. See ss. 53-58 for requirements as to eligible voters.
8. (NB) *Condominium Property Act*, S.N.B. 2009, c. C-16.05, s. 27(4)

   (NL) *Condominium Act, 2009*, S.N.L. 2009, c. C-29.1, s. 27(1)

   (ON) *Condominium Act, 1998*, S.O. 1998, c. 19, s. 28(1).

9. (ON) *Condominium Act, 1998*, S.O. 1998, c. 19, s. 30.
10. (AB) *Condominium Property Act*, R.S.A. 2000, c. C-22, App. 1, s. 6; (SK) Condominium Property Regulations, 2001, R.R.S. c. C-26.1, Reg. 2, App., Part II, Bylaws, s. 7.
11. (AB) Condominium Property Regulation, Alta. Reg. 168/2000, ss. 52(1)-(2), 54

(NB) *Condominium Property Act*, S.N.B. 2009, c. C-16.05, s. 14(1)(g), 14(3)

(NL) *Condominium Act, 2009*, S.N.L. 2009, c. C-29.1, s. 67(1)(f), (4) (not yet in force)

(ON) *Condominium Act, 1998*, S.O. 1998, c. 19, s. 121(1)(e), (3)

(SK) *Condominium Property Act, 1993*, S.S. 1993, c. C-26.1, s. 15(7)

(NT) *Condominium Act*, R.S.N.W.T. 1988, c. C-15, s. 6.2(7)(h).

12. (AB) *Condominium Property Act*, R.S.A. 2000, c. C-22, App. 1, s. 4(3)

    (NB) *Condominium Property Act*, S.N.B. 2009, c. C-16.05, s. 29(1)

    (NL) *Condominium Act, 2009*, S.N.L. 2009, c. C-29.1, s. 28(1)(a) (not yet in force)

    (NS) *Condominium Act*, R.S.N.S. 1989, c. 85, s. 15A(1)(a)

    (ON) *Condominium Act, 1998*, S.O. 1998, c. 19, s. 29(1)(a)

    (SK) Condominium Property Regulations, 2001, R.R.S. c. C-26.1, Reg. 2, App., Part II, Bylaws, s. 5(3).

13. (AB) *Condominium Property Act*, R.S.A. 2000, c. C-22, s. 28(10), App. 1, s. 5(1)-(2)(a), App. 2, s. 4

    (BC) *Strata Property Act*, S.B.C. 1998, c. 43, s. 28(1)

    (NB) *Condominium Property Act*, S.N.B. 2009, c. C-16.05, s. 29(1)-(2)

    (NL) *Condominium Act, 2009*, S.N.L. 2009, c. C-29.1, s. 28(1)(b) (not yet in force)

    (NS) *Condominium Act*, R.S.N.S. 1989, c. 85, s. 15A(1)(b)

    (SK) Condominium Property Regulations, 2001, R.R.S. c. C-26.1, Reg. 2, App., Part II, Bylaws, s. 6(1).

14. (ON) *Condominium Act, 1998*, S.O. 1998, c. 19, s. 29(1)(b); (SK) Condominium Property Regulations, 2001, R.R.S. c. C-26.1, Reg. 2, App., Part II, Bylaws, s. 6(3)(a).

15. (AB) *Condominium Property Act*, R.S.A. 2000, c. C-22, App. 1, s. 5(2)(b); (SK) Condominium Property Regulations, 2001, R.R.S. c. C-26.1, Reg. 2, App., Part II, Bylaws, s. 6(2).

16. (ON) *Condominium Act, 1998*, S.O. 1998, c. 19, s. 29(1)(c); (SK) Condominium Property Regulations, 2001, R.R.S. c. C-26.1, Reg. 2, App., Part II, Bylaws, s. 6(3)(b).

17. (SK) Condominium Property Regulations, 2001, R.R.S. c. C-26.1, Reg. 2, App., Part II, Bylaws, s. 6(3)(c).

18. (AB) *Condominium Property Act*, R.S.A. 2000, c. C-22, App. 1, s. 9

    (ON) *Condominium Act, 1998*, S.O. 1998, c. 19, s. 29(2)

    (QC) *Civil Code of Québec*, L.R.Q. c. C-1991, art. 1086

    (SK) Condominium Property Regulations, 2001, R.R.S. c. C-26.1, Reg. 2, App., Part II, Bylaws, s. 10.

19. (BC) *Strata Property Act*, S.B.C. 1998, c. 43, Schedule of Standard Bylaws, s. 11

    (NB) *Condominium Property Act*, S.N.B. 2009, c. C-16.05, s. 27(13)

    (NL) *Condominium Act, 2009*, S.N.L. 2009, c. C-29.1, s. 30(1) (not yet in force)

    (NS) *Condominium Act*, R.S.N.S. 1989, c. 85, s. 15B(1)

    (ON) *Condominium Act, 1998*, S.O. 1998, c. 19, ss. 33(1), 51(8)

    (PE) *Condominium Act,* R.S.P.E.I. 1988, c. C-16, s. 10(7).

20. (AB) *Condominium Property Act*, R.S.A. 2000, c. C-22, App. 1, s. 8, App. 2, s. 5; (SK) Condominium Property Regulations, 2001, R.R.S. c. C-26.1, Reg. 2, App., Part II, Bylaws, s. 9.
21. *Condominium Corp. No. 0111505 v. Anders*, [2005] A.J. No. 653, 2005 ABQB 401 (Alta. Q.B.).

---

3. Conduct of Business

▼HCD-42▼ Business to be transacted at meeting with quorum. A board of directors may only transact business of the corporation at a meeting of directors at which a quorum of the board is present.[1] In several jurisdictions, a quorum for the transaction of business is a majority of board members or such greater number as the declaration or by-laws may provide.[2] The "indoor management rule" has no application to condominium corporations; a single board member cannot bind the corporation, and all board decisions must be taken at board meetings where a quorum has been established.[3]

Meetings. In some jurisdictions, the Act provides that the board must hold meetings as provided in the declaration or by-laws.[4] In Alberta, subject to an exception, all board meetings must be held within the municipality in which the units are located.[5] In Alberta and Saskatchewan, the board must meet to conduct its business at the call of the president and when a board member gives other members seven days' notice of a proposed meeting together with the reason for the meeting; all matters at board meetings are determined by majority vote; the chair may cast an additional vote in the event of a tie vote; a written board resolution signed by all board members has the same effect as a resolution passed at a board meeting; and all board meetings must be conducted according to the board's rules of procedure.[6] In British Columbia, there are detailed provisions regarding waiver of meetings, notice of meetings, agenda and resolutions at meetings, electronic attendance and voting.[7] In Ontario, in addition to the meetings of directors required by the by-laws, a quorum of directors may call a meeting at any time for the transaction of business.[8] The person calling the meeting must give every director 10 days' written notice of the meeting by delivering the prescribed notice in the prescribed manner.[9] In certain situations, meetings may be conducted by teleconference.[10]

Vacancy. In New Brunswick and Nova Scotia, where a vacancy arises on the board, the board must elect a new member.[11] In other jurisdictions, the board may appoint an individual to fill the office. In Alberta, British Columbia and Prince Edward Island, the replacement is appointed for the remainder of the term,[12] whereas in Newfoundland and Labrador and Saskatchewan, the replacement is appointed until the next meeting or annual meeting.[13] In Ontario, requirements differ depending on whether a quorum of the board remains in office. If a quorum remains, the remaining directors may exercise all board powers, and the majority of remaining members may appoint a replacement until the next annual general meeting.[14] If a quorum does not remain, the remaining directors must call and hold an owner meeting within 30 days of losing the quorum to fill all board vacancies.[15]

Notes

1. (BC) *Strata Property Act*, S.B.C. 1998, c. 43, s. 48(1); (ON) *Condominium Act, 1998*, S.O. 1998, c. 19, s. 32(1).
2. (AB) *Condominium Property Act*, R.S.A. 2000, c. C-22, App. 1, s. 12(2)

   (BC) *Strata Property Act*, S.B.C. 1998, c. 43, Schedule of Standard Bylaws, s. 16(1)

   (NB) *Condominium Property Act*, S.N.B. 2009, c. C-16.05, s. 27(3)

   (NS) *Condominium Act*, R.S.N.S. 1989, c. 85, s. 15(4)

   (ON) *Condominium Act, 1998*, S.O. 1998, c. 19, s. 32(2)

   (PE) *Condominium Act,* R.S.P.E.I. 1988, c. C-16, s. 10(8)

   (SK) Condominium Property Regulations, 2001, R.R.S. c. C-26.1, Reg. 2, App., Part II, Bylaws, s. 13(2).
3. *Rogers Cable Communications Inc. v. Carleton Condominium Corp. No. 53*, [2005] O.J. No. 921, 137 A.C.W.S. (3d) 1031 (Ont. S.C.J.).
4. (MB) *Condominium Act*, C.C.S.M. c. C170, s. 11(2)

   (PE) *Condominium Act,* R.S.P.E.I. 1988, c. C-16, s. 10(10)

   (NT) *Condominium Act*, R.S.N.W.T. 1988, c. C-15, s. 16(2)

   (NU) *Condominium Act*, R.S.N.W.T. (Nu.) 1988, c. C-15, s. 16(2)

   (YT) *Condominium Act*, R.S.Y. 2002, c. 36, s. 11(2).
5. (AB) *Condominium Property Act*, R.S.A. 2000, c. C-22, s. 31.
6. (AB) *Condominium Property Act*, R.S.A. 2000, c. C-22, App. 1, ss. 12(1), 13, 16(1), 18; (SK) Condominium Property Regulations, 2001, R.R.S. c. C-26.1, Reg. 2, App., Part II, Bylaws, ss. 13(1), 14(1), 17(1)(a)-(b), 19.
7. (BC) *Strata Property Act*, S.B.C. 1998, c. 43, ss. 40-52; (BC) *Strata Property Act*, S.B.C. 1998, c. 43, Schedule of Standard Bylaws, ss. 14, 17-18.
8. (ON) *Condominium Act, 1998*, S.O. 1998, c. 19, s. 35(1).
9. (ON) *Condominium Act, 1998*, S.O. 1998, c. 19, s. 35(2)-(3).
10. (ON) *Condominium Act, 1998*, S.O. 1998, c. 19, s. 35(5).
11. (NB) *Condominium Property Act*, S.N.B. 2009, c. C-16.05, s. 27(11); (NS) *Condominium Act*, R.S.N.S. 1989, c. 85, s. 15(3).
12. (AB) *Condominium Property Act*, R.S.A. 2000, c. C-22, App. 1, s. 10

(BC) *Strata Property Act*, S.B.C. 1998, c. 43, Schedule of Standard Bylaws, s. 12(1)

(PE) *Condominium Act,* R.S.P.E.I. 1988, c. C-16, s. 10(6).

13. (NL) *Condominium Act, 2009*, S.N.L. 2009, c. C-29.1, s. 27(5) (not yet in force); (SK) Condominium Property Regulations, 2001, R.R.S. c. C-26.1, Reg. 2, App., Part II, Bylaws, s. 11.
14. (ON) *Condominium Act, 1998*, S.O. 1998, c. 19, s. 34(1)-(2).
15. (ON) *Condominium Act, 1998*, S.O. 1998, c. 19, s. 34(4).

---

4. Standard of Care

▼HCD-43▼ General duties. In exercising the powers and discharging the duties of office, every director and officer must act honestly and in good faith and must exercise the care, diligence and skill that a reasonably prudent person would exercise in comparable circumstances.[1] In accordance with the business judgment rule, deference should be accorded to business decisions of directors taken in good faith and in the performance of the functions they were elected to perform.[2]

Specific duties. Some jurisdictions provide more detailed duties for board members. In some jurisdictions, the Act provides that the board must perform functions and carry out duties as provided in the declaration or bylaws.[3] In Alberta and Saskatchewan, the board must:[4]

- keep proper books of account with respect to all moneys received and expended by the board and the matters with respect to which the receipts and expenditures relate
- for each annual general meeting, prepare financial statements with respect to all moneys of the corporation, including the moneys received and expended by the corporation
- maintain financial records of all assets, liabilities and equity of the corporation
- submit to the annual general meeting an annual report that consists of financial statements and any other information determined by the board or required by a resolution passed at a general meeting
- keep minutes of its proceedings and proceedings at general meetings and
- make the books of account available for inspection at all reasonable times on the application of an owner, mortgagee or person authorized in writing

Saskatchewan's regulation also provides further specific duties of the board.[5]

Validity of acts. The acts of a board member done in good faith are valid notwithstanding a defect in the election, appointment, qualification or continuance in office of the board or council member.[6] In some jurisdictions, a director is not liable for a breach of the duty of good faith if the breach arose because the director relied in good faith on financial statements, reports or opinions prepared by certain qualified individuals.[7] In British Columbia, a council member who acts honestly and in good faith is not personally liable because of anything done or omitted in the exercise or intended exercise of any power or the performance or intended performance of any duty of the council.[8]

Notes

1. (AB) *Condominium Property Act*, R.S.A. 2000, c. C-22, s. 28(2), although that section only refers to the duty of good faith

   (BC) *Strata Property Act*, S.B.C. 1998, c. 43, ss. 6, 31

   (NB) *Condominium Property Act*, S.N.B. 2009, c. C-16.05, s. 30(1)

   (NL) *Condominium Act, 2009*, S.N.L. 2009, c. C-29.1, s. 32(1) (not yet in force)

   (NS) *Condominium Act*, R.S.N.S. 1989, c. 85, s. 15D(1)

   (ON) *Condominium Act, 1998*, S.O. 1998, c. 19, s. 37(1)

   (SK) Condominium Property Regulations, 2001, R.R.S. c. C-26.1, Reg. 2, App., Part II, Bylaws, s. 17(4).
2. *BCE Inc. v. 1976 Debentureholders*, [2008] S.C.J. No. 37, 2008 SCC 69 (S.C.C.). See also *York Condominium Corp. No. 382 v. Dvorchik*, [1997] O.J. No. 378, 12 R.P.R. (3d) 148 (Ont. C.A.); *Muskoka Condominium Corp. No. 39 v. Kreutzweiser*, [2010] O.J. No. 1720, 2010 ONSC 2463 (Ont. S.C.J.); *Metropolitan Toronto Condominium Corp. No. 985 v. Vanduzer*, [2010] O.J. No. 571, 2010 ONSC 900 (Ont. S.C.J.).
3. (MB) *Condominium Act*, C.C.S.M. c. C170, s. 11(2)

   (PE) *Condominium Act,* R.S.P.E.I. 1988, c. C-16, s. 10(10)

   (NT) *Condominium Act*, R.S.N.W.T. 1988, c. C-15, s. 16(2)

   (NU) *Condominium Act*, R.S.N.W.T. (Nu.) 1988, c. C-15, s. 16(2)

   (YT) *Condominium Act*, R.S.Y. 2002, c. 36, s. 11(2).
4. (AB) *Condominium Property Act*, R.S.A. 2000, c. C-22, App. 1, s. 17, App. 2, s. 11; (SK) *Condominium Property Act, 1993*, S.S. 1993, c. C-26.1, s. 39(2).
5. (SK) Condominium Property Regulations, 2001, R.R.S. c. C-26.1, Reg. 2, App., Part II, Bylaws, s. 17(1).
6. (AB) *Condominium Property Act*, R.S.A. 2000, c. C-22, s. 28(9)

   (BC) *Strata Property Act*, S.B.C. 1998, c. 43, s. 30(1)

   (MB) *Condominium Act*, C.C.S.M. c. C170, s. 11(3)

   (NB) *Condominium Property Act*, S.N.B. 2009, c. C-16.05, s. 29(3)

(NL) *Condominium Act, 2009*, S.N.L. 2009, c. C-29.1, s. 31 (not yet in force)
(NS) *Condominium Act*, R.S.N.S. 1989, c. 85, ss. 15(5), 15C
(ON) *Condominium Act, 1998*, S.O. 1998, c. 19, s. 37(2)
(PE) *Condominium Act*, R.S.P.E.I. 1988, c. C-16, s. 10(9)
(SK) *Condominium Property Act, 1993*, S.S. 1993, c. C-26.1, s. 37(2)
(NT) *Condominium Act*, R.S.N.W.T. 1988, c. C-15, s. 16(3)
(NU) *Condominium Act*, R.S.N.W.T. (Nu.) 1988, c. C-15, s. 16(3)
(YT) *Condominium Act*, R.S.Y. 2002, c. 36, s. 11(3).

7. (NB) *Condominium Property Act*, S.N.B. 2009, c. C-16.05, s. 30(2)
(NL) *Condominium Act, 2009*, S.N.L. 2009, c. C-29.1, s. 32(2) (not yet in force)
(NS) *Condominium Act*, R.S.N.S. 1989, c. 85, s. 15D(2)
(ON) *Condominium Act, 1998*, S.O. 1998, c. 19, s. 37(3).

8. (BC) *Strata Property Act*, S.B.C. 1998, c. 43, Schedule of Standard Bylaws, s. 22(1).

---

5. Disclosure of Interest

▼HCD-44▼ Duty to disclose direct or indirect interest. A director who has a direct or indirect interest in an actual or proposed contract or transaction to which the corporation is a party must disclose the nature and extent of the interest.[1] Subject to certain exceptions, such a director may not vote with respect to the contract or transaction and may not be counted in the quorum with respect to the contract or transaction.[2] The duty to disclose and the restrictions on directors voting and being counted in quorums do not apply unless both the contract and transaction and the director's interest in the contract and transaction are material.[3]

Manner of disclosure. In some jurisdictions, disclosure must be in writing.[4] In some jurisdictions, there are specific requirements regarding the content and timing of disclosure, including where the contract or transaction involves the purchase or sale of property.[5]

Effects of disclosure. In Newfoundland and Labrador and Nova Scotia, a director who complies with the requirements for disclosure and who is acting honestly and in good faith at the time a contract or transaction is entered into is not accountable to the corporation or owners for any profit or gain realized from the contract or transaction by reason only of holding the office of director, and the contract or transaction is not voidable by reason only of the director's interest in it, provided there is owner confirmation, which requires that the contract or transaction be confirmed or approved by at least two-thirds of the votes cast at an owner meeting called for that purpose and that the nature and extent of the director's interest in the contract or transaction be declared and disclosed in reasonable detail in the notice calling the meeting.[6] In New Brunswick, owner confirmation is not required to render the director not accountable for profit or gain, but is required to render the contract or transaction not voidable.[7] In Ontario and Saskatchewan, a director who complies and is acting honestly and in good faith is entitled to both effects of disclosure without owner confirmation, and a director who does not comply but is acting honestly and in good faith is entitled to both effects of disclosure with owner confirmation.[8]

Notes

1. (AB) *Condominium Property Act*, R.S.A. 2000, c. C-22, s. 28(3)(a)
   (BC) *Strata Property Act*, S.B.C. 1998, c. 43, s. 32(c)
   (NB) *Condominium Property Act*, S.N.B. 2009, c. C-16.05, s. 31(1)
   (NL) *Condominium Act, 2009*, S.N.L. 2009, c. C-29.1, s. 34(1) (not yet in force)
   (NS) *Condominium Act*, R.S.N.S. 1989, c. 85, s. 15F(1)
   (ON) *Condominium Act, 1998*, S.O. 1998, c. 19, s. 40(1); see also s. 41 for officers' duty of disclosure
   (SK) *Condominium Property Act, 1993*, S.S. 1993, c. C-26.1, s. 48(1)(a)
   (NT) *Condominium Act*, R.S.N.W.T. 1988, c. C-15, s. 16(4)(a).
2. (AB) *Condominium Property Act*, R.S.A. 2000, c. C-22, s. 28(3)(b)-(c), (4)
   (BC) *Strata Property Act*, S.B.C. 1998, c. 43, s. 32(d)
   (NB) *Condominium Property Act*, S.N.B. 2009, c. C-16.05, s. 31(6)
   (NL) *Condominium Act, 2009*, S.N.L. 2009, c. C-29.1, s. 34(7) (not yet in force)
   (NS) *Condominium Act*, R.S.N.S. 1989, c. 85, s. 15F(7)
   (ON) *Condominium Act, 1998*, S.O. 1998, c. 19, s. 40(6)
   (SK) *Condominium Property Act, 1993*, S.S. 1993, c. C-26.1, s. 48(1)(b)-(c), (2)
   (NT) *Condominium Act*, R.S.N.W.T. 1988, c. C-15, s. 16(4)(b)-(c), (5).
3. (AB) *Condominium Property Act*, R.S.A. 2000, c. C-22, s. 28(4)
   (NB) *Condominium Property Act*, S.N.B. 2009, c. C-16.05, s. 31(1)
   (NL) *Condominium Act, 2009*, S.N.L. 2009, c. C-29.1, s. 34(3) (not yet in force)
   (NS) *Condominium Act*, R.S.N.S. 1989, c. 85, s. 15F(3)
   (ON) *Condominium Act, 1998*, S.O. 1998, c. 19, s. 40(2)
   (SK) *Condominium Property Act, 1993*, S.S. 1993, c. C-26.1, s. 48(2)
   (NT) *Condominium Act*, R.S.N.W.T. 1988, c. C-15, ss. 16(6).
4. (NL) *Condominium Act, 2009*, S.N.L. 2009, c. C-29.1, s. 34(1) (not yet in force)
   (NS) *Condominium Act*, R.S.N.S. 1989, c. 85, s. 15F(1)
   (ON) *Condominium Act, 1998*, S.O. 1998, c. 19, s. 40(1).
5. (NB) *Condominium Property Act*, S.N.B. 2009, c. C-16.05, s. 31(2)-(5)

(NL) *Condominium Act, 2009*, S.N.L. 2009, c. C-29.1, s. 34(2), (4)-(6) (not yet in force)

(NS) *Condominium Act*, R.S.N.S. 1989, c. 85, s. 15F(2), (4)-(6)

(ON) *Condominium Act, 1998*, S.O. 1998, c. 19, s. 40(3)-(5)

(SK) *Condominium Property Act, 1993*, S.S. 1993, c. C-26.1, ss. 49-50, 53.

6. (NL) *Condominium Act, 2009*, S.N.L. 2009, c. C-29.1, s. 34(8) (not yet in force); (NS) *Condominium Act*, R.S.N.S. 1989, c. 85, s. 15F(8)
7. (NB) *Condominium Property Act*, S.N.B. 2009, c. C-16.05, s. 31(7)-(8).
8. (ON) *Condominium Act, 1998*, S.O. 1998, c. 19, s. 40(7)-(8)

   (SK) *Condominium Property Act, 1993*, S.S. 1993, c. C-26.1, ss. 51-52.

---

6. Financial Matters

▼HCD-45▼ Remuneration, indemnification and insurance. In several jurisdictions, there are provisions regarding remuneration of the board of the directors. In some jurisdictions, there are also provisions regarding optional indemnification and mandatory insurance.

Remuneration. In several jurisdictions, the Act specifies that the board's compensation is provided for in the declaration or by-laws.[1] Even where the board is required to pass a by-law for remuneration of directors, the board need not pass a by-law for remuneration of officers or agents.[2] In British Columbia, any remuneration paid to a council member must be approved in advance in the budget, in the by-laws and by a resolution passed by a 3/4 vote at an annual or special general meeting.[3] In Ontario, a by-law relating to remuneration must fix the remuneration and the period, not exceeding three years, for which it is to be paid.[4] Directors are entitled to be reimbursed for reasonable costs in connection with work performed for the corporation based on restitutionary principles, even where there was no contract in connection with the costs and work.[5]

Indemnification. In some jurisdictions, a corporation's by-laws may provide that every director and officer and that person's heirs, executors, administrators, estate trustees and other legal personal representatives may be indemnified and saved harmless by the corporation from and against: liability, costs, charges and expenses that the director or officer sustains or incurs in respect of an action, suit or proceeding proposed or commenced against that person respecting anything done, omitted or permitted by the person in respect of the execution of the duties of office; and all other costs, charges and expenses the person sustains or incurs in respect of the condominium's affairs.[6] In Ontario, indemnification is not permitted in respect of an action, suit or other proceeding as a result of which the person is adjudged to have breached the duty to act honestly and in good faith.[7]

Insurance. In Ontario, if insurance is reasonably available, a corporation must purchase and maintain insurance for the benefit of a director or officer except insurance against a liability, cost, charge or expense of the director or officer incurred as a result of a breach of the duty to act honestly and in good faith.[8] An insurance policy that is arranged after a director's time on the board cannot be extended to provide coverage for claims where, at the effective date of the policy, the director knew of a problem and could reasonably foresee that the problem might result in a claim.[9]

Notes

1. (MB) *Condominium Act*, C.C.S.M. c. C170, s. 11(1)
   (NL) *Condominium Act, 2009*, S.N.L. 2009, c. C-29.1, s. 27(8) (not yet in force)
   (ON) *Condominium Act, 1998*, S.O. 1998, c. 19, s. 56(1)
   (PE) *Condominium Act*, R.S.P.E.I. 1988, c. C-16, s. 10(10)
   (QC) *Civil Code of Québec*, L.R.Q. c. C-1991, art. 1084
   (SK) *Condominium Property Act, 1993*, S.S. 1993, c. C-26.1, s. 47(1)
   (NT) *Condominium Act*, R.S.N.W.T. 1988, c. C-15, s. 16(1)
   (NU) *Condominium Act*, R.S.N.W.T. (Nu.) 1988, c. C-15, s. 16(1)
   (YT) *Condominium Act*, R.S.Y. 2002, c. 36, s. 11(1).
2. *Smithers v. York Condominium Corp. No. 60*, [2003] O.J. No. 851, 169 O.A.C. 178 (Ont. Div. Ct.).
3. (BC) *Strata Property Act*, S.B.C. 1998, c. 43, s. 34.
4. (ON) *Condominium Act, 1998*, S.O. 1998, c. 19, s. 56(2).
5. *Extra Gift Exchange Inc. v. Chung*, [2006] B.C.J. No. 697, 2006 BCSC 526 (B.C.S.C.).
6. (NB) *Condominium Property Act*, S.N.B. 2009, c. C-16.05, s. 30(3)
   (NL) *Condominium Act, 2009*, S.N.L. 2009, c. C-29.1, s. 33 (not yet in force)
   (NS) *Condominium Act*, R.S.N.S. 1989, c. 85, s. 15E
   (ON) *Condominium Act, 1998*, S.O. 1998, c. 19, s. 38(1).
7. (ON) *Condominium Act, 1998*, S.O. 1998, c. 19, s. 38(2).
8. (ON) *Condominium Act, 1998*, S.O. 1998, c. 19, s. 39.
9. *Boland v. Allianz Insurance Co. of Canada*, [2006] O.J. No. 2002, [2006] O.T.C. 460 (Ont. S.C.J.).

V. Transfer of Control and Sale and Lease of Units

1. Transfer of Control by Owner/Declarant

(1) First Board of Directors or Council HCD-46
(2) The Owner-Developer and the Corporation HCD-47
(3) Election of New Board of Directors and Turn-over of Records and Other Items HCD-48

2. Sale of Units

(1) Disclosure Requirements for Condominium Corporation HCD-50
(2) Access to Information and Records Regarding the Corporation HCD-53
(3) Implied Covenants and Conditions and Statutory Duties HCD-54
(4) Interim Occupancy HCD-55
(5) Money Held in Trust HCD-56
(6) Interest HCD-57

3. Lease of Units

(1) Notification by Owner.. HCD-58
(2) Deemed Covenant or Conditions HCD-59
(3) Deposits HCD-60

---

1. Transfer of Control by Owner/Declarant

(1) First Board of Directors or Council HCD-46
(2) The Owner-Developer and the Corporation HCD-47
(3) Election of New Board of Directors and Turn-over of Records and Other Items HCD-48

---

(1) First Board of Directors or Council

▼HCD-46▼ Overview. The registration of a condominium's declaration and description creates a corporation, the members of which are the owners of the condominium units. Until the units are sold the owner developer/declarant (the "declarant") owns the units and therefore controls the condominium corporation. To transfer control from the declarant to the unit owners, a meeting must be held within a prescribed period of time at which time the unit owners elect a board of directors. Until control can be transferred to the unit owners through the election of a board of directors, Ontario and Newfoundland require the declarant to appoint a first board of directors to manage the condominium's affairs in the interim. By providing for the transfer of control from the declarant to the unit owners, condominium legislation places a number of limitations on a declarant's ability to indefinitely control the condominium corporation subsequent to the registration of the condominium plan or the declarant's ownership of a majority of units.

Appointment of first board. In Ontario, within ten days after the registration of the condominium's declaration and description, the declarant must appoint a first board of directors of the condominium corporation (the "first board").[1] In Nova Scotia and Newfoundland, a first board must be appointed where the declarant still owns a majority of the units.[2] The first board is unique in that the directors are appointed and not elected and members may therefore be removed and replaced at the declarant's discretion.[3] The first board holds office until a new board is elected at a meeting of the owners, known as a turn-over meeting.[4] The purpose of the first board is to conduct the business affairs of the condominium corporation, including enacting the corporation's by-laws and entering into various service agreements to operate the condominium, until a new board of directors is elected by the condominium owners.

Owners' meeting. In Ontario, once the first board is appointed, it must hold an owners' meeting within a prescribed period of time after the declarant has transferred ownership of a certain number of units.[5] Where legislation does not require the appointment of a first board, the declarant must hold an owners meeting within a prescribed period of time after the registration of the condominium's declaration and description or after the declarant ceases to own a majority of the condominium units.[6]

Notes

1. (ON) *Condominium Act, 1998*, S.O. 1998, c. 19, s. 42(1).
2. (NL) *Condominium Act, 2009*, S.N.L. 2009, c. C-29.1, s. 27(2) (not yet in force); (NS) *Condominium Act*, R.S.N.S. 1989, c. 85, s. 15(1A), (1B).
3. (ON) *Condominium Act, 1998*, S.O. 1998, c. 19, s. 42(2).
4. (ON) *Condominium Act, 1998*, S.O. 1998, c. 19, s. 42(3).
5. (ON) *Condominium Act, 1998*, S.O. 1998, c. 19, s. 42(6).
6. (AB) *Condominium Property Act,* R.S.A. 2000, c. C-22, s. 29(1), application to first phase: (AB) Condominium Property Regulation, Alta. Reg. 168/2000, s. 44

(BC) *Strata Property Act*, S.B.C. 1998, c. 43, s. 16
(MB) *Condominium Act*, C.C.S.M. c. C170, s. 11(4)
(PE) *Condominium Act,* R.S.P.E.I. 1988, c. C-16, s. 12(1)
(SK) *Condominium Property Act, 1993*, S.S. 1993, c. C-26.1, s. 38(1)
(NT) *Condominium Act*, R.S.N.W.T. 1988, c. C-15, s. 16.1.

---

(2) The Owner-Developer and the Corporation

▼HCD-47▼ Control of condominium/strata corporation. The owner-developer of a condominium initially controls the condominium corporation and is vested with all the rights and duties of a board of directors, as enumerated in the governing legislation. In exercising the powers and performing the duties of a board of directors, the owner-developer need not comply with by-law requirements respecting the constitution of the board or the holding or conduct of board meetings.[1] In exercising its powers and performing its duties, the owner-developer is subject to a statutory standard of care to act in the best interest of the corporation and to reasonably exercise care, diligence and skill. The owner-developer must also make reasonable efforts to pursue any remedies under warranties with respect to the construction of the condominium's common property and common assets.[2]

Before lots are conveyed. In British Columbia, before strata lots are conveyed, the owner-developer must pay the strata corporation's actual expenses, as prescribed. During this period, the owner-developer is also permitted to pass any resolution of the strata corporation that is permitted or required by legislation, including a resolution to amend the corporation's by-laws, without holding a special general meeting.[3]

After the first conveyance. In the period after the first conveyance of a strata lot to a purchaser, before the first annual general meeting, the owner-developer may be subject to directions or restrictions, as if it were a council.[4] Specifically, the owner-developer cannot enter into any contract or transaction on behalf of the strata corporation with any person who is not at arm's length from the owner-developer unless it is approved at a special general meeting.[5] The owner-developer is also required to establish a contingency reserve fund, prepare an interim budget and ensure the term of any insurance policy entered into by or on behalf of the strata corporation continues for the prescribed period of time.[6]

Notes

1. (BC) *Strata Property Act*, S.B.C. 1998, c. 43, ss. 5(1), (2) board of directors referred to as council.
2. (BC) *Strata Property Act*, S.B.C. 1998, c. 43, s. 6.
3. (BC) *Strata Property Act*, S.B.C. 1998, c. 43, ss. 7-8.
4. (BC) *Strata Property Act*, S.B.C. 1998, c. 43, s. 9.
5. (BC) *Strata Property Act*, S.B.C. 1998, c. 43, s. 10.
6. (BC) *Strata Property Act*, S.B.C. 1998, c. 43, ss. 12-15.

---

(3) Election of New Board of Directors and Turn-over of Records and Other Items

▼HCD-48▼ Turn-over meeting. The unit owners must elect a board of directors to manage the affairs of the condominium corporation.[1] In jurisdictions where a declarant appoints a first board, the first board must be replaced with individuals elected by the owners. In Ontario, within twenty-one days after the declarant ceases to be the registered owner of the majority of the condominium units, the first board must call a meeting of the unit owners to elect a new board.[2] The turn-over meeting must then be held within twenty-one days from the time it is called.[3] The agenda for the turn-over meeting may list various topics but must include an election of a new board of directors whereby the unit owners (not tenants) are entitled to elect directors. The term "new" board of directors is perhaps a misnomer. While the purpose of the turn-over meeting is to transfer control of the condominium corporation to the owners through the democratic election of a board of directors, directors who had been appointed by the declarant to the first board may run for re-election to the new board at the turn-over meeting. However, if directors who had been appointed by the declarant to the first board are elected to the new board of directors, there is an increased risk of a conflict of interest between the owner-developer and the condominium corporation.[4]

Turn-over of records. In addition to turning over control of the corporation to a new board of directors elected by the owners, the declarant is required to deliver to the corporation certain documents, plans and information deemed necessary for the operation of the condominium within a prescribed period of time. Provincial legislation enumerates certain material that must be delivered to the new board of directors during a prescribed period of time, which may include but not be limited to:

- the corporate seal
- a copy of the registered declaration, by-laws, current rules and minutes of any board meeting
- copies of all agreements entered into by the corporation or the declarant on behalf of the corporation
- copies of all insurance policies, all certificates, approvals and permits issued by local authority
- all structural, electrical, mechanical and architectural working drawings and specifications for the common property
- records of owners, mortgagees and lessees and
- all records related to the units or to the employees.[5]

Before the corporation receives the mandatory documents to be disclosed, the legislation enables the corporation to make a written request to the declarant for a copy of the documents. If a written request is received, the developer must provided the requested documents, if they are in his possession, within a prescribed period of time, at the declarant's expense.[6]

Notes

1. See Section IV.2. ("Number, Term, Election, Qualification and Removal").
2. (ON) *Condominium Act, 1998*, S.O. 1998, c. 19, s. 43(1).
3. (ON) *Condominium Act, 1998*, S.O. 1998, c. 19, s. 43(3). Procedure for electing directors differs for a phased condominium corporation: s. 152(6).
4. See Section IV.5. ("Disclosure of Interest") and Section VIII.3. ("Purchase and Sale of Units and Development of the Condominium Property").
5. (AB) *Condominium Property,* R.S.A. 2000, c. C-22, s. 46(1)

   (MB) *Condominium Act*, C.C.S.M. c. C170, s. 11(5)

   (NL) *Condominium Act, 2009*, S.N.L. 2009, c. C-29.1, s. 22(1) (not yet in force). All documents relating to a phase must be turned over for a phased condominium corporation: s. 78

   (NS) *Condominium Act*, R.S.N.S. 1989, c. 85, s. 17

   (ON) *Condominium Act, 1998*, S.O. 1998, c. 19, s. 43(4), (5), (7). For a phased condominium corporation, additional information must be turned over: s. 152(1), (2)

   (SK) *Condominium Property Act, 1993*, S.S. 1993, c. C-26.1, s. 12(1)

   (NT) *Condominium Act*, R.S.N.W.T. 1988, c. C-15, s. 12.1(1), (2).
6. (AB) *Condominium Property,* R.S.A. 2000, c. C-22, s. 46(2)

   (ON) *Condominium Act, 1998*, S.O. 1998, c. 19, s. 43(6)

   (SK) *Condominium Property Act, 1993*, S.S. 1993, c. C-26.1, s. 12(2).

2. Sale of Units

(1) Disclosure Requirements for Condominium Corporations
(a) Disclosure Statement
(i) Freehold Condominium Corporation... HCD-50
(ii) Leasehold Condominium Corporation HCD-51
(b) Material Changes to Disclosure Statements HCD-52
(2) Access to Information and Records Regarding the Corporation HCD-53
(3) Implied Covenants and Conditions and Statutory Duties HCD-54
(4) Interim Occupancy HCD-55
(5) Money Held in Trust........ HCD-56
(6) Interest HCD-57

---

(1) Disclosure Requirements for Condominium Corporations

(a) Disclosure Statement

▼HCD-49▼ Disclosure statement required. When a buyer signs the agreement of purchase and sale for a new unit, the developer must provide the buyer with prescribed information with respect to the condominium corporation which manages the affairs of the condominium property that the unit forms part of.[1] This package of documents is known in Ontario, and other jurisdictions, as a disclosure statement, the contents of which vary for freehold and leasehold condominium corporations. A disclosure statement is not required for the resale of a unit.

Rescission of agreement of purchase and sale. Once the buyer has received the disclosure statement and has accepted the agreement of purchase and sale for the new unit, legislation provides a "cooling-off" period during which time the buyer can rescind the purchase agreement without cause.[2]

Notes

1. (AB) *Condominium Property Act,* R.S.A. 2000, c. C-22, s. 12(1)
(MB) *Condominium Act*, C.C.S.M. c. C170, s. 8(1.1)
(NL) *Condominium Act, 2009*, S.N.L. 2009, c. C-29.1, s. 40(1) (not yet in force)

(ON) *Condominium Act, 1998*, S.O. 1998, c. 19, s. 72(1)
(SK) *Condominium Property Act, 1993*, S.S. 1993, c. C-26.1, s. 26(1)(g)
(NT) *Condominium Act*, R.S.N.W.T. 1988, c. C-15, s. 6.4(1).

2. See Chapter VIII. ("Compliance, Enforcement, Remedies and Dispute Resolution").
(AB) *Condominium Property*, R.S.A. 2000, c. C-22, s. 13(a)
(MB) *Condominium Act*, C.C.S.M. c. C170, s. 8(1)
(NB) *Condominium Property Act*, S.N.B. 2009, c. C-16.05, s. 52(2)
(SK) *Condominium Property Act, 1993*, S.S. 1993, c. C-26.1, s. 28(a)(iii)
(NT) Condominium Regulation, N.W.T. Reg. 098-2008, s. 4(a).

(i) Freehold Condominium Corporation

▼HCD-50▼ Contents of disclosure statement. The contents of the disclosure statement to be provided by the developer vary depending on whether the condominium property is a standard, phased, vacant land or common elements condominium.

Standard condominium. In the case of a standard condominium, the developer must provide a disclosure statement that includes, but is not limited to:

- a table of contents; the mailing address of the developer and the property
- a description of the property
- a list of amenities the developer proposes to provide
- if construction of amenities is not completed, a schedule of the proposed commencement and completion dates
- a brief description of the significant features of all agreements or proposed agreements
- a copy of the corporation's budget
- any material required by statute or regulations[1]

Phased condominium. In addition to the contents of the disclosure statement required for a standard condominium, the disclosure statement that must be provided in relation to a phased condominium must include additional information with respect to the phases. This information includes, but is not limited to the following statements:

- whether the developer intends to create one or more phases after the creation of the unit

- that the developer is not required to create a phase after the creation of the unit
- the projected year of registration of the amendments to the declaration and description required for creating each phase
- specific information, such as the number of units and location of the building for each phase the developer intends to create[2]

Vacant land condominium. In addition to the contents of the disclosure statement required for a standard condominium, the disclosure statement to be provided in relation to a vacant land condominium must include any statement that the developer has received from the municipality in response to a request, and any other prescribed information.[3]

Common elements condominium. In addition to the contents of the disclosure statement required for a standard condominium, the disclosure statement to be provided *in relation to* a common elements condominium must include a statement that the owner's common interest attaches to the owner's parcel of tied land, as described in the corporation's declaration, and that it cannot be severed from this parcel upon its sale.[4]

Notes

1. (AB) *Condominium Property Act*, R.S.A. 2000, c. C-22, s. 13

   (MB) *Condominium Act*, C.C.S.M. c. C170, s. 8(1.1)

   (NB) *Condominium Property Act,* S.N.B. 2009, c. C-16.05, s. 51(1)

   (NL) *Condominium Act, 2009*, S.N.L. 2009, c. C-29.1, ss. 41, 44 (not yet in force)

   (ON) *Condominium Act, 1998*, S.O. 1998, c. 19, s. 72(3), (4), (5), (6); (ON) General Regulation, O. Reg. 48/01, s. 17

   (SK) *Condominium Property Act, 1993*, S.S. 1993, c. C-26.1, ss. 26(1)(g), 28

   (NT) *Condominium Act*, R.S.N.W.T. 1988, c. C-15, s. 6.4(1), Condominium Regulation, N.W.T. Reg. 098-2008, s. 4.
2. (AB) *Condominium Property Act,* R.S.A. 2000, c. C-22; (AB) Condominium Property Regulation, Alta. Reg. 168/2000, ss. 35, 43

   (NL) *Condominium Act, 2009*, S.N.L. 2009, c. C-29.1, s. 75 (not yet in force)

   (NS) *Condominium Act*, R.S.N.S. 1989, c. 85; (NS) Condominium Regulations, N.S. Reg. 60/71, s. 75(2)

   (ON) *Condominium Act, 1998*, S.O. 1998, c. 19, s. 147(1), (5); (ON) General Regulation, O. Reg. 48/01, s. 55.
3. (NL) *Condominium Act, 2009*, S.N.L. 2009, c. C-29.1, s. 84 (not yet in force); (ON) *Condominium Act, 1998*, S.O. 1998, c. 19, s. 161.
4. (NL) *Condominium Act, 2009*, S.N.L. 2009, c. C-29.1, s. 72 (not yet in force)

   (ON) *Condominium Act, 1998*, S.O. 1998, c. 19, s. 143.

(ii) Leasehold Condominium Corporation

▼HCD-51▼ Contents of disclosure statement. In addition to the contents of the disclosure statement required for a standard condominium corporation, the disclosure statement to be provided in relation to a leasehold condominium includes a statement by the developer as to whether the provisions of the leasehold interests in the property are in good standing and have not been breached, and any other prescribed information.[1]

Note

1. (ON) *Condominium Act, 1998*, S.O. 1998, c. 19, s. 169.

(b) Material Changes to Disclosure Statements

▼HCD-52▼ Revised disclosure statutement or notice of material change. If there is a material change to the information contained in a disclosure statement already delivered to the purchaser of a unit, the developer must also deliver a revised disclosure statement or notice of the material change within a prescribed period of time.[1] The contents of a revised disclosure statement[2] and the definition of what constitutes a material change[3] vary by jurisdiction.

Notes

1. (ON) *Condominium Act, 1998*, S.O. 1998, c. 19, s. 74(1), (4); (NT) Condominium Act, R.S.N.W.T. 1988, c. C-15, s. 6.5(2),(4).
2. (ON) *Condominium Act, 1998*, S.O. 1998, c. 19, s. 74(3); (NT) *Condominium Act*, R.S.N.W.T. 1988, c. C-15, s. 6.5(3).
3. (ON) *Condominium Act, 1998*, S.O. 1998, c. 19, ss. 74(2), 180(2); (NT) *Condominium Act*, R.S.N.W.T. 1988, c. C-15, s. 6.5(1).

---

(2) Access to Information and Records Regarding the Corporation[1]

▼HCD-53▼ Status certificate. In some jurisdictions, a condominium corporation must give to each person who requests it a status certificate. The condominium corporation may charge a prescribed fee for the status certificate and must deliver the certificate within a prescribed period of time after receiving a request for it and payment of the fee.[2] In Newfoundland, the certificate must be delivered by an existing unit owner to a purchaser when entering into an agreement of purchase and sale.[3]

The status certificate must be in the prescribed form, specify the date on which it may contain, among other things:

- a statement of the common expenses — including arrears and increases — for the unit
- assessments made by the board to increase the contribution to the reserve fund and the reason for the assessments
- the address for service of the corporation
- the names and address for service of the directors and officers of the corporation
- a copy of the current declaration, by-laws and rules
- a statement of all outstanding judgments against the corporation and the status of all legal actions to which the corporation is a party
- a statement with respect to the amount of the reserve fund and whether there are any plans to increase it
- statement of the number of units for which the corporation has received notice that such units are leased during the fiscal year preceding the date of the status certificate
- a certificate or memorandum of insurance for each of the current insurance policies and
- a statement of the amounts, if any, that the legislation requires to be added to the common expenses payable for a unit[4]

If a status certificate omits material information that it is required to contain, the certificate is deemed to include a statement that there is no such information.[5] In Ontario, if the condominium corporation does not deliver a status certificate, as required, the corporation is deemed to have given a certificate stating that:

- there has been no default in the payment of common expenses for the unit
- the board has not declared any increase in the common expenses for the unit since the date of the budget of the corporation for the current fiscal year and
- the board has not levied any assessments against the unit since the date of the budget of the corporation for the current fiscal year to increase the contribution to the reserve fund[6]

A purchaser, mortgagee or owner of a unit, and other prescribed persons, are entitled to request a status certificate and regardless of who requests the certificate a purchaser or mortgagee is entitled to rely on the responses to the certificate or the absence of responses. The status certificate binds the condominium corporation, however, only as against a purchaser or mortgagee of a unit who relies on the certificate. The certificate does not bind the corporation against any other individual, including the current owner of a unit who may request one.[7]

Notes

1. See Section III.8. ("Records").
2. (AB) *Condominium Property Act,* R.S.A. 2000, c. C-22; (AB) Condominium Property Regulation, Alta. Reg. 168/2000, ss. 26(2), 29, 31(2)

   (ON) *Condominium Act, 1998*, S.O. 1998, c. 19, s. 76(3); (ON) General Regulation, O. Reg 48/01, s. 18, where any individual can request status certificate

   (SK) *Condominium Property Act, 1993*, S.S. 1993, c. C-26.1, s. 64(1), referred to as estoppel certificate

   (NT) *Condominium Act*, R.S.N.W.T. 1988, c. C-15, s. 19.17(1), (4) where individual other than purchaser or mortgagee must obtain consent of the owner to request certificate

   (YT) *Condominium Act*, R.S.Y. 2002, c. 36, s. 14(1)(g).
3. (NL) *Condominium Act, 2009*, S.N.L. 2009, c. C-29.1, ss. 40(2), (3) (not yet in force), referred to as estoppels certificate. But see exception at s. 91(3).
4. (AB) *Condominium Property Act,* R.S.A. 2000, c. C-22; (AB) Condominium Property Regulation, Alta. Reg. 168/2000, ss. 26(2), 29, 31(2)

   (NS) *Condominium Act*, R.S.N.S. 1989, c. 85, s. 29B(3)

   (ON) *Condominium Act, 1998*, S.O. 1998, c. 19; (ON) General Regulation, O. Reg 48/01, s. 18, Form 3

   (SK) *Condominium Property Act, 1993*, S.S. 1993, c. C-26.1, s. 64(1); (SK) Condominium Property Regulations, 2001, R.R.S. c. C-26.1 Reg. 2, s. 53

   (NT) *Condominium Act*, R.S.N.W.T. 1988, c. C-15, s. 19.17(1). See s. 19.17(2) for additional documents that may be inspected by mortgagee on request

   (YT) *Condominium Act*, R.S.Y. 2002, c. 36, s. 14(1)(g).
5. (NL) *Condominium Act, 2009*, S.N.L. 2009, c. C-29.1, s. 42(3) (not yet in force); (ON) *Condominium Act, 1998*, S.O. 1998, c. 19, s. 76(4).
6. (ON) *Condominium Act, 1998*, S.O. 1998, c. 19, s. 76(5).
7. (NL) *Condominium Act, 2009*, S.N.L. 2009, c. C-29.1, s. 42(4) (not yet in force)

   (ON) *Condominium Act, 1998*, S.O. 1998, c. 19, s. 76(6)

   (NT) *Condominium Act*, R.S.N.W.T. 1988, c. C-15, s. 19.17(3).

---

(3) Implied Covenants and Conditions and Statutory Duties

▼HCD-54▼ Covenants implied into agreement of purchase and sale. In certain jurisdictions, every agreement of purchase and sale for a proposed unit entered into by a developer before the registration of the condominium declaration and plan is deemed to contain the following covenants by the developer:

- If the proposed unit is for residential purposes, a covenant to take all reasonable steps to sell the other residential units included in the property without delay, except for the units that the developer intends to lease
- A covenant to take all reasonable steps to deliver to the purchaser without delay a deed to the unit that is in registerable form and
- A covenant to hold in trust for the corporation the money, if any, that the developer collects from the purchaser on behalf of the corporation

These covenants do not merge on the delivery to the purchaser of a transfer that is in registerable form.[1]

Duty to register declaration and description. In Ontario, a developer who has entered into an agreement of purchase and sale of a proposed unit must take all reasonable steps to complete the buildings provided for in the agreement and register, without delay, a declaration and description in respect of the property in which the proposed unit will be included.[2]

Notes

1. (AB) *Condominium Property Act,* R.S.A. 2000, c. C-22, s. 11, where developer has statutory duty of fair dealing

   (ON) *Condominium Act, 1998*, S.O. 1998, c. 19, s. 78(1), (2). For a phased condominium corporation, see s. 145(4)

   (NT) *Condominium Act*, R.S.N.W.T. 1988, c. C-15, s. 6.3(1).
2. (ON) *Condominium Act, 1998*, S.O. 1998, c. 19, s. 79(1). But see s. 180(1) where corporation has entered into multiple agreements of purchase and sale.

---

(4) Interim Occupancy

▼HCD-55▼ Agreement of purchase and sale. In Ontario, an agreement of purchase and sale may permit or require interim occupancy of a proposed unit. Purchase payments, reserve fund contributions and rates of interest are adjusted for such interim occupancy. If a purchaser assumes interim occupancy of a proposed unit, the *Condominium Act, 1998*[1] enumerates certain rights and duties of the developer.

Note

1. (ON) S.O. 1998, c. 19, s. 80; (ON) General Regulation, O. Reg. 48/01, s. 19(1). For a phased condominium corporation see s. 145(4).

---

(5) Money Held in Trust[1]

▼HCD-56▼ Prescribed money to be held. Legislation in a number of jurisdictions prescribes certain money paid to prescribed classes of people to be held in trust. Upon receiving the money that is required to be held in trust, legislation further prescribes that the money is to be deposited into a prescribed trust account and evidence of compliance with this legislative requirement must also be provided within a prescribed period of time.[2]

Notes

1. (ON) *Condominium Act, 1998*, S.O. 1998, c. 19. See Subsection VIII.3.(7) ("Remedies Related to Money Held in Trust").
2. (AB) *Condominium Property Act,* R.S.A. 2000, c. C-22, ss. 14, 16; (AB) Condominium Property Regulations, Alta. Reg. 168/2000, s. 1(2). But see exemption at s. 15 and note transitional provision at s. 61(1), where s. 14 of the legislation was formerly s. 11

   (BC) *Strata Property Act*, S.B.C. 1998, c. 43, ss. 114-115

   (ON) *Condominium Act, 1998*, S.O. 1998, c. 19, s. 81(1)-(7); (ON) General Regulation, O. Reg. 48/01, ss. 20, 39. But see exception at s. 180(1)

   (NT) *Condominium Act*, R.S.N.W.T. 1988, c. C-15, s. 6.3(3), (4).

---

(6) Interest

▼HCD-57▼ Interest to be paid by declarant. In Alberta, Ontario and Northwest Territories, a developer is required to pay interest at a prescribed rate to the purchaser on all money that a person pays on account of the purchase price of a proposed unit or that the declarant credits to the purchase price of a proposed unit. The interest is to be paid to the purchaser by way of payment or set-off within a prescribed period of time.[1]

Note

1. (AB) *Condominium Property Act,* R.S.A. 2000, c. C-22, s. 14(6), (7)

   (ON) *Condominium Act, 1998*, S.O. 1998, c. 19, s. 82; (ON) General Regulation, O. Reg. 48/01, s. 19(2), (3). Where declarant has entered into one ore more proposed agreements of purchase and sale, see s. 180(1)

   (NT) *Condominium Act*, R.S.N.W.T. 1988, c. C-15, s. 6.3(5), (6).

---

3. Lease of Units

(1) Notification by Owner HCD-58
(2) Deemed Covenant or Conditions HCD-59
(3) Deposits HCD-60

---

(1) Notification by Owner

▼HCD-58▼ Notice of lease to condominium corporation. Unless restricted from doing so by the declaration or the rules of the condominium corporation, an owner is permitted to lease his unit to another tenant. In order to lease a unit, the owner must notify the corporation of his intention to lease, setting out: the tenant's name, the owner's address at which an application or other documents may be served and such other information as required by statute, such as a copy of the lease.[1] If a unit's lease is terminated or not renewed, the owner must also notify the corporation in writing that the unit is no longer rented.[2] The registration of a declaration or a description does not constitute grounds for an owner landlord to give notice of a termination of a tenancy.[3]

Notes

1. (AB) *Condominium Property Act,* R.S.A. 2000, c. C-22, s. 53(1), (5), where notice to the corporation is to be provided in writing. See also (AB) *Residential Tenancies Act*, S.A. 2004, c. R-17.1, s. 57

   (BC) *Strata Property Act*, S.B.C. 1998, c. 43, Part 8

   (NB) *Condominium Property Act,* S.N.B. 2009, c. C-16.05, s. 53

   (ON) *Condominium Act, 1998*, S.O. 1998, c. 19, s. 83(1). See also (ON) General Regulation, O. Reg. 49/01, s. 40(1), (2). For the purpose of s. 83(1), "lease" includes a sublease or assignment of lease: (ON) General Regulation, O. Reg. 48/01, s. 23

   (SK) *Condominium Property Act, 1993*, S.S. 1993, c. C-26.1, ss. 75, 78(1), where notice to the corporation is to be provided in writing

   (NT) *Condominium Act*, R.S.N.W.T. 1988, c. C-15, ss. 19 and 19.1(1), where notice to the corporation is to be provided in writing.

2. (AB) *Condominium Property Act,* R.S.A. 2000, c. C-22, s. 53(6)

   (ON) *Condominium Act, 1998*, S.O. 1998, c. 19, s. 83(2)

   (SK) *Condominium Property Act, 1993*, S.S. 1993, c. C-26.1, s. 78(2)

   (NT) *Condominium Act*, R.S.N.W.T. 1988, c. C-15, s. 19.1(2).

3. (ON) *Condominium Act, 1998*, S.O. 1998, c. 19, ss. 4(2), (3).

---

(2) Deemed Covenant or Conditions

▼HCD-59▼ Duty to comply with legislation and condominium documents.[1] A tenant is bound by the same governing legislation and condominium documents as the unit owner.[2] Notwithstanding an agreement or waiver to the contrary, it is therefore an implied covenant of a tenancy agreement that any person in possession of the unit will not contravene the legislation or the declaration, by-laws and rules of the condominium corporation.[3] An owner must take all reasonable steps to ensure that an occupier of the owner's unit, lessess of the common elements as well as all invitees, agents and employees of the owner or occupier, likewise comply with the legislation and the declaration, by-laws and rules of the corporation.[4] The corporation, the owner and every person having a registered mortgage against a unit and its appurtenant common interest also have the right to require the owners and the occupiers of a unit to comply with the legislation and the corporation's governing documents.[5]

Notes

1. See Section VIII.2. ("Compliance with the Act, Declaration, By-Laws and Rules").
2. (ON) *Condominium Act, 1998*, S.O. 1998, c. 19, s. 119(1). An occupier's duty to comply applies to the proposed declaration by-laws and rules of the condominium corporation until the declaration and description are registered and the by-laws and rules come into force: s. 119(4); (SK) *Condominium Property Act, 1993*, S.S. 1993, c. C-26.1, s. 76.
3. (AB) *Condominium Property Act,* R.S.A. 2000, c. C-22, s. 53(2). See also (AB) *Residential Tenancies Act*, S.A. 2004, c. R-17.1, s. 57.

   (BC) *Strata Property Act*, S.B.C. 1998, c. 43, s. 146

   (NB) *Condominium Property Act,* S.N.B. 2009, c. C-16.05, s. 53(4)

   (NL) *Condominium Act, 2009*, S.N.L. 2009, c. C-29.1, s. 53

   (SK) *Condominium Property Act, 1993*, S.S. 1993, c. C-26.1, s. 76

   (NT) *Condominium Act*, R.S.N.W.T. 1988, c. C-15, s. 19.2
4. (NB) *Condominium Property Act*, S.N.B. 2009, c. C-16.05, s. 53(5); (ON) *Condominium Act, 1998*, S.O. 1998, c. 19, ss. 17(3), 119(2). A declarant must also take all reasonable steps to ensure an occupier complies with the legislation and the proposed by-laws and rules of the condominium corporation until the declaration and description are registered and the by-laws and rules come into force: s. 119(4).
5. (ON) *Condominium Act, 1998*, S.O. 1998, c. 19, s. 119(3). An occupier has a right to require occupiers of the other units in the proposed condominium corporation to comply with the legislation and the proposed by-laws and rules of the condominium corporation until the declaration and description are registered and the by-laws and rules come into force: s. 119(5).

(3) Deposits

▼HCD-60▼ Deposit paid to condominium corporation. The condominium corporation may collect a deposit from the owner of a unit who leases the unit for the maintenance, repair or replacement of the assets of the corporation or of the common elements that is damaged, destroyed, lost or removed by any person in possession of the rented unit.[1] A corporation may only impose or collect a deposit, however, if it is authorized by its by-law.[2] Once the tenancy is terminated, the corporation must return the deposit.[3]

Notes

1. (AB) *Condominium Property Act,* R.S.A. 2000, c. C-22, s. 53(3), (4)
   (SK) *Condominium Property Act, 1993*, S.S. 1993, c. C-26.1, ss. 77(1), (2)
   (NT) *Condominium Act*, R.S.N.W.T. 1988, c. C-15, ss. 19.3(1), (2).
2. (SK) *Condominium Property Act, 1993*, S.S. 1993, c. C-26.1, s. 82(1)(a); (SK) Condominium Property Regulations 2001, R.R.S. c. C-26.1, Reg. 2, s. 33; (NT) *Condominium Act*, R.S.N.W.T. 1988, c. C-15, ss. 19.8(1)(a).
3. (AB) *Condominium Property Act*, R.S.A. 2000, c. C-22, s. 53(7)(a)
   (SK) *Condominium Property Act, 1993*, S.S. 1993, c. C-26.1, s. 79(a)
   (NT) *Condominium Act*, R.S.N.W.T. 1988, c. C-15, s. 19.4(1)(a).

VI. Unit Owners

1. Meetings

(1) Types of Meetings HCD-61
(2) Procedure for Calling Meetings HCD-62

2. Voting

(1) General HCD-63
(2) Persons Entitled to Vote HCD-64
(3) Loss of Right to Vote HCD-66
(4) Method of Voting HCD-67
(5) Number of Votes Required.................................. HCD-68

---

1. Meetings

(1) Types of Meetings HCD-61
(2) Procedure for Calling Meetings HCD-62

---

(1) Types of Meetings

▼HCD-61▼ Overview. Unit owners have the right to attend two types of meetings of the corporation: meetings called by the board of directors for the transaction of specified business, and the annual general meeting. In appropriate circumstances, however, the courts have made orders restraining the holding of condominium meetings.[1]

General meetings. Once the condominium corporation has been created, an initial meeting must be held within a prescribed period of time after the registration of the declaration, description and/or condominium plan.[2] General meetings may then be called by the board of directors thereafter within prescribed periods of time.[3] Subject to other statutory requirements, anything that the legislation requires to be approved by a vote of any or all of the owners must only be approved at a general meeting called for that purpose.[4] All meetings, both general and annual, are to be conducted according to the rules of procedure adopted by the board.[5]

Annual general meetings. The board of directors must hold one annual general meeting every year. These annual general meetings are to be convened within a prescribed period of time after the end of the condominium corporation's fiscal year or the end of the preceding annual general meeting.[6] These meetings are held to discuss, among other things, the financial statements of the previous fiscal year, to appoint an auditor as well as for discussion of any matter relevant to the affairs and business of the condominium corporation. The documents to be provided to owners before the meeting vary by jurisdiction. Generally speaking, before each annual general meeting, the board must provide to the owners, among other things: financial statements approved by the board, the auditor's report and all further information respecting the financial position of the corporation that the by-laws of the corporation require.[7] An election is also held at the annual general meeting for a prescribed number of directors to serve for a prescribed term.[8]

Notes

1. *York Condominium Corporation No. 128 v. McKenzie*, [1996] O.J. No. 2878 (Ont. Gen. Div.); *York Condominium Corp. No. 206 v. Almeida & Almeida Landscaping Co.*, [1992] O.J. No. 1073 (Ont. Gen. Div.)
2. See Section V.1. ("Transfer of Control by Owner/Declarant").
3. (AB) *Condominium Property Act,* R.S.A. 2000, c. C-22, App. 1, ss. 16, 19

   (BC) *Strata Property Act*, S.B.C. 1998, c. 43, ss. 42, 43 (referred to as "special meetings")

   (ON) *Condominium Act, 1998*, S.O. 1998, c. 19, s. 45(2), (4).
4. (ON) *Condominium Act, 1998*, S.O. 1998, c. 19, s. 45(1); (PE) *Condominium Act*, R.S.P.E.I. 1988, c. C-16, s. 11(2).
5. (AB) *Condominium Property Act*, R.S.A. 2000, c. C-22, App. 1, s. 18
6. (AB) *Condominium Property Act*, R.S.A. 2000, c. C-22, ss. 30(1), (2)

   (BC) *Strata Property Act*, S.B.C. 1998, c. 43, s. 40

   (ON) *Condominium Act, 1998*, S.O. 1998, c. 19, s. 45(2), (3)

   (PE) *Condominium Act,* R.S.P.E.I. 1988, c. C-16, s. 11(1)

   (SK) *Condominium Property Act, 1993*, S.S. 1993, c. C-26.1, ss. 40(1), (2). But see exception at (SK) Condominium Property Regulations, 2001, R.R.S. c. C-26.1 Reg. 2, s. 11.

   (NT) *Condominium Act*, R.S.N.W.T. 1988, c. C-15, s. 16.2(1), (2), (3).
7. (AB) *Condominium Property Act,* R.S.A. 2000, c. C-22, s. 30(3), App. 1, s. 17, App. 2, s. 11; (AB) Condominium Property Regulation, Alta. Reg. 168/2000, s. 29(1)

   (NL) *Condominium Act, 2009*, S.N.L. 2009, c. C-29.1, 39(8) (not yet in force). See s. 37(3) for properties consisting of less than 10 units

   (ON) *Condominium Act, 1998*, S.O. 1998, c. 19, s. 69(1), (2)

   (SK) *Condominium Property Act, 1993*, S.S. 1993, c. C-26.1, ss. 39, 51.5, 65(4.1); (SK) Condominium Property Regulations, 2001, R.R.S. c. C-26.1 Reg. 2, Condominium Bylaws, s. 17(1), (2)

   (NT) *Condominium Act*, R.S.N.W.T. 1988, c. C-15, s. 16.2(3).

8. (AB) *Condominium Property Act,* R.S.A. 2000, c. C-22, App. 1, s. 7(1)
(BC) *Strata Property Act*, S.B.C. 1998, c. 43, s. 25
(SK) *Condominium Property Act, 1993*, S.S. 1993, c. C-26.1; (SK) Condominium Property Regulations, 2001, R.R.S. c. C-26.1 Reg. 2, Condominium Bylaws, s. 8.

---

(2) Procedure for Calling Meetings

▼HCD-62▼ Requisition for meeting. A meeting may be requisitioned by owners who, at the time the board receives the requisition, meet prescribed requirements, such as: owning a prescribed percentage of condominium units, being listed in the prescribed records of the corporation and being entitled to vote on business at meetings.[1] Condominium legislation prescribes the form a requisition must take and, in most provinces and territories, the requisition must be provided in writing.[2] Upon receiving a requisition, the board has a duty to call and hold a meeting of the owners of the corporation within a prescribed period of time failing which the owners who signed the requisition may call and hold the meeting.[3]

Notice of meeting and service on owners and mortgagees. A written notice of meeting must be given within a prescribed period of time to each owner who has notified the corporation in writing of the owner's name and address for service and prescribed mortgagees. The notice of meeting must be given within the prescribed period of time, in the prescribed manner, and must specify, among other things, the place, date and time of the meeting and the nature of the business to be presented.[4] If a by-law is to be amended, repealed or replaced, the persons entitled to vote on the amendment must be given written copies of the text of the proposed amendment, repeal or replacement of the by-law within a prescribed period of time.[5] A matter may only be voted upon at a meeting if it was clearly disclosed in the notice of meeting.[6]

Agenda. Various legislation require the board to draft an agenda for specific or special meetings and/or annual general meetings, which may also be included in the notice of meeting.[7] Northwest Territories *Condominium Act* specifically enumerates the matters to be included in an agenda for an annual general meeting as follows:

(a) Approval of the financial statements for the corporation's preceding fiscal year.
(b) Approval of an annual operating budget for the corporation's present fiscal year.

(c) A review of the capital reserve fund plan and annual report in respect of the capital reserve fund, and approval of the owner's contribution to the capital reserve fund for the corporation's present fiscal year.
(d) A review of the corporation's current insurance requirements;
(e) The election of members of the board.
(f) Such other matters as the board considers to be relevant to the affairs and business of the corporation.[8]

In Québec, upon receiving notice of a general meeting, co-owners may cause a question to be placed on the agenda.[9]

Quorum. Condominium legislation prescribes the formula for determining the minimum number of unit owners who must be present at an owner's meeting, or represented by proxy, to form a quorum for the purposes of constituting the meeting. A quorum may be based on the percentage of units owned by the owners to be present or represented, the percentage of common elements owned, a percentage of individuals entitled to receive the notice of meeting or the majority of individuals entitled to vote. No business can be transacted at a meeting of the members of the corporation unless quorum has been established.[10]

Venue. All board meetings and all general meetings of the corporation must be held within the municipality in which the units are located unless a majority of the owners agree to hold the meetings in another location. Such an agreement may be passed by means of an ordinary resolution at the corporation's annual general meeting.[11]

Notes

1. (BC) *Strata Property Act*, S.B.C. 1998, c. 43, s. 43. Meeting called by strata corporation: s. 42; (ON) *Condominium Act, 1998*, S.O. 1998, c. 19, s. 46(1).
2. (ON) *Condominium Act, 1998*, S.O. 1998, c. 19, s. 46(2). Where nature of the business to be presented at meeting includes the removal of one or more director, additional information is required: s. 46(3); (PE) *Condominium Act,* R.S.P.E.I. 1988, c. C-16, s. 11(4).
3. (ON) *Condominium Act, 1998*, S.O. 1998, c. 19, s. 46(4), where board may also add the business to be presented at the meeting to the meeting agenda for the next annual general meeting; (PE) *Condominium Act,* R.S.P.E.I. 1988, c. C-16, s. 11(3).
4. (AB) *Condominium Property Act*, R.S.A. 2000, c. C-22, s. 20(1), (2)

   (BC) *Strata Property Act*, S.B.C. 1998, c. 43, ss. 45, 47

   (MB) *Condominium Act*, C.C.S.M. c. C170, s. 12(1.1)-(1.4)

   (ON) *Condominium Act, 1998*, S.O. 1998, c. 19, ss. 47(1), (3), (6), (7), (8), (11), 54(11). See s. 120(3) for notice of meeting with respect to amalgamation.

   (PE) *Condominium Act,* R.S.P.E.I. 1988, c. C-16, s. 11(5), (6)

(QC) *Civil Code of Québec*, L.R.Q., c. C-1991, c. 64, art. 1087, where the notice must be accompanied with the balance sheet and income statement for the preceding year, statement of debts and claims, budget forecast, any draft amendment to the declaration of co-ownership and a note on the general terms and conditions of any proposed contract or planned work.

(SK) *Condominium Property Act, 1993*, S.S. 1993, c. C-26.1; (SK) Condominium Property Regulations, 2001, R.R.S. c. C-26.1 Reg. 2, Condominium Bylaws, s. 21.

5. (AB) *Condominium Property Act,* R.S.A. 2000, c. C-22, s. 35.

6. (ON) *Condominium Act, 1998*, S.O. 1998, c. 19, s. 47(10); (SK) *Condominium Property Act, 1993*, S.S. 1993, c. C-26.1, s. 23(1).

7. (BC) *Strata Property Act*, S.B.C. 1998, c. 43, s. 46

   (SK) *Condominium Property Act, 1993*, S.S. 1993, c. C-26.1; (SK) Condominium Property Regulations, 2001, R.R.S. c. C-26.1 Reg. 2, s. 19(3)

   (NT) *Condominium Act*, R.S.N.W.T. 1988, c. C-15, s. 16.2(2).

8. (NT) *Condominium Act*, R.S.N.W.T. 1988, c. C-15, s. 16.2(2).

9. (QC) *Civil Code of Québec*, L.R.Q. c. C-1991, art. 1088.

10. See H. Nathan, *Wainberg's Company Meetings* (Toronto: C.C.H. Canadian Ltd., 1998) at 41-44.

    (AB) *Condominium Property Act,* R.S.A. 2000, c. C-22, App. 1, s. 21(1)-(3). See also App. 2, ss. 18, 19

    (BC) *Strata Property Act*, S.B.C. 1998, c. 43, s. 48

    (MB) *Condominium Act*, C.C.S.M. c. C170, s. 12(1.5)

    (NB) *Condominium Property Act,* S.N.B. 2009, c. C-16.05, s. 26

    (NL) *Condominium Act, 2009*, S.N.L. 2009, c. C-29.1, ss. 20(1), (2) (not yet in force)

    (NS) *Condominium Act*, R.S.N.S. 1989, c. 85, s. 14A(1), (2)

    (ON) *Condominium Act, 1998*, S.O. 1998, c. 19, s. 50(1), where reference may be made to the registered by-laws

    (QC) *Civil Code of Québec*, L.R.Q., c. C-1991, art. 1089

    (SK) *Condominium Property Act, 1993*, S.S. 1993, c. C-26.1; (SK) Condominium Property Regulations, 2001, R.R.S. c. C-26.1 Reg. 2, s. 22(1)-(4).

11. (AB) *Condominium Property Act,* R.S.A. 2000, c. C-22, s. 31.

---

2. Voting

(1) General HCD-63

(2) Persons Entitled to Vote

    (a) Owner HCD-64

    (b) Mortgagee HCD-65

(3) Loss of Right to Vote HCD-66

(4) Method of Voting HCD-67

(5) Number of Votes Required HCD-68

(1) General

▼HCD-63▼ Matters at meeting. Any matter to be voted on at an owner's meeting must be clearly disclosed in the notice of meeting as distributed. If a matter was not clearly disclosed in the notice of meeting, only votes on routine procedure can be taken.[1] To determine who is eligible to receive notice and subsequently vote at a meeting, the corporation keeps a register of owners and mortgagees.

Note

1. (ON) *Condominium Act, 1998*, S.O. 1998, c. 19, s. 47(10)

---

(2) Persons Entitled to Vote

(a) Owner

▼HCD-64▼Voting rights. An owner has voting rights in the corporation in the proportions specified by the governing condominium legislation, subject to a mortgagee and a tenant's right to vote. The proportion of an owner's voting rights varies by jurisdiction. In Newfoundland and Ontario, for example, all voting by owners is on the basis of one vote per unit. In Alberta and Saskatchewan, the voting rights of owners are determined by the unit factor of the owner's unit. While in Yukon and Northwest Territories, owners have voting rights in the proportions provided in the corporation's declaration.[1] Provincial and territorial legislation may also prescribe the matters on which owners are entitled to vote.[2]

Notes

1. (AB) *Condominium Property Act,* R.S.A. 2000, c. C-22, s. 26(1). Where a vote is taken by a show of hands, however, each person entitled to vote has one vote: App. 1, s. 26(2). See App. 1, s. 31(1), (2) for voting by co-owners. Voting where owner incapable: s. 27.

   (BC) *Strata Property Act*, S.B.C. 1998, c. 43, ss. 53, 54

   (MB) *Condominium Act*, C.C.S.M. c. C170, s. 15(1).

   (NB) *Condominium Property Act*, S.N.B. 2009, c. C-16.05, s. 25(1)

   (NL) *Condominium Act, 2009*, S.N.L. 2009, c. C-29.1, s. 21(1) (not yet in force). See ss. 21(2), (3) for consolidated units.

   (NS) *Condominium Act*, R.S.N.S. 1989, c. 85, s. 37

   (ON) *Condominium Act, 1998*, S.O. 1998, c. 19, ss. 45, 48(4), 51(1), (2). See s. 51(3) for voting by joint owners.

   (PE) *Condominium Act,* R.S.P.E.I. 1988, c. C-16, s. 11(7)

(QC) *Civil Code of Québec*, L.R.Q., c. C-1991, arts. 1090-1093. See also art. 1076

(SK) *Condominium Property Act, 1993*, S.S. 1993, c. C-26.1, s. 41(1). See (SK) Condominium Property Regulations, 2001, R.R.S. c. C-26.1 Reg. 2, s. 27 for voting by co-owners. Where owner lacks capacity: s. 43(1)

(NT) *Condominium Act*, R.S.N.W.T. 1988, c. C-15, s. 20(1)

(NU) *Condominium Act*, R.S.N.W.T. (Nu.) 1988, c. C-15, s. 20(1)

(YT) *Condominium Act*, R.S.Y. 2002, c. 36, s. 15(1).

2. (ON) *Condominium Act, 1998*, S.O. 1998, c. 19, s. 49(3). Owners entitled to vote may also vote for each member of the board up for election. But see exception for owner-occupied units at (ON) Ontario Regulation, O. Reg. 48/01, s. 44.

(b) Mortgagee

▼HCD-65▼ Voting rights. Where a mortgage or a charge of a unit and common interest contains a provision that authorizes the mortgagee or chargee to exercise the right of the owner to vote or to consent, the mortgageee or charge may exercise that right in place of the owner. If a unit is subject to more than one mortgage for which the mortgagee has the right to vote at a meeting of owners, or if two or more mortgages contain a provision authorizing the mortgagee to exercise the right of the owner to vote, the mortgagee who has priority is entitled to exercise the right. In some jurisdictions a mortgagee must notify the owner and corporation in writing in advance of the meeting in order to be able to exercise the right to vote.[1]

Note

1. (AB) *Condominium Property Act,* R.S.A. 2000, c. C-22, s. 26(2), (3)

(BC) *Strata Property Act*, S.B.C. 1998, c. 43, s. 54

(MB) *Condominium Act*, C.C.S.M. c. C170, s. 15(2)

(NB) *Condominium Property Act,* S.N.B. 2009, c. C-16.05, s. 25(1)

(NL) *Condominium Act, 2009*, S.N.L. 2009, c. C-29.1, s. 21 (not yet in force)

(ON) *Condominium Act, 1998*, S.O. 1998, c. 19, s. 48(1)

(PE) *Condominium Act,* R.S.P.E.I. 1988, c. C-16, s. 28

(SK) *Condominium Property Act, 1993*, S.S. 1993, c. C-26.1, s. 42(1)

(NT) *Condominium Act*, R.S.N.W.T. 1988, c. C-15, s. 20(3)

(NU) *Condominium Act,* R.S.N.W.T. (Nu.) 1988, c. C-15, s. 20(2)

(YT) *Condominium Act*, R.S.Y. 2002, c. 36, s. 15(2)

---

(3) Loss of Right to Vote

▼HCD-66▼ Restrictions and prohibitions on the right to vote. Neither an owner nor a mortgagee is entitled to exercise the right to vote if any contribution payable in respect of an owner's unit, or any other obligation owing to the corporation in respect of the owner's unit or the common property, is in arrears for 30 days or more prior to the meeting at which the power to vote would be exercised.[1]

Note

1. (AB) *Condominium Property Act,* R.S.A. 2000, c. C-22, s. 26(5), App. 1, s. 30

   (ON) *Condominium Act, 1998*, S.O. 1998, c. 19, s. 49

   (QC) *Civil Code of Québec*, L.R.Q., c. C-1991, art. 1094

   (SK) *Condominium Property Act, 1993*, S.S. 1993, c. C-26.1, s. 41(8), however restriction does not apply if the subject-matter of the vote is one that requires a unanimous resolution pursuant to the Act. See also s. 41(9)-(12) and (SK) Condominium Property Regulations, 2001, R.R.S. c. C-26.1 Reg. 2, s. 30

   (NT) *Condominium Act*, R.S.N.W.T. 1988, c. C-15, s. 20(5).

---

(4) Method of Voting

▼HCD-67▼ Overview. The Supreme Court of Canada has stated that: "the best interests of the corporation centre solely on the maintenance of the integrity and propriety of the voting procedure."[1] The enforcement provisions of condominium legislation have therefore been used by the courts to compel compliance with the spirit of the voting and election laws. In one case, the enforcement provision was used to overturn the election of five directors because of suspicious voting procedure irregularities.[2]

Proxies and substitute voting. A person entitled to vote at a meeting of owners may appoint a proxy to vote in his place. An instrument appointing a proxy must be in writing in the prescribed form.[3] A person's right to vote may be voluntarily designated to another person, pursuant to prescribed conditions or may be exercised by another person if the person with the right to vote is incapable.[4]

Notes

1. *Blair v. Consolidated Enfield Corp.*, [1995] S.C.J. No. 29 at para. 43, [1995] 4 S.C.R. 5 (S.C.C.)
2. *Rohoman v. York Condominium Corp. No. 141*, [2001] O.J. No. 4927, [2001] O.T.C. 899 (Ont. S.C.J.) (court also ordered that the meeting was to be chaired by

an independent person agreed-upon by the parties and that this neutral chair was to approve the notice of meeting and form of proxy).

3. (AB) *Condominium Property Act,* R.S.A. 2000, c. C-22, s. 26(4), App. 1, s. 29

   (BC) *Strata Property Act*, S.B.C. 1998, c. 43, s. 56

   (ON) *Condominium Act, 1998*, S.O. 1998, c. 19, s. 52(1),(3); (ON) General Regulation, O. Reg. 48/01, s. 13

   (QC) *Civil Code of Québec*, L.R.Q., c. C-1991, art. 1095

   (SK) *Condominium Property Act, 1993*, S.S. 1993, c. C-26.1, s. 41.1(1)

   (NT) *Condominium Act*, R.S.N.W.T. 1988, c. C-15, s. 20(4)

   See *Keyes v. Metropolitan Toronto Condominium Corp. No. 876*, [1990] O.J. No. 1006, 73 O.R. (2d) 568 (Ont. H.C.J.) (unit owners were misled by proxy holders who solicited their vote, the court held that the proxies were invalid unless a written notice was sent to the unit owners rectifying the misleading advice given with the original solicitation); *Campbell v. Metropolitan Toronto Condominium Corp. No. 694*, [2002] O.J. No. 3879, 117 A.C.W.S. (3d) 42 (Ont. C.A.) (corporation banned the use of proxies and court refused to give compliance order allowing use of proxies).

4. (AB) *Condominium Property Act,* R.S.A. 2000, c. C-22, s. 27(1)

   (BC) *Strata Property Act*, S.B.C. 1998, c. 43, s. 58

   (MB) *Condominium Act*, C.C.S.M. c. C170, s. 15(3)

   (NL) *Condominium Act, 2009*, S.N.L. 2009, c. C-29.1, s. 21(4) (not yet in force)

   (NS) *Condominium Act*, R.S.N.S. 1989, c. 85, s. 37(3)

   (ON) *Condominium Act, 1998*, S.O. 1998, c. 19, s. 52(1), (3)

   (SK) *Condominium Property Act, 1993*, S.S. 1993, c. C-26.1, s. 43(1)

   (NT) *Condominium Act*, R.S.N.W.T. 1988, c. C-15, s. 20(6)

   (NU) *Condominium Act,* R.S.N.W.T. (Nu.) 1988, c. C-15, s. 20(3)

   (YT) *Condominium Act*, R.S.Y. 2002, c. 36, s. 15(3).

(5) Number of Votes Required

▼HCD-68▼ Majority vote. Legislation in Ontario, Saskatchewan and Québec provide that, subject to other legislative provisions, all questions proposed for the consideration of owners at a meeting of owners must be determined by a majority of the votes cast by the owners present at the meeting, in person or by proxy.[1]

Note

1. (ON) *Condominium Act, 1998*, S.O. 1998, c. 19, s. 53

   (QC) *Civil Code of Québec*, L.R.Q., c. C-1991, arts. 1096 and 1097. But see different proportions required: arts. 1098, 1099, 1101, 1102

   (SK) *Condominium Property Act, 1993*, S.S. 1993, c. C-26.1, s. 41(3). But by-laws may provide for a proportion in excess of a majority vote: s. 41(4).

VII. Common Expenses, Repair and Maintenance and Changes to the Condominium

1. Common Expenses

(1) Contribution of Owners HCD-69
(2) Special Levies, Assessments and User Fees HCD-70
(3) Additions to Common Expenses HCD-71
(4) No Avoidance of Common Expenses HCD-72

2. Repair and Maintenance

(1) Repair After Damages HCD-73
(2) Maintenance HCD-75
(3) Common Law Application of Statutory Duty HCD-77
(4) Work Done for Owner HCD-78
(5) Vacant Land Condominium Corporation HCD-79
(6) Common Elements Condominium Corporation HCD-80
(7) Contingency Reserve Fund HCD-81
(8) Warranties HCD-82

3. Changes to the Condominium Property, Assets and Services

(1) Changes Made by Corporation HCD-83
(2) Changes Made by Owners HCD-84

---

1. Common Expenses

(1) Contribution of Owners HCD-69
(2) Special Levies, Assessments and User Fees HCD-70
(3) Additions to Common Expenses HCD-71
(4) No Avoidance of Common Expenses HCD-72

---

(1) Contribution of Owners[1]

▼HCD-69▼ Statutory definition of common expense. Pursuant to provincial and territorial legislation, unit owners must contribute to the corporation's common expenses in the proportions prescribed.[2] What constitutes a common expense, however, varies by jurisdiction and includes a variety of costs and expenses. In Ontario, Newfoundland and Yukon, common expenses mean the expenses related to the performance of the objects and duties of a corporation and all expenses specified as common expenses in the legislation or the corporation's declaration. In addition, in some jurisdictions, legislation specifically provides that, among other things, the cost of an addition, alteration or improvement to, or renovation of, the common elements and the cost of a substantial change in the assets of the corporation are considered common expenses.[3] If the corporation obtains an insurance policy that has a deductible clause limiting the amount payable by the insurer, the portion of a loss that is excluded from coverage may be considered a common expense.[4] Notwithstanding the statutory definitions of common expenses in the various legislation, boards may make, amend or repeal by-laws to govern the assessment and collection of contributions to the common expenses.[5]

Definition of common expenses at common law. The scope of the statutory definition of common expense has been considered by various courts. To the extent that the common expenses are defined as expenses related to the performance of the objects and duties of a corporation, the statutory provisions defining the "objects" of a corporation have been interpreted as conferring broad powers on a condominium corporation.[6] In *Mancuso v. York Condominium Corp. No. 216*, the court considered whether unit owners could be compelled to pay a cable television service charge as a common expense. The corporation's by-laws provided that its duties were "not limited to the operation and maintenance of the common elements and the supply of utilities to the units". While the expenses were not related to the performance of the "objects" or "duties" of the corporation, as defined by the statute, the court found that the corporation's by-laws could reasonably include entering into cable television contracts, a common action taken by corporations.[7]

Allocation of common expenses at common law. As not all condominium legislation provides a specific formula for calculating the allocation of common expenses amongst the corporation's owners, various courts have provided guidance. The court has stated that the reasonable expectation of owners is that there will be a rough degree of consistency in the allocation of common expenses, so that an owner's allocation is proportionate to his use.[8] The Court of Appeal considered this issue of equitable allocation in *York Region Condominium Corp. No. 771 v. Year Full Investment (Canada) Inc.* where it dismissed an appeal of an order requiring the commercial unit owners of a mixed-use condominium to pay for excessive water consumption. While there were less commercial units than residential units in the building, the commercial units utilized 190% of the water budgeted for the entire corporation's use. In ordering the commercial unit owners to pay for the excessive water use, the court stated that the intent of a corporation's declaration is to apportion common expenses amongst unit holders in percentages as close as possible to the percentage of use of, and enjoyment by, each unit holder from the services and charges included in the common expenses. The court concluded that it was therefore unfair for the commercial unit owners to obtain the benefit of water use and not pay for it.[9]

Notes

1. See Section III.6. ("Corporation's Money").
2. (AB) *Condominium Property Act,* R.S.A. 2000, c. C-22, s. 39(1), where common are referred to as "administrative expenses", and owner's duty is inferred from reciprocal duty of the corporation to maintain common expense fund and collect owner contributions

   (BC) *Strata Property Act*, S.B.C. 1998, c. 43

   (NL) *Condominium Act, 2009*, S.N.L. 2009, c. C-29.1, ss. 48(a), 44(3) (not yet in force), where owner's duty is owner contributions

   (ON) *Condominium Act, 1998*, S.O. 1998, c. 19, s. 84(1)

   (SK) *Condominium Property Act, 1993*, S.S. 1993, c. C-26.1, ss. 54(1), 55(1), 56(1), 57(1); (SK) Condominium Property Regulations, 2001, R.R.S. c. C-26.1 Reg. 2, ss. 47, 48

   (NT) *Condominium Act*, R.S.N.W.T. 1988, c. C-15, s. 19.9(1)(a)-(c), where owner's duty is inferred from reciprocal duty of the corporation to maintain common expense fund and collect owner contributions. See s. 19.9(1)(e) for common expenses for leasehold condominiums

   (YT) *Condominium Act*, R.S.Y. 2002, c. 36, s. 14(1)(a), (b), (g), where owner's duty is owner contributions.
3. (NL) *Condominium Act, 2009*, S.N.L. 2009, c. C-29.1, ss. 2(1)(g), 52(2) (not yet in force)

   (ON) *Condominium Act, 1998*, S.O. 1998, c. 19, ss. 1(1), 94(7), 97(7). See s. 171(1)-(3) for common expenses for leasehold condominiums

   (SK) *Condominium Property Act, 1993*, S.S. 1993, c. C-26.1, ss. 55(2), 65(1.2), 101(3)

   (YT) *Condominium Act*, R.S.Y. 2002, c. 36, s. 1.
4. (AB) *Condominium Property Act,* R.S.A. 2000, c. C-22, App. 1, By-laws, s. 2(b)(ii); (ON) *Condominium Act, 1998*, S.O. 1998, c. 19, s. 105(1).

5. (ON) *Condominium Act, 1998*, S.O. 1998, c. 19, s. 56(1)(g).
6. *Eglinton Place Inc. v. Ontario (Ministry of Consumer & Corporate Relations)*, [2000] O.J. No. 498, 47 O.R. (3d) 344 (Ont. S.C.J.).
7. *Mancuso v. York Condominium Corp. No. 216*, [2008] O.J. No. 1737 at para. 33, 292 D.L.R. (4th) 737 (Ont. S.C.J.) (court was also influenced by the length of the contract).
8. *Camrost York Development Corp. v. Metropolitan Condominium Corp. No. 989* (unreported) 1996, Lane J. (Ont. Div. Ct.); *York Condominium Corp., No. 482 v. Christansen*, [2003] O.J. No. 343, 64 O.R. (3d) 65 (Ont. S.C.J.) (a principal object of the Act is to achieve fairness among the parties: the owners, their tenants, their mortgagees and the corporation itself).
9. *York Condominium Corp. No. 771 v. Year Full Investment (Canada) Inc.*, [1993] O.J. No. 769, 12 O.R. (3d) 641 (Ont. C.A.).

---

(2) Special Levies, Assessments and User Fees

▼HCD-70▼ Overview. A board may, by resolution, make amend or repeal by-laws that are not contrary to the governing legislation or the corporation's declaration to govern the assessment and collection of contributions to the common expenses. This permits the corporation to levy further expenses on owners above the prescribed contributions for common expenses.[1]

Note

1. (AB) *Condominium Property Act,* R.S.A. 2000, c. C-22, ss. 39(1)(c), 47(1) where authority to levy contributions must be provided for in the bylaws on a basis other than in proportion to the unit factors of the owners' respective units

   (NL) *Condominium Act, 2009*, S.N.L. 2009, c. C-29.1, s. 18(3)(h) (not yet in force), where consent of the owners of at least 66% of the common elements is required; (ON) *Condominium Act, 1998*, S.O. 1998, c. 19, s. 56(1).

---

(3) Additions to Common Expenses

▼HCD-71▼ Statutory basis. Legislation specifically prescribes a number of expenses that may be added to the common expenses, payable for an owner's unit. These include costs of repair and maintenance, and interest and expenses resulting from an owner's failure to meet a requisite obligation.[1] Various decisions have also supplemented the statutory provisions by providing a framework within which to assess whether a given expense can be added to the common expenses. Legislation in some jurisdictions includes a catch-all provision, allowing the corporation to pass by-laws governing the assessment and collection of contribution towards the common expenses, subject to the governing statutory regulations.[2] In Ontario, the legal and court costs in a court application that the corporation commences against an owner or occupant of a unit may be added to the common expenses for that unit.[3] Furthermore, in *Italiano v. Toronto Standard Condominium Corp. No. 1507*, the costs of an arbitration arising out of an owner's failure to comply with the corporation's by-laws respecting noise were added to his common expenses.[4] The courts have recognized that the proportions of common expenses cannot be examined under a microscope or assessed and allocated on an exact per usage basis. Rather the common expenses must be assessed with regards to a corporation as a whole while ensuring that their allocation does not cause unjust enrichment or undue hardship for any parties.[5]

Notes

1. (NL) *Condominium Act, 2009*, S.N.L. 2009, c. C-29.1, s. 58(2), (3) (damage), s. 85(4)-(6) (vacant land condominium corporation) (not yet in force)

   (ON) *Condominium Act, 1998*, S.O. 1998, c. 19, s. 57.5 (part of common expenses, re: occupancy standard by-law), s. 92(4) (standard condominium corporation costs), s. 98(4) (lien for default), s. 105(2), (3) (owner's responsibility), s. 162(4), (6) (vacant land condominium costs), s. 125(7) (common expenses of other owners), s. 134(5) (compliance order)

   (SK) *Condominium Property Act, 1993*, S.S. 1993, c. C-26.1, s. 65(1.3), (1.4) (damage).
2. (AB) *Condominium Property Act,* R.S.A. 2000, c. C-22, App. 1, By-laws, s. 2(b)(ii)

   (ON) *Condominium Act, 1998*, S.O. 1998, c. 19, s. 56(1)(g)

   (SK) *Condominium Property Act, 1993*, S.S. 1993, c. C-26.1, s. 47(1)(i).
3. (ON) *Condominium Act, 1998*, S.O. 1998, c. 19, s. 134(5).
4. [2008] O.J. No. 2642, 168 A.C.W.S. (3d) 239 (Ont. S.C.J.). See also *York Condominium Corp. No. 482 v. Christiansen*, [2003] O.J. No. 343, 64 O.R. (3d) 65 (S.C.J.) (owners' contributions to the common expenses are the "life blood" of the corporation, as such, the legislature has provided means whereby these corporations are assured of collecting such contributions, along with interest and reasonable legal and other costs incurred in such collection).
5. *York Region Condominium Corp. No. 771 v. Year Full Investment (Canada) Inc.*, [1993] O.J. No. 769, 12 O.R. (3d) 641 (Ont. C.A.) (no adjustment to the common expenses for hydro until there has been excessive use of the water by a certain party); *York Condominium Corporation No. 59 v. York Condominium Corp. No. 87*, [1983] O.J. No. 3088, 42 O.R. (2d) 337 (Ont. C.A.) (declaration interpreted to mean that excess water usage not part of common expenses). But see (ON) *Energy Consumer Protection Act, 2009*, S.O. 2010, c. 8, s. 33(1)-(3) providing that all new condominium developments in Ontario must have sub-metering for hydro-electricity and the board of older condominiums may choose to install sub-meters for hydro-electricity.

(4) No Avoidance of Common Expenses

▼HCD-72▼ Owner not exempt. An owner is not exempt from the obligation to contribute to the common expenses and this statutory obligation cannot be waived or abandoned.[1] While different owners may have different usage requirements in relation to the common elements, they are still obligated to pay the entire sum of their respective proportionate share of the common expenses. As the Ontario Court of Appeal has noted, while persons occupying a unit on the first floor may not use the elevator, they cannot avoid the inclusion of its costs in the common expenses payable.[2]

Notes

1. (NL) *Condominium Act,* S.N.L. 2009, c. C-29.1, s. 49(12)
   (ON) *Condominium Act, 1998*, S.O. 1998, c. 19, s. 84(3)
   (NT) *Condominium Act*, R.S.N.W.T. 1988, c. C-15, s. 19.9(2)
   (YT) *Condominium Act*, R.S.Y. 2002, c. 36, s. 14(2).
2. *York Region Condominium Corp. No. 771 v. Year Full Investment (Canada)*, [1993] O.J. No. 769, 12 O.R. (3d) 641 (Ont. C.A.)

---

2. Repair and Maintenance

(1) Repair After Damages
  (a) General HCD-73
  (b) Condominium Property HCD-74
(2) Maintenance
  (a) General HCD-75
  (b) Condominium Property HCD-76
(3) Common Law Application of Statutory Duty HCD-77
(4) Work Done for Owner HCD-78
(5) Vacant Land Condominium Corporation HCD-79
(6) Common Elements Condominium Corporation HCD-80
(7) Reserve Fund HCD-81
(8) Warranties HCD-82

---

(1) Repair After Damages

(a) General

▼HCD-73▼ Statutory duty. Legislation in a number of jurisdictions obligates a corporation and/or an owner to repair portions of the condominium property (*i.e.*, the units and common elements) after damage. The extent to which a corporation or an owner must repair condominium property after damage, however, varies. In most jurisdictions, the statutory obligation to repair condominium property after damage and the obligation to maintain are mutually exclusive.[1]

Note

1. (BC) *Strata Property Act*, S.B.C. 1998, c. 43, s. 72(1).

   (MB) *Condominium Act*, C.C.S.M. c. C170, s. 18(1)

   (NB) *Condominium Property Act,* S.N.B. 2009, c. C-16.05, s. 48(1)

   (NL) *Condominium Act, 2009*, S.N.L. 2009, c. C-29.1, s. 54(1) (not yet in force)

   (NS) *Condominium Act*, R.S.N.S. 1989, c. 85, s. 35(1)

   (ON) *Condominium Act, 1998*, S.O. 1998, c. 19, s. 90(2). See also s. 97(1). If the corporation has an obligation to repair the units or common elements after damage or to maintain them and the corporation carries out the obligation using materials that are as reasonably close in quality to the original as is appropriate in accordance with current construction standards, the work shall be deemed not to be an addition, alteration or improvement to the common elements.

   (PE) *Condominium Act,* R.S.P.E.I. 1988, c. C-16, s. 21(1)

   (NT) *Condominium Act*, R.S.N.W.T. 1988, c. C-15, s. 23(4)

   (NU) *Condominium Act,* R.S.N.W.T. (Nu.) 1988, c. C-15, s. 23(4)

   (YT) *Condominium Act*, R.S.Y. 2002, c. 36, s. 18(4).

(b) Condominium Property

▼HCD-74▼ Units. Pursuant to certain provincial and territorial legislation, it is the corporation that is responsible for repairing units after damage.[1] This obligation to repair units, however, may not include any obligation to repair improvements made to units.[2] Legislation further provides differing mechanisms for determining what constitutes damage and who is responsible for repairing it. For example, in Manitoba, where damage to the units occurs, the board must determine whether there has been substantial damage pursuant to a prescribed formula, after which time owners vote on whether repairs should be undertaken.[3] Conversely, in other jurisdictions, such as Alberta and Saskatchewan, the duty to repair unit damage depends on what in the unit has been damaged, and whether such repair has been directed by the by-laws or by a municipal or other public authority.[4]

Common elements. As with units, certain provincial and territorial legislation obligate the corporation to repair damage to common elements.[5] A corporation's obligation, however, is limited by prescribed exceptions and, as with units, it is not required to repair damage to improvements made to a unit.[6] Where a corporation has obtained the use or benefit of common element forming part of another condominium property, the party who benefits from the use of that common element bears the burden of repairing any damage to it.[7]

Exclusive-use common elements. In Saskatchewan, subject to the its by-laws, the corporation is responsible for repairing damage to exclusive-use common elements and the unit owner must provide the corporation with access to the exclusive-use common element area that the owner is entitled to, in order to allow for such repair.[8] Legislation in other jurisdictions qualifies the corporation's responsibility for repairing damage to exclusive-use common elements. While the corporation generally has an obligation to repair damage to common elements in Ontario, the declaration may alter this obligation by providing that each owner is responsible for repairing the exclusive-use common element areas that the owner is entitled to.[9] In Alberta, the corporation may collect a deposit from an owner who rents a unit for the repair of damage to any common property, including exclusive-use common property, caused by the lessee.[10]

Substantial damage. In some jurisdictions, substantial damage may be excluded from the corporation's duty to repair.[11] In other jurisdictions, owners may vote on whether the corporation should repair substantial damage to condominium property. For example, in Manitoba, when damage to condominium property occurs, the corporation's board must determine within a prescribed period of time whether such damage qualifies as substantial damage pursuant to the definition of the governing legislation. Where there has been a determination that substantial damage has occurred, owners owning a prescribed percentage of the condominium property vote on whether the corporation should repair the damage. If there is a vote in favour of repairs, the corporation must repair the damage within a prescribed period of time.[12]

Notes

1. (MB) *Condominium Act*, C.C.S.M. c. C170, s. 18(2). A declaration may alter this duty to repair by imposing an obligation on the unit owner: s. 18(5)(a)

   (BC) *Strata Property Act*, S.B.C. 1998, c. 43, s. 72(1). By-laws may alter this duty: s. 72(2)

   (NB) *Condominium Property Act,* S.N.B. 2009, c. C-16.05, s. 48(2). But see exception for substantial damage: s. 49

   (NL) *Condominium Act, 2009*, S.N.L. 2009, c. C-29.1, ss. 35(1)(g) and 54(1), but obligation does not include repairs to substantial damage or wilful damage caused by an owner: s. 54(2)-(5) (not yet in force)

   (ON) *Condominium Act, 1998*, S.O. 1998, c. 19, s. 89(1). A declaration may, and usually does, alter this duty to repair by imposing an obligation on the unit owner to repair his or her unit: s. 91

   (NT) *Condominium Act*, R.S.N.W.T. 1988, c. C-15, s. 23(3). A declaration may alter this duty to repair by imposing an obligation on the unit owner: s. 23(5)

   (YT) *Condominium Act*, R.S.Y. 2002, c. 36, s. 18(3). A declaration may alter this duty to repair by imposing an obligation on the unit owner: s. 18(5).
2. (MB) *Condominium Act*, C.C.S.M. c. C170, s. 18(1), no obligation for improvements made after the registration of the corporation's declaration and plan.

   (ON) *Condominium Act, 1998*, S.O. 1998, c. 19, s. 89(2)-(5)

   (NT) *Condominium Act*, R.S.N.W.T. 1988, c. C-15, s. 23(4)

   (YT) *Condominium Act*, R.S.Y. 2002, c. 36, s. 18(4).
3. (MB) *Condominium Act*, C.C.S.M. c. C170, s. 19(1).
4. (AB) *Condominium Property Act,* R.S.A. 2000, c. C-22, App. 1, s. 2(b) and App. 2, s. 1(b), (c)

   (SK) *Condominium Property Act, 1993*, S.S. 1993, c. C-26.1; (SK) Condominium Property Regulations, 2001, R.R.S. c. C-26.1 Reg. 2, Condominium Bylaws, s. 2(b). But see (SK) Condominium Property Regulations, 2001, R.R.S. c. C-26.1 Reg. 2, Condominium Bylaws, s. 2(a).
5. (AB) *Condominium Property Act,* R.S.A. 2000, c. C-22, s. 37(2) and App. 2, Sch. A, s. 2(b), (d). But see s. 53(3)

   (BC) *Strata Property Act*, S.B.C. 1998, c. 43, s. 72

   (MB) *Condominium Act*, C.C.S.M. c. C170, ss. 18(2), 19(1), (2), 20(1), (2)

   (NB) *Condominium Property Act,* S.N.B. 2009, c. C-16.05, s. 48(2). But see exception for substantial damage: s. 49

   (NL) *Condominium Act, 2009*, S.N.L. 2009, c. C-29.1, s. 19(1)(b) (not yet in force)

   (ON) *Condominium Act, 1998*, S.O. 1998, c. 19, s. 89(1)

   (SK) *Condominium Property Act, 1993*, S.S. 1993, c. C-26.1, s. 35(2)(a), (b)

   (YT) *Condominium Act*, R.S.Y. 2002, c. 36, s. 18(3).
6. (NL) *Condominium Act, 2009*, S.N.L. 2009, c. C-29.1, s. 54(1) (not yet in force), where the duty to repair does not include repair to substantial damage; (ON) *Condominium Act, 1998*, S.O. 1998, c. 19, s. 89(2).
7. *Wentworth Condominium Corp. No. 12 v. Wentworth Condominium Corp. No. 59*, [2007] O.J. No. 2741, 57 R.P.R. (4th) 128 (Ont. S.C.J.).
8. (SK) *Condominium Property Act, 1993*, S.S. 1993, c. C-26.1, s. 72(2).

9. (ON) *Condominium Act, 1998*, S.O. 1998, c. 19, s. 91(c).
10. (AB) *Condominium Property Act,* R.S.A. 2000, c. C-22, s. 53(3)-(7). See also App. 1, s. 34 and the (AB) *Residential Tenancies Act,* S.A. 2004, c. R-17.1, s. 57.
11. (NB) *Condominium Property Act,* S.N.B. 2009, c. C-16.05, ss. 48(2), 49; (NL) *Condominium Act, 2009*, S.N.L. 2009, c. C-29.1, s. 54(1) (not yet in force).
12. (MB) *Condominium Act*, C.C.S.M. c. C170, ss. 19(1), (2), 20(1), (2)

    (NL) *Condominium Act, 2009*, S.N.L. 2009, c. C-29.1, s. 62(1), (2) (not yet in force), but see s. 62(6)

    (ON) *Condominium Act, 1998*, S.O. 1998, c. 19, s. 123(2)-(4), (7), (10). But see exception at (ON) General Regulation, O. Reg. 48/01, s. 26 (where prescribed owners can vote for termination of corporation's governance under the Act)

    (NT) *Condominium Act*, R.S.N.W.T. 1988, c. C-15, s. 24(1), (2). See s. 28.1(1) for leasehold condominiums

    (YT) *Condominium Act*, R.S.Y. 2002, c. 36, s. 19(1), (2).

---

(2) Maintenance

(a) General

▼HCD-75▼ Statutory duty. Legislation in a number of jurisdictions obligates a corporation and/or an owner to maintain portions of the condominium property (*i.e.*, the units and common elements) The statutory duty to maintain includes the obligation to repair after normal wear and tear, but may not include an obligation to repair after damage, or to repair improvements made to units after registration of the corporation's declaration and condominium plan.[1]

Note

1. (NL) *Condominium Act, 2009*, S.N.L. 2009, c. C-29.1, s. 55(2) (not yet in force)

   (ON) *Condominium Act, 1998*, S.O. 1998, c. 19, s. 90(2). See also s. 97(1)

   (YT) *Condominium Act*, R.S.Y. 2002, c. 36, s. 18(4).

(b) Condominium Property

▼HCD-76▼ Unit. In Alberta, Newfoundland, Ontario, Saskatchewan, Northwest Territories and Yukon, each owner is responsible for maintaining his own unit. Legislation in Ontario and Yukon, however, provides that a corporation's by-laws or declaration may transfer an owner's obligation to maintain his unit onto the corporation.[1] In British Columbia,

Manitoba and New Brunswick, it is the corporation who must maintain the units.[2]

Common elements. In Newfoundland and Ontario, it is the corporation that must maintain the common elements. As with units, legislation in some jurisdictions provides that a corporation's declaration may transfer the corporation's obligation to maintain the common elements, or any part of them, to the owners. The definition of "maintain" for the purposes of discharging this statutory duty differs between jurisdictions.[3]

Exclusive-use common elements. In Saskatchewan, subject to the by-laws, the corporation is responsible for maintaining exclusive-use common elements and the entitled unit owner must provide the corporation with access to the exclusive-use common element area for the purpose of such maintenance.[4] In Ontario, while the corporation has the obligation to maintain the common elements, the corporation's declaration may provide that each owner must maintain the common elements or any part of them.[5] In Alberta, the corporation may collect a deposit from an owner who rents a unit for the maintenance of any common property, including exclusive-use common property.[6]

Notes

1. (AB) *Condominium Property Act*, R.S.A. 2000, c. C-22, s. 33, App. 1, ss. 2(b)(i), 2(c), 34, App. 2, s. 1(b), (c), (d)

   (NL) *Condominium Act, 2009*, S.N.L. 2009, c. C-29.1, s. 55(1) (not yet in force)

   (ON) *Condominium Act, 1998*, S.O. 1998, c. 19, s. 90(1), (2)

   (SK) *Condominium Property Act, 1993*, S.S. 1993, c. C-26.1; (SK) Condominium Property Regulations, 2001, R.R.S. c. C-26.1 Reg. 2, Bylaws, s. 2(d)

   (NT) *Condominium Act*, R.S.N.W.T. 1988, c. C-15, s. 23(1), (5)

   (YT) *Condominium Act*, R.S.Y. 2002, c. 36, ss. 18(1), (5).
2. (BC) *Strata Property Act*, S.B.C. 1998, c. 43, s. 72(1), but by-laws may make owner responsible for maintenance of certain elements and the corporation only responsible for a part of the common elements: s. 72(2), (3)

   (MB) *Condominium Act*, C.C.S.M. c. C170, s. 18(3)

   (NB) *Condominium Property Act*, S.N.B. 2009, c. C-16.05, s. 48(3).
3. (AB) *Condominium Property Act*, R.S.A. 2000, c. C-22, ss. 34, 37(2), App. 1, s. 2(b), (c), (d)

   (NL) *Condominium Act, 2009*, S.N.L. 2009, c. C-29.1, ss. 19(1)(b), 55(1) (not yet in force)

   (ON) *Condominium Act, 1998*, S.O. 1998, c. 19, ss. 90(1), 91(b)

   (SK) *Condominium Property Act, 1993*, S.S. 1993, c. C-26.1, s. 35(2). See also s. 35(2)

   (NT) *Condominium Act*, R.S.N.W.T. 1988, c. C-15, s. 23(2), (5)

(YT) *Condominium Act*, R.S.Y. 2002, c. 36, s. 18(1), (5).

4. (SK) *Condominium Property Act, 1993*, S.S. 1993, c. C-26.1, s. 72(2).
5. (ON) *Condominium Act, 1998*, S.O. 1998, c. 19, s. 91(c).
6. (AB) *Condominium Property Act,* R.S.A. 2000, c. C-22, s. 53(3)-(7). See also s. 33, App. 1, s. 34 and the (AB) *Residential Tenancies Act,* S.A. 2004, c. R-17.1, s. 57.

---

(3) Common Law Application of Statutory Duty

▼HCD-77▼ Reasonableness standard. In determining whether a corporation has discharged its statutory duty to repair and maintain units and common elements, courts apply a test of reasonableness.[1] A corporation will not be found liable for damage to condominium property or expenses for the repair if the corporation took all reasonable steps and acted without negligence. To meet the standard of reasonableness in Alberta and British Columbia, a corporation must both assess a problem in a timely manner[2] and retain the proper professionals to inspect damage or conduct repairs.[3] Courts have rejected a strict liability or absolute perfection standard in interpreting a corporation's statutory duty. If a corporation takes all reasonable steps to repair damage and inspect and maintain the condominium property, consistent with the practice of other such associations generally, courts have found that they should not be held responsible for damages arising as a result of any strict statutory liability. Although corporations may be required to obtain and maintain insurance with respect to the condominium property,[4] the courts have held that the condominium corporation itself is not to be treated as an insurer of the property.[5]

Overlap of obligations between owners and corporation. Where the statutory duties of both owners and the corporation are engaged, the rights and obligations of both parties must be balanced. There is no statutory or principled reason why deference should be afforded to a corporation's actions or decisions above an owner's. However, where an owner is carrying on activity that is likely to cause damage to the condominium property or to an individual, the corporation is permitted by statute to intervene.[6] The corporation must provide sufficient evidence that the owner's activities present a real risk to the condominium property or to other individuals on a balance of probabilities. Where an owner undertakes actions deemed unnecessary to repair damage or maintain the property, the owner is responsible for the payments related to such unnecessary actions.[7]

Notes

1. *Wright v. Strata Plan No. 205*, [1996] B.C.J. No. 381 at para. 30, 20 B.C.L.R. (3d) 343 (B.C.S.C.), affd [1998] B.C.J. No. 105, 103 B.C.A.C. 249 (B.C.C.A.); *Baer v. Condominium Plan 9123697*, [2000] A.J. No. 534, 2000 ABQB 293 (Alta. Q.B.); *Buskell v. Linden Real Estate Services Inc.*, [2003] M.J. No. 328, 2003 MBQB 211 (M.B.Q.B.); *Richardson v. Strata Plan LMS2435*, [2005] B.C.J. No. 948, 2005 BCSC 636 (B.C.S.C.), where obtaining inspection report in response to complaints was an appropriate but insufficient response to meet reasonableness standard where report called for further action.
2. *Baer v. Condominium Plan 9123697*, [2000] A.J. No. 534, 2000 ABQB 293 (Alta. Q.B.). Failure to act promptly was unreasonable in *Oldaker v. Strata Plan VR 1008*, [2008] B.C.J. No. 493, 2008 BCSC 346 (B.C.S.C.) and see also *Oldaker v. Strata Plan VR 1008*, [2009] B.C.J. No. 1061, 2009 BCSC 697 (B.C.S.C.) regarding costs.
3. Every strata corporation faced with problems of water ingress must rely upon adviced received from professionals: *Taychuk v. Strata Plan LMS744*, [2002] B.C.J. No. 2653, 2002 BCSC 1638 (BCSC). But see exception in *Wright v. Strata Plan No. 205*, [1996] B.C.J. No. 381, 20 B.C.L.R. (3d) 343 (B.C.S.C.), affd [1998] B.C.J. No. 105, 103 B.C.A.C. 249 (B.C.C.A.) where corporation is not held responsible for faulty work of third party professionals if corporation acted reasonably in circumstances without negligence.
4. (AB) *Condominium Property Act,* R.S.A. 2000, c. C-22, s. 47

   (BC) *Strata Property Act*, S.B.C. 1998, S.B.C. 1998, c. 43, Part 9

   (MB) *Condominium Act*, C.C.S.M. c. C170, s. 17(1)

   (NB) *Condominium Property Act,* S.N.B. 2009, c. C-16.05, s. 50(1)

   (NS) *Condominium Act*, R.S.N.S. 1989, c. 85, s. 34(1)

   (ON) *Condominium Act, 1998*, S.O. 1998, c. 19, s. 99

   (PE) *Condominium Act*, R.S.P.E.I. 1988, c. C-16, s. 18(1)

   (SK) *Condominium Property Act, 1993*, S.S. 1993, c. C-26.1, s. 65

   (NU) *Condominium Act*, R.S.N.W.T. (Nu.) 1988, c. C-15, s. 22(1)

   (YT) *Condominium Act*, R.S.Y. 2002, c. 36, s. 17(1).
5. *John Campbell Law Corp. v. Strata Plan 1350*, [2001] B.C.J. No. 2037, 2001 BCSC 1342 (B.C.S.C.), where the court considers the test for strict liability created in *Rylands v. Fletcher* (1868), L.R. 3 H.L. 330, [1861-1873] All E.R. Rep. 1 (H.L.).
6. (ON) *Condominium Act, 1998*, S.O. 1998, c. 19, s. 117; *Metropolitan Toronto Condominium Corp. No. 545 v. Stein* (2005), 53 C.L.R. (3d) 155 (Ont. C.A.), where the Court of Appeal upheld the decision of a trial judge in dismissing an application under s. 117 of the Act regarding mould contamination in the heating and cooling system of certain units. There was insufficient evidence that the mould constituted a risk of damage to property. The court narrowly construed a corporation's ability to interfere with an owner's actions to circumstances where the unit owner failed in his obligation to such a degree so as to create a risk or a condition that is likely to damage the property or cause injury to an individual.
7. *Summerside v. Le Turnberry,* [2003] J.Q. no. 2285, REJB 2003-40003 (Qué. Sup. Ct.).

(4) Work Done for Owner

▼HCD-78▼ Owner fails to carry out obligation. If an owner has an obligation to: (i) repair any portion of the condominium property after damage, and/or (ii) maintain the any portion of the condominium property, and the owner fails to carry out any of these obligation within a reasonable time, the corporation must do the work necessary to carry out the obligation. The repair and/or maintenance costs may be added to the common expenses payable for the owner's unit.[1]

Note

1. (MB) *Condominium Act*, C.C.S.M. c. C170, s. 18(6)
   (NB) *Condominium Property Act,* S.N.B. 2009, c. C-16.05, s. 48(6)
   (ON) *Condominium Act, 1998*, S.O. 1998, c. 19, s. 92(1)-(4)
   (NT) *Condominium Act*, R.S.N.W.T. 1988, c. C-15, s. 23(7), (8)
   (YT) *Condominium Act*, R.S.Y. 2002, c. 36, s. 18(7), (8).

---

(5) Vacant Land Condominium Corporation

▼HCD-79▼ Repair and maintenance. In Newfoundland and Ontario, the owner of a unit in a vacant land condominium must maintain his unit and repair it after damages while the corporation must maintain the common elements and repair them after damage.[1] The board of a vacant land condominium corporation may make, amend or repeal by-laws specifying the minimum maintenance requirements for a unit or a building structure located on a unit.[2] In Northwest Territories and Yukon, if there are one or more bare land units, the declaration must contain provisions respecting the repair and improvements constructed or added to a bare land unit after the registration of the corporation's declaration and plan after those improvements have been damaged.[3]

Substantial damage. In Newfoundland and Ontario, if the board of a vacant land condominium corporation determines that substantial damage has occurred to a building located on a unit, the owner of the unit may elect to repair the damage or to replace the building with a different building.[4]

Work done for owner. In Ontario, if the owner of a unit in a vacant land corporation fails to maintain his unit within a reasonable time or to repair it within a reasonable time after damage, the corporation may maintain or repair the unit.[5]

Notes

1. (NL) *Condominium Act, 2009*, S.N.L. 2009, c. C-29.1, ss. 19(1)(b), 85(1)-(6) (not yet in force); (ON) *Condominium Act, 1998*, S.O. 1998, c. 19, s. 162(1)-(4). See also s. 155(4).
2. (NL) *Condominium Act, 2009*, S.N.L. 2009, c. C-29.1, s. 83 (not yet in force). The declaration may also specify minimum maintenance requirements: s. 80(d)

   (ON) *Condominium Act, 1998*, S.O. 1998, c. 19, s. 160. See also s. 156(1)(d).
3. (NT) *Condominium Act*, R.S.N.W.T. 1988, c. C-15, s. 23(6); (YT) *Condominium Act*, R.S.Y. 2002, c. 36, s. 18(6).
4. (NL) *Condominium Act, 2009*, S.N.L. 2009, c. C-29.1, s. 86 (not yet in force); (ON) *Condominium Act, 1998*, S.O. 1998, c. 19, s. 163(1)-(4).
5. (ON) *Condominium Act, 1998*, S.O. 1998, c. 19, s. 162(5), (6).

---

(6) Common Elements Condominium Corporation

▼HCD-80▼ Repair and maintenance. In Newfoundland and Ontario, a common elements condominium corporation must repair and replace common elements after damage or failure and must also maintain them.[1]

Note

1. (NL) *Condominium Act, 2009*, S.N.L. 2009, c. C-29.1, s. 73(1), (2) (not yet in force), where repair and maintenance of substantial damage is excluded; (ON) *Condominium Act, 1998*, S.O. 1998, c. 19, s. 144 (1), (2).

---

(7) Reserve Fund

▼HCD-81▼ Overview. The corporation must establish one or more reserve funds used solely for the purpose of major repair and replacement of the common elements and assets of the corporation.[1] In the absence of a statutory requirement, however, the Alberta Court of Appeal has held that an owner/developer does not owe a fiduciary obligation to establish a reserve fund sufficient to pay future capital replacements.[2] Where a reserve fund is required by statute, the corporation must collect contributions to the reserve fund from the owners, in a prescribed amount, as part of the owners' contributions to the common expenses.[3] In Ontario, the board does not require owners' consent to make an expenditure out of the reserve fund.[4] The amount of the reserve fund constitutes an asset of the corporation and is only distributed to mortgagees or owners of the units when the corporation is terminated or the owners and property cease to be governed by their respective condominium legislation.[5]

Reserve fund study/depreciation report and plan for future funding. The corporation must conduct periodic studies to determine whether the amount of money in the reserve fund and the amount of contributions collected by the corporation are adequate for the purposes which the fund was established. The timing and methodology for conducting the reserve fund study is prescribed by legislation and varies by jurisdition.[6] In Alberta, Ontario and Northwest Territories, the board must review the reserve fund study and propose a plan for future funding of the reserve fund within a prescribed time period.[7] Legislation in Newfoundland and Saskatchewan also provides that the corporation must assess owners' contributions and adjust them as required.[8] The corporation's statutory obligation to obtain a reserve fund study within the prescribed time limits is a minimum requirement only and a board may arrange a new study before the prescribed time period has passed and the next reserve fund study is required.[9] While the prescribed time limit is merely an outside deadline, it does not relieve the board from its statutory obligation to review a reserve fund study within a prescribed period of time.

Use of the reserve fund. The courts have held that an unexpected repair expenditure is not a capital improvement and that preparing a reserve fund plan that projects many years into the future is always going to be "a bit of a guessing game".[10] As such, the exact timing and quantum of an expenditure is always an estimate only. Corporations are permitted to spend the reserve fund on major repairs, even if the repairs are completely unexpected and unanticipated. Expenditures of this nature from the fund are within the decision-making powers of the board. As unexpected expenditures may put the reserve fund in a deficit position, the board has a duty to revisit the reserve fund plan and make any necessary adjustments to the reserve fund levy in order to accommodate the unexpected expenditure. In addressing a reserve fund deficit the board may: (i) institute a special assessment or levy, (ii) fund expenditures from its general operating account, or (iii) increase the reserve fund levy. In most cases, the board will use a combination of these techniques to move the reserve fund out of a deficit position. The British Columbia *Strata Property Act* contains requirements for reserve fund expenses to be allocated to certain types of strata lots within the strata corporation only.[11] The courts, however, have held that the scheme of the legislation, in relation to existing strata corporations that had allocated both operating and contingent expenses by type, was to permit the corporation to continue such allocation provided that it had passed and followed a by-law to that effect prior to July 1, 2000, the day the Act came into force.[12]

Notes

1. (AB) *Condominium Property Act*, R.S.A. 2000, c. C-22, s. 38(1). See also s. 38(2) and (AB) Condominium Property Regulation, Alta. Reg. 168/2000, Part 2, ss. 25, 28, 55

   (BC) *Strata Property Act*, S.B.C. 1998, c. 43, s. 92

   (NL) *Condominium Act, 2009*, S.N.L. 2009, c. C-29.1, s. 49(1), (10) (not yet in force). The corporation may also establish a contingency fund: s. 50

   (ON) *Condominium Act, 1998*, S.O. 1998, c. 19, ss. 93(1)-(4), 95(1)

   (SK) *Condominium Property Act, 1993*, S.S. 1993, c. C-26.1, ss. 2(1), 55(1)(b), (3)-(6). For exceptions for units intended or used for agricultural purposes see (SK) Condominium Property Regulations, 2001, R.R.S. c. C-26.1 Reg. 2, s. 11(c)

   (NT) *Condominium Act*, R.S.N.W.T. 1988, c. C-15, s. 19.10(1)-(4). The board must prepare an annual report with respect to the fund: s. 19.12(1), (2).
2. *Condominium Plan No. 822 2630 v. Danray Alberta Ltd.*, [2007] A.J. No. 32, 2007 ABCA 11 (Alta. C.A.).
3. (AB) *Condominium Property Act,* R.S.A. 2000, c. C-22; (AB) Condominium Property Regulation, Alta. Reg. 168/2000, Part 2, ss. 21(1)(d), 27(1)-(3). See also Section III.6. ("Corporation's Money").

   (BC) *Strata Property Act*, S.B.C. 1998, c. 43, Part 6. See *Wilfert v. Ward*, [2004] B.C.J. No. 423, 2004 BCSC 289 (B.C.S.C.), where the court held that the provisions in the Act for operating expenses relating to specific types of strata lots to be shared exclusively by the owners of those lots do not apply to reserve fund expenses. Reserve fund expenses can only be allocated to a subset of strata lots if the strata lots have been divided into sections for purposes of cost-sharing.

   (NL) *Condominium Act, 2009*, S.N.L. 2009, c. C-29.1, s. 49(2), (8), (9) (not yet in force)

   (ON) *Condominium Act, 1998*, S.O. 1998, c. 19, s. 93(5)-(7)

   (SK) *Condominium Property Act, 1993*, S.S. 1993, c. C-26.1, ss. 56(1)(b), 58(1), (2), 59(1)-(3), 60(1), (2); (SK) Condominium Property Regulations, 2001, R.R.S. c. C-26.1 Reg. 2, ss. 47, 48-51

   (NT) *Condominium Act*, R.S.N.W.T. 1988, c. C-15, ss. 19.13(1)-(3), 19.14(2), 19.15(1)-(3).
4. (ON) *Condominium Act, 1998*, S.O. 1998, c. 19, s. 95(2).
5. (AB) *Condominium Property Act,* R.S.A. 2000, c. C-22, s. 38(3)

   (NL) *Condominium Act, 2009*, S.N.L. 2009, c. C-29.1, s. 49(11) (not yet in force)

   (ON) *Condominium Act, 1998*, S.O. 1998, c. 19, s. 95(3)

   (SK) *Condominium Property Act, 1993*, S.S. 1993, c. C-26.1, s. 61(1), (3)

   (NT) *Condominium Act*, R.S.N.W.T. 1988, c. C-15, s. 19.10(4).
6. (AB) *Condominium Property Act*, R.S.A. 2000, c. C-22; (AB) Condominium Property Regulation, Alta. Reg. 168/2000, Part 2, ss. 21(1)-(2), 22, 23(1)-(3), 24(2), 25, 26(1), (2), 30, 55

(NL) *Condominium Act, 2009*, S.N.L. 2009, c. C-29.1, s. 2, s. 49(3)-(5) (not yet in force) where reserve-fund study is required when there are 10 or more units. For amalgamated corporation, see ss. 65, 67.

(ON) *Condominium Act, 1998*, S.O. 1998, c. 19, ss. 1, 94(1)-(7); (ON) General Regulation, O. Reg. 48/01, ss. 27-32. For phased condominium corporations, see s. 153(4). For amalgamated corporations, see (ON) General Regulation, O. Reg. 48/01, s. 38

(SK) *Condominium Property Act, 1993*, S.S. 1993, c. C-26.1, ss. 58.1(1)-(10), 58.2(1), (2); (SK) Condominium Property Regulations, 2001, R.R.S. c. C-26.1 Reg. 2, s. 11, ss. 51.1-51.7

(NT) *Condominium Act*, R.S.N.W.T. 1988, c. C-15, s. 19.11(2)-(9), (12)-(15); (NT) Condominium Regulations, N.W.T. Reg. 098-2008, ss. 1, 7(1)-7(3), 8-11(2).

7. (AB) *Condominium Property Act,* R.S.A. 2000, c. C-22; (AB) Condominium Property Regulation Alta. Reg. 168/2000, Part 2, ss. 23(1), (4)-(7), 24(1)-(3), 25, 26(1), (2), 29(1), (2), 30, 31(1), (2), 55

   (ON) *Condominium Act, 1998*, S.O. 1998, c. 19, ss. 90(1), 94(8)-(10); (ON) General Regulation, O. Reg. 48/01, ss. 33(1)-(3), 38(1)-(6)

   (NT) *Condominium Act*, R.S.N.W.T. 1988, c. C-15, ss. 19.11(10)-(11), (13)-(15).

8. (NL) *Condominium Act, 2009*, S.N.L. 2009, c. C-29.1, ss. 2, 49(2), (6), (7), 63(3) (not yet in force); (SK) *Condominium Property Act, 1993*, S.S. 1993, c. C-26.1, s. 51. But note there is no specific provision for plan for future funding.

9. *Scotwick Realty Services Inc. v. Condominium Plan No. 7510479*, [2003] A.J. No. 831, 2003 ABQB 550 (Alta. Q.B.); *Little v. Metropolitan Toronto Condominium Corp. No. 590*, [2006] O.J. No. 3294, 50 R.P.R. (4th) 128 (Ont. C.J.)

   (AB) *Condominium Property Act,* R.S.A. 2000, c. C-22; (AB) Condominium Property Regulation, Alta. Reg. 168/2000, Part 2, s. 30

   (NL) *Condominium Act, 2009,* S.N.L. 2009, c. C-29.1, s. 49(3), (5) (not yet in force)

   (ON) *Condominium Act, 1998*, S.O. 1998, c. 19, s. 94(4); (ON) General Regulation, O. Reg. 48/01, s. 31(2)

   (SK) *Condominium Property Act, 1993*, S.S. 1993, c. C-26.1; (SK) Condominium Property Regulations, 2001, R.R.S. c. C-26.1 Reg. 2, s. 51.2

   (NT) *Condominium Act*, R.S.N.W.T. 1988, c. C-15, s. 19.11(5), (6).

10. *Scotwick Realty Services Inc. v. Condominium Plan No. 7510479*, [2003] A.J. No. 831 at para. 15, 2003 ABQB 550 (Alta. Q.B.).

11. (B.C.) *Strata Property Act*, S.B.C. 1998, c. 43, ss. 99, 109; Strata Property Regulation, B.C. Reg. 43/2000, s. 64; *Strata Plan VR 2654 v. Mason*, [2004] B.C.J. No. 1061 (B.C.S.C.), where the court found that such a by-law had been passed and filed and concluded that the condominium by-law authorizes the strata corporation to allocate operating fund expenses and contingency reserve expenses, including those raised by special levy, according to type of strata lot (*i.e.*, townhouse or apartment) both before and after January 1, 2002. Under s. 17.11(1) and (2) of the regulation, the standard by-laws under the Act did not apply up to January 1, 2002 while the by-laws created prior to July 1, 2000, including the by-law in this case, did apply.

12. *Strata Plan VR 2654 v. Mason*, [2004] B.C.J. No. 1061 (B.C.S.C.).

(8) Warranties

▼HCD-82▼ Benefit of warranties. In Ontario, all warranties given with respect to work and materials furnished for a unit are for the benefit of the owner, while all warranties given with respect to the work and materials furnished for the common elements are for the benefit of the corporation. The corporation may enforce an owner's warranties on behalf of the owner if the corporation does work on the owner's behalf.[1]

Note

1. See Chapter VIII. ("Compliance, Enforcement Remedies and Dispute Resolution") (ON) *Condominium Act, 1998*, S.O. 1998, c. 19, s. 96(1)-(3).

---

3. Changes to the Condominium Property, Assets and Services

(1) Changes Made by Corporation HCD-83
(2) Changes Made by Owners HCD-84

---

(1) Changes Made by Corporation

▼HCD-83▼ Changes/modifications to common elements or assets. Legislation in Newfoundland, Nova Scotia, Ontario provide that a corporation requires approval from a prescribed percentage of owners to make a substantial addition, alteration, improvement to the common elements, a substantial change in the assets of the corporation or a substantial change in a service that the corporation provides to the owners. The definition of what constitutes a substantial change varies by jurisdiction. Legislation further provides a mechanism for corporations to make non-substantial additions, alterations, improvements to the common elements, changes in the assets of the corporation or changes in a service that the corporation provides. For example, a corporation in Nova Scotia requires a vote by the majority of owners while in Ontario, a corporation may undertake such changes, with our without notice, by meeting prescribed requirements.[1] The costs of above changes made by the corporation are common expenses in some jurisdictions.[2]

Notes

1. (AB) *Condominium Property Act*, R.S.A. 2000, c. C-22, ss. 1(1)(x), 38(1)-(3), 61(4), App. 1, ss. 1(1)-(4), 3(f), App. 2, s. 3(e); (AB) Condominium Property Regulation, Alta. Reg. 168/2000, Part 2, ss. 21(1), 28

   (BC) *Strata Property Act*, S.B.C. 1998, c. 43, s. 71, where there must be reasonable grounds to believe that immediate change is necessary to ensure safety or prevent significant loss or damage

   (MB) *Condominium Act,* C.C.S.M. c. C170, ss. 16(1), 16(1.1)-(1.6), (3), (4)

   (NB) *Condominium Property Act*, S.N.B. 2009, c. C-16.05, s. 14(1), (3), (4)

   (NL) *Condominium Act, 2009*, S.N.L. 2009, c. C-29.1, s. 52(1) (not yet in force)

   (NS) *Condominium Act*, R.S.N.S. 1989, c. 85, s. 32(1)

   (ON) *Condominium Act, 1998*, S.O. 1998, c. 19, s. 97(1)-(6)

   (PE) *Condominium Act*, R.S.P.E.I. 1988, c. C-16, s. 17(1), (4), (5)

   (SK) *Condominium Property Act, 1993*, S.S. 1993, c. C-26.1; (SK) Condominium Property Regulations, 2001, R.R.S. c. C-26.1 Reg. 2, ss. 44, 44.1, Condominium Bylaws (s. 44), ss. 1(1)-(4), 4(f)

   (NT) *Condominium Act*, R.S.N.W.T. 1988, c. C-15, s. 21(1), (3). See s. 28.1(1) for changes to leasehold condominium corporations

   (YT) *Condominium Act*, R.S.Y. 2002, c. 36, s. 16(1), (3).

2. (MB) *Condominium Act,* C.C.S.M. c. C170, s. 16(2)

   (NB) *Condominium Property Act*, S.N.B. 2009, c. C-16.05, s. 14(2)

   (NL) *Condominium Act, 2009*, S.N.L. 2009, c. C-29.1, s. 52(2) (not yet in force)

   (NS) *Condominium Act*, R.S.N.S. 1989, c. 85, s. 32(2)

   (ON) *Condominium Act, 1998*, S.O. 1998, c. 19, s. 97(7)

   (PE) *Condominium Act*, R.S.P.E.I. 1988, c. C-16, s. 17(3)

   (NT) *Condominium Act*, R.S.N.W.T. 1988, c. C-15, s. 21(2)

   (YT) *Condominium Act*, R.S.Y. 2002, c. 36, s. 16(2).

---

(2) Changes Made by Owners

▼HCD-84▼ Changes/modifications to common elements or assets. An owner may only make an addition, alteration or improvement to the common elements with the consent of the board, or a prescribed number of owners owning common elements; and such consent cannot be unreasonably withheld.[1] The board is given wide latitude as to how it will exercise its discretion in granting or withholding consent and the Alberta Court of Appeal has stated that there is nothing objectionable to the board setting down rules and regulations as to how its discretion will be exercised in the normal course.[2] Specifically, withholding consent is not unreasonable when the corporation acts in the interest of the entire community in enforcing the corporation's by-laws.[3] Alternatively, an owner may make an addition, alteration or improvement to parts of the common elements over which he has exclusive use, without notice or approval from the board, if the changes meet a prescribed criteria.[4] An owner's right to make changes has also been informed by the common law. The Supreme Court has ruled that owners do not waive their religious rights and freedoms in purchasing a unit in a corporation or by signing the declaration. In *Syndicat Northcrest v. Amselem*, owners were permitted to put succahs (a temporary hut constructed for temporary use for the week-long Jewish holiday of Sukkot) on their balconies so long as they complied with the corporation's safety restrictions and constructed their succahs in a manner that conformed, as much as possible, with the general aesthetics of the property in order to respect the co-owner's property interests.[5] Where an addition violates a corporation's declaration and rules, its removal cannot be delayed until after the next owner's meeting where the merits of such additions will be considered.[6]

Notes

1. (AB) *Condominium Property Act*, R.S.A. 2000, c. C-22, s. 33, App. 1, ss. 1(1), 2(e). Written consent required for structural, mechanical or electrical alterations to common property.

   (ON) *Condominium Act, 1998*, S.O. 1998, c. 19, s. 98(1), (3), (4), (5); (ON) General Regulation, O. Reg. 48/01, s. 25(1), (2); see *Wentworth Condominium Corp. No. 198 v. McMahon*, [2009] O.J. No. 5298, 2009 ONCA 870 (Ont. C.A.) regarding definition of "addition", alteration" and "improvement")

   (SK) *Condominium Property Act, 1993*, S.S. 1993, c. C-26.1; (SK) Condominium Property Regulations, 2001, R.R.S. c. C-26.1 Reg. 2, ss. 44, 44.1, Interpretation, ss. 1(1)-(4), 2(f) Written consent required for mechanical or electrical alterations to common property or unit that affect common property or another unit.
2. *Maverick Equities Inc. v. Condominium Plan No. 9422336*, [2008] A.J. No. 616, 2008 ABCA 221 (Alta. C.A.); see also *Metropolitan Toronto Condominium Corp. No. 985 v. Vanduzer*, [2010] O.J. No. 571 at para. 26 (Ont. S.C.) where the Ontario Superior Court noted that there are no statutory criteria limiting the scope of discretion reposed in condominium boards in approving or denying owner request to make alterations, additions and improvements.
3. *AW-NM Ventures Ltd. v. Strata Plan LMS 2856*, [2004] B.C.J. No. 1004, 2004 BCSC 666 (B.C.S.C.), where corporation was entitled to insist on removal of commercial sign erected by an owner on the common elements.
4. (ON) *Condominium Act, 1998*, S.O. 1998, c. 19, s. 98(2).
5. *Syndicat Northcrest v. Amselem*, [2004] S.C.J. No. 46, 2004 SCC 47 (S.C.C.) where the court found that a prohibition of a religious addition to an exclusive use common element infringed an owner's right to freedom of religion guaranteed under the (QC) *Charter of Human Rights*, R.S.Q., c. C-12 and the *Canadian Charter of Rights and Freedoms*, Part I of the *Constitution Act, 1982*, being Schedule B to the *Canada Act 1982* (U.K.), 1982, c. 11 (the "Charter").

6. *Peel Condominium Corp. No. 283 v. Genik*, [2007] O.J. No. 2544, 2007 CanLII 23915 (Ont. S.C.J.).

VIII. Compliance, Enforcement, Remedies and Dispute Resolution

1. Introduction HCD-85

2. Compliance with the Act, Declaration, By-Laws and Rules HCD-86

3. Purchase and Sale of Units and Development of the Condominium Property

(1) Rescission of Agreement of Purchase and Sale by Purchaser HCD-87
(2) Termination of Agreement of Purchase and Sale by Developer HCD-88
(3) Termination of Other Types of Agreements HCD-89
(4) Damages for Developer's Statement or Information HCD-90
(5) Warranties and Performance Audit Related to Construction of the Condominium Property HCD-91
(6) Remedies Related to Developer's Turn-Over Obligations HCD-92
(7) Remedies Related to Money Held in Trust HCD-93
(8) Obligations Related to First-Year Deficit HCD-94
(9) Remedies for Other Obligations HCD-95
(10) Obligations and Remedies Related to Phased Development HCD-96

4. Non-Payment of Common Expenses or Other Contributions by Owners

(1) Statutory Lien HCD-97
(2) Court Proceedings HCD-98
(3) Payment of Arrears by Tenant HCD-99
(4) Mortgagee's Rights HCD-100

5. Occupation and Use of Units and Common Elements

(1) Use of Common Elements and Changes to Units and Common Elements HCD-101
(2) Repair and Maintenance HCD-102

(3) Noise, Nuisance and Harassment HCD-103
(4) Tenants and Occupants HCD-104
(5) Pets HCD-105
(6) Dangerous Activities HCD-106

6. Court-Appointed Officers

(1) Appointment of Inspector HCD-107
(2) Appointment of Investigator HCD-108
(3) Appointment of Administrator HCD-109

7. Oppression Remedy

(1) Statutory Basis HCD-110
(2) Application of Oppression Remedy HCD-111

8. Costs and Indemnification HCD-112

9. Alternative Dispute Resolution

(1) Optional Alternative Dispute Resolution HCD-113
(2) Mandatory Alternative Dispute Resolution HCD-114

10. Offences HCD-115

---

1. Introduction

▼HCD-85▼ Remedial nature of condominium legislation. Condominium legislation is remedial and is not to be rigidly or narrowly construed to the extent that it confers rights on the condominium.[1] As far as possible and with due regard for the particular mutual covenants of individual owners, courts should bring a broad and equitable approach to the resolution of their problems.[2] Nothing in the condominium statutes restricts the remedies otherwise available for failure to perform a duty imposed by the legislation.[3]

Remedies covered elsewhere. This chapter aims to cover all remedies contained in the legislation and case law specific to condominiums, with the exception of remedies regarding amendments to a declaration, description or plan[4] and remedies regarding termination of the condominium scheme,[5] which are covered in other chapters.

Notes

1. *Middlesex Condominium Corp. No. 87 v. 600 Talbot Street London Ltd.*, [1998] O.J. No. 450, 37 O.R. (3d) 22 (Ont. C.A.).
2. *York Condominium Corp. No. 59 v. York Condominium Corp. No. 87*, [1983] O.J. No. 3088, 42 O.R. (2d) 337 (Ont. C.A.).
3. (AB) *Condominium Property Act*, R.S.A. 2000, c. C-22, ss. 36(7), 80(2)
   (BC) *Strata Property Act*, S.B.C. 1998, c. 43, ss. 165, 173
   (MB) *Condominium Act*, C.C.S.M. c. C170, s. 24(4)
   (NB) *Condominium Property Act*, S.N.B. 2009, c. C-16.05, s. 60(5)
   (NL) *Condominium Act, 2009*, S.N.L. 2009, c. C-29.1, s. 64(6) (not yet in force)
   (NS) *Condominium Act*, R.S.N.S. 1989, c. 85, s. 38(4)
   (ON) *Condominium Act, 1998*, S.O. 1998, c. 19, s. 136
   (PE) *Condominium Act,* R.S.P.E.I. 1988, c. C-16, s. 29(4)
   (SK) *Condominium Property Act, 1993*, S.S. 1993, c. C-26.1, s. 99(6)
   (NT) *Condominium Act*, R.S.N.W.T. 1988, c. C-15, ss. 17.2(7), 30(4)
   (NU) *Condominium Act*, R.S.N.W.T. 1988 (Nu.), c. C-15, s. 30(4)
   (YT) *Condominium Act*, R.S.Y. 2002, c. 36, s. 24(4).
4. See Subsection II.4.(3) ("Amendments").
5. See Section IX.2. ("Termination of Condominium or Corporation").

---

2. Compliance with the Act, Declaration, By-Laws and Rules

▼HCD-86▼ Obligation to comply. Every owner is bound by, must comply with and has a right to compliance by the owners with the Act, declaration, by-laws and, in some jurisdictions, rules.[1] The condominium corporation and every person having an encumbrance against a unit and common interest has a right to compliance and, in some jurisdictions, to the performance of any duty of the corporation specified by the statute, declaration, by-laws and rules.[2] In some jurisdictions, the obligation to comply extends to tenants renting a unit from an owner.[3] In Alberta, improper conduct includes non-compliance by a developer, corporation, employee, board member or owner.[4] In Ontario, the obligation to comply extends to condominium corporations, the directors, officers and employees of the corporation, developers, lessors of leasehold condominiums, occupiers of units and proposed units and persons having an encumbrance against a unit and its appurtenant common interest.[5] The declaration, description, by-laws and rules of a corporation are vital to the integrity of the title acquired by a unit owner; a unit owner is bound by their terms and provisions and is entitled to insist that other unit owners be similarly bound.[6]

Duty to effect compliance. The corporation has a duty to effect compliance by the owners with the Act, declaration, by-laws and rules.[7] In Manitoba, this duty extends to compliance by tenants renting a unit from an owner.[8] In Newfoundland and Labrador and Ontario, this duty extends to compliance by occupiers of units, lessees of common elements and the corporation's agents and employees.[9] In Ontario, an owner must take all reasonable steps to ensure that an occupier of the owner's unit and all invitees, agents and employees of the owner or occupier comply, and a developer must take all reasonable steps to ensure that occupiers of proposed units comply.[10] The major advantage of requiring compliance is the message to current and prospective owners that the declaration, by-laws and rules are in place for a good reason and that the courts will support the board where it acts reasonably in carrying out its duty to enforce the declaration, by-laws and rules.[11]

Application for compliance order. In most jurisdictions, if a duty imposed by the statute, declaration, by-laws or rules is not performed, the corporation, any owner or any person having an encumbrance against a unit and common interest may apply to court for an order directing the performance of the duty.[12] In Alberta, a corporation, board member, owner, registered mortgagee or any other person with a registered interest in a unit may apply to court for a compliance order.[13] In British Columbia, a corporation, owner, tenant, mortgagee or interested person may apply to court for a compliance order.[14] In Ontario, a corporation, owner, occupier of a proposed unit, developer, lessor of a leasehold condominium or mortgagee of a unit may apply to court for an order enforcing compliance with any provision of the statute, declaration, by-laws or rules or an agreement between two or more corporation for the mutual use, provision, maintenance or cost-sharing of facilities or services of any of the parties to the agreement.[15] However, in Ontario, if the mediation and arbitration processes described in the statute are available, a person is not entitled to apply for a compliance order until the person has failed to obtain compliance through using those processes.[16]

Terms of compliance order. In most jurisdictions, the court may direct performance of the duty by order and may include in the order any provisions the court considers appropriate in the circumstances, including the payment of costs and the appointment of an administrator for any time and on any terms and conditions as it considers necessary.[17] In Alberta, the court may: direct that an investigator be appointed; direct that a person cease carrying on improper conduct; give directions so that the conduct will not reoccur or continue; award compensation in respect of a loss; award costs; give any other directions or order it considers appropriate; and grant interim relief.[18] In British Columbia, the court may order the performance of the duty and the cessation of the contravention and may make any other orders it considers necessary to give effect to those orders.[19] In Ontario, the court may grant the order applied for, may require named persons to pay damages and costs, or may grant such other relief as is fair and equitable in the circumstances. The court may also make an order requiring a person convicted of an offence to comply with the provisions of the statute that the person has contravened, if the court has competent jurisdiction to make the order.[20]

Sanctions for by-laws. In Alberta, a corporation may by by-law impose reasonable monetary or other sanctions on owners, tenants and invitees of the owners or tenants who fail to comply with the by-laws.[21] A by-law under which sanctions are imposed must set out the possible sanctions and, in the case of monetary sanctions, the amount or range of monetary sanctions.[22] A sanction may not have the effect of prohibiting or restricting the devolution of units or any transfer, lease, mortgage or other dealing with the units or of destroying or modifying any easement implied or created by the act.[23] If a person fails to comply with a sanction, the condominium corporation may take proceedings in two different courts and, depending on the court, a court may award damages to a maximum of $10,000 or may award injunctive relief, other appropriate relief, costs and legal expenses.[24] In Saskatchewan, if an owner, tenant or other person who resides in a unit contravenes a by-law, the corporation may take proceedings in small claims court to recover a maximum penalty of $500 for the contravention, and the court may award damages and costs.[25] A corporation may not recover a penalty where it fails to properly follow the procedures in its by-laws regarding claims for such a penalty.[26]

Deference to duly elected boards. As a matter of general application, courts should defer to the decisions of duly elected boards acting within their jurisdiction and should not lightly interfere with such decisions and substitute their own opinion, unless the decisions are clearly oppressive, capricious, unreasonable or contrary to the legislative scheme.[27] However, this deference is not absolute.[28]

Notes

1. (AB) *Condominium Property Act*, R.S.A. 2000, c. C-22, s. 32(2)
   (MB) *Condominium Act*, C.C.S.M. c. C170, s. 13(1)
   (NB) *Condominium Property Act*, S.N.B. 2009, c. C-16.05, s. 23(1)-(2)
   (PE) *Condominium Act,* R.S.P.E.I. 1988, c. C-16, s. 15(1)-(2)

(NT) *Condominium Act*, R.S.N.W.T. 1988, c. C-15, s. 18(1)

(NU) *Condominium Act*, R.S.N.W.T. 1988 (Nu.), c. C-15, s. 18(1)

(YT) *Condominium Act*, R.S.Y. 2002, c. 36, s. 13(1).

For cases in which owners breached the duty to comply with a declaration, by-law or rule by failing to obtain permission or approval before making changes to property or by exceeding the permission or approval given, see *e.g.*, *Syndicat des copropriétaires Copropriété du Square St-David I c. Chevalier*, [2005] J.Q. no 9815 (Que C.S.); *Summerville Condominium Corp. v. Dynamic Physiotherapy Services Ltd.*, [2003] N.J. No. 332, 2003 NLSCTD 182 (Nfld. S.C.); *East Gate Estates Essex Condominium Corp. No. 2 v. Kimmerly*, [2003] O.J. No. 582 (Ont. S.C.J.); *Ciddio v. York Region Condominium Corp. No. 730*, [2002] O.J. No. 553 (Ont. S.C.J.).

2. (MB) *Condominium Act*, C.C.S.M. c. C170, s. 13(2)-(3)

(NB) *Condominium Property Act*, S.N.B. 2009, c. C-16.05, s. 23(3)

(NS) *Condominium Act*, R.S.N.S. 1989, c. 85, s. 30(3)

(PE) *Condominium Act,* R.S.P.E.I. 1988, c. C-16, s. 15(3)

(NT) *Condominium Act*, R.S.N.W.T. 1988, c. C-15, s. 18(2)-(3)

(NU) *Condominium Act*, R.S.N.W.T. 1988 (Nu.), c. C-15, s. 18(2)-(3)

(YT) *Condominium Act*, R.S.Y. 2002, c. 36, s. 13(2)-(3).

3. (AB) *Condominium Property Act*, R.S.A. 2000, c. C-22, s. 53(2)

(MB) *Condominium Act*, C.C.S.M. c. C170, s. 13(1.1)

(NL) *Condominium Act, 2009*, S.N.L. 2009, c. C-29.1, s. 53 (not yet in force)

(NS) *Condominium Act*, R.S.N.S. 1989, c. 85, s. 44A

(PE) *Condominium Act,* R.S.P.E.I. 1988, c. C-16, s. 29(3)

(NT) *Condominium Act*, R.S.N.W.T. 1988, c. C-15, s. 19.2.

Carleton Condominium Corp. No. 555 v. Lagacé, [2004] O.J. No. 1480, [2004] O.T.C. 318 (Ont. S.C.J.) (condominium corporations have a direct legal relationship with unit owners, not tenants, and unit owners have a direct legal relationship with tenants and are responsible for their behaviour while occupying units; corporations look to owners to live up to the terms of declarations, by-laws and rules, and owners require tenants under a tenancy agreement to agree to comply with those documents; on a breach, corporations demand compliance from owners, who in turn demand compliance from tenants).

4. (AB) *Condominium Property Act*, R.S.A. 2000, c. C-22, s. 67(1)(a)(i).

5. (ON) *Condominium Act, 1998*, S.O. 1998, c. 19, s. 119(1), (4)-(5).

6. *Carleton Condominium Corp. No. 279 v. Rochon*, [1987] O.J. No. 417, 59 O.R. (2d) 545 (Ont. C.A.).

7. (AB) *Condominium Property Act*, R.S.A. 2000, c. C-22, s. 37(1)

(MB) *Condominium Act*, C.C.S.M. c. C170, s. 13(1)

(NB) *Condominium Property Act*, S.N.B. 2009, c. C-16.05, s. 19(4)

(NL) *Condominium Act, 2009*, S.N.L. 2009, c. C-29.1, s. 19(1)(c) (not yet in force)

(NS) *Condominium Act*, R.S.N.S. 1989, c. 85, s. 18(2)

(ON) *Condominium Act, 1998*, S.O. 1998, c. 19, s. 17(3)

(PE) *Condominium Act,* R.S.P.E.I. 1988, c. C-16, s. 10(12)

(SK) *Condominium Property Act, 1993*, S.S. 1993, c. C-26.1, s. 35(1)

(NT) *Condominium Act*, R.S.N.W.T. 1988, c. C-15, s. 18(1)

(NU) *Condominium Act*, R.S.N.W.T. 1988 (Nu.), c. C-15, s. 18(1)

(YT) *Condominium Act*, R.S.Y. 2002, c. 36, s. 13(1).

8. (MB) *Condominium Act*, C.C.S.M. c. C170, s. 13(1.1).

9. (NL) *Condominium Act, 2009*, S.N.L. 2009, c. C-29.1, s. 19(1)(c) (not yet in force)

   (ON) *Condominium Act, 1998*, S.O. 1998, c. 19, s. 17(3).

10. (ON) *Condominium Act, 1998*, S.O. 1998, c. 19, s. 119(2), (4).

11. *Metropolitan Toronto Condominium Corp. No. 776 v. Gifford*, [1989] O.J. No. 1691, 6 R.P.R. (2d) 217 (Ont. Dist. Ct.).

12. (MB) *Condominium Act*, C.C.S.M. c. C170, s. 24(1)

    (NB) *Condominium Property Act*, S.N.B. 2009, c. C-16.05, s. 60(1)

    (PE) *Condominium Act,* R.S.P.E.I. 1988, c. C-16, s. 29(1)

    (NT) *Condominium Act*, R.S.N.W.T. 1988, c. C-15, s. 30(1)

    (NU) *Condominium Act*, R.S.N.W.T. 1988 (Nu.), c. C-15, s. 30(1)

    (YT) *Condominium Act*, R.S.Y. 2002, c. 36, s. 24(1).

13. (AB) *Condominium Property Act*, R.S.A. 2000, c. C-22, s. 67(1)(b).

14. (BC) *Strata Property Act*, S.B.C. 1998, c. 43, ss. 165, 173.

15. (ON) *Condominium Act, 1998*, S.O. 1998, c. 19, s. 134(1).

16. (ON) *Condominium Act, 1998*, S.O. 1998, c. 19, s. 134(2).

17. (BC) *Strata Property Act*, S.B.C. 1998, c. 43, ss. 165, 173

    (MB) *Condominium Act*, C.C.S.M. c. C170, s. 24(2)

    (NB) *Condominium Property Act*, S.N.B. 2009, c. C-16.05, s. 60(2)

    (PE) *Condominium Act,* R.S.P.E.I. 1988, c. C-16, s. 29(2)

    (NT) *Condominium Act*, R.S.N.W.T. 1988, c. C-15, s. 30(2)

    (NU) *Condominium Act*, R.S.N.W.T. 1988 (Nu.), c. C-15, s. 30(2)

    (YT) *Condominium Act*, R.S.Y. 2002, c. 36, s. 24(2).

18. (AB) *Condominium Property Act*, R.S.A. 2000, c. C-22, s. 67(2)-(3). See also *Condominium Plan 7722911 v. Marnel*, [2008] A.J. No. 305, 2008 ABQB 195 (Alta. Q.B.) (ordering ceasing of improper conduct and costs); *Condominium Plan No. 022 1347 v. N.Y.*, [2003] A.J. No. 1227, 2003 ABQB 790 (Alta. Q.B.) (s. 67 permits eviction of an owner for breach of by-laws).

19. (BC) *Strata Property Act*, S.B.C. 1998, c. 43, ss. 165, 173.

20. (ON) *Condominium Act, 1998*, S.O. 1998, c. 19, s. 134(3)-(4). See also *Orr v. Metropolitan Toronto Condominium Corp. No. 1056*, [2011] O.J. No. 3898, 2011 ONSC 4876 (Ont. S.C.J.).

21. (AB) *Condominium Property Act*, R.S.A. 2000, c. C-22, s. 35(1), (4).

22. (AB) *Condominium Property Act*, R.S.A. 2000, c. C-22, s. 35(2).

23. (AB) *Condominium Property Act*, R.S.A. 2000, c. C-22, s. 35(6).

24. (AB) *Condominium Property Act*, R.S.A. 2000, c. C-22, s. 36(1), (3), (4), (5). See also *Condominium Corp. No. 8110264 v. Farkas*, [2009] A.J. No. 911, 2009 ABQB 488 (Alta. Q.B.) (s. 36 remedies are exclusively monetary and do not include eviction of an owner).

25. (SK) *Condominium Property Act, 1993*, S.S. 1993, c. C-26.1, s. 99(1), (3).

26. *Dunn v. Condominium Plan No. 89PA14638*, [2003] S.J. No. 76, 2003 SKQB 53 (Sask. Q.B.).

27. See *e.g.*, *Muskoka Condominium Corp. No. 39 v. Kreutzweiser*, [2010] O.J. No. 1720, 2010 ONSC 2463 (Ont. S.C.J.); *Weir v. Strata Plan NW 17*, [2010] B.C.J. No. 1057, 2010 BCSC 784 (B.C.S.C.); *934859 Alberta Inc. v. Condominium Corp. No. 0312180*, [2007] A.J. No. 1233, 2007 ABQB 640 (Alta. Q.B.); *Schaper-Kotter v. Strata Plan 148*, [2006] B.C.J. No. 924, 2006 BCSC 634 (B.C.S.C.); *York Condominium Corp. No. 382 v. Dvorchik*, [1997] O.J. No. 378, 12 R.P.R. (3d) 148 (Ont. C.A.); *Condominium Plan No. 932 2887 v. Redweik*, [1994] A.J. No. 1020, 43 R.P.R. (2d) 154 (Alta. Q.B.); *Desjardins v. Winnipeg Condominium Corp. No. 75*, [1990] M.J. No. 523, [1991] 2 W.W.R. 193 (Man. Q.B.).

28. See, *e.g.*, *934859 Alberta Inc. v. Condominium Corp. No. 0312180*, [2007] A.J. No. 1233, 2007 ABQB 640 (Alta. Q.B.) (although courts should defer to elected boards as a matter of general application, if a court is satisfied that improper conduct has taken place, the court may direct or grant any of the remedies set out in s. 67(2)); *Metropolitan Toronto Condominium Corp. No. 949 v. Staib*, [2005] O.J. No. 5131, 205 O.A.C. 15 (Ont. C.A.); *Metropolitan Toronto Condominium Corp. No. 601 v. Hadbavny*, [2001] O.J. No. 4176, [2001] O.T.C. 770 (Ont. S.C.J.); *Niagara North Condominium Corp. No. 46 v. Chassie*, [1999] O.J. No. 1201, 173 D.L.R. (4th) 524 (Ont. Gen. Div.) (lack of enforcement, capricious enforcement or delay of enforcement of a rule can make a rule unreasonable for owners who have a reasonable expectation that the rule will not be enforced).

---

3. Purchase and Sale of Units and Development of the Condominium Property

(1) Rescission of Agreement of Purchase and Sale by Purchaser HCD-87
(2) Termination of Agreement of Purchase and Sale by Developer HCD-88
(3) Termination of Other Types of Agreements HCD-89
(4) Damages for Developer's Statement or Information HCD-90
(5) Warranties and Performance Audit Related to Construction of the Condominium Property HCD-91
(6) Remedies Related to Developer's Turn-Over Obligations HCD-92
(7) Remedies Related to Money Held in Trust HCD-93
(8) Obligations Related to First-Year Deficit HCD-94
(9) Remedies for Other Obligations HCD-95
(10) Obligations and Remedies Related to Phased Development HCD-96

---

(1) Rescission of Agreement of Purchase and Sale by Purchaser

▼HCD-87▼ Right to rescind on notice. In some jurisdictions, a purchaser of a unit may rescind the agreement of purchase and sale on written notice without incurring liability for doing so.[1] In Alberta, Saskatchewan and Northwest Territories, the purchaser may rescind the agreement in writing within 10 days after the agreement was signed, but may not do so if all required documents and information were delivered to the purchaser not less than 10 days before the agreement was signed.[2] In Alberta, the developer must include in the agreement a specific clause regarding the purchaser's right to rescind.[3] In Newfoundland and Labrador, the purchaser must give the written notice within 10 days of the later of the date the purchaser receives the disclosure statement or required estoppel certificate and the date the agreement is executed.[4] In Ontario, the written notice may be given by the purchaser or purchaser's solicitor to the developer or developer's solicitor, and the developer must receive the notice within 10 days of the later of the date the purchaser receives the disclosure statement and the date the purchaser receives a copy of the executed agreement.[5]

Where no right to rescind on notice. In Saskatchewan and Northwest Territories, the purchaser may not rescind the agreement of purchase and sale where the units and common facilities have been completed and the developer has provided certain documents to the condominium and convened the first annual meeting.[6] In Saskatchewan only, a purchaser may waive the right to rescind where he or she has obtained a certificate of independent legal advice,[7] and a purchaser of a unit intended for agricultural purposes may not rescind the agreement on the basis that the developer has not satisfied certain provisions related to the sale of units for agricultural purposes.[8]

Refund upon rescission on notice. Within 10 days after receiving written notice of rescission from the purchaser, a developer must refund to the purchaser all of the money paid in respect of the purchase of the unit.[9] In Ontario, the developer must also refund interest on the money paid, calculated at the prescribed rate from the date the developer received the money until the date the developer refunds the money.[10] In Newfoundland and Labrador, no time limit is specified for the refund, but the developer must refund the money promptly.[11]

Rescission after material change. In Ontario and Northwest Territories, within 10 days of receiving revised information in a revised disclosure statement or notice, a purchaser may apply to court for a determination whether a change or series of changes set out in the revised information is a material change.[12] In Ontario, the developer may also apply to court for the same determination within 10 days after receiving a notice of rescission, if the purchaser has not already made an application.[13] In Ontario and Northwest Territories, if a change or series of changes set out in revised information delivered to a purchaser is a material change, or if a material change occurs that the developer does not disclose in revised information, the purchaser may, before accepting a transfer of the unit being purchased, rescind the agreement of purchase and sale within 10 days after the latest of:[14]

- the date the purchaser receives the revised information, if the developer delivered revised information to the purchaser
- the date the purchaser becomes aware of a material change, if the developer did not deliver revised information to the purchaser as required with respect to the change and
- the date the court makes a determination that the change is material, if the purchaser, or the purchaser or developer in Ontario, has applied for the determination

Refund upon rescission after material change. In Ontario, within 10 days after the court makes a determination, a developer must refund to the purchaser all of the money paid in respect of the purchase of the unit together with interest on the money paid, calculated at the prescribed rate from the date the developer received the money until the date the developer refunds the money.[15]

Notes

1. (AB) *Condominium Property Act*, R.S.A. 2000, c. C-22, s. 12(3)

   (NL) *Condominium Act, 2009*, S.N.L. 2009, c. C-29.1, s. 43(1) (not yet in force)

   (ON) *Condominium Act, 1998*, S.O. 1998, c. 19, s. 73(1)

   (SK) *Condominium Property Act, 1993*, S.S. 1993, c. C-26.1, s. 26(2)

   (NT) *Condominium Act*, R.S.N.W.T. 1988, c. C-15, s. 6.4(2)

   See also *Abdool v. Somerset Place Developments of Georgetown Ltd.*, [1992] O.J. No. 2115, 10 O.R. (3d) 120 (Ont. C.A.), leave to appeal to S.C.C. refused [1992] S.C.C.A. No. 575, [1993] 2 S.C.R. v (S.C.C.); *Rogers Cove Ltd. v. Sloot*, [1991] O.J. No. 1937, 19 R.P.R. (2d) 154 (Ont. Gen. Div.); *Ormond v. Richmond Square Development Corp.*, [2003] O.J. No. 668, 8 R.P.R. (4th) 234 (Ont. S.C.J.); *Buyanovsky v. Townsgate 1 Ltd.*, [1993] O.J. No. 518, 30 R.P.R. (2d) 269 (Ont. Gen. Div.), additional reasons at (1993), 30 R.P.R. (2d) 269n (Ont. Gen. Div.); *Ho v. Camrost York Development Corp.*, [1994] O.J. No. 592 (Ont. Gen. Div.), affd [1996] O.J. No. 950 (Ont. C.A.); *Scaroni v. Rosepol Holdings Ltd.*, [1995] O.J.

No. 3212, 48 R.P.R. (2d) 276 (Ont. Gen. Div); *Towne Meadow Development Corp v. Chong*, [1993] O.J. No. 693, 30 R.P.R. (2d) 228 (Ont. Gen Div.); *Bondy v. P.C. Cove Builders Inc.*, [1991] O.J. No. 2185, 22 R.P.R. (2d) 217 (Ont. Gen. Div.); *Skyrise Developments Ltd v. Aldrovandi*, [1997] O.J. No. 393 (Ont. Gen. Div.), affd [1999] O.J. No. 983 (Ont. C.A.); *Christie Corp. v. Lawrence*, [1995] O.J. No. 4532 (Ont. Gen. Div), affd [1997] O.J. No. 3776, 35 O.R. (3d) 412 (Ont. C.A.); *500 Glencairn v. Farkas*, [1994] O.J. No. 138, 36 R.P.R. (2d) 270 (Ont. Gen. Div.); *Landmark of Thornhill Ltd. v. Jacobson*, [1995] O.J. No. 2819, 47 R.P.R. (2d) 211 (Ont. C.A.). For Alberta and Saskatchewan cases, see *Bugar v. 928028 Alberta Ltd.*, [2006] A.J. No. 1254, 2006 ABPC 268 (Alta. Prov. Ct.); *Lyon v. Apex Lifestyle Communities Inc.*, [2006] A.J. No. 1331 (Alta. Master); *Buchar v. Birchwood Village Greens Ltd.*, 1997 CarswellAlta 292 (Alta. Q.B.); *Sabine v. Excelsior Loft Enterprises Corp.*, [1994] A.J. No. 384, 39 R.P.R. (2d) 86 (Alta. Master); *Foster v. MFD Warehouse Restorations Ltd.*, [2008] S.J. No. 122, 2008 SKCA 28 (Sask. C.A.); *Condominium Plan N. 86-S-36901 v. Remai Construction (1981) Inc.*, [1991] S.J. No. 410, 84 D.L.R. (4th) 6 (Sask. C.A.).

2. (AB) *Condominium Property Act*, R.S.A. 2000, c. C-22, s. 12(3)-(4)

   (SK) *Condominium Property Act, 1993*, S.S. 1993, c. C-26.1, s. 26(2)-(3)

   (NT) *Condominium Act*, R.S.N.W.T. 1988, c. C-15, s. 6.4(2)-(3).
3. (AB) *Condominium Property Act*, R.S.A. 2000, c. C-22, s. 13.
4. (NL) *Condominium Act, 2009*, S.N.L. 2009, c. C-29.1, s. 43(2) (not yet in force).
5. (ON) *Condominium Act, 1998*, S.O. 1998, c. 19, s. 73(2).
6. (SK) *Condominium Property Act, 1993*, S.S. 1993, c. C-26.1, s. 26(5); (NT) *Condominium Act*, R.S.N.W.T. 1988, c. C-15, s. 6.4(5).
7. (SK) *Condominium Property Act, 1993*, S.S. 1993, c. C-26.1, s. 27.
8. (SK) Condominium Property Regulations, 2001, R.R.S. c. C-26.1, Reg. 2, s. 10.
9. (AB) *Condominium Property Act*, R.S.A. 2000, c. C-22, s. 12(5)

   (ON) *Condominium Act, 1998*, S.O. 1998, c. 19, s. 74(9)-(10)(a)

   (SK) *Condominium Property Act, 1993*, S.S. 1993, c. C-26.1, s. 26(4)

   (NT) *Condominium Act*, R.S.N.W.T. 1988, c. C-15, s. 6.4(4).
10. (ON) *Condominium Act, 1998*, S.O. 1998, c. 19, s. 74(9).
11. (NL) *Condominium Act, 2009*, S.N.L. 2009, c. C-29.1, s. 43(3) (not yet in force).
12. (ON) *Condominium Act, 1998*, S.O. 1998, c. 19, s. 74(5); (NT) *Condominium Act*, R.S.N.W.T. 1988, c. C-15, s. 6.5(5).
13. (ON) *Condominium Act, 1998*, S.O. 1998, c. 19, s. 74(8).
14. (ON) *Condominium Act, 1998*, S.O. 1998, c. 19, s. 74(6); (NT) *Condominium Act*, R.S.N.W.T. 1988, c. C-15, s. 6.5(6).
15. (ON) *Condominium Act, 1998*, S.O. 1998, c. 19, s. 74(9)-(10). See also *Abdool v. Somerset Place Developments of Georgetown Ltd.*, [1992] O.J. No. 2115, 10 O.R. (3d) 120 (Ont. C.A.), leave to appeal to S.C.C. refused [1992] S.C.C.A. No. 575, [1993] 2 S.C.R. v (S.C.C.); *Buyanovsky v. Townsgate 1 Ltd.*, [1993] O.J. No. 518, 30 R.P.R. (2d) 269 (Ont. Gen. Div.), additional reasons at (1993), 30 R.P.R. (2d) 269n (Ont. Gen. Div.); *Ormond v. Richmond Square Development Corp.*, [2003] O.J. No. 668, 8 R.P.R. (4th) 234 (Ont. S.C.J.); *Rogers Cove Ltd. v. Sloot*, [1991] O.J. No. 1937, 19 R.P.R. (2d) 154 (Ont. Gen. Div.); *Brooker v. Silver*, [2006] O.J. No. 5553 (Ont. S.C.J.), revd on other grounds 2007 CarswellOnt 7790 (Ont. Div. Ct.); *Atkinson v. TWS Developments Inc.*, [2005] O.J. No. 2300, 32 R.P.R. (4th) 38

(Ont. S.C.J.); *Bugar v. 928028 Alberta Ltd.*, [2006] A.J. No. 1254, 2006 ABPC 268 (Alta. Prov. Ct.); *Belcourt v. 860619 Alberta Ltd.*, [2005] A.J. No. 1276, 2005 ABPC 272 (Alta. Prov. Ct.); *Foster v. MFD Warehouse Restorations Ltd.*, [2008] S.J. No. 122, 2008 SKCA 28 (Sask. C.A.). For decisions finding a material change under Ontario's predecessor rescission provisions, see *Atkinson v. TWS Developments Inc.*, [2005] O.J. No. 2300, 32 R.P.R. (4th) 38 (Ont. S.C.J.); *Ormond v. Richmond Square Development Corp.*, [2003] O.J. No. 668, 8 R.P.R. (4th) 234 (Ont. S.C.J.); *Grinberg v. Law Development Group (Thornhill) Ltd.*, [1996] O.J. No. 1722, 2 R.P.R. (3d) 209 (Ont. Gen. Div.). For decisions finding no material change, see *Abdool v. Somerset Place Developments of Georgetown Ltd.*, [1992] O.J. No. 2115, 10 O.R. (3d) 120 (Ont. C.A.), leave to appeal to S.C.C. refused [1992] S.C.C.A. No. 575, [1993] 2 S.C.R. v (S.C.C.); *Gore Plaza Inc. v. Bains*, [2007] O.J. No. 5023, 162 A.C.W.S. (3d) 1046 (Ont. S.C.J.); *Brooker v. Silver*, [2006] O.J. No. 5553 (Ont. S.C.J.), revd on other grounds 2007 CarswellOnt 7790 (Ont. Div. Ct.); *Milgram v. York Humber Ltd.*, [1992] O.J. No. 283, 22 R.P.R. (2d) 102 (Ont. Gen. Div.); *Cheung v. Greens at Tam O'Shanter Inc.*, [1993] O.J. No. 821, 31 R.P.R. (2d) 52 (Ont. C.A.); *Aiken v. Dockside Village Inc.*, [1993] O.J. No. 369 (Ont. Gen. Div.); *500 Glencairn Ltd. v. Farkas*, [1994] O.J. No. 138, 36 R.P.R. (2d) 270 (Ont. Gen. Div.); *Kozourek v. Carlyle Residence (III) Inv.*, [1996] O.J. No. 1467, 2 R.P.R. (3d) 175 (Ont. Div. Ct.), affd [1998] O.J. No. 4175 (Ont. C.A.).

---

(2) Termination of Agreement of Purchase and Sale by Developer

▼HCD-88▼ Termination only on court order. In Ontario and Prince Edward Island, a developer may not terminate an agreement of purchase and sale of a proposed unit by reason only of the failure to register the declaration and description within the period of time specified in the agreement, unless the purchaser consents to the termination in writing.[1] However, if a declaration and description have not been registered, a developer may apply to court for an order terminating the agreement.[2] In Ontario only, the developer must provide 15 days' written notice of the application to the purchasers of all proposed units in the property affected by the declaration and description.[3] In Ontario and Prince Edward Island, on an application, the court must consider whether the developer has taken all reasonable steps to register a declaration and description, whether the registration can occur within a reasonable period of time and whether the failure to register is caused by circumstances beyond the developer's control.[4] In its order, the court may provide that a declaration and description may not be registered in respect of the property in which the proposed units will be included during a period specified in the order.[5]

Termination related to phased development. In Alberta, a purchaser may enforce an agreement of purchase and sale even if the developer fails to comply with the statute.[6] However, where a building or land is to be developed in phases and the developer is unable or unwilling to register or complete the project or becomes bankrupt before all phases making up the development are registered or completed, the developer, the condominium corporation or an interested party may apply to court for an order terminating the development and giving directions or a determination in respect of any matter arising out of the termination.[7]

Notes

1. (ON) *Condominium Act, 1998*, S.O. 1998, c. 19, s. 79(2); see also *Dinicola v. Huang & Danczkay Properties*, [1996] O.J. No. 1733, 29 O.R. (3d) 161 (Ont. Gen. Div.), affd [1998] O.J. No. 2570, 40 O.R. (3d) 252 (Ont. C.A.)

   (PE) *Condominium Act*, R.S.P.E.I. 1988, c. C-16, s. 30(2).
2. (ON) *Condominium Act, 1998*, S.O. 1998, c. 19, s. 79(3); (PE) *Condominium Act*, R.S.P.E.I. 1988, c. C-16, s. 30(3).
3. (ON) *Condominium Act, 1998*, S.O. 1998, c. 19, s. 79(3).
4. (ON) *Condominium Act, 1998*, S.O. 1998, c. 19, s. 79(5); (PE) *Condominium Act*, R.S.P.E.I. 1988, c. C-16, s. 30(3).
5. (ON) *Condominium Act, 1998*, S.O. 1998, c. 19, s. 79(4); (PE) *Condominium Act*, R.S.P.E.I. 1988, c. C-16, s. 30(4).
6. (AB) *Condominium Property Act*, R.S.A. 2000, c. C-22, s. 80(3). See also *Regehr v. Camrose Crown Care Corp.*, [2006] A.J. No. 466, 2006 ABQB 296 (Alta. Q.B.).
7. (AB) Condominium Property Regulation, Alta. Reg. 168/2000, s. 37.

---

(3) Termination of Other Types of Agreements

▼HCD-89▼ Types of agreements that may be terminated. In some jurisdictions, the following types of agreements may be terminated in certain circumstances: management agreements; shared facilities and cost-sharing agreements; insurance trust agreements; and other agreements.

Management agreements. In Alberta, Saskatchewan and Northwest Territories, a condominium may terminate a developer's management agreement at any time after the developer ceases to own the majority of the units or common elements, but may not do so without cause until one year has elapsed from the day on which the parties signed the agreement, unless the agreement permits earlier termination.[1] In British Columbia, a strata management contract may be cancelled without liability or penalty by either party, but if the condominium corporation is cancelling the contract, the cancellation must first be approved by a resolution passed by a

3/4 vote at an annual or special general meeting, except if the cancellation is done in accordance with the contract's terms.[2] In Prince Edward Island, a condominium corporation may terminate a management agreement by a vote of members owning two-thirds of the common elements.[3] In Ontario, a condominium corporation may, by board resolution, terminate an agreement for the management of the property that it entered into with a person before the owners elected a new board at a meeting.[4] In addition, after the registration of the amendments to the declaration and description required for creating a phase, a corporation may, by board resolution, terminate an agreement for the management of the property contained in a phase that the developer entered into on behalf of the corporation before the registration of the amendments.[5] In all of these jurisdictions, the corporation or board must provide at least 60 days' written notice to the person with whom the corporation entered into the agreement.[6] In Alberta, Saskatchewan and Northwest Territories, a corporation that terminates a developer's management agreement is not liable to the other party by reason only of the termination of the agreement.[7]

Shared facilities and cost-sharing agreements. In Ontario, if a corporation and a person have entered into an agreement, other than certain telecommunications agreements, for the mutual use, provision, maintenance or cost-sharing of facilities or services before the owners elected a new board at a meeting, any party to the agreement may, within 12 months following the election, apply to court for an order terminating or amending the agreement or any of its provisions.[8] The court may make such an order or any other order it deems necessary if it is satisfied that the disclosure statement did not clearly and adequately disclose the provisions of the agreement and that the agreement or any of its provisions produces a result that is oppressive or unconscionably prejudicial to the corporation or any of the unit owners.[9] The same applies if a developer on behalf of a condominium has entered into an agreement for the mutual use, provision, maintenance or cost-sharing of facilities or services before the registration of the amendments to the declaration and description required for creating a phase, if the agreement affects the property contained in the phase.[10]

Insurance trust agreements. In Ontario, despite anything in the declaration and anything contained in an insurance trust agreement that a corporation has entered into with an insurance trustee, the corporation may terminate the insurance trust agreement by giving at least 60 days' written notice of the termination date to the trustee.[11]

Other agreements. In Ontario, a corporation may, by board resolution within 12 months following the election of a new board at a meeting, terminate the following agreements, other than certain telecommunications agreements, that the corporation has entered into with a person other than another condominium corporation before the election of the new board: an agreement for the provision of goods or services on a continuing basis; an agreement for the provision of facilities to the condominium on other than a non-profit basis; and a lease of all or part of the common elements for business purposes.[12] The board must provide at least 60 days' written notice of the date of termination to the person with whom the corporation entered into the agreement.[13] The same applies within 12 months following the first election of the board after the registration of the amendments to the declaration and description required for creating a phase to an agreement that a developer entered into on behalf of the corporation before the registration of the amendments and that affects the property contained in the phase.[14] The termination of an easement created by an instrument in writing is not permitted except in accordance with the instrument.[15] The right to terminate these agreements does not include the right to terminate the legal obligations arising from a declaration.[16]

Notes

1. (AB) *Condominium Property Act*, R.S.A. 2000, c. C-22, s. 17(2), (3)(a). See also *York Region Condominium Corp. No. 921 v. ATOP Communications Inc.*, [2003] O.J. No. 5255, [2003] O.T.C. 1116 (Ont. S.C.J.).

   (SK) *Condominium Property Act, 1993*, S.S. 1993, c. C-26.1, s. 29(2), (3)(a)

   (NT) *Condominium Act*, R.S.N.W.T. 1988, c. C-15, s. 12.2(2), (3)(a).
2. (BC) *Strata Property Act*, S.B.C. 1998, c. 43, s. 39(1)-(2).
3. (PE) *Condominium Act*, R.S.P.E.I. 1988, c. C-16, s. 19.
4. (ON) *Condominium Act, 1998*, S.O. 1998, c. 19, s. 111(1). For decisions regarding management agreements, see *Miehm v. Doering*, [2001] O.J. No. 5187, [2001] O.T.C. 1021 (Ont. S.C.J.), additional reasons at [2002] O.J. No. 3752, 117 A.C.W.S. (3d) 35 (Ont. S.C.J.); *Rossi v. York Condominium Corp. No. 123*, [1989] O.J. No. 1424 (Ont. H.C.J.), affd [1991] O.J. No. 3174 (Ont. C.A.); *York Condominium Corp. No. 167 v. Newrey Holdings Ltd.*, [1981] O.J. No. 2965, 32 O.R. (2d) 458 (Ont. C.A.), leave to appeal to S.C.C. refused [1981] 1 S.C.R. xi, 32 O.R. (2d) 458n (S.C.C.); *York Condominium Corp No. 162 v. Noldan Investment Ltd.*, [1977] O.J. No. 300, 1 R.P.R. 236 (Ont. H.C.J.).
5. (ON) *Condominium Act, 1998*, S.O. 1998, c. 19, s. 154(1).
6. (AB) *Condominium Property Act*, R.S.A. 2000, c. C-22, s. 17(3)(b)

   (BC) *Strata Property Act*, S.B.C. 1998, c. 43, s. 39(1). See also s. 37 and Strata Property Regulation, B.C. Reg. 43/2000, s. 43 regarding failure of strata manager to return records.

   (ON) *Condominium Act, 1998*, S.O. 1998, c. 19, ss. 111(2), 154(2)

   (PE) *Condominium Act*, R.S.P.E.I. 1988, c. C-16, s. 19

(SK) *Condominium Property Act, 1993*, S.S. 1993, c. C-26.1, s. 29(3)(b)

(NT) *Condominium Act*, R.S.N.W.T. 1988, c. C-15, s. 12.2(3)(b).

7. (AB) *Condominium Property Act*, R.S.A. 2000, c. C-22, s. 17(3)

   (SK) *Condominium Property Act, 1993*, S.S. 1993, c. C-26.1, s. 29(4)

   (NT) *Condominium Act*, R.S.N.W.T. 1988, c. C-15, s. 12.2(4).

8. (ON) *Condominium Act, 1998*, S.O. 1998, c. 19, s. 113(1)-(2). For cases on the nature and fairness of shared facilities and cost-sharing agreements, see, *e.g.*, *Metropolitan Toronto Condominium Corp. No. 1021 v. Metropolitan Toronto Condominium Corp. No. 1008*, [2006] O.J. No. 479, 145 A.C.W.S. (3d) 827 (Ont. C.A.); *Metropolitan Toronto Condominium Corp. No. 1272 v. Beach Development (Phase II) Corp.*, [2010] O.J. No. 5025, 2010 ONSC 6090 (Ont. S.C.J.); *York Region Condominium Corp. No. 889 v. York Region Condominium Corp. No. 878*, [2008] O.J. No. 1743, 167 A.C.W.S. (3d) 241 (Ont. S.C.J.); *Simcoe Condominium Corp. No. 78 v. Simcoe Condominium Corp. Nos. 50, 52, 53, 56, 59, 63 and 64*, [2006] O.J. No. 605, [2006] O.T.C. 157 (Ont. S.C.J.).
9. (ON) *Condominium Act, 1998*, S.O. 1998, c. 19, s. 113(3).
10. (ON) *Condominium Act, 1998*, S.O. 1998, c. 19, s. 154(5)-(6).
11. (ON) *Condominium Act, 1998*, S.O. 1998, c. 19, s. 114.
12. (ON) *Condominium Act, 1998*, S.O. 1998, c. 19, s. 112(1)-(3).
13. (ON) *Condominium Act, 1998*, S.O. 1998, c. 19, s. 112(4).
14. (ON) *Condominium Act, 1998*, S.O. 1998, c. 19, s. 154(3)-(4).
15. (ON) *Condominium Act, 1998*, S.O. 1998, c. 19, s. 112(5).
16. *Lexington on the Green Inc. v. Toronto Standard Condominium Corp. No. 1930*, [2010] O.J. No. 4853, 2010 ONCA 751 (Ont. C.A.).

---

(4) Damages for Developer's Statement or Information

▼HCD-90▼ Statutory right to recover damages. In Ontario and Saskatchewan, there is a statutory right to recover damages with respect to a developer's statement or information. In Ontario, a corporation or owner may bring an application to court to recover damages for any loss sustained as a result of relying on a statement or information that a developer is required to provide if the statement or information contains a material statement or material information that is false, deceptive or misleading or if the statement or information does not contain a material statement or material information that the developer is required to provide.[1] In Saskatchewan, a corporation or developer may bring an action or proceeding to recover damages for any misrepresentation by or on behalf of a developer in a declaration or in information provided to a purchaser.[2]

Common law remedy of common intention preserved. Under the common law, where a developer intended a reasonable purchaser to believe or to justifiably assume that a superintendent's suite, guest suite or other property is a common element or asset of the corporation, the developer must convey that property to the corporation.[3] The enactment of the statutory right to recover damages with respect to a developer's statement or information did not eliminate the common law remedy of common intention; both remedies are available.[4]

Statement or information related to phased development. In Alberta, if in accordance with a phased development disclosure statement or agreement between a developer and corporation the developer must transfer facilities and property intended for common use to a corporation after registration of one or more phases and the developer fails to do so within the time provided, an owner, corporation or interested party may bring an action for damages or for an order giving directions.[5] In Ontario, within 15 days of registering amendments to a declaration and description required for creating a phase, a developer must send a copy of the amendments to the corporation and owners.[6] A person who purchased a unit or proposed unit before the registration of the amendments may apply to court to recover damages from the developer for any difference between the registered amendments and specified matters disclosed in the disclosure statement delivered to the person if the difference is material and detrimentally affects the use and enjoyment of the person's unit.[7]

Notes

1. (ON) *Condominium Act, 1998*, S.O. 1998, c. 19, s. 133(2). See also *Peel Condominium Corp. No. 505 v. Cam-Valley Homes Ltd.*, [2001] O.J. No. 714, 53 O.R. (3d) 1 (Ont. C.A.); *Abdool v. Somerset Place Developments of Georgetown Ltd.*, [1992] O.J. No. 2115, 10 O.R. (3d) 120 (Ont. C.A.), leave to appeal to S.C.C. refused [1992] S.C.C.A. No. 575, [1993] 2 S.C.R. v (S.C.C.); *Lamarche v. Mastercraft Development Corp.*, [1995] O.J. No. 620 (Ont. Gen. Div.); *Benner v. HLS York Developments Ltd.*, [1985] O.J. No. 2647, 52 O.R. (2d) 243 (Ont. H.C.J.). For decisions finding material misrepresentation and/or non-disclosure, see *Wellington Condominium Corp. No. 61 v. Marilyn Drive Holdings Ltd.*, [1998] O.J. No. 448, 37 O.R. (3d) 1 (Ont. C.A.); *Jaremko v. Shipp Corp.*, [1995] O.J. No. 2015, 47 R.P.R. (2d) 229 (Ont. Gen. Div.), affd [1996] O.J. No. 2155 (Ont. C.A.); *Chapman v. HLS York Development Ltd.*, [1988] O.J. No. 722, 64 O.R. (2d) 498 (Ont. H.C.J.); *Grinberg v. Law Development Group (Thornhill) Ltd.*, [1996] O.J. No. 1722, 2 R.P.R. (3d) 209 (Ont. Gen. Div.). For decisions finding no material misrepresentation and/or non-disclosure, see *Essex Condominium Corp. No. 89 v. Glengarda Residences*, [2010] O.J. No. 822, 2010 ONCA 167 (Ont. C.A.); *Landmark of Thornhill Ltd. v. Sobhi*, [1995] O.J. No. 1733 (Ont. C.A.), leave to appeal to S.C.C. refused [1995] S.C.A.A. No. 404, 94 O.A.C. 320*n* (S.C.C.); *Israel v. Townsgate 1 Ltd.*, [1994] O.J. No. 3187 (Ont. Gen. Div.); *Skyrise Developments Ltd. v. Aldrovandi*, [1997] O.J. No. 393 (Ont. Gen. Div.), affd [1999] O.J. No. 983 (Ont. C.A.).
2. (SK) *Condominium Property Act, 1993*, S.S. 1993, c. C-26.1, s. 24. See also *Condominium Plan N. 86-S-36901 v. Remai Construction (1981) Inc.*, [1991] S.J. No.

410, 84 D.L.R. (4th) 6 (Sask. C.A.); *Holmes v. Jastek Master Builder 2004 Inc.*, [2008] S.J. No. 590, 2008 SKQB 367 (Sask. Q.B.); *Holmes v. Jastek Master Builder 2004 Inc.*, [2009] S.J. No. 680, 2009 SKQB 421 (Sask. Q.B.); *Foster v. MFD Warehouse Restorations Ltd.*, [2008] S.J. No. 122, 2008 SKCA 28 (Sask. C.A.).

3. *Middlesex Condominium Corp. No. 87 v. 600 Talbot Street London Ltd*, [1998] O.J. No. 450, 37 O.R. (3d) 22 (Ont. C.A.); *Wellington Condominium Corp. No. 61 v. Marilyn Drive Holdings Ltd.*, [1998] O.J. No. 448, 37 O.R. (3d) 1 (Ont. C.A.).
4. *Middlesex Condominium Corp. No. 87 v. 600 Talbot Street London Ltd*, [1998] O.J. No. 450, 37 O.R. (3d) 22 (Ont. C.A.); *Wellington Condominium Corp. No. 61 v. Marilyn Drive Holdings Ltd.*, [1998] O.J. No. 448, 37 O.R. (3d) 1 (Ont. C.A.).
5. (AB) Condominium Property Regulation, Alta. Reg. 168/2000, s. 36(5).
6. (ON) *Condominium Act, 1998*, S.O. 1998, c. 19, s. 150(1).
7. (ON) *Condominium Act, 1998*, S.O. 1998, c. 19, s. 150(2).

---

(5) Warranties and Performance Audit Related to Construction of the Condominium Property

▼HCD-91▼ Warranties. In Ontario, all warranties given with respect to work and materials for a unit are for the benefit of an owner, and a corporation may enforce the warranties on behalf of an owner if the corporation does work on behalf of the owner after the owner fails to meet his or her obligation to repair damage, maintain the common elements or maintain the owner's unit within a reasonable time.[1] In Saskatchewan, a corporation or owner may bring a proceeding against a developer for damages for the failure to reasonably pursue remedies under warranties in existence with respect to the construction of common property and common facilities.[2]

Performance audit. In Ontario, all warranties given with respect to work and materials furnished for the common elements are for the benefit of the corporation.[3] If the condominium property includes one or more units for residential purposes or if the condominium is a common elements condominium, the board must retain a person who holds a specified professional certificate to conduct a performance audit of the common elements described in the description on behalf of the corporation.[4] The person who conducts the audit must determine whether there are any deficiencies in the performance of the common elements described in the description after construction has been completed on them that may give rise to a claim for payment to the corporation out of the guarantee fund under the *Ontario New Home Warranties Plan Act* or that would give rise to such a claim if the condominium property were subject to that act.[5]

Ontario's condominium legislation sets out several requirements with respect to the performance audit, including the time and cost of the audit, the auditor's duties and powers, the contents and submission of the auditor's report and the application of the performance audit to phased condominiums.[6]

Notes

1. (ON) *Condominium Act, 1998*, S.O. 1998, c. 19, s. 96(1)-(2). See also *Carleton Condominium Corp. No. 32 v. Camdev Corp.*, [1999] O.J. No. 3448 (Ont. C.A.).
2. (SK) *Condominium Property Act, 1993*, S.S. 1993, c. C-26.1, s. 24(b). See also *Condominium Plan N. 86-S-36901 v. Remai Construction (1981) Inc.*, [1991] S.J. No. 410, 84 D.L.R. (4th) 6 (Sask. C.A.); *Holmes v. Jastek Master Builder 2004 Inc.*, [2008] S.J. No. 590, 2008 SKQB 367 (Sask. Q.B.); *Holmes v. Jastek Master Builder 2004 Inc.*, [2009] S.J. No. 680, 2009 SKQB 421 (Sask. Q.B.).
3. (ON) *Condominium Act, 1998*, S.O. 1998, c. 19, s. 96(3).
4. (ON) *Condominium Act, 1998*, S.O. 1998, c. 19, s. 44(1).
5. (ON) *Condominium Act, 1998*, S.O. 1998, c. 19, s. 44(4); (ON) *Ontario New Home Warranties Plan Act*, R.S.O. 1990, c. O.31.
6. (ON) *Condominium Act, 1998*, S.O. 1998, c. 19, ss. 44(2)-(3), (5)-(6), (8)-(9), 153(1)-(2); (ON) General Regulation, O. Reg. 48/01, s. 12. See also *MTCC No. 1250 v. Mastercraft Group*, [2006] O.J. No. 3600, 151 A.C.W.S. (3d) 403 (Ont. S.C.J.); *Metropolitan Toronto Condominium Corp. No. 1250 v. Mastercraft Group Inc.*, [2009] O.J. No. 3104, 2009 OCA 584 (Ont. C.A.); *Ottawa-Carleton Standard Condominium Corp. No. 650 v. Claridge Homes Corp.*, [2009] O.J. No. 2139 (Ont. S.C.J.).

---

(6) Remedies Related to Developer's Turn-Over Obligations

▼HCD-92▼ Damages, costs, additional amount and compliance order. In Ontario, not more than 21 days after a developer ceases to be the registered owner of the majority of units, the board must call an owner meeting to elect a new board.[1] The developer must then turn over to the new board several specified items at the meeting and several specified items within 30 and 60 days of the meeting.[2] If the developer fails to turn over an item, the corporation may apply to court for an order, and the court must grant the application if it is satisfied that the developer failed to turn over the item without reasonable excuse.[3] The court must order the developer to pay the corporation damages for the loss it incurred as a result of the developer's acts of non-compliance and must order the developer to pay the corporation's costs of the application.[4] The court may also order the developer to pay the corporation an additional amount up to $10,000 and may order the developer to comply with its turn-over obligations.[5]

Same remedies for phased development. In Ontario, on the registration of the amendments to the declaration and description required for creating a phase, the developer must turn over to the board several specified items.[6] If the developer fails to turn over an item, the corporation may apply to court for an order, and the court must grant the application if it is satisfied that the developer failed to turn over the item without reasonable excuse.[7] The same remedies of mandatory damages and costs and an optional additional amount and compliance order apply.[8]

Notes

1. (ON) *Condominium Act, 1998*, S.O. 1998, c. 19, s. 43(1). See also *Keyes v. Metropolitan Toronto Condominium Corp. No. 876*, [1990] O.J. No. 1006, 73 O.R. (2d) 568 (Ont. H.C.J.).
2. (ON) *Condominium Act, 1998*, S.O. 1998, c. 19, s. 43(4), (5), (7).
3. (ON) *Condominium Act, 1998*, S.O. 1998, c. 19, s. 43(8)-(9).
4. (ON) *Condominium Act, 1998*, S.O. 1998, c. 19, s. 43(9)(a)-(b).
5. (ON) *Condominium Act, 1998*, S.O. 1998, c. 19, s. 43(9)(c)-(d).
6. (ON) *Condominium Act, 1998*, S.O. 1998, c. 19, s. 152(1)-(2).
7. (ON) *Condominium Act, 1998*, S.O. 1998, c. 19, s. 152(4)-(5).
8. (ON) *Condominium Act, 1998*, S.O. 1998, c. 19, s. 152(5).

---

(7) Remedies Related to Money Held in Trust

▼HCD-93▼ Order to pay out money, compliance order and sanctions for offences. Depending on the jurisdiction, the remedies for breach of the duty to hold money in trust include an order to pay out the money, a compliance order, and sanctions for offences.

Order to pay out money. In Alberta, where, with respect to a unit or related common property or both, money is held in trust or held, secured or otherwise dealt with under a plan, agreement, scheme or arrangement approved by the minister and the developer has not met the requirements under which that money is to be paid out of the trust or otherwise disbursed, a corporation or interested party may apply to court for an order that the money be paid out for the purposes of substantially completing the unit or related common property or be used as directed by the court.[1] On hearing the application, a court may give directions as to the use of the money, appoint an administrator, receiver or receiver and manager and/or award costs.[2] In Saskatchewan, where titles are not issued pursuant to a condominium plan within the specified time and a person who receives moneys to be held in trust fails to refund the moneys as required within 15 days after receiving a written demand for the moneys, the failure is, in the absence of evidence to the contrary, proof that the person used or applied the moneys for a purpose other than the purpose for which the moneys were entrusted to the person, and the moneys are recoverable with costs in a civil action by the person from whom they were received.[3]

Compliance order. In Ontario and Northwest Territories, a corporation may apply for an order of compliance with the obligation to hold money in trust pursuant to the general right to apply for an order enforcing compliance with any provision of the statute, declaration or by-laws.[4]

Sanctions for offences. In Newfoundland and Labrador, anyone who contravenes a provision of the statute or regulations commits an offence and is liable on summary conviction to a fine or to imprisonment for up to six months or both.[5] In Ontario, the provision creating the duty to hold money in trust is specifically listed among the provisions whose breach constitutes an offence subjecting persons to a fine.[6] Directors and officers who knowingly cause, authorize, permit, participate in or acquiesce in the corporation's commission of an offence also commit an offence.[7]

Notes

1. (AB) *Condominium Property Act*, R.S.A. 2000, c. C-22, s. 14(13).
2. (AB) *Condominium Property Act*, R.S.A. 2000, c. C-22, s. 14(14). See also *Bare Land Condominium Plan 8820814 v. Birchwood Village Greens Ltd.*, [1998] A.J. No. 1300, 1998 ABQB 1023 (Alta. Q.B.); *Condominium Plan No. 0020701 v. Investplan Properties Inc.*, [2006] A.J. No. 368, 2006 ABQB 224 (Alta. Q.B.); *Condominium Plan No. 0020701 v. Investplan Properties Inc.*, [2007] A.J. No. 1478, 162 A.C.W.S. (3d) 908 (Alta. Q.B.); *Condominium Plan No. 982-2595 v. Fantasy Homes Ltd.*, [2006] A.J. No. 495, 2006 ABQB 325 (Alta. Q.B.); *Condominium Plan No. 982 2595 v. Fantasy Homes Ltd.*, [2007] A.J. No. 50, 2007 ABQB 32 (Alta. Q.B.); *Condominium Plan No. 982 2595 v. Fantasy Homes Ltd.*, [2008] A.J. No. 1057, 2008 ABQB 584 (Alta. Q.B.).
3. (SK) *Condominium Property Act, 1993*, S.S. 1993, c. C-26.1, s. 13(6)-(8).
4. (ON) *Condominium Act, 1998*, S.O. 1998, c. 19, s. 134(1); (NT) *Condominium Act*, R.S.N.W.T. 1988, c. C-15, s. 30(1).
5. (NL) *Condominium Act, 2009*, S.N.L. 2009, c. C-29.1, s. 90(c) (not yet in force).
6. (ON) *Condominium Act, 1998*, S.O. 1998, c. 19, s. 137(1).
7. (ON) *Condominium Act, 1998*, S.O. 1998, c. 19, s. 137(2).

(8) Obligations Related to First-Year Deficit

▼HCD-94▼ Accountability for budget statement. In Newfoundland and Labrador, a developer is accountable to the corporation for the budget statement that covers the one-year period immediately following the conveyance of the first unit.[1] Immediately following that conveyance, the developer's solicitor must hold in trust from the sale proceeds of the first unit, or subsequent units if necessary, an amount equal to at least 10% of the budgeted statement.[2] In Ontario, a developer is accountable to the corporation for the budget statement that covers the one-year period immediately following the registration of the declaration and description.[3]

Common expenses, revenue and set-off. In Newfoundland and Labrador and Ontario, a developer must pay the corporation the amount by which the total actual amount of common expenses incurred for the period covered by the budget statement exceeds the total budgeted amount.[4] The developer must also pay the corporation the amount by which the total actual amount of fees, charges, rents and other revenue paid or to be paid to the corporation during the period covered by the budget statement for the use of any part of the common elements or assets or of any other facilities related to the property is less than the total budgeted amount.[5] In both provinces, if the total actual amount of revenue exceeds the total budgeted amount, the developer may deduct the excess from any amount payable in relation to the common expenses.[6]

Notice of payment. In Newfoundland and Labrador and Ontario, after receiving the audited financial statements for the period covered by the budget statement, the board must compare the actual amount of common expenses and revenue for the period covered by the budget statement with the budgeted amounts and must, within 30 days of receiving the audited financial statements, provide written notice of the amount the developer is required to pay the corporation.[7] In Newfoundland and Labrador, the board must provide the notice to the developer's solicitor, and in Ontario, the board must provide the notice to the developer.[8]

Time for payment. In Newfoundland and Labrador, where notice is not given to the developer's solicitor within 30 days of the board's receipt of the financial statement, the solicitor may release the funds held in trust to the developer.[9] In Ontario, the developer must pay the corporation the required amount within 30 days of receiving the notice.[10]

Notes

1. (NL) *Condominium Act, 2009*, S.N.L. 2009, c. C-29.1, s. 45(1) (not yet in force).
2. (NL) *Condominium Act, 2009*, S.N.L. 2009, c. C-29.1, s. 45(2) (not yet in force).
3. (ON) *Condominium Act, 1998*, S.O. 1998, c. 19, s. 75(1).
4. (NL) *Condominium Act, 2009*, S.N.L. 2009, c. C-29.1, s. 45(3) (not yet in force)

   (ON) *Condominium Act, 1998*, S.O. 1998, c. 19, s. 75(2), but this is subject to an exception for common expenses attributable to the termination of certain agreements. See also *York Condominium Corp. No. 435 v. Starburst Investments Ltd.*, [1984] O.J. No. 3481 (Ont. Co. Ct.); *Metropolitan Toronto Condominium Corp. No. 1250 v. Mastercraft Group Inc.*, [2007] O.J. No. 603, 2007 CarswellOnt 921 at paras. 16-35 (Ont. S.C.J.), vard [2009] O.J. No. 3104 (Ont. C.A.); *York Condominium Corp. No. 162 v. Noldon Investment Ltd.*, [1977] O.J. No. 300, 1 R.P.R. 236 (Ont. H.C.J.); *Dazol Developments Ltd. v. York Condominium Corp. No. 329*, [1979] O.J. No. 4149, 24 O.R. (2d) 46 (Ont. H.C.J.); *Benner v. HLS York Developments Ltd.*, [1985] O.J. No. 2647, 52 O.R. (2d) 243 (Ont. H.C.J.).
5. (NL) *Condominium Act, 2009*, S.N.L. 2009, c. C-29.1, s. 45(4) (not yet in force); (ON) *Condominium Act, 1998*, S.O. 1998, c. 19, s. 75(3).
6. (NL) *Condominium Act, 2009*, S.N.L. 2009, c. C-29.1, s. 45(5) (not yet in force); (ON) *Condominium Act, 1998*, S.O. 1998, c. 19, s. 75(4).
7. (NL) *Condominium Act, 2009*, S.N.L. 2009, c. C-29.1, s. 45(6) (not yet in force); (ON) *Condominium Act, 1998*, S.O. 1998, c. 19, s. 75(5).
8. (NL) *Condominium Act, 2009*, S.N.L. 2009, c. C-29.1, s. 45(6) (not yet in force); (ON) *Condominium Act, 1998*, S.O. 1998, c. 19, s. 75(5).
9. (NL) *Condominium Act, 2009*, S.N.L. 2009, c. C-29.1, s. 45(7) (not yet in force).
10. (ON) *Condominium Act, 1998*, S.O. 1998, c. 19, s. 75(6).

---

(9) Remedies for Other Obligations

▼HCD-95▼ Certificates, implied covenants, records and common property and facilities. In some jurisdictions, the legislation creates obligations and remedies with respect to status or information certificates, breach of implied covenants, access to corporation records and completion of common property or common facilities.

Order regarding inaccurate certificate. In Newfoundland and Labrador, Ontario and Northwest Territories, a status or information certificate binds a corporation, as of the date it is given or deemed to be given, with respect to the information it contains or is deemed to contain, as against a purchaser or mortgagee of a unit who relies on the certificate.[1] In British Columbia, on an application by a corporation, owner or person affected by an inaccurate certificate, the court may make any order it considers just in the circumstances to give effect to or relieve the corporation from some or all of the consequences of the inaccurate certificate.[2]

Order for compliance by purchaser with implied covenants. In Ontario, if a developer breaches one of the following implied covenants, a purchaser under an agreement of purchase and sale may apply to court for an order to comply with the covenants:[3]

- if the proposed unit is for residential purposes, a covenant to take all reasonable steps to sell the other residential units included in the property without delay, except for the units the developer intends to lease
- a covenant to take all reasonable steps to deliver to the purchaser without delay a deed to the unit in registrable form and
- a covenant to hold in trust for the condominium any money the developer collects from the purchaser on behalf of the condominium

Fine for failure to permit access to condominium records. In Ontario, a corporation that, without reasonable excuse, does not permit an owner or owner's agent to examine its records or copy them must pay the owner $500 on receiving the owner's written request for payment.[4] The owner may recover the sum from the condominium in small claims court, which may also order the condominium to produce the records for examination.[5]

Remedies for failure to complete common property or common facilities. In Alberta, the regulations create a purchaser's protection program to address loss by a purchaser resulting from a developer's failure to complete the construction of units, related common property or both.[6] In Saskatchewan, a person may apply to the minister for a certificate of acceptance by providing evidence that the developer obtained the prescribed security to provide a remedy to owners where the developer fails to complete the common property or common facilities described in the condominium plan.[7] The minister may endorse a declaration with a certificate of acceptance where there is satisfactory evidence that the developer has obtained the prescribed security and that the declaration adequately describes the common property and common facilities on the parcel that the developer undertakes to provide.[8]

Notes

1. (NL) *Condominium Act, 2009*, S.N.L. 2009, c. C-29.1, s. 42(4) (not yet in force)

   (ON) *Condominium Act, 1998*, S.O. 1998, c. 19, s. 76(6). See also *Citifinancial Mortgage Corp. v. Simcoe Condominium Corp. No. 27*, [2005] O.J. No. 2755 (Ont. S.C.J.), additional reasons at 2005 CarswellOnt 4649 (Ont. S.C.J.); *Bilorosek v. Vaitkus*, [2004] O.J. No. 5072, 135 A.C.W.S. (3d) 734 (Ont. Sm. Cl. Ct.); *Armstrong v. London Life Insurance Co.*, [1999] O.J. No. 3507, 103 O.T.C. 192 (Ont.

S.C.J.), affd [2001] O.J. No. 2080, 149 O.A.C. 201 (Ont. C.A.); *Boschetti v. Sanzo*, [2003] O.J. No. 5227, [2003] O.T.C. 1109 (Ont. S.C.J.), affd [2006] O.J. No. 3318, 49 R.P.R. (4th) 61 (Ont. C.A.); *Jasinski v. Trinchini*, [1994] O.J. No. 576, 37 R.P.R. (2d) 240 (Ont. Gen. Div.); *1240233 Ontario Inc. v. York Region Condominium Corp. No. 852*, [2009] O.J. No. 1 (Ont. S.C.J.); *Elkishawi v. Metro Toronto Condominium Corp. No. 1130*, [2004] O.J. No. 6264 (Ont. Sm. Cl. Ct.); *Stafford v. Frontenac Condominium Corp. No. 11*, [1994] O.J. No. 2072, 41 R.P.R. (2d) 7 (Ont. Gen. Div.); *Condominium Plan 832 1384 v. McDonald*, [1998] A.J. No. 885, 1998 ABQB 7677 (Alta. Q.B.); *Fisher v. Metropolitan Toronto Condominium Corp. No. 596*, [2004] O.J. No. 5758, 31 R.P.R. (4th) 273 (Ont. Div. Ct.); *Durham Condominium Corp. No. 63 v. On-Cite Solutions Ltd.*, [2010] O.J. No. 5214, 2010 ONSC 6342 (Ont. S.C.J.); *Lightner v. Condominium Plan No. 772 3097*, [2009] A.J. No. 9, 2009 ABQB 3 (Alta. Q.B.); *Little v. Condominium Plan No. 82S15667*, [2006] S.J. No. 307, 2006 SKCA 56 (Sask. C.A.); *Yanos v. Darkeff*, [2008] O.J. No. 5559, 77 R.P.R. (4th) 316 (Ont. Sm. Cl. Ct.).

(NT) *Condominium Act*, R.S.N.W.T. 1988, c. C-15, s. 19.17(3).

2. (BC) *Strata Property Act*, S.B.C. 1998, c. 43, s. 59(6).

3. (ON) *Condominium Act, 1998*, S.O. 1998, c. 19, s. 78(3). See also *Remo Valente Real Estate (1990) Ltd v. Portofino Riverside Tower Inc.*, [2008] O.J. No. 1887 (Ont. S.C.J.), additional reasons to [2007] O.J. No. 3271 (Ont. S.C.J.); *Essex Condominium Corp. No. 5 v. Rose-Ville Community Center Assn.*, [2007] O.J. No. 2067, 51 C.P.C. (6th) 89 (Ont. S.C.J.); *Carleton Condominium Corp. No. 347 v. Trendsetter Developments Ltd.*, [1992] O.J. No. 1767, 9 O.R. (3d) 481 (Ont. C.A.); *Scaroni v. Rosepol Holdings Ltd.*, [1995] O.J. No. 3212, 48 R.P.R. (2d) 276 (Ont. Gen. Div.); *Scanlon v. Castlepoint Development Corp.*, [1992] O.J. No. 2692, 11 O.R. (3d) 744 (Ont. C.A.); *Justein v. 3900 Yonge St. Ltd.*, [1983] O.J. No. 1177, 29 R.P.R. 80 (Ont. H.C.J.); *Singer v. Reemark Sterling I Ltd.*, [1992] O.J. No. 1083 (Ont. Gen. Div.), affd [1997] O.J. No. 653 (Ont. C.A.); *Russ-Cad Management Ltd. v. Bayview 400 Industrial Developments Inc.*, [1992] O.J. No. 695, 24 R.P.R. (2d) 6 (Ont. Gen. Div.); *Harding v. Wyldewyn Village Inc.*, [1994] O.J. No. 578, 38 R.P.R. (2d) 268 (Ont. Gen. Div.); *Ally v. Harding Addison Properties Ltd.*, [1990] O.J. No. 2213, 1 O.R. (3d) 167 (Ont. Gen. Div.); *Kierdorf v. Reemark East Hamptons Ltd.*, [1992] O.J. No. 1902, 26 R.P.R. (2d) 16 (Ont. Gen. Div.); *Aita v. Silverstone Towers Ltd.*, [1978] O.J. No. 3362, 19 O.R. (2d) 681 (Ont. C.A.); *Wong v. Reemark Sterling II Ltd.*, [1992] O.J. No. 2105, 26 R.P.R. (2d) 93 (Ont. Gen. Div.); *Harding Addison Properties Ltd. v. Campbell*, [1992] O.J. No. 2732, 28 R.P.R. (2d) 284 (Ont. Gen. Div.); *Kratz v. Parkside Hill Ltd.*, [1995] O.J. No. 2890, 48 R.P.R. (2d) 98 (Ont. C.A.); *Chawla v. Hayter Street Development Inc.*, [1994] O.J. 1908, 41 R.P.R. (2d) 94 (Ont. Gen. Div.), affd [1997] O.J. No. 1997, 10 R.P.R. (3d) 33 (Ont. C.A.); *Landmark of Thornhill Ltd v. Maleki-Yazdi*, [1995] O.J. No. 759, 45 R.P.R. (2d) 280 (Ont. Gen. Div.), affd [1998] O.J. No. 2300 (Ont. C.A.); *Newman v. Law Development Group (Georgetown) Ltd.*, [1996] O.J. No. 393 (Ont. Gen. Div.); *Kozourek v. Carlyle Residence (III) Inc.*, [1996] O.J. No. 1467 (Ont. Gen. Div.), affd [1998] O.J. No. 4175 (Ont. C.A.); *Morris v. Cam-Nest Developments Ltd.*, [1988] O.J. No. 720, 64 O.R. (2d) 475 (Ont. H.C.J.); *Gyulay v. Kenderry Corp.*, [1998] O.J. No. 5328, 24 R.P.R. (3d) 84 (Ont. Gen. Div.); *Goetz v. Whitehall Development Corp.*, [1978] O.J. No. 3277, 19 O.R. (2d) 33 (Ont. C.A.); *Di Cecco v. 733725 Ontario Inc.*, [1990] O.J. No. 2559 (Ont. Gen Div.), affd [1991] O.J. No. 3126 (Ont. C.A.); *Shoihet v. 110 Bloor West Development Corp.*, [1984] O.J. No. 411, 32 R.P.R. 179 (Ont. H.C.J.); *Chung v. 741501 Ontario Ltd.*, [1996] O.J. No. 3731 (Ont. C.A.); *Sokoloff v. 5 Rosehill Avenue Development Inc.*, [1998] O.J. No. 4911, 21 R.P.R. (3d) 176 (Ont. Gen. Div.); *Grinberg v. Law*

Development Group (Thornhill) Ltd., [1996] O.J. No. 1722, 2 R.P.R. (3d) 209 (Ont. Gen. Div.); *Borthwick v. St. James Square Associates Inc.*, [1989] O.J. No. 172 (Ont. H.C.J.), additional reasons at [1989] O.J. No. 279 (Ont. H.C.J.); *Peel Condominium Corp. No. 199 v. Sanrose Construction (Dixie) Ltd.*, [1989] O.J. No. 766, 68 O.R. (2d) 513 (Ont. H.C.J.), affd [1992] O.J. No. 3223, 10 O.R. (3d) 640 (Ont. C.A.).

4. (ON) *Condominium Act, 1998*, S.O. 1998, c. 19, s. 55(8). See also *Lahrkamp v. Metropolitan Toronto Condominium Corp. No. 932*, unreported (2010) (Ont. Sm. Cl. Ct.), awarding the $500 penalty; *McKay v. Waterloo North Condominium Corp. No.* 23, [1992] O.J. No. 2435, 11 O.R. (3d) 341 (Ont. Gen. Div.); *Fisher v. Metropolitan Toronto Condominium Corp. No. 596*, [2004] O.J. No. 5758, 31 R.P.R. (4th) 273 (Ont. Div. Ct.) *Miehm v. Doering*, [2001] O.J. No. 5187, [2001] O.T.C. 1021 (Ont. S.C.J.); *Metropolitan Toronto Condominium Corp. No. 932 v. Lahrkamp*, [2009] O.J. No. 1785, 2009 ONCA 362 (Ont. C.A.); *Rohoman v. York Condominium Corp. No. 141*, [2000] O.J. No. 2356 (Ont. S.C.J.); *York Condominium Corp. No. 60 v. Brown*, [2001] O.J. No. 4927 (Ont. S.C.J.).
5. (ON) *Condominium Act, 1998*, S.O. 1998, c. 19, s. 55(9)-(10).
6. (AB) Condominium Property Regulation, Alta. Reg. 168/2000, ss. 63-69.
7. (SK) *Condominium Property Act, 1993*, S.S. 1993, c. C-26.1, s. 5.2(3).
8. (SK) *Condominium Property Act, 1993*, S.S. 1993, c. C-26.1, s. 5.2(4).

---

(10) Obligations and Remedies Related to Phased Development

▼HCD-96▼ Available obligations and remedies. The condominium obligations related to phased development include performance audits and notice on termination of certain agreements. The remedies related to phased development include injunctions, damages, directions, termination of an agreement of purchase and sale, termination or amendment of other agreements and extensions of time.

Condominium obligations. In Ontario, if a developer registers amendments to a declaration and description required for creating a phase and the phase contains one or more units for residential purposes, the board must have a performance audit of the common elements contained in the phase conducted on behalf of the corporation.[1] In Ontario, on 60 days' written notice of the date of termination to the person with whom the developer has entered into an agreement, a corporation may, by board resolution, terminate an agreement for the management of the property contained in the phase or other specified agreements that the developer entered into on behalf of the corporation before the registration of the amendments.[2]

Injunctions. In Ontario, before the earlier of the registration date of proposed amendments to the declaration and description required for creating a phase and 60 days after receiving certain documents, the corporation may apply to court for an injunction to prevent the registration if any of the differences described in a statement specifying all differences between the proposed amendment and certain matters are material and detrimentally affect the corporation or the use and enjoyment of the property by the owners.[3] The court hearing the application may grant the injunction or award the corporation damages and may include all provisions it considers appropriate in its order.[4] If the corporation applies for an injunction, the developer may not register a declaration and description to create a condominium on the land to be included in the phase, instead of registering the amendments required for creating the phase, unless 120 days have passed after the court has made a final disposition of the application.[5]

Damages. In Alberta, if in accordance with a phased development disclosure statement or agreement between a developer and corporation the developer must transfer facilities and property intended for common use to a corporation after registration of one or more phases and the developer fails to do so within the time provided, an owner, corporation or interested party may bring an action for damages or an order giving directions.[6] In British Columbia, unless otherwise agreed between an owner developer and a corporation, if an owner developer elects not to proceed with a phase, on application of the owner developer or corporation, a court may order that the owner developer contribute to the corporation's expenses attributable to the common facilities as if the owner developer had elected to proceed and that the owner developer pay money, post a bond, provide a letter of credit or provide other security for the owner developer's share of the corporation's expenses.[7] In Manitoba, a corporation or one or more owners or both are entitled to damages for any detrimental effect to the corporation or to the use or enjoyment of the property by unit owners resulting from the developer's failure to complete a phase as described in the declaration.[8] In Ontario, a person who purchased a unit or proposed unit before the registration of the amendments may apply to court to recover damages from the developer for any difference between the registered amendments and specified matters disclosed in the disclosure statement delivered to the person if the difference is material and detrimentally affects the use and enjoyment of the person's unit.[9] In Ontario, a corporation may also apply to court to recover damages from a developer for loss incurred as a result of the developer's non-compliance of its turnover obligations with respect to the creation of a phase; if the developer failed to comply without reasonable excuse, the court must also order costs and may order compliance and an additional amount up to $10,000.[10]

Directions. In Alberta, in addition to directions regarding facilities and property intended for common use, if after the registration of one or more phases the developer does not proceed with one or more other phases that were to have been included and common property that was to be available for the use of the owners in the registered phases was to have been included in the phases not being proceeded with, a developer, corporation or interested party may apply to court for an order giving directions as to how the common property may be made available and as to the application of any funds provided to secure the provision of that common property.[11] In addition, if after the registration of one or more phases the developer does not proceed with one or more other phases that were to have been included and land on which the phases not being proceeded with were to have been located remains part of the condominium plan, a developer, corporation or interested party may apply to court for an order removing the unused land from under the condominium plan; the court may, among other things, give any directions it considers appropriate respecting the transfer of the land, the vesting of ownership in the land, the issuance, cancellation or modification of any certificate of title to the land, the reallocation of unit factors and any other matter relating to the transaction.[12] In British Columbia, if a court determines that an owner developer's election not to proceed with a phase is unfair, the court may order that the owner developer complete whatever common facilities the court considers equitable and that some or all of the security provided for the common facilities be paid.[13] In Manitoba, a court hearing an application regarding the completion of a phase may make an order giving a direction or making a determination in relation to any matter arising out of the cancellation of a proposed phase.[14]

Termination of agreement of purchase and sale. In Alberta, where a building or land is to be developed in phases and the developer is unable or unwilling to register or complete the project or becomes bankrupt before all phases making up the development are registered or completed, a developer, corporation or interested party may apply to court for an order terminating the development and giving directions or a determination in respect of any matter arising out of the termination.[15]

Termination of other agreements. In Ontario, after the registration of the amendments to the declaration and description required for creating a phase, a corporation may, by board resolution, terminate an agreement for the management of the property contained in a phase that the developer entered into on behalf of the corporation before the registration of the amendments.[16] The board must provide at least 60 days' written notice of the date of termination to the person with whom the corporation entered into the agreement.[17] In Ontario, if a developer on behalf of a corporation has entered into an agreement for the mutual use, provision, maintenance or cost-sharing of facilities or services before the registration of the amendments to the declaration and description required for creating a phase and the agreement affects the property contained in the phase, any party to the agreement may, within 12 months following the first election of the board after the registration of the amendments, apply to court for an order terminating or amending the agreement or any of its provisions.[18] The court may make such an order or any other order it deems necessary if it is satisfied that the disclosure statement did not clearly and adequately disclose the provisions of the agreement and that the agreement or any of its provisions produces a result that is oppressive or unconscionably prejudicial to the corporation or any of its owners.[19] In Ontario, a corporation may, by board resolution within 12 months following the first election of the board after the registration of the amendments to the declaration and description required for creating a phase, terminate the following agreements, other than certain telecommunications agreements, that a developer entered into on behalf of the corporation before the registration of the amendments and that affects the property contained in the phase: an agreement for the provision of goods or services on a continuing basis; an agreement for the provision of facilities to the condominium on other than a non-profit basis; and a lease of all or part of the common elements for business purposes.[20] The board must provide at least 60 days' written notice of the date of termination to the person with whom the corporation entered into the agreement.[21] In connection with these agreements, the termination of an easement created by an instrument in writing is not permitted except in accordance with the instrument.[22]

Extension of time. In Saskatchewan, within one year after the expiration of time for obtaining titles pursuant to a replacement plan, a developer may apply to court for an order amending a declaration or extending the time for obtaining titles pursuant to the replacement plan.[23] The application must be served on the corporation, the local authority, the minister and any other person the court considers appropriate, and the court may make any order it considers appropriate.[24]

Notes

1. (ON) *Condominium Act, 1998*, S.O. 1998, c. 19, s. 153(1).

2. (ON) *Condominium Act, 1998*, S.O. 1998, c. 19, s. 154(1)-(4).
3. (ON) *Condominium Act, 1998*, S.O. 1998, c. 19, s. 149(2).
4. (ON) *Condominium Act, 1998*, S.O. 1998, c. 19, s. 149(3)-(4).
5. (ON) *Condominium Act, 1998*, S.O. 1998, c. 19, s. 149(5).
6. (AB) Condominium Property Regulation, Alta. Reg. 168/2000, s. 36(5).
7. (BC) *Strata Property Act*, S.B.C. 1998, c. 43, s. 235(3). See also *Strata Plan LMS 1564 v. Lark Odyssey Project Ltd. (c.o.b. Lark Group)*, [2008] B.C.J. No. 2407, 2008 BCCA 509 (B.C.C.A.); *Kornfeld v. Intrawest Corp.*, [2005] B.C.J. No. 230, 2005 BCSC 162 (B.C.S.C.); *Kornfeld v. Intrawest Corp.*, [2005] B.C.J. No. 1824, 2005 BCSC 1187 (B.C.S.C.).
8. (MB) *Condominium Act*, C.C.S.M. c. C170, s. 5.11(4)(e).
9. (ON) *Condominium Act, 1998*, S.O. 1998, c. 19, s. 150(2).
10. (ON) *Condominium Act, 1998*, S.O. 1998, c. 19, s. 152(2), (4)-(5).
11. (AB) Condominium Property Regulation, Alta. Reg. 168/2000, s. 36(6).
12. (AB) Condominium Property Regulation, Alta. Reg. 168/2000, s. 36(7)-(8).
13. (BC) *Strata Property Act*, S.B.C. 1998, c. 43, s. 235(6).
14. (MB) *Condominium Act*, C.C.S.M. c. C170, s. 5.11(4)(d).
15. (AB) Condominium Property Regulation, Alta. Reg. 168/2000, s. 37.
16. (ON) *Condominium Act, 1998*, S.O. 1998, c. 19, s. 154(1).
17. (ON) *Condominium Act, 1998*, S.O. 1998, c. 19, s. 154(2).
18. (ON) *Condominium Act, 1998*, S.O. 1998, c. 19, s. 154(5).
19. (ON) *Condominium Act, 1998*, S.O. 1998, c. 19, s. 154(6).
20. (ON) *Condominium Act, 1998*, S.O. 1998, c. 19, s. 154(3).
21. (ON) *Condominium Act, 1998*, S.O. 1998, c. 19, s. 154(4).
22. (ON) *Condominium Act, 1998*, S.O. 1998, c. 19, s. 112(5).
23. (SK) *Condominium Property Act, 1993*, S.S. 1993, c. C-26.1, s. 20(1).
24. (SK) *Condominium Property Act, 1993*, S.S. 1993, c. C-26.1, s. 20(2)-(3).

---

4. Non-Payment of Common Expenses or Other Contributions by Owners

(1) Statutory Lien HCD-97
(2) Court Proceedings.. HCD-98
(3) Payment of Arrears by Tenant.............................. HCD-99
(4) Mortgagee's Rights... HCD-100

---

(1) Statutory Lien

▼HCD-97▼ Creation of lien. If an owner defaults in the obligation to contribute to the common expenses or other required expenses, the corporation has a lien against the owner's unit and its appurtenant common interest for the unpaid amount together, in some jurisdictions, with all interest owing and all reasonable legal costs and reasonable expenses incurred by the corporation in connection with the collection or attempted collection of the unpaid amount.[1]

Registration of lien. The corporation may register the lien as an encumbrance over the owner's unit and common interest.[2] In Alberta, the corporation registers a lien by filing a caveat against the certificate of title to an owner's unit.[3] In other jurisdictions, the corporation registers a lien by registering a notice of lien,[4] and in other jurisdictions, the corporation registers a lien by registering a certificate of lien.[5] In New Brunswick, Ontario and Prince Edward Island, the corporation must register the lien within three months of the default that gave rise to the lien to prevent the lien from expiring.[6] In Ontario, when registered, the certificate of lien covers: the amount owing under all of the corporation's liens against the owner's unit that have not expired at the time of registration; the amount by which the owner defaults in the obligation to contribute to the common expenses after the registration; and all interest owing and all reasonable legal costs and reasonable expenses that the corporation incurs in connection with the collection or attempted collection of the unpaid amounts, including the costs of preparing and registering the certificate of lien and a discharge of it.[7] In New Brunswick and Ontario, the corporation must give and serve written notice of the lien to the owner whose unit is affected by it in the required timeframe and manner.[8]

Certificate of lien by persons with interest in unit. In Prince Edward Island, any person who acquires an interest in a unit from an owner may, with the owner's consent, request that the corporation give a certificate in the prescribed form in respect of the owner's common expenses and any default in their payment.[9] The certificate binds the corporation as against the person requesting it in respect of any default shown in the certificate as of the day it is given.[10] The corporation must give the requested certificate within seven days of receiving the request, failing which the corporation is deemed, as against the person who requested the certificate, to have given a certificate stating no default.[11]

Enforcement and priority of lien. The lien may be enforced in the same manner as a mortgage.[12] In Alberta, the lien has the same priority from the date of filing as a mortgage and has priority over a subsequent foreclosure action, subsequent action for specific performance and subsequent public action.[13] In other provinces, the lien has priority over all other encumbrances, subject to certain exceptions.[14] In British Columbia, there are exceptions for a unit's share of a judgment against a corporation, liens or charges in favour of the Crown that are not a mortgage of land and liens or charges under the *Builders Lien Act*.[15] In Newfoundland and Labrador, there is an exception for taxes.[16] In Nova Scotia, there are exceptions for taxes and liens of money due for the supply of electric power and energy.[17] In Ontario and Saskatchewan, there are exceptions for claims for taxes, charges, rates or assessments levied or recoverable and for liens or claims that are prescribed.[18] In Ontario, there is a further exception for Crown claims other than by way of a mortgage.[19] In Manitoba, Northwest Territories, Nunavut and Yukon, there is an exception for provisions made in the declaration.[20]

Notice of lien to encumbrancers. In British Columbia, a corporation must give an owner at least two weeks' written notice demanding payment and indicating that a lien may be registered if payment is not made within the two-week period.[21] In New Brunswick, Ontario and Saskatchewan, on or before the day the lien is registered, the corporation must give and serve written notice of the lien in the prescribed form to every encumbrancer whose encumbrance is registered against the title of the unit affected by the lien.[22] In Ontario and Saskatchewan, if the corporation does not give the required notice to the encumbrancer, the lien loses its priority over the encumbrance.[23] In Ontario and Saskatchewan, if the corporation gives the required notice after the day the certificate of lien is registered, the lien has priority over the encumbrance to the extent of the arrears of common expenses, and reserve fund expenses in Saskatchewan, that accrued during the three months before the day notice is given and that continue to accrue subsequent to that day.[24] In Ontario only, the lien also has priority over all interest owing on the arrears and all reasonable legal costs and reasonable expenses incurred by the corporation in connection with the collection or attempted collection of the arrears.[25]

Discharge of lien. On payment of the unpaid amount, the corporation must give the owner a discharge of the lien in the prescribed form.[26] In New Brunswick and Ontario, the corporation must register a discharge of the certificate of lien,[27] and in Ontario, the corporation must advise the owner in writing of the particulars of the registration.[28] In Manitoba, Prince Edward Island, Nunavut and Yukon, in addition to payment of the unpaid amount, the corporation must demand a discharge for a discharge to occur.[29]

Lien for common elements condominium. In Newfoundland and Labrador and Ontario, if an owner defaults in the obligation to contribute to the common expenses of a common elements condominium, the corporation has a lien against the owner's parcel of land.[30] The same provisions applicable to other liens apply, but the lien does not have priority over an encumbrance registered against an owner's parcel of land before the owner's common interest attached to it unless the encumbrancer agrees otherwise in writing.[31]

Notes

1. (AB) *Condominium Property Act*, R.S.A. 2000, c. C-22, ss. 39(7)-(8), 41, 42
(BC) *Strata Property Act*, S.B.C. 1998, c. 43, ss. 116(1), 118
(MB) *Condominium Act*, C.C.S.M. c. C170, s. 14(1)(e)
(NB) *Condominium Property Act*, S.N.B. 2009, c. C-16.05, s. 46(1)
(NL) *Condominium Act, 2009*, S.N.L. 2009, c. C-29.1, s. 51(1) (not yet in force)
(NS) *Condominium Act*, R.S.N.S. 1989, c. 85, s. 31(6)
(ON) *Condominium Act, 1998*, S.O. 1998, c. 19, s. 85(1)
(PE) *Condominium Act*, R.S.P.E.I. 1988, c. C-16, s. 16(4)
(SK) *Condominium Property Act, 1993*, S.S. 1993, c. C-26.1, s. 63(1), (2), (4)
(NT) *Condominium Act*, R.S.N.W.T. 1988, c. C-15, ss. 19.9(1)(f), 19.15, 19.16
(NU) *Condominium Act*, R.S.N.W.T. (Nu.) 1988, c. C-15, s. 19(1)(e)
(YT) *Condominium Act*, R.S.Y. 2002, c. 36, s. 14(1)(e).
2. (AB) *Condominium Property Act*, R.S.A. 2000, c. C-22, s. 39(7)
(BC) *Strata Property Act*, S.B.C. 1998, c. 43, s. 116(1)-(2)
(MB) *Condominium Act*, C.C.S.M. c. C170, s. 14(1.1)
(NL) *Condominium Act, 2009*, S.N.L. 2009, c. C-29.1, s. 51(1) (not yet in force)
(NS) *Condominium Act*, R.S.N.S. 1989, c. 85, s. 31(7B)
(ON) *Condominium Act, 1998*, S.O. 1998, c. 19, s. 85(2)
(SK) *Condominium Property Act, 1993*, S.S. 1993, c. C-26.1, s. 63(1)
(NU) *Condominium Act*, R.S.N.W.T. (Nu.) 1988, c. C-15, s. 19(1)(e)
(NT) *Condominium Act*, R.S.N.W.T. 1988, c. C-15, s. 19.9(1)(f)
(YT) *Condominium Act*, R.S.Y. 2002, c. 36, s. 14(1)(e).
3. (AB) *Condominium Property Act*, R.S.A. 2000, c. C-22, s. 39(7).
4. (MB) *Condominium Act*, C.C.S.M. c. C170, s. 14(1.1)
(NB) *Condominium Property Act*, S.N.B. 2009, c. C-16.05, s. 46(7)
(PE) *Condominium Act*, R.S.P.E.I. 1988, c. C-16, s. 16(5)
(NT) *Condominium Act*, R.S.N.W.T. 1988, c. C-15, s. 19.9(1)(f)
(NU) *Condominium Act*, R.S.N.W.T. (Nu.) 1988, c. C-15, s. 19(1)(e)
(YT) *Condominium Act*, R.S.Y. 2002, c. 36, s. 14(1)(e).
5. (BC) *Strata Property Act*, S.B.C. 1998, c. 43, s. 116(1)

(NL) *Condominium Act, 2009*, S.N.L. 2009, c. C-29.1, s. 51(1), (3) (not yet in force)

(NS) *Condominium Act*, R.S.N.S. 1989, c. 85, s. 31(7A)

(ON) *Condominium Act, 1998*, S.O. 1998, c. 19, s. 85(2).

6. (NB) *Condominium Property Act*, S.N.B. 2009, c. C-16.05, s. 46(2)

   (ON) *Condominium Act, 1998*, S.O. 1998, c. 19, s. 85(2)

   (PE) *Condominium Act,* R.S.P.E.I. 1988, c. C-16, s. 16(5).

7. (ON) *Condominium Act, 1998*, S.O. 1998, c. 19, s. 85(3).

8. (NB) *Condominium Property Act*, S.N.B. 2009, c. C-16.05, s. 46(5)-(6); (ON) *Condominium Act, 1998*, S.O. 1998, c. 19, ss. 85(4)-(5).

9. (PE) *Condominium Act,* R.S.P.E.I. 1988, c. C-16, s. 16(6).

10. (PE) *Condominium Act,* R.S.P.E.I. 1988, c. C-16, s. 16(6).

11. (PE) *Condominium Act,* R.S.P.E.I. 1988, c. C-16, s. 16(7).

12. (AB) *Condominium Property Act*, R.S.A. 2000, c. C-22, s. 39(9)

    (MB) *Condominium Act*, C.C.S.M. c. C170, s. 14(1)(f)

    (NB) *Condominium Property Act*, S.N.B. 2009, c. C-16.05, s. 46(10)

    (NL) *Condominium Act, 2009*, S.N.L. 2009, c. C-29.1, s. 51(5) (not yet in force)

    (NS) *Condominium Act*, R.S.N.S. 1989, c. 85, s. 31(9)

    (ON) *Condominium Act, 1998*, S.O. 1998, c. 19, s. 85(6)

    (PE) *Condominium Act,* R.S.P.E.I. 1988, c. C-16, s. 16(8)

    (SK) *Condominium Property Act, 1993*, S.S. 1993, c. C-26.1, s. 63(2)(b)

    (NT) *Condominium Act*, R.S.N.W.T. 1988, c. C-15, s. 19.9(1)(g)

    (NU) *Condominium Act*, R.S.N.W.T. (Nu.) 1988, c. C-15, s. 19(1)(f)

    (YT) *Condominium Act*, R.S.Y. 2002, c. 36, s. 14(1)(f).

13. (AB) *Condominium Property Act*, R.S.A. 2000, c. C-22, s. 39(9), (12).

14. (BC) *Strata Property Act*, S.B.C. 1998, c. 43, s. 116(5)

    (MB) *The Condominium Act*, C.C.S.M. c. C170, s. 14(2)

    (NB) *Condominium Property Act*, S.N.B. 2009, c. C-16.05, s. 46(4)

    (NL) *Condominium Act, 2009*, S.N.L. 2009, c. C-29.1, s. 51(2) (not yet in force)

    (NS) *Condominium Act*, R.S.N.S. 1989, c. 85, s. 31(7)

    (ON) *Condominium Act, 1998*, S.O. 1998, c. 19, s. 86(1)

    (SK) *Condominium Property Act, 1993*, S.S. 1993, c. C-26.1, s. 63.1(1)

    (NT) *Condominium Act*, R.S.N.W.T. 1988, c. C-15, s. 19.9(1)(f)

    (NU) *Condominium Act*, R.S.N.W.T. (Nu.) 1988, c. C-15, s. 19(1)(e)

    (YT) *Condominium Act*, R.S.Y. 2002, c. 36, s. 14(1)(e).

15. (BC) S.B.C. 1997, c. 45; (BC) *Strata Property Act*, S.B.C. 1998, c. 43, s. 116(5).

16. (NL) *Condominium Act, 2009*, S.N.L. 2009, c. C-29.1, s. 51(2) (not yet in force).

17. (NS) *Condominium Act*, R.S.N.S. 1989, c. 85, s. 31(7).

18. (ON) *Condominium Act, 1998*, S.O. 1998, c. 19, s. 86(1)(b)-(c); (SK) *Condominium Property Act, 1993*, S.S. 1993, c. C-26.1, s. 63.1(2).

19. (ON) *Condominium Act, 1998*, S.O. 1998, c. 19, s. 86(1)(a).

20. (MB) *Condominium Act*, C.C.S.M. c. C170, s. 14(2)

(NT) *Condominium Act*, R.S.N.W.T. 1988, c. C-15, s. 19.9(1)(f)

(NU) *Condominium Act*, R.S.N.W.T. (Nu.) 1988, c. C-15, s. 19(1)(e)

(YT) *Condominium Act*, R.S.Y. 2002, c. 36, s. 14(1)(e).

21. (BC) *Strata Property Act*, S.B.C. 1998, c. 43, s. 112(2).

22. (NB) *Condominium Property Act*, S.N.B. 2009, c. C-16.05, s. 46(8)-(9)

(ON) *Condominium Act, 1998*, S.O. 1998, c. 19, s. 86(3)-(4)

(SK) *Condominium Property Act, 1993*, S.S. 1993, c. C-26.1, s. 63.1(3)-(4).

23. (ON) *Condominium Act, 1998*, S.O. 1998, c. 19, s. 86(5); (SK) *Condominium Property Act, 1993*, S.S. 1993, c. C-26.1, s. 63.1(5).

24. (ON) *Condominium Act, 1998*, S.O. 1998, c. 19, s. 86(6); (SK) *Condominium Property Act, 1993*, S.S. 1993, c. C-26.1, s. 63.1(6).

25. (ON) *Condominium Act, 1998*, S.O. 1998, c. 19, s. 86(6).

26. (AB) *Condominium Property Act*, R.S.A. 2000, c. C-22, s. 39(11)

(BC) *Strata Property Act*, S.B.C. 1998, c. 43, s. 116(6)

(MB) *Condominium Act*, C.C.S.M. c. C170, s. 14(4)

(NB) *Condominium Property Act*, S.N.B. 2009, c. C-16.05, s. 46(13)-(14)

(NL) *Condominium Act, 2009*, S.N.L. 2009, c. C-29.1, s. 51(6) (not yet in force)

(NS) *Condominium Act*, R.S.N.S. 1989, c. 85, s. 31(10)

(ON) *Condominium Act, 1998*, S.O. 1998, c. 19, s. 85(7)

(PE) *Condominium Act,* R.S.P.E.I. 1988, c. C-16, s. 16(9)

(SK) *Condominium Property Act, 1993*, S.S. 1993, c. C-26.1, s. 63(3)

(NT) *Condominium Act*, R.S.N.W.T. 1988, c. C-15, s. 19.9(3)

(NU) *Condominium Act*, R.S.N.W.T. (Nu.) 1988, c. C-15, s. 19(3)

(YT) *Condominium Act*, R.S.Y. 2002, c. 36, s. 14(3).

27. (NB) *Condominium Property Act*, S.N.B. 2009, c. C-16.05, s. 46(14); (ON) *Condominium Act, 1998*, S.O. 1998, c. 19, s. 85(7).

28. (ON) *Condominium Act, 1998*, S.O. 1998, c. 19, s. 85(7).

29. (MB) *The Condominium Act*, C.C.S.M. c. C170, s. 14(4)

(PE) *Condominium Act,* R.S.P.E.I. 1988, c. C-16, s. 16(9)

(NU) *Condominium Act*, R.S.N.W.T. (Nu.) 1988, c. C-15, s. 19(3)

(YT) *Condominium Act*, R.S.Y. 2002, c. 36, s. 14(3).

30. (NL) *Condominium Act, 2009*, S.N.L. 2009, c. C-29.1, s. 69(5) (not yet in force); (ON) *Condominium Act, 1998*, S.O. 1998, c. 19, s. 139(5).

31. (NL) *Condominium Act, 2009*, S.N.L. 2009, c. C-29.1, s. 69(6)-(7) (not yet in force); (ON) *Condominium Act, 1998*, S.O. 1998, c. 19, s. 139(6)-(7).

---

(2) Court Proceedings

▼HCD-98▼ Action for debt in most jurisdictions. In most jurisdictions, a corporation has a right to recover with respect to a lien for common expenses or other contributions through an action for debt.[1]

Forced sale and compliance orders. In British Columbia, a condominium's rights with respect to a lien are enforced through an application for an order for the sale of the unit.[2] In Ontario, the condominium's rights with respect to a lien are enforced through an application for an order enforcing compliance with the lien provisions of the Act.[3]

Notes

1. (AB) *Condominium Property Act*, R.S.A. 2000, c. C-22, s. 39(1)(d), 39(2)
   (MB) *Condominium Act*, C.C.S.M. c. C170, s. 14(1)(d)(i)
   (NB) *Condominium Property Act*, S.N.B. 2009, c. C-16.05, s. 37(5)(a)
   (NL) *Condominium Act, 2009*, S.N.L. 2009, c. C-29.1, s. 48(d)(i) (not yet in force)
   (NS) *Condominium Act*, R.S.N.S. 1989, c. 85, s. 31(1)(e)(i)
   (SK) *Condominium Property Act, 1993*, S.S. 1993, c. C-26.1, ss. 57(2), 58(4)
   (NT) *Condominium Act*, R.S.N.W.T. 1988, c. C-15, s. 19.9(1)(d)(i)
   (NU) *Condominium Act*, R.S.N.W.T. (Nu.) 1988, c. C-15, s. 19(1)(d)(i)
   (YT) *Condominium Act*, R.S.Y. 2002, c. 36, s. 14(1)(d)(i).
2. (BC) *Strata Property Act*, S.B.C. 1998, c. 43, s. 117.
3. (ON) *Condominium Act, 1998*, S.O. 1998, c. 19, s. 134.

---

(3) Payment of Arrears by Tenant

▼HCD-99▼ Tenant to pay amount of rent. In some jurisdictions, where an owner who has rented a unit defaults in the owner's obligation to contribute to the common expenses, the corporation may require the tenant to pay to the corporation the rent otherwise due to the owner.[1] In Saskatchewan and Northwest Territories, the same applies where a corporation obtains a judgment requiring an owner to pay an amount to the corporation and the owner has not paid the full amount.[2] In Ontario, Saskatchewan and Northwest Territories, the corporation must provide written notice to the tenant and owner,[3] and in Northwest Territories, the corporation must also provide written notice to the mortgagee.[4] In Ontario, the tenant must pay the lesser of the amount of the default and the amount of the rent due.[5]

Rent deemed to be paid to owner. Where a tenant pays the rent to the corporation, the tenant is deemed to have paid the rent to the owner.[6] In Ontario, the tenant cannot by reason only of the payment to the corporation be considered to be in default of an obligation in the lease.[7] In Saskatchewan and Northwest Territories, the tenant deducts the amount of the payment from the rent to be paid to the owner, the corporation deducts the amount of the payment from the arrears or judgment debt owed by the owner to the corporation, and the owner is not liable to the corporation for the amount of the payment.[8]

Actions prohibited unless authorized by by-law. In Saskatchewan and Northwest Territories, a corporation may not impose or collect deposits or apply to a rental officer unless those actions are authorized by by-law.[9] In Northwest Territories, a corporation also may not collect common expenses from a tenant under certain statutory provisions or apply to obtain possession of a rented unit unless authorized by by-law.[10]

Notes

1. (AB) *Condominium Property Act*, R.S.A. 2000, c. C-22, s. 39(4)
   (NS) *Condominium Act*, R.S.N.S. 1989, c. 85, s. 31(8)
   (ON) *Condominium Act, 1998*, S.O. 1998, c. 19, s. 87(1)
   (SK) *Condominium Property Act, 1993*, S.S. 1993, c. C-26.1, s. 81(1)
   (NT) *Condominium Act*, R.S.N.W.T. 1988, c. C-15, s. 19.7(1).
2. (SK) *Condominium Property Act, 1993*, S.S. 1993, c. C-26.1, s. 81(1.1); (NT) *Condominium Act*, R.S.N.W.T. 1988, c. C-15, s. 19.7(2).
3. (ON) *Condominium Act, 1998*, S.O. 1998, c. 19, s. 87(1)-(4)
   (SK) *Condominium Property Act, 1993*, S.S. 1993, c. C-26.1, s. 81(1)-(1.1).
4. (NT) *Condominium Act*, R.S.N.W.T. 1988, c. C-15, s. 19.7(1)-(2).
5. (ON) *Condominium Act, 1998*, S.O. 1998, c. 19, s. 87(1).
6. (AB) *Condominium Property Act*, R.S.A. 2000, c. C-22, s. 39(5)
   (ON) *Condominium Act, 1998*, S.O. 1998, c. 19, s. 87(6)
   (SK) *Condominium Property Act, 1993*, S.S. 1993, c. C-26.1, s. 81(3)(c)
   (NT) *Condominium Act*, R.S.N.W.T. 1988, c. C-15, s. 19.7(3)(b).
7. (ON) *Condominium Act, 1998*, S.O. 1998, c. 19, s. 87(6)
8. (SK) *Condominium Property Act, 1993*, S.S. 1993, c. C-26.1, s. 81(2)-(3); (NT) *Condominium Act*, R.S.N.W.T. 1988, c. C-15, s. 19.7(3)(a), (c), (d).
9. (SK) *Condominium Property Act, 1993*, S.S. 1993, c. C-26.1, s. 82(1); (SK) Condominium Property Regulations, 2001, R.R.S. c. C-26.1, Reg. 2, App. 1, Part II, Bylaws, 33(c); (NT) *Condominium Act*, R.S.N.W.T. 1988, c. C-15, s. 19.8(1)(a)-(b).
10. (NT) *Condominium Act*, R.S.N.W.T. 1988, c. C-15, s. 19.8(1)(c)-(d).

---

(4) Mortgagee's Rights

▼HCD-100▼ Right to pay owner's contribution to common expenses. In some jurisdictions, where an owner fails to pay its contribution to the common expenses, the mortgagee may pay the amount owing in respect of the contribution as well as all interest owing, reasonable costs and reasonable expenses incurred in connection with the collection or attempted collection of the unpaid amount; the mortgagee may add the amount owing, interest owing, reasonable costs and reasonable expenses to the amount owing to the mortgagee under the mortgage.[1]

Additional rights. In Ontario and Saskatchewan, the mortgagee may collect the owner's contribution to the common expenses and must promptly pay the amount collected to the corporation on behalf of the owner; the owner's default in the obligation to contribute to the common expenses constitutes default under the mortgage; and if after demand the owner fails to fully reimburse the mortgagee, the mortgage immediately becomes due and payable at the option of the mortgagee.[2] On receipt of a request from a mortgagee of a unit, a corporation must provide a written statement to the mortgagee, at no charge, setting out the common expenses in respect of the unit and, if there is a default in the payment of them, the amount owing, interest owing, reasonable costs and reasonable expenses in respect of the unit.[3]

Notes

1. (AB) *Condominium Property Act*, R.S.A. 2000, c. C-22, ss. 39(3), 41
   (NL) *Condominium Act, 2009*, S.N.L. 2009, c. C-29.1, s. 51(4) (not yet in force)
   (NS) *Condominium Act*, R.S.N.S. 1989, c. 85, s. 31(8)
   (ON) *Condominium Act, 1998*, S.O. 1998, c. 19, s. 88(1)(c)-(d)
   (SK) *Condominium Property Act, 1993*, S.S. 1993, c. C-26.1, s. 63.2(1)(c)-(d).
2. (ON) *Condominium Act, 1998*, S.O. 1998, c. 19, s. 88(1)(a), (b), (e); (SK) *Condominium Property Act, 1993*, S.S. 1993, c. C-26.1, s. 63.2(1)(a), (b), (e).
3. (ON) *Condominium Act, 1998*, S.O. 1998, c. 19, s. 88(2); (SK) *Condominium Property Act, 1993*, S.S. 1993, c. C-26.1, s. 63.2(2).

---

5. Occupation and Use of Units and Common Elements

(1) Use of Common Elements and Changes to Units and Common Elements HCD-101
(2) Repair and Maintenance HCD-102
(3) Noise, Nuisance and Harassment HCD-103
(4) Tenants and Occupants HCD-104
(5) Pets HCD-105
(6) Dangerous Activities HCD-106

---

(1) Use of Common Elements and Changes to Units and Common Elements

▼HCD-101▼ Reasonable use of common elements. In several jurisdictions, an owner may make reasonable use of the common elements, subject to the statute, declaration, by-laws and rules.[1] In Alberta, British Columbia and Saskatchewan, the by-laws provide a list of restrictions for owners, including the general restriction that an owner may not use or enjoy the corporation's real or personal property or the common property in a manner that unreasonably interferes with its use and enjoyment by other owners or by occupants.[2] In Newfoundland and Labrador, the Act provides that the by-laws may provide for the making of rules by the corporation respecting the use of the common elements for the purpose of preventing unreasonable interference with the use and enjoyment of the units and common elements.[3] The rules must be reasonable and consistent with the act, declaration and by-laws and must be approved by 66% of the condominium members.[4]

Written consent required for changes to units and common elements. In Alberta and Saskatchewan, the by-laws provide that an owner may not make mechanical or electrical alterations to the owner's unit or to the common property without the prior written consent of the board, and in Alberta, the same applies to structural changes.[5] In British Columbia, the by-laws set out a detailed list of structural alterations to a unit that require the corporation's written consent; the by-laws also provide that an owner must obtain the corporation's written consent before making an alteration to common property or common assets.[6] Consent must not be unreasonably withheld with respect to units and common property in Alberta and with respect to units in British Columbia.[7]

Notes

1. (MB) *Condominium Act*, C.C.S.M. c. C170, s. 8(3)
   (NB) *Condominium Property Act*, S.N.B. 2009, c. C-16.05, s. 16(4)
   (NS) *Condominium Act*, R.S.N.S. 1989, c. 85, s. 28(4)
   (ON) *Condominium Act, 1998*, S.O. 1998, c. 19, s. 116
   (NT) *Condominium Act*, R.S.N.W.T. 1988, c. C-15, s. 8(3)
   (NU) *Condominium Act*, R.S.N.W.T. (Nu.) 1988, c. C-15, s. 8(3)
   (YT) *Condominium Act*, R.S.Y. 2002, c. 36, s. 8(3).
2. (AB) *Condominium Property Act*, R.S.A. 2000, c. C-22, App. 1, s. 36(2)(a), App. 2, s. 1(d)
   (BC) *Strata Property Act*, S.B.C. 1998, c. 43, Schedule of Standard Bylaws, s. 3

(SK) Condominium Property Regulations, 2001, R.R.S. c. C-26.1, Reg. 2, App. 1, Part II, Bylaws, s. 34(2)(a).

3. (NL) *Condominium Act, 2009*, S.N.L. 2009, c. C-29.1, s. 36(1) (not yet in force).
4. (NL) *Condominium Act, 2009*, S.N.L. 2009, c. C-29.1, s. 36(2) (not yet in force).
5. (AB) *Condominium Property Act*, R.S.A. 2000, c. C-22, App. 1, s. 2(e); (SK) Condominium Property Regulations, 2001, R.R.S. c. C-26.1, Reg. 2, App. 1, Part II, Bylaws, s. 2(f).
6. (BC) *Strata Property Act*, S.B.C. 1998, c. 43, Schedule of Standard Bylaws, ss. 5(1), 6(1).
7. (AB) *Condominium Property Act*, R.S.A. 2000, c. C-22, App. 1, s. 2(e); (BC) *Strata Property Act*, S.B.C. 1998, c. 43, Schedule of Standard Bylaws, s. 5(2).

---

(2) Repair and Maintenance

▼HCD-102▼ Action for debt. In most jurisdictions, a corporation has a right to recover, through an action for debt, any sum of money for repairs done by it for the owner and for repairs to or work done by it or at its direction in complying with any notice or order by a competent public or local authority in respect of the portion of the building comprising the owner's unit.[1]

Potential deposit requirement. In Alberta, a corporation may require an owner who rents the owner's unit to pay to and maintain with the corporation a deposit that the corporation may use for the following purposes where property is damaged, destroyed, lost or removed by any person in possession of a rented unit: the repair or replacement of the corporation's real and personal property or the common property; and the maintenance, repair or replacement of any common property that is subject to a lease granted to a unit owner permitting the owner to exercise exclusive possession in respect of an area or areas of the common property.[2] Alberta's legislation also contains provisions regarding the amount of the deposit and written notice with respect to the deposit.[3]

Settlement scheme. In Alberta and Saskatchewan, if a building is damaged but the condominium status is not terminated, a corporation, owner or registered mortgagee of a unit may apply to court to settle a scheme; in Alberta, a vendor under an agreement for sale of a unit may also apply to court, and in Saskatchewan an application to settle a scheme may also be made in respect of a fixture on land or landscaping.[4] On an application, a court may by order settle a scheme, including provisions for the reinstatement in whole or in part of the building, fixture on land or landscaping or for transfer of the interests of owners of units that have been wholly or partially destroyed to the other owners in proportion to their unit factors.[5] The court may make any orders it considers necessary or expedient for giving effect to the scheme, including orders directing the application of insurance money received by the corporation with respect to damage to the building, fixture on land or landscaping, orders directing the payment of money by the corporation or owners or one or more of them, orders directing an amendment of the condominium plan so as to include in the common property any accretion to it, and orders imposing any terms and conditions the court thinks fit.[6]

Manner of repair. In performing its duty to repair and maintain its common property, a corporation must act reasonably in the circumstances.[7] Deference is due to decisions made by the boards and strata councils, and courts should be wary of intervening where the issue is the manner in which necessary repairs are to be effected.[8] Choosing a more cautious approach to resolving a repair or maintenance issue does not render the approach unreasonable.[9]

Repair in the context of shared facilities agreements. In a dispute between corporation with respect to liability for sharing in the payment of shared facility repairs, the concept of repair should not be approached in a narrow legalistic manner.[10] Courts should take into account several considerations, including the relationship of the parties, the wording of their contractual obligations, the nature of the total development, the total replacement cost of the facility to be repaired, the nature of the work required to effect the repairs, the facility to be repaired and the benefit that may be acquired by all parties if the repairs are effected compared to the detriment that may be occasioned by the failure to undertake the repairs.[11]

Notes

1. (AB) *Condominium Property Act*, R.S.A. 2000, c. C-22, s. 39(1)(d), 39(2)
   (MB) *Condominium Act*, C.C.S.M. c. C170, s. 14(1)(d)(ii)-(iii)
   (NB) *Condominium Property Act*, S.N.B. 2009, c. C-16.05, s. 37(5)(b)-(c)
   (NL) *Condominium Act, 2009*, S.N.L. 2009, c. C-29.1, s. 48(d)(i)(ii) (not yet in force)
   (NS) *Condominium Act*, R.S.N.S. 1989, c. 85, s. 31(1)(e)(ii)-(iii)
   (SK) *Condominium Property Act, 1993*, S.S. 1993, c. C-26.1, s. 98
   (NT) *Condominium Act*, R.S.N.W.T. 1988, c. C-15, s. 19.9(1)(d)(ii)-(iii)
   (NU) *Condominium Act*, R.S.N.W.T. (Nu.) 1988, c. C-15, s. 19(1)(d)(ii)-(iii)
   (YT) *Condominium Act*, R.S.Y. 2002, c. 36, s. 14(1)(d)(ii)-(iii).
2. (AB) *Condominium Property Act*, R.S.A. 2000, c. C-22, s. 53(3).

3. (AB) *Condominium Property Act*, R.S.A. 2000, c. C-22, s. 53(4)-(7).
4. (AB) *Condominium Property Act*, R.S.A. 2000, c. C-22, s. 59(1); (SK) *Condominium Property Act, 1993*, S.S. 1993, c. C-26.1, s. 102(1).
5. (AB) *Condominium Property Act*, R.S.A. 2000, c. C-22, s. 59(2); (SK) *Condominium Property Act, 1993*, S.S. 1993, c. C-26.1, s. 102(2).
6. (AB) *Condominium Property Act*, R.S.A. 2000, c. C-22, s. 59(3); (SK) *Condominium Property Act, 1993*, S.S. 1993, c. C-26.1, s. 102(3).
7. *Weir v. Strata Plan NW 17*, [2010] B.C.J. No. 1057, 2010 BCSC 784 (B.C.S.C.); *Orr v. Metropolitan Toronto Condominium Corporation No. 1056*, [2011] O.J. No. 3898, 2011 ONSC 4876 (Ont. S.C.J.).
8. *Weir v. Strata Plan NW 17*, [2010] B.C.J. No. 1057, 2010 BCSC 784 (B.C.S.C.).
9. *Weir v. Strata Plan NW 17*, [2010] B.C.J. No. 1057, 2010 BCSC 784(B.C.S.C.).
10. *York Condominium Corp. No. 59 v. York Condominium Corp. No. 87*, [1983] O.J. No. 3088, 42 O.R. (2d) 337 (Ont. C.A.).
11. *York Condominium Corp. No. 59 v. York Condominium Corp. No. 87*, [1983] O.J. No. 3088, 42 O.R. (2d) 337 (Ont. C.A.).

---

(3) Noise, Nuisance and Harassment

▼HCD-103▼ Basis for action. Under the common law, an owner is entitled to be compensated for a nuisance, of which noise is one type. In addition, a corporation's declaration, by-laws or rules may contain provisions restricting owners from unreasonably interfering with the use and enjoyment of property through noise, nuisance or harassment. In Alberta and Saskatchewan, the by-laws provide that an owner may not use or enjoy the corporation's real or personal property or the common property in such a manner as to unreasonably interfere with its use and enjoyment by other owners or by occupants, that an owner may not make undue noise in or on the owner's unit or on or about the corporation's real property or common property, and that an owner may not use the owner's unit in a manner or for a purpose that will cause a nuisance or hazard to any other owner or occupant.[1] In British Columbia, the by-laws provide that an owner, tenant, occupant or visitor may not use a unit, the common property or common assets in a way that unreasonably interferes with the rights of other persons to use and enjoy the common property, common assets or another unit, that such a person may not cause unreasonable noise, and that such a person may not cause a nuisance or hazard to another person.[2]

Grounds for remedy. With respect to noise, a remedy may only be granted if there is sufficient evidence of a defect in a unit or action by an owner that is the cause of noise problems.[3] With respect to nuisance, a remedy may only be granted if there is an unreasonable interference with the use and enjoyment of land by another, whether the interference is intentional, negligent or non-faulty.[4] With respect to harassment, although a strained relationship between a unit owner and corporation may justify an order regulating how the owner exercises rights under condominium legislation, where the owner's behaviour does not amount to actionable harassment, an order prohibiting the owner from exercising statutory rights should not be granted.[5]

Notes

1. (AB) *Condominium Property Act*, R.S.A. 2000, c. C-22, App. 1, s. 36(2)(a), (b), (d), App. 2, Sch. A, s. 1(d)-(e), Sch. B, s. 1(b); (SK) Condominium Property Regulations, 2001, R.R.S. c. C-26.1, Reg. 2, App. 1, Part II, Bylaws, s. 34(2)(a), (b), (d).
2. (BC) *Strata Property Act*, S.B.C. 1998, c. 43, Schedule of Standard Bylaws, s. 3(1)(a)-(c).
3. For decisions finding insufficient evidence, see, *e.g.*, *Pelletier v. Couture*, [2003] J.Q. No 3355, J.E. 2003-1056 (Qué Sup. Ct.); *Chiang v. Yang*, [1999] B.C.J. No. 966 (B.C. Prov. Ct.). For decisions finding sufficient evidence, see, *e.g.*, *Italiano v. Toronto Standard Condominium Corp. No. 1507*, [2008] O.J. No. 2642, 168 AC.W.S. (3d) 239 (Ont. S.C.J.); *York Region Condominium Corp. No. 622 v. Pisman*, [2001] O.J. No. 2913 (Ont. S.C.J.), affd [2002] O.J. No. 105 (Ont. C.A.); *Bond v. Strata Plan VR2538*, [1996] B.C.J. No. 2137 (B.C.S.C.); *York Condominium Corp. No. 166 v. Nunez*, [1990] O.J. No. 649 (Ont. Dist. Ct.); *Strata Plan NW87 v. Karamanian*, [1989] B.C.J. No. 629 (B.C.S.C.).
4. *Chiang v. Yang*, [1999] B.C.J. No. 966 (B.C. Prov. Ct.).
5. *Metropolitan Toronto Condominium Corp. No. 932 v. Lahrkamp*, [2009] O.J. No. 1785, 2009 ONCA 362 (Ont. C.A.).

---

(4) Tenants and Occupants

▼HCD-104▼ Termination of lease. In Manitoba, a corporation may give a tenant renting from an owner notice of termination if the tenant fails to remedy a contravention or breach of the corporation's declaration, by-laws or rules within a reasonable time after having received written notice to do so from the corporation.[1] In Ontario, a court may not grant an order terminating a lease of a unit for residential purposes unless the court is satisfied that the lessee has contravened a compliance order and that the lessee has received a notice requiring the lessee to pay the corporation an amount with respect to the owner's default to contribute to common expenses and has not paid the required amount.[2] Where there is a longstanding pattern of conduct on the part of a tenant and his or her guests that unreasonably interferes with the quiet enjoyment of other residents, a court will order termination of a lease.[3] In Prince Edward Island, where a lessee contravenes an order to comply with a duty imposed by the statute declaration or by-laws, a court may terminate the lease.[4] In Saskatchewan and Northwest Territories, if a by-law so authorizes, a corporation may apply to a designated rental officer under the relevant residential tenancies legislation for an order for possession of a rented residential unit if a person who occupies the unit causes excessive damage to the corporation's real or personal property, common property or common facilities, causes excessive noise, or is a danger to or intimidates persons who occupy other units.[5]

Termination of lease in Alberta. In Alberta, in addition to a corporation's right to require an owner to maintain a deposit,[6] a corporation may give a tenant renting a unit notice to give up possession of the unit if any person in possession of the unit causes damage, other than normal wear and tear, to the corporation's real or personal property or to the common property, or contravenes a by-law; if the tenant does not give up possession as required, the corporation or the landlord may apply to court for an order requiring the tenant to give up possession, and the court may order the tenant to give up possession and may make any other order it considers proper.[7] Notwithstanding whether a tenant renting a unit has been given notice to give up possession, a corporation may apply to court for an order requiring the tenant to give up possession if any person in possession of the unit being rented has caused or is causing excessive damage to the corporation's real or personal property or to the common property or is a danger to or is intimidating the owners or any persons in possession of the other units located on the parcel.[8] The court may make an order requiring the tenant to give up possession if the court is satisfied that the grounds for the application are met and that there are reasonable and probable grounds to believe that further damage may be done or that the danger or intimidation will not cease if the tenant is allowed to remain in possession of the rented unit; the court may also make any other order it considers proper in the circumstances.[9]

Short-term leases. In several cases, courts have found that the short-term, hotel-like lease of a unit contravenes a condominium's enforceable declaration or rules restricting the use of units to private single family residences or providing a minimum term for the lease or tenancy of a unit.[10] Whether a short-term lease contravenes a condominium's declaration or rules is a question of fact.[11]

Notes

1. (MB) *Condominium Act*, C.C.S.M. c. C170, s. 13.1(1).
2. (ON) *Condominium Act, 1998*, S.O. 1998, c. 19, s. 134(4).
3. *Metropolitan Toronto Condominium Corp. No. 706 v. Quinto*, [1990] O.J. No. 2981 (Ont. Dist. Ct.), affd [1991] O.J. No. 2776 (Ont. C.A.).
4. (PE) *Condominium Act,* R.S.P.E.I. 1988, c. C-16, s. 29(3).
5. (NT) *Condominium Act*, R.S.N.W.T. 1988, c. C-15, ss. 19.5(1), 19.8(1); (SK) *Condominium Property Act, 1993*, S.S. 1993, c. C-26.1, ss. 80(1), 82(1); Saskatchewan's legislation authorizes this in its by-laws: (SK) Condominium Property Regulations, 2001, R.R.S. c. C-26.1, Reg. 2, App. 1, Part II, Bylaws, s. 33(b).
6. See Section VII.2. ("Repair and Maintenance").
7. (AB) *Condominium Property Act*, R.S.A. 2000, c. C-22, ss. 54(1), 55(1), (4).
8. (AB) *Condominium Property Act*, R.S.A. 2000, c. C-22, s. 56(1).
9. (AB) *Condominium Property Act*, R.S.A. 2000, c. C-22, s. 56(4).
10. See *e.g.*, *Skyline Executive Properties Inc. v. Metropolitan Toronto Condominium Corp. No. 1385*, [2002] O.J. No. 5117, 17 R.P.R. (4th) 152 (Ont. S.C.J.); *Apartments International Inc. v. Metropolitan Toronto Condominium Corp. No. 1170*, [2002] O.J. No. 3821, [2007] O.T.C. 733 (Ont. S.C.J.); *Skyline Executive Properties Inc. v. Metropolitan Toronto Condominium Corp. No. 1280*, [2001] O.J. No. 3512, [2001] O.T.C. 677 (Ont. S.C.J.); *Metropolitan Toronto Condominium Corp. No. 1170 v. Zeidan*, [2001] O.J. No. 2785, [2001] O.T.C. 517 (Ont. S.C.J.); *Metropolitan Toronto Condominium Corp. No. 850 v. Oikle*, [1994] O.J. No. 3055, 44 R.P.R. (2d) 55 (Ont. Gen. Div.).
11. *Metropolitan Toronto Condominium Corp. No. 850 v. Oikle*, [1994] O.J. No. 3055, 44 R.P.R. (2d) 55 (Ont. Gen. Div.).

---

(5) Pets

▼HCD-105▼ Basis for action. A corporation's declaration, by-laws or rules may contain provisions restricting the number, size or nature of pets. In Alberta, the by-laws provide that an owner may not keep an animal on the owner's unit or the common property after a date specified in a notice given to the owner by the board.[1] In British Columbia, the statute provides that a by-law that prohibits a pet does not apply to a pet living with an owner, tenant or occupant at the time the by-law is passed and which continues to live there after the by-law in passed.[2] The by-laws provide that an owner, tenant, occupant or visitor must ensure that all animals are leashed or otherwise secured when on the common property or on land that is a common asset.[3] The by-laws also provide that an owner, tenant or occupant may not keep any pets on a unit other than one or more of the following: a reasonable number of fish or other small aquarium animals; a reasonable number of small caged mammals; up to two caged birds; and one dog or one cat.[4]

Prohibitions and restrictions generally enforceable. Courts generally find that restrictions on pets are enforceable on the basis that deference is due to the decisions of duly elected boards acting within their jurisdiction in enacting their declarations, by-laws and rules and that courts should not lightly interfere with such decisions and substitute their own opinions, unless the decisions are clearly oppressive, capricious, unreasonable or contrary to the legislative scheme.[5]

Exceptions to enforceability. The deference due to the declarations, by-laws and rules of boards is not absolute. Courts will not defer where the lack of enforcement, capricious enforcement or delay of enforcement of restrictions on pets makes a rule unreasonable for owners, who had a reasonable expectation that the rule would not be enforced.[6] In addition, in one case the court held that conditions and restrictions in a declaration banning all pets were void and unenforceable on the basis that they exceeded the permitted ambit of declarations and rules under the condominium legislation.[7]

Notes

1. (AB) *Condominium Property Act*, R.S.A. 2000, c. C-22, App. 1, s. 36(2)(e), App. 2, s. 1(c).
2. (BC) *Strata Property Act*, S.B.C. 1998, c. 43, s. 123(1).
3. (BC) *Strata Property Act*, S.B.C. 1998, c. 43, Schedule of Standard Bylaws, s. 3(3).
4. (BC) *Strata Property Act*, S.B.C. 1998, c. 43, Schedule of Standard Bylaws, s. 3(4).
5. See, *e.g.*, *Muskoka Condominium Corporation No. 39 v. Kreutzweiser*, [2010] O.J. No. 1720, 2010 ONSC 2463 (Ont. S.C.J.); *York Condominium Corp. No. 382 v. Dvorchik*, [1997] O.J. No. 378, 12 R.P.R. (3d) 148 (Ont. C.A.); *Metropolitan Toronto Condominium Corp. No. 776 v. Gifford*, [1989] O.J. No. 1691, 6 R.P.R. (2d) 217 (Ont. Dist. Ct.).
6. See, *e.g.*, *Metropolitan Toronto Condominium Corp. No. 949 v. Staib*, [2005] O.J. No. 5131, 205 O.A.C. 15 (Ont. C.A.); *Metropolitan Toronto Condominium Corp. No. 601 v. Hadbavny*, [2001] O.J. No. 4176, [2001] O.T.C. 770 (Ont. S.C.J.); *Niagara North Condominium Corp. No. 46 v. Chassie*, [1999] O.J. No. 1201, 173 D.L.R. (4th) 524 (Ont. Gen. Div.).
7. *215 Glenridge Ave. Ltd. Partnership v. Waddington*, [2005] O.J. No. 665, 75 O.R. (3d) 46 (Ont. S.C.J.). This decision is unusual in finding a prohibition on pets unenforceable.

(6) Dangerous Activities

▼HCD-106▼ Dangerous condition or activity. In several jurisdictions, no condition may be permitted to exist and no activity may be carried on that is likely to damage the property.[1] In British Columbia, an owner, tenant, occupant or visitor may not cause damage, other than reasonable wear and tear, to the common property, common assets or parts of a unit that the condominium must repair and maintain.[2] In Ontario, no person may permit a condition to exist or carry on an activity in a unit or in the common elements if the condition or activity is likely to damage the property or cause injury to an individual.[3] The use of vulgar, offensive, demeaning, foul or obscene language and aggressive glaring and yelling is threatening conduct that constitutes a condition or activity likely to cause injury to an individual.[4] In extreme cases, courts will order the eviction of a unit owner or resident and/or the sale of the unit.[5]

Illegal or injurious use, hazard and increased risk and insurance. In Alberta, an owner may not use the owner's unit for any purpose that may be illegal or injurious to the regulation of the building.[6] In British Columbia, an owner, tenant, occupant or visitor may not use a unit, the common property or common assets in a way that causes a hazard to another person or is illegal.[7] In Alberta and Saskatchewan, an owner cannot use the owner's unit in a manner or for a purpose that will cause a hazard to any other owner or occupant and cannot do anything in respect of the owner's unit, the corporation's real or personal property or the common property or bring or keep anything on it that will in any way increase the risk of fire or result in an increase of any insurance premiums payable by the corporation.[8]

Dangerous activities in relation to leases. In Alberta, it is a condition of a tenancy that any person in possession of a rented unit cannot cause damage to the corporation's real or personal property or the common property, and the deposit requirement applies where property is damaged, destroyed, lost or removed by any person in possession of a rented unit.[9] In Saskatchewan and Northwest Territories, if a by-law so authorizes, a corporation may apply to a designated rental officer under the relevant residential tenancies legislation for an order for possession of a rented residential unit if a person who occupies the unit causes excessive damage to the corporation's real or personal property, common property or common facilities, causes excessive noise, or is a danger to or intimidates persons who occupy other units.[10]

Notes

1. (MB) *Condominium Act*, C.C.S.M. c. C170, s. 7(3)
   (NB) *Condominium Property Act*, S.N.B. 2009, c. C-16.05, s. 15(3)
   (NL) *Condominium Act, 2009*, S.N.L. 2009, c. C-29.1, s. 55(3) (not yet in force)
   (NS) *Condominium Act*, R.S.N.S. 1989, c. 85, s. 27(3)
   (ON) *Condominium Act, 1998*, S.O. 1998, c. 19, s. 117
   (PE) *Condominium Act,* R.S.P.E.I. 1988, c. C-16, s. 6(3)
   (NT) *Condominium Act*, R.S.N.W.T. 1988, c. C-15, s. 7(3)
   (NU) *Condominium Act*, R.S.N.W.T. 1988 (Nu.), c. C-15, s. 7(3)
   (YT) *Condominium Act*, R.S.Y. 2002, c. 36, s. 7(3).
2. (BC) *Strata Property Act*, S.B.C. 1998, c. 43, Schedule of Standard Bylaws, s. 3(2).
3. (ON) *Condominium Act, 1998*, S.O. 1998, c. 19, s. 117.
4. *Carleton Condominium Corp. No. 291 v. Weeks*, [2003] O.J. No. 1204, [2003] O.T.C. 239 (Ont. S.C.J.).
5. *Metropolitan Toronto Condominium Corp. No. 747 v. Korolekh*, [2010] O.J. No. 3491, 2010 ONSC 4448 (Ont. S.C.J.); *Waterloo North Condominium Corp. No. 168 v. Webb*, [2011] O.J. No. 2195, 2011 ONSC 2365 (Ont. S.C.J.); *Toronto Standard Condominium Corp. No. 1443 v. Cecutti*, [2003] O.J. No. 4144 (Ont. S.C.J.) and [2003] O.J. No. 4145 (Ont. S.C.J.).
6. (AB) *Condominium Property Act*, R.S.A. 2000, c. C-22, App. 2, Sch. B, s. 1(a).
7. (BC) *Strata Property Act*, S.B.C. 1998, c. 43, Schedule of Standard Bylaws, s. 3(1)(a), (d).
8. (AB) *Condominium Property Act*, R.S.A. 2000, c. C-22, App. 1, s. 36(2)(b), (g), App. 2, Sch. A, s. 1(e); (SK) Condominium Property Regulations, 2001, R.R.S. c. C-26.1, Reg. 2, App. 1, Part II, Bylaws, ss. 34(2)(b), (e).
9. (AB) *Condominium Property Act*, R.S.A. 2000, c. C-22, ss. 53(2)-(3).
10. (NT) *Condominium Act*, R.S.N.W.T. 1988, c. C-15, ss. 19.5(1), 19.8(1); (SK) *Condominium Property Act, 1993*, S.S. 1993, c. C-26.1, ss. 80(1), 82(1); Saskatchewan's legislation authorizes this in its by-laws: (SK) Condominium Property Regulations, 2001, R.R.S. c. C-26.1, Reg. 2, App. 1, Part II, Bylaws, s. 33(b).

---

6. Court-Appointed Officers

(1) Appointment of Inspector HCD-107
(2) Appointment of Investigator HCD-108
(3) Appointment of Administrator HCD-109

---

(1) Appointment of Inspector

▼HCD-107▼ When inspector may be appointed. In Ontario and Prince Edward Island, a corporation, lessor of a leasehold condominium, owner, mortgagee or chargee may apply to court for an order appointing an inspector.[1] The court may grant the order if it is satisfied that the application is made in good faith and that the order is in the best interests of the applicant.[2] The inspector has certain powers of a commissioner appointed under the relevant Acts respecting public inquiries.[3]

Contents of order. In Ontario, the court may order the inspector to investigate the items the developer must give the board under its turn-over obligations, to investigate the corporation's records, to investigate the affairs of a person who receives money on behalf of or for the benefit of the corporation, or to conduct an audit of accounts and records.[4] In its order, the court must require the inspector to make a written report within a specified time to the applicant and corporation on the activities the order requires the inspector to perform, and the court may make an order as to the costs of the investigation or audit or as to any other matter it deems proper.[5] The board must send a summary of the report to the owners.[6] In Prince Edward Island, the court may order the inspector to make such investigation of the affairs of any person in receipt of money paid by or on behalf of an owner for the payment of common expenses and may order the inspector to make such audit of the accounts and records of such person as the court considers necessary.[7] The court may make its order on such terms as to the costs of the investigation or audit as the court considers proper.[8]

Notes

1. (ON) *Condominium Act, 1998*, S.O. 1998, c. 19, s. 130(1); (PE) *Condominium Act*, R.S.P.E.I. 1988, c. C-16, s. 20(2).
2. (ON) *Condominium Act, 1998*, S.O. 1998, c. 19, s. 130(2); (PE) *Condominium Act*, R.S.P.E.I. 1988, c. C-16, s. 20(2).
3. (ON) *Condominium Act, 1998*, S.O. 1998, c. 19, s. 130(3); (PE) *Condominium Act*, R.S.P.E.I. 1988, c. C-16, s. 20(3).
4. (ON) *Condominium Act, 1998*, S.O. 1998, c. 19, s. 130(1).
5. (ON) *Condominium Act, 1998*, S.O. 1998, c. 19, s. 130(4).
6. (ON) *Condominium Act, 1998*, S.O. 1998, c. 19, s. 130(5).
7. (PE) *Condominium Act,* R.S.P.E.I. 1988, c. C-16, s. 20(2).
8. (PE) *Condominium Act,* R.S.P.E.I. 1988, c. C-16, s. 20(2).

(2) Appointment of Investigator

▼HCD-108▼ When investigator may be appointed. In Alberta, where on an application by an interested party a court is satisfied that improper conduct has taken place, the court may direct that an investigator be appointed to review the improper conduct and report to the court.[1]

Note

1. (AB) *Condominium Property Act*, R.S.A. 2000, c. C-22, s. 67(2)(a).

---

(3) Appointment of Administrator

▼HCD-109▼ When administrator may be appointed. In Alberta and Saskatchewan, a corporation or a person having an interest in a unit may apply to court for the appointment of an administrator.[1] In Alberta, the appointment of an administrator, receiver or receiver and manager is also one of the remedies a court may order where, with respect to a unit or related common property or both, money is held in trust or is otherwise held, secured or dealt with and the developer has not met the requirements under which that money is to be paid out of the trust or otherwise disbursed.[2] In British Columbia, a corporation, owner, tenant, mortgagee or other person having an interest in a unit may apply to court for the appointment of an administrator to exercise the powers and perform the duties of the corporation, and a court may appoint an administrator if, in the court's opinion, the appointment is in the best interests of the corporation.[3] In Manitoba, New Brunswick, Nova Scotia, Northwest Territories, Nunavut and Yukon, the court appointment of an administrator is one of the remedies a court may order in connection with the performance of a duty imposed by the act, declaration or by-laws.[4]

Terms and conditions of appointment. The court may appoint an administrator for any time and on any terms and conditions as it considers necessary.[5] An administrator has, to the exclusion of the board and condominium, the powers and duties of the corporation that the court orders, may delegate any of its powers or duties, and must be paid for services by the corporation out of the common expenses fund.[6] The powers of the administrator cannot exceed the regular powers of the board of directors.[7]

Appointment of administrator in Ontario. In Ontario, on an application by a corporation, lessor of a leasehold condominium, owner or mortgagee of a unit, a court may appoint an administrator if at least 120 days have passed since the holding of a turn-over meeting and the court is of the opinion that it would be just or convenient, having regard to the scheme and intent of the act and the best interests of the owners.[8] The order must specify the powers of the administrator, state which powers and duties, if any, of the board will be transferred to the administrator, and contain the directions and impose the terms the court considers just.[9] An administrator may apply to court for the court's opinion, advice or direction on any question regarding the corporation's management or administration.[10]

Replacement of administrator. In Alberta, British Columbia and Saskatchewan, on the application of an administrator, corporation or person having an interest in a unit, the court may remove or replace an administrator.[11]

Notes

1. (AB) *Condominium Property Act*, R.S.A. 2000, c. C-22, s. 58(1); (SK) *Condominium Property Act, 1993*, S.S. 1993, c. C-26.1, s. 101(1).
2. (AB) *Condominium Property Act*, R.S.A. 2000, c. C-22, s. 14(13)-(14).
3. (BC) *Strata Property Act*, S.B.C. 1998, c. 43, s. 174(1)-(2). For the factors to be considered in determining whether the appointment of an administrator is in the best interests of the condominium, see *Oldaker v. Strata Plan VR 1008*, [2007] B.C.J. No. 991, 2007 BCSC 669 (B.C.S.C.).
4. (MB) *Condominium Act*, C.C.S.M. c. C170, s. 24(2)

   (NB) *Condominium Property Act*, S.N.B. 2009, c. C-16.05, s. 60(2)

   (NS) *Condominium Act*, R.S.N.S. 1989, c. 85, s. 38(2)(a)

   (NT) *Condominium Act*, R.S.N.W.T. 1988, c. C-15, s. 30(2)

   (NU) *Condominium Act*, R.S.N.W.T. 1988 (Nu.), c. C-15, s. 30(2)

   (YT) *Condominium Act*, R.S.Y. 2002, c. 36, s. 24(2).
5. (AB) *Condominium Property Act*, R.S.A. 2000, c. C-22, s. 58(2)

   (BC) *Strata Property Act*, S.B.C. 1998, c. 43, s. 174(3)

   (MB) *Condominium Act*, C.C.S.M. c. C170, s. 24(2)

   (NB) *Condominium Property Act*, S.N.B. 2009, c. C-16.05, s. 60(2)

   (NS) *Condominium Act*, R.S.N.S. 1989, c. 85, s. 38(2)(a)

   (SK) *Condominium Property Act, 1993*, S.S. 1993, c. C-26.1, s. 101(2)

   (NT) *Condominium Act*, R.S.N.W.T. 1988, c. C-15, s. 30(2)

   (NU) *Condominium Act*, R.S.N.W.T. 1988 (Nu.), c. C-15, s. 30(2)

   (YT) *Condominium Act*, R.S.Y. 2002, c. 36, s. 24(2)(a).
6. (AB) *Condominium Property Act*, R.S.A. 2000, c. C-22, s. 58(3)-(5)

   (BC) *Strata Property Act*, S.B.C. 1998, c. 43, s. 174(3)-(5)

   (MB) *Condominium Act*, C.C.S.M. c. C170, s. 24(3)

   (NB) *Condominium Property Act*, S.N.B. 2009, c. C-16.05, s. 60(3)-(4)

   (NS) *Condominium Act*, R.S.N.S. 1989, c. 85, s. 38(3)

(SK) *Condominium Property Act, 1993*, S.S. 1993, c. C-26.1, s. 101(3)-(5)
(NT) *Condominium Act*, R.S.N.W.T. 1988, c. C-15, s. 30(3)
(NU) *Condominium Act*, R.S.N.W.T. 1988 (Nu.), c. C-15, s. 30(3)
(YT) *Condominium Act*, R.S.Y. 2002, c. 36, s. 24(3).

7. *Aviawest Resort Club v. Strata Plan LMS1863*, [2005] B.C.J. No. 2748, 2005 BCSC 1728 (B.C.S.C.).
8. (ON) *Condominium Act, 1998*, S.O. 1998, c. 19, s. 131(1)-(2).
9. (ON) *Condominium Act, 1998*, S.O. 1998, c. 19, s. 131(3).
10. (ON) *Condominium Act, 1998*, S.O. 1998, c. 19, s. 131(4).
11. (AB) *Condominium Property Act*, R.S.A. 2000, c. C-22, s. 58(6)
(BC) *Strata Property Act*, S.B.C. 1998, c. 43, s. 174(6)
(SK) *Condominium Property Act, 1993*, S.S. 1993, c. C-26.1, s. 101(6).

---

7. Oppression Remedy

(1) Statutory Basis HCD-110
(2) Application of Oppression Remedy...................... HCD-111

---

(1) Statutory Basis

▼HCD-110▼ Statutory remedy. Condominium legislation provides owners and other prescribed persons with a statutory right to bring an action against a corporation for improper conduct. This extraordinary right of relief is called the oppression remedy. The definition of improper conduct varies by jurisdiction but generally includes a condominium's conduct of business or exercise of power in a manner that is oppressive or unfairly prejudicial to or that unfairly disregards the interests of an interested party. The legislation prescribes the persons who may apply to court for an oppression remedy.[1]

Common law test of oppression. In *BCE Inc. v. 1976 Debentureholders*, the Supreme Court of Canada set out a two-part test for establishing oppression. First, there must be a breach of a reasonable expectation of conduct. Second, the breach must amount to "oppression", "unfair practice", or "unfair disregard of a shareholder" within the meaning of the relevant statute.[2]

Definition of oppression. In determining whether improper conduct meets the governing statutory threshold for the purposes of the oppression remedy, courts have provided different definitions of oppression. In *BCE*

Inc., the Supreme Court defined oppression as conduct that is "burdensome, harsh and wrongful" and that is "a visible departure from standards of fair dealing".[3] In British Columbia, the term "significantly unfair", which is the basis of improper conduct, has been held to encompass oppressive and unfairly prejudicial conduct, while the term "unfairly prejudicial" has been held to mean conduct that is unjust and inequitable.[4] Because the oppression remedy provisions in condominium legislation are similarly worded to those in the federal business corporations act and some provincial business corporations acts, courts have referred to the interpretations of these and other similarly worded legislation.[5] Since the purpose of the oppression remedy is to protect legitimate expectations, courts must balance a unit owner's objectively reasonable expectations with the board's ability to exercise judgment and secure the safety, security and welfare of all owners and the condominium's property and assets. The oppression remedy provisions should therefore not be unduly restricted and should be given a broad and flexible interpretation that gives effect to the remedy they created.[6]

Notes

1. (AB) *Condominium Property Act,* R.S.A. 2000, c. C-22, ss. 67-68

   (BC) *Strata Property Act*, S.B.C. 1998, c. 43, s. 164(1)

   (ON) *Condominium Act, 1998*, S.O. 1998, c. 19, s. 135. For mutual use agreements, see s. 113

   (NT) *Condominium Act*, R.S.N.W.T. 1988, c. C-15, ss. 5(7)-(10), 6(10)-(13), 17(6)-(10).
2. *BCE Inc. v. 1976 Debentureholders*, [2008] S.C.J. No. 37, [2008] 3 S.C.R. 560 (S.C.C.).
3. *BCE Inc. v. 1976 Debentureholders*, [2008] S.C.J. No. 37, [2008] 3 S.C.R. 560 (S.C.C.).
4. For other cases addressing the meaning of "unfairly prejudicial", see, *e.g.*, *Blue-Red Holdings Ltd. v. Strata Plan VR 857*, [1994] B.C.J. No. 2293, 42 R.P.R. (3d) 421 (B.C.S.C.); *Reid v. Strata Plan LMS 2503*, [2003] B.C.J. No. 417, 2003 BCCA 126 (B.C.S.C.). See also *Gentis v. Strata Plan VR 368*, [2003] B.C.J. No. 140, 2003 BCSC 120 (B.C.S.C.) ("significantly" modifies "unfair", indicating that courts should only interfere with a condominium's discretion if it was exercised oppressively or in a way that transcends mere prejudice or trifling unfairness).
5. (CAN) *Canada Business Corporations Act*, R.S.C. 1985, c. C-44, s. 241

   (AB) *Business Corporations Act*, R.S.A. 2000, c. B-9, s. 242

   (BC) *Business Corporations Act*, S.B.C. 2002, c. 57, s. 227

   Condominium Plan No. 982-2595 v. Fantasy Homes Ltd., [2006] A.J. No. 495, 2006 ABQB 325 (Alta. Q.B.); *Diligenti v. RWMD Operations Kelowna Ltd.*, [1976] B.J. No. 38, 1 B.C.L.R. 36 (B.C.S.C.) (adopting the dictionary definition of oppressive as "burdensome, harsh and wrongful"); *Ferguson v. Imax Systems Corp.*, [1983] O.J. No. 3156, 43 O.R. (2d) 128 (Ont. C.A.) (evaluating the meaning of fairness); *Goldex Mines Ltd. v. Revill*, [1974] O.J. No. 2245, 7 O.R. (2d) 216

(Ont. C.A.) (when the test of fairness is not met, the court's equitable jurisdiction can be invoked to prevent or remedy injustice); *Esteem Investments Ltd. v. Strata Plan No. VR 1513*, [1987] B.C.J. No. 2505, 46 D.L.R. (4th) 577 (B.C.S.C.) (the meaning of oppression and unfairly prejudicial should be liberally construed).

6. *McKinstry v. York Condominium Corp. No. 472*, [2003] O.J. No. 5006, 68 O.R. (3d) 557 (Ont. S.C.J.).

---

(2) Application of Oppression Remedy

▼HCD-111▼ Oppressive conduct found. Although an assessment of oppression is a fact-specific inquiry, the following cases are instructive of instances in which the oppression remedy may be granted. In Alberta, requiring an owner to remove his satellite dish when the by-laws provided no such prohibition was held to be oppressive conduct that was unfairly prejudicial to the owner.[1] A by-law restricting access to commercial units in a building shared with residential units for the security of residents was found to be oppressive and prejudicial to the commercial owner's interest.[2] In British Columbia, where new by-laws imposed a substantial change, significantly affected an owner's rights and provided no guarantee of representation on the strata council to the affected owner, the by-laws were held to be unfairly prejudicial to the owner and were therefore void.[3] Where a contingency reserve fund was allocated equally between townhomes and the apartments in a condominium but the townhomes could only be partially remediated after resulting damage, the result was found to be significantly unfair to the townhome owners.[4] In Ontario, an oppression remedy action was permitted to proceed where a company terminated its chief executive officer to reorganize its corporate operations.[5] The court held that while the conduct may not have constituted oppression in the classic sense of conduct that is "lacking probity" or that is "burdensome, harsh and wrongful", it was nonetheless conduct that was unfairly prejudicial to or that unfairly disregarded the interests of the minority shareholder; although unfairly prejudicial conduct may constitute less rigorous grounds for invoking an oppression remedy, it will still trigger statutory relief.[6]

No oppressive conduct found. The following cases are instructive of instances in which the oppression remedy may not be granted. In Alberta, a special assessment levied against one unit was held not to be oppressive conduct under the Act.[7] In addition, prohibiting an owner from placing a film on her window to prevent excessive heat was found not to be oppressive conduct, since the corporation had a history of maintaining the consistency of the building's external appearance and was waiting for information concerning the effectiveness of the film.[8] In British Columbia, a company that owned eight units in a residential condominium building was subject to a special levy approved by the strata council to finance a legal action claiming compensation for defects in the building's common property; in applying the then in force *Condominium Act*, the court found that the strata council's actions were neither oppressive nor unfairly prejudicial, since the assessment was imposed on all unit owners in proportion to their unit holdings.[9] Under the new *Strata Property Act*, the court has held that phased repairs of water ingress due to economic constraints was not significantly unfair, since there was no evidence that any strata council member acted in furtherance of his or her own interests and since owners expect that their ability to finance repairs is always a consideration in deciding whether to undertake the repairs.[10] In Ontario, denying access to common elements to an owner with an outstanding debt was held not to be oppressive conduct, since there was no abuse of power or harsh and wrongful conduct by the condominium.[11]

Notes

1. *Condominium Plan No. 8111679 v. Elekes*, [2003] A.J. No. 329, 2003 ABQB 219 (Alta. Q.B.).
2. *Point of View Marketing & Management Inc. v. Condominium Corp. No. 0111661*, [2003] A.J. No. 1371, 2003 ABQB 883 (Alta. Q.B.) (visitors to commercial units must be granted the same access as visitors to residential units in the same building).
3. *Blue-Red Holdings Ltd. v. Strata Plan 857*, [1994] B.C.J. No. 2293, 42 R.P.R. (3d) 421 (B.C.S.C.).
4. *Chow v. Strata Plan LMS 1277*, [2006] B.C.J. No. 430, 2006 BCSC 335 (B.C.S.C.). But see *Strata Plan LMS 1537 v. Alvarez*, [2003] B.C.J. No. 1610, 17 B.C.L.R. (4th) 63 (B.C.S.C.); *Coupal v. Strata Plan LMS 2503*, [2004] B.C.J. No. 2276, 36 B.C.L.R. (4th) 238 (B.C.C.A.) (lack of distinction between units was not unfair).
5. *Deluce Holdings Inc. v. Air Canada*, [1992] O.J. No. 2382, 98 D.L.R. (4th) 509 (Ont. Gen. Div.).
6. *Deluce Holdings Inc. v. Air Canada*, [1992] O.J. No. 2382, 98 D.L.R. (4th) 509 (Ont. Gen. Div.) (the defendant's holding corporation, which was its minority shareholder, had a reasonable expectation that the chief executive officer would only be terminated where this was in the best interests of the company as a whole). See also *Mason v. Intercity Properties Ltd.*, [1987] O.J. No. 448, 59 O.R. (2d) 631 (Ont. C.A.); *Jermyn Street Turkish Baths Ltd. (Re)*, [1971] 3 All E.R. 184, [1971] 1 W.L.R. 1042 (C.A.); *Ernest & Twins Ventures (PP) Ltd. v. Strata Plan LMS 3259*, [2004] B.C.J. No. 2455, 2004 BCCA 597 (B.C.C.A.).
7. *Condominium Plan No. 982-2595 v. Fantasy Homes Ltd.*, [2006] A.J. No. 495, 2006 ABQB 325 (Alta. Q.B.). See also *934859 Alberta Inc. v. Condominium Corp. No. 0312180*, [2007] A.J. No. 1233, 2007 ABQB 640 (Alta. Q.B.).
8. *Condominium Plan 7722911 v. Marnel*, [2008] A.J. No. 305, 2008 ABQB 195 (Alta. Q.B.).

9. *Esteem Investments Ltd. v. Strata Plan No. VR 1513*, [1988] B.C.J. No. 1956, 53 D.L.R. (4th) 377 (B.C.C.A.) (there was no oppression in the absence of a suggestion of bad faith). See also *Schaper-Kotter v. Strata Plan 148*, [2006] B.C.J. No. 924, 2006 BCSC 634 (B.C.S.C.) (equal sharing to unit entitlement was not significantly unfair); *Strata Plan LMS 1537 v. Alvarez*, [2003] B.C.J. No. 1610, 17 B.C.L.R. (4th) 63 (B.C.S.C.); *Coupal v. Strata Plan LMS 2503*, [2004] B.C.J. No. 2276, B.C.L.R. (4th) 238 (B.C.C.A.) (lack of distinction between units was not unfair); *Terry v. Strata Plan LMS 2153*, [2006] B.C.J. No. 1404, 2006 BCSC 950 (B.C.S.C.).
10. See *Oldaker v. Strata Plan VR 1008*, [2008] B.C.J. No. 493, 2008 BCSC 346 (B.C.S.C.) and cost award at [2009] B.C.J. No. 1061, 2009 BCSC 697 (B.C.S.C.); (BC) *Strata Property Act*, S.B.C. 1998, c. 43.
11. *Niedermeier v. York Condominium Corp. No. 50*, [2006] O.J. No. 2612, 45 R.P.R. (4th) 182 (Ont. S.C.J.). See also *Metropolitan Toronto Condominium Corp. 551 v. Adam*, [2006] O.J. No. 4836, 153 A.C.W.S. (3d) 296 (Ont. S.C.J.) (excessive requests by a unit owner to photocopy a condominium's records was not oppressive and the condominium's photocopying charges for providing the records was also not oppressive); *Orr v. Metropolitan Toronto Condominium Corp. No. 1056*, [2011] O.J. No. 3898, 2011 ONSC 4876 (Ont. S.C.J.) (the board's behaviour must be measured against the duty to balance the private and communal interests of unit owners, and its conduct was not oppressive).

---

8. Costs and Indemnification

▼HCD-112▼ Statutory right to costs. In all jurisdictions, a corporation has a statutory right to recover from an owner in an action for debt:

- the unpaid amount of any assessment
- money expended by it for repairs to or work done by it that the owner was required to undertake at its direction in complying with any notice or order
- money expended by it for repairs to or work done by it at its direction in complying with any notice or order and
- legal costs incurred in the collection of debt[1]

Costs and indemnification under common law. Where a corporation remedies a unit owner's by-law contravention but fails to provide the owner with particulars of the complaint in writing as required by the Act, the corporation may be entitled to remedy the contravention at the owner's expense but is not entitled to costs of the enforcement proceeding.[2] Costs are not permitted to a successful defendant corporation where the case is akin to a public interest case.[3] Solicitor-client costs may be awarded to a corporation where an owner contravenes the corporation's rules and fails to follow a compliance request, since it is unfair and inequitable to force other condominium owners to subsidize the corporation's enforcement proceedings against a non-compliant owner.[4] Where a corporation is successful in obtaining an order against an owner who installs a sign on common property and plugs it into the condominium's power source, the owner must pay the corporation the cost of all electrical power used in relation to the sign, the costs of the application and all reasonable legal expenses incurred by the corporation to the extent that the legal expenses exceed the costs of recovery.[5]

Statutory right in relation to compliance orders in Ontario. In Ontario, for compliance orders only, if a corporation obtains an award of damages or costs in an order made against an owner or occupier of a unit, the damages or costs, together with any actual additional costs to the corporation in obtaining the order, are added to the common expenses for the unit.[6] These costs may include: the actual legal costs owing by the corporation to its lawyer, including costs beyond those a court may have ordered the owner to pay; all costs incurred in relation to an appeal in the matter; and any other costs, such as administrative or managerial costs, incurred by the condominium in the matter, if the costs were incurred in obtaining the order.[7] The costs of obtaining an order, including the costs defending the order obtained on appeal, are included, but the costs of enforcement are not included.[8] The costs claimed by the corporation must be reasonable.[9]

Notes

1. (AB) *Condominium Property Act*, R.S.A. 2000, c. C-22, ss. 36(3)(d), (5), 67(2)

   (BC) *Strata Property Act*, S.B.C. 1998, c. 43, ss. 133, 135(1)(b)

   (MB) *Condominium Act*, C.C.S.M. c. C170, s. 24

   (NB) *Condominium Property Act*, S.N.B. 2009, c. C-16.05, s. 60(4)

   (NL) *Condominium Act, 2009*, S.N.L. 2009, c. C-29.1, s. 48(d)(iii) (not yet in force)

   (NS) *Condominium Act*, R.S.N.S. 1989, c. 85, s. 38(2)(c)

   (ON) *Condominium Act, 1998*, S.O. 1998, c. 19, s. 134(5)

   (SK) *Condominium Property Act, 1993*, S.S. 1993, c. C-26.1, s. 98

   (NT) *Condominium Act*, R.S.N.W.T. 1988, c. C-15, ss. 17.2(5), 19.16

   (NU) *Condominium Act*, R.S.N.W.T. (Nu.) 1988, c. C-15, s. 19(1)(d)

   (YT) *Condominium Act*, R.S.Y. 2002, c. 36, s. 24(2)(b).
2. *Strata Plan VR19 v. Collins*, [2004] B.C.J. No. 2757, 2004 BCSC 1743 (B.C.S.C.) (condominium had to bear its own costs of the enforcement proceeding).
3. *Sauve v. McKeage*, [2006] B.C.J. No. 1144, 2006 BCSC 781 (B.C.S.C.) (plaintiff's interest was not solely limited to her private interest, since she represented the interests of others).

4. For other cases in which solicitor-client costs were granted, see, *e.g.*, *York Condominium Corp. No. 219 v. Naumovich*, unreported decision of Taliano J., released January 3, 1985 (consideration of fairness is separate and apart from consideration of whether there is an indemnification clause in a declaration), *York Condominium Corp. No. 42 v. Miller*, unreported decision of German J., released January 5, 1988, *Eva Osvath v. Carleton Condominium Corp. No. 237* (Small Claims Court, January 11, 2005) (condominium was entitled to costs above small claims court limit in its defence of a discrimination and harassment claim that was "completely and entirely without merit" to obtain partial indemnification for counsel costs that would "undoubtedly be passed on the all owners"), *Maverick Equities Inc. v. Condominium Plan No. 9422336*, [2008] A.J. No. 616, 2008 ABCA 221 (Alta. C.A.) (the appellant was entitled to solicitor-and-client appellate costs, as provided for in the condominium's by-laws), *Condominium Plan No. 0221347 v. N.Y.*, [2003] A.J. No. 1227, 2003 ABQB 790 (Alta. Q.B.) (condominium was entitled to solicitor-and-client costs, since the sole reason for court proceedings was the appellant's failure to comply with the condominium's by-laws and leave the premises when she was evicted).
5. *Summerville Condominium Corp. v. Dynamic Physiotherapy Services Ltd.*, [2003] N.J. No. 332, 2003 NLSCTD 182 (Nfld. S.C.).
6. (ON) *Condominium Act, 1998*, S.O. 1998, c. 19, s. 134(5).
7. *York Condominium Corp. No. 98 v. Jeffers*, [2008] O.J. No. 2646, 168 A.C.W.S. (3d) 297 (Ont. Div. Ct.) (where a condominium obtained a dismissal with costs of a plaintiff's slander of title claim, it could not obtain full indemnity costs, since the action was not an application by the condominium for an order enforcing compliance with any provision of the act, declaration or by-laws). But see *Peel Condominium Corp. No. 449 v. Hogg,* [1997] O.J. No. 623, 25 O.T.C. 304 (Ont. Gen. Div.) (costs were awarded to condominium on a solicitor-client basis as a result of an indemnification clause in the declaration) and *Peel Condominium Corp. No. 338 v. Young*, [1996] O.J. No. 1478, 62 A.C.W.S. (3d) 670 (Ont. Gen. Div.).
8. *Metropolitan Toronto Condominium Corp. No. 1385 v. Skyline Executive Properties Inc.*, [2005] O.J. No. 1604, 253 D.L.R. (4th) 656 (Ont. C.A.).
9. *Jankowski v. 990088 Ontario Inc.*, [1998] O.J. No. 2764, 72 O.T.C. 375 (Ont. Gen. Div.), affd [2000] O.J. No. 444 (Ont. C.A.).

---

9. Alternative Dispute Resolution

(1) Optional Alternative Dispute Resolution............. HCD-113
(2) Mandatory Alternative Dispute Resolution.......... HCD-114

---

(1) Optional Alternative Dispute Resolution

▼HCD-113▼ Where alternative dispute resolution is optional. Mediation and arbitration are optional in Alberta, British Columbia and Newfoundland and Labrador. Arbitration is optional for a broad range of matters in British Columbia, Manitoba, New Brunswick, Nova Scotia and Saskatchewan and is optional for specific matters in several jurisdictions.

Optional mediation and arbitration. In Alberta, with the agreement of the parties to a dispute, any dispute in respect of a matter arising under the act or in respect of the corporation's by-laws may be dealt with by means of mediation, conciliation or similar techniques to encourage settlement of the dispute, or may be arbitrated; a dispute may also be arbitrated after an unsuccessful attempt to deal with the dispute by means of mediation, conciliation or a similar technique.[1] In British Columbia, a dispute among owners, tenants, the corporation or any combination of them may be referred to a dispute resolution committee by a party to the dispute if all the parties to the dispute consent and the dispute involves the Act, regulations, by-laws or rules.[2] In Manitoba, a tenant or corporation may apply under the *Residential Tenancies Act* to have the director investigate, endeavour to mediate a settlement and determine a matter arising from an alleged breach by the tenant of the duty to comply with the act, declaration and by-laws.[3] In Newfoundland and Labrador, where both parties consent, a dispute may be submitted to a certified mediator selected by the parties where the dispute arises between an owner and a corporation, two or more owners, a developer and a corporation, a developer and an owner, or an owner of a unit and an occupier of another unit.[4] Where the parties do not agree to refer the matter to mediation, cannot agree on the appointment of a mediator, or referred the matter to mediation and the mediation was unsuccessful, the dispute may be referred to an arbitrator if both parties consent, or the parties may make an application to court.[5] The provisions with respect to mediation and arbitration do not restrict the legal remedies otherwise available for failure to perform a duty imposed by the statute.[6]

Optional arbitration for broad range of matters. In British Columbia, where there is a dispute between an owner or tenant and a corporation, another owner or another tenant, the dispute may be referred to arbitration if it concerns: the interpretation or application of the Act, regulations, by-laws or rules; the common property or common assets; the use or enjoyment of a unit; money owing under the Act, by-laws or rules; an action or threatened action by or decision of the corporation in relation to an owner or tenant; or the exercise of voting rights by a person who holds at least 50% of the votes at an annual or special general meeting.[7] The arbitrator's decision is final and binding but may be reviewed and may be appealed with the required consent and leave.[8] In Manitoba, where there is a dispute respecting the performance of a duty or satisfaction of a right under the Act, declaration or by-laws whose resolution may proceed by way of an application in court, the parties to the dispute may agree in writing to submit the dispute to arbitration; the arbitrator's award is final and binding and not subject to review or appeal.[9] In New Brunswick and Nova Scotia, where there is a dispute between a corporation and an owner, a corporation and a person who has agreed with the corporation to manage the condominium property, a corporation and any other corporation created or continued under the Act or two or more owners, a party to the dispute may give notice to the other party and to the director that the party intends to have the dispute arbitrated and, when notice is given, the parties are deemed to have entered into an arbitration agreement;[10] disputes regarding termination of the property do not qualify for arbitration, but disputes between a board and an owner as to whether a board decision or proposed action is prejudicial to the condominium property qualify for arbitration.[11] In Nova Scotia, the arbitration provisions also apply to disputes between a corporation and an occupier of a unit and between an owner and an occupier of another unit.[12] In Saskatchewan, where there is a dispute between owners or between the corporation and one or more owners respecting any matter relating to the corporation, the parties to the dispute may agree in writing to submit the dispute to arbitration, and the decision of an appointed arbitrator is final and binding.[13]

Optional arbitration for specific matters. In Manitoba, Prince Edward Island, Northwest Territories, Nunavut and Yukon Territory, a declaration may provide that if any substantial addition, alteration or improvement to or renovation of the common elements is made or if any substantial change in the corporation's assets is made, the corporation must, on demand of any owner who dissented, purchase that owner's unit and common interest; if the corporation and the dissenting owner do not agree as to the purchase price of the unit and common interest, the dissenting owner may elect to have the fair market value of the unit and common interest determined by arbitration by serving a notice to that effect on the corporation.[14] In addition, in these jurisdictions and in New Brunswick and Nova Scotia, on a sale of the property or common elements, any dissenting owner may elect to have the fair market value of the property at the time of the sale determined by arbitration by serving notice to that effect on the corporation within 10 days after a vote.[15] In New Brunswick, if an owner fails to comply with his or her obligations with respect to a tenancy agreement, a corporation may serve notice on the owner that the corporation intends to submit the dispute to arbitration.[16]

Notes

1. (AB) *Condominium Property Act*, R.S.A. 2000, c. C-22, s. 69(1)-(2).
2. (BC) *Strata Property Act*, S.B.C. 1998, c. 43, Schedule of Standard Bylaws, s. 29(1).
3. (MB) *Condominium Act*, C.C.S.M. c. C170, s. 13.1(7); (MB) *Residential Tenancies Act*, C.C.S.M. c. R119.
4. (NL) *Condominium Act, 2009*, S.N.L. 2009, c. C-29.1, s. 64(1).
5. (NL) *Condominium Act, 2009*, S.N.L. 2009, c. C-29.1, s. 64(3)-(4) (not yet in force).
6. (NL) *Condominium Act, 2009*, S.N.L. 2009, c. C-29.1, s. 64(4).
7. (BC) *Strata Property Act*, S.B.C. 1998, c. 43, s. 177.
8. (BC) *Strata Property Act*, S.B.C. 1998, c. 43, ss. 187-188.
9. (MB) *Condominium Act*, C.C.S.M. c. C170, s. 25(1), (3).
10. (NB) *Condominium Property Act*, S.N.B. 2009, c. C-16.05, s. 59(1)-(2); (NS) *Condominium Act*, R.S.N.S. 1989, c. 85, s. 33(2).
11. (NB) *Condominium Property Act*, S.N.B. 2009, c. C-16.05, s. 59(3)-(4); (NS) *Condominium Act*, R.S.N.S. 1989, c. 85, s. 33(2).
12. (NS) *Condominium Act*, R.S.N.S. 1989, c. 85, s. 33(2)(d)-(e).
13. (SK) *Condominium Property Act, 1993*, S.S. 1993, c. C-26.1, s. 100(1), (3).
14. (MB) *Condominium Act*, C.C.S.M. c. C170, s. 16(3)-(4)
    (PE) *Condominium Act,* R.S.P.E.I. 1988, c. C-16, s. 17(5)
    (NT) *Condominium Act*, R.S.N.W.T. 1988, c. C-15, s. 21(3)-(4)
    (NU) *Condominium Act*, R.S.N.W.T. 1988 (Nu.), c. C-15, s. 21(3)-(4)
    (YT) *Condominium Act*, R.S.Y. 2002, c. 36, s. 16(3)-(4).
15. (MB) *Condominium Act*, C.C.S.M. c. C170, s. 21(7)
    (NB) *Condominium Property Act*, S.N.B. 2009, c. C-16.05, s. 47(6)
    (NS) *Condominium Act*, R.S.N.S. 1989, c. 85, s. 40(5)
    (PE) *Condominium Act,* R.S.P.E.I. 1988, c. C-16, s. 24(5)
    (NT) *Condominium Act*, R.S.N.W.T. 1988, c. C-15, s. 27(1)
    (NU) *Condominium Act*, R.S.N.W.T. 1988 (Nu.), c. C-15, s. 27(1)
    (YT) *Condominium Act*, R.S.Y. 2002, c. 36, s. 21(8).
16. (NB) *Condominium Property Act*, S.N.B. 2009, c. C-16.05, s. 53(6).

---

(2) Mandatory Alternative Dispute Resolution

▼HCD-114▼ Mandatory mediation and arbitration in Ontario. In Ontario, mediation and arbitration are mandatory for several types of disagreements, including disagreements with respect to certain agreements, disagreements with respect to budget statements, disagreements with respect to the declaration, by-laws and rules, disagreements with respect to the interpretation of leasehold interests and disagreements with respect to sale of the property or a part of the common elements. Mediation is mandatory unless the parties have previously submitted the dispute to mediation.[1] Unless the mediator obtains a settlement between the parties with respect to the dispute, arbitration becomes mandatory 30 days after the mediator selected by the parties delivers a notice stating that the mediation has failed, or 60 days after the parties submit the dispute to arbitration if the parties do not select a mediator.[2] If mediation and arbitration processes are available, a person may not apply to court for a compliance order until the person has failed to obtain compliance through using those processes.[3] The legislative objective of the mandatory alternative dispute resolution provisions is to enable the resolution of disputes within the condominium community quickly and efficiently through the more informal procedures of mediation and arbitration.[4]

Disagreements with respect to certain agreements. Every agreement between a developer and a corporation, between two corporations, between a corporation and a unit owner with respect to additions, alterations or improvements by the owner to the common elements and between a corporation and a person for the management of property is deemed to contain a provision to submit a disagreement between the parties to mediation and arbitration.[5] Where there is no actual agreement between the owner and corporation with respect to additions, alterations or improvements to common elements, a disagreement on that issue need not proceed to mediation and arbitration.[6]

Disagreements with respect to budget statements. A developer and a board are deemed to have agreed in writing to submit to mediation and arbitration a disagreement between the parties with respect to the developer's obligation to provide a purchaser of a unit with a budget statement for the one-year period immediately following registration of the declaration and description and with respect to the developer's accountability for that budget statement.[7]

Disagreements with respect to declaration, by-laws and rules. Every declaration is deemed to contain a provision that the corporation and owners agree to submit to mediation and arbitration a disagreement between the parties with respect to the declaration, by-laws or rules.[8] The term "disagreements" encompasses claims for damages arising from the subject matter of the disagreement.[9] The phrase "with respect to the declaration, by-laws or rules" applies to disagreements about the application or non-application of the declaration, by-law and rules,[10] but there is some question as to whether it applies to disagreements about the legal validity and interpretation of the declaration, by-laws and rules.[11]

Disagreements with respect to the interpretation of leasehold provisions. A lessor and a corporation are deemed to have agreed that either party may submit to mediation and arbitration a disagreement on the interpretation of the provisions of the leasehold interests in the property that bind the property.[12]

Disagreements with respect to sale of the property or part of the common elements. Every owner and a corporation that sells the condominium property or a part of the common elements are deemed to have made an agreement that an owner who has dissented on the vote authorizing the sale may submit to mediation and arbitration a dispute over the fair market value of the property or the part of the common elements that has been sold, determined as of the time of the sale.[13] An owner who serves a notice of intention is entitled to receive from the proceeds of the sale the amount the owner would have received if the sale price had been the fair market value as determined by the arbitration.[14]

Situations in which mediation and arbitration are not required. Courts have held that mediation and arbitration are not required where a party seeks an oppression remedy,[15] where the evidence establishes a clear violation of the statute, declaration and rules,[16] where the dispute relates to a breach of the statute[17] and where the conduct of an owner is not merely a nuisance but is likely to damage property or cause injury to an individual.[18]

Notes

1. (ON) *Condominium Act, 1998*, S.O. 1998, c. 19, s. 132(1)(a).
2. (ON) *Condominium Act, 1998*, S.O. 1998, c. 19, s. 132(1)(b).
3. (ON) *Condominium Act, 1998*, S.O. 1998, c. 19, s. 134(2).
4. *McKinstry v. York Condominium Corp. No. 472*, [2003] O.J. No. 5006, 68 O.R. (3d) 557 (Ont. S.C.J.).
5. (ON) *Condominium Act, 1998*, S.O. 1998, c. 19, s. 132(2).
6. *Peel Condominium Corp. No. 33 v. Johnson*, [2005] O.J. No. 2875, 35 R.P.R. (4th) 300 (Ont. S.C.J.).
7. (ON) *Condominium Act, 1998*, S.O. 1998, c. 19, s. 132(3). See also Subsection VIII.3.(8) ("Obligations Related to First-Year Deficit").
8. (ON) *Condominium Act, 1998*, S.O. 1998, c. 19, s. 132(4).
9. *McKinstry v. York Condominium Corp. No. 472*, [2003] O.J. No. 5006, 68 O.R. (3d) 557 (Ont. S.C.J.); *Kovats v. M.F. Property Management Ltd.*, [2009] O.J. No. 1972 (Ont. S.C.J.).

10. *McKinstry v. York Condominium Corp. No. 472*, [2003] O.J. No. 5006, 68 O.R. (3d) 557 (Ont. S.C.J.).
11. See *McKinstry v. York Condominium Corp. No. 472*, [2003] O.J. No. 5006, 68 O.R. (3d) 557 (Ont. S.C.J.). But see also *Nipissing Condominium Corp. No. 4 v. Simard*, [2009] O.J. No. 4430, 2009 ONCA 743 (Ont. C.A.).
12. (ON) *Condominium Act, 1998*, S.O. 1998, c. 19, s. 168(3)-(4).
13. (ON) *Condominium Act, 1998*, S.O. 1998, c. 19, s. 125(1)-(2).
14. (ON) *Condominium Act, 1998*, S.O. 1998, c. 19, s. 125(4).
15. *McKinstry v. York Condominium Corp. No. 472*, [2003] O.J. No. 5006, 68 O.R. (3d) 557 (Ont. S.C.J.).
16. *Peel Condominium Corp. No. 283 v. Genik*, [2007] O.J. No. 2544, 158 A.CW.S. (3d) 665 (Ont. S.C.J.).
17. *Metro Toronto Condominium Corp. No. 545 v. Stein*, [2006] O.J. No. 2473, 212 O.A.C. 100 (Ont. C.A.).
18. *Carleton Condominium Corp. No. 291 v. Weeks*, [2003] O.J. No. 1204, [2003] O.T.C. 239 (Ont. S.C.J.).

---

10. Offences

▼HCD-115▼ Offences subject to fines. In Alberta, a person who fails to comply with certain provisions regarding sale of units by developers and conversion to condominium units is guilty of an offence and liable to a fine.[1] In addition, a person who fails to comply with the statute and each board member who is knowingly a party to a corporation's failure is guilty of an offence and liable to a fine.[2] In Ontario, every corporation and other person who knowingly contravenes certain provisions relating to turn-over meetings and obligations, records, disclosure statements, money held in trust, the condominium's money, entry by canvassers and false and misleading statements is guilty of an offence and liable to a fine.[3] Directors and officers who knowingly cause, authorize, permit, participate in or acquiesce in the commission by the corporation also commit an offence.[4] In Prince Edward Island, every person who knowingly contravenes certain provisions relating to investigation of records and sale of units or who knowingly purports to enter into a lease in contravention of certain provisions relating to lease of units is guilty of an offence and liable on summary conviction to a fine.[5] In Saskatchewan, every corporation that contravenes certain provisions relating to board duties, annual meetings, reserve funds and notice of termination of condominium status or that contravenes any duty to a local authority imposed on a corporation by the statute is guilty of an offence and liable on summary conviction to a fine.[6] In addition, every developer who contravenes certain provisions relating to turn-over obligations, sale of units by the developer and requirements for purchase agreements is guilty of an offence and liable on summary conviction to a fine;[7] every officer or board member who directed, authorized, assented to, acquiesced in or participated in the commission of a corporation's offence is a party to the offence and liable on summary conviction to a fine; and every person who fails to comply with any duty imposed by the act is guilty of an offence and liable on summary conviction to a fine.[8]

Offences subject to fines or imprisonment. In British Columbia, an individual who knowingly makes a false statement in a certificate commits an offence and is liable on conviction to a fine or to imprisonment for up to 6 months or to both.[9] In Newfoundland and Labrador, an individual who knowingly makes a false statement in a certificate, sells as a condominium individual units in a building that are not registered as a condominium under the Act, or contravenes a provision of the act or regulations commits an offence and is liable on summary conviction to a fine or to imprisonment for up to six months or to both.[10]

Limitation periods. In Ontario and Saskatchewan, the legislation provides a two-year limitation period for proceedings regarding contraventions of the Act.[11]

Notes

1. (AB) *Condominium Property Act*, R.S.A. 2000, c. C-22, s. 79(1).
2. (AB) *Condominium Property Act*, R.S.A. 2000, c. C-22, s. 79(2)-(3).
3. (ON) *Condominium Act, 1998*, S.O. 1998, c. 19, s. 137(1).
4. (ON) *Condominium Act, 1998*, S.O. 1998, c. 19, s. 137(2).
5. (PE) *Condominium Act,* R.S.P.E.I. 1988, c. C-16, s. 35.
6. (SK) *Condominium Property Act, 1993*, S.S. 1993, c. C-26.1, s. 111(1).
7. (SK) *Condominium Property Act, 1993*, S.S. 1993, c. C-26.1, s. 111(2).
8. (SK) *Condominium Property Act, 1993*, S.S. 1993, c. C-26.1, s. 111(3)-(4).
9. (BC) *Strata Property Act*, S.B.C. 1998, c. 43, s. 290.
10. (NL) *Condominium Act, 2009*, S.N.L. 2009, c. C-29.1, s. 90 (not yet in force).
11. (ON) *Condominium Act, 1998*, S.O. 1998, c. 19, s. 137(3)
    (SK) *The Condominium Property Act, 1993*, S.S. 1993, c. C-26.1, s. 111.1.

IX. Amalgamation and Termination of Condominiums

1. Amalgamation

(1) Requirements for Amalgamation HCD-116
(2) Effect of Amalgamation HCD-117

2. Termination or Winding Up of Condominium or Strata Corporation

(1) Termination HCD-119
(2) Expropriation HCD-123
(3) Effect of Termination or Expropriation HCD-124
(4) Leasehold Condominium Corporations HCD-125

---

1. Amalgamation

(1) Requirements for Amalgamation HCD-116
(2) Effect of Amalgamation HCD-117

---

(1) Requirements for Amalgamation

▼HCD-116▼ Procedure. Subject to the regulations of the governing legislation, two or more condominiums of the same type may amalgamate. To amalgamate, the amalgamating condominiums must comply with prescribed requirements. In most jurisdictions, this includes registering a declaration and description of the amalgamated condominium with written consent. The declaration of an amalgamated condominiums cannot not be registered unless the officers of each amalgamating corporation, who are authorized to sign on behalf of the corporation, have signed the declaration. The board of each amalgamating corporation must also call an owners meeting for the purpose of considering a declaration and plan amalgamating the condominiums. The board is required to give the owners a notice of the meeting which includes:

- a copy of the proposed declaration and plan of the amalgamated condominium and a copy of the proposed budget for the amalgamated corporation's first year of operation

- a copy of all proposed by-laws and rules of the amalgamated corporation
- a certificate as to the status for each amalgamating corporation in the prescribed form
- for each amalgamating corporation, the auditor's report on the last annual financial statements of the corporation, if it is not included in the above-referenced certificate and
- all additional statements and information that the regulations made under the governing Act require[1]

Note

1. (AB) *Condominium Property Act,* R.S.A. 2000, c. C-22; (AB) Condominium Property Regulation, Alta. Reg. 168/2000, ss. 46-51

   (BC) *Strata Property Act*, S.B.C. 1998, c. 43, ss. 269-270

   (NB) *Condominium Property Act*, S.N.B. 2009, c. C-16.05, s. 13; (NB) General Regulation, N.B. Reg. 2009-169, ss. 5, 6

   (NL) *Condominium Act, 2009*, S.N.L. 2009, c. C-29.1, ss. 65, 66 (not yet in force)

   (NS) *Condominium Act*, R.S.N.S. 1989, c. 85, ss. 29A, B; (NS) Condominium Regulations, N.S. Reg. 60/71, s. 54AA

   (ON) *Condominium Act, 1998*, S.O. 1998, c. 19, s. 120; (ON) General Regulation, O. Reg. 48/01 ss. 7, 34-37; (ON) Description and Registration Regulation, O. Reg. 49/01, ss. 4, 18, 28, 42

   (SK) *Condominium Property Act, 1993*, S.S. 1993, c. C-26.1, s. 15; (SK) Condominium Property Regulations, 2001, R.R.S. c. C-26.1 Reg. 2, ss. 30, 36

   (NT) *Condominium Act*, R.S.N.W.T. 1988, c. C-15, s. 6.2(1)-(6); (NT) Condominium Regulations, N.W.T. Reg. 098-2008, ss. 2, 3

---

(2) Effect of Amalgamation

▼HCD-117▼ Amalgamated condominium and corporation. Pursuant to legislation, upon receipt of an application for amalgamation in the proper form, the local land titles authority must:

- advise the amalgamated corporation of the new condominium corporation number
- cancel the ownership registers for the units described in the existing condominium plan
- establish an ownership register for unit in the approved plan
- register interests affecting a unit for which titles were cancelled against the titles for the same unit issued and register in the pre-

scribed manner against all titles any interest that affects all of the owners

On the issuance of titles in accordance with the foregoing requirements:

- any condominium plan pursuant to which titles had issued respecting the parcels affected by the amalgamation ceases to apply
- the amalgamating corporations are amalgamated and continued as one corporation
- the amalgamated corporation possesses all the assets, rights and privileges and is subject to all the liabilities including civil, criminal and quasi-criminal, and all the contracts, agreements and debts of each amalgamating corporation
- a conviction against, or a ruling, order or judgment in favour of or against an amalgamating corporation may be enforced by or against the amalgamated corporation
- the amalgamated corporation shall be deemed to be the plaintiff or defendant, as the case may be, in any civil action commenced by or against an amalgamating corporation before the amalgamation becomes effective
- units and common interests in an amalgamating condominium are units and common interests in the amalgamated condominium
- on the issuance of titles, the members of the boards of the amalgamating corporations constitute the members of the board of the amalgamated corporation and shall hold office until the election of the members of the board at the first annual meeting of owners of the amalgamated corporation[1]

Note

1. (AB) *Condominium Property Act,* R.S.A. 2000, c. C-22; (AB) Condominium Property Regulation, Alta. Reg. 168/2000, ss. 47(2), 51(3), (4), 52-56

   (BC) *Strata Property Act*, S.B.C. 1998, c. 43, s. 271

   (NB) *Condominium Property Act*, S.N.B. 2009, c. C-16.05, s. 14

   (NL) *Condominium Act, 2009*, S.N.L. 2009, c. C-29.1, ss. 65, 67 (not yet in force)

   (NS) *Condominium Act*, R.S.N.S. 1989, c. 85, s. 29C

   (ON) *Condominium Act, 1998*, S.O. 1998, c. 19, s. 121; (ON) Description and Registration Regulation, O. Reg. 49/01, s. 27(6). In Ontario, the reserve fund study requirements differ for an amalgamated condominium corporation; see (ON) General Regulation, O. Reg. 48/01, s. 38 and see Subsection VII.2.(7) ("Reserve Fund").

   (SK) *Condominium Property Act, 1993*, S.S. 1993, c. C-26.1, s. 15(5.1), (6), (7); (SK) Condominium Property Regulations, 2001, R.R.S. c. C-26.1 Reg. 2, s. 41.8

(NT) *Condominium Act*, R.S.N.W.T. 1988, c. C-15, s. 6.2(7).

---

2. Termination or Winding Up of Condominium or Strata Corporation

(1) Termination
(a) With Consent HCD-119
(b) Upon Substantial Damage HCD-120
(c) By Sale HCD-121
(d) By the Court HCD-122
(2) Expropriation HCD-123
(3) Effect of Termination or Expropriation HCD-124
(4) Leasehold Condominium Corporations HCD-125

---

(1) Termination

▼HCD-118▼ Overview. The governance of a condominium property by the relevant condominium legislation may be terminated by various means, including: with the requisite consent of the corporation's owners, upon substantial damage to the property, by the sale of the property, by court order and in some jurisdictions, by expropriation.

(a) With Consent

▼HCD-119▼ Termination by notice without sale. A corporation may register a notice terminating the governance of the property by the relevant condominium legislation with the consent of a prescribed number of owners and the consent of prescribed persons having registered claims against the property created after the registration of the declaration and description/plan.[1] The notice of termination must be in the prescribed form, signed by the prescribed classes of people. Once submitted, the Registrar must accept such notice for registration.[2] In Alberta and Saskatchewan, however, the condominium status of a building or land may be terminated by a special resolution or a unanimous resolution respectively.[3]

Notes

1. (MB) *Condominium Act,* C.C.S.M. c. C170, ss. 16(1), 22(1)

(NB) *Condominium Property Act,* S.N.B. 2009, c. C-16.05, s. 54

(NL) *Condominium Act, 2009*, S.N.L. 2009, c. C-29.1, s. 63(1) (not yet in force). But see exception for amalgamation at ss. 65, 66(7)

(NS) *Condominium Act*, R.S.N.S. 1989, c. 85, s. 41(1)

(ON) *Condominium Act, 1998*, S.O. 1998, c. 19, s. 122(1). But see exceptions at (ON) General Regulation, O. Reg. 48/01, s. 26 and (ON) Description and Registration Regulation, O. Reg. 49/01, s. 34. For phased condominium corporations, see s. 145(4), (5)

(PE) *Condominium Act*, R.S.P.E.I. 1988, c. C-16, s. 25(1)

(NT) *Condominium Act*, R.S.N.W.T. 1988, c. C-15, s. 28(1)

(NU) *Condominium Act*, R.S.N.W.T. (Nu.) 1988, c. C-15, s. 28(1)

(YT) *Condominium Act*, R.S.Y. 2002, c. 36, s. 22(1).

2. (MB) *Condominium Act,* C.C.S.M. c. C170, ss. 16(1), 22(2)

(NL) *Condominium Act*, 2009, S.N.L. 2009, c. C-29.1, s. 63(2) (not yet in force)

(NS) *Condominium Act*, R.S.N.S. 1989, c. 85, s. 41(2)

(ON) *Condominium Act, 1998*, S.O. 1998, c. 19, s. 122(2); (ON) Description and Registration Regulation, O. Reg. 49/01, ss. 47(1), (3), (4), (5)

(PE) *Condominium Act*, R.S.P.E.I. 1988, c. C-16, s. 25(2)

(NT) *Condominium Act*, R.S.N.W.T. 1988, c. C-15, s. 28(2)

(NU) *Condominium Act*, R.S.N.W.T. (Nu.) 1988, c. C-15, s. 28(2)

(YT) *Condominium Act*, R.S.Y. 2002, c. 36, s. 22(2).

3. (AB) *Condominium Property Act,* R.S.A. 2000, c. C-22, ss. 1(1)(x), 60

(SK) *Condominium Property Act, 1993*, S.S. 1993, c. C-26.1, ss. 2(1)(aa), 83.

(b) Upon Substantial Damage

▼HCD-120▼ Determination of damage. The unit owners of a condominium property may terminate the governance of the property under the Act because of substantial damage. Substantial damage is defined by condominium legislation as damage for which the cost of repair is estimated or equal to a prescribed percentage of the replacement cost of all buildings and structures located on the property.[1] If damage occurs to a building or a structure located on the property the board must determine within a prescribed period of time of the occurrence whether there has been substantial damage. Where there has been a determination that there has been substantial damage, the owners vote for repair of the damage or termination of the corporation. If a prescribed number of owners vote in favour of termination, the board must register a notice terminating the government of the property within a prescribed period of time and in the prescribed form. If there is no vote in favour of termination, the corporation must repair the damage to the building or structure located on the property within a prescribed period of time.[2]

Notes

1. (MB) *Condominium Act,* C.C.S.M. c. C170, s. 19(1)

   (NL) *Condominium Act, 2009,* S.N.L. 2009, c. C-29.1, s. 62(1) (not yet in force)

   (NS) *Condominium Act*, R.S.N.S. 1989, c. 85, s. 36(1)

   (ON) *Condominium Act, 1998*, S.O. 1998, c. 19, s. 123(2)

   (PE) *Condominium Act*, R.S.P.E.I. 1988, c. C-16, s. 22(1)

   (QC) *Civil Code of Québec*, L.R.Q., c. C-1991, art. 1108

   (NT) *Condominium Act*, R.S.N.W.T. 1988, c. C-15, s. 24(1)

   (NU) *Condominium Act*, R.S.N.W.T. (Nu.) 1988, c. C-15, s. 24(1)

   (YT) *Condominium Act*, R.S.Y. 2002, c. 36, s. 19(1).

2. (MB) *Condominium Act,* C.C.S.M. c. C170, ss. 19, 20

   (NL) *Condominium Act, 2009*, S.N.L. 2009, c. C-29.1, s. 62 (not yet in force)

   (NS) *Condominium Act*, R.S.N.S. 1989, c. 85, s. 36(1)-(5)

   (ON) *Condominium Act, 1998*, S.O. 1998, c. 19, s. 123(1)-(10). See exceptions at (ON) General Regulation, O. Reg. 48/01, s. 26 and (ON) Description and Registration Regulation, O. Reg. 49/01, ss. 34, 47(2)-(5)

   (PE) *Condominium Act*, R.S.P.E.I. 1988, c. C-16, ss. 22, 23

   (QC) *Civil Code of Québec*, L.R.Q., c. C-1991, art. 1108

   (NT) *Condominium Act*, R.S.N.W.T. 1988, c. C-15, ss. 24, 25

   (NU) *Condominium Act*, R.S.N.W.T. (Nu.) 1998, c. C-15, ss. 24, 25

   (YT) *Condominium Act*, R.S.Y. 2002, c. 36, ss. 19, 20.

   See Subsection VII.2.(1) ("Repair After Damages").

(c) By Sale

▼HCD-121▼ Sale of all or part of a condominium property. Condominium legislation authorizes a corporation to sell the condominium property or a part of the common elements. Once the property is sold, it is no longer governed by the applicable condominium Act. The legislation provides conditions upon which condominium property can be sold. In most jurisdictions, a corporation cannot sell the condominium property, or a portion of the common elements, unless: (i) a prescribed percentage of owners vote in favour of the sale, and (ii) individuals who have registered claims against the property being sold, that were created after the registration of the declaration and description applicable to the property being sold, vote in favour of the sale and consent in writing. In Manitoba, Newfoundland, Ontario, Prince Edward Island and Northwest

Territories, the prescribed number of owners and individuals with registered claims must be at least 80%.[1] Once the sale is authorized, prescribed documents must be executed, delivered and registered by the relevant Registrar.[2] Subject to the rights of dissenters, the owners then share the net proceeds of the sale in the same proportions as their common interests.[3]

Right of dissenters. Every corporation that makes a sale of the condominium property or a portion of the common elements is deemed to have made an agreement with an owner who did not vote in favour of the vote to submit to mediation a disute over the fair market value of the property or part of the common element that has been sold. A dissenting owner is entitled to receive, from the proceeds of the sale, the amount the owner would have received if the sale price had been the fair market value as determined at the mediation or subsequent arbitration, if any. Where the proceeds of the sale are inadequate to pay the fair market value amount as determined at mediation or arbitration, each owner who voted for the sale is liable for the amount of the deficiency in proportion to their common interest.[4] The Nova Scotia Court of Appeal considered the fiduciary duty, of the majority owners approving a sale, to the dissenters. According to the court, a sale authorized by a majority of voters, in most circumstances, provides adequate assurance that the sale is in the collective best interests of the unit owners and the corporation. However, where a single individual has a controlling interest in the corporation, that individual is subject to a fiduciary duty which requires objective assurances that the sale is in the best interest of the corporation as a whole.[5]

Notes

1. (AB) *Condominium Property Act*, R.S.A. 2000, c. C-22, ss. 1(1)(x), 49(1)-(3) (persons with interests in the property must consent in writing to the release of those interests). See also s. 63(1), (2)

   (MB) *Condominium Act,* C.C.S.M. c. C170, s. 21(1)

   (NL) *Condominium Act, 2009*, S.N.L. 2009, c. C-29.1, s. 61(1) (not yet in force)

   (ON) *Condominium Act, 1998*, S.O. 1998, c. 19, s. 124(1), (2). If the sale is for only part of the common elements and includes exclusive-use common elements, those owners of the exclusive-use common elements must also consent in writing to the sale. See exception at (ON) Description and Registration Regulation, O. Reg. 49/01, s. 4. For phased condominium corporations, see ss. 145(4), (5)

   (PE) *Condominium Act*, R.S.P.E.I. 1988, c. C-16, s. 24(1)

   (SK) *Condominium Property Act, 1993*, S.S. 1993, c. C-26.1, s. 70(1), (2) (but provision does not apply to parking spaces that become parking units, ss. 70(5)), 88(1)

   (NT) *Condominium Act*, R.S.N.W.T. 1988, c. C-15, s. 26(1)

   (YT) *Condominium Act*, R.S.Y. 2002, c. 36, s. 21(1).

2. (AB) *Condominium Property Act*, R.S.A. 2000, c. C-22, s. 49(4)-(6). See also s. 63(3)-(6) and (AB) Condominium Property Regulation, Alta. Reg. 168/2000, ss. 13-18

   (MB) *Condominium Act,* C.C.S.M. c. C170, s. 21(2)-(4)

   (NL) *Condominium Act, 2009*, S.N.L. 2009, c. C-29.1, s. 61(2), (3) (not yet in force)

   (ON) *Condominium Act, 1998*, S.O. 1998, c. 19, s. 124(3). See (ON) Description and Registration Regulation, O. Reg. 49/01, s. 48, for deed for sale and other documentary requirements

   (PE) *Condominium Act*, R.S.P.E.I. 1988, c. C-16, s. 24(2)

   (SK) *Condominium Property Act, 1993*, S.S. 1993, c. C-26.1, ss. 70(3)-(5), 70.1, 71(1), (2), 88(2)-(4), 88.1, 89; (SK) Condominium Property Regulations, 2001, R.R.S. c. C-26.1 Reg. 2, ss. 61, 62

   (NT) *Condominium Act*, R.S.N.W.T. 1988, c. C-15, s. 26(2)-(4)

   (YT) *Condominium Act*, R.S.Y. 2002, c. 36, s. 21(2)-(4).
3. (MB) *Condominium Act,* C.C.S.M. c. C170, s. 21(6)

   (NL) *Condominium Act, 2009*, S.N.L. 2009, c. C-29.1, s. 40(4) (not yet in force)

   (ON) *Condominium Act, 1998*, S.O. 1998, c. 19, s. 124(5).
4. (MB) *Condominium Act,* C.C.S.M. c. C170, s. 21(7), (8)

   (NL) *Condominium Act, 2009*, S.N.L. 2009, c. C-29.1, s. 40(5), (6) (not yet in force)

   (ON) *Condominium Act, 1998*, S.O. 1998, c. 19, s. 125.
5. *2475813 Nova Scotia Ltd. v. Rodgers,* [2001] N.S.J. No. 21, 2001 NSCA 12 (N.S.C.A.) (where a controlling owner wants to sell his units, he has a fiduciary duty to act in the best transfer of the remaining unit owners as his broad, discretionary power gave him the right to affect the property rights of others and dispossess them of their home. While a duty not to unreasonably withhold consent may not be read into a statute, it can be found to exist on a case-by-case basis).

(d) By the Court

▼HCD-122▼ Court order. A corporation, an owner, a person having an encumbrance against a unit and common interest or other prescribed individuals, may make an application to the court for an order terminating the governance of the condominium property by the Act. Legislation in Yukon and Northwest Territories specifies that an application for termination may be brought if damage to the condominium property occurs or all or part of the property is expropriated. The court may order that the governance of the property by terminated if it is of the opinion that it would be just and equitable to do so having regard to prescribed grounds, including:

- the scheme and intent of the governing Act

- the rights and interests of the owners individually and as a whole
- what course of action would be most just and equitable
- the probability of confusion and uncertainty in the affairs of the corporation or the owners if the court does not make the order[1]

Note

1. (AB) *Condominium Property Act*, R.S.A. 2000, c. C-22, ss. 61, 64(1), (2)
   (MB) *Condominium Act,* C.C.S.M. c. C170, s. 23
   (NS) *Condominium Act*, R.S.N.S. 1989, c. 85, s. 43
   (ON) *Condominium Act, 1998*, S.O. 1998, c. 19, s. 128 and (ON) Description and Registration Regulation, O. Reg. 49/01, ss. 34, 50
   (PE) *Condominium Act*, R.S.P.E.I. 1988, c. C-16, s. 26
   (SK) *Condominium Property Act, 1993*, S.S. 1993, c. C-26.1, ss. 84, 90(1), (2)
   (NT) *Condominium Act*, R.S.N.W.T. 1988, c. C-15, s. 29
   (NU) *Condominium Act*, R.S.N.W.T. (Nu.) 1988, c. C-15, s. 29
   (YT) *Condominium Act*, R.S.Y. 2002, c. 36, s. 23.

---

(2) Expropriation

▼HCD-123▼ Act ceases to govern property in Newfoundland and Ontario. In Newfoundland and Ontario, upon the expropriation of all or part of the condominium property under the *Expropriations Act*, the expropriated property is no longer governed by the provincial condominium legislation. As with the sale of part of the common elements in Newfoundland and Ontario, if part of the common elements is expropriated, the owners share the proceeds in the same proportions as their common interests.[1] Legislation prescribes the manner in which notices under the *Expropriation Act* and the *Planning Act* must be served by the expropriating authority on the owners of the land to be expropriated.[2]

Act does not cease to govern property. While expropriation is a means of terminating the governance of the condominium property by the relevant Act in Newfoundland and Ontario, such governance does not automatically terminate in other jurisdictions. The *Condominium Act* in Nova Scotia specifically states that "the expropriation of all or part of the property shall not terminate the government of the property by (the) Act".[3] In Yukon, prescribed persons may bring an application to the court for an order terminating the government of the property under the relevant condominium legislation, or an order amending the declaration or plan, if all or part of the property is expropriated.[4]

Notes

1. (NL) *Condominium Act, 2009*, S.N.L. 2009, c. C-29.1, s. 60(1) (not yet in force)
   (ON) *Condominium Act, 1998*, S.O. 1998, c. 19, s. 126(1)-(3).
2. (ON) *Condominium Act, 1998*, S.O. 1998, c. 19, ss. 24, 25; (ON) Description and Registration Regulation, O. Reg. 49/01, ss. 34, 49(1).
3. (NS) *Condominium Act*, R.S.N.S. 1989, c. 85, s. 39.
4. (YT) *Condominium Act*, R.S.Y. 2002, c. 36, s. 23(1), (3)-(5).

---

(3) Effect of Termination or Expropriation

▼HCD-124▼ Overview. Provincial and territorial legislation enumerate a number of effects resulting from the termination and/or expropriation of condominium property. While these effects vary by jurisdictions and by the type of termination, they include but are not limited to, the following:

- the relevant condominium legislation ceases to govern the property
- the owners are tenants in common of the land and interests appurtenant to the land described in the description in the same proportions as their common interests
- claims against the land and the interests appurtenant to the land described in the description, that were created before the registration of the declaration and description that made the relevant Act applicable to the land, are as effective as if the declaration and description or plan had not been registered
- encumbrances against each unit and common interest, that were created after the registration of the declaration and description or plan that made the relevant Act applicable to the unit, are claims against the interests of the owner in the land and interests appurtenant to the land described in the description and have the same priority as they had before the registration of the notice of termination and
- all other claims against the property that were created after the registration of the declaration and description or plan that made the relevant Act applicable to the property are extinguished
- the assets of the corporation are used to pay all claims for the payment of money against the corporation and

- the remainder of the assets of the corporation are distributed among the owners in the same proportions as the proportions of their common interests[1]

Subject to the right of dissenters and the presence of exclusive-use common elements, the owners at the time of registration of documentation for the sale of the condominium property share the net proceeds of the sale in the same proportion as their common interests. Similarly, subject to the presence of exclusive-use common elements, if part of the common elements is expropriated, the owners share the proceeds in the same proportions as their common interests.[2]

Notes

1. (AB) *Condominium Property Act,* R.S.A. 2000, c. C-22, s. 62(1) (termination by special resolution and/or application to court), s. 63 (termination by sale); (AB) Condominium Property Regulation, Alta. Reg. 168/2000, ss. 16(1), (2) (termination upon consent and application to court). See also ss. 2, 3 for application of (AB) *Municipal Government Act*, R.S.A. 2000, c. M-26

   (MB) *Condominium Act,* C.C.S.M. c. C170, s. 22(3) (termination by notice without sale), s. 20(3) (termination upon substantial damage), s. 21(5) (termination by sale), s. 10(12) (disposition of assets)

   (NL) *Condominium Act, 2009*, S.N.L. 2009, c. C-29.1, ss. 59, 62(2)-(5), 63(3) (destruction of property) (not yet in force)

   (ON) *Condominium Act, 1998*, S.O. 1998, c. 19, s. 42 (termination upon consent or substantial damage), s. 127(2) (termination by sale or expropriation), s. 129 (distribution of assets), but note that effects enumerated in s. 127 do not apply to leasehold corporations, s. 175(2)

   (PE) *Condominium Act*, R.S.P.E.I. 1988, c. C-16, ss. 23(3), 24(3), 25(3) (termination upon consent), s. 10(19) (disposition of assets)

   (QC) *Civil Code of Québec*, L.R.Q., c. C-1991, art. 1109

   (SK) *Condominium Property Act, 1993*, S.S. 1993, c. C-26.1, s. 71(3) (sale of property), ss. 85, 87; (SK) Condominium Property Regulations, 2001, R.R.S. c. C-26.1 Reg. 2, ss. 63, 64 (termination by special resolution and/or application to court), s. 86(1) (disposition of assets), ss. 88, 88.1 (transfer of parts of parcels). See also s. 3 for application of other laws

   (NT) *Condominium Act*, R.S.N.W.T. 1988, c. C-15, ss. 25(3), 26(5)-(7), 28(3) (termination upon substantial damage), s. 15 (owners and property cease to be governed by Act)

   (NU) *Condominium Act*, R.S.N.W.T. (Nu.) 1988, c. C-15, ss. 25(3), 26(5)-(6), 28(3) (termination by notice without sale), s. 15 (disposition of assets)

   (YT) *Condominium Act*, R.S.Y. 2002, c. 36, s. 10(13) (termination upon substantial damage), s. 20 (termination by sale) ss. 21(5), (6), 22(3).

2. (NL) *Condominium Act, 2009*, S.N.L. 2009, c. C-29.1, s. 60(2), (3), 61(5)-(13) (not yet in force)

   (ON) *Condominium Act, 1998*, S.O. 1998, c. 19, ss. 124(4), (5), 125, 126(2), (3). See also (ON) Description and Registration Regulation, O. Reg. 49/01 s. 51. For phased condominium corporations, see s. 145(4), (5)

   (NT) *Condominium Act*, R.S.N.W.T. 1988, c. C-15, s. 26(7), s. 27

   (NU) *Condominium Act*, R.S.N.W.T. (Nu.) 1988, c. C-15, ss. 26(7), 27

   (YT) *Condominium Act*, R.S.Y. 2002, c. 36, s. 1, s. 21(7)-(9).

---

(4) Leasehold Condominium Corporations

▼HCD-125▼ Termination. In Newfoundland and Ontario, a leasehold condominium corporation cannot register a notice of termination for termination of the property's governance by the Act by consent, upon substantial damage or upon the sale of the property, unless the lessor has consented to and executed the notice or the agreement of purchase and sale.[1] A lessor cannot terminate a leasehold interest in a unit in a leasehold corporation unless the lessor has been granted an order terminating the leasehold interests in all the units.[2] Termination of the property's governance by the Act by any means, including expropriation, results in the following:

- the Act ceases to govern the property, which also means that the condominium corporation is terminated
- the leasehold interests are terminated
- claims against the leasehold interests that do not secure the payment of money are extinguished, unless the lessor consented to their registration, in which case they are continued against the lessor's interest and
- claims against the leasehold interests that secure the payment of money are claims against the persons who were owners of the leasehold interests immediately before the termination of those interest, and not against the land[3]

Notes

1. (NL) *Condominium Act, 2009*, S.N.L. 2009, c. C-29.1, s. 28.1(2) (not yet in force); (ON) *Condominium Act, 1998*, S.O. 1998, c. 19, s. 172 and (ON) Description and Registration Regulation, O. Reg. 49/01, ss. 44(2), 47(4)-(6), 49(1)-(2).
2. (NL) *Condominium Act, 2009*, S.N.L. 2009, c. C-29.1, s. 28.2(1)-(5), (7) (not yet in force); (ON) *Condominium Act, 1998*, S.O. 1998, c. 19, ss. 173, 174; (ON) General Regulation, O. Reg. 48/01, s. 62(2), (4); (ON) Description and Registration Regulation, O. Reg. 49/01, ss. 44(2), 47(4)-(6), 48(1), (3), (4), s. 50.

3. (NL) *Condominium Act, 2009*, S.N.L. 2009, c. C-29.1, s. 28.2(6), (8), (9) (not yet in force); (ON) *Condominium Act, 1998*, S.O. 1998, c. 19, s. 175.

Halsbury's
Laws of Canada
First Edition

Constitutional Law — Division of Powers

Contributed by

Martin William Mason
B.A., M.A., LL.B.

Guy Régimbald
LL.B., B.C.L. (Oxon.)

Contributing Editor

Charlene Quincey
B.A., J.D.

Ambit of Title

The title **Constitutional Law – Division of Powers** examines the constitutional documents and cases which determine the allocation of jurisdiction between the federal and provincial governments in Canada, and govern the rules of constitutional interpretation. Topics covered include: sources of constitutional law and institutions; constitutional conventions and unwritten principles of the constitution; constitutional interpretation; peace, order and good government; the regulation of trade and commerce; the raising of revenue, the spending power and federal authority in relation to financial matters; works and undertakings, communications and transportation and labour relations; and property and civil rights and provincial authority in relation to local and private matters.

Statement of Currency

The law stated in this title is in general that in force on October 1, 2011. Subsequent developments may be located by referring to this volume's Annual Cumulative Supplement.

Related Titles

Please refer to the following titles (when published) for related and complementary information:

Banking and Finance
Conflict of Laws (2011 Reissue)
Constitutional Law – Charter of Rights
Criminal Offences and Defences
Criminal Procedure
Elections
Environment
Judges and Courts
Legislation
Legislatures
Police, Security and Emergencies
Public International Law
Public Utilities
Transportation

References and Abbreviations

AB	Alberta
BC	British Columbia
CAN	Canada
Charter	*Canadian Charter of Rights and Freedoms*
MB	Manitoba
NB	New Brunswick
NL	Newfoundland and Labrador
NS	Nova Scotia
NT	Northwest Territories
NU	Nunavut
ON	Ontario
PE	Prince Edward Island
POGG	Peace, Order and Good Government
QC	Québec
SK	Saskatchewan
YT	Yukon

Table of Contents — Constitutional Law — Division of Powers

Page

Table of Cases 37

Table of Statutes 83

Table of Statutory Instruments 87

Ambit of Title, Statement of Currency, Related Titles 331

References and Abbreviations 333

I. Sources of Constitutional Law and Institutions

1. Overview 343

2. Major Sources

(1) *The Constitution Act, 1867* 345
(2) *The Constitution Act, 1982* 346
(3) Section 52(2) of the *Constitution Act, 1982* 347
(4) Founding Statute of the Crown and Parliament of Great Britain 348

3. Canadian Statutes that have Quasi-Constitutional Nature 349

4. Crown Prerogative

(1) Overview 350
(2) The Role of the Prime Minister 352
(3) Judicial Review of Decisions Made Pursuant to a Crown Prerogative 353

5. Parliament 355

Page

6. Senate 356

7. House of Commons 357

II. Constitutional Conventions and the Unwritten Principles of the Constitution

1. Constitutional Conventions

(1) General 359
(2) Between Law and Usage 362
(3) Convention Formation 363
(4) Convention Components 364
(5) Convention and the Law 365

2. Ultimate Significance 366

3. Unwritten Principles of the Constitution

(1) General 367
(2) Specific Unwritten Principles
(a) The Principle of Parliamentary Sovereignty 372
(b) The Rule of Law 375
(c) Democracy 379
(d) Judicial Independence 382
(e) The Protection of Minorities 384
(f) The Principle of Constitutionalism 385
(g) The Neutrality of the Public Service 386
(h) No Taxation Without Representation 387
(i) Separation of Powers 388
(j) Solicitor-client Privilege 390
(k) Parliamentary Privileges 391
(l) Full Faith and Credit Doctrine 398

III. Courts, Independence of Judiciary and Judicial Review

1. Establishment of Courts 401

Page

2. Independence of the Judiciary

(1) Three Conditions for Judicial Independence
(a) Security of Tenure 408
(b) Financial Security 408
(c) Institutional Independence 409
(2) Independence of Judges 411

3. Judicial Review

(1) General 412
(2) Section 96 of the *Constitution Act, 1867*
(a) Whether Power Conforms to Required Jurisdiction
(i) Characterization of the Power 415
(ii) Three Preliminary Questions 416
(b) Whether a "Judicial" Function 417
(c) Whether Function "Merely Ancillary" 418
(3) Section 101: Supreme Court, Exchequer Court and Federal Court of Canada
(a) Test for Federal Court Jurisdiction
(i) Statutory Grant of Jurisdiction 420
(ii) Existing Body of Federal Law 421
(iii) Whether a "Law of Canada" 422

IV. Constitutional Interpretation: Pith and Substance, Double Aspect, Paramountcy and Interjurisdictional Immunity

1. The Division of Legislative Authority 425

2. Presumption of Constitutionality 426

3. The Judicial Approach to Determining Constitutional Validity of Legislation

(1) Pith and Substance
(a) Effect of the Statute 428
(b) Purpose of the Statute 429
(2) Assignment to a Legislative Head of Power 431

Page

4. **Principle of Exclusivity** 431

5. **Double Aspect** 432

6. **Ancillary Effects** 433

7. **Paramountcy** 436

8. **Interjurisdictional Immunity** 438

9. **Reading Down** 441

10. **Severance** 442

V. Peace Order and Good Government

1. **General** 443

2. **POGG as a Residual Clause or for New Matters** 444

3. **The National Interest Context** 445

4. **The Emergency Context** 446

VI. Criminal Law – Federal and Provincial Jurisdiction

1. **Introduction** 449

2. **Criminal Law Power**

(1) Components 451
(2) Health and the Environment 452
(3) Tobacco and Drugs 453
(4) Gun Control 455
(5) Jurisdiction over the Establishment of Criminal Courts 456

Page

(6) Criminal Procedure and Evidence 457
(7) Criminal Justice and Policing 458
(8) Prosecution of Offences 458

3. Civil Law Remedies under the Criminal Law Power 459

4. Provincial Power to Enact Penal Laws 460

5. Punishment and Prevention of Crime 460

6. Young Offenders 462

VII. The Regulation of Trade and Commerce

1. General 463

2. Two Branches of the Trade and Commerce Power

(1) International and Interprovincial Trade and Commerce 464
(2) The General Regulation of Trade and Commerce 466

VIII. The Raising of Revenue, the Spending Power and Federal Authority in Relation to Financial Matters

1. The Raising of Revenue

(1) Introduction 470
(2) Section 125 of the *Constitution Act, 1867* 472
(3) Raising Revenue Through the Imposition of Taxes
(a) Direct vs. Indirect Taxes 476

Page

(b) Direct Taxation Within the Province for a Provincial Purpose 479
(c) Established Types of Direct Taxes 480
(4) Raising Revenue Through Regulatory Charges ... 484
(5) Raising Revenue through Licences 489
(6) Section 92A of the *Constitution Act, 1867* 491

2. The Spending Power 491

3. Banking 493

4. Bankruptcy 497

5. Interest 499

IX. Works and Undertakings, Communications and Transportation and Labour Relations

1. Works and Undertakings

(1) Section 92(10)(a) 502
(2) Section 92(10)(c) 504

2. Communication and Transportation

(1) Communication 506
(2) Transportation 508

3. Labour Relations 511

X. Property and Civil Rights and Provincial Authority in Relation to Local and Private Matters

1. Provincial Power to Make Laws in Relation to Property and Civil Rights 515

Page

2. Provincial Power to Legislate Matters of a Local or Private Nature 516

3. Double Aspect Doctrine in Relation to s. 92(13) and s. 92(16)

(1) Provincial Powers over Trade and Commerce 519
(2) Provincial Powers over Public Order and Morality 521

XI. The Environment and Natural Resources

1. The Environment

(1) Federal Regulation of Extra-Provincial Actions........ 526
(2) Peace, Order and Good Government........ 527
(3) Effect on Federal Jurisdiction........ 527
(4) Criminal Law Power 528

2. Natural Resources

(1) Mines and Minerals
  (a) Taxation 532
  (b) Trade and Commerce Power........ 532
  (c) Works and Undertakings under s. 92(10)(a)........ 533
  (d) Peace, Order and Good Government 533
  (e) Offshore Minerals 534
(2) Federal Declaratory Power........ 534
(3) Forestry........ 535
(4) Fisheries........ 537

Page

Index 553

Selected Secondary Sources 573

Glossary of Defined Terms in Selected Legislation Relevant to Constitutional Law — Division of Powers 633

I. Sources of Constitutional Law and Institutions

1. **Overview** HCL-1

2. **Major Sources** HCL-2
   - (1) *Constitution Act, 1867* HCL-3
   - (2) *Constitution Act, 1982* HCL-4
   - (3) Section 52(2) of the *Constitution Act, 1982* HCL-5
   - (4) Founding Statute of the Crown and Parliament of Great Britain HCL-6

3. **Canadian Statutes that have Quasi-Constitutional Nature** HCL-7

4. **Crown Prerogative**
   - (1) Overview HCL-8
   - (2) The Role of the Prime Minister HCL-9
   - (3) Judicial Review of Decisions Made Pursuant to a Crown Prerogative HCL-10

5. **Parliament** HCL-13

6. **Senate** HCL-14

7. **The House of Commons** HCL-15

---

1. Overview

▼HCL-1▼ Constitution of Canada. A fundamental principle of law in Canada is the supremacy of the Constitution which is enshrined in the *Constitution Act, 1982.*[1] All laws, whether common or legislative, must comply with the Constitution. Furthermore, all government action must also comply with the Constitution. The Supreme Court of Canada has clarified that the executive branch of our government is not exempt from this principle, stating that "their sole claim to exercise lawful authority rests in the powers allocated to them under the Constitution, and can come from no other source".[2] This principle guides the development and application of laws in Canada, and therefore the daily lives of its citizens. The enactment of the *Constitution Act, 1982*[3] allows courts to invalidate laws that are either in breach of the Charter,[4] or contravene the Division of Powers.[5] With the introduction of the Charter,[6] Canada went from a system of Parliamentary supremacy to one of constitutional supremacy.[7]

Notes

1. *Constitution Act, 1982*, being Schedule B to the *Canada Act 1982* (U.K.), 1982, c. 11, s. 52(1), provides that "any law that is inconsistent with the provisions of the Constitution is, to the extent of the inconsistency, of no force or effect".
2. *Reference re Secession of Québec*, [1998] S.C.J. No. 61, [1998] 2 S.C.R. 217 at para. 17 (S.C.C.).
3. Particularly, s. 52 of the *Constitution Act, 1982*, being Schedule B to the *Canada Act 1982* (U.K.), 1982, c. 11.
4. *Canadian Charter of Rights and Freedoms*, Part I of the *Constitution Act, 1982*, being Schedule B to the *Canada Act 1982* (U.K.), 1982, c. 11.
5. *Canadian Charter of Rights and Freedoms*, Part I of the *Constitution Act, 1982*, being Schedule B to the *Canada Act 1982* (U.K.), 1982, c. 11, s. 52; see discussion in *Chaoulli v. Québec (Attorney General)*, [2005] S.C.J. No. 33, [2005] 1 S.C.R. 791 at paras. 85-95 (S.C.C.).
6. *Canadian Charter of Rights and Freedoms*, Part I of the *Constitution Act, 1982*, being Schedule B to the *Canada Act 1982* (U.K.), 1982, c. 11.
7. R.G.B. Dickson, "Keynote Address", *The Cambridge Lectures 1985* at 3-4; see also *Vriend v. Alberta*, [1998] S.C.J. No. 29, [1998] 1 S.C.R. 493 (S.C.C.).

---

2. Major Sources

(1) *Constitution Act, 1867* HCL-3
(2) *Constitution Act, 1982* HCL-4
(3) Section 52(2) of the *Constitution Act, 1982* HCL-5
(4) Founding Statute of the Crown and Parliament of Great Britain HCL-6

▼HCL-2▼ Overview. The sources of constitutional law originate from the past historical events, and especially from the tensions between the Crown and its subjects. The sources have evolved in a set of rules governing our democracy. Some of these have been written while others are not. Another category of unwritten principles have evolved and became constitutional conventions. The written sources of the Canadian Constitution are numerous. Unlike the Constitution of the United States, the Canadian Constitution is not found in one or two founding documents, but in numerous Imperial statutes adopted by Parliament in Westminster, in statutes adopted by the Parliament of Canada, as well as in unwritten principles. Normally, however, the sources of constitutional law would be comprised of the Constitutional document itself and potentially amendments made to it; some special statutes that acquire quasi-constitutional form; unwritten rules that have been followed by governmental actors since time immemorial and that have crystallized in norms of fundamental importance; and may also include judicial decisions interpreting the Constitution, where the common law may have confirmed unwritten rules or principles, such as that of democracy, the separation of powers and the principle of responsible government. The *Constitution Act, 1982*[1] provides a schedule of constitutional documents. The list provided pursuant to the *Constitution Act, 1982*[2] was held to be exhaustive.[3]

Notes

1. *Constitution Act, 1982*, being Schedule B to the *Canada Act 1982* (U.K.), 1982, c. 11.
2. *Constitution Act, 1982*, being Schedule B to the *Canada Act 1982* (U.K.), 1982, c. 11, s. 53.
3. See *New Brunswick Broadcasting Co. v. Nova Scotia (Speaker of the House of Assembly)*, [1993] S.C.J. No. 2, [1993] 1 S.C.R. 319 (S.C.C.).

---

(1) The *Constitution Act, 1867*

▼HCL-3▼ Overview. The *Constitution Act, 1867*,[1] or the *British North America Act, 1867*[2] as it was known, is the most important constitutional source of the Canadian Constitution, along with the *Constitution Act, 1982*.[3] The *Constitution Act, 1867*[4] provides for the rules of government by establishing the principle institutions of the Canadian government, including the powers of the Executive, the Parliament of Canada and the provincial legislatures. The *Constitution Act, 1867*[5] provided for a constitutional federation, and divided the legislative powers or jurisdictions between the Federal and Provincial governments. It also established the Canadian courts system, provided for an economic union and provided rules governing the admission of new colonies into the federation. Notably, however, the *Constitution Act, 1867*[6] did not create the country of Canada. Such was done in 1931, with the adoption of an Imperial statute, the *Statute of Westminster*.[7]

Notes

1. (U.K.), 30 & 31 Vict., c. 3.

2. (U.K.), 30 & 31 Vict., c. 3.
3. *Constitution Act, 1982*, being Schedule B to the *Canada Act 1982* (U.K.), 1982, c. 11.
4. (U.K.), 30 & 31 Vict., c. 3.
5. (U.K.), 30 & 31 Vict., c. 3.
6. (U.K.), 30 & 31 Vict., c. 3.
7. *Statute of Westminster, 1931* (U.K.), 22 & 23 Geo. V., c. 4.

---

(2) *Constitution Act, 1982*

▼HCL-4▼ Overview. The *Constitution Act, 1982*[1] is the second most important constitutional written document. It mainly filled some gaps that had been omitted[2] in the *Constitution Act, 1867*.[3] The *Constitution Act, 1982*[4] includes the *Canadian Charter of Rights and Freedoms*[5] and confirms the rights of the First Nations.[6] Notably, the *Constitution Act, 1982*[7] provides for an amendment formula[8] and provides that the Constitution of Canada is now the supreme law of Canada, and any law that is inconsistent with the provisions of the Constitution is, to the extent of the inconsistency, of no force or effect.[9] The *Constitution Act, 1982*[10] grants to the courts the power to strike any statute adopted by Parliament or any provincial legislature if they are against any provision of the Canadian Constitution,[11] and provides an exhaustive list of all those constitutional documents which must be respected for a statute to conform with the Canadian Constitution.[12]

Legislation that is constitutional may be found to violate the Charter. A finding that legislation does not offend the division of powers doctrine will not doom a Charter challenge to that legislation. There is no conflict between finding that a federal law is validly adopted under s. 91 of the *Constitution Act, 1867*, and asserting that the same law, in purpose or effect, deprives individuals of rights guaranteed by the Charter. The Charter applies to all valid federal and provincial laws. Laws must conform to the constitutional division of powers and to the Charter.[13]

Notes

1. *Constitution Act, 1982*, being Schedule B to the *Canada Act 1982* (U.K.), 1982, c. 11.
2. These had not really been "omitted" or forgotten, but rather it was a conscious decision not to provide for an amendment formula.

3. (U.K.), 30 & 31 Vict., c. 3.
4. *Constitution Act, 1982*, being Schedule B to the *Canada Act 1982* (U.K.), 1982, c. 11.
5. Part I of the *Constitution Act, 1982*, being Schedule B to the *Canada Act 1982* (U.K.), 1982, c. 11.
6. Part I of the *Constitution Act, 1982*, being Schedule B to the *Canada Act 1982* (U.K.), 1982, c. 11, s. 35.
7. *Constitution Act, 1982*, being Schedule B to the *Canada Act 1982* (U.K.), 1982, c. 11.
8. Part I of the *Constitution Act, 1982*, being Schedule B to the *Canada Act 1982* (U.K.), 1982, c. 11, ss. 40-44.
9. Part I of the *Constitution Act, 1982*, being Schedule B to the *Canada Act 1982* (U.K.), 1982, c. 11, s. 52(1).
10. *Constitution Act, 1982*, being Schedule B to the *Canada Act 1982* (U.K.), 1982, c. 11.
11. *Constitution Act, 1982*, being Schedule B to the *Canada Act 1982* (U.K.), 1982, c. 11, s. 52(1).
12. *Constitution Act, 1982*, being Schedule B to the *Canada Act 1982* (U.K.), 1982, c. 11, s. 52(2).
13. *Canada (Attorney General) v. PHS Community Services Society*, [2011] S.C.J. No. 44, 2011 SCC 44 (S.C.C.).

---

(3) Section 52(2) of the *Constitution Act, 1982*

▼HCL-5▼ Overview. The *Constitution Act, 1982*[1] provides a list of the Imperial and Canadian statutes which are recognized as being part of the Canadian Constitution. The list of documents includes: (a) the *Canada Act 1982*,[2] including this Act; (b) the Acts and Orders referred to in the Schedule; and (c) any amendment to any Act or Order referred to in paragraph (a) or (b). The Constitution will include the Acts and orders referred in the Schedule. The schedule lists 24 Acts and Orders.[3] The Constitution will also include the amendments to any Act or order listed in the schedule[4] or to the *Canada Act, 1982*[5] and the *Constitution Act, 1982*.[6]

Notes

1. *Constitution Act, 1982*, being Schedule B to the *Canada Act 1982* (U.K.), 1982, c. 11, s. 52(2).
2. *Canada Act 1982* (U.K.), 1982, c. 11.
3. *Constitution Act, 1867* (U.K.), 30 & 31 Vict., c. 3; *Manitoba Act, 1870*, 33 Vict., c. 3; Rupert's Land and North-Western Territory Order, R.S.C. 1985, App. II, No. 9; British Columbia Terms of Union, R.S.C. 1985, App. II, No. 10; *Constitution*

Act, 1871 (U.K.), 34 & 35 Vict., c. 28; Prince Edward Island Terms of Union, R.S.C. 1985, App. II, No. 12; *Parliament of Canada Act, 1875* (U.K.), 38 & 39 Vict., c. 38; Adjacent Territories Order, R.S.C. 1985, App. II, No. 14; *Constitution Act, 1886* (U.K.), 49 & 50 Vict., c. 35; *Canada (Ontario Boundary) Act, 1889* (U.K.), 52 & 53 Vict., c. 28; *Alberta Act* (U.K.), 4 & 5 Edw. VII, c. 3; *Saskatchewan Act* (U.K.) 4 & 5 Edw. VII, c. 42; *Constitution Act, 1907* (U.K.) 7 Edw. VII, c. 11; *Constitution Act, 1915* (U.K.), 5 & 6 Geo. V, c. 45; *Constitution Act, 1930* (U.K.), 20 & 21 Geo. V, c. 26; *Statute of Westminster*, 1931 (U.K.) 22 Geo. V, c. 4; *Constitution Act, 1940* (U.K.) 3 & 4 Geo. VI, c. 36; *Newfoundland Act* (U.K.), 12 & 13 Geo. VI, c. 22; *Constitution Act, 1960* (U.K.), 9 Eliz. II, c. 2; *Constitution Act, 1964* (U.K.), 12 & 13 Eliz. II, c. 73; *Constitution Act, 1965*, R.S.C. 1985, App. II, No. 39; *Constitution Act, 1974*, R.S.C. 1985, App. II, No. 40; *Constitution Act (No. 1), 1975*, R.S.C. 1985, App. II, No. 41; *Constitution Act (No. 2), 1975*, R.S.C. 1985, App. II, No. 42.

4. *Constitution Act, 1982*, being Schedule B to the *Canada Act 1982* (U.K.), 1982, c. 11, s. 52(2)(c).
5. *Canada Act 1982* (U.K.), 1982, c. 11.
6. *Constitution Amendment Proclamation, 1983*, S.I./84-102, reprinted in R.S.C. 1985, App. II, No. 46; *Constitution Act, 1985 (Representation)*, S.C. 1986, c. 8, reprinted in R.S.C. 1985, App. II, No. 47; *Constitution Amendment, 1987 (Newfoundland Act)*, S.I./88-11; *Constitution Amendment, 1993 (New Brunswick)*, S.I./93-54; *Constitution Amendment, 1993 (Prince Edward Island)*, S.I./94-50; *Constitution Amendment, 1997 (Newfoundland Act)*, S.I./97-55; *Constitution Amendment, 1997 (Quebec)*, S.I./97-141; *Constitution Amendment, 1998 (Newfoundland Act)*, S.I./98-25; *Constitution Act, 1999 (Nunavut)*, S.C. 1998, c. 15, Part II; *Constitution Amendment, 2001 (Newfoundland and Labrador)*, S.I./2002-117.

---

(4) Founding Statute of the Crown and Parliament of Great Britain

▼HCL-6▼ Statutes promulgated by the King or Queen of England. Some statutes or other documents that contain sources of the Canadian Constitution were promulgated by the King or Queen of England. An example of a document promulgated by the King is the Royal Proclamation of 1763,[1] where King George III proclaimed North America as a new territory of Great Britain. Examples of statutes include the *Constitution Act, 1867*[2] which is now patriated and entrenched pursuant to the *Constitution Act, 1982*.[3] Interestingly, to patriate the Constitution, Canada needed a formal statute to be adopted by the Parliament of Great Britain: the *Canada Act, 1982*.[4]

Statutes adopted by the Parliament of Great Britain. There are many statutes adopted by the Parliament of Great Britain, which are sources of the Canadian Constitution. For example, the *Statute of Westminster, 1931*[5] granted full independence and autonomy to Canada. The *Colonial*

Laws Validity Act 1865,[6] previously, had essentially upheld the validity of colonial laws that were in contradiction with the laws of the Imperial Parliament. In effect, it granted paramountcy to colonial laws, unless those statutes contained powers which extended beyond the boundaries of the colony and affected Great Britain. This is one limitation that was repealed by the *Statute of Westminster, 1931*.[7] The *Act of Settlement 1701*[8] and the *Bill of Rights 1689*[9] are other sources of the Canadian Constitution. They are important to the extent that they provide for the succession of the Crown and have also laid the groundwork for some of the individual rights which were later entrenched in the *Charter*. The provisions related to the Monarchy are sources of the Canadian Constitution, and are important because of the *Constitution Act, 1982*,[10] as well as the *Constitution Act, 1867*.[11] The final example of a document which is a source of the Canadian Constitution, but was issued in Great Britain, is the Letters Patent of 1947,[12] which established the office of the Governor General.

Notes

1. George R., Proclamation, 7 October 1763 (3 Geo. III), reprinted in R.S.C. 1985, App. II, No. 1.
2. (U.K.), 30 & 31 Vict., c. 3.
3. *Constitution Act, 1982*, being Schedule B to the *Canada Act 1982* (U.K.), 1982, c. 11, s. 52(2).
4. (U.K.), 1982, c. 11.
5. (U.K.), 22 Geo. V, c. 4.
6. (U.K.), 28 & 29 Vict., c. 63.
7. (U.K.), 22 Geo. V, c. 4.
8. (U.K.), 12 & 13 Will. III, c. 2.
9. *Act Declaring the Rights and Liberties of the Subject and Settling and Succession of the Crown, 1689* (U.K.), 1 Will. & Mar. sess. 2, c. 2.
10. *Constitution Act, 1982*, being Schedule B to the *Canada Act 1982* (U.K.), 1982, c. 11, s. 41(a).
11. (U.K.), 30 & 31 Vict., c. 3, preamble and ss. 9, 12, 17.
12. George R., Letters Patent constituting the office of Governor General of Canada (1947), 1 October 1947, reprinted in R.S.C. 1985, App. II, No. 31.

---

3. Canadian Statutes that have Quasi-Constitutional Nature

▼HCL-7▼ Overview. Some statutes, while not entrenched in the Constitution *per se*, have acquired a quasi-constitutional nature. These statutes include the *Supreme Court Act*[1] the existence of which is guaranteed by the *Constitution Act, 1982*,[2] the *Canadian Bill of Rights*[3] and the

Official Languages Act,[4] the use of which is guaranteed pursuant to the *Constitution Act, 1982*.[5]

Notes

1. (CAN) *Supreme Court Act*, R.S.C. 1985, c. S-26.
2. *Constitution Act, 1982*, being Schedule B to the *Canada Act 1982* (U.K.), 1982, c. 11, s. 41(d).
3. (CAN) *Canadian Bill of Rights*, S.C. 1960, c. 44.
4. (CAN) *Official Languages Act*, R.S.C. 1985, c. 31 (4th) Supp.).
5. *Constitution Act, 1982*, being Schedule B to the *Canada Act 1982* (U.K.), 1982, c. 11, ss. 41(c) and 43.

---

4. Crown Prerogative

(1) Overview HCL-8
(2) The Role of the Prime Minister HCL-9
(3) Judicial Review of Decisions Made Pursuant to a Crown Prerogative HCL-10

---

(1) Overview

▼HCL-8▼ Power vested in the Queen. The *Constitution Act, 1867* provides that the Executive Government and Authority of and over Canada is vested in the Queen.[1] In turn, the *Constitution Act, 1867*[2] provides that all the powers vested in the Governor General will be exercisable with the advice and consent of the Privy Council which are persons chosen from time to time by the Governor General and sworn in as Privy Councillors.[3] Effectively, the executive decisions are made by Cabinet, which represents the Governor-in-Council. Despite the principle of the Crown's indivisibility,[4] a distinction must be made between the Queen in right of Canada and the Queen in right of a province. In these distinct capacities, the Crown acts as separate persons in the sense that the act of one cannot engage the responsibility of the other.[5] In other words, the decisions of the federal executive and the provincial executives are distinct and unrelated.

Crown prerogative defined. The Crown prerogative exists as an element of the common law and forms a residual category including the residual powers and privileges which rest with the Crown at any given time.[6] Crown prerogatives only include the powers and privileges which are unique to the Crown, *i.e.*, which are not also possessed by private persons. Thus, powers that are exercisable by individuals, such as owning property or entering into contracts, do not form part of the prerogative. The royal prerogative may be limited by statute and it may be delegated to some extent, but the Crown may not voluntarily abdicate its prerogatives.[7]

Crown prerogative today. Some of the more consequential prerogative powers still in effect today are the conduct of foreign affairs including the declaration of war, the making of treaties, the appointment of the Prime Minister and other cabinet ministers, the issuing of passports and the granting of honours. The scope of Crown prerogatives have diminished over the course of history with the advancing role of statute and the rise of democratic norms. However, it is by means of the principle of responsible government that the Crown prerogative and democracy are brought into harmonious conjunction: the Cabinet is appointed by the monarch but is responsible to the popularly elected House of Commons. Crown prerogatives are now exercised by the Governor-in-Council, perhaps with the exception with the granting of honours by the Governor General of Canada.[8] Although the areas in which Parliament has not chosen to intervene by statute are generally shrinking, this statement of the Crown prerogative remains accurate today.

Notes

1. *Constitution Act, 1867* (U.K.), 30 & 31 Vict., c. 3, s. 9.
2. *Constitution Act, 1867* (U.K.), 30 & 31 Vict., c. 3, s. 12.
3. *Constitution Act, 1867* (U.K.), 30 & 31 Vict., c. 3, s. 11.
4. *Theodore v. Duncan*, [1919] A.C. 696 (Aust. P.C.).
5. *J.R. Théberge Ltée v. R.*, [1970] Ex. C.R. 649 (Ex. Ct.).
6. *Canada (Prime Minister) v. Khadr*, [2010] S.C.J. No. 3, [2010] 1 S.C.R. 44 at para. 34 (S.C.C.).
7. See *Ross River Dena Council Band v. Canada*, [2002] S.C.J. No. 54, [2002] 2 S.C.R. 816 at paras. 63-64 (S.C.C.); *Canada (Attorney General) v. Ontario (Attorney General)*, [1894] S.C.J. No. 54, 23 S.C.R. 458 (S.C.C.).
8. Note, however, *Black v. Canada (Prime Minister)*, [2001] O.J. No. 1853, 54 O.R. (3d) 215 (Ont. C.A.), where the Prime Minister refused that Mr. Black be granted a peerage by the Queen of England.

(2) The Role of the Prime Minister

▼HCL-9▼ Appointment of the Prime Minister. In Canada, the Governor General, the Queen's personal representative, appoints the Prime Minister,[1] who in turn appoints the members of the Cabinet. The choice of Prime Minister is notable in that it is one of the very few decisions that is made by the Governor General upon his or her own discretion, rather than upon the advice of a minister. Notwithstanding this important conceptual difference, the Governor General typically exercises no meaningful choice, as the person appointed Prime Minister must be a person capable of forming a government which will enjoy the confidence of the House of Commons, and this person is, nearly without exception, the parliamentary leader of the political party enjoying a majority, or a plurality, of the seats in the House of Commons.

Responsibilities of Prime Minister. While the executive authority rests with Cabinet, the Prime Minister has a special authority in relation to it. For example, the Prime Minister is the one responsible for appointing and dismissing the ministers (the Prime Minister of course recommends the appointments to the Governor General who, by convention, will follow with the appointment).[2] In that sense, the Prime Minister controls the individuals forming the Cabinet, and consequently the voice of the Prime Minister will be most influential. This results in the Prime Minister also controlling the executive, its agenda and its meetings. While the appointment of ministers to Cabinet is a Crown prerogative, it is exercised with the advice of the Prime Minister.

Powers of the Prime Minister. The Prime Minister also controls two fundamental aspects of the executive power and Crown prerogatives: that of declaring elections or dissolving Parliament and summoning Parliament into session. The Governor General, under the advice of the Prime Minister, will dissolve the House of Commons for an election, and will also prorogue the House of Commons and later summon the House for another legislative session. The Crown prerogatives are not executed by the Governor General-in-Council following the advice of Cabinet, but by the Governor General following the advice of the Prime Minister. The Prime Minister thus holds a specific place, with personal powers and responsibilities not shared with the Cabinet.

Notes

1. Craig Forcese and Aaron Freeman, *The Laws of Government: The Legal Foundations of Canadian Democracy* (Toronto: Irwin Law, 2005) at 34. See also *Figueroa v. Canada (Attorney General)*, [2003] S.C.J. No. 37, [2003] 1 S.C.R. 912,

2003 SCC 37 (S.C.C.); *Angus v. Canada*, [1990] F.C.J. No. 610, 72 D.L.R. (4th) 672 (F.C.A.).

2. Constitutional conventions will be discussed in Chapter 2 ("Constitutional Conventions and the Unwritten Principles of the Constitution").

---

(3) Judicial Review of Decisions Made Pursuant to a Crown Prerogative

▼HCL-10▼ Overview. The negotiation, signing and ratification of treaties are Crown prerogatives and thus function exclusively within the jurisdiction of the Executive. The exercise of such prerogatives or of any power delegated by a statute may be subject to the courts' oversight power. In all circumstances, acts of the Executive must be in accordance with the Constitution, and, in particular, with the *Canadian Charter of Rights and Freedoms*.[1] Moreover, other rules may affect the validity of actions taken pursuant to the prerogative, such as the fundamental principles of administrative law and procedural fairness.[2] The federal government's foreign policy can also be subject to this oversight power, to some extent.[3]

Scope of review. The jurisdiction and powers of the courts are not clearly defined. Not all decisions made by the Executive or the Crown in the name of a prerogative are subject to judicial review. The approach that the courts have taken has been to respect the sphere of unreviewable discretion of Crown and Parliament while tempering it in two ways. First, the courts have claimed unto themselves the jurisdiction to determine the scope and the extent of that sphere. In other words, while there exists a definite boundary beyond which the courts may not step, the task of determining the proper location of that limit falls to the courts. Once their boundary is thus defined, the courts may not interfere with those legislative and executive spheres of decision-making. Secondly, the Supreme Court of Canada has emphasized that a sphere immune from judicial review is not a sphere immune from the rule of law. All branches of government are bound to act constitutionally and democratically. The jurisdiction of the courts and the rule of law are not coterminous: all branches of government remain bound to the rule of law regardless of whether their actions are open to judicial review.[4]

Notes

1. *Canadian Charter of Rights and Freedoms*, Part I of the *Constitution Act, 1982*, being Schedule B to the *Canada Act 1982* (U.K.), 1982, c. 11.

2. *Operation Dismantle Inc. v. Canada*, [1985] S.C.J. No. 22, [1985] 1 S.C.R. 441 at paras. 28 and 50 (S.C.C.); *Khadr v. Canada (Attorney General)*, [2006] F.C.J. No. 888, [2007] 2 F.C.R. 218 at para. 92 (F.C.); *Khadr v. Canada (Prime Minister)*, [2009] F.C.J. No. 462, [2010] 1 F.C.R. 34 (F.C.), affd. [2009] F.C.J. No. 893, 2009 FCA 246, [2010] 1 F.C.R. 73 (F.C.A.), vard [2010] S.C.J. No. 3, 2010 SCC 3, [2010] 1 S.C.R. 44 (S.C.C.); *Vancouver Island Peace Society v. Canada*, [1993] F.C.J. No. 601, [1994] 1 F.C. 102 (F.C.T.D.), affd [1995] F.C.J. No. 70, 179 N.R. 106 (F.C.A.); *Smith v. Canada (Attorney General)*, [2009] F.C.J. No. 234, [2010] 1 F.C.R. 3 at para. 23 (F.C.), supp. reasons [2009] F.C.J. No. 522, 348 F.T.R. 290 (F.C.); P. W. Hogg & P.J. Monahan, *Liability of the Crown*, 3d ed. (Toronto: Carswell, 2000) at 19.
3. *Operation Dismantle Inc. v. Canada*, [1985] S.C.J. No. 22, [1985] 1 S.C.R. 441 at paras. 38 and 50 (S.C.C.); *Black v. Canada (Prime Minister)*, [2001] O.J. No. 1853, 54 O.R. (3d) 215 at paras. 30 and 47 (Ont. C.A.); *Smith v. Canada (Attorney General)*, [2009] F.C.J. No. 234, [2010] 1 F.C.R. 3 (F.C.), supp. reasons [2009] F.C.J. No. 522, 348 F.T.R. 290 (F.C.); *Khadr v. Canada (Prime Minister)*, [2009] F.C.J. No. 462, [2010] 1 F.C.R. 34 (F.C.), affd. [2009] F.C.J. No. 893, 2009 FCA 246, [2010] 1 F.C.R. 73 (F.C.A.), vard [2010] S.C.J. No. 3, 2010 SCC 3, [2010] 1 S.C.R. 44 (S.C.C.).
4. *Canada (Prime Minister) v. Khadr*, [2010] S.C.J. No. 3, [2010] 1 S.C.R. 44 at paras. 36-37 (S.C.C.).

▼HCL-11▼ Specific Crown prerogatives. Certain Crown prerogatives – more specifically, those with a "highly political" tenor, will be further immunized as compared to others regarding judicial review which can be exercised against them by the courts. For example, the issuance of a Canadian passport is a Crown prerogative, which cannot be refused to a person. If it is, the Federal Court could be justified in intervening.[1] On the other hand, it would be difficult to obtain access to an intervention of this kind in a case involving national defence or in a case involving expulsion of a foreign diplomat from Canada.[2] A decision based on a purely strategic or political choice, such as a Crown prerogative, generally escapes judicial review: their object does not lend itself to judicial review by the courts. However, if the object of the decision directly affects a person's rights or legitimate expectations, the courts have jurisdiction to rule on its legality.[3] For example, the awarding of honours was not a justiciable prerogative whereas a petition for clemency filed with a State regarding a Canadian citizen was judged to be a prerogative subject to the judicial review of the court.[4]

Notes

1. *Khadr v. Canada (Attorney General),* [2006] F.C.J. No. 888, [2007] 2 F.C.R. 218 (F.C.); *Abdelrazik c. Canada (Ministre des Affaires étrangères),* [2009] F.C.J. No. 656, [2010] 1 R.C.F. 267 (C.F.).

2. *Copello v. Canada (Minister of Foreign Affairs)*, [2001] F.C.J. No. 1835, [2002] 3 F.C. 24 (F.C.), affd [2003] F.C.J. No. 1056, 308 N.R. 175 (F.C.A.).
3. *Smith v. Canada (Attorney General)*, [2009] F.C.J. No. 234, [2010] 1 F.C.R. 3 at para. 26 (F.C.), supp. reasons [2009] F.C.J. No. 522, 348 F.T.R. 290 (F.C.).
4. *Smith v. Canada (Attorney General)*, [2009] F.C.J. No. 234, [2010] 1 F.C.R. 3 at para. 26 (F.C.), supp. reasons [2009] F.C.J. No. 522, 348 F.T.R. 290 (F.C.).

▼HCL-12▼ Crown immunity. Since 1561, there has existed a presumption at common law that a statute does not apply to the prejudice of the Crown. This presumption may be rebutted by express statutory language. The rule may accurately be stated as a Crown immunity, and in this sense constitutes a prerogative. Thus, express and precise statutory language is required to revoke a prerogative of the Crown.[1] It should be noted that the presumption of Crown immunity enjoys little judicial or academic support. The historical reasons for the presumption seem strained and unconvincing and modern commentators are hard pressed to find any current justification.[2]

Notes

1. *Operation Dismantle Inc. v. Canada*, [1983] F.C.J. No. 1095, [1983] 1 F.C. 745 (F.C.A.), affd [1985] S.C.J. No. 22, [1985] 1 S.C.R. 441 (S.C.C.).
2. Ruth Sullivan, *Sullivan and Driedger on the Construction of Statutes*, 4th ed. (Markham, ON: Butterworths, 2002) at 603.

---

5. Parliament

▼HCL-13▼ Overview. Pursuant to the *Constitution Act, 1867*,[1] Parliament consists of the Sovereign, the House of Commons and the Senate. Parliament enjoys the power to legislate, and no legislation may be made except by Parliament or a provincial legislature.[2] Parliament also controls its procedure. As with Crown prerogatives, parliamentary privilege shields decisions made by the Parliament from court supervision, as it enjoys constitutional protection.[3] Parliamentary privileges arise in the Canadian Parliament under the *Constitution Act, 1867*.[4]

Notes

1. *Constitution Act, 1867* (U.K.), 30 & 31 Vict., c. 3, s. 17.
2. *Reference re: Initiative and Referendum Act (Man.)*, [1919] J.C.J. No. 5, [1919] A.C. 935 (P.C.).

3. *New Brunswick Broadcasting Co. v. Nova Scotia (Speaker of the House of Assembly)*, [1993] S.C.J. No. 2, [1993] 1 S.C.R. 319 at 374, 384-85 (S.C.C.); *Canada (House of Commons) v. Vaid*, [2005] S.C.J. No. 28, [2005] 1 S.C.R. 667 (S.C.C.).
4. *Constitution Act, 1867* (U.K.), 30 & 31 Vict., c. 3, preamble and s. 18.

---

6. Senate

▼HCL-14▼ Overview. Pursuant to the *Constitution Act, 1867*,[1] the Senate consists of 105 senators. Senators are appointed by the Governor General upon the advice of the Prime Minister. The regions of Canada are represented in the Senate according to a four-way division between Ontario, Québec, the Maritime Provinces (not including Newfoundland), and the Western Provinces.[2] The four divisions are "equally represented in the Senate".[3] "In the Case of Quebec each of the Twenty-four Senators representing that Province shall be appointed for One of the Twenty-four Electoral Divisions of Lower Canada specified in Schedule A."[4]

Qualifications. The qualifications to be a senator are listed in the *Constitution Act, 1867*.[5] Senators must be at least 30 years of age, must be resident of the province in respect of which he or she is appointed, and must own a minimum amount of property in that province. A special requirement is imposed upon Senators from Québec: they must not only own property in Québec, but specifically must own property in the electoral division for which they are appointed. The historical purpose of this requirement was to ensure fair linguistic representation for Québec. A Senator may hold office until the age of 75 years.[6] In regards to the issue of whether women were considered "qualified persons" in the *Constitution Act, 1867*,[7] the Privy Council held that women are eligible for appointment to the Senate of Canada.[8]

Powers of the Senate. The powers of the Senate are the same as those of the House of Commons. In fact, for a Bill to receive Royal Assent and become law pursuant to the *Constitution Act, 1867*,[9] both Houses of Parliament must pass the Bill. There are two main differences between the House of Commons and the Senate. The first is that Bills that incur any expenditure of money from the public revenue must originate in the House of Commons pursuant to the *Constitution Act, 1867*.[10] The second has only been seen once, and it is for constitutional amendments which require resolutions from both Houses. If such resolution is passed by the House of Commons but, within 180 days, has not been passed by the Senate, the amendment will be adopted if the House of Commons again votes on and adopts the same resolution pursuant to the *Constitution Act, 1867*.[11] This has only been used once, for The Meech Lake Accord in 1987.[12]

Appointment of additional senators. The Senate normally will make its role subordinate to that of the House of Commons, which is directly elected by the people. If, however, the Senate decides to block legislation, but only by a small majority, the Governor General may, with the advice of the Prime Minister, resolve the political deadlock in the Senate by appointing additional Senators pursuant to the *Constitution Act, 1867*.[13] There is, however, one limit to this power. The *Constitution Act, 1867*[14] provides that the number of Senators must not exceed 113.

Notes

1. *Constitution Act, 1867* (U.K.), 30 & 31 Vict., c. 3, s. 21.
2. *Constitution Act, 1867* (U.K.), 30 & 31 Vict., c. 3, s. 22.
3. *Constitution Act, 1867* (U.K.), 30 & 31 Vict., c. 3, s. 22: Ontario by 24 Senators; Quebec by 24 Senators; the Maritime Provinces and Prince Edward Island by 24 Senators, ten thereof representing Nova Scotia, ten thereof representing New Brunswick, and four thereof representing Prince Edward Island; the Western Provinces by 24 Senators, six thereof representing Manitoba, six thereof representing British Columbia, six thereof representing Saskatchewan, and six thereof representing Alberta; Newfoundland shall be entitled to be represented in the Senate by six members; the Yukon Territory and the Northwest Territories shall be entitled to be represented in the Senate by one member each.
4. *Constitution Act, 1867* (U.K.), 30 & 31 Vict., c. 3, s. 22.
5. (U.K.), 30 & 31 Vict., c. 3, s. 23.
6. *Constitution Act, 1867* (U.K.), 30 & 31 Vict., c. 3, s. 29.
7. (U.K.), 30 & 31 Vict., c. 3, s. 24.
8. *Edwards v. Canada (Attorney General)*, [1930] A.C. 124 (Can. P.C.).
9. *Constitution Act, 1867* (U.K.), 30 & 31 Vict., c. 3, s. 55.
10. *Constitution Act, 1867* (U.K.), 30 & 31 Vict., c. 3, s. 53.
11. *Constitution Act, 1867* (U.K.), 30 & 31 Vict., c. 3, s. 47(1).
12. Canada, Special Joint Committee of the Senate and House of Commons, *The 1987 Constitutional Accord* (Ottawa: Queen's Printer, 1987).
13. *Constitution Act, 1867* (U.K.), 30 & 31 Vict., c. 3, s. 26.
14. *Constitution Act, 1867* (U.K.), 30 & 31 Vict., c. 3, s. 28.

---

7. The House of Commons

▼HCL-15▼ Overview. The *Constitution Act, 1867*[1] provides for a House of Commons consisting of elected officials from each province and territory. Pursuant to the *Constitution Act, 1867*[2] and the *Canadian Charter of Rights and Freedoms*,[3] the House of Commons will continue for five years from the day of the return of the writs for choosing the House (subject to an earlier dissolution by the Governor General), and no longer. The number of seats in the House will be readjusted after each decennial census.[4] However, each province is guaranteed at least to a number of seats in the House of Commons that is equal to the number of senators representing such province.[5] The number of seats in the House of Commons may be increased by Parliament, provided the proportionate representation of the provinces prescribed by the *Constitution Act, 1867*[6] is not disturbed.[7] Finally, the *Constitution Act, 1867*[8] and the Charter,[9] the Governor General shall, in the Queen's Name, summon and call together the House of Commons, but there must be one such sitting of Parliament and of each legislature at least once every 12 months.

Powers. The House of Commons possesses the same powers as the Senate to pass legislation. However, it possesses two additional powers. Pursuant to the *Constitution Act, 1867*,[10] any Bill for appropriating any part of the public revenue, or for imposing any tax or impost, must originate in the House of Commons. In addition, pursuant to the *Constitution Act, 1867*[11] and for constitutional amendments which require resolutions from both Houses, if such resolution is passed by the House of Commons but is not adopted by the Senate within 180 days, the amendment will be enacted if the House of Commons again adopts the same resolution enacting the constitutional amendment.

Notes

1. *Constitution Act, 1867* (U.K.), 30 & 31 Vict., c. 3, s. 37.
2. *Constitution Act, 1867* (U.K.), 30 & 31 Vict., c. 3, s. 50.
3. *Canadian Charter of Rights and Freedoms*, Part I of the *Constitution Act, 1982*, being Schedule B to the *Canada Act 1982* (U.K.), 1982, c. 11, s. 4(1).
4. *Constitution Act, 1867* (U.K.), 30 & 31 Vict., c. 3, s. 51.
5. *Constitution Act, 1867* (U.K.), 30 & 31 Vict., c. 3, s. 51(a).
6. *Constitution Act, 1867* (U.K.), 30 & 31 Vict., c. 3.
7. *Constitution Act, 1867* (U.K.), 30 & 31 Vict., c. 3, s. 52.
8. *Constitution Act, 1867* (U.K.), 30 & 31 Vict., c. 3, s. 38.
9. *Canadian Charter of Rights and Freedoms*, Part I of the *Constitution Act, 1982*, being Schedule B to the *Canada Act 1982* (U.K.), 1982, c. 11, s. 5.
10. *Constitution Act, 1867* (U.K.), 30 & 31 Vict., c. 3, s. 53(a).
11. *Constitution Act, 1867* (U.K.), 30 & 31 Vict., c. 3, s. 47(1).

II. Constitutional Conventions and the Unwritten Principles of the Constitution

1. Constitutional Conventions

(1) General HCL-16
(2) Between Law and Usage HCL-18
(3) Convention Formation... HCL-20
(4) Convention Components HCL-21
(5) Convention and the Law..................................... HCL-22

2. Ultimate Significance HCL-24

3. Unwritten Principles of the Constitution

(1) General HCL-25
(2) Specific Unwritten Principles.............................. HCL-28

---

1. Constitutional Conventions

(1) General HCL-16
(2) Between Law and Usage HCL-18
(3) Convention Formation... HCL-20
(4) Convention Components HCL-21
(5) Convention and the Law..................................... HCL-22

---

(1) General

▼HCL-16▼ Overview. Conventions have been described as rules of conduct in the political community that are accepted by those political actors as "binding" or "obligatory".[1] They are also described as non-legal rules because, while they demand compliance, they are not enforceable by the courts.[2] Conventions are informal as they are rarely acknowledged in written form, but nevertheless they form part of the guiding doctrine of the Constitution. They may impose duties or, in some circumstances, bestow rights or privileges upon political actors in the Canadian government. For instance, the Governor General is appointed by the British Crown as required by the *Constitution Act, 1867*[3] and the Letters Patent of King George (1947).[4] The Governor General, as the Queen's representative, plays a key role in Canadian governance.[5] The Governor General appoints

Cabinet ministers, the House Speaker, and the Lieutenant Governors. The signature of the Governor General is also required to pass any law in Parliament. Most importantly, the Governor General has the power to appoint or dismiss the Prime Minister. However, while the Queen technically has the authority to choose whomever she deems appropriate to act as the Governor General, by convention she is bound to select the individual recommended by the Canadian government.

Two heads of state. Canada's system is one of a responsible government in which two heads of state hold the power to govern. Like other commonwealth countries, the formal head of state is the British monarchy and the political head is the Prime Minister. At the federal level, the Governor General acts in place of the Queen, while Lieutenant Governors act at the provincial level. There are conventions at both levels, and the provincial conventions concerning Lieutenant Governors tend to mirror those of the Governor General.

Purpose of constitutional conventions. The purpose behind constitutional conventions is to uphold and support the guiding constitutional principles of representative democracy and responsible government in the context of modern values and expectations. A representative democracy ensures that the best interests of the people are taken into account as the administrators of the country are chosen by the people. Responsible government requires two things: (1) the responsibility of individual ministers and their respective departments for their activities; and (2) the responsibility and accountability of the executive to the House of Commons, which involves the Prime Minister maintaining the confidence of the Legislative Assembly. In a responsible government, the executive branch is required to have the confidence of the legislative assembly. As per convention, if the Prime Minister loses a vote of confidence, he or she must resign from office or seek the dissolution of the assembly by the Governor General and call for an election. This is all achieved through an advisory process by which the Prime Minister advises the Governor General who by convention always complies.

Notes

1. G. Marshall, *Constitutional Conventions: The Rules and Forms of Political Accountability* (Oxford: Clarendon Press, 1984) at 11.
2. See Albert Venn Dicey, *Introduction to the Study of the Law of the Constitution*, 10th ed. (London: Macmillan, 1965) at ch. 14, 15; I. Jennings, *The Law and the Constitution*, 5th ed. (London: University of London Press Ltd., 1959) at ch. 3; K.C. Wheare, *Modern Constitutions*, 2nd ed. (Toronto: Oxford University Press, 1966) at ch. 8; A. Heard, *Canadian Constitutional Conventions: The Marriage o*

Law and Politics (Toronto: Oxford University Press, 1991); A.W. Bradley & K.D. Ewing, *Constitutional and Administrative Law* (London: Pearson Longman, 2003) at ch. 2.

3. (U.K.), 30 & 31 Vict., c. 3.
4. *Constitution Act, 1982*, being Schedule B to the *Canada Act 1982* (U.K.), 1982, c. 11; *Letters Patent Constituting the Office of Governor General of Canada*, 1947, George R., reprinted in R.S.C. 1985, App. II, No. 31. The Letters Patent, (1947), transferred the power of the monarch to the Governor General as per the royal prerogative. As such, the Letters Patent cannot be repealed or modified by the Canadian Parliament.
5. *Constitution Act, 1867* (U.K.), 30 & 31 Vict., c. 3, s. 17 provides that the single Parliament of Canada must consist of the House of Commons, the Senate and the Queen.

▼HCL-17▼ Formal legal rules contrary to convention. Some existing formal legal rules have the potential to undermine these principles if they are strictly applied. For example, the Governor General has the formal capacity to veto any bill that is brought before Parliament by withholding Royal Assent. This is a lingering corollary of Canada's link to the British Crown. Such a rule was once a logical extension of the Crown's colonial sovereignty; however, the exercise of such a paternalistic power in today's setting would be unacceptable. By convention, this power of disallowance is never exerted as it would flout the principle of representative democracy; the Governor General is appointed by the Queen and is not an elected Canadian representative.[1] The Constitution is littered with similar provisions. Constitutional conventions are therefore in place to override the use of such archaic powers.

Conventions used to fill gaps in Constitution. Conventions are also used to fill gaps found throughout Canada's formal Constitution. For instance, there is no legal rule requiring the government to resign its post if the opposition party garners a majority of seats in a general election. The implication is that, legally, the Prime Minister could refuse to resign, denying office to the individuals selected by the people of Canada. It is by convention only that the Prime Minister is compelled to relinquish his or her position, not by a formal rule of the Constitution.[2]

Notes

1. *Constitution Act, 1982*, being Schedule B to the *Canada Act 1982* (U.K.), 1982, c. 11, s. 55, allows the Governor General to assent, withhold assent or reserve a bill brought before Parliament. Reservation involves sending the bill to the British Crown for determination of whether the bill is a valid law.

2. The convention requires the Governor General to appoint to the office of Prime Minister an individual who could realistically endure a confidence vote. This does not require a majority government, but a government who has lost an election to the majority opposition would not be able to maintain the confidence of the House of Commons.

---

(2) Between Law and Usage

▼HCL-18▼ Constitutional conventions are not formal legal rules. Constitutional conventions are not formal legal rules. They are typically not found in statutes and have not been incorporated into the common law.[1] This means that they are unenforceable by the courts. If, for example, the Prime Minister refused to vacate office upon a successful opposition majority in an election, the courts would have no authority to intervene. The courts are duty bound to apply the letter of the law. Conventions, by definition, fall outside the ambit of judicial reach. As such, if an issue concerning a convention arises, the courts typically shy away from intervening on the basis of justiciability. If a legal rule is pitted against a contradictory convention, the court would be required to decide in favour of the written legal rule, even if the effect of this would be undesirable.

Note

1. Some conventions have been recognized concretely in written form in such places as the preamble of the *Statute of Westminster, 1931* (U.K.), 22 Geo. V, c. 4, or conference proceedings and documents. The majority of conventions are unwritten rules, which can make them difficult to identify with any certainty.

▼HCL-19▼ Consequences of a constitutional convention violation. Although courts cannot intervene to enforce a constitutional convention if violated, a breach does carry considerable consequences. These repercussions cannot be considered legal remedies as they are political in nature. Regardless, a breach of a convention is termed "unconstitutional".[1] However, it cannot be said that all conventions are deemed equal and, as such, apportioned equal weight.[2] Various constitutional conventions fall on a spectrum of significance, which should be placed in accordance with the impact of its breach.[3]

Convention vs. usage. A convention is also distinct from a "usage", which is a custom or practice that normally instructs the behaviour of government officials. A usage merely guides behaviour and does not oblige the actor to follow it strictly. A usage may over time be deemed obligatory through years of strict adherence, thereby assuming the status of convention. There has been confusion as to what criteria separates a convention from a usage but it is well established that a convention cannot, even through long and rigorous usage, "crystallize" into law.[4]

Notes

1. *Re Amendment of Constitution of Canada*, [1981] S.C.J. No. 58, [1981] 1 S.C.R. 753 at 883 (S.C.C.).
2. R. MacGregor Dawson, *The Government of Canada*, 5th ed. (Toronto: University of Toronto Press, 1970) at 67.
3. A. Heard, "Constitutional Conventions and Parliament" (2005) Can. Parl. Rev. 22.
4. *Re Amendment of Constitution of Canada*, [1981] S.C.J. No. 58, [1981] 1 S.C.R. 753 (S.C.C.).

---

(3) Convention Formation

▼HCL-20▼ Natural formation. Many conventions evolve naturally from usages over time through their faithful observance. For example, the power of disallowance applies to Lieutenant Governors of the provinces, as it does to the Governor General of Canada.[1] It affords the federal government the power to veto provincial bills. This power had been exercised extensively in the decades leading up to the Second World War, but has not been employed since 1943.[2] The intrusion into the increasingly autonomous governance of the provinces by the federal government became less desirable, leading to formal abolishment proposals for both the powers of disallowance and reservation by some provincial premiers.[3] Though the Constitution was not formally amended to reflect these proposals, they have effectively been barred from being used. Decades of political obsolescence has transformed this abstinence from a practice, or usage, into a constitutional convention.

Formation through agreement. Another method in which a convention may be formed is through an agreement of relevant officials representing each level of government. This method is vastly different from the natural evolution of usages as these conventions are not derived from historical practices or customs.[4] There are no precedents that inform the development of these conventions, and their onset is comparatively sudden.

Notes

1. *Constitution Act, 1982*, being Schedule B to the *Canada Act 1982* (U.K.), 1982, c. 11, s. 58, allows for the appointment of Lieutenant Governors by the Governor General of Canada.
2. A. Heard, *Canadian Constitutional Conventions: The Marriage of Law and Politics* (Toronto: Oxford University Press, 1991) at 103.
3. Reservation power refers to a process in which the Lieutenant Governor can refer a provincial bill to the Federal Cabinet to determine its validity.
4. G. Marshall, *Constitutional Conventions: The Rules and Forms of Political Accountability* (Oxford: Clarendon Press, 1984) at 9.

---

(4) Convention Components

▼HCL-21▼ Conventions as positive rules. The existence of a convention is not always clear to all parties. There have been disputes over the scope and application of a proposed convention. In some circumstances, it is uncertain whether a convention exists at all. Conventions under contention have been brought before the judiciary to shed light on their existence and scope. The Court has stated that conventions, though not legal rules, "are positive rules the existence of which has to be ascertained by reference to objective standards".[1]

Test to determine whether a convention exists. To discern whether a constitutional convention exists, three questions must be asked: First, "what are the precedents; secondly, did the actors in the precedents believe that they were bound by the rule; and thirdly, is there a reason for the rule?"[2] The second step is an essential and normative element of conventions. It allows one to "distinguish a constitutional rule from a rule of convenience or from political expediency".[3] In other words, a convention cannot be implied without any explicit acceptance, whether in the form of written recognition or through statements of political actors.[4] Moreover, "a single precedent with a good reason may be good enough to establish the rule. A whole string of precedents without such a reason will be of no avail, unless it is perfectly certain that the persons concerned regarded them as bound by it".[5]

Notes

1. *Re: Amendment of Canadian Constitution*, [1982] S.C.J. No. 101, [1982] 2 S.C.R. 793 at 803 (S.C.C.).
2. *Re: Amendment of Canadian Constitution*, [1982] S.C.J. No. 101, [1982] 2 S.C.R. 793 at 816 (S.C.C.).

3. *Re: Amendment of Canadian Constitution*, [1982] S.C.J. No. 101, [1982] 2 S.C.R. 793 at 794 (S.C.C.).
4. *Re: Amendment of Canadian Constitution*, [1982] S.C.J. No. 101, [1982] 2 S.C.R. 793 at 817 (S.C.C.).
5. I. Jennings, *The Law and the Constitution*, 5th ed. (London: University of London Press Ltd., 1959) at 136; see also *Re Amendment of Constitution of Canada*, [1981] S.C.J. No. 58, [1981] 1 S.C.R. 753 at 888 (S.C.C.).

---

(5) Convention and the Law

▼HCL-22▼ Conversion of convention in a law. It is possible for a convention to be transplanted into the legal realm, making it accessible to the courts to intervene where one is breached. However, a constitutional convention may only be recognized as a legal rule through its formal adoption into statute.[1] The courts do not have the authority to enforce conventions, which precludes conventions from evolving into legal rules alongside common law. If the courts could enforce a convention, it would not, by definition, be a convention. They may only become laws via statutory adoption and not through the evolution of common law, to which conventions do not belong. While it is generally accepted that legal rules and conventional rules must remain separate entities, one cannot be mutually exclusive of the other.

Note

1. *Re Amendment of Constitution of Canada*, [1981] S.C.J. No. 58, [1981] 1 S.C.R. 753 at 856 (S.C.C.).

▼HCL-23▼ Domestic conventions vs. international conventions. The international sphere has no governing constitution, no legislating authority, no executive enforcement authority and no generally accepted judicial organ through which international law could be developed.[1] In that context, it may be possible for a convention to crystallize into law. Within Canada, where a constitution and three-branch government are firmly in place, the same possibility does not apply.[2]

Notes

1. *Re Amendment of Constitution of Canada*, [1981] S.C.J. No. 58, [1981] 1 S.C.R. 753 at 778 (S.C.C.).

2. *Re Amendment of Constitution of Canada*, [1981] S.C.J. No. 58, [1981] 1 S.C.R. 753 at 776 (S.C.C.).

---

2. Ultimate Significance

▼HCL-24▼ Overview. Constitutional conventions are essential to the functioning of Canadian government.[1] Conventions fill the gaps where the constitution falls silent and overrule the constitution where it no longer holds relevance. It is arguable that some conventions are more important than formal legal rules. For instance, the Prime Minister is not mentioned anywhere in the *Constitution Act, 1867*,[2] though he or she is the head of the government. Further, if one were to look solely at the written constitution and common law to decipher the inner workings of our government, it would appear as though Canada was ruled by a foreign dictator acting through the Governor General. The Governor General has even been granted full executive authority over the naval and military forces of Canada.[3] Constitutional conventions exist to quash outdated legal powers underlying our representative system of government. Moreover, conventions evolve naturally as the Canadian political atmosphere shifts in new directions. Conventions are like most fundamental rules of any constitution in that they rest essentially upon general acquiescence. A written constitution is not law because somebody drafted it, but because it has been adopted.[4] That means that any change that occurs in the operation of our constitution would reflect the consensus of the modern political scene and, therefore, the people of our representative democracy.[5]

Notes

1. I. Jennings, *The Law and the Constitution*, 5th ed. (London: University of London Press Ltd., 1959) at 81.
2. (U.K.), 30 & 31 Vict., c. 3.
3. *Constitution Act, 1867* (U.K.), 30 & 31 Vict., c. 3, s. 15.
4. I. Jennings, *The Law and the Constitution*, 5th ed. (London: University of London Press Ltd., 1959) at 117.
5. *Reference re Secession of Quebec*, [1998] S.C.J. No. 61, [1998] 2 S.C.R. 217 at para. 49 (S.C.C.).

---

3. Unwritten Principles of the Constitution

(1) General HCL-25
(2) Specific Unwritten Principles
(a) The Principle of Parliamentary Sovereignty HCL-29
(b) The Rule of Law HCL-33
(c) Democracy HCL-37
(d) Judicial Independence HCL-41
(e) The Protection of Minorities HCL-42
(f) The Principle of Constitutionalism HCL-43
(g) Neutrality of the Public Service HCL-45
(h) No Taxation without Representation HCL-46
(i) Separation of Powers HCL-47
(j) Solicitor-client Privilege HCL-48
(k) Parliamentary Privilege HCL-49
(l) Full Faith and Credit Doctrine HCL-58

---

(1) General

▼HCL-25▼ Overview. The *Constitution Act, 1982*[1] defines the "*Constitution of Canada*" in a non-exhaustive manner, providing that "The Constitution of Canada includes: (a) the *Canada Act 1982*, including this Act; (b) the Acts and orders referred to in the schedule; and (c) any amendment to any Act or order referred to in paragraph (a) or (b)."[2]

Acts referred to in the Canadian Constitution. The Canadian Constitution includes a series of statutes, such as the *Constitution Act, 1867*,[3] the *Constitution Act, 1982*[4] and the *Canadian Charter of Rights and Freedoms*.[5] The Constitution also includes a variety of statutes and Imperial Orders in Council, such as the *Manitoba Act, 1870*,[6] the *Constitution Act, 1871*,[7] the Imperial Order in Council admitting British Columbia into the Union, the Imperial Order in Council admitting Prince Edward Island into the Union, the *Alberta Act*,[8] the *Constitution Act, 1930*,[9] the *Statute of Westminster, 1931*[10] and the *Newfoundland Act, 1949*.[11] The *Constitution Act, 1982*[12] was not meant to be exhaustive and the Constitution includes unwritten or implied principles.[13] Other layers of the Constitution must be added to the written texts consisting of common law rules, constitutional conventions and, finally, unwritten principles. The unwritten principles are part of the Constitution's "internal architecture" or its basic constitutional structure.[14]

Notes

1. *Constitution Act, 1982*, being Schedule B to the *Canada Act 1982* (U.K.), 1982, c. 11, s. 52(2).
2. *Constitution Act, 1982*, being Schedule B to the *Canada Act 1982* (U.K.), 1982, c. 11, s. 52(2).
3. *Constitution Act, 1867* (U.K.), 30 & 31 Vict., c. 3, reprinted in R.S.C. 1985, App. II, No. 5.
4. *Constitution Act, 1982*, being Schedule B to the *Canada Act 1982* (U.K.), 1982, c. 11.
5. *Canadian Charter of Rights and Freedoms*, Part I of the *Constitution Act, 1982*, being Schedule B to the *Canada Act 1982* (U.K.), 1982, c. 11.
6. 33 Vict., c. 3, reprinted in R.S.C. 1985, App. II, No. 8.
7. (U.K.), 34 & 35 Vict., c. 28, reprinted in R.S.C. 1985, App. II, No. 11.
8. 4 & 5 Edw. VII, c. 3, reprinted in R.S.C. 1985, App. II, No. 20.
9. (U.K.), 20 & 21 Geo. V, c. 26, reprinted in R.S.C. 1985, App. II, No. 26.
10. (U.K.), 22 Geo. V, c. 4, reprinted in R.S.C. 1985, App. II, No. 27.
11. (U.K.), 212 & 213 Geo. VI, c. 22, reprinted in R.S.C. 1985, App. II, No. 32.
12. *Constitution Act, 1982*, being Schedule B to the *Canada Act 1982* (U.K.), 1982, c. 11, s. 52(2).
13. *New Brunswick Broadcasting Co. v. Nova Scotia (Speaker of the House of Assembly)*, [1993] S.C.J. No. 2, [1993] 1 S.C.R. 319 at 376-77 (S.C.C.). See also Marc Cousineau, "*Le Renvoi relatif à la sécession du Québec: La résurrection des droits linguistiques au Canada*" (1999) 11 N.J.C.L. 147 at 151.
14. See *O.P.S.E.U. v. Ontario (Attorney General)*, [1987] S.C.J. No. 48, [1987] 2 S.C.R. 2 at 57 (S.C.C.); see also *Ref. re Amendment of the Constitution of Canada*, [1981] S.C.J. No. 58, [1981] 1 S.C.R. 753 at 852-53, 876-77 (S.C.C.).

▼HCL-26▼ Preamble. The express provisions of the Constitution should be understood as elaborations of the underlying, unwritten and organizing principles found in the preamble to the *Constitution Act, 1867*.[1] While the unwritten principles originate from the preamble of the *Constitution Act, 1867*, the preamble has no enacting force. Consequently, while the unwritten principles have no proper legal force, the preamble "invites the courts to turn those principles into the premises of a constitutional argument that culminates in the filling of gaps" between the express terms of the constitutional text.[2] Unwritten principles, some of which are identifiable "by the oblique reference in the preamble to the *Constitution Act, 1867*",[3] are vital unstated assumptions that inform and sustain the constitutional text. The principles function in symbiosis; they cannot "be defined in isolation from the others", and no one principle trumps or excludes the operation of any other.[4] The Constitution has an internal architecture and structure, and the principles are linked to the other individual elements of the Constitution. The elements must all be considered in the proper interpretation of the Constitution as a whole. They, in effect, breathe life into it.[5] Properly construed, the principles assist in "the delineation of spheres of jurisdiction, the scope of rights and obligations, and the role of our political institutions".[6] The preamble "is not only a key to construing the express provisions of the *Constitution Act, 1867,* but also invites the use of those organizing principles to fill out gaps in the express terms of the constitutional scheme. It is the means by which the underlying logic of the Act can be given the force of law".[7]

Notes

1. *Beauregard v. Canada*, [1986] S.C.J. No. 50, [1986] 2 S.C.R. 56 at para. 29 S.C.C.); *Reference re Remuneration of Judges of the Provincial Court of Prince Edward Island; Reference re Independence and Impartiality of Judges of the Provincial Court of Prince Edward Island*, [1997] S.C.J. No. 75, [1997] 3 S.C.R. 3 at para. 107 (S.C.C.).
2. *Reference re Remuneration of Judges of the Provincial Court of Prince Edward Island; Reference re Independence and Impartiality of Judges of the Provincial Court of Prince Edward Island*, [1997] S.C.J. No. 75, [1997] 3 S.C.R. 3 at para. 104 (S.C.C.).
3. *Reference re Secession of Quebec*, [1998] S.C.J. No. 61, [1998] 2 S.C.R. 217 at para. 51 (S.C.C.).
4. *Reference re Secession of Quebec*, [1998] S.C.J. No. 61, [1998] 2 S.C.R. 217 at para. 49 (S.C.C.).
5. *Reference re Secession of Quebec*, [1998] S.C.J. No. 61, [1998] 2 S.C.R. 217 at para. 50 (S.C.C.).
6. *Reference re Secession of Quebec*, [1998] S.C.J. No. 61, [1998] 2 S.C.R. 217 at para. 52 (S.C.C.).
7. *Reference re Remuneration of Judges of the Provincial Court of Prince Edward Island; Reference re Independence and Impartiality of Judges of the Provincial Court of Prince Edward Island*, [1997] S.C.J. No. 75, [1997] 3 S.C.R. 3 at para. 95 (S.C.C.).

▼HCL-27▼ Unwritten principles and substantive obligations. The unwritten principles may in certain circumstances give rise to substantive legal obligations which constitute substantive limitations upon government action. "These principles may give rise to very abstract and general obligations, or they may be more specific and precise in nature. The principles are not merely descriptive, but are also invested with a powerful normative force, and are binding upon both courts and governments."[1] Nevertheless, the probative value of the unwritten principles of the Constitution is limited.[2]

Notes

1. *Reference re Secession of Quebec*, [1998] S.C.J. No. 61, [1998] 2 S.C.R. 217 at para. 54 (S.C.C.); approved in *Babcock v. Canada (Attorney General)*, [2002] S.C.J. No. 58, [2002] 3 S.C.R. 3 at para. 54 (S.C.C.) and in *British Columbia v. Imperial Tobacco Canada Ltd.*, [2005] S.C.J. No. 50, [2005] 2 S.C.R. 473 at para. 60 (S.C.C.).
2. *O.P.S.E.U. v. Ontario (Attorney General)*, [1987] S.C.J. No. 48, [1987] 2 S.C.R. 2 at 57 (S.C.C.).

---

(2) Specific Unwritten Principles

▼HCL-28▼ Specific unwritten principles. Unwritten principles of the Constitution include: Parliamentary Sovereignty;[1] the rule of law;[2] democracy;[3] independence of the judiciary;[4] the protection of minorities;[5] constitutionalism;[6] the neutrality of the public service;[7] the principle of no taxation without representation;[8] the separation of powers;[9] the solicitor-client privilege;[10] the Parliamentary privilege;[11] and the full faith and credit doctrine.[12] Other principles, such as freedom of religion[13] and freedom of speech and the press[14] existed prior to the *Canadian Charter of Rights and Freedoms*[15] ("Charter") in the form of unwritten principles, and were subsequently entrenched in the Charter.

Notes

1. The principle of Parliamentary Sovereignty means neither more nor less than this, namely, that Parliament thus defined has, under the English Constitution, the right to make or unmake any law whatever; and, further, that no person or body is recognized by the law of England as having a right to override or set aside the legislation of Parliament. See Albert Venn Dicey, *Introduction to the Study of the Law of the Constitution*, 8th ed. (London: Macmillan, 1915) at 3-5; *Reference re: Liquor License Act of 1877* (Ont.), [1883] J.C.J. No. 2, 9 App. Cas. 117 (P.C.); *Ontario (Attorney General) v. Canada (Attorney General)*, [1912] A.C. 571 (P.C.); *R. v. Mercure*, [1988] S.C.J. No. 11, [1988] 1 S.C.R. 234 (S.C.C.); *Canada (Auditor Gen.) v. Canada (Min. of Energy, Mines and Resources)*, [1989] S.C.J. No. 80, [1989] 2 S.C.R. 49 (S.C.C.); *Reference Re Canada Assistance Plan (B.C.)*, [1991] S.C.J. No. 60, [1991] 2 S.C.R. 525 (S.C.C.); *Babcock v. Canada (Attorney General)*, [2002] S.C.J. No. 58, [2002] 3 S.C.R. 3 (S.C.C.).
2. See Albert Venn Dicey, *Introduction to the Study of the Law of the Constitution*, 10th ed. (London: Macmillan, 1965) at 202-203. The Supreme Court recently defined the concept, in *British Columbia v. Imperial Tobacco Canada Ltd.*, [2005] S.C.J. No. 50, [2005] 2 S.C.R. 473 at paras. 57-58 (S.C.C.), as follows:

   > The rule of law is 'a fundamental postulate of our constitutional structure' (*Roncarelli v. Duplessis*, [1959] S.C.R. 121, at 142) that lies 'at the root of our system of government' (*Reference re Secession of Quebec*, [1998] 2 S.C.R. 217, at para. 70). It is expressly acknowldeged by the preamble to the *Constitution Act, 1982*, and implicitly recognized in the preamble to the

> *Constitution Act, 1867*: see *Reference re Manitoba Language Rights*, [1985] 1 S.C.R. 721 at 750. ... [The] Court has described the rule of law as embracing three principles. The first recognizes that 'the law is supreme over officials of the government as well as private individuals, and thereby preclusive of the influence of arbitrary power': *Reference re Manitoba Language Rights*, [1985] 1 S.C.R. 721 at 748. The second 'requires the creation and maintenance of an actual order of positive laws which preserves and embodies the more general principle of normative order': *Reference re Manitoba Language Rights*, [1985] 1 S.C.R. 721 at 749. The third requires that 'the relationship between the state and the individual ... be regulated by law': *Reference re Secession of Quebec*, at para. 71.

The rule of law in the context of Parliamentary sovereignty was the subject of a detailed analysis in Warren J. Newman, "The Principle of the Rule of Law and Parliamentary Sovereignty in Constitutional Theory and Litigation" (2005) 16 N.J.C.L. 175; P.W. Hogg & C.F. Zwibel, "The Rule of Law in the Supreme Court of Canada" (2005) 55 U.T.L.J. 715 at 717-18. See also *Ref. re Amendment of Constitution of Canada*, [1981] S.C.J. No. 58, [1981] 1 S.C.R. 753 at 805-806 (S.C.C.).

3. *Re Amendment of Constitution of Canada*, [1981] S.C.J. No. 58, [1981] 1 S.C.R. 753 at 880 (S.C.C.); *O.P.S.E.U. v. Ontario (Attorney General)*, [1987] S.C.J. No. 48, [1987] 2 S.C.R. 2 (S.C.C.); *Reference re Secession of Quebec*, [1998] S.C.J. No. 61, [1998] 2 S.C.R. 217 at para. 66 (S.C.C.); *Figueroa v. Canada (Attorney General)*, [2003] S.C.J. No. 37, [2003] 1 S.C.R. 912 at para. 28 (S.C.C.).

4. *Beauregard v. Canada*, [1986] S.C.J. No. 50, [1986] 2 S.C.R. 56 (S.C.C.); *R. v. Valente*, [1985] S.C.J. No. 77, [1985] 2 S.C.R. 673 (S.C.C.); *Reference re Remuneration of Judges of the Provincial Court of Prince Edward Island; Reference re Independence and Impartiality of Judges of the Provincial Court of Prince Edward Island*, [1997] S.C.J. No. 75, [1997] 3 S.C.R. 3 at 84-85 (S.C.C.); *Mackin v. New Brunswick (Minister of Finance); Rice v. Nouveau Brunswick*, [2002] S.C.J. No. 13, [2002] 1 S.C.R. 405 (S.C.C.); *Ell v. Alberta*, [2003] S.C.J. No. 35, [2003] 1 S.C.R. 857 (S.C.C.); *Application under s. 83.28 of the Criminal Code (Re)*, [2004] S.C.J. No. 40, [2004] 2 S.C.R. 248 at paras. 83-92 (S.C.C.); *Provincial Court Judges' Assn. of New Brunswick v. New Brunswick (Minister of Justice)*; *Ontario Judges' Assn. v. Ontario (Management Board)*; *Bodner v. Alberta*; *Conférence des juges du Québec v. Quebec (Attorney General)*; *Minc v. Quebec (Attorney General)*, [2005] S.C.J. No. 47, [2005] 2 S.C.R. 286 (S.C.C.); *British Columbia v. Imperial Tobacco Canada Ltd.*, [2005] S.C.J. No. 50, [2005] 2 S.C.R. 473 at paras. 44-56 (S.C.C.).

5. *Reference re Secession of Quebec*, [1998] S.C.J. No. 61, [1998] 2 S.C.R. 217 at paras. 79-82 (S.C.C.); *Vriend v. Alberta*, [1998] S.C.J. No. 29, [1998] 1 S.C.R. 493 at para. 176 (S.C.C.); *Lalonde v. Ontario (Commission de restructuration des services de santé)*, [2001] O.J. No. 4767, 56 O.R. (3d) 505 (Ont. C.A.).

6. *Reference re Secession of Quebec*, [1998] S.C.J. No. 61, [1998] 2 S.C.R. 217 at paras. 70-78(S.C.C.).

7. *O.P.S.E.U. v. Ontario (Attorney General)*, [1987] S.C.J. No. 48, [1987] 2 S.C.R. 2 (S.C.C.); *Osborne v. Canada (Treasury Board)*, [1991] S.C.J. No. 45, [1991] 2 S.C.R. 69 (S.C.C.).

8. *Eurig Estate (Re)*, [1998] S.C.J. No. 72, [1998] 2 S.C.R. 565 (S.C.C.); *Ontario English Catholic Teachers' Assn. v. Ontario (Attorney General)*, [2001] S.C.J. No. 14, [2001] 1 S.C.R. 470 (S.C.C.).

9. *Reference re Remuneration of Judges of the Provincial Court of Prince Edward Island; Reference re Independence and Impartiality of Judges of the Provincial Court of Prince Edward Island*, [1997] S.C.J. No. 75, [1997] 3 S.C.R. 3 (S.C.C.); *Reference re Secession of Quebec*, [1998] S.C.J. No. 61, [1998] 2 S.C.R. 217 (S.C.C.).
10. *Lavallee, Rackel & Heintz v. Canada (Attorney General); White, Ottenheimer & Baker v. Canada (Attorney General); R. v. Fink*, [2002] S.C.J. No. 61, [2002] 3 S.C.R. 209 (S.C.C.).
11. See *Canada (House of Commons) v. Vaid*, [2005] S.C.J. No. 28, [2005] 1 S.C.R. 667 (S.C.C.); *New Brunswick Broadcasting Co. v. Nova Scotia (Speaker of the House of Assembly)*, [1993] S.C.J. No. 2, [1993] 1 S.C.R. 319 (S.C.C.).
12. *Hunt v. T & N plc*, [1993] S.C.J. No. 125, [1993] 4 S.C.R. 289 (S.C.C.); *Morguard Investments Ltd. v. De Savoye*, [1990] S.C.J. No. 135, [1990] 3 S.C.R. 1077 (S.C.C.).
13. *Switzman v. Elbling*, [1957] S.C.J. No. 13, [1957] S.C.R. 285 (S.C.C.); *Saumur v. Quebec (City)*, [1953] S.C.J. No. 49, [1953] 2 S.C.R. 299 (S.C.C.); *R. v. Boucher*, [1950] S.C.J. No. 41, [1951] S.C.R. 265 (S.C.C.).
14. See *R.W.D.S.U. v. Dolphin Delivery Ltd.*, [1986] S.C.J. No. 75, [1986] 2 S.C.R. 573 at 584 (S.C.C.); *Reference re: Alberta Legislation*, [1938] S.C.J. No. 2, [1938] S.C.R. 100 (S.C.C.).
15. Part I of the *Constitution Act, 1982*, being Schedule B to the *Canada Act 1982* (U.K.), 1982, c. 11.

(a) The Principle of Parliamentary Sovereignty

▼HCL-29▼ Parliamentary sovereignty. One of the most important features of our constitutional foundation is that, through the *Constitution Act, 1867*,[1] Canada inherited a constitution similar to that of the United Kingdom.[2] The sovereignty of Parliament is the dominant characteristic of Canada's political institutions[3] and the cornerstone of the law of the Constitution.[4] It is also the foundation of the unwritten principles, as all unwritten principles must be balanced against the principle of Parliamentary sovereignty.[5] The unwritten principle of Parliamentary sovereignty means that Parliament thus defined has, under the English constitution, the right to make or unmake any law whatsoever; and, further, that no person or body is recognized by the law of England as having a right to override or set aside the legislation of Parliament.[6] Parliamentary sovereignty represents the exercise by Parliament and the provincial legislatures of their legislative powers within the boundaries provided pursuant to the Constitution of Canada. Within the legislative spheres identified by the *Constitution Act, 1867*,[7] Parliament and the legislatures are sovereign. The principle has been implicitly recognized by the preamble of the *Constitution Act, 1867*,[8] and by the Supreme Court in several cases.[9]

Notes

1. (U.K.), 30 & 31 Vict., c. 3, reprinted in R.S.C. 1985, App. II, No. 5.
2. Preamble of the *Constitution Act, 1867* (U.K.), 30 & 31 Vict., c. 3, reprinted in R.S.C. 1985, App. II, No. 5.
3. See Albert Venn Dicey, *Introduction to the Study of the Law of the Constitution*, 8th ed. (London: Macmillan, 1915) at 39.
4. See Albert Venn Dicey, *Introduction to the Study of the Law of the Constitution*, 8th ed. (London: Macmillan, 1915) at 70.
5. *Babcock v. Canada (Attorney General)*, [2002] S.C.J. No. 58, [2002] 3 S.C.R. 3 at para. 55 (S.C.C.).
6. See Albert Venn Dicey, *Introduction to the Study of the Law of the Constitution*, 8th ed. (London: Macmillan, 1915) at 39-40; *Reference re: Liquor License Act of 1877 (Ont.)*, [1883] J.C.J. No. 2, 9 App. Cas. 117 (P.C.); *Ontario (Attorney General) v. Canada (Attorney General)*, [1912] A.C. 571 (P.C.); *R. v. Mercure*, [1988] S.C.J. No. 11, [1988] 1 S.C.R. 234 (S.C.C.); *Canada (Auditor Gen.) v. Canada (Min. of Energy, Mines & Resources)*, [1989] S.C.J. No. 80, [1989] 2 S.C.R. 49 (S.C.C.); *Reference Re Canada Assistance Plan (B.C.)*, [1991] S.C.J. No. 60, [1991] 2 S.C.R. 525 (S.C.C.); *Babcock v. Canada (Attorney General)*, [2002] S.C.J. No. 58, [2002] 3 S.C.R. 3 (S.C.C.).
7. (U.K.), 30 & 31 Vict., c. 3.
8. (U.K.), 30 & 31 Vict., c. 3.
9. [1912] A.C. 571 at 581 (P.C.).

▼HCL-30▼ Restrictions on Parliamentary sovereignty. Parliamentary sovereignty is not absolute. In Canada, the powers of Parliament and of the legislatures are attenuated by the *Constitution Act, 1867*,[1] as well as the Charter.[2] The role of reviewing the validity of legislation and governmental action has been entrusted to courts. The constitutional role of the judiciary with regard to the validity of laws is influenced by the federal division of powers as well as the Constitutional substantive protection of the Charter[3] and the *Constitution Act, 1982*.[4] Nevertheless, absent any constitutional issue, "in the residual area reserved for the principle of Parliamentary sovereignty in Canadian constitutional law, it is Parliament and the legislatures, not the courts, that have ultimate constitutional authority to draw the boundaries. It is the prerogative of a sovereign Parliament to make its intention known as to the role the courts are to play in interpreting, applying and enforcing its statutes".[5] The principle "with which the courts must work in this context is that of the sovereignty of Parliament".[6]

Notes

1. *Constitution Act, 1867* (U.K.), 30 & 31 Vict., c. 3.

2. *Canadian Charter of Rights and Freedoms*, Part I of the *Constitution Act, 1982*, being Schedule B to the *Canada Act 1982* (U.K.), 1982, c. 11.
3. *Canadian Charter of Rights and Freedoms*, Part I of the *Constitution Act, 1982*, being Schedule B to the *Canada Act 1982* (U.K.), 1982, c. 11.
4. *Constitution Act, 1982*, being Schedule B to the *Canada Act 1982* (U.K.), 1982, c. 11, s. 52; *Canada (Auditor General) v. Canada (Minister of Energy, Mines and Resources)*, [1989] S.C.J. No. 80, [1989] S.C.R. 49 at 91 (S.C.C.).
5. *Canada (Auditor Gen.) v. Canada (Min. of Energy, Mines and Resources)*, [1989] S.C.J. No. 80, [1989] 2 S.C.R. 49 at 91.
6. *Canada (Auditor Gen.) v. Canada (Min. of Energy, Mines and Resources)*, [1989] S.C.J. No. 80, [1989] 2 S.C.R. 49 at 103 (S.C.C.).

▼HCL-31▼ Parliamentary sovereignty vs. Parliamentary supremacy. Due to the constitutional limits imposed on the principle, it would be in error to confuse the principle of Parliamentary sovereignty with that of Parliamentary supremacy. In the United Kingdom, where the courts do not have any powers of judicial review[1] of Parliament and where there is no federal system, the terms "sovereignty" and "supremacy" can be used interchangeably. In Canada however, the division of powers and the Charter makes it preferable to use the term "Parliamentary sovereignty". The principle of Parliamentary sovereignty was also enacted into a federal statute and provides that, "[e]very Act shall be so construed as to reserve to Parliament the power of repealing or amending it, and of revoking, restricting or modifying any power, privilege or advantage thereby vested in or granted to any person."[2] Even without the provision, however, a government "could not bind Parliament from exercising its powers to legislate amendments"[3] to statutes. Any contrary argument would negate the sovereignty of Parliament. Parliamentary sovereignty prevents a legislature from binding itself to future legislation.[4]

Notes

1. See *Reference re Remuneration of Judges of the Provincial Court of Prince Edward Island; Reference re Independence and Impartiality of Judges of the Provincial Court of Prince Edward Island*, [1997] S.C.J. No. 75, [1997] 3 S.C.R. 3 at paras. 308-309 (S.C.C.), *per* La Forest J., dissenting.
2. (CAN) *Interpretation Act*, R.S.C. 1985, c. I-21, s. 42(1).
3. *Reference Re Canada Assistance Plan (B.C.)*, [1991] S.C.J. No. 60, [1991] 2 S.C.R. 525 at 548 (S.C.C.).
4. *Reference Re Canada Assistance Plan (B.C.)*, [1991] S.C.J. No. 60, [1991] 2 S.C.R. 525 at 548 (S.C.C.).

▼HCL-32▼ Powers of the legislature. Courts must interpret, apply and enforce statutes. Parliament and the legislatures, to the extent that they remain within their limits, may express their intentions through statutes. To that extent, it is "well within the power of the legislature to enact laws, even laws which some would consider draconian, as long as it does not fundamentally alter or interfere with the relationship between the courts and the other branches of government".[1] Consequently, the principle of Parliamentary sovereignty is fundamental to the law of the Canadian Constitution. Nevertheless, it is somewhat limited when compared to the current British Parliament in the United Kingdom. First, the *Constitution Act, 1867*,[2] provides for a division of powers between Parliament and the provincial legislatures. Thus, Parliament is sovereign within its jurisdiction, pursuant to the *Constitution Act, 1867*,[3] while the provincial legislatures are sovereign within theirs.[4] Moreover, as a result of the *Constitution Act, 1982*,[5] and especially the *Canadian Charter of Rights and Freedoms*,[6] Canada went from a system of Parliamentary supremacy to constitutional supremacy.[7] Parliamentary sovereignty implies that Parliament is superior to any other institution, or omnipotent, and courts are bound by the acts of Parliament and must apply them.[8]

Notes

1. *Babcock v. Canada (Attorney General)*, [2002] S.C.J. No. 58, [2002] 3 S.C.R. 3 at para. 57 (S.C.C.).
2. *Constitution Act, 1867* (U.K.), 30 & 31 Vict., c. 3.
3. *Constitution Act, 1867* (U.K.), 30 & 31 Vict., c. 3, s. 91.
4. *Constitution Act, 1867* (U.K.), 30 & 31 Vict., c. 3, s. 92.
5. Part I of the *Constitution Act, 1982*, being Schedule B to the *Canada Act 1982* (U.K.), 1982, c. 11.
6. Part I of the *Constitution Act, 1982*, being Schedule B to the *Canada Act 1982* (U.K.), 1982, c. 11.
7. R.G.B. Dickson, "Keynote Address", *The Cambridge Lectures 1985* (Montréal: Yvon Blais, 1985); *Constitution Act, 1982*, being Schedule B to the *Canada Act 1982* (U.K.), 1982, c. 11, s. 52(1) provides that: "The Constitution of Canada is the supreme law of Canada, and any law that is inconsistent with the provisions of the Constitution is, to the extent of the inconsistency, of no force or effect".
8. Albert Venn Dicey, *Lectures introductory to the study of the law of the constitution*, 2d ed. (London: Macmillan, 1886) at 36.

(b) The Rule of Law

▼HCL-33▼ Overview. The *rule of law*[1] is a fundamental postulate of Canada's constitutional structure[2] that is explicitly recognized in the preamble to the *Constitution Act, 1982*,[3] and implicitly mentioned in the preamble to the *Constitution Act, 1867*.[4] The principle of the rule of law is also "clearly implicit in the very nature of the Constitution".[5] The rule of law means the absolute supremacy or predominance of regular law as opposed to the influence of arbitrary power, and excludes the existence of arbitrariness, or prerogative, or even of wide discretionary authority on the part of the government.[6] "The 'rule of law' is a highly textured expression ... conveying ... a sense of orderliness, of subjection to known legal rules and of executive accountability to legal authority."[7] The rule of law lies at the root of Canada's system of government, "vouchsafes to the citizens and residents of the country a stable, predictable and ordered society in which to conduct their affairs", and provides a shield for individuals from arbitrary state action.[8]

Elements. The rule of law means that the law is supreme over officials of the government as well as private individuals, and thereby preclusive of the influence of arbitrary power. Second, the rule of law requires the creation and maintenance of an actual order of positive laws which preserves and embodies the more general principle of normative order. Law and order are indispensable elements of civilized life. The rule of law expresses a preference for law and order within a community rather than anarchy, warfare and constant strife. In this sense, the rule of law is a philosophical view of society which in the Western tradition is linked with basic democratic notions.[9] A third element of the content of the rule of law is that "the exercise of all public power must find its ultimate source in a legal rule".[10] In other words, the relationship between the state and the individual is subject to legal requirements. These three considerations make the rule of law "a principle of profound constitutional and political significance".[11]

Notes

1. Albert Venn Dicey, *Introduction to the Study of the Law of the Constitution*, 10th ed. (London: Macmillan, 1965) at 202. See also *Roncarelli v. Duplessis*, [1959] S.C.J. No. 1, [1959] S.C.R. 121 (S.C.C.); *Reference re: Manitoba Language Rights*, [1985] S.C.J. No. 36, [1985] 1 S.C.R. 721 at 748-49 (S.C.C.). The rule of law in the context of Parliamentary sovereignty was the subject of a detailed analysis in Warren J. Newman, "The Principle of the Rule of Law and Parliamentary Sovereignty in Constitutional Theory and Litigation" (2005) 16 N.J.C.L. 175; P.W. Hogg & C.F. Zwibel, "The Rule of Law in the Supreme Court of Canada" (2005) 55 U.T.L.J. 715 at 717-18. See also *Re Amendment of Constitution of Canada*, [1981] S.C.J. No. 58, [1981] 1 S.C.R. 753 at 805-806 (S.C.C.).
2. *Roncarelli v. Duplessis*, [1959] S.C.J. No. 1, [1959] S.C.R. 121 at 142 (S.C.C.); see also *Reference re: Manitoba Language Rights*, [1985] S.C.J. No. 36, [1985] 1

S.C.R. 721 at 748, 750 (S.C.C.); *British Columbia v. Imperial Tobacco Canada Ltd.*, [2005] S.C.J. No. 50, [2005] 2 S.C.R. 473 at para. 57 (S.C.C.).

3. (U.K.), 30 & 31 Vict., c. 3.
4. See *Reference re: Manitoba Language Rights*, [1985] S.C.J. No. 36, [1985] 1 S.C.R. 721 at 750 (S.C.C.); see also *British Columbia v. Imperial Tobacco Canada Ltd.*, [2005] S.C.J. No. 50, [2005] 2 S.C.R. 473 at para. 57 (S.C.C.); *British Columbia (Attorney General) v. Christie*, [2007] S.C.J. No. 21, [2007] 1 S.C.R. 873 at para. 19 (S.C.C.); see also *R. v. Campbell*, [1999] S.C.J. No. 16, [1999] 1 S.C.R. 565 at para. 18 (S.C.C.).
5. *Reference re: Manitoba Language Rights*, [1985] S.C.J. No. 36, [1985] 1 S.C.R. 721 at 750 (S.C.C.).
6. *Pearson v. Canada*, [2000] F.C.J. No. 1444 at para. 10, 195 F.T.R. 31 (F.C.T.D.), quoting Prof. A.V. Dicey in his *Introduction to the Study of the Law of the Constitution*, first published by MacMillan & Co., Ltd. in 1885.
7. *Re Amendment of Constitution of Canada*, [1981] S.C.J. No. 58, [1981] 1 S.C.R. 753 at 805-806 (S.C.C.); see also *Reference re Secession of Quebec*, [1998] S.C.J. No. 61, [1998] 2 S.C.R. 217 at para. 70 (S.C.C.).
8. *Reference re Secession of Quebec*, [1998] S.C.J. No. 61, [1998] 2 S.C.R. 217 at para. 70 (S.C.C.).
9. Wade & Phillips, *Constitutional and Administrative Law*, 9th ed. (London: Longman, 1977) at 89.
10. *Reference re Remuneration of Judges of the Provincial Court of Prince Edward Island; Reference re Independence and Impartiality of Judges of the Provincial Court of Prince Edward Island*, [1997] S.C.J. No. 75, [1997] 3 S.C.R. 3 at para. 10 (S.C.C.).
11. *Reference re Secession of Quebec*, [1998] S.C.J. No. 61, [1998] 2 S.C.R. 217 at para. 71 (S.C.C.); *British Columbia v. Imperial Tobacco Canada Ltd.*, [2005] S.C.J. No. 50, [2005] 2 S.C.R. 473 at para. 58 (S.C.C.); *British Columbia (Attorney General) v. Christie*, [2007] S.C.J. No. 21, [2007] 1 S.C.R. 873 at para. 19 (S.C.C.); *Charkaoui v. Canada (Citizenship and Immigration)*, [2007] S.C.J. No. 9, [2007] 1 S.C.R. 350 at para. 134 (S.C.C.).

▼HCL-34▼ Citizens and public bodies subject to rule of law. Governmental powers, or any authority delegated by Parliament, must be exercised pursuant to valid laws, either directly or indirectly permitted by an act of Parliament or of a legislature. If the governmental power is not authorized by legislation, affected individuals may resort to courts, as the rule of law requires that both citizens and public bodies (and the government) are equally subject to the law.[1]

Note

1. *Operation Dismantle Inc. v. Canada*, [1985] S.C.J. No. 22, [1985] 1 S.C.R. 441 (S.C.C.); *Slaight Communications Inc. v. Davidson*, [1989] S.C.J. No. 45, [1989] 1 S.C.R. 1038 (S.C.C.).

▼HCL-35▼ Rule of law, arbitrary decisions and abuse of government. The rule of law also protects against arbitrary decisions or abuses by the government. If the only requirement of the rule of law was for governmental actions to be provided by statute, Parliament could delegate extreme executive and discretionary powers to public officials, so that any action may be within the boundaries of the legislation.[1] The rule of law thus sets out limits to discretionary power. It establishes a system of rules for preventing abuse of discretion, and allows ordinary courts of law to overrule administrative actions which they deem arbitrary.

Note

1. See *Slaight Communications Inc. v. Davidson*, [1989] S.C.J. No. 45, [1989] 1 S.C.R. 1038 at 1078 (S.C.C.); *Eldridge v. British Columbia (Attorney General)*, [1997] S.C.J. No. 86, [1997] 3 S.C.R. 624 at paras. 21-22 (S.C.C.).

▼HCL-36▼ Normative force of rule of law. The unwritten principle of the rule of law has normative force. Courts have invoked it to preclude the government from transforming discretionary powers into arbitrary ones. However, as discussed above, those "governmental" actions limited by the rule of law are normally those of the executive branch of government. As for the legislative branch, the rule of law only constrains it to the extent that it "must comply with legislated requirements as to manner and form" (*i.e.*, the procedures by which legislation is to be enacted, amended and repealed).[1] This dynamic aspect of the rule of law enables the courts to increase their powers of review and eliminate arbitrariness. This will allow the courts to reduce arbitrariness by requiring governments to comply with the letter and intent of the statutes. In doing so, governments will act reasonably, in good faith, relying on relevant grounds, and without discrimination, errors or lack of evidence.[2]

Notes

1. *British Columbia v. Imperial Tobacco Canada Ltd.*, [2005] S.C.J. No. 50, [2005] 2 S.C.R. 473 at para. 60 (S.C.C.); see also *R. v. Mercure*, [1988] S.C.J. No. 11, [1988] 1 S.C.R. 234 (S.C.C.).
2. P. Garant, *Droit Administratif*, 4th ed., vol. 2 (Montréal: Yvon Blais, 1991) at 4-5.

(c) Democracy

▼HCL-37▼ Foundations of democracy. Democracy[1] is probably the most important principle underlying any political and juridical system, a fundamental value in Canada's constitutional and political structure, and the most important rampart in protecting civil liberties.[2] It is commonly understood as being a political system of majority rule, and can be traced back to the *Magna Carta* (1215) through the long struggle for Parliamentary supremacy culminating in the English *Bill of Rights of 1689*.[3] The "commitment to Parliamentary democracy was incorporated into the Canadian Constitution by the *Constitution Act, 1867*,[4] through that provision's reference to a constitution 'similar in Principle to that of the United Kingdom'".[5] The principle of Parliamentary sovereignty could not exist if it was not for democracy. Democracy does not only relate to the process of government, but is linked with substantive goals such as the promotion of self-government and the accommodation of cultural and group identities.[6] Democracy must allow for the participation of the people through public institutions created under the Constitution, as democracy requires continuous discussions leading to compromises, negotiation and deliberation, and the consideration of dissenting voices.[7]

Democracy and federalism. "The relationship between democracy and federalism means, for example, that in Canada there may be different and equally legitimate majorities in different provinces and territories and at the federal level. No one majority is more or less 'legitimate' than the others as an expression of democratic opinion, although, of course, the consequences will vary with the subject matter. A federal system of government enables different provinces to pursue policies responsive to the particular concerns and interests of people in that province. At the same time, Canada as a whole is also a democratic community in which citizens construct and achieve goals on a national scale through a federal government acting within the limits of its jurisdiction. The function of federalism is to enable citizens to participate concurrently in different collectivities and to pursue goals at both a provincial and a federal level."[8] Democracy can thus be considered to be a constraint to the principle of

Parliamentary sovereignty, in the sense that Parliament or a provincial legislature could not enact legislation which would limit our democratic and elected political system.[9]

Notes

1. *Ref Re Amendment of Constitution of Canada*, [1981] S.C.J. No. 58, [1981] 1 S.C.R. 753 at 880 (S.C.C.); *O.P.S.E.U. v. Ontario (Attorney General)*, [1987] S.C.J. No. 48, [1987] 2 S.C.R. 2 at para. 40 (S.C.C.); *Reference re Secession of Quebec*, [1998] S.C.J. No. 61, [1998] 2 S.C.R. 217 at para. 66 (S.C.C.); *Figueroa v. Canada (Attorney General)*, [2003] S.C.J. No. 37, [2003] 1 S.C.R. 912 at para. 28 (S.C.C.).
2. P.H. Russel, "A democratic Approach to Civil Liberties" (1969) 19 U.T.L.J. 109; see also *Reference re Secession of Quebec*, [1998] S.C.J. No. 61, [1998] 2 S.C.R. 217 at para. 61 (S.C.C.).
3. *Act Declaring the Rights and Liberties of the Subject and Settling and Succession of the Crown, 1689* (U.K.), 1 Will. & Mar. sess. 2, c. 2; see also *Reference re Secession of Quebec*, [1998] S.C.J. No. 61, 1998] 2 S.C.R. 217 at para. 61 (S.C.C.).
4. (U.K.), 30 & 31 Vict., c. 3.
5. *Cooper v. Canada (Canadian Human Rights Commission)*, [1996] S.C.J. No. 115, [1996] 3 S.C.R. 854 at para. 22 (S.C.C.).
6. *Reference re Secession of Quebec*, [1998] S.C.J. No. 61, [1998] 2 S.C.R. 217 at para. 64 (S.C.C.).
7. *Reference re Secession of Quebec*, [1998] S.C.J. No. 61, [1998] 2 S.C.R. 217 at paras. 67-68 (S.C.C.).
8. *Reference re Secession of Quebec*, [1998] S.C.J. No. 61, [1998] 2 S.C.R. 217 at para. 66 (S.C.C.).
9. It should also be noted that judicial independence, specifically its institutional character, results in part from the "preservation of the democratic process": *Beauregard v. Canada*, [1986] S.C.J. No. 50, [1986] 2 S.C.R. 56 at 70; *Reference re Remuneration of Judges of the Provincial Court of Prince Edward Island; Reference re Independence and Impartiality of Judges of the Provincial Court of Prince Edward Island*, [1997] S.C.J. No. 75, [1997] 3 S.C.R. 3 at 84 (S.C.C.).

▼HCL-38▼ Principle of federalism — overview. The "enactment of the B.N.A. (*British North America Act, 1867*)[1] Act created a federal Constitution of Canada which confined the whole area of self-government within Canada to the Parliament of Canada and the provincial legislatures each being supreme within its own defined sphere and area. It can fairly be said, therefore, that the dominant principle of Canadian constitutional law is federalism. The implications of that principle are clear. Each level of government should not be permitted to encroach on the other, either directly or indirectly".[2] Only the preamble of the *Constitution Act, 1867*[3] mentions this fundamental principle, but the *Constitution Act, 1867*[4] confirmed this vision by distributing the legislative powers between the federal government and the provincial legislatures to form a federation. The principle of federalism is a central organizational theme of the Constitution and represents a "political and legal response to underlying social and political realities".[5] The principle of federalism was followed and respected by political and constitutional practice, and has allowed an interpretation of the written provisions of the Constitution in this light.[6]

Notes

1. (U.K.), 12 & 13 Geo. VI, c. 22.
2. *Ref re Amendment of Constitution of Canada*, [1981] S.C.J. No. 58, [1981] 1 S.C.R. 753 at 821 (S.C.C.).
3. (U.K.), 30 & 31 Vict., c. 3.
4. (U.K.), 30 & 31 Vict., c. 3, ss. 91, 92.
5. *Reference re Secession of Quebec*, [1998] S.C.J. No. 61, [1998] 2 S.C.R. 217 at para. 57 (S.C.C.).
6. *Reference re Secession of Quebec*, [1998] S.C.J. No. 61, [1998] 2 S.C.R. 217 at para. 55 (S.C.C.).

▼HCL-39▼ Federalism on a provincial level. The principle of federalism also enables provinces to enact specific statutes to pursue specific collective goals, and may promote different cultures and linguistic minorities within specific provinces or areas.[1] At the same time, federalism allows "citizens to construct and achieve goals on a national scale through a federal government acting within the limits of its jurisdiction". Consequently, federalism is key to enable citizens to participate in different collectivities and to pursue goals at local, provincial and national levels.[2] "The principle of federalism recognizes the diversity of the component parts of Confederation, and the autonomy of provincial governments to develop their societies within their respective spheres of jurisdiction. The federal structure of our country also facilitates democratic participation by distributing power to the government thought to be most suited to achieving the particular societal objective having regard to this diversity."[3]

Notes

1. *Reference re Secession of Quebec*, [1998] S.C.J. No. 61, [1998] 2 S.C.R. 217 at para. 59 (S.C.C.); see also *Canadian Western Bank v. Alberta*, [2007] S.C.J. No. 22, [2007] 2 S.C.R. 3 at para. 22 (S.C.C.).
2. *Reference re Secession of Quebec*, [1998] S.C.J. No. 61, [1998] 2 S.C.R. 217 at para. 66 (S.C.C.).

3. *Reference re Secession of Quebec*, [1998] S.C.J. No. 61, [1998] 2 S.C.R. 217 at paras. 57-58 (S.C.C.).

▼HCL-40▼ Democracy as an interpretive tool. "The principle of democracy has always informed the design of our [Canada's] constitutional structure, and continues to act as an essential interpretive consideration to this day. ... [T]he democracy principle can best be understood as a sort of baseline against which the framers of our Constitution, and subsequently, our elected representatives under it, have always operated. It is perhaps for this reason that the principle was not explicitly identified in the text of the *Constitution Act*, 1867 itself."[1] The possibility to use the unwritten principles as a tool for statutory interpretation is consistent with the use of Charter[2] values when interpreting statutes in other contexts.[3]

Notes

1. *Reference re Secession of Quebec*, [1998] S.C.J. No. 61, [1998] 2 S.C.R. 217 at para. 62 (S.C.C.).
2. *Canadian Charter of Rights and Freedoms*, Part I of the *Constitution Act, 1982*, being Schedule B to the *Canada Act 1982* (U.K.), 1982, c. 11.
3. See *Bell ExpressVu Limited Partnership v. Rex*, [2002] S.C.J. No. 43, [2002] 2 S.C.R. 559 (S.C.C.) for a discussion of Charter values. It may be possible to use the unwritten principles in the same manner and rely on them in statutory interpretation.

(d) Judicial Independence

▼HCL-41▼ Origins of judicial independence. The principle of the independence of the judiciary[1] is implicitly found in the preamble of the *Constitution Act, 1867*.[2] The existence of this principle in English law goes back to the *Act of Settlement*[3] of 1701. It is also explicitly referenced in the *Constitution Act, 1867*[4] and in the Charter,[5] and is "implicitly recognized as a residual right" protected under s. 7 of the Charter.[6] The independence of the judiciary allows the courts to act as a shield against abuses by governments of individual rights and freedoms. Judicial independence also represents the cornerstone of the common law duty of procedural fairness and is an unwritten principle of the Constitution.[7] Judicial independence has "grown into a principle that now extends to all courts, not just the superior courts of this country".[8]

The individual, the collective and judicial independence. Judicial independence "involves both individual and institutional relationships: the individual independence of a judge, as reflected in such matters as security of tenure, and the institutional independence of the court or tribunal over which he or she presides, as reflected in its institutional or administrative relationships to the executive and legislative branches of government".[9] There is, therefore, "an individual and a collective or institutional aspect to judicial independence".[10]

Institutional or collective independence. Institutional independence of the judiciary arises "out of the position of the courts as organs of and protectors 'of the Constitution and the fundamental values embodied in it'".[11] Judicial independence is also fundamental when courts are called upon to settle disputes between the federal and provincial governments. Without such independence, judgments would be stripped of the necessary impartiality to maintain the confidence of the population. In other words, the concept of independence accordingly "refers essentially to the nature of the relationship between a court and others. This relationship must be marked by a form of intellectual separation that allows the judge to render decisions based solely on the requirements of the law and justice".[12]

Notes

1. See *Beauregard v. Canada*, [1986] S.C.J. No. 50, [1986] 2 S.C.R. 56 (S.C.C.); *R. v. Valente*, [1985] S.C.J. No. 77, [1985] 2 S.C.R. 673 (S.C.C.); *Reference re Remuneration of Judges of the Provincial Court of Prince Edward Island; Reference re Independence and Impartiality of Judges of the Provincial Court of Prince Edward Island*, [1997] S.C.J. No. 75, [1997] 3 S.C.R. 3 at 84-85 (S.C.C.); *Mackin v. New Brunswick (Minister of Finance); Rice v. New Brunswick*, [2002] S.C.J. No. 13, [2002] 1 S.C.R. 405 (S.C.C.); *Ell v. Alberta*, [2003] S.C.J. No. 35, [2003] 1 S.C.R. 857 (S.C.C.); *Application under s. 83.28 of the Criminal Code (Re)*, [2004] S.C.J. No. 40, [2004] 2 S.C.R. 248 at paras. 83-92 (S.C.C.); *Provincial Court Judges' Assn. of New Brunswick v. New Brunswick (Minister of Justice); Ontario Judges' Assn. v. Ontario (Management Board); Bodner v. Alberta; Conférence des juges du Québec v. Quebec (Attorney General); Minc v. Quebec (Attorney General)*, [2005] S.C.J. No. 47, [2005] 2 S.C.R. 286 (S.C.C.), reconsideration denied [2005] S.C.J. No. 60, [2005] 3 S.C.R. 41 (S.C.C.); *British Columbia v. Imperial Tobacco Canada Ltd.*, [2005] S.C.J. No. 50, [2005] 2 S.C.R. 473 at paras. 44-56 (S.C.C.).
2. (U.K.), 30 & 31 Vict., c. 3; *Beauregard v. Canada*, [1986] S.C.J. No. 50, [1986] 2 S.C.R. 56 at 72 (S.C.C.); *Reference re Remuneration of Judges of the Provincial Court of Prince Edward Island; Reference re Independence and Impartiality of Judges of the Provincial Court of Prince Edward Island*, [1997] S.C.J. No. 75, [1997] 3 S.C.R. 3 at paras. 83, 109 (S.C.C.); see also *Ell v. Alberta*, [2003] S.C.J. No. 35, [2003] 1 S.C.R. 857 at para. 19 (S.C.C.); *Cooper v. Canada (Canadian Human Rights Commission)*, [1996] S.C.J. No. 115, [1996] 3 S.C.R. 854 at para. 12 (S.C.C.).

3. (U.K.), 12 & 13 Will., sess. 3, c. 2.
4. (U.K.), 30 & 31 Vict., c. 3, ss. 96-100.
5. *Canadian Charter of Rights and Freedoms*, Part I of the *Constitution Act, 1982*, being Schedule B to the *Canada Act 1982* (U.K.), 1982, c. 11, s. 11(d).
6. *Application under s. 83.28 of the Criminal Code (Re)*, [2004] S.C.J. No. 40, [2004] 2 S.C.R. 248 at para. 81 (S.C.C.).
7. *Reference re Remuneration of Judges of the Provincial Court of Prince Edward Island; Reference re Independence and Impartiality of Judges of the Provincial Court of Prince Edward Island*, [1997] S.C.J. No. 75, [1997] 3 S.C.R. 3 at para. 109 (S.C.C.); *Application under s. 83.28 of the Criminal Code (Re)*, [2004] S.C.J. No. 40, [2004] 2 S.C.R. 248 at paras. 80-81 (S.C.C.).
8. *Reference re Remuneration of Judges of the Provincial Court of Prince Edward Island; Reference re Independence and Impartiality of Judges of the Provincial Court of Prince Edward Island*, [1997] S.C.J. No. 75, [1997] 3 S.C.R. 3 at para. 106 (S.C.C.).
9. *Valente v. The Queen*, [1985] S.C.J. No. 77, [1985] 2 S.C.R. 673 at 685, 687 (S.C.C.).
10. *Beauregard v. Canada*, [1986] S.C.J. No. 50, [1986] 2 S.C.R. 56 at para. 23 (S.C.C.).
11. *Reference re Remuneration of Judges of the Provincial Court of Prince Edward Island; Reference re Independence and Impartiality of Judges of the Provincial Court of Prince Edward Island*, [1997] S.C.J. No. 75, [1997] 3 S.C.R. 3 at para. 123 (S.C.C.), citing *Beauregard v. Canada*, [1986] S.C.J. No. 50, [1986] 2 S.C.R. 56 at 69 (S.C.C.).
12. *Mackin v. New Brunswick (Minister of Finance)*, [2002] S.C.J. No. 13, [2002] 1 S.C.R. 405 at para. 37 (S.C.C.).

(e) The Protection of Minorities[1]

▼HCL-42▼ Protection of minorities. The principle of the protection of minorities is an unwritten principle of the Constitution based on the product of negotiations and historical compromises,[2] "reflects an important underlying constitutional value",[3] and has been part of the design of our constitutional structure since Confederation.[4] Protection of minorities remains an unwritten principle despite there being a number of specific constitutional provisions protecting minorities, such as linguistic minorities, religious minorities and education rights. The unwritten principle of protection of minorities must continue to exercise influence in the interpretation of the Constitution.[5] The minorities protected by the unwritten principle include those already protected by the Charter[6] and the "analogous ground" criteria, as well as aboriginal rights under the *Constitution Act, 1982*.[7]

Notes

1. *Reference re Secession of Quebec*, [1998] S.C.J. No. 61, [1998] 2 S.C.R. 217 at paras. 79-82 (S.C.C.); *Vriend v. Alberta*, [1998] S.C.J. No. 29, [1998] 1 S.C.R. 493 at para. 176 (S.C.C.); *Lalonde v. Ontario (Commission de restructuration des services soins de santé)*, [2001] O.J. No. 4767, 56 O.R. (3d) 577 (Ont. C.A.).
2. *Reference re Secession of Quebec*, [1998] S.C.J. No. 61, [1998] 2 S.C.R. 217 at paras. 79-80 (S.C.C.).
3. *Reference re Secession of Quebec*, [1998] S.C.J. No. 61, [1998] 2 S.C.R. 217 at para. 82 (S.C.C.).
4. *Reference re Secession of Quebec*, [1998] S.C.J. No. 61, [1998] 2 S.C.R. 217 at para. 81 (S.C.C.).
5. *Reference re Secession of Quebec*, [1998] S.C.J. No. 61, [1998] 2 S.C.R. 217 at para. 81 (S.C.C.).
6. *Canadian Charter of Rights and Freedoms*, Part I of the *Constitution Act, 1982*, being Schedule B to the *Canada Act 1982* (U.K.), 1982, c. 11, s. 15.
7. *Constitution Act, 1982*, being Schedule B to the *Canada Act 1982* (U.K.), 1982, c. 11, s. 35.

(f) The Principle of Constitutionalism

▼HCL-43▼ Principle of constitutionalism. The "constitutionalism principle"[1] is similar to that of the rule of law. The principle of constitutionalism requires that all government action comply with the Constitution. On the other hand, the principle of the rule of law requires that all government action must comply with the law, including the Constitution. It is now entrenched in the *Constitution Act, 1982*,[2] which provides that "the Constitution of Canada is the supreme law of Canada, and any law that is inconsistent with the provisions of the Constitution is, to the extent of the inconsistency, of no force or effect."[3]

Notes

1. *Reference re Secession of Quebec*, [1998] S.C.J. No. 61, [1998] 2 S.C.R. 217 at paras. 70-78 (S.C.C.).
2. *Constitution Act, 1982*, being Schedule B to the *Canada Act 1982* (U.K.), 1982, c. 11, s. 52(1).
3. *Reference re Secession of Quebec*, [1998] S.C.J. No. 61, [1998] 2 S.C.R. 217 at para. 72 (S.C.C.).

▼HCL-44▼ Purpose of an entrenched constitution. There are three overlapping reasons why an entrenched Constitution beyond the reach of the majority is required, which in turn provides an explanation of the scope and importance of the principles of constitutionalism and the rule of law.[1] The first reason is that a constitution may provide an extra layer of protection for fundamental human rights and freedoms which might otherwise be susceptible to government interference when the majority will be tempted to ignore those rights in accomplishing collective goals. Second, a constitution may ensure that minorities will be protected from assimilative forces and provided with the institutions and rights necessary to maintain and promote their identities. Finally, a constitution, and particularly a federation or confederation, may allocate political power amongst different levels of government. Without a constitution, one level of government "could usurp the powers of the other simply by exercising its legislative power to allocate additional political power to itself unilaterally".[2] The principle of constitutionalism also allows greater protection to minorities. By requiring an enhanced majority prior to any constitutional amendment, the Constitution ensures that the interests of all groups must be considered and accommodated prior to changes being enacted.[3] Although fundamental to our Constitution, the principle of constitutionalism has never been formally used to limit governmental action. The main reason is likely the adoption of the Charter[4] which brought us "from a system of Parliamentary supremacy to constitutional supremacy".[5]

Notes

1. *Reference re Secession of Quebec*, [1998] S.C.J. No. 61, [1998] 2 S.C.R. 217 at para. 73 (S.C.C.).
2. *Reference re Secession of Quebec*, [1998] S.C.J. No. 61, [1998] 2 S.C.R. 217 at para. 74 (S.C.C.).
3. See *Reference re Secession of Quebec*, [1998] S.C.J. No. 61, [1998] 2 S.C.R. 217 at para. 77 (S.C.C.).
4. *Canadian Charter of Rights and Freedoms*, Part I of the *Constitution Act, 1982*, being Schedule B to the *Canada Act 1982* (U.K.), 1982, c. 11.
5. R.G.B. Dickson, "Keynote Address", *The Cambridge Lectures 1985* (Montréal: Yvon Blais, 1985) at 3-4; see *Vriend v. Alberta*, [1988] S.C.J. No. 29, [1998] 1 S.C.R. 493 (S.C.C.).

(g) Neutrality of Public Service

▼HCL-45▼ Overview. It has been recognized that the political neutrality of the public service[1] and the employees of government is a fundamental pillar of a democratic government and is essential for its efficient operation.[2] It is one of the features of a responsible government. The principle of political neutrality of public servants existed at the time of Confederation and the reasoning in support of such principle has been consistent throughout the subsequent years. Such historical practice has resulted in public confidence in the civil service, and this confidence requires political neutrality and impartial service, regardless of the party in power.[3] If restrictions on the political activities of public servants were withdrawn, the public might cease to believe in the impartiality of Crown servants and Ministers might cease to have confidence in the loyal and faithful support of their official subordinates. If such was the case, the result would be that Ministers would prefer hiring individuals in whom they have confidence, rather than the system of recruitment by open competition favouring greater competence. In that case, the Civil Service would cease to be an impartial and non-political body, capable of loyal service to all Ministers and parties alike. That change could affect the public estimation of the Service and negate one of the greatest advantages of our administrative system.[4]

Notes

1. *O.P.S.E.U. v. Ontario (Attorney General)*, [1987] S.C.J. No. 48, [1987] 2 S.C.R. 2 (S.C.C.); *Osborne v. Canada (Treasury Board)*, [1991] S.C.J. No. 45, [1991] 2 S.C.R. 69 (S.C.C.).
2. *O.P.S.E.U. v. Ontario (Attorney General)*, [1987] S.C.J. No. 48, [1987] 2 S.C.R. 2 at para. 98 (S.C.C.).
3. *O.P.S.E.U. v. Ontario (Attorney General)*, [1987] S.C.J. No. 48, [1987] 2 S.C.R. 2 at para. 99 (S.C.C.).
4. *Fraser v. Canada (Public Service Staff Relations Board)*, [1985] S.C.J. No. 71, [1985] 2 S.C.R. 455 at 470-71 (S.C.C.).

(h) No Taxation without Representation

▼HCL-46▼ Overview. The "principle of no taxation without representation"[1] has been imported in Canadian law in the preamble of the Constitution,[2] as well as in the *Constitution Act, 1867*.[3] There is thus "a constitutional guarantee of 'no taxation without representation' in Canada".[4] The rationale of the *Constitution Act, 1867*[5] was to codify the principle of no taxation without representation by requiring any taxation bill that raised revenue to originate with the legislature. Thus, only the directly elected legislature could impose a tax. This "ensures parliamentary control over, and accountability for, taxation".[6] Consequently, the principle of no taxation without representation is a constitutional imperative recognized by the preamble as well as the *Constitution Act, 1867*,[7] and "is enforceable by the courts".[8]

Notes

1. *Eurig Estate (Re)*, [1998] S.C.J. No. 72, [1998] 2 S.C.R. 565 (S.C.C.); *Ontari English Catholic Teachers' Assn. v. Ontario (Attorney General)*, [2001] S.C.J. No 14, [2001] 1 S.C.R. 470 (S.C.C.).
2. *Ontario English Catholic Teachers' Assn. v. Ontario (Attorney General)*, [2001 S.C.J. No. 14, [2001] 1 S.C.R. 470 at para. 69 (S.C.C.).
3. (U.K.), 30 & 31 Vict., c. 3, s. 53.
4. *Ontario English Catholic Teachers' Assn. v. Ontario (Attorney General)*, [2001 S.C.J. No. 14, [2001] 1 S.C.R. 470 at para. 70 (S.C.C.).
5. (U.K.), 30 & 31 Vict., c. 3, s. 53.
6. *Eurig Estate (Re)*, [1998] S.C.J. No. 72, [1998] 2 S.C.R. 565 at paras. 30, 3 (S.C.C.).
7. (U.K.), 30 & 31 Vict., c. 3.
8. *Eurig Estate (Re)*, [1998] S.C.J. No. 72, [1998] 2 S.C.R. 565 at para. 34 (S.C.C.).

(i) Separation of Powers

▼HCL-47▼ Overview. One of the main features of the Canadian Constitution is the separation of powers.[1] While the Canadian separation of powers is not definite as compared with the United States of America the three branches of government are independent from each other.[2] Thei roles are all different, the judiciary interprets and applies the law, and ac as judicial arbiters;[3] the legislature chooses the appropriate response t social problems, makes policy decisions and enacts legislation;[4] and th executive administers and implements policy.[5] The separation of power requires that the three branches must be responsible for some specifi functions, and exercise them exclusively.[6] The principle of the separation of powers also "requires that the different branches of government onl interact, as much as possible, in particular ways". The "relationships between the different branches of government should have a particular character".[7]

Not a strict separation of powers. The separation of powers under th Canadian Constitution is not strict because the judicial functions "may b vested in non-judicial bodies such as tribunals, and ... the judiciary ma be vested with non-judicial functions".[8] Parliament and the provincial legislatures may properly confer legal functions on the courts, and may confer certain judicial functions on bodies that are not courts, subject only t the requirements of the *Constitution Act, 1867*.[9]

Separation between legislative and executive. The separation of powers between the legislative and the executive is incomplete, as the members of the executive (or cabinet) are also members of the legislature. One of the main principles of that relationship is the hierarchical relationship between the executive and the legislature, in that the executive must execute, implement or effectuate legislative intent. Sometimes, however, legislative intent is so broad that it is difficult to speak of any legislative intent at all. Moreover, the broadness or vagueness may have been intended in order to leave a broad role to the executive to develop and shape the boundaries of a regulatory regime. Nevertheless, the "fundamental matters of political choice rest with the legislature, and the executive is bound to adhere to those choices".[10] Hence, once the legislature has made a political decision and enacted legislation, it is the constitutional duty of the executive to implement those choices.

Depoliticized. The separation of powers also means that, in theory, the relationships between the legislative and executive, on one side, and the judiciary, on the other, should be depoliticized. The "legislature and executive cannot, and cannot appear to, exert political pressure on the judiciary, and conversely, ... members of the judiciary should exercise reserve in speaking out publicly" on public policy issues that could potentially come before the courts.[11]

Notes

1. *Reference re Remuneration of Judges of the Provincial Court of Prince Edward Island; Reference re Independence and Impartiality of Judges of the Provincial Court of Prince Edward Island*, [1997] S.C.J. No. 75, [1997] 3 S.C.R. 3 (S.C.C.); *Reference re Secession of Quebec*, [1998] S.C.J. No. 61, [1998] 2 S.C.R. 217 at para. 15 (S.C.C.).
2. *Cooper v. Canada (Canadian Human Rights Commission)*, [1996] S.C.J. No. 115, [1996] 3 S.C.R. 854 at para. 10 (S.C.C.); *Fraser v. Canada (Public Service Staff Relations Board)*, [1985] S.C.J. No. 71, [1985] 2 S.C.R. 455 at 469-70 (S.C.C.); *New Brunswick Broadcasting Co. v. Nova Scotia (Speaker of the House of Assembly)*, [1993] S.C.J. No. 2, [1993] 1 S.C.R. 319 at 389 (S.C.C.); *Doucet-Boudreau v. Nova Scotia (Minister of Education)*, [2003] S.C.J. No. 63, [2003] 3 S.C.R. 3 at para. 33 (S.C.C.).
3. *Doucet-Boudreau v. Nova Scotia (Minister of Education)*, [2003] S.C.J. No. 63, [2003] 3 S.C.R. 3 at para. 34 (S.C.C.).
4. *RJR-MacDonald Inc. v. Canada (Attorney General)*, [1995] S.C.J. No. 68, [1995] 3 S.C.R. 199 at para. 136 (S.C.C.).
5. *Fraser v. Canada (Public Service Staff Relations Board)*, [1985] S.C.J. No. 71, [1985] 2 S.C.R. 455 at 469-70 (S.C.C.); see *R. v. Power*, [1994] S.C.J. No. 29, [1994] 1 S.C.R. 601 at 620 (S.C.C.).
6. See *Cooper v. Canada (Canadian Human Rights Commission)*, [1996] S.C.J. No. 115, [1996] 3 S.C.R. 854 at para. 13 (S.C.C.); *Reference re Remuneration of*

Judges of the Provincial Court of Prince Edward Island; Reference re Independence and Impartiality of Judges of the Provincial Court of Prince Edward Island, [1997] S.C.J. No. 75, [1997] 3 S.C.R. 3 at para. 139 (S.C.C.).

7. *Reference re Remuneration of Judges of the Provincial Court of Prince Edward Island; Reference re Independence and Impartiality of Judges of the Provincial Court of Prince Edward Island*, [1997] S.C.J. No. 75, [1997] 3 S.C.R. 3 at para. 139 (S.C.C.).
8. *Reference Re Residential Tenancies Act, 1979*, [1981] S.C.J. No. 57, [1981] 1 S.C.R. 714 at 728 (S.C.C.); see *Douglas/Kwantlen Faculty Assn. v. Douglas College*, [1990] S.C.J. No. 124, [1990] 3 S.C.R. 570 at 601 (S.C.C.); *Cooper v. Canada (Canadian Human Rights Commission)*, [1996] S.C.J. No. 115, [1996] 3 S.C.R. 854 at para. 10 (S.C.C.).
9. (U.K.), 30 & 31 Vict., c. 3, s. 96; *Reference re Secession of Quebec*, [1998] S.C.J. No. 61, [1998] 2 S.C.R. 217 at para. 15 (S.C.C.).
10. *Cooper v. Canada (Human Rights Commission)*, [1996] S.C.J. No. 115, [1996] 3 S.C.R. 854 at para. 23 (S.C.C.); *Reference re Remuneration of Judges of the Provincial Court of Prince Edward Island; Reference re Independence and Impartiality of Judges of the Provincial Court of Prince Edward Island*, [1997] S.C.J. No. 75, [1997] 3 S.C.R. 3 at para. 139 (S.C.C.).
11. *Reference re Remuneration of Judges of the Provincial Court of Prince Edward Island*, [1997] S.C.J. No. 75, [1997] 3 S.C.R. 3 at paras. 139-140 (S.C.C.).

(j) Solicitor-client Privilege

▼HCL-48▼ Overview. The solicitor-client privilege is a principle of fundamental justice and a civil right of the utmost importance in Canadian law.[1] The Court described the principle as one of the most ancient and powerful privileges known to our jurisprudence which is supported by and impressed with the values underlying the Charter.[2] However, while a "principle of fundamental justice", its constitutional protection is still unconfirmed.[3] The privilege favours a fair, just and efficient law enforcement process, as well as the privacy interests of a potential accused. "The *prima facie* protection for solicitor-client communications is based on the fact that the relationship and the communications between solicitor and client are essential to the effective operation of the legal system."[4]

Exceptions. The privilege, however, does not apply in absolutely every case. For example, "if a client seeks guidance from a lawyer in order to facilitate the commission of a crime or a fraud, the communication will not be privileged".[5] Moreover, the courts have concluded that solicitor-client privilege does not apply where the effect would be to preclude the accused on a criminal charge from bringing forward relevant evidence, or to make full answer and defence to criminal charges.[6] The solicitor-client privilege had to be as close to absolute as possible to ensure public confidence and retain relevance, and should only yield in certain clearly defined circumstances. Moreover, the privilege should "not involve a balancing of interests on a case-by-case basis".[7]

Notes

1. *Lavallee, Rackel & Heintz v. Canada (Attorney General); White, Ottenheimer & Baker v. Canada (Attorney General); R. v. Fink*, [2002] S.C.J. No. 61, [2002] 3 S.C.R. 209 at para. 36 (S.C.C.); *Smith v. Jones*, [1999] S.C.J. No. 15, [1999] 1 S.C.R. 455 at para. 45, *per* Cory J. (S.C.C.); *Canada v. Solosky*, [1979] S.C.J. No. 130, [1980] 1 S.C.R. 821 at 833 (S.C.C.); *A. (L.L.) v. B (A.)*, [1995] S.C.J. No. 102, [1995] 4 S.C.R. 536 at para. 69 (S.C.C.).
2. *Canadian Charter of Rights and Freedoms*, Part I of the *Constitution Act, 1982*, being Schedule B to the *Canada Act 1982* (U.K.), 1982, c. 11, s. 7; *R. v. National Post*, [2010] S.C.J. No. 16, [2010] 1 S.C.R. 477 at para. 39 (S.C.C.).
3. *R. v. National Post*, [2010] S.C.J. No. 16, [2010] 1 S.C.R. 477 (S.C.C.).
4. *R. v. Gruenke*, [1991] S.C.J. No. 80, [1991] 3 S.C.R. 263 at 289 (S.C.C.); see also *Smith v. Jones*, [1999] S.C.J. No. 15, [1999] 1 S.C.R. 455 at para. 46, *per* Cory J., at para. 5, *per* Major J., dissenting (S.C.C.); see also *Descôteaux v. Mierzwinski*, [1982] S.C.J. No. 43, [1982] 1 S.C.R. 860 at 872 (S.C.C.); *Wigmore on Evidence*, vol. 8 (McNaughton rev. 1961) § 2292 at 554.
5. *Solosky v. The Queen*, [1979] S.C.J. No. 130, [1980] 1 S.C.R. 821 at 835 (S.C.C.); *R. v. Campbell*, [1999] S.C.J. No. 16, [1999] 1 S.C.R. 565 at para. 55 (S.C.C.).
6. See *R. v. Seaboyer; R. v. Gayme*, [1991] S.C.J. No. 62, [1991] 2 S.C.R. 577 (S.C.C.); *Canada (Solicitor General) v. Ontario (Royal Commission of Inquiry into the Confidentiality of Health Records)*, [1981] S.C.J. No. 95, [1981] 2 S.C.R. 494 (S.C.C.); *R. v. Dunbar*, [1982] O.J. No. 581, 68 C.C.C. (2d) 13 at 43-45 (Ont. C.A.); *A. (L.L.) v. B. (A.)*, [1995] S.C.J. No. 102, [1995] 4 S.C.R. 536 at paras. 37, 69 (S.C.C.).
7. *Goodis v. Ontario (Ministry of Correctional Services)*, [2006] S.C.J. No. 31, [2006] 2 S.C.R. 32 at paras. 15-16 (S.C.C.).

(k) Parliamentary Privileges

▼HCL-49▼ Definition. Parliamentary privilege is the necessary immunity that the law provides for members of Parliament, and for members of the legislatures of each of the 10 provinces and two territories, in order for these legislators to do their legislative work. It is also the necessary immunity that the law provides for anyone while taking part in a proceeding in Parliament or in a legislature. Finally, it is the authority and power of each House of Parliament and of each legislature to enforce that immunity.[1]

Rationale. The rationale of the principle was that in order to perform their functions, legislative bodies and parliamentarians require certain privileges relating to the performance of their duties and the conduct of their business. It had also long been accepted that those privileges had to be held absolutely and constitutionally if they were to be effective, and that those privileges were so important that even the Crown and the courts could not touch them. Thus privilege, though part of the law of the land, is to a certain extent an exemption from the general law.[2] Parliamentary privileges were held by the assemblies as against the Crown and the judiciary. Parliamentary privileges are the "sum of the fundamental rights of the House and of its individual members as against the prerogatives of the Crown, the authority of the ordinary Courts of Law, and the special rights of the House of Lords".[3]

Origin. Parliamentary privilege has its roots in the preamble to our *Constitution Act, 1867* which calls for "'a Constitution similar in Principle to that of the United Kingdom'. Each of the branches of the State is vouchsafed a measure of autonomy from the others. Parliamentary privilege was partially codified in art. 9 of the U.K. *Bill of Rights* of 1689, 1 Will. & Mar. sess. 2, c. 2, but the freedom of speech to which it refers was asserted at least as early as 1523. ... Parliamentary privilege is a principle common to all countries based on the Westminster system, and has a loose counterpart in the Speech or Debate Clause of the United States Constitution."[4] It is in part because of the preamble that the Supreme Court of Canada has held that parliamentary privileges are necessary for the functioning of Parliament and have a constitutional status.[5] The implied principles of the *Bill of Rights*[6] are thus part of the Constitution of Canada.[7] Parliament plays an essential role in determining which privileges apply to the House of Commons, pursuant to the *Constitution Act, 1867*,[8] the *Parliament of Canada Act*,[9] as well as the principles underlying the *Bill of Rights* of 1689.[10]

Notes

1. Joseph Maingot, *Parliamentary Privilege in Canada* (Toronto: Butterworths, 1982) at 12.
2. *New Brunswick Broadcasting Co. v. Nova Scotia (Speaker of the House of Assembly)*, [1993] S.C.J. No. 2, [1993] 1 S.C.R. 319 at 378-80 (S.C.C.).
3. *New Brunswick Broadcasting Co. v. Nova Scotia (Speaker of the House of Assembly)*, [1993] S.C.J. No. 2, [1993] 1 S.C.R. 319 at 342 (S.C.C.).
4. *Canada (House of Commons) v. Vaid*, [2005] S.C.J. No. 28, [2005] 1 S.C.R. 667 at paras. 20-21 (S.C.C.); see also *Villeneuve v. Northwest Territories (Legislative Assembly)*, [2008] N.W.T.J. No. 40, [2008] 10 W.W.R. 704 at para. 17 (N.W.T.S.C.).
5. *New Brunswick Broadcasting Co. v. Nova Scotia (Speaker of the House of Assembly)*, [1993] S.C.J. No. 2, [1993] 1 S.C.R. 319 at 374, 385 (S.C.C.).

6. *Act Declaring the Rights and Liberties of the Subject and Settling and Succession of the Crown, 1689* (U.K.), 1 Will. & Mar. sess. 2, c. 2, art. 9.
7. *Canada (House of Commons) v. Vaid*, [2005] S.C.J. No. 28, [2005] 1 S.C.R. 667 at para. 21 (S.C.C.); *New Brunswick Broadcasting Co. v. Nova Scotia (Speaker of the House of Assembly)*, [1993] S.C.J. No. 2, [1993] 1 S.C.R. 319 at 385 (S.C.C.); J.P. Maingot, *Le privilège parlementaire au Canada*, 2d ed. (Montréal: Presses universitaires McGill-Queen's, 1997) at 315.
8. (U.K.), 30 & 31 Vict, c. 3, s. 18.
9. (CAN) *Parliament of Canada Act*, R.S.C. 1985, c. P-1, s. 4.
10. *Act Declaring the Rights and Liberties of the Subject and Settling and Succession of the Crown, 1689* (U.K.), 1 Will. & Mar. sess. 2, c. 2, art. 9. See *New Brunswick Broadcasting Co. v. Nova Scotia (Speaker of the House of Assembly)*, [1993] S.C.J. No. 2, [1993] 1 S.C.R. 319 at 385 (S.C.C.); see also *Canada (Attorney General) v. P.E.I. (Legislative Assembly)*, [2003] P.E.I.J. No. 7 at paras. 23, 24, 32 (P.E.I. S.C. (T.D.)).

▼HCL-50▼ Parliamentary privileges and s. 18 of the *Constitution Act, 1867*. The extent of the parliamentary privileges must also be analyzed taking into account the provisions of the *Constitution Act, 1867*.[1] This section grants to Parliament the power to enact legislation to determine the extent of the privileges, immunities and powers of the Senate and the House of Commons, as well as their members and committees. This power is plenary, with one exception: Parliament cannot grant privileges, immunities or powers that exceed the powers held by the House of Commons of the United Kingdom in 1867.[2] Nevertheless, these powers must be allowed to adapt to the changing circumstances that exist today.[3] Consequently, to determine the extent of the privileges, one must first determine the privileges that existed in 1867 and applied to the House of Commons in the United Kingdom.[4]

Notes

1. (U.K.), 30 & 31 Vict., c. 3, s. 18.
2. *Constitution Act, 1867* (U.K.), 30 & 31 Vict., c. 3, s. 18.
3. *Canada (House of Commons) v. Vaid*, [2005] S.C.J. No. 28, [2005] 1 S.C.R. 667 at para. 39 (S.C.C.); *Gagliano v. Canada*, [2005] F.C.J. No. 683, 253 D.L.R. (4th) 701 at para. 32 (F.C.).
4. *Canada (House of Commons) v. Vaid*, [2005] S.C.J. No. 28, [2005] 1 S.C.R. 667 at para. 37 (S.C.C.).

▼HCL-51▼ Parliamentary privileges and s. 4 of the *Parliament of Canada Act*. The Canadian Parliament exercised its powers under the

Constitution Act, 1867[1] and enacted s. 4 of the *Parliament of Canada Act*.[2] The *Parliament of Canada Act*[3] refers to the privileges, immunities and powers enjoyed and exercised by the Commons House of Parliament of the United Kingdom in 1867, and provides that Parliament may define these privileges, but may not exceed those enjoyed by the House of Commons of the United Kingdom in 1867. Consequently, it is the principles underlying the *Bill of Rights, 1689*[4] that apply, rather than the provision itself.[5]

Notes

1. (U.K.), 30 & 31 Vict., c. 3, s. 18.
2. (CAN) *Parliament of Canada Act*, R.S.C. 1985, c. P-1, s. 4.
3. (CAN) *Parliament of Canada Act*, R.S.C. 1985, c. P-1.
4. *Act Declaring the Rights and Liberties of the Subject and Settling and Succession of the Crown, 1689* (U.K.), 1 Will. & Mar. sess. 2, c. 2, art. 9.
5. *New Brunswick Broadcasting Co. v. Nova Scotia (Speaker of the House of Assembly)*, [1993] S.C.J. No. 2, [1993] 1 S.C.R. 319 at 385 (S.C.C.); *Gagliano v. Canada*, [2005] F.C.J. No. 683, 253 D.L.R. (4th) 701 at para. 33 (F.C.).

▼HCL-52▼ Inherent privileges. Certain "inherent" privileges include:

(a) freedom of speech, including immunity from civil proceedings with respect to any matter arising from the carrying out of the duties of a member of the House;
(b) exclusive control over the House's own proceedings;
(c) ejection of strangers from the House and its precincts; and
(d) control of publication of debates and proceedings in the House.[1]

Historically, case law has clearly recognized the necessity of the categories of privileges linked to the powers of inquiry of the House and its committees, as well as freedom of expression without any risk to be questioned outside Parliament on the content of the expression. "What is said or done within the walls of Parliament cannot be inquired into in a court of law."[2] Furthermore, the House of Commons is not subject to the control of Her Majesty's Courts in its administration of that part of the statute-law, which has relation to its own internal proceedings.

Notes

1. *New Brunswick Broadcasting Co. v. Nova Scotia (Speaker of the House of Assembly)*, [1993] S.C.J. No. 2 at para. 129, [1993] 1 S.C.R. 319 (S.C.C.).

2. *New Brunswick Broadcasting Co. v. Nova Scotia (Speaker of the House of Assembly)*, [1993] S.C.J. No. 2, [1993] 1 S.C.R. 319 at 342 (S.C.C.).

▼HCL-53▼ Boundaries of inherent privileges. Legislative bodies created by the *Constitution Act, 1867*[1] do not constitute enclaves shielded from the ordinary law of the land. The "tradition of curial deference does not extend to everything a legislative assembly might do, but is firmly attached to certain specific activities — the privileges — of legislative assemblies".[2] Privilege does not embrace and protect activities of individuals, whether members or non-members, simply because they take place within the precincts of Parliament.[3] Parliamentary privilege is the sum of the privileges, immunities and powers enjoyed by the Senate, the House of Commons and provincial legislative assemblies, and by each member individually, without which they could not discharge their functions.[4] Third, parliamentary privilege does not create a gap in the general public law of Canada but is an important part of it, inherited from the Parliament at Westminster by virtue of the preamble to the *Constitution Act, 1867*,[5] and in the case of the Canadian Parliament, through the same Act.[6]

Notes

1. (U.K.), 30 & 31 Vict., c. 3.
2. *New Brunswick Broadcasting Co. v. Nova Scotia (Speaker of the House of Assembly)*, [1993] S.C.J. No. 2, [1993] 1 S.C.R. 319 at 370-71 (S.C.C.).
3. U.K., Joint Committee on Parliamentary Privilege, *Report and Proceedings of the Committee*, vol. 1 (London: Her Majesty's Stationery Office, 1999) ("British Joint Committee Report") at para. 242.
4. Alistair Fraser, W.F. Dawson & John A. Holtby, eds., *Beauchesne's Rules & Forms of the House of Commons of Canada*, 6th ed. (Toronto: Carswell, 1989) at 11; Erskine May, *Parliamentary Practice*, 20th ed. (London: Butterworths, 1983) at 75; *New Brunswick Broadcasting Co. v. Nova Scotia (Speaker of the House of Assembly)*, [1993] S.C.J. No. 2, [1993] 1 S.C.R. 319 at 380 (S.C.C.).
5. (U.K.), 30 & 31 Vict., c. 3.
6. *Constitution Act, 1867*, (U.K.), 30 & 31 Vict., c. 3, s. 18. *New Brunswick Broadcasting Co. v. Nova Scotia (Speaker of the House of Assembly)*, [1993] S.C.J. No. 2, [1993] 1 S.C.R. 319 at 374-78 (S.C.C.); *Telezone Inc. v. Canada (Attorney General)*, [2004] O.J. No. 5, 69 O.R. (3d) 161 at 165 (Ont. C.A.); and *Samson Indian Nation and Band v. Canada*, [2003] F.C.J. No. 1238, [2004] 1 F.C.R. 556 (F.C.).

▼HCL-54▼ Determining existence of privilege. The first step in determining the existence of a privilege consists in determining whether the alleged privilege, as well as its extent, has already been authoritatively established as applying to Parliament.[1] If that is the case, there is no need to inquire as to the necessity of the claimed privilege.[2] Certain categories, like the freedom of speech in the House of Commons, the power of the House to control its procedure and debates, as well as the power of discipline over its members, have been recognized for some time as privileges required for the adequate functioning of Parliament.[3]

Notes

1. *Canada (House of Commons) v. Vaid*, [2005] S.C.J. No. 28, [2005] 1 S.C.R. 667 at para. 39 (S.C.C.); *Villeneuve v. Northwest Territories (Legislative Assembly)*, [2008] N.W.T.J. No. 40, [2008] 10 W.W.R. 704 at para. 19 (N.W.T.S.C.).
2. *Canada (House of Commons) v. Vaid*, [2005] S.C.J. No. 28, [2005] 1 S.C.R. 667 at para. 37 (S.C.C.).
3. *Canada (House of Commons) v. Vaid*, [2005] S.C.J. No. 28, [2005] 1 S.C.R. 667 at para. 29 (S.C.C.).

▼HCL-55▼ Power to enact privileges. Unlike the provinces, "the federal Parliament has an express legislative power to enact privileges which may exceed those 'inherent' in the creation of the Senate and the House of Commons, although such legislated privileges must not 'exceed' those 'enjoyed and exercised' by the U.K. House of Commons and its members at the date of the enactment".[1] Pursuant to the *Parliament of Canada Act*,[2] Parliament has exercised its powers under the *Constitution Act, 1867*[3] and has granted to the Senate and House of Commons all privileges authorized by the Constitution. Parliament has not enumerated or described what those privileges were, or what was their extent, with the exception of the reference to those privileges enjoyed by the House of Commons or the United Kingdom in 1867.[4] In order to determine whether a privilege exists or not pursuant to the *Parliament of Canada Act*,[5] a court must verify whether the existence and the extent of the privilege "have been authoritatively established in relation to our own Parliament or to the House of Commons" of the United Kingdom.[6]

Notes

1. *Canada (House of Commons) v. Vaid*, [2005] S.C.J. No. 28, [2005] 1 S.C.R. 667 at para. 33 (S.C.C.).
2. (CAN) *Parliament of Canada Act*, R.S.C. 1985, c. P-1, s. 4.
3. (U.K.), 30 & 31 Vict., c. 3.
4. *Canada (House of Commons) v. Vaid*, [2005] S.C.J. No. 28, [2005] 1 S.C.R. 667 at para. 35 (S.C.C.).

5. (CAN) R.S.C. 1985, c. P-1.
6. *Canada (House of Commons) v. Vaid*, [2005] S.C.J. No. 28, [2005] 1 S.C.R. 667 at para. 39 (S.C.C.).

▼HCL-56▼ Necessity. When a claim to privilege is relied upon to immunize a Parliamentarian, and the validity and scope of the specific privilege sought in relation to the U.K. House of Commons and its members has not been already authoritatively established, the courts will test the claim against the doctrine of necessity, the foundation of all parliamentary privileges. In making that determination, courts will owe great deference to "Parliament's view of the scope of autonomy it considers necessary to fulfill its functions".[1] As for necessity, it has been held that, while the privileges may not exceed those that existed in 1867 in the United Kingdom, the respective Parliaments are not necessarily in lock step. Parliamentary privilege is limited to the extent of what is necessary to allow and enable the House of Commons and its members to discharge their constitutional functions.

Test for necessity. "In order to sustain a claim of parliamentary privilege, the assembly or member seeking its immunity must show that the sphere of activity for which privilege is claimed is so closely and directly connected with the fulfilment by the assembly or its members of their functions as a legislative and deliberative body, including the assembly's work in holding the government to account, that outside interference would undermine the level of autonomy required to enable the assembly and its members to do their work with dignity and efficiency."[2]

Notes

1. *Canada (House of Commons) v. Vaid*, [2005] S.C.J. No. 28, [2005] 1 S.C.R. 667 at para. 40 (S.C.C.).
2. *Canada (House of Commons) v. Vaid*, [2005] S.C.J. No. 28, [2005] 1 S.C.R. 667 at para. 46 (S.C.C.).

▼HCL-57▼ Constitutional protection. The Charter[1] cannot limit or deny the application of the privileges, "on the principle that one part of the Constitution cannot abrogate another part of the Constitution".[2] Parliamentary privilege may benefit from the same constitutional status as the Charter[3] itself.[4] Moreover, given that the privileges have a constitutional status, Parliament or a legislature may only withdraw them by a constitutional act providing clearly and expressly that the privileges are to be abrogated.[5]

Notes

1. *Canadian Charter of Rights and Freedoms*, Part I of the *Constitution Act, 1982*, being Schedule B to the *Canada Act 1982* (U.K.), 1982, c. 11.
2. *New Brunswick Broadcasting Co. v. Nova Scotia (Speaker of the House of Assembly)*, [1993] S.C.J. No. 2, [1993] 1 S.C.R. 319 at 390 (S.C.C.).
3. *Canadian Charter of Rights and Freedoms*, Part I of the *Constitution Act, 1982*, being Schedule B to the *Canada Act 1982* (U.K.), 1982, c. 11.
4. *Canada (House of Commons) v. Vaid*, [2005] S.C.J. No. 28, [2005] 1 S.C.R. 667 at paras. 33-34 (S.C.C.).
5. *Canada (House of Commons) v. Vaid*, [2005] S.C.J. No. 28, [2005] 1 S.C.R. 667 at para. 26 (S.C.C.); *Duke of Newcastle v. Morris* (1870), L.R. 4 H.L. 661 (H.L.); *New Brunswick Broadcasting Co. v. Nova Scotia (Speaker of the House of Assembly)*, [1993] S.C.J. No. 2, [1993] 1 S.C.R. 319 at 374, 379-81 (S.C.C.); *Fielding v. Thomas*, [1896] A.C. 600 (P.C.).

(l) Full Faith and Credit Doctrine

▼HCL-58▼ Overview. The "full faith and credit" principle relates to the recognition and enforcement of judgments in any province of Canada, regardless of the province where the judgment was rendered. In other words, the courts of one province are under a constitutional duty to recognize the decisions of the courts of another province.[1] The faith and credit doctrine rested on the obvious intention of the Constitution to create a single country[2] and on the legal interdependence of our judicial system, as well as the federal principle "under the scheme of confederation established in 1867".[3] The necessity to recognize and enforce judgments of other provinces include the fact that the Canadian judicial structure is composed of superior court judges appointed pursuant to the *Constitution Act, 1867*,[4] and those judges have superintending control over other provincial courts and tribunals. Moreover, all judgments in Canada are "subject to the final review of the Supreme Court of Canada".[5]

Shared jurisdiction over recognition of judgments. The recognition of judgments is to a certain extent a shared jurisdiction, and a provincial legislature is not debarred from enacting any legislation that may have some effect on litigation in other provinces if it respects minimum standards of order and fairness. Thus, nothing precludes a province from legislating in the area subject except, of course, if the measure adopted is unconstitutional.[6]

Recognition of foreign judgments. The principle of international comity, as well as the prevalence of international cross-border transactions and movement called for a modernization of private international law. Therefore, the recognition and enforcement of interprovincial judgments has been expanded to foreign judgments.[7] Thus, unless the provincial legislatures adopted a different approach, the "real and substantial connection" test which applied to interprovincial judgments should also be applied to the recognition and enforcement of foreign judgments.[8]

Notes

1. *Hunt v. T&N plc*, [1993] S.C.J. No. 125, [1993] 4 S.C.R. 289 at 331 (S.C.C.).
2. *Morguard Investments Ltd. v. De Savoye*, [1990] S.C.J. No. 135, [1990] 3 S.C.R. 1077 at 1099 (S.C.C.).
3. *Hunt v. T&N plc*, [1993] S.C.J. No. 125, [1993] 4 S.C.R. 289 at 292 (S.C.C.).
4. (U.K.), 30 & 31 Vict., c. 3, s. 96.
5. *Morguard Investments Ltd. v. De Savoye*, [1990] S.C.J. No. 135, [1990] 3 S.C.R. 1077 at 1100 (S.C.C.).
6. *Hunt v. T&N plc*, [1993] S.C.J. No. 125, [1993] 4 S.C.R. 289 at 327 (S.C.C.).
7. *Morguard Investments Ltd. v. De Savoye*, [1990] S.C.J. No. 135, [1990] 3 S.C.R. 1077 (S.C.C.).
8. *Morguard Investments Ltd. v. De Savoye*, [1990] S.C.J. No. 135, [1990] 3 S.C.R. 1077 (S.C.C.).

III. Courts, Independence of Judiciary and Judicial Review

1. **Establishment of Courts** HCL-59

2. **Independence of the Judiciary**
   (1) Three Conditions for Judicial Independence........ HCL-64
   (2) Independence of Judges.. HCL-69

3. **Judicial Review**
   (1) General HCL-71
   (2) Section 96 of the *Constitution Act, 1867*.............. HCL-73
   (3) Section 101: Supreme Court, Exchequer Court and Federal Court of Canada................................ HCL-80

---

1. Establishment of Courts

▼HCL-59▼ Provincial courts. Section 92(14) of the *Constitution Act, 1867*[1] allocates to the provinces the jurisdiction to enact laws in relation to the administration of justice in the province. This includes the power to constitute, maintain and organize provincial courts of civil and of criminal jurisdiction, even if criminal law is under federal jurisdiction pursuant to s. 91(27).[2] Section 92(14) also includes the power over procedure in civil matters before those courts, and covers administration of justice and provincial jurisdiction. Courts established pursuant to provincial jurisdiction also have jurisdiction over provincial and federal statutes. On the contrary, the courts established pursuant to s. 92(14) confer jurisdiction to provincial courts over a wide range of cases regardless of whether the statute was enacted pursuant to federal or provincial jurisdiction.[3] While s. 92(14) allows provinces to establish provincial courts, s. 92(4) allows each province to enact laws for the "Establishment and Tenure of Provincial Offices and the Appointment and Payment of Provincial Officers".[4] Pursuant to this power, provinces may nominate judges to provincial courts and this power allows them to pay the judges of the provincial courts.

Notes

1. (U.K.), 30 & 31 Vict., c. 3.
2. *Constitution Act, 1867* (U.K.), 30 & 31 Vict., c. 3.

3. *Valin v. Langlois*, [1879] S.C.J. No. 2, 3. S.C.R. 1 at 19 (S.C.C.); and *Ontario (Attorney General) v. Pembina Exploration Canada Ltd.*, [1989] S.C.J. No. 9, [1989] 1 S.C.R. 206 at 217 (S.C.C.).
4. *Constitution Act, 1867* (U.K.), 30 & 31 Vict., c. 3, s. 92(14).

▼HCL-60▼ Superior courts. Section 96 of the *Constitution Act, 1867* guarantees the existence of "superior courts" as one of the ultimate safeguards of the rule of law.[1] Section 96 was designed to ensure existence of the rule of law, and the independence of the judiciary. It gives the Governor General the power to appoint all superior court judges, and "establishes the primary and specially entrenched place of the superior courts of the country in the function of interpreting and applying law".[2] Section 96 also protects "the 'core' jurisdiction of the superior courts so as to provide for some uniformity throughout the country in the judicial system".[3] The "core" jurisdiction only includes the critically important powers "which are essential to the existence of a superior court of inherent jurisdiction and to the preservation of its foundational role within our legal system".[4] The full range of powers which comprise the inherent jurisdiction of a superior court are, together, its "essential character" or "immanent attribute".[5] These "core" jurisdictions cannot be removed from the superior courts by either level of government because if they could, s. 96 could not be said either to ensure uniformity in the judicial system throughout the country or to protect the independence of the judiciary.[6]

Remuneration of superior court judges. If superior court judges are appointed by the Governor General in Council pursuant to s. 96 of the *Constitution Act, 1867*, they are also paid from the federal consolidated revenue fund, pursuant to s. 100 of the *Constitution Act, 1867*,[7] under a statute enacted by Parliament. Because the federal government is responsible for appointing and remunerating the judges of the superior courts across the country, these courts have served as a unifying force in Canada, and their constitutionally guaranteed existence "may be seen as one of the ultimate safeguards of the rule of law".[8]

Notes

1. *Constitution Act, 1867* (U.K.), 30 & 31 Vict., c. 3, s. 96; *Reference re Amendments to the Residential Tenancies Act (N.S.)*, [1996] S.C.J. No. 13, [1996] 1 S.C.R. 186 at para. 72 (S.C.C.).

2. *Reference re Amendments to the Residential Tenancies Act (N.S.)*, [1996] S.C.J. No. 13, [1996] 1 S.C.R. 186 at para. 26 (S.C.C.); citing W.R. Lederman, "The Independence of the Judiciary" (1956) 34 Can. Bar Rev. 1139 at 1178.
3. *Reference re Young Offenders Act (P.E.I.)*, [1990] S.C.J. No. 60, [1991] 1 S.C.R. 252 at 264 (S.C.C.).
4. *Reference re Amendments to the Residential Tenancies Act (N.S.)*, [1996] S.C.J. No. 13, [1996] 1 S.C.R. 186 at para. 56 (S.C.C.). See also in *MacMillan Bloedel Ltd. v. Simpson*, [1995] S.C.J. No. 101, [1995] 4 S.C.R. 725 (S.C.C.).
5. *MacMillan Bloedel Ltd. v. Simpson*, [1995] S.C.J. No. 101, [1995] 4 S.C.R. 725 at para. 30 (S.C.C.).
6. *MacMillan Bloedel Ltd. v. Simpson*, [1995] S.C.J. No. 101, [1995] 4 S.C.R. 725 at para. 15 (S.C.C.).
7. (U.K.) 30 & 31, Vict., c. 3.
8. *Reference re Amendments to the Residential Tenancies Act (N.S.)*, [1996] S.C.J. No. 13, [1996] 1 S.C.R. 186 at paras. 11 and 72 (S.C.C.).

▼HCL-61▼ Dichotomy between federal and provincial jurisdiction. This dichotomy between federal and provincial jurisdiction to constitute courts and pay judges also can create problems. The provincial authority pursuant to s. 92(14) of the *Constitution Act, 1867*[1] to constitute courts is very wide, and permits, theoretically, legislatures to create levels of courts or administrative tribunals. However, this power is subject to ss. 96 to 101 of the *Constitution Act, 1867*,[2] which protects the jurisdiction of "superior" courts. Section 92(14) and ss. 96 to 101 represent an important compromise of the Fathers of Confederation, because the intended effect of s. 96 — a unitary judicial system maintaining the rule of law — would be destroyed if a province could pass legislation creating a tribunal, appoint members thereto, and then confer on the tribunal the jurisdiction of the superior courts.[3] It follows from the constitutional status of the s. 96 superior courts that neither Parliament nor the legislatures may impair the status of "superior" courts by transferring their jurisdiction, and work, to inferior tribunals. Only the delegation of ancillary powers of the superior court, or found to be subsidiary to a valid administrative scheme or necessarily incidental to an otherwise *intra vires* legislative objective are allowed. Moreover, the attempt to delegate powers to an administrative tribunal may not be colourable as to create shadow courts and tribunals usurping the functions of the superior courts.[4] On the other hand, ss. 96 to 101 do not prevent Parliament or the legislatures from creating other courts and tribunals, provided they do not threaten the constitutional position of the s. 96 courts.[5] Section 96 should not stand in the way of new institutional, adjudicative and administrative approaches and solutions to social or political problems.[6] In fact, s. 101

was relied upon by Parliament in creating the Supreme Court of Canada in 1875, and the Exchequer Court, now known as the Federal Court of Canada.

Notes

1. (U.K.), 30 & 31, Vict., c. 3, s. 92(14).
2. (U.K.), 30 & 31, Vict., c. 3, ss. 96-101.
3. *Yeomans v. Sobeys Stores Ltd.*, [1989] S.C.J. No. 13, [1989] 1 S.C.R. 238 at 264-65 (S.C.C.); and *MacMillan Bloedel Ltd. v. Simpson*, [1995] S.C.J. No. 101, [1995] 4 S.C.R. 725 at para. 51 (S.C.C.).
4. *Reference re Amendments to the Residential Tenancies Act (N.S.)*, [1996] S.C.J. No. 13, [1996] 1 S.C.R. 186 at para. 73 (S.C.C.).
5. *MacMillan Bloedel Ltd. v. Simpson*, [1995] S.C.J. No. 101, [1995] 4 S.C.R. 725 at para. 52 (S.C.C.).
6. *Yeomans v. Sobeys Stores Ltd.*, [1989] S.C.J. No. 13, [1989] 1 S.C.R. 238 at 253 (S.C.C.).

---

2. Independence of the Judiciary

(1) Three Conditions for Judicial Independence
(a) Security of Tenure HCL-65
(b) Financial Security HCL-66
(c) Institutional Independence HCL-67
(2) Independence of Judges HCL-69

▼HCL-62▼ Overview. The principle of the independence of the judiciary[1] is implicitly found in the preamble of the *Constitution Act, 1867*.[2] The existence of this principle in English law goes back to the *Act of Settlement* of 1701. It is also explicitly referenced in ss. 96 to 100 of the *Constitution Act, 1867* and in s. 11(d) of the Charter, and is implicitly recognized as a residual right protected under s. 7 of the Charter.[3] Judicial independence is considered to be the lifeblood of constitutionalism in democratic societies,[4] is one of the original principles of the English Constitution,[5] and is of the utmost importance in protecting, preserving and promoting the rule of law. The independence of the judiciary allows the courts to act as a shield against abuses by governments of individual rights and freedoms. If it wasn't for an independent judiciary, it would be impossible to ensure that the power of the state is exercised in accordance with the Constitution and the rule of law.[6] Judicial independence also represents the cornerstone of the common-law duty of procedural fairness and is an unwritten principle of the Constitution.[7] Judicial independence "has grown into a principle that now extends to all courts, not just the superior courts of this country".[8]

Notes

1. See *Beauregard v. Canada*, [1986] S.C.J. No. 50, [1986] 2 S.C.R. 56 (S.C.C.); *R. v. Valente*, [1985] S.C.J. No. 77, [1985] 2 S.C.R. 673 (S.C.C.); *Reference re Remuneration of Judges of the Provincial Court of Prince Edward Island; Reference re Independence and Impartiality of Judges of the Provincial Court of Prince Edward Island*, [1997] S.C.J. No. 75, [1997] 3 S.C.R. 3 at paras. 84-85 (S.C.C.); *Mackin v. New Brunswick (Minister of Finance); Rice v. New Brunswick*, [2002] S.C.J. No. 13, [2002] 1 S.C.R. 405 (S.C.C.); *Ell v. Alberta*, [2003] S.C.J. No. 35, [2003] 1 S.C.R. 857 (S.C.C.); *Application under s. 83.28 of the Criminal Code (Re)*, [2004] S.C.J. No. 40, [2004] 2 S.C.R. 248 at paras. 83-92 (S.C.C.); *Provincial Court Judges' Assn. of New Brunswick v. New Brunswick (Minister of Justice)*; *Ontario Judges' Assn. v. Ontario (Management Board)*; *Bodner v. Alberta; Conférence des juges du Québec v. Quebec (Attorney General); Minc v. Quebec (Attorney General)*, [2005] S.C.J. No. 47, [2005] 2 S.C.R. 286 (S.C.C.); and *British Columbia v. Imperial Tobacco Canada Ltd.*, [2005] S.C.J. No. 50, [2005] 2 S.C.R. 473 at paras. 44-56 (S.C.C.).
2. *Beauregard v. Canada*, [1986] S.C.J. No. 50, [1986] 2 S.C.R. 56 at 72 (S.C.C.); and *Reference re Remuneration of Judges of the Provincial Court of Prince Edward Island; Reference re Independence and Impartiality of Judges of the Provincial Court of Prince Edward Island*, [1997] S.C.J. No. 75, [1997] 3 S.C.R. 3 at paras. 83 and 109 (S.C.C.). See also *Ell v. Alberta*, [2003] S.C.J. No. 35, [2003] 1 S.C.R. 857 at para. 19 (S.C.C.); and *Cooper v. Canada (Canadian Human Rights Commission)*, [1996] S.C.J. No. 115, [1996] 3 S.C.R. 854 at para. 12 (S.C.C.); *Constitution Act, 1867*, (U.K.), 30 & 31 Vict., c. 3.
3. *Application under s. 83.28 of the Criminal Code (Re)*, [2004] S.C.J. No. 40, [2004] 2 S.C.R. 248 at para. 81 (S.C.C.).
4. *Beauregard v. Canada*, [1986] S.C.J. No. 50, [1986] 2 S.C.R. 56 at 70 (S.C.C.); and *Application under s. 83.28 of the Criminal Code (Re)*, [2004] S.C.J. No. 40, [2004] 2 S.C.R. 248 at para. 80 (S.C.C.).
5. W.R. Lederman, "The Independence of the Judiciary" in Allen M. Linden, ed., *The Canadian Judiciary* (Toronto: York University Law Library, 1976) 1 at 2.
6. *Ell v. Alberta*, [2003] S.C.J. No. 35, [2003] 1 S.C.R. 857 at para. 22 (S.C.C.), *per* Major J.
7. *Reference re Remuneration of Judges of the Provincial Court of Prince Edward Island; Reference re Independence and Impartiality of Judges of the Provincial Court of Prince Edward Island*, [1997] S.C.J. No. 75, [1997] 3 S.C.R. 3 at para. 109 (S.C.C.); and *Application under s. 83.28 of the Criminal Code (Re)*, [2004] S.C.J. No. 40, [2004] 2 S.C.R. 248 at paras. 80-81 (S.C.C.).
8. *Reference re Remuneration of Judges of the Provincial Court of Prince Edward Island; Reference re Independence and Impartiality of Judges of the Provincial Court of Prince Edward Island*, [1997] S.C.J. No. 75, [1997] 3 S.C.R. 3 at para. 106 (S.C.C.).

▼HCL-63▼ Scope of judicial independence. The principles of impartiality and independence also form part the rules of natural justice in administrative law, *e.g.*, the right to a hearing before an unbiased decision-maker.[1] Historically, the requirement for judicial independence developed to demarcate the fundamental division between the judiciary and the executive. The requirement for "institutional independence" applies to courts and, in a more flexible manner, to quasi-judicial and other administrative tribunals which must function at arm's length from the executive government.[2] It protects the impartiality of judges, both in fact and perception, "by insulating them from external influence, most notably the influence of the executive".[3] While primarily having to do with independence from government, the principle has been extended also to mean independence from "any other external force, such as business or corporate interests or other pressure groups".[4] The requirement of independence has also been applied to administrative tribunals, but adapted in a flexible manner and subject to statutory direction.[5]

Notes

1. *Bell Canada v. Canadian Telephone Employees Assn.*, [1998] F.C.J. No. 313, [1998] 3 F.C. 244 (F.C.T.D.).
2. See *International Woodworkers of America, Local 2-69 v. Consolidated-Bathurst Packaging Ltd.*, [1990] S.C.J. No. 20, [1990] 1 S.C.R. 282 (S.C.C.); *Canadian Pacific Ltd. v. Matsqui Indian Band*, [1995] S.C.J. No. 1, [1995] 1 S.C.R. 3 (S.C.C.); *Katz v. Vancouver Stock Exchange*, [1996] S.C.J. No. 95, [1996] 3 S.C.R. 405 (S.C.C.); *2747-3174 Québec Inc. v. Quebec (Régie des permis d'alcool)*, [1996] S.C.J. No. 112, [1996] 3 S.C.R. 919 (S.C.C.); *Bell Canada v. Canadian Telephone Employees Assn.*, [2003] S.C.J. No. 36, [2003] 1 S.C.R. 884 (S.C.C.); and *Ocean Port Hotel Ltd. v. British Columbia (General Manager, Liquor Control and Licensing Branch)*, [2001] S.C.J. No. 17, [2001] 2 S.C.R. 781 (S.C.C.).
3. *Ocean Port Hotel Ltd. v. British Columbia (General Manager, Liquor Control and Licensing Branch)*, [2001] S.C.J. No. 17, [2001] 2 S.C.R. 781 at para. 23 (S.C.C.).
4. *R. v. Généreux*, [1992] S.C.J. No. 10, [1992] 1 S.C.R. 259 (S.C.C.); and *R. v. Lippé*, [1991] S.C.J. No. 128, [1991] 2 S.C.R. 114 (S.C.C.).
5. See *Ocean Port Hotel Ltd. v. British Columbia (General Manager, Liquor Control and Licensing Branch)*, [2001] S.C.J. No. 17, [2001] 2 S.C.R. 781 at para. 22 (S.C.C.); *Canadian Pacific Ltd. v. Matsqui Indian Band*, [1995] S.C.J. No. 1, [1995] 1 S.C.R. 3 (S.C.C.); *2747-3174 Québec Inc. v. Quebec (Régie des permis d'alcool)*, [1996] S.C.J. No. 112, [1996] 3 S.C.R. 919 (S.C.C.); and *Bell Canada v. Canadian Telephone Employees Assn.*, [2003] S.C.J. No. 36, [2003] 1 S.C.R. 884 (S.C.C.).

(1) Three Conditions for Judicial Independence

▼HCL-64▼ Overview. The three conditions for judicial independence found in ss. 96-100 of the *Constitution Act, 1867*[1] and s. 11(d) of the *Canadian Charter of Rights and Freedoms*[2] are security of tenure, financial security and institutional independence of the tribunal with regard to matters of administration bearing directly on the exercise of the judicial function. The purpose of these objective elements is to ensure that the judge can reasonably be perceived as independent and that any apprehension of bias will thus be eliminated. Independence is in short a guarantee of impartiality.[3] Historically, the principle of judicial independence represented the complete liberty of individual judges to hear and decide the cases. There is, therefore, "an individual and a collective or institutional aspect to judicial independence".[4] The independence of a particular court includes an individual dimension and an institutional dimension. The former relates especially to the person of the judge and involves his or her independence from any other entity, whereas the latter relates to the court to which the judge belongs and involves its independence from the executive and legislative branches of the government.[5] The status of a tribunal must guarantee not only its freedom from interference by the executive and legislative branches of government but also by any other external force, such as business or corporate interests or other pressure groups.[6]

Notes

1. (U.K.), 30 & 31 Vict., c. 3, ss. 96-100.
2. *Canadian Charter of Rights and Freedoms*, Part I of the *Constitution Act, 1982*, being Schedule B to the *Canada Act 1982* (U.K.), 1982, c. 11, s. 11(d).
3. *Beauregard v. Canada*, [1986] S.C.J. No. 50, [1986] 2 S.C.R. 56 at 69 (S.C.C.). See also *2747-3174 Québec Inc. v. Quebec (Régie des permis d'alcool)*, [1996] S.C.J. No. 112, [1996] 3 S.C.R. 919 at para. 61 (S.C.C.).
4. *Beauregard v. Canada*, [1986] S.C.J. No. 50, [1986] 2 S.C.R. 56 at 70 (S.C.C.).
5. *Mackin v. New Brunswick (Minister of Finance); Rice v. New Brunswick*, [2002] S.C.J. No. 13, [2002] 1 S.C.R. 405 at paras. 39-40 (S.C.C.).
6. *R. v. Généreux*, [1992] S.C.J. No. 10, [1992] 1 S.C.R. 259 at 283-84 (S.C.C.). See also *Canadian Pacific Ltd. v. Matsqui Indian Band*, [1995] S.C.J. No. 1, [1995] 1 S.C.R. 3 at para. 62 (S.C.C.), *Mackin v. New Brunswick (Minister of Finance); Rice v. New Brunswick*, [2002] S.C.J. No. 13, [2002] 1 S.C.R. 405 at para. 38 (S.C.C.).

(a) Security of Tenure

▼HCL-65▼ Overview. The essentials of security of tenure for purposes of s. 11(d) of the Charter[1] are that the judge be removable only for cause, and that cause be subject to independent review and determination by a process at which the judge affected is afforded a full opportunity to be heard. The essence of security of tenure for purposes of s. 11(d) of the Charter is a tenure, whether until an age of retirement, for a fixed term, or for a specific adjudicative task, that is secure against interference by the Executive or other appointing authority in a discretionary or arbitrary manner.[2] In order for the individual dimension of security of tenure to be constitutionally protected, it was sufficient that a judge could be removed from office only for a reason relating to his or her capacity to perform his or her judicial duties. Any arbitrary removal is accordingly prohibited.[3]

Tenure of Superior Court Judges. Section 99 of the *Constitution Act, 1867*[4] guarantees the tenure of judges of the superior courts. Pursuant to the Act, a judge will hold office during good behaviour, but may be removable by the Governor in Council on address of the Senate and the House of Commons. That section only applies to superior courts, as provincial court judges are regulated by provincial law.

Notes

1. *Canadian Charter of Rights and Freedoms*, Part I of the *Constitution Act, 1982*, being Schedule B to the *Canada Act 1982* (U.K.), 1982, c. 11, s. 11(d).
2. *R. v. Valente*, [1985] S.C.J. No. 77, [1985] 2 S.C.R. 673 at 698 (S.C.C.).
3. *Mackin v. New Brunswick (Minister of Finance); Rice v. New Brunswick*, [2002] S.C.J. No. 13, [2002] 1 S.C.R. 405 at paras. 42-44 (S.C.C.).
4. (U.K.), 30 & 31 Vict., c. 3, s. 99.

(b) Financial Security

▼HCL-66▼ Overview. The second essential condition of judicial independence for purposes of s. 11(d) of the Charter[1] is financial security. That means security of salary or other remuneration, and, where appropriate, security of pension. The essence of such security is that the right to salary and pension should be established by law and not be subject to arbitrary interference by the Executive in a manner that could affect judicial independence.[2] In the case of pension, the essential distinction is between a right to a pension and a pension that depends on the grace or favour of the Executive. Each of the elements of financial independence at the institutional level results from the constitutional imperative that, as far as possible, the relationship between the judiciary and the other two branches of government should be depoliticized.[3]

Salary of provincial court judges. Provincial court judges may be reasonably perceived to have the essential security of salary required for independence within the meaning of s. 11(d) of the Charter.[4] The essential point is that the right to salary of a provincial court judge is established by law, and there is no way in which the Executive could interfere with that right in a manner to affect the independence of the individual judge.

Notes

1. *Canadian Charter of Rights and Freedoms*, Part I of the *Constitution Act, 1982*, being Schedule B to the *Canada Act 1982* (U.K.), 1982, c. 11, s. 11(d).
2. *Mackin v. New Brunswick (Minister of Finance); Rice v. New Brunswick*, [2002] S.C.J. No. 13, [2002] 1 S.C.R. 405 at paras. 51 and 54 (S.C.C.).
3. *Mackin v. New Brunswick (Minister of Finance); Rice v. New Brunswick*, [2002] S.C.J. No. 13, [2002] 1 S.C.R. 405 at paras. 51 and 54 (S.C.C.).
4. *R. v. Valente*, [1985] S.C.J. No. 77, [1985] 2 S.C.R. 673 at 706 (S.C.C.).

(c) Institutional Independence

▼HCL-67▼ Institutional independence. The third essential condition of judicial independence for purposes of s. 11(d) of the Charter[1] is the institutional independence of the tribunal with respect to matters of administration bearing directly on the exercise of its judicial function. Judicial control over assignment of judges, sittings of the court, and court lists as well as the related matters of allocation of court rooms and direction of the administrative staff engaged in carrying out these functions, has generally been considered the essential or minimum requirement for institutional or "collective" independence.[2] Institutional independence of the judiciary arises out of the position of the courts as organs of and protectors of the Constitution and the fundamental values embodied in it — rule of law, fundamental justice, equality, preservation of the democratic process.[3] The test of the independence of the judiciary was whether an informed person viewing the matter realistically and practically would have a reasonable apprehension of bias.[4]

Notes

1. *Canadian Charter of Rights and Freedoms*, Part I of the *Constitution Act, 1982* being Schedule B to the *Canada Act 1982* (U.K.), 1982, c. 11, s. 11(d).
2. *R. v. Valente*, [1985] S.C.J. No. 77, [1985] 2 S.C.R. 673 at 708 and 709 (S.C.C.).
3. *Reference re Remuneration of Judges of the Provincial Court of Prince Edward Island; Reference re Independence and Impartiality of Judges of the Provincial Court of Prince Edward Island*, [1997] S.C.J. No. 75, [1997] 3 S.C.R. 3 at para 123 (S.C.C.), citing *Beauregard v. Canada*, [1986] S.C.J. No. 50, [1986] 2 S.C.R 56 at 70 (S.C.C.).
4. See also *Committee for Justice and Liberty v. Canada (National Energy Board)* [1976] S.C.J. No. 118, [1978] 1 S.C.R. 369 at 394 (S.C.C.), applied in *R. v. Bain* [1992] S.C.J. No. 3, [1992] 1 S.C.R. 91 (S.C.C.); *Newfoundland Telephone Co. v Newfoundland (Board of Commissioners of Public Utilities)*, [1992] S.C.J. No. 21 [1992] 1 S.C.R. 623 (S.C.C.); *Idziak v. Canada (Minister of Justice)*, [1992] S.C.J No. 97, [1992] 3 S.C.R. 631 (S.C.C.); and *Ruffo v. Conseil de la magistrature* [1995] S.C.J. No. 100, [1995] 4 S.C.R. 267 (S.C.C.).

▼HCL-68▼ Independence of judiciary of all courts. In 1982 with the adoption of the *Canadian Charter of Rights and Freedoms*,[1] s. 11(d) protected the independence of judiciary. However, that independence was guaranteed only in the criminal jurisdiction, as s. 11(d) of the Charter specifically applied to an accused person.[2] The Supreme Court of Canada extended this protection to all judges of every court, as the Constitution contained an unwritten principle providing that the independence of judges was guaranteed in all courts regardless of the underlying issues they were deciding.[3] Consequently, judicial independence is guaranteed at all levels of courts, and includes security of tenure, financial security and administrative freedom from the executive branch of government.[4] The Supreme Court confirmed that this unwritten principle applied to all courts no matter which cases they heard.[5]

Notes

1. Part I of the *Constitution Act, 1982*, being Schedule B to the *Canada Act 1982* (U.K.), 1982, c. 11, s. 11(d).
2. *Canadian Charter of Rights and Freedoms*, Part I of the *Constitution Act, 1982*, being Schedule B to the *Canada Act 1982* (U.K.), 1982, c. 11, s. 11(d).
3. *Reference re Remuneration of Judges of the Provincial Court of Prince Edward Island; Reference re Independence and Impartiality of Judges of the Provincial Court of Prince Edward Island*, [1997] S.C.J. No. 75, [1997] 3 S.C.R. 3 at paras. 106-107 (S.C.C.).
4. *R. v. Valente*, [1985] S.C.J. No. 77, [1985] 2 S.C.R. 673 (S.C.C.); and *Reference re Remuneration of Judges of the Provincial Court of Prince Edward Island*,

Reference re Independence and Impartiality of Judges of the Provincial Court of Prince Edward Island, [1997] S.C.J. No. 75, [1997] 3 S.C.R. 3 (S.C.C.).

5. *Reference re Remuneration of Judges of the Provincial Court of Prince Edward Island; Reference re Independence and Impartiality of Judges of the Provincial Court of Prince Edward Island*, [1997] S.C.J. No. 75, [1997] 3 S.C.R. 3 at paras. 106-107 (S.C.C.).

---

(2) Independence of Judges

▼HCL-69▼ Independence of inferior court judges. The independence of provincial court judges is not specifically guaranteed by the Constitution. Section 99 of the *Constitution Act, 1867*[1] protects the tenure and independence of superior court judges and s. 11(d) of the Charter[2] confirms the same for any tribunal executing criminal jurisdiction. Consequently, inferior court judges are not explicitly included by those provisions unless they are performing a criminal jurisdiction. The issue in *Re Remuneration of Judges*[3] turned on the guarantee of independence of those judges exercising civil jurisdictions while sitting on a provincial or an "inferior" court. In that case, the Supreme Court of Canada extended this protection to all judges of every court, as the Constitution contained an "unwritten" principle providing that the independence of judges was guaranteed on all courts regardless of the underlying issue they were deciding.[4] Consequently, judicial independence is guaranteed at all levels of courts, and includes security of tenure, financial security and administrative freedom from the executive branch of government.[5]

Notes

1. (U.K.), 30 & 31 Vict., c. 3, s. 99.
2. *Canadian Charter of Rights and Freedoms*, Part I of the *Constitution Act, 1982*, being Schedule B to the *Canada Act 1982* (U.K.), 1982, c. 11, s. 11(d).
3. *Reference re Remuneration of Judges of the Provincial Court of Prince Edward Island; Reference re Independence and Impartiality of Judges of the Provincial Court of Prince Edward Island*, [1997] S.C.J. No. 75, [1997] 3 S.C.R. 3 (S.C.C.).
4. *Reference re Remuneration of Judges of the Provincial Court of Prince Edward Island; Reference re Independence and Impartiality of Judges of the Provincial Court of Prince Edward Island*, [1997] S.C.J. No. 75, [1997] 3 S.C.R. 3 at paras. 106-107 (S.C.C.).
5. *R. v. Valente*, [1985] S.C.J. No. 77, [1985] 2 S.C.R. 673 (S.C.C.); and *Reference re Remuneration of Judges of the Provincial Court of Prince Edward Island; Reference re Independence and Impartiality of Judges of the Provincial Court of Prince Edward Island*, [1997] S.C.J. No. 75, [1997] 3 S.C.R. 3 (S.C.C.).

▼HCL-70▼ Independence of military court judges. The principle of the independence of the judiciary also applies to military courts. In *R. v. Généreux*,[1] the Supreme Court confirmed that the principle of judicial independence applied to a Court Martial under the *National Defence Act*.[2] In trying a member of the armed forces, a Court Martial was an independent and impartial tribunal pursuant to s. 11(d) of the Charter.[3]

Notes

1. [1992] S.C.J. No. 10, [1992] 1 S.C.R. 259 (S.C.C.).
2. (CAN) R.S.C. 1985, c. N-5.
3. *Canadian Charter of Rights and Freedoms*, Part I of the *Constitution Act, 1982* being Schedule B to the *Canada Act 1982* (U.K.), 1982, c. 11, s. 11(d).

---

3. Judicial Review

(1) General HCL-71
(2) Section 96 of the *Constitution Act, 1867* HCL-73
(a) Whether Power Conforms to Required Jurisdiction .... HCL- 75
(i) Characterization of the Power HCL-76
(ii) Three Preliminary Questions HCL-77
(b) Whether a "Judicial" Function HCL-78
(c) Whether Function "Merely Ancillary" HCL-79
(3) Section 101: Supreme Court, Exchequer Court and Federal Court of Canada HCL-80
(a) Test for Federal Court Jurisdiction
(i) Statutory Grant of Jurisdiction HCL-82
(ii) Existing Body of Federal Law HCL-83
(iii) Whether a "Law of Canada" HCL-85

---

(1) General

▼HCL-71▼ Overview. Judicial review is the procedure allowing superior courts to look at a decision of a public body and determine if the decision is within the scope of the power delegated to it by Parliament or a provincial legislature. The inherent power of superior courts to review administrative action is constitutionally protected by ss. 96 to 101 of the *Constitution Act, 1867*.[1] The result of this combination is that administrative action may sometimes not be appealed, but may always be judicially reviewed by the courts of inherent jurisdiction. Judicial review is rooted in the basic tenets of constitutional law as a consequence of the relationship between the principles of parliamentary sovereignty, the *rule of law*, and the inherent power of the courts to review the legality of actions in order to maintain an adequate balance between these two principles. "Judicial review seeks to address an underlying tension between the rule of law and the foundational democratic principle, which finds an expression in the initiatives of Parliament and legislatures to create various administrative bodies and endow them with broad powers."[2]

Notes

1. (U.K.), 30 & 31 Vict., c. 3, ss. 96-101; *Crevier v. Québec (Attorney General)*, [1981] S.C.J. No. 80, [1981] 2 S.C.R 220 (S.C.C.); and *Union des employés de service, local 298 v. Bibeault*, [1988] S.C.J. No. 101, [1988] 2 S.C.R. 1048 (S.C.C.).
2. *Dunsmuir v. New Brunswick*, [2008] S.C.J. No. 9, [2008] 1 S.C.R. 190 at para. 27 (S.C.C.).

▼HCL-72▼ Review of administrative actions. Parliament or the legislature may, for purposes of expertise, economy, efficiency or other *bona fide* reasons, intend to preclude any right to appeal any administrative decision to the superior courts. However, judicial review allows superior courts, entrusted with an "inherent" jurisdiction under the rule of law to supervise the legality of any action, to perform its supervisory function and even quash decisions that are *ultra vires*. Intervention is thus possible, on judicial review, even where a strong privative clause was put in place by the legislature. As guardian of the rule of law and legislative supremacy, superior courts cannot have their authority diminished by any legislative attempt to shield an administrative decision from their supervisory powers. The inherent power of superior courts to review administrative action is constitutionally protected by ss. 96 to 101 of the *Constitution Act, 1867*.[1] The result of this combination is that administrative action may sometimes not be appealed, but may always be judicially reviewed by the courts of inherent jurisdiction.

Note

1. (U.K.), 30 & 31 Vict., c. 3, ss. 96-101.

---

(2) Section 96 of the *Constitution Act, 1867*

▼HCL-73▼ Superior courts. Section 92(14) of the *Constitution Act, 1867*[1] grants the provinces the jurisdiction to constitute, maintain and administer courts in the province. However, this power is subject to ss. 96 to 101 of the *Constitution Act, 1867*,[2] in the sense that the creation by provinces of provincial courts, or administrative tribunals for that matter, cannot have the effect of negating the effect of s. 96 of the *Constitution Act, 1867*[3] and impair the status of superior courts by transferring their work to inferior tribunals. The same issue applies, to a certain extent, to federal administrative tribunals even if the federal administrative decision-makers are appointed by the Governor in Council, the same authority that appoints judges pursuant to s. 96 of the *Constitution Act, 1867*.[4] Nevertheless, these decision-makers do not benefit from any protection in their tenure or the same extent of judicial independence. That power enjoyed by superior courts at Confederation could be removed and conferred to inferior courts or administrative tribunals, provided that those jurisdictions were also the type generally exercised by courts of summary jurisdiction.[5]

Notes

1. (U.K.), 30 & 31 Vict., c. 3, s. 92(14).
2. (U.K.), 30 & 31 Vict., c. 3, ss. 96-101.
3. (U.K.), 30 & 31 Vict., c. 3, s. 96.
4. (U.K.), 30 & 31 Vict., c. 3, s. 96.
5. *Reference re: Adoption Act*, [1938] S.C.J. No. 21, [1938] S.C.R. 398 at 418 and 421 (S.C.C.), *per* Duff C.J.

▼HCL-74▼ Three-step test. The leading case on s. 96 of the *Constitution Act, 1867*[1] and its impact on federal and provincial administrative tribunals is *Reference re Residential Tenancies Act, 1979*.[2] The case sets out a three-step test[3] in order to determine whether legislation that confers adjudicative functions to a provincial administrative tribunal is unconstitutional in that it delegates to an "inferior court" a jurisdiction exercised by a s. 96[4] court at Confederation.

Notes

1. (U.K.), 30 & 31 Vict., c. 3, s. 96.
2. [1981] S.C.J. No. 57, [1981] 1 S.C.R. 714 (S.C.C.).

3. *Reference re: Adoption Act*, [1938] S.C.J. No. 21, [1938] S.C.R. 398 (S.C.C.); *Labour Relations Board of Saskatchewan v. John East Iron Works, Ltd.*, [1949] A.C. 134 (P.C.); and *Tomko v. Nova Scotia (Labour Relations Board)*, [1975] S.C.J. No. 111, [1977] 1 S.C.R. 112 (S.C.C.).
4. *Constitution Act, 1867* (U.K.), 30 & 31 Vict., c. 3, s. 96.

(a) Whether Power Conforms to Required Jurisdiction

▼HCL-75▼ First step. The first step of the test is to consider "whether the power or jurisdiction conforms to the ... jurisdiction exercised by superior, district or county courts at the time of Confederation".[1] If the historical evidence indicates that, at Confederation, the power in question was exercised exclusively by a superior or court of the *Constitution Act, 1867*,[2] then it is necessary to proceed to the second step of the inquiry. If the power is not one that was exercised exclusively by a superior court, then there is no constitutional impediment to the statutory delegation.

Notes

1. *Reference re Residential Tenancies Act, 1979*, [1981] S.C.J. No. 57, [1981] 1 S.C.R. 714 (S.C.C.).
2. (U.K.), 30 & 31 Vict., c. 3, s. 96.

(i) Characterization of the Power

▼HCL-76▼ Power or jurisdiction at issue. Before embarking into the first part of the three-step test, one must properly characterize the contentious power or jurisdiction at issue exercised by the administrative tribunal, and determine whether this authority had to be exercised exclusively by a section 96 court at Confederation. In characterizing the delegated jurisdiction, general statutory principles of interpretation apply. The essential test is to ask the question as to whether "the challenged power or jurisdiction broadly conform[s] to the power or jurisdiction exercised by Superior, District or County Courts".[1] Like any other constitutional provision, however, the general principle for the interpretation of s. 96 of the *Constitution Act, 1867*[2] remains the same: "Notwithstanding the importance of s. 96 in its institutional context (*i.e.*, the protection of the independence and the 'core' jurisdiction of superior courts), [it is] recognized that a constitution is a 'living tree' which must be capable of accommodating new areas and new interests. Consequently, a flexible approach has been adopted in determining when judicial power may be transferred to inferior courts and tribunals."[3]

Notes

1. *Massey-Ferguson Industries Ltd. v. Government of Saskatchewan*, [1981] S.C.J. No. 90, [1981] 2 S.C.R. 413 at 429 (S.C.C.), *per* Laskin C.J.; *Re: Family Relations Act (B.C.)*, [1982] S.C.J. No. 112, [1982] 1 S.C.R. 62 at 104 (S.C.C.), *per* Estey J.
2. *Constitution Act, 1867* (U.K.), 30 & 31 Vict., c. 3, s. 96.
3. *Reference re Amendments to the Residential Tenancies Act (N.S.)*, [1996] 1 S.C.R. 186 at para. 27. See also *Reference re: Adoption Act*, [1938] S.C.J. No. 21, [1938] S.C.R. 398 (S.C.C.); *Labour Relations Board of Saskatchewan v. John East Iron Works, Ltd.*, [1949] A.C. 134 (P.C.); *Renvoi re: Juridiction de la Cour de Magistrat (Loi Concernant) (Québec)*, 55 D.L.R. (2d) 701, [1965] S.C.R. 772 (S.C.C.); *Reference Re Residential Tenancies Act, 1979*, [1981] S.C.J. No. 57 [1981] 1 S.C.R. 714 (S.C.C.); *Reference re Family Relations Act*, [1982] S.C.J. No. 112, [1982] 1 S.C.R. 62 at 112-13 (S.C.C.).

(ii) Three Preliminary Questions

▼HCL-77▼ Preliminary questions. There are three preliminary questions to help in characterizing the power:

(1) How broadly should the power or jurisdiction be characterized for purposes of the historical analysis?
(2) Do the words "broadly conform" to Superior Court jurisdiction mean that such jurisdiction must have been exclusive to those courts at Confederation?
(3) Should the court look only at the jurisdiction of the courts of the province in which the case arose or should the inquiry embrace all or most of the provinces?[1]

As for the first question, "while the jurisdiction of the inferior courts will not be frozen as of the date of Confederation, neither will it be substantially expanded so as to undermine the independence of the judiciary which s. 96 protects".[2] As for the second preliminary question, for the delegation of jurisdiction to an "inferior" court or tribunal to be unconstitutional, it must have been exercised exclusively by the superior courts at Confederation.[3] In determining this question, however, the focus must not be overly technical, and minor concurrency in subsidiary aspects of the power may be insufficient to negate the fact that the type of dispute fell principally within the purview of the superior courts.[4] Clearly, s. 96 of the *Constitution Act, 1867*[5] will be violated if provincial tribunals are delegated a jurisdiction that belonged exclusively to s. 96 courts at Confederation. It is equally clear that there will be no violation if the power was exclusive to the inferior courts. The difficulty arises when a jurisdiction was shared or concurrent between the two levels of court. Lastly, the third question suggests that consistency at the level of historical analysis would seem to be desirable and that it is best achieved by measuring each s. 96 challenge against the same historical yardstick and therefore, the test at this stage should be national, not provincial.[6]

Notes

1. *Yeomans v. Sobeys Stores Ltd.*, [1989] S.C.J. No. 13, [1989] 1 S.C.R. 238 at 251-52 (S.C.C.).
2. *Yeomans v. Sobeys Stores Ltd.*, [1989] S.C.J. No. 13, [1989] 1 S.C.R. 238 at 253 (S.C.C.); *Reference re: Adoption Act*, [1938] S.C.J. No. 21, [1938] S.C.R. 398 (S.C.C.); *Reference re Family Relations Act*, [1982] S.C.J. No. 112, [1982] 1 S.C.R. 62 at 68 (S.C.C.); *Séminaire de Chicoutimi v. Quebec (Attorney General)*, [1972] S.C.J. No. 99, [1973] S.C.R. 681 (S.C.C.); *Renvoi re: Juridiction de la Cour de Magistrat (Loi Concernant) (Québec)*, [1965] S.C.R. 772, 55 D.L.R. (2d) 701 (S.C.C.); and *Canadian Broadcasting Corp. v. Quebec (Police Commission)*, [1979] S.C.J. No. 60, [1979] 2 S.C.R. 618 (S.C.C.).
3. *Yeomans v. Sobeys Stores Ltd.*, [1989] S.C.J. No. 13, [1989] 1 S.C.R. 238 at 256 (S.C.C.).
4. *Reference re Amendments to the Residential Tenancies Act (N.S.)*, [1996] S.C.J. No. 13, [1996] 1 S.C.R. 186 at para. 77 (S.C.C.); and *Yeomans v. Sobeys Stores Ltd.*, [1989] S.C.J. No. 13, [1989] 1 S.C.R. 238 at 255 (S.C.C.).
5. *Constitution Act, 1867* (U.K.), 30 & 31 Vict., c. 3, s. 96.
6. *Yeomans v. Sobeys Stores Ltd.*, [1989] S.C.J. No. 13, [1989] 1 S.C.R. 238 at 256 (S.C.C.).

(b) Whether a "Judicial" Function

▼HCL-78▼ Second step. The second step in the *Residential Tenancies* analysis is to determine whether the function of the provincial tribunal within its institutional setting is a "judicial" function.[1] The first issue to consider here is the nature of the question which the tribunal must decide. Usually, its function will be judicial if it is faced with the adjudication of private disputes through the "application of a recognized body of rules in a manner consistent with fairness and impartiality".[2] On the other hand, if the tribunal assesses broader policy concerns and considers polycentric issues in its decision-making process, the tribunal will likely be considered not to be exercising a judicial function. If the power is not a judicial one, then that is the end of the inquiry and the provincial administrative tribunal will be constitutionally valid.

Notes

1. *Reference re: Residential Tenancies Act, 1979 (Ontario)*, [1981] S.C.J. No. 57, [1981] 1 S.C.R. 714 (S.C.C.).
2. See *Reference re: Residential Tenancies Act, 1979 (Ontario)*, [1981] S.C.J. No. 57, [1981] 1 S.C.R. 714 at 735 (S.C.C.).

(c) Whether Function "Merely Ancillary"

▼HCL-79▼ Third step. If the power is a judicial one, it is necessary to proceed to the third step of the *Residential Tenancies* analysis which involves the determination of whether the s. 96 power of the *Constitution Act, 1867*[1] in question is either subsidiary or ancillary to a predominantly administrative function or necessarily incidental to the overall functions of the tribunal.[2] The third part of the test requires a consideration of the "context" in which this power is exercised. While it is possible for administrative tribunals to exercise powers and jurisdiction which were once exercised by the s. 96 courts, the impugned "judicial powers" must be merely subsidiary or ancillary[3] or necessarily incidental[4] to the achievement of a broader policy objective assigned to the tribunal by the legislature. The delegation will only be invalid if the adjudicative, or judicial function of the administrative tribunal is a sole or central function of the tribunal.[5] If it can be determined that the power, in its institutional setting, is ancillary or necessary to the policy objective of the scheme in which it is exercised, the power will have changed its character sufficiently to negate the broad conformity with superior court jurisdiction.[6] In other words, the judicial aspect will have changed colour when considered in the factual setting in which the court will operate.[7] The derogation from s. 96 powers established by the first and second inquiries of the test is validated by its administrative function. In such circumstances, there can be no fear that the constitutional status of the s. 96 courts will be threatened, as a tribunal exercising a judicial power ancillary or necessary to a broader administrative scheme is still performing an administrative function[8] and is not "acting like a court".[9]

Rationale for third part of test. The rationale for this third step is that, in determining the true character of a statute, one must focus on its essence or "pith and substance". Therefore, where the pith and substance of a legislation is valid, or in this case, where a delegation of power, in its pith and substance, does not trump superior court jurisdictions, the delegation remains valid despite minor incidental or ancillary intrusions on s. 96 jurisdictions. Consequently, even if an administrative tribunal is authorized to do what would otherwise be considered to be a s. 96 power, the scheme will be valid if it is fundamentally administrative, even if some processes are judicial in nature.

Notes

1. *Constitution Act, 1867* (U.K.), 30 & 31 Vict., c. 3, s. 96.
2. *Reference re: Residential Tenancies Act, 1979 (Ontario)*, [1981] S.C.J. No. 57, [1981] 1 S.C.R. 714 at 733-34 (S.C.C.); and *MacMillan Bloedel Ltd. v. Simpson*, [1995] S.C.J. No. 101, [1995] 4 S.C.R. 725 at paras. 62-65 (S.C.C.).
3. *Labour Relations Board of Saskatchewan v. John East Iron Works, Ltd.* (1948), [1949] A.C. 134 (P.C.); and *Tomko v. Nova Scotia (Labour Relations Board)*, [1976] S.C.J. No. 111, [1977] 1 S.C.R. 112 (S.C.C.).
4. *Mississauga (City) v. Peel (Regional Municipality)*, [1979] S.C.J. No. 46, [1979] 2 S.C.R. 244 (S.C.C.).
5. *Farrah v. Quebec (Attorney General)*, [1978] S.C.J. No. 24, [1978] 2 S.C.R. 638 (S.C.C.). See also *Reference re: Residential Tenancies Act, 1979 (Ontario)*, [1981] S.C.J. No. 57, [1981] 1 S.C.R. 714 at 735-36 (S.C.C.).
6. *MacMillan Bloedel Ltd. v. Simpson*, [1995] S.C.J. No. 101, [1995] 4 S.C.R. 725 at para. 64 (S.C.C.); Peter W. Hogg, *Constitutional Law of Canada*, 5th ed., looseleaf (Toronto: Carswell, 2007) at 7-48 to 7-52; and John M. Evans, "Administrative Tribunals and Charter Challenges" (1989) 2 Can. J. Admin. L. & Prac. 13 at 36.
7. *McEvoy v. New Brunswick (Attorney General)*, [1983] S.C.J. No. 51, [1983] 1 S.C.R. 704 at 717 (S.C.C.).
8. *MacMillan Bloedel Ltd. v. Simpson*, [1995] S.C.J. No. 101, [1995] 4 S.C.R. 725 at paras. 64-65 (S.C.C.).
9. *Reference re: Residential Tenancies Act, 1979 (Ontario)*, [1981] S.C.J. No. 57, [1981] 1 S.C.R. 714 at 733-34 (S.C.C.).

---

(3) Section 101: Supreme Court, Exchequer Court and Federal Court of Canada

▼HCL-80▼ Section 101 of the *Constitution Act, 1867*. Pursuant to s. 101 of the *Constitution Act, 1867*,[1] Parliament may establish a general court of appeal for Canada, as well as "additional Courts for the better administration of the Laws of Canada".[2] Section 101 was used for the first time to create the Supreme Court of Canada, in 1875, as a general court of appeal of Canada as provided by the first branch of s. 101. At the same time, Parliament created an additional court, the Exchequer Court of Canada, and gave it jurisdiction over revenue and the Crown in right of Canada.[3] The Exchequer Court's jurisdiction was later expanded to include copyrights, trade marks, patents, admiralty, tax, and citizenship, and was later continued as the Federal Court of Canada. While the jurisdiction of the Supreme Court of Canada is plenary, in the sense that it is the final court of appeal in Canada for any type of litigation, the Federal Court's jurisdiction is limited by statute, and does not possess any inherent jurisdiction.

Notes

1. (U.K.), 30 & 31 Vict., c. 3, s. 101.
2. (U.K.), 30 & 31 Vict., c. 3, s. 101.
3. See (CAN) *Supreme and Exchequer Court Act*, S.C. 1875, c. 11; also quoted in *Canada (Human Rights Commission) v. Canadian Liberty Net*, [1998] S.C.J. No. 31, [1998] 1 S.C.R. 626 at para. 28 (S.C.C.).

(a) Test for Federal Court Jurisdiction

▼HCL-81▼ Test for Federal Court jurisdiction. There are three fundamental requirements for establishing Federal Court jurisdiction. There must be a statutory grant of jurisdiction by Parliament, there must be an existing body of federal law which is essential to the disposition of the case and which nourishes the statutory grant of jurisdiction and the law on which the case is based must be a "Law of Canada" as the phrase is used in s. 101 of the *Constitution Act, 1867.*[1]

Note

1. *Constitution Act, 1867* (U.K.), 30 & 31 Vict., c. 3, s. 101.

(i) Statutory Grant of Jurisdiction

▼HCL-82▼ Statutory grant of jurisdiction by Parliament. Since the Federal Court possesses no inherent and general jurisdiction, there must be a specific statutory conferral of jurisdiction in relation to the particular subject-matter by Parliament to the Court. This is currently achieved through the *Federal Courts Act*[1] itself or another federal statute. Notably, the Federal Court is not a court of general jurisdiction of federal matters.[2] However, any jurisdiction conferred must be interpreted broadly,[3] and may be given implied jurisdiction to the extent that the existence and exercise of such powers are necessary for the Court to exercise fully the jurisdiction expressly conferred.[4] This requirement is exactly the opposite of provincial superior courts, which have a presumed jurisdiction, unless removed explicitly by statute.

Notes

1. (CAN) R.S.C. 1985, c. F-7.
2. *Ordon Estate v. Grail*, [1998] S.C.J. No. 84, [1998] 3 S.C.R. 437 at para. 46 (S.C.C.); and *Roberts v. Canada*, [1989] S.C.J. No. 16, [1989] 1 S.C.R. 322 at 331 (S.C.C.).
3. *Canada (Human Rights Commission) v. Canadian Liberty Net*, [1998] S.C.J. No. 31, [1998] 1 S.C.R. 626 at 657-58 (S.C.C.).
4. *New Brunswick (Electric Power Commission) v. Maritime Electric Co.*, [1985] S.C.J. No. 93, [1985] 2 F.C. 13 at 25 (Fed. C.A.), leave to appeal refused [1985] S.C.C.A. No. 314, [1985] S.C.R. ix (S.C.C.). See also David Sgayias *et al.*, *Federal Court Practice* (Toronto: Carswell, 2004) at 4.

(ii) Existing Body of Federal Law

▼HCL-83▼ Grant of jurisdiction by federal law. The statutory grant of jurisdiction must be "nourished" by an existing body of federal law which is essential to the disposition of the case. This requirement stems from the wording of s. 101 of the *Constitution Act, 1867*,[1] requiring that additional courts be created for the better administration of the "Laws of Canada". Therefore, not only must the Federal Court of Canada be granted jurisdiction by an Act, but it must be over another Act. This requirement is met if the subject-matter of the court's jurisdiction is over a federal statute, over regulations or other delegated powers, and even over the administration of federal laws.[2]

Notes

1. (U.K.) 30 & 31 Vict., c. 3, s. 101.
2. *Tétrault-Gadoury v. Canada (Employment & Immigration Commission)*, [1991] S.C.J. No. 41, [1991] 2 S.C.R. 22 at 37-38 (S.C.C.). See also *Canada (Attorney General) v. Law Society of British Columbia*, [1982] S.C.J. No. 70, [1982] 2 S.C.R. 307 at 326-28 (S.C.C.).

▼HCL-84▼ Constitution of Canada. As for the Constitution of Canada, provincial superior court jurisdiction to consider constitutional questions could not be removed and transferred exclusively to the Federal Court.[1] The Federal Court could consider the constitutional validity or applicability of a federal statute. The Federal Court does possess the jurisdiction to consider constitutional questions, at least insofar as the constitutionality relates to the context of the execution and administration of a federal statute. However, it remains open whether the Federal Court has jurisdiction to determine the constitutionality of federal statutes, not as a threshold question of an administrative proceeding but in a vacuum without express jurisdiction to do so. Surely a provincial superior court may make those determinations and declare statutes to be unconstitutional, and that power cannot be removed from them or granted solely to the Federal Court.[2] The Federal Court's jurisdiction over that type of question must always be a part of an administrative matter. Proceedings for a bare declaration of unconstitutionality, absent an administrative matter, should be brought before provincial superior courts because they would be founded on the *Constitution Act, 1867*[3] or the Charter,[4] which are not federal statutes.

Notes

1. *Canada (Attorney General) v. Law Society of British Columbia*, [1982] S.C.J. No. 70, [1982] 2 S.C.R. 307 at 326-29 (S.C.C.).
2. *Canada (Attorney General) v. Law Society of British Columbia*, [1982] S.C.J. No. 70, [1982] 2 S.C.R. 307 at 326-29 (S.C.C.); and *Canada (Labour Relations Board) v. Paul L'Anglais Inc.*, [1983] S.C.J. No. 12, [1983] 1 S.C.R. 147 at 153-62 (S.C.C.).
3. (U.K.), 30 & 31 Vict., c. 3.
4. *Canadian Charter of Rights and Freedoms*, Part I of the *Constitution Act, 1982*, being Schedule B to the *Canada Act 1982* (U.K.), 1982, c. 11.

(iii) Whether a "Law of Canada"

▼HCL-85▼ "Law of Canada". Thirdly, the federal law underpinning the case must be a "Law of Canada", as that phrase is used in s. 101 of the *Constitution Act, 1867*.[1] In other words, the legislation in question must be valid, *i.e.*, within the jurisdiction of Parliament. Thus, the third step of the test will be met if the Act is a valid exercise of the powers of Parliament. There has always been a question as to whether federal common law was "Law of Canada" for the purposes s. 101 of the *Constitution Act, 1867*. The Supreme Court has held that the phrase did not include the common law, even if the subject-matter would ultimately be within the jurisdiction of Parliament. For the Federal Court to have jurisdiction, there must be an existing and applicable federal law upon which the jurisdiction of the court can be exercised. Thus, it can be said that the matter comes within the expression "administration of the Laws of Canada" in s. 101 of the *Constitution Act, 1867* only if there is an act of Parliament.[2]

Notes

1. *Constitution Act, 1867* (U.K.) 30 & 31 Vict., c. 3, s. 101.
2. David Sgayias *et al.*, *Federal Court Practice* (Toronto: Carswell, 2004) at 6-7.

IV. Constitutional Interpretation: Pith and Substance, Double Aspect, Paramountcy and Interjurisdictional Immunity

1. **The Division of Legislative Authority** HCL-86

2. **Presumption of Constitutionality** HCL-87

3. **The Judicial Approach to Determining Constitutional Validity of Legislation**

   (1) Pith and Substance... HCL-89
   (2) Assignment to a Legislative Head of Power HCL-94

4. **Principle of Exclusivity** HCL-95

5. **Double Aspect** HCL-96

6. **Ancillary Effects** HCL-97

7. **Paramountcy** HCL-99

8. **Interjurisdictional Immunity** HCL-102

9. **Reading Down** HCL-105

10. **Severance** HCL-106

---

1. The Division of Legislative Authority

▼HCL-86▼ Overview. In Canada, the division of legislative powers between Parliament and the provincial legislatures is principally set out in ss. 91 and 92 of the *Constitution Act, 1867*.[1] Section 91 of the *Constitution Act, 1867*, lists the areas of legislative authority which are within the jurisdiction of Parliament, whereas s. 92 of the Act lists the subject-matters over which the provincial legislatures have authority to enact laws. Sections 91 and 92 of the Act proscribe that the respective levels of government may "exclusively" make laws in relation to "matters" coming within the "classes of subjects" set out within those particular sections.

Note

1. Other sections which confer law-making powers to the respective levels of governments include ss. 92A, 93, 94, 94A, 95, 101, 132 of the *Constitution Act, 1867* (U.K.) 30 & 31 Vict., c. 3; *Constitution Act, 1871* (U.K.) 34 & 35, c. 28, ss. 2, 3, 4; and the *Statute of Westminster, 1931* (U.K.), 22 Geo. V, c. 4, ss. 2 and 3.

---

2. Presumption of Constitutionality

▼HCL-87▼ Overview. There is a presumption that statutes enacted by Parliament or the legislature are constitutionally valid.[1] The court cannot ignore the rule implicit in the proposition stated as early as 1878 that "any question as to the validity of provincial legislation is to be approached on the assumption that it was validly enacted".[2] As a consequence of the presumption of constitutionality, the onus of proving that a statute is unconstitutional lies with the party that is challenging the legislation.[3] In addition, the presumption of constitutionality requires that where there are competing characterizations of a specific statute, a court should choose a characterization that is consistent with the framework of the Constitution.[4] Where a statute is open to both a wide and narrow interpretation in terms of its application, and if a wide or broad interpretation of the law's applicability would remove it from the enacting body's jurisdictional power, the court should interpret the legislation in such a manner such that the statute's application is confined to the lawful constitutional powers of the enacting legislative body. Arguably, this presumption, that statutes enacted by legislatures are constitutionally valid, reduces the potential for intervention by the courts in the affairs of the legislative branch of government.[5]

Notes

1. *Nova Scotia Board of Censors v. McNeil*, [1978] S.C.J. No. 25, [1978] 2 S.C.R. 662 (S.C.C.).
2. *Nova Scotia Board of Censors v. McNeil*, [1978] S.C.J. No. 25, [1978] 2 S.C.R. 662 at 687-88 (S.C.C.); see also J.E. Magnet, "The Presumption of Constitutionality" (1980) 18 Osgoode Hall L.J. 87.
3. See *Reference re: Firearms Act (Can.)*, [2000] S.C.J. No. 31, [2000] 1 S.C.R. 783 at para. 25 (S.C.C.).
4. *Reference re: Firearms Act*, [2000] S.C.J. No. 31, [2000] 1 S.C.R. 783 at para. 25 (S.C.C.); *Siemens v. Manitoba (Attorney General)*, [2002] S.C.J. No. 69, [2003] 1 S.C.R. 6 at para. 33 (S.C.C.).
5. *Nova Scotia Board of Censors v. McNeil*, [1978] S.C.J. No. 25, [1978] 2 S.C.R. 662 at 687-88 (S.C.C.).

---

3. The Judicial Approach to Determining Constitutional Validity of Legislation

(1) Pith and Substance
(a) Effect of the Statute...................................... HCL-90
(b) Purpose of the Statute HCL-91
(2) Assignment to a Legislative Head of Power HCL-94

▼HCL-88▼ Two-step approach. There are two general steps involved in the process by which a court determines whether a statute falls within the scope of the legislative authority attributable to a level of government. First, the "matter" of the legislation in question must be identified by the court. Following identification of the matter of the statute, the second step is for the court to allocate that matter to a specific "class of subject" or legislative power provided for within s. 91 or 92 of the *Constitution Act, 1867*.[1] This process of judicial review of an impugned statute ultimately determines the constitutional validity of that law.

Note

1. (U.K.) 30 & 31 Vict., c. 3, ss. 91, 92; *Saumur v. Quebec*, [1953] S.C.J. No. 49, [1953] 2 S.C.R. 299 at 333 (S.C.C.); *R. v. Morgentaler*, [1993] S.C.J. No. 95, [1993] 3 S.C.R. 463 at 481 (S.C.C.); *R. v. Hydro-Québec*, [1997] S.C.J. No. 76, [1997] 3 S.C.R. 213 at para. 23 (S.C.C.); *Global Securities Corp. v. British Columbia (Securities Commission)*, [2000] S.C.J. No. 5, [2000] 1 S.C.R. 494 at paras. 21-22 (S.C.C.); *Kitkatla Band v. British Columbia (Minister of Small Business, Tourism and Culture)*, [2002] S.C.J. No. 33, [2002] 2 S.C.R. 146 at para. 52 (S.C.C.); *Canadian Western Bank v. Alberta*, [2007] S.C.J. No. 22, [2007] 2 S.C.R. 3 at para. 26 (S.C.C.).

---

(1) Pith and Substance

▼HCL-89▼ Identifying the matter of a law. The first step undertaken by the courts in reviewing an impugned statute for validity under the Constitution is to determine the "matter" of the law. To determine the "matter" of the statute, courts undertake an analysis of the "pith and substance" doctrine. The "pith and substance" doctrine is founded on the recognition that it is nearly impossible for a legislature to exercise its power over a matter without incidentally affecting matters within the jurisdiction of the other level of government.[1] In essence, the court must identify the true, dominant or most important characteristic of the challenged statute in order to assign the law to one of the provisions of the Constitution which allocates law-making authority to the legislative bodies.[2]

Determining pith and substance. In determining the pith and substance of a legislation, the court looks to: (1) the purpose of the legislation as well as (2) its effect in identifying the "matter" of a statute, or its true character. There is no single test and the approach used must be flexible and technical, rather than formalistic.[3] Problems and difficulties may arise, however, where a law has more than one feature and one of those features comes within a federal jurisdiction, while another falls within the scope of a provincial power. This dilemma can be avoided simply by the court selecting one feature over another to be the pith and substance of the statute. In cases where there are potentially numerous subject-matters inherent within the statute, the court will decide which is the most important or dominant aspect of the statute and characterize that aspect as being the pith and substance or matter of the law. The other features within the statute become merely incidental or ancillary, and are irrelevant for the purposes of constitutional interpretation.[4]

Notes

1. *Canadian Western Bank v. Alberta*, [2007] S.C.J. No. 22, [2007] 2 S.C.R. 3 at para. 29 (S.C.C.).
2. *R. v. Hydro-Quèbec*, [1997] S.C.J. No. 76, [1997] 3 S.C.R. 213 at para. 23 (S.C.C.); *R. v. Morgentaler*, [1993] S.C.J. No. 95, [1993] 3 S.C.R. 463 at 481 (S.C.C.); *Global Securities Corp. v. British Columbia (Securities Commission)*, [2000] S.C.J. No. 5, [2000] 1 S.C.R. 494 at paras. 21-22 (S.C.C.); *Kitkatla Band v. British Columbia (Minister of Small Business, Tourism and Culture)*, [2002] S.C.J. No. 33, [2002] 2 S.C.R. 146 at para. 52 (S.C.C.); *Canadian Western Bank v. Alberta*, [2007] S.C.J. No. 22, [2007] 2 S.C.R. 3 at para. 26 (S.C.C.).
3. *Quebec (Attorney General) v. Lacombe*, [2010] S.C.J. No. 38, [2010] 2 S.C.R. 453 at para. 20 (S.C.C.); *R. v. Morgentaler*, [1993] S.C.J. No. 95, [1993] 3 S.C.R. 463 at 481 (S.C.C.).
4. *Canadian Western Bank v. Alberta*, [2007] S.C.J. No. 22, [2007] 2 S.C.R. 3 at para. 28 (S.C.C.).

(a) Effect of the Statute

▼HCL-90▼ Overview. When identifying the matter or pith and substance of a statute, the courts must be cognizant of the effects that a statute has on those who are subject to it. The effects that a statute has in its application will generally serve as an indication of the reasons for enacting the legislation and assist a court in identifying the matter or pith and substance of the impugned statute. In looking at the effect of the legislation, the court may consider both its legal effect and its practical effect. In other words, the court looks to see, first, what effect flows directly from the provisions of the statute itself; then, second, what "side" effects flow from the application of the statute that are not direct effects of the provisions of the statute itself.[1]

Note

1. *Kitkatla Band v. British Columbia (Minister of Small Business, Tourism and Culture)*, [2002] S.C.J. No. 33, [2002] 2 S.C.R. 146 at paras. 53-54 (S.C.C.); *Global Securities Corp. v. British Columbia (Securities Commission)*, [2000] S.C.J. No. 5, [2000] 1 S.C.R. 494 at para. 23 (S.C.C.); *R. v. Morgentaler*, [1993] S.C.J. No. 95, [1993] 3 S.C.R. 463 at 482-83 (S.C.C.).

(b) Purpose of the Statute

▼HCL-91▼ True purpose. If the main purpose of the statute is within the powers of the enacting body, the constitutional validity of the statute will be confirmed. In an effort to determine whether legislation is consistent with the division of powers within the Constitution, the court will often look beyond the direct legal effects of a law to examine the underlying purposes that a law is meant to serve or achieve.[1] The underlying purpose of a statute will often reveal whether it is within the authority of its enacting legislative body. In assessing the true purpose of an impugned statute (as opposed to a mere stated or apparent purpose), the courts may consider intrinsic or extrinsic evidence, such as the legislation's preamble or purpose clauses, Hansard and minutes of parliamentary debates.[2]

Notes

1. *Reference re: Firearms Act (Can.)*, [2000] S.C.J. No. 31, [2000] 1 S.C.R. 783 at para. 16 (S.C.C.); *Canadian Western Bank v. Alberta*, [2007] S.C.J. No. 22, [2007] 2 S.C.R. 3 at para. 27 (S.C.C.).
2. *Attorney-General for Ontario v. Reciprocal Insurers*, [1924] A.C. 328 at 337 (P.C.); *R. v. Morgentaler*, [1993] S.C.J. No. 95, [1993] 3 S.C.R. 463 at 483-84 (S.C.C.); *Kitkatla Band v. British Columbia (Minister of Small Business, Tourism and Culture)*, [2002] S.C.J. No. 33, [2002] 2 S.C.R. 146 at para. 53 (S.C.C.); *Canadian Western Bank v. Alberta*, [2007] S.C.J. No. 22, [2007] 2 S.C.R. 3 at para. 27 (S.C.C.).

▼HCL-92▼ Colourability. In certain circumstances, a statute may appear as though it falls within the range of authority of a particular level of government, but in actuality the statute concerns subject-matter which is entirely outside the scope of the enacting body. When a legislature attempts to enact a law outside the scope of its authority but frames the statute in such a way that it appears to fall under one of the legislature's designated heads of power, it can be said that the legislature has "coloured"[1] the statute in such a way as to achieve the objective it had envisioned. The legislature is in essence acting outside of the constraints placed upon it by the Constitution by appearing, at least on a superficial level, to adhere to the division of powers. The legislature cannot venture outside of its permitted legislative sphere by enacting laws which superficially appear to adhere to the provisions of the Constitution. In constitutional cases, particularly where there are allegations of colourability, extrinsic evidence may be considered to ascertain not only the operation and effect of the impugned legislation, but its true object and purpose as well.[2]

Notes

1. *Reference re: Dairy Industry Act (Canada), s. 5(a)*, [1948] S.C.J. No. 42, [1949] S.C.R. 1 (S.C.C.); *Reference re: Upper Churchill Water Rights Reversion Act 1980*, [1984] S.C.J. No. 16, [1984] 1 S.C.R. 297 (S.C.C.); *R. v. Morgentaler*, [1993] S.C.J. No. 95, [1993] 3 S.C.R. 463 (S.C.C.).
2. *Global Securities Corp. v. British Columbia (Securities Commission)*, [2000] S.C.J. No. 5, [2000] 1 S.C.R. 494 at para. 25 (S.C.C.).

▼HCL-93▼ Efficacy of laws. When a court identifies the pith and substance or effect of a statute for the purposes of determining the law's constitutional validity, the court is not to engage in a substantive evaluation of the underlying policy objectives of the statute at issue. Rather, when classifying a law under a particular head of power for the purposes of constitutional review, the courts must confine themselves solely to considering the purpose and effect of the statute by attempting to ascertain the intention of the legislative body that enacted it.[1] An inquiry "into efficacy does not advance the pith and substance inquiry. The purpose of legislation cannot be challenged by proposing an alternate, allegedly better, method for achieving that purpose."[2] In this respect, the courts have consistently held that it is not their institutional function to conduct an inquiry into the efficacy or soundness of policy objectives underlying a statute when making a determination as to the statute's constitutional validity.

Notes

1. *Reference re: Firearms Act (Can.)*, [2000] S.C.J. No. 31, [2000] 1 S.C.R. 783 (S.C.C.).
2. *Ward v. Canada (Attorney General)*, [2002] S.C.J. No. 21, [2002] 1 S.C.R. 569 at para. 26 (S.C.C.).

---

(2) Assignment to a Legislative Head of Power

▼HCL-94▼ Assignment of the statute. Once the pith and substance of an impugned statute has been ascertained by the court, the next step in the process of constitutional interpretation is to assign the statute to a head of power provided for under s. 91 or 92 of the *Constitution Act, 1867.*[1] During this process, it is the role of the courts to interpret the heads of legislative power embodied within ss. 91 and 92 of the Act.

Note

1. (U.K.) 30 & 31 Vict., c. 3, ss. 91, 92; *Canadian Western Bank v. Alberta*, [2007] S.C.J. No. 22, [2007] 2 S.C.R. 3 (S.C.C.).

---

4. Principle of Exclusivity

▼HCL-95▼ Overview. Each of the subject-matters listed within ss. 91 and 92 of the *Constitution Act, 1867*[1] fall within the exclusive jurisdiction of the legislative body to which the subject-matter has been assigned. If either Parliament or a provincial legislature fails to enact laws to the full extent of the power permitted to that level of government under the *Constitution Act, 1867,* this does not result in a corresponding expansion of the powers attributable to the other level of government.[2] Although the subject-matters found within ss. 91 and 92 of the *Constitution Act, 1867* are exclusive to their respective legislative body, this does not mean that similar, or even nearly identical laws cannot be enacted by both levels of government. While it may appear that such laws overlap or duplicate each other in application and scope, this is generally not the case. Rather, similar statutes may have a double aspect or may affect each other in an incidental manner.

Notes

1. (U.K.) 30 & 31 Vict., c. 3, ss. 91, 92.
2. *Union Colliery Co. v. Bryden*, [1899] A.C. 580 at 588 (P.C.).

---

5. Double Aspect

▼HCL-96▼ Overview. Conceptually, the doctrine of double aspect recognizes that some laws, by nature, are impossible to categorize under a single head of power as they contain both federal and provincial subject-matter.[1] Thus, the fact that a matter may for one purpose and in one aspect fall within federal jurisdiction does not mean that it cannot, for another purpose and in another aspect, fall within provincial jurisdiction. Consequently, the matter is potentially within the legislative competency of both Parliament and the provinces, and both levels of government may enact laws on this matter, provided that the "pith and substance" of the statute is within the jurisdiction of the enacting body.[2] Essentially, when the courts view the two matters within a law as being of nearly equal importance, then the double aspect doctrine will apply so that the statute is within the authority of both the federal and provincial levels of government.[3] Securities regulation, for example, is an area of law where the courts have recognized the existence of a double aspect.[4] In the end, when a particular legislative subject-matter can be said to have a "double aspect", so that viewed in one light the subject falls within the legislative competence of Parliament and, viewed in another light, within the legislative competence of the provincial legislature, the federal legislation will only be paramount when there is a direct conflict with the relevant provincial legislation.[5]

Notes

1. *Reference re: Liquor License Act of 1877 (Ont.)*, [1883] J.C.J. No. 2, 9 App. Cas. 117 at 130 (P.C.).
2. For examples see *O'Grady v. Sparling*, [1960] S.C.J. No. 48, [1960] S.C.R. 804 (S.C.C.); *Bell Canada v. Québec (Commission de la santé et de la sécurité du travail du Québec)*, [1988] S.C.J. No. 41, [1988] 1 S.C.R. 749 (S.C.C.); *Canadian Western Bank v. Alberta*, [2007] S.C.J. No. 22, [2007] 2 S.C.R. 3 at para. 30 (S.C.C.).
3. W.R. Lederman, *Continuing Canadian Constitutional Dilemmas* (Toronto: Butterworths, 1981) at 244.
4. *R. v. Smith*, [1960] S.C.J. No. 47, [1960] S.C.R. 776 (S.C.C.).

5. *Rio Hotel Ltd. v. New Brunswick (Liquor Licensing Board)*, [1987] S.C.J. No. 46, [1987] 2 S.C.R. 59 at para. 5 (S.C.C.).

6. Ancillary Effects

▼HCL-97▼ Overview. Despite the principle of exclusivity inherent within the *Constitution Act, 1867*,[1] a degree of overlap tends to occur in the interpretation of the division of powers under ss. 91 and 92. Recognizing that a degree of jurisdictional overlap is inevitable, the law accepts the validity of measures that lie outside a legislature's (or Parliament's) competence, if these measures constitute an integral part of a legislative scheme that comes within provincial (or federal) jurisdiction. The pith and substance analysis provides for this degree of overlap and Parliament and the legislatures may avail themselves of ancillary legislative power.[2] Legislation in which the pith and substance falls within the jurisdiction of the legislature that enacted it may, to a certain extent, affect matters beyond the legislature's jurisdiction, without necessarily being unconstitutional.[3] The ancillary powers doctrine permits one level of government to trench on the jurisdiction of the other in order to enact a comprehensive regulatory scheme. The secondary objectives and effects of the legislation have no impact on its constitutional validity[4] (even if those effects are of significant practical importance to the matter), if those effects are collateral and secondary to the mandate of the enacting legislature.[5] These secondary collateral effects are considered to be ancillary to the dominant purpose of the legislation. In pith and substance, provisions enacted pursuant to the ancillary powers doctrine fall outside the enumerated powers of their enacting body. Consequently, the invocation of ancillary powers runs contrary to the notion that Parliament and the legislatures have sole authority to legislate within the jurisdiction allocated to them by the *Constitution Act, 1867*. Because of this, the availability of ancillary powers is limited to situations in which the intrusion on the powers of the other level of government is justified by the important role that the extrajurisdictional provision plays in a valid legislative scheme. In the end, a law that is found to be invalid under the pith and substance analysis may still be saved under the ancillary effects doctrine.[6] The ancillary powers doctrine is not to be confused with the incidental effects rule. The ancillary powers doctrine applies where a provision is, in pith and substance, outside the competence of its enacting body. The potentially invalid provision will be saved where it is an important part of a broader legislative scheme that is within the competence of the enacting body. The incidental effects rule, by contrast, applies when a provision, in pith and substance, lies within the competence of the enacting body but touches on a subject assigned to the other level of government. It holds that such a provision will not be invalid merely because it has an incidental effect on a legislative competence that falls beyond the jurisdiction of its enacting body. Mere incidental effects will not warrant the invocation of ancillary powers. The ancillary powers doctrine should also not be confused with the double aspect doctrine. The double aspect doctrine recognizes the overlapping jurisdiction of the two levels of government: "... some matters are by their very nature impossible to categorize under a single head of power: they may have both provincial and federal aspects. Thus, the fact that a matter may for one purpose and in one aspect fall within federal jurisdiction does not mean that it cannot, for another purpose and in another aspect, fall within provincial competence ....".[7] By contrast, ancillary powers apply only where a legislative provision does not come within those heads of power assigned to its enacting body under the *Constitution Act, 1867*.

Notes

1. (U.K.) 30 & 31 Vict., c. 3.
2. *Quebec (Attorney General) v. Lacombe*, [2010] S.C.J. No. 38, [2010] 2 S.C.R. 453 at para. 34; For example, see *Workmen's Compensation Board v. Canadian Pacific Railway Co.*, [1920] A.C. 184 (P.C.); and *Lymburn v. Mayland*, [1932] A.C. 318 (P.C.).
3. *Canadian Western Bank v. Alberta*, [2007] S.C.J. No. 22, [2007] 2 S.C.R. 3 at para. 28 (S.C.C.).
4. *Global Securities Corp. v. British Columbia (Securities Commission)*, [2000] S.C.J. No. 5, [2000] 1 S.C.R. 494 at para. 23 (S.C.C.); *Canadian Western Bank v. Alberta*, [2007] S.C.J. No. 22, [2007] 2 S.C.R. 3 at para. 28 (S.C.C.).
5. *British Columbia v. Imperial Tobacco Canada Ltd.*, [2005] S.C.J. No. 50, [2005] 2 S.C.R. 473 at para. 28 (S.C.C.); *General Motors of Canada Ltd. v. City National Leasing*, [1989] S.C.J. No. 28, [1989] 1 S.C.R. 641 at 670 (S.C.C.); *Bank of Toronto v. Lambe* (1887), L.R. 12 App. Cas. 575 (P.C.); *Canadian Western Bank v. Alberta*, [2007] S.C.J. No. 22, [2007] 2 S.C.R. 3 at para. 28 (S.C.C.).
6. *General Motors of Canada Ltd. v. City National Leasing*, [1989] S.C.J. No. 28, [1989] 1 S.C.R. 641 at 669 (S.C.C.). See also *Canada (Attorney General) v. PHS Community Services Society*, [2011] S.C.J. No. 44, 2011 SCC 44 (S.C.C.).
7. *Canadian Western Bank v. Alberta*, [2007] 2 S.C.R. 3 at para. 30 (S.C.C.).

▼HCL-98▼ Seriousness of the encroachment. Finding that a provision standing alone, in its pith and substance, intrudes on federal or provincial powers does not determine its ultimate constitutional validity. "It is necessary to consider both the impugned provision and the Act as a whole when undertaking constitutional analysis".[1] "If the legislation is valid and the provision is sufficiently integrated within the scheme, it can be upheld by virtue of that relationship."[2] To determine whether an intruding provision can be saved pursuant to the ancillary effects doctrine, the application of a three-step test is required.

First step. The first part of the test asks whether the impugned provision encroaches on a provincial (or federal) head of power, and to what extent.[3] This step seeks to determine the seriousness of the encroachment into the legislative sphere of the other level of government.[4]

Second step. The second part of the test asks if the impugned provision encroaches on a provincial (or federal) head of power, "is it nevertheless part of a valid federal (or provincial) legislative scheme?"[5] With respect to the second step, the court must determine whether the impugned provision can be justified by reason of its connection to an overall valid legislative scheme.[6]

Third step. The final step of the analysis is to determine if the impugned provision is part of a valid federal (or provincial) scheme and whether it sufficiently integrated with that scheme?[7] To do so, "it is necessary to determine the appropriate test of 'fit', namely 'how well the provision is integrated into the scheme of the legislation and how important it is for the efficacy of the legislation.'"[8] If the provision passes this integration test, it is *intra vires* Parliament's (or a provincial legislature's) power. If the provision is not sufficiently integrated into the scheme of regulation, it cannot be sustained. To determine the degree of integration required, it is necessary to consider the extent to which the provision encroaches on provincial powers: the degree of relationship that is required is a function of the extent of the provision's intrusion into provincial powers. If the encroachment is minimal, then a "functional relationship" is sufficient to sustain the constitutionality of the provision. If the provision is highly intrusive, a stricter test is applied: the provision must be "truly necessary" or "integral" to the federal scheme. "Consideration of the seriousness of the encroachment on provincial powers and of the proper standard for the relationship between a legislative provision and a valid federal scheme ensures that the balance of constitutional powers is maintained and focuses the analysis on the 'pith and substance' of the provision".[9]

Notes

1. *Kirkbi AG v. Ritvik Holdings Inc.*, [2005] S.C.J. No. 66, [2005] 3 S.C.R. 302 at para. 20 (S.C.C.).

2. *Kirkbi AG v. Ritvik Holdings Inc.*, [2005] S.C.J. No. 66, [2005] 3 S.C.R. 302 a para. 20 (S.C.C.).
3. *Kirkbi AG v. Ritvik Holdings Inc.*, [2005] S.C.J. No. 66, [2005] 3 S.C.R. 302 a para. 21 (S.C.C.); *Kitkatla Band v. British Columbia (Minister of Small Business Tourism and Culture*, [2002] S.C.J. No. 33, [2002] 2 S.C.R. 146 (S.C.C.); *Genera Motors of Canada Ltd. v. City National Leasing Ltd.*, [1989] S.C.J. No. 28, [1989 1 S.C.R. 641 (S.C.C.).
4. *General Motors of Canada Ltd. v. City National Leasing Ltd.*, [1989] S.C.J. No 28, [1989] 1 S.C.R. 641 at 671 (S.C.C.).
5. *Kirkbi AG v. Ritvik Holdings Inc.*, [2005] S.C.J. No. 66, [2005] 3 S.C.R. 302 a para. 21 (S.C.C.).
6. *General Motors of Canada Ltd. v. City National Leasing Ltd.*, [1989] S.C.J. No 28, [1989] 1 S.C.R. 641 at 668 (S.C.C.).
7. *Kirkbi AG v. Ritvik Holdings Inc.*, [2005] S.C.J. No. 66, [2005] 3 S.C.R. 302 a para. 21 (S.C.C.).
8. *Kirkbi AG v. Ritvik Holdings Inc.*, [2005] S.C.J. No. 66, [2005] 3 S.C.R. 302 a para. 32 (S.C.C.).
9. *Kirkbi AG v. Ritvik Holdings Inc.*, [2005] S.C.J. No. 66, [2005] 3 S.C.R. 302 a para. 32 (S.C.C.).

---

7. Paramountcy

▼HCL-99▼ Overview. The principle of federal paramountcy dictates that where there is an inconsistency, a conflict or an incompatible operational effect between validly enacted but overlapping provincial and federal legislation, the provincial legislation is inoperative to the extent o any inconsistency.[1] The validity of the legislation at issue is first dependent upon the outcome of the pith and substance analysis. In determining whether the principle of paramountcy applies, the first determination mus be whether both opposing statutes were within the jurisdiction of thei respective enacting body. The court must then determine whether there is an express or obvious conflict between both statutes, or whether one statute merely duplicates the other. If that is the case, both statutes are valid.[2] If there is no obvious conflict between the impugned statutes, the cour must analyze whether there could be an operational conflict such that it is impossible to comply with both laws.[3] Finally, if there is no obvious conflict and if there is no operational conflict, the court must examine the objective and purpose of the federal statute to ensure that the applicatior of the provincial statute will not frustrate or be inconsistent with the legislative purpose of the federal law.[4] The doctrine applies to statutes where the provincial legislature has legislated pursuant to its ancillary power to intrude on an area of federal jurisdiction and for situations in which the legislature acts within its primary powers, and Parliament acts pursuant to its ancillary powers.[5]

Notes

1. *Rothmans, Benson & Hedges Inc. v. Saskatchewan*, [2005] S.C.J. No. 1, [2005] 1 S.C.R. 188 at para. 11 (S.C.C.); *Canadian Western Bank v. Alberta*, [2007] S.C.J. No. 22, [2007] 2 S.C.R. 3 at para. 69 (S.C.C.); *Quebec (Attorney General) v. Canadian Owners and Pilots Assn.*, [2010] S.C.J. No. 39, [2010] 2 S.C.R. 536 at paras. 62-66 (S.C.C.).
2. *Multiple Access Ltd. v. McCutcheon*, [1982] S.C.J. No. 66, [1982] 2 S.C.R. 161 (S.C.C.).
3. *M & D Farm Ltd. v. Manitoba Agricultural Credit Corp.*, [1999] S.C.J. No. 4, [1999] 2 S.C.R. 961 (S.C.C.).
4. *Bank of Montreal v. Hall*, [1990] S.C.J. No. 9, [1990] 1 S.C.R. 121 (S.C.C.); *Law Society of British Columbia v. Mangat*, [2001] S.C.J. No. 66, [2001] 3 S.C.R. 113 (S.C.C.).
5. *Canadian Western Bank v. Alberta*, [2007] S.C.J. No. 22, [2007] 2 S.C.R. 3 at para. 69 (S.C.C.).

▼HCL-100▼ Inconsistency. An inconsistency may arise when two laws, one enacted by Parliament and another enacted by a provincial legislature, contradict one another so as to make dual compliance with both statutes impossible. In this respect, compliance with one law would necessarily involve a breach of the other.[1] The impossibility of dual compliance with provincial and federal laws is not the sole mark of inconsistency.[2] Provincial legislation that displaces or frustrates Parliament's legislative purpose has also been determined to be inconsistent for the purposes of the federal paramountcy doctrine.[3]

Notes

1. *R. v. Smith,* [1960] S.C.J. No. 47, [1960] S.C.R. 776 at 800 (S.C.C.); *Multiple Access Ltd. v. McCutcheon*, [1982] S.C.J. No. 66, [1982] 2 S.C.R. 161 (S.C.C.).
2. *Rothmans, Benson & Hedges Inc. v. Saskatchewan*, [2005] S.C.J. No. 1, [2005] 1 S.C.R. 188 at para. 12 (S.C.C.).
3. *Law Society of British Columbia v. Mangat*, [2001] S.C.J. No. 66, [2001] 3 S.C.R. 113 at para. 72 (S.C.C.).

▼HCL-101▼ Dual compliance. The focus of the inquiry must be on the broader question of whether operation of the provincial Act is compatible with the federal legislative purpose. Without this compatibility, dual compliance is impossible.[1] The mere existence of a duplication o norms at the federal and provincial levels does not in itself constitute a degree of incompatibility capable of triggering the application of the doc trine. Moreover, provincial statutes may also add requirements that sup plement the requirements of federal legislation.[2]

Onus of proof. The onus of proving the doctrine of federal paramountcy and demonstrating that federal and provincial laws are incompatible ei ther because it is impossible to comply with both laws or that to apply the provincial law would frustrate the purpose of the federal law, rests with the party claiming it. Moreover, constitutional interpretation and reading down are available in favour of an interpretation suggesting that both sta tutes may apply.[3] "When a federal statute can be properly interpreted so as not to interfere with a provincial statute, such an interpretation is to be applied in preference to another applicable construction which would bring about a conflict between the two statutes".[4]

Notes

1. *Bank of Montreal v. Hall*, [1990] S.C.J. No. 9, [1990] 1 S.C.R. 121 at 15 (S.C.C.).
2. *Canadian Western Bank v. Alberta*, [2007] S.C.J. No. 22, [2007] 2 S.C.R. 3 a para. 72 (S.C.C.); *114957 Canada Ltée (Spraytech, Société d'arrosage) v. Hudson (Town)*, [2001] S.C.J. No. 42, [2001] 2 S.C.R. 241 (S.C.C.).
3. *Canadian Western Bank v. Alberta*, [2007] S.C.J. No. 22, [2007] 2 S.C.R. 3 a para. 75 (S.C.C.).
4. *Canada (Attorney General) v. Law Society of British Columbia*, [1982] S.C.J. No 70, [1982] 2 S.C.R. 307 at 356 (S.C.C.); *Canadian Western Bank v. Alberta*, [2007] S.C.J. No. 22, [2007] 2 S.C.R. 3 at para. 75 (S.C.C.).

---

8. Interjurisdictional Immunity

▼HCL-102▼ Overview. The doctrine of interjurisdictional immunity has its roots in cases involving federally regulated companies. Historically, provincial laws that asserted power so as to "impair" or "sterilize" a federal activity were held to be inapplicable to that federally regulated work or undertaking. The Supreme Court of Canada abandoned the language of sterilization and formulated a test that instead focused on whether the provincial statute affected a "vital part" of the federal undertaking.[1] Interjuridictional immunity is a doctrine of constitutional interpretation that emphasizes exclusive federal jurisdiction over shared jurisdiction with the provinces. The doctrine applies where an otherwise valid provincial law impairs the core or vital aspects of a subject-matter within the exclusive jurisdiction of the federal legislature.[2] The first step is to determine whether the provincial law trenches on the protected "core" of a federal competence. If it does, the second step is to determine whether the provincial law's effect on the exercise of the protected federal power is sufficiently serious to invoke the doctrine of interjurisdictional immunity. The test is whether the subject comes within the essential jurisdiction — the "basic, minimum and unassailable content" — of the legislative power in question. The core of a federal power is the authority that is absolutely necessary to enable Parliament "to achieve the purpose for which exclusive legislative jurisdiction was conferred". Under these circumstances, the provincial law is held to be inapplicable to the extent that it impairs the vital part of the federal subject-matter. The doctrine is rooted in references to "exclusivity" throughout ss. 91 and 92 of the *Constitution Act, 1867*.[3] The rationale for this doctrine is that if a jurisdiction is to be "exclusive", it cannot be invaded by provincial legislation even if the federal power remains unexercised. The doctrine is reciprocal, in that it may also protect provincial jurisdictions from federal intrusion or federal encroachment.[4] However, jurisprudence shows that the application of the doctrine has produced "asymmetrical" results.

Notes

1. *Québec (Commission du Salaire Minimum) v. Bell Telephone Co. of Canada*, [1966] S.C.J. No. 51, [1966] S.C.R. 767 (S.C.C.).
2. *Canadian Western Bank v. Alberta*, [2007] S.C.J. No. 22, [2007] 2 S.C.R. 3 at para. 48 (S.C.C.). See also *Newfoundland and Labrador (Workplace Health, Safety and Compensation Commission) v. Ryan Estate*, [2011] N.J. No. 207, 2011 NLCA 42 (Nfld. C.A.).
3. (U.K.) 30 & 31 Vict., c. 3, ss. 91, 92.
4. *Canada (Attorney General) v. PHS Community Services Society*, [2011] S.C.J. No. 44, 2011 SCC 44 (S.C.C.).

▼HCL-103▼ Impairment test. In determining whether the doctrine of interjurisdictional immunity applies, the courts will need to determine whether the provincial law *impairs* the federal exercise of the core competence or whether the federal law *impairs* the provincial exercise of the core competence. It is not enough for the provincial or federal legislation simply to "affect" that which makes a federal or provincial subject or object of rights specifically of federal or provincial jurisdiction. It is when the adverse impact of a law adopted by one level of government increases in severity from "affecting" to "impairing" (without necessarily "sterilizing" or "paralyzing") that the "core" competence of the other level of government (or the vital or essential part of an undertaking it duly constitutes) is placed in jeopardy, and not before.[1] The impact of the provincial or federal statute must not only affect the core power, but must do so in a way that seriously or significantly trammels the federal or provincial power. In an era of co-operative, flexible federalism, application of the doctrine of interjurisdictional immunity requires a significant or serious intrusion on the exercise of the federal power. It need not paralyze it, but it must be serious. In the end, interjurisdictional immunity is a doctrine of limited application which should generally be reserved for situations already covered by precedent.[2] The doctrine of interjurisdictional immunity should not be a doctrine of first recourse and should be "applied with restraint".[3]

Qualifications on the "core" or "vital part" test. The "vital part" test applies only to laws that intrude on the "core" of the power of the other level of government. Where provincial (or federal) legislation indirectly affects a federal undertaking (or provincial jurisdiction), the statute will still be found to apply, unless it impairs a vital part of the "core" power of the other level of government.[4]

Notes

1. *Canadian Western Bank v. Alberta*, [2007] S.C.J. No. 22, [2007] 2 S.C.R. 3 at para. 48 (S.C.C.); *Quebec (Attorney General) v. Canadian Owners and Pilots Assn.*, [2010] S.C.J. No. 39, [2010] 2 S.C.R. 536 at para. 45 (S.C.C.). See also *Canada (Attorney General) v. PHS Community Services Society*, [2011] S.C.J. No. 44, 2011 SCC 44 (S.C.C.); *Newfoundland and Labrador (Workplace Health, Safety and Compensation Commission) v. Ryan Estate*, [2011] N.J. No. 207, 2011 NLCA 42 (Nfld. C.A.).
2. *Canadian Western Bank v. Alberta*, [2007] S.C.J. No. 22, [2007] 2 S.C.R. 3 at para. 77 (S.C.C.); *Quebec (Attorney General) v. Canadian Owners and Pilots Assn.*, [2010] S.C.J. No. 39, [2010] 2 S.C.R. 536 at paras. 26, 36 (S.C.C.); *Canada (Attorney General) v. PHS Community Services Society*, [2011] S.C.J. No. 44, 2011 SCC 44 (S.C.C.).
3. *Canadian Western Bank v. Alberta*, [2007] S.C.J. No. 22, [2007] 2 S.C.R. 3 at paras. 47 and 67 (S.C.C.); *Canada (Attorney General) v. PHS Community Services Society*, [2011] S.C.J. No. 44, 2011 SCC 44 (S.C.C.).
4. *Canadian Western Bank v. Alberta*, [2007] S.C.J. No. 22, [2007] 2 S.C.R. 3 at para. 48 (S.C.C.). See also *Newfoundland and Labrador (Workplace Health, Safety and Compensation Commission) v. Ryan Estate*, [2011] N.J. No. 207, 2011 NLCA 42 (Nfld. C.A.).

▼HCL-104▼ Interjurisdictional immunity and pith and substance. Oftentimes it is difficult to differentiate between the circumstances when the doctrine of interjurisdictional immunity applies and when the pith and substance doctrine applies so that a statute in relation to a provincial matter can validly affect a federal matter. Generally, where possible, the pith and substance doctrine allowing the provincial statute to remain valid and affect the federal jurisdiction will be preferred by the courts over the doctrine of interjurisdictional immunity, which excludes the application of the provincial law from the federal matter.[1]

Note

1. *Bell Canada v. Québec (Commission de Santé et de la Sécurité du Travail du Québec)*, [1988] S.C.J. No. 41, [1988] 1 S.C.R. 749 at 762 (S.C.C.). The same approach is applied with respect to the impact of criminal law legislation on areas of core provincial competence: *Canada (Attorney General) v. PHS Community Services Society*, [2011] S.C.J. No. 44, 2011 SCC 44 (S.C.C.).

9. Reading Down

▼HCL-105▼ Overview. Where possible, the language in a statute is to be narrowly construed so that the statute remains within the permissible scope of authority of the legislative body which enacted it. This doctrine of constitutional interpretation is known as “reading down”. In practical terms, reading down means that the provisions of a statute that could potentially be interpreted to extend beyond the jurisdictions of Parliament or a legislature is interpreted in such a manner so as to keep the statute within the permissible scope of legislative authority.[1] The doctrine of reading down is only available to a court where the language used within the statute will support both a broad interpretation and a limited interpretation of the statute. However, it is the limited interpretation which is given to the statute by the courts. Reading down is based upon the presumption of constitutionality. That is, the legislative body that enacted the provisions is presumed to be acting within the purview of its constitutional authority. “Reading down” the provisions of a statute in a manner to confine it to the jurisdictions of the enacting body allows the constitutional validity of the legislation and ensures consistency with the boundaries of the Constitution. Reading down can be contrasted with the doctrine of severance, but unlike reading down which is a method of statutory interpretation, severance involves a court ruling that a portion of a statute is not constitutionally valid.

Note

1. See, for example, the discussions in *R. v. Dick*, [1985] S.C.J. No. 62, [1985] 2 S.C.R. 309 (S.C.C.); *Derrickson v. Derrickson*, [1986] S.C.J. No. 16, [1986] 1 S.C.R. 285 (S.C.C.); *Ordon Estate v. Grail*, [1998] S.C.J. No. 84, [1998] 3 S.C.R. 437 (S.C.C.); *British Columbia (Attorney General) v. Lafarge Canada Inc.*, [2007] S.C.J. No. 23, [2007] 2 S.C.R. 86 (S.C.C.); *Canadian Western Bank v. Alberta*, [2007] S.C.J. No. 22, [2007] 2 S.C.R. 3 at para. 35 (S.C.C.).

---

10. Severance

▼HCL-106▼ Overview. When a court concludes that a provision of a statute is contrary to the Constitution, generally the court strikes down the statute in its entirety. Nevertheless, in certain circumstances, it is possible that only part of the statute will be invalidated, while the remainder will be permitted to continue standing on its own. Removing the infringing provisions from a statute as a whole is known as "severance" of provisions which offend the Constitution. The rule that has been developed by the courts is that severance is inappropriate when the non-infringing portion of the statute is so inextricably bound up with the part declared invalid that what remains cannot independently survive.[1] When this is the case, a court may assume that the legislature would not have enacted the remaining portion of the statute.[2] When the two parts of the statute could potentially exist independently of one another, though, then severance is an appropriate course of judicial action because it may be assumed that the legislative body would have enacted one portion of the statute even if it could not validly enact the other.[3]

Notes

1. *Alberta (Attorney General) v. A.G. Canada*, [1947] A.C. 503 at 518 (P.C.).
2. *Alberta (Attorney General) v. A.G. Canada*, [1947] A.C. 503 at 518 (P.C.).
3. W.R. Lederman, *Continuing Canadian Constitutional Dilemmas* (Toronto: Butterworths 1981), 247-48; B.L. Strayer, *Canadian Constitution and the Courts*, 3d ed. (Toronto: Butterworths 1988) 301-303. For examples of contemporary cases where severance was ordered by the Supreme Court of Canada: *MacDonald v. Vapor Canada*, [1976] S.C.J. No. 60, [1977] 2 S.C.R. 134 (S.C.C.); *Nova Scotia (Board of Censors) v. McNeil*, [1978] S.C.J. No. 25, [1978] 2 S.C.R. 622 (S.C.C.); *Reference re: Agricultural Products Marketing Act, 1970 (Canada)*, [1978] S.C.J. No. 58, [1978] 2 S.C.R. 1198 (S.C.C.); *Peel (Regional Municipality) v. MacKenzie*, [1982] S.C.J. No. 58, [1982] 2 S.C.R. 9 (S.C.C.).

V. Peace, Order and Good Government

1. **General** HCL-107

2. **POGG as a Residual Clause or for New Matters** HCL-108

3. **The National Interest Context** HCL-109

4. **The Emergency Context** HCL-110

---

1. General

▼HCL-107▼ Overview. The *Constitution Act, 1867*[1] provides that, "[i]t shall be lawful for the Queen, by and with the Advice and Consent of the Senate and House of Commons, to make Laws for the Peace, Order, and good Government of Canada, in relation to all Matters not coming within the Classes of Subjects by this Act assigned exclusively to the Legislatures of the Provinces".[2] The nature of the power has been debated amongst commentators and within jurisprudence to the extent that is not entirely clear what the power of Peace, Order, and Good Government ("POGG") grants to Parliament. Decisions of the Judicial Committee of the Privy Council, as well as the Supreme Court of Canada, have suggested that the POGG power represented a residual clause granting legislative power to Parliament over matters that were not listed under the *Constitution Act, 1867*,[3] and over any "new" matter not existing at Confederation. Other cases of the Privy Council and the Supreme Court have limited the scope of the POGG power to matters of "national interest" and to matters properly characterized as an "emergency".

Notes

1. *Constitution Act, 1867* (U.K.), 30 & 31 Vict., c. 3.
2. *Constitution Act, 1867* (U.K.), 30 & 31 Vict., c. 3, s. 91.
3. (U.K.), 30 & 31 Vict., c. 3, s. 92.

---

2. POGG as a Residual Clause or for New Matters

▼HCL-108▼ Residual clause. The first suggestion that the POGG power might be the residual clause of the *Constitution Act, 1867*[1] came from the Judicial Committee of the Privy Council[2] which observed that it was not necessary to ground the authority to incorporate federal companies on a specific enumerated ground like the regulation of trade and commerce.[3] In the first case where POGG was really relied upon to ground a federal statute, a statute was upheld having concluded that the *Canada Temperance Act, 1878*[4] was a matter not properly falling within property and civil rights in the province.[5] In that case, it was unnecessary to consider whether the Act could fall within an enumerated head under the *Constitution Act, 1867*[6] because the matter was necessarily within the jurisdiction of the Dominion Parliament through its general POGG power by virtue of it not being listed in the *Constitution Act, 1867*.[7] [8] More recent cases evoking the POGG power as a residuary clause include Canada's exclusive jurisdiction to explore and exploit the continental shelf which rested on the *British North America Act, 1871*[9] "or under the residual power in s. 91"[10] and the enactment of the *Official Languages Act*[11] as being a law "for the peace, order and Good Government of Canada in relation to [a matter] not coming within the classes of subjects … assigned exclusively to the Legislatures of the Provinces".[12]

New matters. There have also been examples of matters that were allocated to the powers of Parliament because they were new matters that did not exist at the time of Confederation. The constitutional validity of the *Narcotic Control Act*,[13] for example, rested on the peace, order and good government power of Parliament, rather than on its jurisdiction with respect to criminal law. The majority in that case said that the principal consideration in support of that view was that the abuse of narcotic drugs, with which the Act dealt, was a new problem which did not exist at the time of Confederation, and that since it did not come within matters of a merely local or private nature in the province, it fell within the "general residual power" in the same manner as aeronautics[14] and radio.[15]

Notes

1. (U.K.), 30 & 31 Vict., c. 3.
2. *Citizens Insurance Company of Canada v. Parsons* (1881), 7 App. Cas. 96 (H.L.).
3. *Citizens Insurance Company of Canada v. Parsons* (1881), 7 App. Cas. 96 at 116, 117 (H.L.).
4. (CAN) *Canada Temperance Act*, R.S.C. 1927, c. 196.
5. *Russell v. The Queen* (1882), 7 App. Cas. 829 (P.C.).

6. (U.K.), 30 & 31 Vict., c. 3, s. 91.
7. (U.K.), 30 & 31 Vict., c. 3, s. 92.
8. *Russell v. The Queen* (1882), 7 App. Cas. 829 at 836, 838-42 (P.C.).
9. (U.K.), 34 & 35 Vict., c. 28, s. 91(1)(a).
10. *Reference re: Ownership of Off Shore Mineral Rights (British Columbia)*, [1967] S.C.J. No. 70, [1967] S.C.R. 792 at 816 (S.C.C.).
11. R.S.C. 1985, c. 31 (4th Supp.).
12. *Jones v. New Brunswick (A.G.)*, [1974] S.C.J. No. 91, [1975] 2 S.C.R. 182 at 189 (S.C.C.).
13. (CAN) *Narcotic Control Act*, R.S.C. 1985, c. N-1, repealed by the *Controlled Drugs and Substances Act*, S.C. 1996, c. 19.
14. *Regulation and Control of Aeronautics in Canada (Re)*, [1932] A.C. 54 (P.C.); *Johannesson v. West St. Paul (Rural Mun.)*, [1951] S.C.J. No. 50, [1952] 1 S.C.R. 292 (S.C.C.).
15. *R. v. Hauser*, [1979] S.C.J. No. 18, [1979] 1 S.C.R. 984 at 986 (S.C.C.).

---

3. The National Interest Context

▼HCL-109▼ Matters of national concern. The national concern doctrine was suggested by Lord Watson in the *Local Prohibition* case[1] and given its modern formulation by Viscount Simon in *Attorney-General for Ontario v. Canada Temperance Federation.*[2] It is now firmly established that the "national concern doctrine is separate and distinct from the national emergency doctrine ... which is chiefly distinguishable by the fact that it provides a constitutional basis for what is necessarily legislation of a temporary nature"[3] and that the "national concern doctrine applies to both new matters which did not exist at Confederation and to matters which, although originally matters of a local or private nature in a province, have since, in the absence of national emergency, become matters of national concern".[4] Furthermore, for a matter "to qualify as a matter of national concern in either sense it must have a singleness, distinctiveness and indivisibility that clearly distinguishes it from matters of provincial concern and a scale of impact on provincial jurisdiction that is reconcilable with the fundamental distribution of legislative power under the Constitution".[5]

Singleness, distinctiveness and indivisibility. "In determining whether a matter has attained the required degree of singleness, distinctiveness and indivisibility that clearly distinguishes it from matters of provincial concern it is relevant to consider what would be the effect on extra-provincial interests of a provincial failure to deal effectively with the control or regulation of the intra-provincial aspects of the matter."[6] The above is often referred to as the "provincial inability" test.[7]

Notes

1. *Local Prohibition* case *(Attorney-General for Ontario v. Attorney-General for the Dominion)*, [1896] A.C. 348 (H.L.).
2. *Ontario (Attorney General) v. Canada Temperance Federation*, [1946] A.C. 193 (P.C.).
3. *R. v. Crown Zellerbach Canada Ltd.*, [1988] S.C.J. No. 23, [1988] 1 S.C.R. 401 at para. 33 (S.C.C.).
4. *R. v. Crown Zellerbach Canada Ltd.*, [1988] S.C.J. No. 23, [1988] 1 S.C.R. 401 at para. 33 (S.C.C.).
5. *R. v. Crown Zellerbach Canada Ltd.*, [1988] S.C.J. No. 23, [1988] 1 S.C.R. 401 at para. 33 (S.C.C.).
6. *R. v. Crown Zellerbach Canada Ltd.*, [1988] S.C.J. No. 23, [1988] 1 S.C.R. 401 at para. 33 (S.C.C.).
7. *R. v. Crown Zellerbach Canada Ltd.*, [1988] S.C.J. No. 23, [1988] 1 S.C.R. 401 at para. 33 (S.C.C.).

---

4. The Emergency Context

▼HCL-110▼ Overview. In the earliest cases, the POGG power was only available where some extraordinary peril threatened the national life of Canada, such as the case arising out of famine and war.[1] The peril had to be "so great and so general that at least for the period it was a menace to the national life of Canada so serious and pressing that the National Parliament was called on to intervene to protect the nation from disaster."[2] In recent years, the POGG power has broadened and has, for example, applied in peacetime to justify the control of rampant inflation.[3] In other words, the POGG power may be available "where there can be said to be an urgent and critical situation adversely affecting all Canadians and being of such proportions as to transcend the authority vested in the Legislatures of the Provinces and thus presenting an emergency which can only be effectively dealt with by Parliament in the exercise of the powers conferred upon it by s. 91 of the *British North America Act*".[4] In an emergency, the power of Parliament is dictated by the nature of the crisis, and has the ability to trump provincial jurisdiction.[5] The existence of an emergency however does not automatically confer unfettered powers to the federal government; the legislation must be "necessary" to address the emergency.[6] In order to determine whether legislation was enacted to combat such an emergency as demanded of the POGG power, it is necessary to examine the legislation itself. The first observation regarding POGG that emerges from this is that Parliament is given power over "distinct subject matters which do not fall within any of the enumerated heads of s. 92 and which, by nature, are of national concern".[7] Second, the power gives Parliament *temporary* jurisdiction over all subject-matters needed to deal with an emergency, and which "in practice … operates as a partial and temporary alteration of the distribution of powers between Parliament and the provincial legislatures". All in all, the emergency power under POGG supports the federal emergency power, but only to the extent that it implements temporary measures.[8]

Notes

1. *Toronto Electric Commissioners v. Snider*, [1925] A.C. 396 at 412 (P.C.).
2. *Toronto Electric Commissioners v. Snider*, [1925] A.C. 396 at 412 (P.C.).
3. *Reference re: Anti Inflation Act*, [1976] S.C.J. No. 12, [1976] 2 S.C.R. 373 (S.C.C.).
4. *Reference re: Anti Inflation Act*, [1976] S.C.J. No. 12, [1976] 2 S.C.R. 373 at para. 437 (S.C.C.).
5. *Reference re: Wartime Leasehold Regulations, P.C. 9029*, [1950] S.C.J. No. 1, [1950] S.C.R. 124 (S.C.C.).
6. *Reference re: Anti Inflation Act*, [1976] S.C.J. No. 12, [1976] 2 S.C.R. 373 at para. 391 (S.C.C.).
7. *Reference re: Anti Inflation Act*, [1976] S.C.J. No. 12, [1976] 2 S.C.R. 373 at 457 (S.C.C.).
8. *Reference re: Anti Inflation Act*, [1976] S.C.J. No. 12, [1976] 2 S.C.R. 373 at para. 427, 437-38, 461 (S.C.C.).

VI. Criminal Law – Federal and Provincial Jurisdiction

1. **Introduction** HCL-111

2. **Criminal Law Power**

(1) Components HCL-113
(2) Health and the Environment HCL-115
(3) Tobacco and Drugs HCL-117
(4) Gun Control HCL-119
(5) Jurisdiction Over the Establishment of Criminal Courts HCL-120
(6) Criminal Procedure and Evidence HCL-121
(7) Criminal Justice and Policing HCL-122
(8) Prosecution of Offences HCL-123

3. **Civil Law Remedies under the Criminal Law Power** HCL-124

4. **Provincial Power to Enact Penal Laws** HCL-125

5. **Punishment and Prevention of Crime** HCL-126

6. **Young Offenders** HCL-128

---

1. Introduction

▼HCL-111▼ Criminal law power. Pursuant to the *Constitution Act, 1867*,[1] the power to make laws in relation to criminal law rests with Parliament. Parliament's jurisdiction over criminal law allows it to enact laws in relation to a number of different matters, as long as the statute may be considered to be in relation to "criminal law". "The federal criminal law power is plenary in nature and has been broadly construed."[2] Parliament will be able to justify its statute under the *Constitution Act, 1867*[3] if the statute presents the three elements identified. These three prerequisites are: (1) a valid criminal law purpose; (2) backed by a prohibition; and (3) a penalty for any infringement. Parliament cannot invade into provincial jurisdiction by enacting a "colourable" criminal statute, but that in reality is within provincial matters.[4]

Notes

1. (U.K.), 30 & 31 Vict., c. 3, s. 91(27).
2. *R. v. Malmo-Levine*, [2003] S.C.J. No. 79, [2003] 3 S.C.R. 571 at para. 73 (S.C.C.) [emphasis added].
3. (U.K.), 30 & 31 Vict., c. 3, s. 91(27).
4. *Scowby v. Glendinning*, [1986] S.C.J. No. 57, [1986] 2 S.C.R. 226 at 237 (S.C.C.).

▼HCL-112▼ Provincial jurisdiction. The *Constitution Act, 1867*[1] grants the provincial legislatures power to create laws in relation to "the Administration of Justice in the Province, including the Constitution, Maintenance, and Organization of Provincial Courts, both of Civil and of Criminal Jurisdiction, and including Procedure in Civil Matters in those Courts". This power is expressly excluded from the federal Parliament.[2] The *Constitution Act, 1867*[3] also grants provincial legislatures the power to create laws in relation to the "Imposition of Punishment by Fine, Penalty, or Imprisonment for enforcing any law of the Province made in relation to any Matter coming within any of the Classes of Subjects enumerated in this section".[4]

Federal and provincial jurisdiction. The provincial and federal governments both have jurisdiction over correctional institutions. Provinces retain jurisdiction over "prisons", which house criminal offenders sentenced to terms of less than two years, while federal "penitentiaries" house offenders sentenced to terms in excess of two years.[5]

Notes

1. (U.K.), 30 & 31 Vict., c. 3, s. 92(14).
2. *Constitution Act, 1867*, (U.K.), 30 & 31 Vict., c. 3, s. 91(27).
3. (U.K.), 30 & 31 Vict., c. 3, s. 92(15).
4. *Constitution Act, 1867* (U.K.), 30 & 31 Vict., c. 3, s. 92(15).
5. *Constitution Act, 1867* (U.K.), 30 & 31 Vict., c. 3, ss. 91(28), 92(6); (CAN) *Criminal Code*, R.S.C. 1985, c. C-46, s. 743.1(1).

---

2. Criminal Law Power

(1) Components HCL-113
(2) Health and the Environment HCL-115
(3) Tobacco and Drugs HCL-117
(4) Gun Control HCL-119

(5) Jurisdiction Over the Establishment of Criminal Courts HCL-120
(6) Criminal Procedure and Evidence HCL-121
(7) Criminal Justice and Policing HCL-122
(8) Prosecution of Offences HCL-123

---

(1) Components

▼HCL-113▼ Overview. There are three requirements that must be met for a law to be criminal in nature. The law must be a prohibition, the prohibition must be accompanied by a punishment, or penal sanctions and the law must be directed toward a public purpose.[1] The prohibition with penal consequences should be directed at an evil or injurious effect on the public.[2] To determine whether a law is enacted with a view to a public purpose, the laws must be "designed to promote public peace, safety, order, health or other legitimate public purpose".[3]

Notes

1. *Reference re: Dairy Industry Act (Canada) s. 5(a)*, [1948] S.C.J. No. 42, [1949] S.C.R. 1 (S.C.C.).
2. *R. v. Malmo-Levine*, [2003] S.C.J. No. 79, [2003] 3 S.C.R. 571 (S.C.C.).
3. *R. v. Malmo-Levine*, [2003] S.C.J. No. 79, [2003] 3 S.C.R. 571 at para. 41 (S.C.C.); see also *R. v. Boggs*, [1981] S.C.J. No. 6, [1981] 1 S.C.R. 49 (S.C.C.).

▼HCL-114▼ No necessity of harm. The "harm principle" stands for the proposition that the *absence* of proven harm creates an unqualified barrier to legislative action.[1] "While there is no constitutional threshold level of harm required before Parliament may use its broad criminal law power, conduct with little or no threat of harm is unlikely to qualify as a 'public health evil'."[2] "Harm need not be shown to the court's satisfaction to be 'serious and substantial' before Parliament can impose a prohibition. Once it is demonstrated ... that the harm is not *de minimis*, or not 'insignificant or trivial', the precise weighing and calculation of the nature and extent of the harm" is within the purview of Parliament.[3] Moreover, a legislator "may sometimes be justified in criminalizing conduct that is either not harmful (in the sense contemplated by the harm principle), or that causes harm only to the accused".[4] "Bestiality and cruelty to animals are examples of crimes that rest on their offensiveness to deeply held social values" rather than on the "harm principle".[5]

Notes

1. *R. v. Malmo-Levine*, [2003] S.C.J. No. 79, [2003] 3 S.C.R. 571 at para. 115 (S.C.C.).
2. *R. v. Malmo-Levine*, [2003] S.C.J. No. 79, [2003] 3 S.C.R. 571 (S.C.C.).
3. *R. v. Malmo-Levine*, [2003] S.C.J. No. 79, [2003] 3 S.C.R. 571 at para. 114 (S.C.C.).
4. *R. v. Malmo-Levine*, [2003] S.C.J. No. 79, [2003] 3 S.C.R. 571 at para. 115 (S.C.C.).
5. *R. v. Malmo-Levine*, [2003] S.C.J. No. 79, [2003] 3 S.C.R. 571 at para. 117 (S.C.C.).

---

(2) Health and the Environment

▼HCL-115▼ Health and criminal law. The criminal law treatment of health and the environment is a special issue in the Constitution — one which is under the responsibility of Parliament or to the provincial legislatures depending on the purpose or effect of a given measure. With respect to health, the provinces have wide-ranging powers over public health under the *Constitution Act, 1867*[1] as a local or private matter. Nevertheless, Parliament may still legislate in relation to health measures. Section 91(27) grants Parliament the power to enact criminal law with respect to conduct that is dangerous to health.[2] In addition, POGG very likely allows for legislation to restrict such conduct where the issue is of national concern or a national emergency.[3] An epidemic might be held to justify criminal legislation in this area. Furthermore, Parliament may enact health measures relating to occupational health and safety for those jurisdictions where labour relations are governed federally. And finally, Parliament may impose national standards on health insurance and medical care programs as a condition of federal contributions to these programs.[4]

Notes

1. (U.K.), 30 & 31 Vict., c. 3, s. 92(16).
2. *Constitution Act, 1867* (U.K.), 30 & 31 Vict., c. 3, s. 91(27); see *Reference re Assisted Human Reproduction Act*, [2010] S.C.J. No. 61, [2010] 3 S.C.R. 457 at para. 52 (S.C.C.); *R.J.R.-MacDonald v. Canada (Attorney General)*, [1995] S.C.J. No. 18, [1995] 3 S.C.R. 199 (S.C.C.); *Canada (Attorney General) v. JTI-Macdonald Corp.*, [2007] S.C.J. No. 30, [2007] 2 S.C.R. 610 (S.C.C.); *R. v. Wetmore (County Court Judge)*, [1983] S.C.J. No. 74, [1983] 2 S.C.R. 284 (S.C.C.); *Canada (Attorney General) v. PHS Community Services Society*, [2011] S.C.J. No. 44, 2011 SCC 44 (S.C.C.).

3. *Schneider v. (British Columbia*, [1982] S.C.J. No. 64, [1982] 2 S.C.R. 112 (S.C.C.).
4. *Québec (Attorney General) v. Canada*, [2011] S.C.J. No. 11, 412 N.R. 115 (S.C.C.).

▼HCL-116▼ Environment and criminal law. The issue of environmental protection, *i.e.*, the protection of air, water and the environment generally extends beyond the protection merely of human health. It is a public purpose and rightfully falls under the jurisdiction of Parliament. The environment has a fundamental value to society and Parliament may use its criminal law power to underline that value.[1] Provinces do not have the jurisdiction to enact criminal legislation, nor can the federal government delegate such jurisdiction to them. "Any environmental legislation enacted by the provinces must, therefore, be of a regulatory nature. Deferring to the provincial regulatory schemes on the basis that they are 'equivalent' to federal regulations made under s. 34(1) creates a strong presumption that the federal regulations are themselves of a regulatory, not criminal, nature".[2]

Notes

1. *R. v. Hydro-Québec*, [1997] S.C.J. No. 76, [1997] 3 S.C.R. 213 at paras. 296-297 (S.C.C.). See also *Halsbury's Laws of Canada – Environment.*
2. *R. v. Hydro-Québec*, [1997] S.C.J. No. 76, [1997] 3 S.C.R. 213 at para. 57 (S.C.C.).

---

(3) Tobacco and Drugs

▼HCL-117▼ Tobacco. The Supreme Court addressed the validity of the *Tobacco Products Control Act.*[1] The Act prohibited the advertising of cigarettes and other tobacco products, and also required that health warnings be printed on the exterior of cigarette packaging. In determining whether there existed a valid criminal purpose, the Court concluded that the package warnings met the requirements of protecting the public from danger. Because it is within the power of Parliament to prohibit the use, sale or manufacture of tobacco products for health reasons, then it necessarily has the power to take lesser steps in limiting or prohibiting the advertisement of these products. A prohibition on advertising had a similar underlying public purpose as the prohibition on smoking — namely, protecting the public from a dangerous product. However, the advertising prohibition was struck down as violating the Charter,[2] as the impact of the prohibition on advertising violated freedom of expression. In response to this judgment, Parliament amended the legislative scheme, which was upheld by the Supreme Court, including the requirement that health warnings be printed on the packaging.

Notes

1. S.C. 1998, c. 20; *R.J.R.-MacDonald Inc. v. Canada (Attorney General)*, [1995] S.C.J. No. 68, [1995] 3 S.C.R. 199 (S.C.C.); *Canada (Attorney General) v. JTI-Macdonald Corp.*, [2007] S.C.J. No. 30, [2007] 2 S.C.R. 610 (S.C.C.).
2. *Canadian Charter of Rights and Freedoms*, Part I of the *Constitution Act, 1982*, being Schedule B to the *Canada Act 1982* (U.K.), 1982, c. 11.

▼HCL-118▼ Drugs. Parliament has jurisdiction to enact laws in relation to narcotics and drugs, and has done so with the federal *Controlled Drugs and Substances Act*[1] which prohibits the production, importation, sale and possession of illicit drugs, and has been upheld as valid criminal law,[2] and the *Food and Drugs Act*[3] which regulates the production and sale of food and medicinal drugs.[4] On the other hand, provincial legislatures have jurisdiction to legislate in relation to social problems arising from drug addiction. British Columbia's *Heroin Treatment Act*,[5] for example, outlined compulsory apprehension, assessment and treatment of drug addicts. Treatment under the Act could include involuntary detention for up to six months. It was argued that, due to the impact on the liberty of a detained person, the Act was actually criminal legislation, and within the exclusive jurisdiction of Parliament. The Court unanimously decided that the Act was *intra vires* the provincial legislature stating that "the 'pith and substance' of the *Heroin Treatment Act*[6] is the medical treatment of heroin addicts and is within the general provincial competence over health matters under s. 92(16) of the *B.N.A. Act*".[7] The Supreme Court of Canada concluded that the "Legislature was endeavouring to cure a medical condition" rather than to punish a criminal activity.[8]

Notes

1. (CAN) S.C. 1996, c. 19.
2. *Canada (Attorney General) v. PHS Community Services Society*, [2011] S.C.J. No. 44, 2011 SCC 44 (S.C.C.).
3. (CAN) R.S.C. 1985, c. F-27.
4. (CAN) *Controlled Drugs and Substances Act*, S.C. 1996, c. 19; (CAN) *Food and Drugs Act*, R.S.C. 1985, c. F-27; see *Canada v. Industrial Acceptance Corp.*, [1953] S.C.J. No. 47, [1953] 2 S.C.R. 273 (S.C.C.); *R. v. Hauser*, [1979] S.C.J. No. 18, [1979] 1 S.C.R. 984 (S.C.C.); *R. v. Wetmore (County Court Judge)*, [1983] S.C.J. No. 74, [1983] 2 S.C.R. 284 (S.C.C.); *R. v. Malmo-Levine*, [2003] S.C.J. No. 79, [2003] 3 S.C.R. 571 (S.C.C.); *Canadian Generic Pharmaceutical Assn. v. Can-*

ada (Minister of Health), [2010] F.C.J. No. 1582, 2010 FCA 334 (F.C.A.), leave to appeal dismissed [2011] S.C.C.A. No. 54 (S.C.C.). See also *Halsbury's Laws of Canada – Drugs and Controlled Substances* and see also *Halsbury's Laws of Canada – Agriculture*.

5. (BC) S.B.C. 1978, c. 24.
6. (BC) S.B.C. 1978, c. 24.
7. *British North America Act, 1867* (U.K.), 30 & 31 Vict., c. 3.
8. *Schneider v. British Columbia*, [1982] S.C.J. No. 64, [1982] 2 S.C.R. 112 at 138 (S.C.C.).

(4) Gun Control

▼HCL-119▼ Overview. The *Firearms Act*[1] made it mandatory for all gun owners to register all guns. Before the passage of this Act, the *Criminal Code*[2] controlled access to firearms by prohibiting some types of guns, such as automatic weapons, and requiring registration and licensing for some other types. The government of Alberta referred the Act to the Alberta Court of Appeal to challenge its constitutionality. Ultimately, the Act was upheld and the province appealed to the Supreme Court.[3] The Supreme Court concluded that the statute was a valid exercise of the criminal law power, as its purpose was to restrict access to an inherently dangerous thing. The legislative history of the *Firearms Act*[4] showed that the drafters were concerned with violent crime, domestic violence, suicides, and accidents as a result of gun use. The Court found that the Act was directed to public safety: registration provisions ensured that each gun had a serial number and that it could be traced to the licence holder; licensing provisions required a gun holder to pass criminal record checks, complete a screening for past violent behaviour, and attend mandatory gun safety courses. The impact on property rights was incidental to the public safety concerns underpinning the Act. In furtherance of this conclusion, the Court pointed to the fact that the Act was not merely regulatory, but carried the hallmarks of a classic criminal law: prohibition and penalty.[5]

Notes

1. (CAN) S.C. 1995, c. 39.
2. (CAN) R.S.C. 1985, c. C-46.
3. *Reference re: Firearms Act*, [2000] S.C.J. No. 31, [2000] 1 S.C.R. 783 (S.C.C.). See also *Halsbury's Laws of Canada – Firearms, Weapons and Explosives*.

4. S.C. 1995, c. 39.
5. *Reference re: Firearms Act*, [2000] S.C.J. No. 31, [2000] 1 S.C.R. 783 (S.C.C.).

---

(5) Jurisdiction Over the Establishment of Criminal Courts

▼HCL-120▼ Overview. The jurisdiction to constitute criminal courts is specifically referred to in the *Constitution Act, 1867*,[1] which grants to the legislature the exclusive powers to make laws in relation to the "Administration of Justice in the Province, including the Constitution, Maintenance, and Organization of Provincial Courts, both of Civil and of Criminal Jurisdiction, and including Procedure in Civil Matters in those Courts."[2] However, this does not fully address the issue as to which level of government has jurisdiction to constitute courts of criminal justice, as the *Constitution Act, 1867*[3] grants to Parliament, notwithstanding anything in the Act, the power to establish any additional courts for the better administration of the laws of Canada. Parliament having jurisdiction over criminal law, the *Criminal Code*[4] is a "law of Canada". Consequently, it can be said that the jurisdiction to constitute courts of criminal jurisdiction is shared between both levels of government. The *Criminal Code*[5] grants to provincial courts the power to adjudicate matters of criminal law, and historically, the majority of cases, including serious offences, are adjudicated before the provincial courts. The exception lies in the *Criminal Code*[6] and exists due to the *Constitution Act, 1867*.[7] Because some crimes were, at Confederation, tried before "superior courts" in the United Kingdom, the jurisdiction over those most serious crimes rests with the Superior Court, where the judges are appointed by the Governor in Council.[8] Consequently, the *Criminal Code*[9] (and Parliament) may delegate the adjudication of most criminal cases to provincial courts, but cannot delegate all criminal cases to those courts because of the *Constitution Act, 1867*.[10] While it can be asserted that the power to constitute courts of criminal jurisdiction may be shared, a more convincing argument would be that the provincial legislatures have a better hold on the jurisdiction to create courts of criminal jurisdiction or courts to adjudicate offences under the *Criminal Code*.[11] However, Parliament could establish courts for any other offences under any federal legislation enacted pursuant to any other head of power under the *Constitution Act, 1867*.[12]

Notes

1. (U.K.), 30 & 31 Vict., c. 3.
2. *Constitution Act, 1867* (U.K.), 30 & 31 Vict., c. 3, s. 92(14).
3. (U.K.), 30 & 31 Vict., c. 3, s. 101.

4. (CAN) R.S.C. 1985, c. C-46. See also *Halsbury's Laws of Canada – Criminal Offences and Defences*.
5. (CAN) R.S.C. 1985, c. C-46.
6. (CAN) R.S.C. 1985, c. C-46.
7. (U.K.), 30 & 31 Vict., c. 3, s. 96.
8. See *McEvoy v. New Brunswick (Attorney General)*, [1983] S.C.J. No. 51, [1983] 1 S.C.R. 704 (S.C.C.); *Reference re Young Offenders Act (P.E.I.)*, [1990] S.C.J. No. 60, [1991] 1 S.C.R. 252 (S.C.C.).
9. (CAN) R.S.C. 1985, c. C-46.
10. (U.K.), 30 & 31 Vict., c. 3, s. 96.
11. (CAN) R.S.C. 1985, c. C-46.
12. (U.K.), 30 & 31 Vict., c. 3, s. 91.

---

(6) Criminal Procedure and Evidence

▼HCL-121▼ Criminal procedure. As noted above, the *Constitution Act, 1867*[1] expressly provides that the procedure in matters of criminal law is within the exclusive jurisdiction of Parliament. Parliament has enacted, in the *Criminal Code*,[2] several provisions in relation to procedure.[3]

Evidence. The *Constitution Act, 1867*[4] expressly provides that the rules of evidence in matters of criminal law is within the exclusive jurisdiction of Parliament, and Parliament has enacted the *Canada Evidence Act*.[5] Because of the rule of paramountcy, provincial rules of evidence that are inconsistent with the federal rules are not applicable in matters of criminal law, and provincial legislatures cannot enact legislation that would shield any evidence from the criminal law process.[6]

Notes

1. (U.K.), 30 & 31 Vict., c. 3, s. 91(27).
2. (CAN) R.S.C. 1985, c. C-46.
3. See also *Halsbury's Laws of Canada – Criminal Procedure*.
4. (U.K.), 30 & 31 Vict., c. 3, s. 91(27).
5. (CAN) R.S.C. 1985, c. C-5.
6. See *Klein v. Bell*, [1955] S.C.J. No. 19, [1955] S.C.R. 309 (S.C.C.); *Di Iorio v. Montreal (City) Common Jail*, [1976] S.C.J. No. 113, [1978] 1 S.C.R. 152 (S.C.C.); *Bisaillon v. Keable*, [1983] S.C.J. No. 65, [1983] 2 S.C.R. 60 (S.C.C.).

---

(7) Criminal Justice and Policing

▼HCL-122▼ Overview. Under its jurisdiction over the "administration of justice in the Province" pursuant to the *Constitution Act, 1867*,[1] provincial legislatures have jurisdiction over criminal justice and policing in the province. Thus, provincial authorities may establish and control a police force for the enforcement of laws and the protection of the public.[2] In turn, this also allows provincial legislatures to delegate to municipalities the authority to establish municipal police forces.[3] Nevertheless, only Québec and Ontario have established their police force. Most provinces have entered into contracts with the federal government for the services of the Royal Canadian Mounted Police (R.C.M.P.). In providing police services in these provinces, the R.C.M.P. enforces both provincial and federal laws.

Secret service. As for the secret service or the security service, the R.C.M.P. used to be in control and provide the services for intelligence or espionage activities. The Canadian Security Intelligence Service (C.S.I.S.) and other agencies were later created, and Parliament's jurisdiction over these "policing" services could likely be found in the *Constitution Act, 1867*[4] and the jurisdiction over national defence, and the P.O.G.G. power pursuant to the opening words of the *Constitution Act, 1867*.[5]

Notes

1. (U.K.), 30 & 31 Vict., c. 3, s. 92(14).
2. See *Di Iorio v. Montreal (City) Common Jail*, [1976] S.C.J. No. 113, [1978] 1 S.C.R. 152 (S.C.C.); *O'Hara v. B.C.*, [1987] S.C.J. No. 69, [1987] 2 S.C.R. 591 (S.C.C.). See also *Halsbury's Laws of Canada – Police, Security and Emergencies*.
3. Provincial legislatures have jurisdiction to create municipalities pursuant to the *Constitution Act, 1867* (U.K.), 30 & 31 Vict., c. 3, s. 92(8).
4. (U.K.), 30 & 31 Vict., c. 3, s. 91(7).
5. (U.K.), 30 & 31 Vict., c. 3, s. 91. There has never been any confirmation of the jurisdiction of Parliament over these activities, although *dicta* in *Quebec (Attorney General) v. Canada (Attorney General)*, [1978] S.C.J. No. 84, [1979] 1 S.C.R. 218 (S.C.C.) and *Alberta (Attorney General) v. Putnam*, [1981] S.C.J. No. 85, [1981] 2 S.C.R. 267 (S.C.C.) support Parliament's jurisdiction.

---

(8) Prosecution of Offences

▼HCL-123▼ Overview. The prosecution of both federal and provincial offences are generally conducted by provincial prosecutors and provincial Crown Attorneys. Provincial jurisdiction can be found in the *Constitution Act, 1867*.[1]

Federal Crown Attorneys. Federal Crown Attorneys also have powers to prosecute crimes for federal offences other than those under the *Criminal Code*.[2] A federal Crown Attorney could prosecute a federal offence under the *Narcotic Control Act*.[3] The Supreme Court affirmed this principle for all federal offences, even if those offences had been adopted pursuant to Parliament's power over criminal law, as opposed to another offence adopted under another head of power.[4] Moreover, a federal prosecutor could prosecute an offence under the *Food and Drugs Act*,[5] a statute enacted pursuant to Parliament's power under the *Constitution Act, 1867*.[6]

Notes

1. (U.K.), 30 & 31 Vict., c. 3, s. 92(14). See *Re Bradley and the Queen*, [1975] O.J. No. 2374, 9 O.R. (2d) 161 (Ont. C.A.); see also *Canada (Attorney General) v. Canadian National Transportation Ltd.*, [1983] S.C.J. No. 73, [1983] 2 S.C.R. 206 (S.C.C.) where Laskin C.J. held that the federal prosecutors had the exclusive jurisdiction to prosecute federal offences, except for those that were already prosecuted by the provincial Crown Attorneys and retained under the *Constitution Act, 1867* (U.K.), 30 & 31 Vict., c. 3, s. 129.
2. (CAN) R.S.C. 1985, c. C-46.
3. (CAN) R.S.C. 1985, c. N-1, repealed by the *Controlled Drugs and Substances Act*, S.C. 1996, c. 19; *R. v. Hauser*, [1979] S.C.J. No. 18, [1979] 1 S.C.R. 984 (S.C.C.).
4. *Canada (Attorney General) v. Canadian National Transportation Ltd.*, [1983] S.C.J. No. 73, [1983] 2 S.C.R. 206 (S.C.C.); *R. v. Wetmore (County Court Judge)*, [1983] S.C.J. No. 74, [1983] 2 S.C.R. 284 (S.C.C.).
5. (CAN) R.S.C. 1985, c. F-27.
6. (U.K.), 30 & 31 Vict., c. 3, s. 91(27).

---

3. Civil Law Remedies under the Criminal Law Power

▼HCL-124▼ Criminal law remedies. The question of whether the criminal law power authorizes Parliament to confer a civil right of action is one made difficult by the very nature of the criminal law power, which contemplates punishment and rehabilitation for public wrongs as opposed to pecuniary redress for private prejudices. The *Criminal Code*[1] grants courts the ability to order a convicted person to pay the victim compensation for any loss or damage.[2] Three restrictions were placed on the granting of such an order: it must be made on the application of the victim, as opposed to the Crown or judge; the amount must be related to the value of the victim's loss, rather than the nature of the crime or the moral blameworthiness of the accused; and the order must be enforced by the victim as if it were a civil remedy.[3] The absence of civil procedures, such as discovery, does not make the provision unconstitutional, but rather suggests to a trier of fact some restraint in exercising his or her discretion.

Notes

1. (CAN) R.S.C. 1985, c. C-46.
2. *R. v. Zelensky*, [1978] S.C.J. No. 48, [1978] 2 S.C.R. 940 (S.C.C.).
3. *R. v. Zelensky*, [1978] S.C.J. No. 48, [1978] 2 S.C.R. 940 at 961 (S.C.C.).

---

4. Provincial Power to Enact Penal Laws

▼HCL-125▼ Overview. Section 92(15) grants provincial legislatures the power to impose "Punishment by Fine, Penalty or Imprisonment"[1] to enforce valid provincial statutes. In assessing provincial penalty provisions, the courts must distinguish between valid provincial law with an ancillary penalty, and laws which are invalid as encroaching on Parliament's exclusive jurisdiction over criminal law. Provincial offences were upheld in the areas of careless driving, failing to remain at the scene of an accident, and giving false information in a prospectus. Each of these related to a *Criminal Code*[2] violation that was upheld as valid criminal law. The Supreme Court will step in if it deems that a provincial or municipal law has gone too far.[3] For example, a municipal by-law that prohibited a person from remaining on the street for the purposes of prostitution was struck down as being criminal law.

Notes

1. *Constitution Act, 1867* (U.K.), 30 & 31 Vict., c. 3, s. 92(15).
2. (CAN) *Criminal Code*, R.S.C. 1985, c. C-46.
3. *R. v. Westendorp*, [1983] S.C.J. No. 6, [1983] 1 S.C.R. 43 (S.C.C.); see also *R. v. Morgentaler*, [1993] S.C.J. No. 95, [1993] 3 S.C.R. 463 (S.C.C.).

---

5. Punishment and Prevention of Crime

▼HCL-126▼ Punishment. Both Parliament and provincial legislatures may provide for punishment, including prison terms, for any offence under their jurisdiction. Parliament may provide for punishment of any federal offence.[1] Provinces may do the same under the *Constitution Act,*

1867[2] and their jurisdiction over the administration of justice, as well as pursuant to the *Constitution Act, 1867*[3] and their jurisdiction, to provide for "Punishment by fine, penalty or imprisonment"[4] to enforce valid provincial statutes. Additional jurisdiction over the matter may be found in each level of government's respective jurisdiction over correction institutions. Parliament has jurisdiction over "the Establishment, Maintenance, and Management of Penitentiaries",[5] and provincial legislatures have jurisdiction over the "Establishment, Maintenance, and Management of Public and Reformatory Prisons in and for the Province".[6]

Notes

1. *Constitution Act, 1867* (U.K.), 30 & 31 Vict., c. 3, s. 91(27). See also *Halsbury's Laws of Canada – Criminal Procedure*.
2. *Constitution Act, 1867* (U.K.), 30 & 31 Vict., c. 3, s. 92(14).
3. *Constitution Act, 1867* (U.K.), 30 & 31 Vict., c. 3, s. 92(15).
4. *Constitution Act, 1867* (U.K.), 30 & 31 Vict., c. 3, s. 92(15).
5. *Constitution Act, 1867* (U.K.), 30 & 31 Vict., c. 3, s. 91(28).
6. *Constitution Act, 1867* (U.K.), 30 & 31 Vict., c. 3, s. 92(6).

▼HCL-127▼ Prevention of crime. Even if a law itself does not have criminal characteristics, it may be validly enacted as long as it is in relation to the criminal law. A law which repealed a criminal law, for example, would be a valid exercise of power by Parliament. The most noteworthy application is in regard to laws designed to prevent crime. The concept of prevention has been used to justify a provision of the *Combines Investigation Act*,[1] for example, which grants the courts the power to order a prohibition of future conduct which would violate the Act.[2] The *Criminal Code*[3] itself contains numerous provisions relating to disposition, assessment, and treatment in relation to accused with mental health issues. Two groups are covered by these provisions: those found "not criminally responsible on account of mental disorder" and those "unfit to stand trial". The *Criminal Code*[4] allows for the continued detention of offenders who fall into the first group and who are considered a significant threat to society despite the fact that they have not been convicted of any crime. Once an accused in this group is deemed to no longer be a significant threat to public safety, then the accused is released.[5] By contrast, those deemed unfit to stand trial by reason of mental health disorder remain in the criminal justice system because they are subject to an unresolved criminal charge.

Notes

1. (CAN) R.S.C. 1927, c. 26.
2. See *R. v. Goodyear Tire and Rubber Co.*, [1956] S.C.J. No. 8, [1956] S.C.R. 303 (S.C.C.).
3. (CAN) R.S.C. 1985, c. C-46.
4. (CAN) R.S.C. 1985, c. C-46.
5. (CAN) *Criminal Code*, R.S.C. 1985, c. C-46, s. 672.54.

---

6. Young Offenders

▼HCL-128▼ Overview. The federal *Juvenile Delinquents Act*[1] was upheld as valid criminal law.[2] This was done despite the fact that there is express language in the Act to the effect that juvenile delinquents are not to be treated as criminals, but are "subjected to such wise care, treatment and control as will tend to check their evil tendencies and strengthen their better instincts".[3] The Act was replaced in 1984 by the *Young Offenders Act*,[4] which was designed to be most closely tailored to our traditional conception of the criminal law. However, the Act maintained much of the curative spirit of its predecessor and, in some instances, allowed for youth diversion programs in place of traditional criminal sanctions. These programs were themselves upheld as an exercise of the preventative aspect of the criminal law power. Today, young offenders are subject to the provisions of the *Youth Criminal Justice Act*,[5] which replaced the *Young Offenders Act* in 2003. There are more detailed provisions for diversion programs in the current Act, including police warnings and cautions, and referrals to community programs. All accused are tried in Youth Justice Courts, which have the discretion to hand down adult sentences for serious offences. The court will choose whether or not to exercise its discretion in this area only at the end of trial.

Notes

1. (CAN) R.S.C. 1952, c. 160.
2. *British Columbia (Attorney General) v. Smith*, [1967] S.C.J. No. 64, [1967] S.C.R. 702 (S.C.C.).
3. *British Columbia (Attorney General) v. Smith*, [1967] S.C.J. No. 64, [1967] S.C.R. 702 (S.C.C.).
4. (CAN) R.S.C. 1985, c. Y-1 (repealed).
5. (CAN) S.C. 2002, c. 1. See also *Halsbury's Laws of Canada – Youth Justice*.

VII. The Regulation of Trade and Commerce

1. General HCL-129

2. Two Branches of the Trade and Commerce Power

(1) International and Interprovincial Trade and Commerce. HCL-131

(2) The General Regulation of Trade and Commerce HCL-134

---

1. General

▼HCL-129▼ Overview. The *Constitution Act, 1867*[1] grants to Parliament the authority to legislate over matters falling within "The Regulation of Trade and Commerce".[2] The phrase "the regulation of trade and commerce", given its plain and ordinary meaning, has the potential of encompassing almost any sphere of activity capable of legislative regulation. Delineating the boundaries of the trade and commerce power has proven to be problematic because it comes into direct opposition and overlaps with several matters of exclusive provincial legislative jurisdiction enumerated in the *Constitution Act, 1867*.[3] The trade and commerce power comes into conflict with the provincial authority over "Property and Civil Rights in the Province".[4] [5] Trade and commerce also has the potential of overlapping with the exclusive provincial authority over "Generally all Matters of a merely local or private Nature in the Province."[6] Analysis of trade and commerce cases should be confined to the facts before the court, as making more general pronouncements on the scope of the trade and commerce power leads to dangerous territory.[7]

Notes

1. (U.K.), 30 & 31 Vict., c. 3, s. 91(2).
2. *Constitution Act, 1867* (U.K.), 30 & 31 Vict., c. 3, s. 91(2).
3. (U.K.), 30 & 31 Vict., c. 3, s. 92.
4. *Constitution Act, 1876* (U.K.), 30 & 31 Vict., c. 3, s. 92(13).
5. *Citizens Insurance Company of Canada v. Parsons* (1881), 7 App. Cas. 96 (P.C.).
6. *Constitution Act, 1876* (U.K.), 30 & 31 Vict., c. 3, s. 92(16).

7. See, for example, *John Deere Plow Co. v. Wharton*, [1915] A.C. 330 at 338-39 (P.C.).

2. Two Branches of the Trade and Commerce Power

(1) International and Interprovincial Trade and Commerce.. HCL-131
(2) The General Regulation of Trade and Commerce.. HCL-134

▼HCL-130▼ Overview. A subject-matter under the trade and commerce power could fall within one of two branches: (1) interprovincial and international trade and commerce; and (2) the general regulation of trade and commerce affecting the whole of Canada.[1] "This interpretation of s. 91(2), which limits the scope of the federal trade and commerce power to these two branches, is intended to ensure a proper constitutional balance between the otherwise overlapping federal power over trade and commerce (s. 91(2)) and the provincial power over property and civil rights in the province (s. 92(13))."[2]

Notes

1. *Citizens Insurance Company of Canada v. Parsons* (1881), 7 App. Cas. 96 at 113 (P.C.).
2. *Kirkbi AG v. Ritvik Holdings Inc.*, [2005] S.C.J. No. 66, [2005] 3 S.C.R. 302 at para. 15 (S.C.C.).

(1) International and Interprovincial Trade and Commerce

▼HCL-131▼ First branch. Initially, the scope for interprovincial trade was very narrowly construed, but the power has broadened over the years. Generally, however, federal regulation of trade and commerce cannot interfere with transactions that are completely intra-provincial. In other words, "the Parliament of Canada may not, in the guise of regulating trade and commerce, reach into fields allocated to the provinces by s. 92(13) and (16) and regulate trading transactions occurring entirely within the provinces".[1] To demonstrate, in the case of wheat, since the trade in wheat is essentially a matter of export and interprovincial trade, the marketing of wheat, both intra-provincial and interprovincial, should be subject to federal regulation.[2] The trade and commerce power does not have independent effect under the *Constitution Act, 1867*[3] when property and civil rights are also at stake[4] although federal regulation may be necessary, and indeed desirable for the economic development of Canada.[5]

Notes

1. *R. v. Dominion Stores Ltd.*, [1979] S.C.J. No. 131, [1980] 1 S.C.R. 844 (S.C.C.).
2. Brian Morgan, "The Trade and Commerce Power" in Joseph Eliot Magnet, *Constitutional Law of Canada*, 9th ed. (Edmonton: Juriliber Limited, 2007) at 522.
3. (U.K.), 30 & 31 Vict., c. 3, s. 91.
4. *Toronto Electric Commissioners v. Snider*, [1925] A.C. 396 at 410 (P.C.).
5. For further discussion on this issue see Brian Morgan, "The Trade and Commerce Power" in Joseph Eliot Magnet, *Constitutional Law of Canada*, 9th ed. (Edmonton: Juriliber Limited, 2007) at 523.

▼HCL-132▼ Matter of local concern. If an industry is "substantially local in character, ... the regulations created are ... confined to the regulation of a trade within a province".[1] Once an article enters into the flow of interprovincial or external trade however, "the subject-matter and all of its attendant circumstances cease to be a mere matter of local concern".[2]

Notes

1. *Labatt Brewing Co. v. Canada*, [1979] S.C.J. No. 134, [1980] 1 S.C.R. 914 at 943 (S.C.C.).
2. *Reference Re: Farm Products Marketing Act*, [1957] S.C.J. No. 11, [1957] S.C.R. 198 at 205 (S.C.C.).

▼HCL-133▼ Provincial laws. Generally, once "a provincial statute aims at 'regulation of trade in matters of interprovincial concern' it is beyond the competence of a Provincial Legislature".[1] However, if provincial regulations only have an incidental effect on interprovincial trade, then such provincial legislation may be valid.[2] "If the federal Parliament cannot regulate local trade because it would be more efficient to regulate it together with the extra-provincial trade, *a fortiori* a provincial Legislature cannot regulate inter-provincial trade in a given product because this appears desirable for the effective control of intra-provincial trade. In other words, the direct regulation of inter-provincial trade is of itself a matter outside the legislative authority of any province and it cannot be treated as an accessory of the local trade."[3]

Notes

1. *Manitoba (Attorney General) v. Manitoba Egg and Poultry Association*, [1971] S.C.J. No. 63, [1971] S.C.R. 689 (S.C.C.).
2. *Carnation Co. v. Quebec (Agricultural Marketing Board)*, [1968] S.C.J. No. 11, [1968] S.C.R. 238 (S.C.C.).
3. *Manitoba (Attorney General) v. Burns Foods Ltd.*, [1973] S.C.J. No. 151, [1975] 1 S.C.R. 494 at 503-504 (S.C.C.).

---

(2) The General Regulation of Trade and Commerce

▼HCL-134▼ Second branch. "The 'general trade and commerce' category requires an assessment of the relative importance of an activity to the national economy as well as an inquiry into whether an activity should be regulated by Parliament as opposed to the provinces."[1] The "following factors are hallmarks of a valid exercise of Parliament's general trade and commerce power: (i) the impugned legislation must be part of a regulatory scheme; (ii) the scheme must be monitored by the continuing oversight of a regulatory agency; (iii) the legislation must be concerned with trade as a whole rather than with a particular industry; (iv) the legislation should be of a nature that provinces jointly or severally would be constitutionally incapable of enacting; and (v) the failure to include one or more provinces or localities in a legislative scheme would jeopardize the successful operation of the scheme in other parts of the country".[2] These *indicia* do not, however, represent an exhaustive list of traits that will tend to characterize general trade and commerce legislation. Nor is the presence or absence of any of these five criteria necessarily determinative.[3] The proper approach to the characterization is a careful case-by-case assessment.[4]

Notes

1. *Kirkbi AG v. Ritvik Holdings Inc.*, [2005] S.C.J. No. 66, [2005] 3 S.C.R. 302 at para. 16 (S.C.C.).
2. *Kirkbi AG v. Ritvik Holdings Inc.*, [2005] S.C.J. No. 66, [2005] 3 S.C.R. 302 at para. 17 (S.C.C.).
3. *Canada (Attorney General) v. Canadian National* Transportation *Ltd.*, [1983] S.C.J. No. 73, [1983] 2 S.C.R. 206 at 267-68 (S.C.C.).
4. *Canada (Attorney General) v. Canadian National Transportation Ltd.*, [1983] S.C.J. No. 73, [1983] 2 S.C.R. 206 at 267-68 (S.C.C.).

▼HCL-135▼ Three-step test. The three-part test for determining whether the impugned provision is within constitutional powers of the enacting legislature seeks to determine whether the impugned provision intrudes into a provincial head of power, and to what extent. If the impugned provision intrudes into a provincial head of power, is it nevertheless part of a valid federal legislative scheme? And lastly, if the impugned provision is part of a valid federal scheme, is it sufficiently integrated with that scheme?[1] The analysis of the second step above is guided by the five *indicia* already identified. With respect to the third step, the degree of integration required is dependent on the extent to which the provision encroaches on provincial powers. For example, if the impugned provision only encroaches marginally on provincial powers, then a "functional" relationship may be sufficient to justify the provision. Alternatively, if the impugned provision is highly intrusive vis-à-vis provincial powers, then a stricter test is appropriate. A careful case-by-case assessment of the proper test is the best approach.[2]

Notes

1. *Kirkbi AG v. Ritvik Holdings Inc.*, [2005] S.C.J. No. 66, [2005] 3 S.C.R. 302 at para. 21 (S.C.C.).
2. *Kirkbi AG v. Ritvik Holdings Inc.*, [2005] S.C.J. No. 66, [2005] 3 S.C.R. 302 at para. 32 (S.C.C.); see also, *General Motors of Canada Ltd. v. City National Leasing*, [1989] S.C.J. No. 28, [1989] 1 S.C.R. 641 at 669 (S.C.C.).

VIII. The Raising of Revenue, the Spending Power and Federal Authority in Relation to Financial Matters

1. **The Raising of Revenue**
   - (1) Introduction HCL-136
   - (2) Section 125 of the *Constitution Act, 1867* HCL-138
   - (3) Raising Revenue Through the Imposition of Taxes HCL-140
   - (4) Raising Revenue Through Regulatory Charges HCL-150
   - (5) Raising Revenue Through Licences HCL-157
   - (6) Section 92A of the *Constitution Act, 1867* HCL-159
2. **The Spending Power** HCL-160
3. **Banking** HCL-163
4. **Bankruptcy** HCL-168
5. **Interest** HCL-171

---

1. **The Raising of Revenue**
   - (1) Introduction HCL-136
   - (2) Section 125 of the *Constitution Act, 1867* HCL-138
   - (3) Raising Revenue Through the Imposition of Taxes
     - (a) Direct vs. Indirect Taxes HCL-142
     - (b) Direct Taxation Within the Province for a Provincial Purpose HCL-144
     - (c) Established Types of Direct Taxes HCL-145
   - (4) Raising Revenue Through Regulatory Charges HCL-150
   - (5) Raising Revenue Through Licences HCL-157
   - (6) Section 92A of the *Constitution Act, 1867* HCL-159

---

(1) Introduction

▼HCL-136▼ Overview. The Canadian federal and provincial governments must all raise revenues to finance national, provincial or even local programs or interests. The *Constitution Act, 1867*[1] provides the grounds pursuant to which the federal and provincial government may raise revenues.[2] Parliament's jurisdiction over taxation is expressed in the *Constitution Act, 1867*,[3] which empowers Parliament to raise money by any mode or system of taxation. This definition includes any conceivable type of taxation, including indirect taxes such as customs and excise and direct taxation such as income taxes and licence fees.[4] On the other hand, provinces are limited to enact taxes that are "Direct", "within the Province" and "for Provincial Purposes".[5] That power is plenary,[6] which means that courts cannot evaluate the policy rationale underlying the tax. For both levels of government to impose a tax, that tax must have been adopted by either Parliament or the provincial legislature, through a Ways and Means measure. In other words, to impose a tax, Parliament or a legislature must have explicitly adopted a tax for the raising of general revenue. On the other hand, both levels of government (a territorial government is akin to a provincial legislature)[7] may adopt regulatory schemes allowing for the adoption of charges, fees or levies, which will be valid despite not having been adopted by Parliament or a legislature, but rather be imposed by a governmental agency. These charges are not taxes, because they are not raised for the general revenue (and to finance general objectives), but rather are imposed to defray the cost of the specific programs to which those specific charges are attached.

Notes

1. (U.K.), 30 & 31 Vict., c. 3.
2. *Constitution Act, 1867* (U.K.), 30 & 31 Vict., c. 3, ss. 53, 91(3), 92(2), 92(9), 92A(4), 125.

   53. Bills for appropriating any Part of the Public Revenue, or for imposing any Tax or Impost, shall originate in the House of Commons.

   ...

   > **91(3).** The raising of Money by any Mode or System of Taxation.

   ...

   > **92(2).** Direct Taxation within the Province in order to [sic] the raising of a Revenue for Provincial Purposes.

   ...

   > **92(9).** Shop, Saloon, Tavern, Auctioneer, and other Licences in order to [sic] the raising of a Revenue for Provincial, Local, or Municipal Purposes.

   ...

92A(4) In each province, the legislature may make laws in relation to the raising of money by any mode or system of taxation in respect of

(a) non-renewable natural resources and forestry resources in the province and the primary production therefrom, and

(b) sites and facilities in the province for the generation of electrical energy and the production therefrom,

whether or not such production is exported in whole or in part from the province, but such laws may not authorize or provide for taxation that differentiates between production exported to another part of Canada and production not exported from the province.

...

125. No Lands or Property belonging to Canada or any Province shall be liable to Taxation.

3. (U.K.), 30 & 31 Vict., c. 3, s. 91(3).
4. *British Columbia (Attorney General) v. Canada (Attorney General)*, [1923] J.C.J. No. 5, [1924] A.C. 222 (P.C.); *Croft v. Dunphy*, [1932] J.C.J. No. 4, [1933] A.C. 156 (P.C.); *British Columbia (Attorney General) v. McDonald Murphy Lumber Co.*, [1930] J.C.J. No. 1, [1930] A.C. 357 (P.C.); *Proprietary Articles Trade Association v. Canada (Attorney General)*, [1931] J.C.J. No. 1, [1931] A.C. 310 (P.C.); *Canada v. Shearwater Co.*, [1934] S.C.J. No. 8, [1934] S.C.R. 197 (S.C.C.); *Reference re: British North America Act, 1867, s. 108 (Can)*, [1898] J.C.J. No. 1, [1898] A.C. 700 (P.C.).
5. (U.K.), 30 & 31 Vict., c. 3, s. 92(2).
6. *Reference re: Liquor License Act of 1877 (Ont.)*, [1883] J.C.J. No. 2, 9 App. Cas. 117 at 132.
7. See *Fédération Franco-Ténoise v. Canada*, [2001] F.C.J. No. 1093, [2001] 3 F.C. 641 (Fed. C.A.); *Fédération Franco-Ténoise v. Canada (Attorney General)*, [2008] N.W.T.J. No. 45, 440 A.R. 56 (N.W.T.C.A.), supp. reasons [2008] N.W.T.J. No. 48, [2009] 12 W.W.R. 376 (N.W.T.C.A.), leave to appeal to S.C.C. refused [2008] S.C.C.A. No. 432, [2008] C.S.C.R. no 432 (S.C.C.); *R. v. St. Jean*, [1986] Y.J. No. 76, 2 Y.R. 116 (Y.T.S.C.).

▼HCL-137▼ No taxation without representation. The *Constitution Act, 1867*[1] codifies the principle of no taxation without representation, by requiring any bill that imposes a tax to originate with the legislature.[2] This principle originated in the *Bill of Rights of 1689*,[3] and represents one of the foundations of democracy, responsible and representative government: the Crown may not raise revenue or require the surrender of property except if authorized by Parliament or a provincial legislature.[4] The *Constitution Act, 1867*[5] is more than a simple procedural matter. For example, it does "not prohibit Parliament or the legislatures from vesting any control over the details and mechanism of taxation in statutory delegates such as the Lieutenant Governor in Council. Rather, it prohibits not only the Senate, but also any other body other than the directly elected legislature, from imposing a tax on its own accord."[6]

Notes

1. (U.K.), 30 & 31 Vict., c. 3, s. 53.
2. *Eurig Estate (Re)*, [1998] S.C.J. No. 72, [1998] 2 S.C.R. 565 at paras. 30-32 (S.C.C.). See also *620 Connaught Ltd. v. Canada (Attorney General)*, [2008] 1 S.C.J. No. 7, [2008] 1 S.C.R. 131 at para. 5 (S.C.C.); *Westbank First Nation v. British Columbia Hydro and Power Authority*, [1999] S.C.J. No. 38, [1999] 3 S.C.R. 134 at para. 19 (S.C.C.); *Confédération des syndicats nationaux v. Canada (Attorney General)*, [2008] S.C.J. No. 69, [2008] 3 S.C.R. 511 at para. 82 (S.C.C.).
3. *Act Declaring the Rights and Liberties of the Subject and Settling and Succession of the Crown, 1689* (U.K.), 1 Will. & Mar. sess. 2, c. 2, art. 4.
4. See *620 Connaught Ltd. v. Canada (Attorney General)*, [2008] S.C.J. No. 7, [2008] 1 S.C.R. 131 at para. 4 (S.C.C.).
5. (U.K.), 30 & 31 Vict., c. 3, s. 53.
6. *Eurig Estate (Re)*, [1998] S.C.J. No. 72, [1998] 2 S.C.R. 565 at para. 30 (S.C.C.). In *Reference re: Agricultural Products Marketing Act, 1970 (Canada)*, [1978] S.C.J. No. 58, [1978] 2 S.C.R. 1198 at 1290-91 (S.C.C.), there was an *obiter dictum* concerning the scope of the *Constitution Act, 1867* (U.K.), 30 & 31 Vict., c. 3, s. 53. Justice Pigeon, writing for the majority, appeared to reduce that provision to a mere rule of internal parliamentary procedure. He opined that "ss. 53 and 54 are not entrenched provisions of the constitution, they are clearly within those parts which the Parliament of Canada is empowered to amend by s. 91(1)". In *Eurig Estate (Re)*, [1998] S.C.J. No. 72, [1998] 2 S.C.R. 565 at para. 34 (S.C.C.), Major J. clarified and stated that "[s]ection 53 is a constitutional imperative" and that the Court may overrule the dictum. See also the discussion in *Confédération des syndicats nationaux v. Canada (Attorney General)*, [2008] S.C.J. No. 69, [2008] 3 S.C.R. 511 at para. 84 (S.C.C.).

---

(2) Section 125 of the *Constitution Act, 1867*

▼HCL-138▼ Restriction on imposition of taxes. Section 125 precludes provinces or the federal government from imposing taxes as understood under the *Constitution Act, 1867*[1] to the other level of government or its agencies or Crown corporations.[2] Section 125 is founded on the principle that imposing a tax on a level of government may significantly harm the ability of that government to raise revenue in order "to exercise its constitutionally mandated governmental functions".[3] In determining whether a levy is constitutionally inapplicable because it offends s. 125 of the *Constitution Act, 1867*, the court will consider whether the levy was enacted pursuant to Parliament or the legislature's taxation power, or whether the levy may be justifiable under another head of power.

Section 125 and regulatory charges. Section 125 does not apply to regulatory charges.[4] Governments are not immune from paying regulatory charges and user fees because those fees are not appropriated for general expenditures, but to defray the costs of the services that the government chooses to use, as opposed to being obligated to pay. Consequently, regulatory charges are applicable to the Crown of the other level of government and its agents. In the cases where regulatory charges are levied against an Agent of the Crown, a Crown corporation or the other Crown, and that charge is sustainable under a different head of power than the taxation powers pursuant to the *Constitution Act, 1867*,[5] the fee is payable.

Notes

1. (U.K.), 30 & 31 Vict., c. 3, ss. 91(3), 92(2).
2. *British Columbia (Attorney General) v. Canada (Attorney General)*, [1923] J.C.J. No. 5, [1924] A.C. 222 (P.C.).
3. *Westbank First Nation v. British Columbia Hydro and Power Authority*, [1999] S.C.J. No. 38, [1999] 3 S.C.R. 134 at paras. 17 and 19 (S.C.C.). See also *Reference re: Proposed Federal Tax on exported Natural Gas*, [1982] S.C.J. No. 52, [1982] 1 S.C.R. 1004 at 1065 (S.C.C.).
4. *Westbank First Nation v. British Columbia Hydro and Power Authority*, [1999] S.C.J. No. 38, [1999] 3 S.C.R. 134 at para. 19 (S.C.C.). See also *Canada (Attorney General) v. Toronto (City)*, [1893] S.C.J. No. 47, 23 S.C.R. 514 (S.C.C.); *Canada (Attorney-General) v. British Columbia (Registrar of Titles, Vancouver)*, [1934] B.C.J. No. 101, [1934] 4 D.L.R. 764 at 771-72 (B.C.C.A.).
5. (U.K.), 30 & 31 Vict., c. 3, ss. 91(3), 92(9).

▼HCL-139▼ Crown property. Federal taxes or provincial taxes cannot apply to lands or property of the Crown. Agents of the Crown also enjoy the same immunity as the Crown and cannot be taxed by the other level of government.[1] Lands and property of Crown corporations, if the corporation is an agent of the Crown, have the same type of immunity over taxes of the other order of government.[2] Any property tax levied on a person occupying a Crown land, if that person is an official or an Agent of the Crown, is prohibited pursuant to the *Constitution Act, 1867*.[3][4] The *Constitution Act, 1867*[5] however, does not preclude the federal or provincial governments from taxing the interest that a private individual may have on a property or land in which the government also has an interest. In other words, if a businessperson leases a property that belongs to the Crown, he or she is subject to the tax that was adopted by the federal, provincial or municipal authority.[6] Any interest that a person may have in a property that belongs to the Crown may be taxed.[7] A property tax cannot be levied against any person that has no legal interest in a Crown property, even if benefits are derived from that Crown property. However, a personal tax may be imposed on an individual that is occupying a Crown property even though that individual has no legal interest in it.[8]

Notes

1. *Westbank First Nation v. British Columbia Hydro and Power Authority*, [1999] S.C.J. No. 38, [1999] 3 S.C.R. 134 at para. 46 (S.C.C.).
2. *Halifax (City) v. Halifax Harbour Commissioners*, [1934] S.C.J. No. 70, [1935] S.C.R. 215 (S.C.C.); *Regina Industries Ltd. v. Regina (City)*, [1947] S.C.J. No. 16, [1947] S.C.R. 345 (S.C.C.); *Westbank First Nation v. British Columbia Hydro*, [1999] S.C.J. No. 38, [1999] 3 S.C.R. 134 (S.C.C.).
3. (U.K.), 30 & 31 Vict., c. 3, s. 125.
4. *Montreal (City) v. Canada (Attorney General)*, [1922] J.C.J. No. 2, [1923] A.C. 136 (P.C.); *Halifax (City) v. Halifax Harbour Commissioners*, [1934] S.C.J. No. 70, [1935] S.C.R. 215 (S.C.C.). See, however, *Montréal (City) v. Montreal Port Authority*, [2010] S.C.J. No. 4, [2010] 1 S.C.R. 427 (S.C.C.).
5. (U.K.), 30 & 31 Vict., c. 3, s. 125.
6. *Smith v. Vermillion Hills (Rural Council)*, [1916] 2 A.C. 569 (P.C.); *Phillips v. Sault St. Marie (City)*, [1954] S.C.J. No. 27, [1954] S.C.R. 404 (S.C.C.).
7. See *Montreal (City) v. Canada (Attorney General)*, [1922] J.C.J. No. 2, [1923] A.C. 136 (P.C.); *Southern Alberta Land Co. v. McLean (Rural Municipality)*, [1916] S.C.J. No. 20, 53 S.C.R. 151 (S.C.C.); *Calgary and Edmonton Land Co. v. Alberta (Attorney-General)*, [1911] S.C.J. No. 36, 45 S.C.R. 170 (S.C.C.); *Halifax (City) v. Halifax Harbour Commissioners*, [1934] S.C.J. No. 70, [1935] S.C.R. 215 (S.C.C.).
8. See *Montreal (City) v. Canada (Attorney General)*, [1922] J.C.J. No. 2, [1923] A.C. 136 (P.C.); *Southern Alberta Land Co. v. McLean (Rural Municipality)*, [1916] S.C.J. No. 20, 53 S.C.R. 151 (S.C.C.); *Calgary and Edmonton Land Co. v. Alberta (Attorney-General)*, [1911] S.C.J. No. 36, 45 S.C.R. 170 (S.C.C.); *Halifax (City) v. Halifax Harbour Commissioners*, [1934] S.C.J. No. 70, [1935] S.C.R. 215 (S.C.C.).

---

(3) Raising Revenue Through the Imposition of Taxes

▼HCL-140▼ Hallmarks of a tax. To be a tax, the levy must be: (1) enforceable by law; (2) imposed pursuant to the authority of Parliament (or a legislature); (3) levied by a public body; (4) imposed for a public purpose.[1] Not every fee or charge that meets the four-prong test is a tax in the constitutional sense.[2] Levies that meet the hallmarks of a tax may nevertheless be adopted under another head of power and be regulatory charges, thereby escaping the limitations of the *Constitution Act, 1867*.[3] For example, in determining whether probate fees imposed by Regulations under the Ontario *Administration of Justice Act*[4] were a regulatory charge or a tax, it was found that the probate levy was enforceable by law, was imposed pursuant to a statute adopted by the legislature, was levied by a public body, was intended for public purposes, and that there was no nexus between the amount of the levy and the cost of the service for granting letters probate. Therefore, the probate levy was a tax, and was unconstitutional because it was not adopted by the legislature in accordance with the requirements set out in the *Constitution Act, 1867*.[5]

Notes

1. *Eurig Estate (Re)*, [1998] S.C.J. No. 72, [1998] 2 S.C.R. 565 at para. 7 (S.C.C.); *Westbank First Nation v. British Columbia Hydro and Power Authority*, [1999] S.C.J. No. 38, [1999] 3 S.C.R. 134 at para. 21 (S.C.C.); *620 Connaught Ltd. v. Canada (Attorney General)*, [2008] S.C.J. No. 7, [2008] 1 S.C.R. 131 at para. 22 (S.C.C.).
2. *Reference re: Agricultural Products Marketing Act, 1970 (Canada)*, [1978] S.C.J. No. 58, [1978] 2 S.C.R. 1198 at 1237, *per* Laskin C.J.C., and at 1291, *per* Pigeon J. (S.C.C.).
3. (U.K.), 30 & 31 Vict., c. 3, ss. 90, 91(3), 92(2), 53, 125.
4. (ON) R.S.O. 1990, c. A.6.
5. (U.K.), 30 & 31 Vict., c. 3, ss. 53, 90; *Eurig Estate (Re)*, [1998] S.C.J. No. 72, [1998] 2 S.C.R. 565 at para. 23 (S.C.C.).

▼HCL-141▼ Delegation of taxes. Taxes must be adopted by Parliament or a provincial legislature pursuant to the *Constitution Act, 1867*,[1] and cannot be adopted by any other body.[2] However, the *Constitution Act, 1867*[3] does not preclude Parliament or a legislature from delegating any control over the details and mechanism of taxation, or the adoption of regulatory charges, to a statutory delegate such as the Governor in Council, a Minister, or a school board.[4] These delegated bodies have no power to impose taxes, unless they have been authorized specifically by an enabling statute. In that sense, the *Constitution Act, 1867*[5] constitutionalizes the principle that taxation powers cannot be incidentally delegated in legislation. The power of taxation otherwise rests exclusively in Parliament.[6] While a tax may not be adopted by regulation,[7] a statute properly enacted by the House of Commons or a provincial legislature may expressly and clearly delegate the power to a regulatory authority to enact taxes. In those cases, the delegated body does not raise a new tax, but only imposes a tax that has been approved by Parliament or the legislatures.[8] In addition to this, the *Constitution Act, 1867*[9] does not limit Parliament or a legislature's authority to vest or delegate control and decision-making power over the details and mechanism of taxation to a body such as the Governor in Council. The *Constitution Act, 1867*[10] only precludes the Senate or any other body from imposing a tax absent any specific delegation of power, because it constitutionalizes the principle that taxation powers cannot arise incidentally in delegated legislation. There must always be parliamentary control and accountability for taxation statutes.[11]

Notes

1. (U.K.), 30 & 31 Vict., c. 3, ss. 53, 90.
2. *620 Connaught Ltd. v. Canada (Attorney General)*, [2008] S.C.J. No. 7, [2008] 1 S.C.R. 131 at paras. 4-5 (S.C.C.).
3. (U.K.), 30 & 31 Vict., c. 3, s. 53.
4. *620 Connaught Ltd. v. Canada (Attorney General)*, [2008] S.C.J. No. 7, [2008] 1 S.C.R. 131 at para. 5 (S.C.C.). In *Connaught*, the regulatory charge was delegated to the Minister of Canadian Heritage pursuant to (CAN) *Parks Canada Agency Act*, S.C. 1998, c. 31. See also *Home Builders'* where it was imposed by the school board (*Ontario Home Builders' Association v. York Region Board of Education*, [1996] S.C.J. No. 80, [1996] 2 S.C.R. 929 (S.C.C.).
5. (U.K.), 30 & 31 Vict., c. 3, s. 53.
6. See *Canada v. National Fish Co.*, [1931] Ex. C.R. 75 at 83 (Ex. Ct.); see also *620 Connaught Ltd. v. Canada (Attorney General)*, [2008] S.C.J. No. 7, [2008] 1 S.C.R. 131 at para. 5 (S.C.C.); E. A. Driedger, "Money Bills and the Senate" (1968) 3 Ottawa L. Rev. 25 at 41.
7. *Eurig Estate (Re)*, [1998] S.C.J. No. 72, [1998] 2 S.C.R. 565 (S.C.C.).
8. *Ontario English Catholic Teachers' Assn. v. Ontario (Attorney General)*, [2001] S.C.J. No. 14, [2001] 1 S.C.R. 470 (S.C.C.). See also *Reference re: Liquor License Act of 1877 (Ont.)*, [1883] J.C.J. No. 2, 9 App. Cas. 117 (P.C.); *Confédération des syndicats nationaux v. Canada (Attorney General)*, [2008] S.C.J. No. 69, [2008] 3 S.C.R. 511 at paras. 86-88 (S.C.C.).
9. (U.K.), 30 & 31 Vict., c. 3, s. 53.
10. (U.K.), 30 & 31 Vict., c. 3, s. 53.
11. *Eurig Estate (Re)*, [1998] S.C.J. No. 72, [1998] 2 S.C.R. 565 at para. 30 (S.C.C.). See also *Confédération des syndicats nationaux v. Canada (Attorney General)*, [2008] S.C.J. No. 69, [2008] 3 S.C.R. 511 at paras. 81-89 (S.C.C.).

(a) Direct vs. Indirect Taxes

▼HCL-142▼ Overview. The determination whether a tax is a direct tax is especially important for provinces and provincial taxes as, unlike Parliament, provincial legislatures may only raise moneys through direct taxation pursuant to the *Constitution Act, 1867*.[1] Thus, when raising revenue, provinces are limited to direct taxation but may also, like Parliament, raise funds through regulatory charges. "A direct tax is one which is demanded from the very persons who it is intended or desired should pay it. Indirect taxes are those which are demanded from one person in the expectation and intention that he shall indemnify himself at the expense of another, such as excise or customs. The producer or importer of a commodity is called upon to pay tax on it, not with the intention to levy a peculiar contribution upon him, but to tax through him the consumers of the commodity, from whom it is supposed that he will recover the amount by means of an advance in price."[2] For the tax to be indirect, the tax itself must have a general tendency to be passed on.[3] "The dividing line between a direct and an indirect tax is referable and ascertainable by the 'general tendencies of the tax and the common understanding of men as to those tendencies. The general tendency of a tax is the relevant criterion'".[4] Normally, when it is determined that the tax is payable by the ultimate customer, and enforceable on the customer, the definition is complete and the tax is considered to be direct in nature. However, where the payer of the tax is able to pass the tax along to the ultimate purchaser of the goods and be in a position to recuperate the tax, the tax is said to be indirect.[5] In determining whether a tax is indirect, the general tendency of the tax will be considered, as opposed to its ultimate incidence.[6] In that sense, there must not be a perfect correlation between the tax and the increased cost of the product for the tax to be indirect. A tax may be indirect even if certain units of a taxed commodity do not reach the market.[7] Consequently, both "the context within which the tax operates as well as the purpose of the tax" are important considerations in determining the type of tax.[8] The test to determine whether a tax is direct or indirect is a legal one, as opposed to being economic in nature.

Notes

1. (U.K.), 30 & 31 Vict., c. 3, s. 92(2).
2. John Stuart Mill, *Principles of Political Economy, with some of their Applications to Social Philosophy* (New York: D. Appleton and Co., 1864) vol. 2, Book V, c. 3, §1 at 418, cited in *Bank of Toronto v. Lambe*, [1887] J.C.J. No. 1, L.R. 12 App. Cas. 575 at 581 (P.C.). See also *Reference re: Liquor License Act s. 51, ss. 2*, [1897] A.C. 231 (P.C.); *Cairns Construction Ltd. v. Saskatchewan*, [1960] S.C.J. No. 35, [1960] S.C.R. 619 (S.C.C.); *Reference re Quebec Sales Tax*, [1994] S.C.J. No. 56, [1994] 2 S.C.R. 715 (S.C.C.); *Cotton v. The King*, [1914] A.C. 176 (P.C.); *Attorney-General for Manitoba v. Attorney-General for Canada*, [1925] A.C. 561 (P.C.).
3. *British Columbia (Attorney General) v. Esquimalt and Nanaimo Railway Co.*, [1949] J.C.J. No. 2, [1950] A.C. 87 (P.C.).
4. *Simpsons-Sears Ltd. v. New Brunswick (Secretary)*, [1978] S.C.J. No. 44, [1978] 2 S.C.R. 869 at 889 (S.C.C.).
5. See *Bank of Toronto v. Lambe*, [1887] J.C.J. No. 1, L.R. 12 App. Cas. 575 (P.C.); *Attorney-General for British Columbia v. Canadian Pacific Railway Co.*, [1927] A.C. 934 (P.C.).

6. *Ontario Home Builders' Association v. York Region Board of Education*, [1996] S.C.J. No. 80, [1996] 2 S.C.R. 929 at para. 41 (S.C.C.).
7. *Allard Contractors Ltd. v. Coquitlam (District)*, [1993] S.C.J. No. 126, [1993] 4 S.C.R. 371 at 397 (S.C.C.); and *Ontario Home Builders' Association v. York Region Board of Education*, [1996] S.C.J. No. 80, [1996] 2 S.C.R. 929 at para. 41 (S.C.C.). See also *Bank of Toronto v. Lambe*, [1887] J.C.J. No. 1, L.R. 12 App. Cas. 575 (P.C.); *Reference re: Liquor License Act s. 51, ss. 2*, [1897] J.C.J. No. 1, [1897] A.C. 231 (P.C.); *Cairns Construction Ltd. v. Saskatchewan*, [1960] S.C.J. No. 35, [1960] S.C.R. 619 (S.C.C.).
8. *Ontario Home Builders' Association v. York Region Board of Education*, [1996] S.C.J. No. 80, [1996] 2 S.C.R. 929 at para. 43 (S.C.C.).

▼HCL-143▼ Elements of a direct tax. One indicium of a direct tax is whether the intention of the legislator as to who should bear the tax is clear. The "taxing authority is not indifferent as to which of the parties to the transaction ultimately bears the burden, but intends it as a 'peculiar contribution' on the particular party selected to pay the tax".[1] A related indicium of direct taxation is whether everyone knows how much tax they really pay. "Though the criterion of accountability may not be the central focus of the more recent jurisprudence pertaining to s. 92(2), transparency still serves to identify a tax as direct."[2] A third indicium is whether "the tax is related or relateable, directly or indirectly, to a unit of the commodity or its price, imposed when the commodity is in the course of being manufactured or marketed".[3] The courts have said that they are not concerned with whether the tax is in fact recouped by the taxpayer in a particular case.[4] The reason why a court will not be concerned with whether a tax is in fact recouped by the taxpayer is that in the course of business, a business will always seek to recoup the tax payable as part of the price of the goods that are sold to its consumers. If a court was concerned with whether the fact that the tax is recouped, then most of the taxes could be considered to be indirect taxes. Consequently, the recoupment cannot be given constitutional significance. The courts must thus distinguish between a tax that will be recouped because it is a cost of doing business, and the tax that will likely be passed on as an element of the good or service or transaction which is taxed.[5]

Notes

1. *Reference re Quebec Sales Tax*, [1994] S.C.J. No. 56, [1994] 2 S.C.R. 715 at 725-26 (S.C.C.).
2. *Reference re Quebec Sales Tax*, [1994] S.C.J. No. 56, [1994] 2 S.C.R. 715 at 725-26 (S.C.C.).

3. *Allard Contractors Ltd. v. Coquitlam (District)*, [1993] S.C.J. No. 126, [1993] 4 S.C.R. 371 (S.C.C.). See also *Canadian Pacific Railway Co. v. Saskatchewan (Attorney General)*, [1952] S.C.J. No. 21, [1952] 2 S.C.R. 231 (S.C.C.).
4. *Bank of Toronto v. Lambe*, [1887] J.C.J. No. 1, L.R. 12 App. Cas. 575 at 581 (P.C.). See also *Reference re: Liquor License Act s. 51, ss. 2*, [1897] J.C.J. No. 1, [1897] A.C. 231 (P.C.); *Cairns Construction Ltd. v. Saskatchewan*, [1960] S.C.J. No. 35, [1960] S.C.R. 619 (S.C.C.).
5. *Allard Contractors Ltd. v. Coquitlam (District)*, [1993] S.C.J. No. 126, [1993] 4 S.C.R. 371 (S.C.C.).

(b) Direct Taxation Within the Province for a Provincial Purpose

▼HCL-144▼ Overview. The provincial legislatures only have the power to make laws in relation to direct taxation, within the province, and for provincial purposes. While the province may only raise levies, taxes or charges for provincial purposes, there is no real limit attached to these words.[1] A province is also limited, pursuant to the *Constitution Act, 1867*,[2] to levy taxation only "within the province". That includes, for example, taxes on property or transactions and purchases in the province as long as the tax is direct.[3] In those cases, it is irrelevant if the individual paying the tax is a resident of the province or not. Provincial taxes are imposable on individual residents of the province and also on persons who are in the province for other purposes such as vacation, business or employment.[4] In contrast, taxes on income, property or transactions outside the province are invalid.[5] Normally, the issue of whether a person or property is within a province does not raise specific issues. For a province to have jurisdiction, there must be a substantial presence in the province to provide a basis for imposing a tax. For example, even if a province has jurisdiction over its airspace, an airline is not subject to the province's *Retail Sales Act*[6] in respect of meals and liquors consumed and sold on board the aircraft while the aircraft is flying over the province.[7]

Notes

1. *Reference re: Employment and Social Insurance Act*, [1936] S.C.J. No. 30, [1936] S.C.R. 427 at 434, *per* Duff C.J., dissenting (S.C.C.).
2. (U.K.), 30 & 31 Vict., c. 3, s. 92(2).
3. *The King v. Lovitt*, [1911] J.C.J. No. 2, [1912] A.C. 212 (P.C.); *Erie Beach Co. v. Ontario (Attorney General)*, [1929] J.C.J. No. 3, [1930] A.C. 161 (P.C.); *Sharples v. Barthe*, [1921] J.C.J. No. 5, [1922] 1 A.C. 215 (P.C.); *Alberta (Provincial Treasurer) v. Kerr*, [1933] J.C.J. No. 2, [1933] A.C. 710 (P.C.); *International Harvester Co. of Canada v. Saskatchewan (Provincial Tax Commission)*, [1948] J.C.J. No. 2, [1949] A.C. 36 (P.C.); *Atlantic Smoke Shops Ltd. v. Conlon*, [1943] J.C.J.

No. 1, [1943] A.C. 550 (P.C.); *Cairns Construction Ltd. v. Saskatchewan*, [1960] S.C.J. No. 35, [1960] S.C.R. 619 (S.C.C.).

4. *Alberta (Provincial Treasurer) v. Kerr*, [1933] J.C.J. No. 2, [1933] A.C. 710 (P.C.); *Re Income Tax Act, 1932 and Proctor and Gamble Co.*, [1937] S.C.J. No. 70, [1938] 2 D.L.R. 597 (Sask. K.B.).
5. *Kerr v. Alberta (Superintendent of Income Tax)*, [1942] S.C.J. No. 36, [1942] S.C.R. 435 (S.C.C.); *Firestone Tire and Rubber Co. of Canada v. Canada (Commissioner of Income Tax)*, [1942] S.C.J. No. 40, [1942] S.C.R. 476 (S.C.C.); *Ontario (Attorney General) v. Woodruff*, [1908] J.C.J. No. 4, [1908] A.C. 508 (P.C.); *Provincial Treasurer of Alberta v. Kerr*, [1933] A.C. 710 (P.C.); *Manitoba (Treasurer v. Bennett Estate*, [1937] S.C.J. No. 5, [1937] S.C.R. 138 (S.C.C.); *Lambe v. Manuel*, [1902] J.C.J. No. 1, [1903] A.C. 68 (P.C.); *Alworth Estate v. British Columbia (Minister of Finance)*, [1977] S.C.J. No. 52, [1978] 1 S.C.R. 44[illegible] (S.C.C.).
6. In this instance, (MB) *Retail Sales Tax Act*, R.S.M. 1970, c. R150.
7. *Manitoba v. Air Canada*, [1980] S.C.J. No. 69, [1980] 2 S.C.R. 303 (S.C.C.). See also *Canadian Pacific Air Lines Ltd. v. British Columbia*, [1989] S.C.J. No. 43, [1989] 1 S.C.R. 1133 (S.C.C.); *Air Canada v. British Columbia*, [1989] S.C.J. No. 44, [1989] 1 S.C.R. 1161 (S.C.C.).

(c) Established Types of Direct Taxes

▼HCL-145▼ Flat fees. It has been generally accepted that, in typical cases of a flat rate licence fee, the flat fee will constitute a form of direct taxation.[1] The issue of whether a tax is direct or indirect arises when the fee is variable. In those cases, there is no automatic conclusion as to the general tendency of the fee that can be drawn, and each case must be examined on its merit to determine the general tendency of the variable fees.[2]

Notes

1. *Bank of Toronto v. Lambe* (1887), L.R.12 App. Cas. 575 (P.C.).
2. See *Allard Contractors Ltd. v. Coquitlam (District)*, [1993] S.C.J. No. 126, [1993] 4 S.C.R. 371 (S.C.C.).

▼HCL-146▼ Land and property taxes. Land taxes are a type of tax that have always been regarded as examples of direct taxes within the meaning of the *Constitution Act, 1867*,[1] regardless of their general incidence. They are imposed on the owner of the land and are collectable against the land itself.[2] They may be assessed as a percentage of the value of the land, as a fixed charge per acre, and be an annual or recurring tax or a one-time charge. Moreover, even if the tax is passed on, as in an owner-lessee relationship for example, it "does not transform the direct nature of the tax into an indirect one".[3] A wide variety of taxes have been held to be taxes on land notwithstanding their ultimate incidence, "simply because they were imposed on land or its owner".[4] A tax on land based on the market value of the timber was a "direct" land tax even if the tax tended to be passed on to the purchasers of the timber cut on the land.

Indirect land taxes. The only types of "land taxes" that have been held to be "indirect" in nature were taxes that were considered by the courts as being export taxes or other types of taxes on land produce that entered the general stream of commerce.[5] The rationale underlying this jurisprudence is that those types of taxes are always considered to be "land taxes" and, as such, are "direct" even if they could have a tendency to be passed on to others. Nevertheless, those taxes against land or its owner on a specific use of the land have always been held to be direct.[6]

Notes

1. (U.K.), 30 & 31 Vict., c. 3. s. 92(2).
2. *British Columbia (Attorney General) v. Esquimalt and Nanaimo Railway Co.*, [1949] J.C.J. No. 2, [1950] A.C. 87 (P.C.); *Ontario Home Builders' Association v. York Region Board of Education*, [1996] S.C.J. No. 80, [1996] 2 S.C.R. 929 at paras. 126-127 (S.C.C.); *Halifax (City) v. Fairbanks Estate*, [1927] J.C.J. No. 1, [1928] A.C. 117 (P.C.); *Rattenbury v. British Columbia (Land Settlement Board)*, [1928] S.C.J. No. 77, [1929] S.C.R. 52 at 73 (S.C.C.); *Canadian Pacific Railway Co. v. Saskatchewan (Attorney General)*, [1952] S.C.J. No. 21, [1952] 2 S.C.R. 231 at 258-59 (S.C.C.).
3. *Ontario Home Builders' Association v. York Region Board of Education*, [1996] S.C.J. No. 80, [1996] 2 S.C.R. 929 at para. 46 (S.C.C.).
4. *Ontario Home Builders' Association v. York Region Board of Education*, [1996] S.C.J. No. 80, [1996] 2 S.C.R. 929 at para. 130 (S.C.C.).
5. *Ontario Home Builders' Association v. York Region Board of Education*, [1996] S.C.J. No. 80, [1996] 2 S.C.R. 929 at para. 133 (S.C.C.). La Forest J. relied on *Canadian Industrial Gas & Oil Ltd. v. Saskatchewan*, [1977] S.C.J. No. 124, [1978] 2 S.C.R. 545 (S.C.C.); *Texada Mines Ltd. v. British Columbia (Attorney General)*, [1960] S.C.J. No. 43, [1960] S.C.R. 713 (S.C.C.).
6. *Canadian Industrial Gas & Oil Ltd. v. Saskatchewan*, [1977] S.C.J. No. 124, [1978] 2 S.C.R. 545 (S.C.C.).

▼HCL-147▼ Taxes on shares. Different rules have been developed for the different types of property. For example, it has been held that shares are situated, for the purposes of provincial taxes, where they can be dealt with between the shareholder and the company. This means that the jurisdiction is not necessarily the same as the one where the share can be sold to a subsequent purchaser.[1] For shares, the first factor to consider is the location of the registry. If the registry of the shares can be in more than one jurisdiction, a rational choice must be made between them. This choice will depend on where the share certificates are physically situated and where the owner is domiciled. Normally, if the share certificates are situated in the same jurisdiction where the owner is domiciled, then that will be the location for the purposes of provincial taxation. If the shares are located in a different jurisdiction from where the individual is domiciled, the location of the share certificates will prevail.[2]

Notes

1. *Ontario v. Williams Estate*, [1942] J.C.J. No. 3, [1942] A.C. 541 (P.C.). See also *Erie Beach Co. v. Ontario (Attorney General)*, [1929] J.C.J. No. 3, [1930] A.C. 161 (P.C.); and *Alberta (Provincial Treasurer) v. Kerr*, [1933] J.C.J. No. 2, [1933] A.C. 710 (P.C.).
2. G.V. La Forest, *The Allocation of Taxing Power Under the Canadian Constitution*, 2d ed. (Toronto: Canadian Tax Foundation, 1981) at 128-30.

▼HCL-148▼ Income and business taxes. There is no doubt that income tax has always been seen as a direct tax open to provincial legislatures.[1] Income taxes are taxes that are imposed on net income earned after the deduction of certain expenses incurred in producing the income. Those types of taxes are direct.[2] Business taxes can take different forms. When a tax is imposed for the mere reason that one is conducting a business, then that tax is a direct tax.[3] The tax will remain direct even if it varies with the size of the capital and the number of places of business is conducted by the owner.[4] Business taxes are also types of direct taxes as long as the tax does not vary on the volume of transactions.[5] These types of business taxes remain direct taxation even though, obviously, the business person will pass on this type of cost of production to the ultimate consumer. This will not, for that sole reason, make the taxes indirect, for the purposes of the *Constitution Act, 1867*.[6] A tax will only be indirect when it can be identified with a specific good during the course of manufacture. Those types of taxes are normally imposed or graduated depending on the good and are a part of the unit cost of the article or of the good in question.

Notes

1. See *Forbes v. Manitoba (Attorney General)*, [1936] J.C.J. No. 1, [1937] A.C. 260 at 268 (P.C.). See also G.V. La Forest, *The Allocation of Taxing Power Under the Canadian Constitution*, 2d ed. (Toronto: Canadian Tax Foundation, 1981) at 101.

2. *Nickel Rim Mines Ltd. v. Attorney-General for Ontario*, [1965] O.J. No. 1177, [1966] 1 O.R. 345 (Ont. C.A.), affd [1967] S.C.J. No. 17, [1967] S.C.R. 270 (S.C.C.). See also G.V. La Forest, *The Allocation of Taxing Power Under the Canadian Constitution*, 2d ed. (Toronto: Canadian Tax Foundation, 1981) at 101-103; *Forbes v. Manitoba (Attorney General)*, [1936] J.C.J. No. 1, [1937] A.C. 260 (P.C.); *Abbott v. St. John (City)*, [1908] S.C.J. No. 44, 40 S.C.R. 597 (S.C.C.); *Kerr v. Alberta (Superintendent of Income Tax)*, [1942] S.C.J. No. 36, [1942] S.C.R. 435 (S.C.C.).
3. *Reference re: Liquor License Act s. 51, ss. 2*, [1897] J.C.J. No. 1, [1897] A.C. 231 (P.C.).
4. See *Bank of Toronto v. Lambe* (1887), L.R. 12 App. Cas. 575 (P.C.).
5. *Reference re: Liquor License Act s. 51, ss. 2*, [1897] J.C.J. No. 1, [1897] A.C. 231 (P.C.); *Bank of Toronto v. Lambe* (1887), L.R. 12 App. Cas. 575 (P.C.); G.V. La Forest, *The Allocation of Taxing Power Under the Canadian Constitution*, 2d ed. (Toronto: Canadian Tax Foundation, 1981) at 103-104.
6. (U.K.), 30 & 31 Vict., c. 3.

▼HCL-149▼ Inheritance of success charges. It has been held that estate taxes cannot be enacted by the provinces because they are considered to be indirect taxation. They are so considered because the tax is levied on the executor or administrator of the estate, as opposed to on the deceased, and the executor or administrator will be reimbursed from the assets of the estate. Consequently, the tax will be passed to the beneficiaries of the estate. Another difficulty associated with estate taxes, is that an estate may include properties that are outside the province and exceed the requirement that the taxes be imposed only in the province. Provinces may, however, enact an inheritance tax or succession duty because they are directly levied on the beneficiaries.[1] Careful consideration, however, must be followed by the provinces in enacting those types of taxes. A province must carefully frame those taxes to avoid the traps of indirectness and extraterritoriality. Many cases have discussed the issue of indirectness with inheritance and such types of taxes.[2] Death and succession duties, to be direct taxation, must be imposed on the deceased, even if they will be paid by an executor or representative. Moreover, where the succession includes properties, it is possible to raise death duties on the transmission of property located in the province, or all property inherited by a person domiciled or resident in the province even if the deceased was domiciled outside the province.[3] It is impossible, however, to levy death duties on properties that are outside the province or inherited by non-residents even if the deceased was domiciled in the province.[4]

Notes

1. *British Columbia (Attorney General) v. Canada Trust Co.*, [1980] S.C.J. No. 86, [1980] 2 S.C.R. 466 at 472 (S.C.C.).
2. *Cotton v. The King*, [1913] J.C.J. No. 3, [1914] A.C. 176 (P.C.); *Burland v. The King*, [1921] J.C.J. No. 5, [1922] 1 A.C. 215 (P.C.); see also *Alberta (Provincial Treasurer) v. Kerr*, [1933] J.C.J. No. 2, [1933] A.C. 710 (P.C.); heard together with *Alleyn Sharples v. Barthe*, [1921] J.C.J. No. 5, [1922] 1 A.C. 215 (P.C.).
3. G.V. La Forest, *The Allocation of Taxing Power Under the Canadian Constitution*, 2d ed. (Toronto: Canadian Tax Foundation, 1981) at 106.
4. G.V. La Forest, *The Allocation of Taxing Power Under the Canadian Constitution*, 2d ed. (Toronto: Canadian Tax Foundation, 1981) at 106. See also *Cotton v. The King*, [1913] J.C.J. No. 3, [1914] A.C. 176 (P.C.).

---

(4) Raising Revenue Through Regulatory Charges

▼HCL-150▼ Overview. A provincial charge that has "indirect" elements to its nature could be valid if it does not present the trappings of a tax, but is rather a "regulatory charge".[1] A regulatory charge is a charge that is raised to pay for the costs of providing the specific service. It may be a charge issued for a licence[2] or for the use of a service.[3] These types of charges are not taxes because they are used to defray the expenses related to the regulatory scheme as opposed to revenues raised for the general expenditures of the government. Regulatory charges may be of two sorts: a regulatory charge may exist to cover the expenses of a regulatory scheme or the regulatory charge themselves may be the means of advancing a regulatory purpose.[4] The main feature of a regulatory charge, that differentiates it from a tax, is that even if it bears all the hallmarks of a tax, it is connected to a form of regulatory scheme.[5] In those cases, it can be concluded that the fee has not been adopted pursuant to Parliament's or a legislature's jurisdiction over taxation, but under another head of power.[6]

Notes

1. *Allard Contractors Ltd. v. Coquitlam (District)*, [1993] S.C.J. No. 126, [1993] 4 S.C.R. 371 (S.C.C.); *Ontario Home Builders' Association v. York Region Board of Education*, [1996] S.C.J. No. 80, [1996] 2 S.C.R. 929 (S.C.C.). See also *620 Connaught Ltd. v. Canada (Attorney General)*, [2008] S.C.J. No. 7, [2008] 1 S.C.R. 131 at para. 18 (S.C.C.).
2. *Shannon v. Lower Mainland Dairy Products Board*, [1938] J.C.J. No. 2, [1938] A.C. 708 (P.C.); *Reference re: Farm Products Marketing Act (Ontario)*, [1957] S.C.J. No. 11, [1957] S.C.R. 198 (S.C.C.).
3. *Dominion of Canada v. Levis (City)*, [1919] A.C. 505 (P.C.).

4. *Westbank First Nation v. British Columbia Hydro and Power Authority*, [1999] S.C.J. No. 38, [1999] 3 S.C.R. 134 at para. 29 (S.C.C.). It is important to mention that in both *Allard* and *Home Builders'*, the issue was not whether the levies in question were fees or taxes. The Court, having concluded that the levies were indirect taxes, had to determine whether the levies were unconstitutional on the basis that the Constitution prohibits indirect taxation by the province. On the other hand, if the charges were regulatory fees that otherwise fell under provincial jurisdiction, they would be constitutional. In any event, both cases concerned fees whose purpose was to defray the expenses of a regulatory scheme. See also *Allard Contractors Ltd. v. Coquitlam (District)*, [1993] S.C.J. No. 126, [1993] 4 S.C.R. 371 (S.C.C.); *Ontario Home Builders' Association v. York Region Board of Education*, [1996] S.C.J. No. 80, [1996] 2 S.C.R. 929 (S.C.C.).
5. *Westbank First Nation v. British Columbia Hydro and Power Authority*, [1999] S.C.J. No. 38, [1999] 3 S.C.R. 134 at para. 43 (S.C.C.).
6. *Confédération des syndicats nationaux v. Canada (Attorney General)*, [2008] S.C.J. No. 69, [2008] 3 S.C.R. 511 at para. 83 (S.C.C.).

▼HCL-151▼ Hallmarks of a regulatory charge. In order to determine whether a charge is a "tax" or a "regulatory charge" for the purposes of the *Constitution Act, 1867*,[1] several key questions must be asked. "Is the charge: (1) compulsory and enforceable by law; (2) imposed under the authority of the legislature; (3) levied by a public body; (4) intended for a public purpose; and (5) unconnected to any form of a regulatory scheme? If the answers to all of these questions are affirmative, then the levy in question will generally be described as a tax."[2] In answering the fifth question, to identify the existence of a relevant regulatory scheme, one must look for the presence of some or all of the following indicia normally present in a regulatory scheme: (1) a complete, complex and detailed code of regulation; (2) a regulatory purpose with the objective to affect some behaviour; (3) the costs, or an appropriate estimation of the costs of the regulation; (4) a relationship between the person being regulated and the regulation, where the person being regulated either benefits from, or causes the need for, the regulation.[3] It is important to note that these elements are not mandatory nor exhaustive, in that there may be a regulatory scheme even if some of these elements cannot be found, and that other elements may be considered.[4] The second step in determining whether a levy is connected to a regulatory scheme is to find a relationship between the charge and the scheme itself. This will be the case when the revenues raised by the charge are tied to the costs of the regulatory scheme, or where the charges have, as a regulatory purpose, the objective to alter or regulate certain behaviour.[5]

Notes

1. (U.K.), 30 & 31 Vict., c. 3, s. 125.
2. *Westbank First Nation v. British Columbia Hydro and Power Authority*, [1999] S.C.J. No. 38, [1999] 3 S.C.R. 134 at para. 43 (S.C.C.).
3. See *Westbank First Nation v. British Columbia Hydro and Power Authority*, [1999] S.C.J. No. 38, [1999] 3 S.C.R. 134 at para. 24 (S.C.C.).
4. *Westbank First Nation v. British Columbia Hydro and Power Authority*, [1999] S.C.J. No. 38, [1999] 3 S.C.R. 134 at para. 24 (S.C.C.); *620 Connaught Ltd. v. Canada (Attorney General)*, [2008] S.C.J. No. 7, [2008] 1 S.C.R. 131 at para. 26 (S.C.C.); and *Confédération des syndicats nationaux v. Canada (Attorney General)*, [2008] S.C.J. No. 69, [2008] 3 S.C.R. 511 at para. 72 (S.C.C.).
5. *Westbank First Nation v. British Columbia Hydro and Power Authority*, [1999] S.C.J. No. 38, [1999] 3 S.C.R. 134 at para. 44 (S.C.C.); *620 Connaught Ltd. v. Canada (Attorney General)*, [2008] S.C.J. No. 7, [2008] 1 S.C.R. 131 at para. 27 (S.C.C.).

▼HCL-152▼ Requisite nexus. A reasonable connection between the cost of the service provided and the amount charged will suffice.[1] "[W]here a regulatory purpose for a levy has been established, the requisite nexus between that levy and the regulatory scheme in which it arises will nonetheless exist even if the quantum of the revenues raised by that levy exceeds the costs of the regulatory scheme in which that levy arises."[2] When a regulatory scheme and a regulatory purpose exist and a charge is levied for a licence, benefit or a privilege, "there is ... no need for a reasonable nexus between, or a linkage to, the quantum of the levy and the costs of the regulatory scheme, whatever epithet or qualifier, i.e. direct, indirect, soft or hard, may be given to that linkage".[3]

Notes

1. *Eurig Estate (Re)*, [1998] S.C.J. No. 72, [1998] 2 S.C.R. 565 at paras. 21-22 (S.C.C.). See also *Allard Contractors Ltd. v. Coquitlam (District)*, [1993] S.C.J. No. 126, [1993] 4 S.C.R. 371 at 411 (S.C.C.).
2. *Canadian Assn. of Broadcasters v. Canada*, [2008] F.C.J. No. 672, [2009] 1 F.C.R. 3 (Fed. C.A.), leave to appeal to S.C.C. granted [2008] S.C.C.A. No. 423 (S.C.C.), appeal discontinued.
3. *Canadian Assn. of Broadcasters v. Canada*, [2008] F.C.J. No. 672, [2009] 1 F.C.R. 3 at para. 103 (Fed. C.A.), leave to appeal to S.C.C. granted [2008] S.C.C.A. No. 423 (S.C.C.), appeal discontinued.

▼HCL-153▼ Pith and substance analysis. In analyzing whether a levy is a tax or a regulatory charge, courts must determine whether, in pith and substance, the fees constitute a "tax" in the constitutional sense, or whether it is a charge levied and used to defray the costs of a regulatory scheme.[1] It is the statute's primary purpose, not its incidental effects, that will determine whether it is a tax or a regulatory fee in the constitutional sense. In determining the pith and substance of the statute, or the "matter" and "effect" that a statute seeks to address, the "approach must be flexible and a technical, formalistic approach is to be avoided."[2] The proper test to be conducted is to look at the "legal effect" and the "practical effect" of the impugned statute.[3] One must look beyond the legal effects of the statute and inquire into the social or economic purposes which the statute was enacted to achieve, the background and circumstances surrounding the adoption of the statute and, if applicable, consider evidence of the practical effect of the legislation.[4] It may be difficult to find a single "pith and substance" of a taxation statute,[5] and a statute raising revenue is not "colourable" merely because it aims at multiple objectives. To that effect, a charge or fee may meet the four-pronged test to be a tax, but "legislation which is in form taxation" may sometimes be upheld on the basis of another head of power where in substance the statute has been "primarily enacted under another head of power".[6] The pith and substance of a law that imposes a charge may have an object other than taxation, such as insurance, banking, trade, labour relations or marketing.[7]

Notes

1. *Westbank First Nation v. British Columbia Hydro and Power Authority*, [1999] S.C.J. No. 38, [1999] 3 S.C.R. 134 at para. 30 (S.C.C.); *620 Connaught Ltd. v. Canada (Attorney General)*, [2008] S.C.J. No. 7, [2008] 1 S.C.R. 131 at para. 21 (S.C.C.). See also *General Motors of Canada Ltd. v. City National Leasing*, [1989] S.C.J. No. 28, [1989] 1 S.C.R. 641 (S.C.C.); *Reference re: Goods and Services Tax*, [1992] S.C.J. No. 62, [1992] 2 S.C.R. 445 (S.C.C.).
2. *R. v. Morgentaler*, [1993] S.C.J. No. 95, [1993] 3 S.C.R. 463 at 481 (S.C.C.).
3. *R. v. Morgentaler*, [1993] S.C.J. No. 95, [1993] 3 S.C.R. 463 at 482-83 (S.C.C.).
4. *R. v. Morgentaler*, [1993] S.C.J. No. 95, [1993] 3 S.C.R. 463 at 483 (S.C.C.). See also *Ontario Home Builders' Association v. York Region Board of Education*, [1996] S.C.J. No. 80, [1996] 2 S.C.R. 929, *per* La Forest J. (S.C.C.).
5. *Reference re: Proposed Federal Tax on exported Natural Gas*, [1982] S.C.J. No. 52, [1982] 1 S.C.R. 1004 at 1074-75 (S.C.C.).
6. *Reference re: Proposed Federal Tax on exported Natural Gas*, [1982] S.C.J. No. 52, [1982] 1 S.C.R. 1004 at 1068 (S.C.C.).
7. *Reference re: Insurance Act*, [1931] J.C.J. No. 3, [1932] A.C. 41 (P.C.); *Canada (Attorney General) v. Ontario (Attorney General)*, [1937] J.C.J. No. 6, [1937] A.C. 355 (P.C.); *Alberta (Attorney General) v. Canada (Attorney General)*, [1938] J.C.J. No. 3, [1939] A.C. 117 (P.C.) (Bank Taxation); *Texada Mines Ltd. v. of British Columbia (Attorney General)*, [1960] S.C.J. No. 43, [1960] S.C.R. 713 (S.C.C.); *Québec (Commission du Salaire Minimum) v. Bell Telephone Co. of Canada*, [1966] S.C.J. No. 51, [1966] S.C.R. 767 (S.C.C.); *Reference re: Agricul-*

tural Products Marketing Act, 1970 (Canada), [1978] S.C.J. No. 58, [1978] 2 S.C.R. 1198 (S.C.C.).

▼HCL-154▼ Whether revenues are part of Consolidated Revenue Fund. The final destination of the revenues is not determinative as to whether the levy is a tax as opposed to a fee.[1] It is an indicia and may be a significant factor. For example, the fact that the revenues raised under a regulatory scheme are deposited in the Consolidated Revenue Fund could not lead automatically to the conclusion that the levy was a tax.[2] Rather, the funds must be traceable, and it is sufficient if an equivalent or higher amount, which is incurred in that regulatory scheme, is withdrawn from the Consolidated Revenue Fund and applied to the regulatory scheme. Case law thus seems to indicate that the destination of the revenues of a regulatory scheme is not significant.[3] Notably, however, the opposite is also true. A charge may be a tax even if does not form part of the Consolidated Revenue Fund, and *vice versa*.[4]

Notes

1. See *Confédération des syndicats nationaux v. Canada (Attorney General)*, [2008] S.C.J. No. 69, [2008] 3 S.C.R. 511 at para. 74 (S.C.C.).
2. *Canadian Assn. of Broadcasters v. Canada*, [2008] F.C.J. No. 672, [2009] 1 F.C.R. 3 at paras. 81-82 (Fed. C.A.), leave to appeal to S.C.C. granted [2008] S.C.C.A. No. 423 (S.C.C.), appeal discontinued.
3. *Ontario Home Builders' Association v. York Region Board of Education*, [1996] S.C.J. No. 80, [1996] 2 S.C.R. 929 at para. 118 (S.C.C.).
4. *Westbank First Nation v. British Columbia Hydro and Power Authority*, [1999] S.C.J. No. 38, [1999] 3 S.C.R. 134 at para. 39 (S.C.C.); *Eurig Estate (Re)*, [1998] S.C.J. No. 72, [1998] 2 S.C.R. 565 at para. 20 (S.C.C.).

▼HCL-155▼ Section 125 and regulatory charges. Section 125 essentially provides that one level of government may not impose a tax on the other level of government. It does not, however, preclude one level from imposing regulatory charges or fees properly enacted within its jurisdiction against the other level of government. In other words, where a tax would not be applicable to another level of government, s. 125 does not apply to regulatory charges, which can in turn be payable by the other level of government. Consequently, in many cases involving s. 125, the issue is whether the levy can be considered to be a tax or a regulatory charge. This characterization, or the pith and substance of the levy, is the central factor in determining its constitutionality.

▼HCL-156▼ User fees. Another category that is considered not to be a tax is that of user fees. A user fee is a levy charged to the user of a service or product, where the value charged generally represents the cost of the service or facility being provided or directly rendered.[1] In the case of user fees, as opposed to other types of regulatory charges, "there must be a clear nexus between the quantum charged and the cost to the government of providing such services or facilities. The fees charged cannot exceed the cost to the government of providing the services or facilities".[2]

Notes

1. *Westbank First Nation v. British Columbia Hydro and Power Authority*, [1999] S.C.J. No. 38, [1999] 3 S.C.R. 134 at para. 30 (S.C.C.); *620 Connaught Ltd. v. Canada (Attorney General)*, [2008] S.C.J. No. 7, [2008] 1 S.C.R. 131 at para. 19 (S.C.C.).
2. *620 Connaught Ltd. v. Canada (Attorney General)*, [2008] S.C.J. No. 7, [2008] 1 S.C.R. 131 at para. 19 (S.C.C.).

---

(5) Raising Revenue Through Licences

▼HCL-157▼ Overview. The provinces may raise revenues by licences pursuant to the *Constitution Act, 1867*.[1] The *Constitution Act, 1867*[2] has consistently been interpreted broadly[3] and has applied to a wide range of activities including insurance, pharmaceutical products, brewers, marketing organizations, trades, billiard halls, bowling alleys, commission agents, barristers, butchers, mobile home parks and other types of trades and occupations.[4] Consequently, the *Constitution Act, 1867*[5] encompasses all licences and is not limited to those that are noted in it.[6] Moneys raised under a licensing regime, or a regulatory scheme, are neither taxes nor necessarily "regulatory charges", but constitute a consideration for the privilege obtained.

Notes

1. (U.K.), 30 & 31 Vict., c. 3, s. 92(9).
2. (U.K.), 30 & 31 Vict., c. 3, s. 92(9).
3. See Bora Laskin, *Canadian Constitutional Law: Cases and Text on Distribution of Legislative Power* (Toronto: Carswell, 1951) at 598.

4. *Ontario (Attorney-General) v. Reciprocal Insurers*, [1924] J.C.J. No. 1, [1924] A.C. 328 (P.C.); *Vadeboncoeur v. Three Rivers (City)*, [1885] S.C.J. No. 6, 11 S.C.R. 25 (S.C.C.); *Molson v. Lambe*, [1888] S.C.J. No. 13, 15 S.C.R. 253 (S.C.C.); *Reference re: Liquor License Act s. 51, ss. 2*, [1897] J.C.J. No. 1, [1897] A.C. 231 (P.C.); *Lawson v. Interior Tree Fruit and Vegetables Committee of Direction*, [1931] S.C.J. No. 84, [1931] S.C.R. 357 (S.C.C.); *Shannon v. Lower Mainland Dairy Products Board*, [1938] J.C.J. No. 2, [1938] A.C. 708 (P.C.); *Reference re: Farm Products Marketing Act (Ontario)*, [1957] S.C.J. No. 11, [1957] S.C.R. 198 (S.C.C.); *Segal v. Montreal (City)*, [1931] S.C.J. No. 19, [1931] S.C.R. 460 (S.C.C.); *Pigeon v. Recorder's Court*, [1890] S.C.J. No. 19, 17 S.C.R. 495 (S.C.C.).
5. (U.K.), 30 & 31 Vict., c. 3, s. 92(9).
6. J. Harvey Perry, *Taxation in Canada*, 2d ed. (Toronto: University of Toronto Press, 1953) at 162. See also, *Allard Contractors Ltd. v. Coquitlam (District)*, [1993] S.C.J. No. 126, [1993] 4 S.C.R. 371 at 404 (S.C.C.); G.V. La Forest, *The Allocation of Taxing Power Under the Canadian Constitution*, 2d ed. (Toronto: Canadian Tax Foundation, 1981) at 159.

▼HCL-158▼ Indirect licence fees. "[Section] 92(9), in combination with ss. 92(13) and (16), comprehends a power of regulation through licences ... which is not confined to the requirement of direct taxation in s. 92(2)".[1] However, where levies have included an element of indirect taxation, the cases have limited the power of indirect taxation to situations where the fees raised could "only be used to defray the costs of regulation".[2] Where the regulatory charges are not related to the specific licence or permit, but are charges raised to defray the cost of a regulatory scheme, these types of regulatory charges must be related to the costs of the regulatory scheme. However, where the levy is charged in exchange for a specific licence or permit granting a benefit or a privilege to the recipient of the licence or permit, and where the purpose or pith and substance of the permit or licence is to raise revenues for "Provincial, Local, or Municipal Purposes" and is unrelated to the "regulatory scheme", the fee is adopted pursuant to s. 92(9). The fee (which represents a cost of engaging in business) may bear the hallmarks of an indirect tax because it will necessarily be passed to the customer if the business is to make any benefit. In that regard, those types of fees are not related to s. 92(13) and (16). The possibility is not foreclosed that regulatory charges, in certain circumstances, could raise revenue unrelated to the costs of the regulatory scheme.[3]

Notes

1. *Constitution Act, 1867* (U.K.), 30 & 31 Vict., c. 3, ss. 92(2), 92(9), 92(13), (16); *Allard Contractors Ltd. v. Coquitlam (District)*, [1993] S.C.J. No. 126, [1993] 4 S.C.R. 371 at 402-405 (S.C.C.); *Shannon v. Lower Mainland Dairy Products Board*, [1938] J.C.J. No. 2, [1938] A.C. 708 at 721 (P.C.); *Ontario Home Builders'*

Association v. York Region Board of Education, [1996] S.C.J. No. 80, [1996] 2 S.C.R. 929 at para. 51 (S.C.C.).

2. *Allard Contractors Ltd. v. Coquitlam (District)*, [1993] S.C.J. No. 126, [1993] 4 S.C.R. 371 at 402 (S.C.C.).
3. *620 Connaught Ltd. v. Canada (Attorney General)*, [2008] S.C.J. No. 7, [2008] 1 S.C.R. 131 at para. 48 (S.C.C.).

---

(6) Section 92A of the *Constitution Act, 1867*

▼HCL-159▼ Provincial power to raise revenue regarding non-renewable resources. In the 1982 constitutional amendment, paragraphs 92A (4) and (5) were added to the *Constitution Act, 1867*,[1] providing that provinces may make laws in relation to the raising of money by any mode or system of taxation in respect of non-renewable natural resources and forestry resources in the province. Essentially, s. 92A simply allows increased provincial power with respect to the raising of "revenues from resources and to regulating the development and production of resources without diminishing Parliament's pre-existing powers".[2] Whereas provincial legislature never had any authority to raise revenues through indirect taxation, this is now possible with regard to non-renewable resources.

Notes

1. (U.K.), 30 & 31 Vict., c. 3, ss. 92A(4) and (5).
2. *Ontario Hydro v. Ontario (Labour Relations Board)*, [1993] S.C.J. No. 99, [1993] 3 S.C.R. 327 at 409-10 (S.C.C.); *Westcoast Energy Inc. v. Canada (National Energy Board)*, [1998] S.C.J. No. 27, [1998] 1 S.C.R. 322 at para. 81 (S.C.C.).

---

2. The Spending Power

▼HCL-160▼ Overview. The constitutional sources of the spending power include the *Constitution Act, 1867*.[1] Other sources of the spending power include the royal prerogatives and the legal rule that the Crown has the same powers as a private person including that of spending its moneys as it decides.[2] Those sources grant jurisdiction to Parliament to make laws in relation to public debt and property, taxation, and the authority to make payments out of the Consolidated Revenue Fund. The spending power has been defined as meaning the power of Parliament to make payments to people or institutions or governments for a purpose the subject-matter of which is not necessarily one in relation to which it may exclusively make laws.[3]

Notes

1. (U.K.), 30 & 31 Vict., c. 3, ss. 19(1A), 91(3), 102, 106.
2. G.V. La Forest, *The Allocation of Taxing Power Under the Canadian Constitution*, 2d ed. (Toronto: Canadian Tax Foundation, 1981) at 196-99; F.R. Scott, "The Constitutional Background of Taxation Agreements" (1955) 2 McGill L.J. 1 at 6.
3. E.A. Driedger, "The Spending Power" (1981) 7 Queen's L.J. 124. See also Pierre Elliot Trudeau, *Les subventions fédérales-provinciales et le pouvoir de dépenser du Parlement canadien* (Ottawa: Imprimeur de la Reine, 1969) at 5.

▼HCL-161▼ Limits to the spending power. There are limits to the spending power, and it is subject to the qualification that it must stop short of a scheme which in its true character is not an exercise of jurisdiction over public property but legislation in respect of provincial matter.[1] Although Parliament can use its spending power and grant subsidies in matters that are under provincial jurisdictions and could also provide for restrictions on the use of those funds, Parliament cannot purport, through the use of its spending power, to regulate or bring a matter which is otherwise provincial into federal competence.[2] In the end, the federal government can spend on any program it chooses as long as it does not regulate the matter if it was in provincial jurisdiction.[3]

Notes

1. G.V. La Forest, *Natural Resources and Public Property under the Canadian Constitution* (Toronto: University of Toronto Press, 1969) at 140.
2. *YMHA Jewish Community Centre of Winnipeg Inc. v. Brown*, [1989] S.C.J. No. 57, [1989] 1 S.C.R. 1532 (S.C.C.); G.V. La Forest, *The Allocation of Taxing Power Under the Canadian Constitution*, 2d ed. (Toronto: Canadian Tax Foundation, 1981) at 45.
3. *Reference re: Employment and Social Insurance Act*, [1936] S.C.J. No. 30, [1936] S.C.R. 427 (S.C.C.).

▼HCL-162▼ Provincial spending power. It is important to note that the provincial legislatures also have the same type of broad spending power.[1] The provincial spending power is derived from the *Constitution Act, 1867*.[2] In other words, provinces may also spend in federal jurisdictions.[3] In using its spending power, however, Parliament can grant conditional grants and indirectly create shared cost social programs such as health care, even if those programs can only be regulated by the provincial legislature.[4]

Notes

1. E.A. Driedger, "The Spending Power" (1981) 7 Queen's L.J. 124 at 131. See also *Lovelace v. Ontario*, [2000] S.C.J. No. 36, [2000] 1 S.C.R. 950 (S.C.C.).
2. (U.K.), 30 & 31 Vict., c. 3, s. 126.
3. Patrick Macklem & Carole Rogerson, exec. eds., *Canadian Constitutional Law*, 4th ed. (Toronto: Emond Montgomery, 2010) at 466.
4. *Eldridge v. British Columbia (Attorney General)*, [1997] S.C.J. No. 86, [1997] 3 S.C.R. 624 at para. 25 (S.C.C.); *Auton (Guardian ad litem of) v. British Columbia (Attorney General)*, [2004] S.C.J. No. 71, [2004] 3 S.C.R. 657 (S.C.C.) at Appendix B: "Under the *Constitution Act, 1867*, delivery of health care services lies primarily with the provinces. The federal government, however, has authority under its spending power to attach conditions to financial grants to the provinces that are used to pay for social programs. This authority is the foundation of the (CAN) *Canada Health Act*, R.S.C. 1985, c. C-6, which allows the federal government to set broad boundaries around the provinces' design and administration of their health insurance plans if the provinces are to access federal funds for health care." See also *Reference Re: Canada Assistance Plan (B.C.)* [1991] S.C.J. No. 60, [1991] 2 S.C.R. 525 at 567 (S.C.C.); *Chaoulli v. Quebec (Attorney General)*, [2005] S.C.J. No. 33, [2005] 1 S.C.R. 791 at para. 16 (S.C.C.); and Andrée Lajoie, "L'impact des Accords du Lac Meech sur le pouvoir de dépenser" in Réal-A. Forest, ed., *L'adhésion du Québec à l'Accord du Lac Meech* (Montréal: Thémis, 1988) at 163.

---

3. Banking

▼HCL-163▼ Overview. Banking is a federal jurisdiction which grants jurisdiction to Parliament over "Banking, Incorporation of Banks, and the Issue of Paper Money" and over "Savings Banks".[1] The reason that the jurisdiction over "Banking, Incorporation of Banks, and the Issue of Paper Money" was allocated to Parliament pursuant to the *Constitution Act, 1867*,[2] was to create an orderly and uniform pan-Canadian financial system, where jurisdiction and control rested exclusively with Parliament, as opposed to a regionalized system which had proven chaotic in the United States of America prior to Confederation.[3] The definition of what constitutes a bank is not to be gleaned merely from an examination of the particular activities carried on by an institution engaged in the provision of financial services, but rather depends on an institutional test, *i.e.*, on the definition of a bank as fixed by Parliament.[4] Parliament's jurisdiction over "banking" extended to whatever "com[es] within the legitimate business of a banker".[5] The business of banking would necessarily embrace the "lending of money on the security of goods, or of documents representing the property of goods".[6] The federal banking power extends to allowing Parliament to confer upon a bank privileges which had "the effect of modifying civil rights in the province".[7] The "federal banking power empowers Parliament to create an innovative form of financing and to define, in a comprehensive and exclusive manner, the rights and obligations of borrower and lender pursuant to that interest".[8]

Notes

1. *Constitution Act, 1867* (U.K.), 30 & 31 Vict., c. 3, s. 91(15)-(16).
2. (U.K.), 30 & 31 Vict., c. 3, s. 91(15).
3. *Canadian Western Bank v. Alberta*, [2007] S.C.J. No. 22, [2007] 2 S.C.R. 3 at para. 83 (S.C.C.), relying on Patrick N. McDonald, "The B.N.A. Act and the Near Banks: A Case Study in Federalism" (1972) 10 Alta. L. Rev. 155 at 156; and Bora Laskin, *Canadian Constitutional Law: Cases and Text on Distribution of Legislative Power*, 3d ed. (Toronto: Carswell, 1969) at 603.
4. *Canadian Pioneer Management Ltd. v. Saskatchewan (Labour Relations Board)*, [1979] S.C.J. No. 15, [1980] 1 S.C.R. 433 at 441 and 465-68 (S.C.C.). See also *Bank of Montreal v. Hall*, [1990] S.C.J. No. 9, [1990] 1 S.C.R. 121 at 132-34 (S.C.C.).
5. *Tennant v. Union Bank of Canada*, [1893] J.C.J. No. 1, [1894] A.C. 31 at 46 (P.C.). See also *Bank of Montreal v. Hall*, [1990] S.C.J. No. 9, [1990] 1 S.C.R. 121 at 132 (S.C.C.); *Merchants' Bank of Canada v. Smith*, [1884] S.C.J. No. 1, 8 S.C.R. 512 at 541 (S.C.C.), where Henry J. held that "everything necessarily connected with banking should be within the powers of Parliament; although interfering, in some respects, with property and civil rights".
6. *Tennant v. Union Bank of Canada*, [1893] J.C.J. No. 1, [1894] A.C. 31 at 46 (P.C.). See also *Bank of Montreal v. Hall*, [1990] S.C.J. No. 9, [1990] 1 S.C.R. 121 at 132 (S.C.C.).
7. *Tennant v. Union Bank of Canada*, [1893] J.C.J. No. 1, [1894] A.C. 31 at 47 (P.C.). See also *Merchants' Bank of Canada v. Smith*, [1884] S.C.J. No. 1, 8 S.C.R. 512 (S.C.C.); *Canada (Attorney General) v. Quebec (Attorney General)*, [1946] J.C.J. No. 11, [1947] A.C. 33 (P.C.); *Alberta (Attorney General) v. Canada (Attorney General)*, [1947] J.C.J. No. 5, [1947] A.C. 503 (P.C.); *Reference re: Alberta Legislation*, [1938] S.C.J. No. 2, [1938] S.C.R. 100 (S.C.C.).
8. *Bank of Montreal v. Hall*, [1990] S.C.J. No. 9, [1990] 1 S.C.R. 121 at 150 (S.C.C.). See also *Canadian Western Bank v. Alberta*, [2007] S.C.J. No. 22, [2007] 2 S.C.R. 3 at para. 89 (S.C.C.).

▼HCL-164▼ Security interest. The "federal banking power extends to allowing Parliament to define a security interest and to permit borrowing on the strength of that interest".[1] Parliament, pursuant to its jurisdiction over "banking", has enacted a complete code that exclusively defines and provides for the realization of a security interest. Provinces may not enact specific measures that would conflict with the federal statute. If that was the case, the legislation would be construed as inapplicable to the extent that it encroached on valid federal banking legislation.[2]

Notes

1. *Bank of Montreal v. Hall*, [1990] S.C.J. No. 9, [1990] 1 S.C.R. 121 at 132-33 (S.C.C.).
2. *Bank of Montreal v. Hall*, [1990] S.C.J. No. 9, [1990] 1 S.C.R. 121 at 155 (S.C.C.).

▼HCL-165▼ What banking does not include. Banking does not include every transaction coming within the legitimate business of a banker because "taken literally such a definition 'would then mean ... that the borrowing of money or the lending of money, with or without security, which come[s] within the legitimate business of a great many other types of institutions as well as of individuals, would, in every respect, fall under the exclusive legislative competence of Parliament. Such a result was never intended'".[1] Rather, "banking" includes the incorporation of banks and the securing of loans by an appropriate collateral.[2] Parliament's jurisdiction over "banking" cannot realistically be interpreted as extending "to every entity engaged in transactions that might ... be described as coming within the 'legitimate business of a banker.'"[3]

Notes

1. *Canadian Western Bank v. Alberta*, [2007] S.C.J. No. 22, [2007] 2 S.C.R. 3 at para. 65 (S.C.C.), citing *Canadian Pioneer Management Ltd. v. Saskatchewan (Labour Relations Board)*, [1979] S.C.J. No. 115, [1980] 1 S.C.R. 433, *per* Beetz J. (S.C.C.).
2. *Canadian Western Bank v. Alberta*, [2007] S.C.J. No. 22, [2007] 2 S.C.R. 3 at para. 85 (S.C.C.).
3. *Bank of Montreal v. Hall*, [1990] S.C.J. No. 9, [1990] 1 S.C.R. 121 at 132 (S.C.C.).

▼HCL-166▼ Provincial power. Parliament's jurisdiction over "banking" does not shield banks from provincial laws. It cannot be argued that Parliament's "banking" power is so wide that doctrines such as inter-jurisdictional immunity or paramountcy will apply against any type of provincial legislation. For example, now that banks participate in the promotion of insurance, which is regulated by the provinces, banks must follow provincial regulations in that matter.[1] Legislatures may enact measures permitting borrowing or other types of loans. Other types of institutions, labelled as "near banks", have now entered the business and entered into competition with the banks. Those institutions are normally credit unions or trust companies, or caisses populaires. While those types of institutions are now competing against banks in the banking field, banks are now beginning operations in fields previously occupied by these institutions. Interestingly, those institutions and activities are regulated by the provinces, which leads to an overlap of regulations.[2]

Notes

1. *Canadian Western Bank v. Alberta*, [2007] S.C.J. No. 22, [2007] 2 S.C.R. 3 at para. 81 (S.C.C.).
2. *Canadian Pioneer Management Ltd. v. Saskatchewan (Labour Relations Board)*, [1979] S.C.J. No. 115, [1980] 1 S.C.R. 433 (S.C.C.).

▼HCL-167▼ Provincial vs. federal incorporation. A bank must be incorporated pursuant to the *Bank Act*,[1] a federal legislation, whereas credit unions, caisses populaires and trust companies are provincially incorporated. Parliament has never attempted to regulate the activities of credit unions, trust companies and caisses populaires. However, the constitutional status of those types of financial institutions has been upheld by the courts in cases related to labour relations. For example, where a federally incorporated trust company engaged in most of the same activities as a bank, the Court held that the labour relations were governed by provincial legislation because the company was not involved in banking as it is understood pursuant to the *Constitution Act, 1867*.[2 3] In that case, "banking" was defined as meaning a business of the institutions authorized by the federal *Bank Act*[4] to hold themselves out as banks.[5] Consequently, it is for Parliament to define the meaning of a "bank" and the scope of "banking".[6]

Notes

1. (CAN) S.C. 1991, c. 46.
2. (U.K.), 30 & 31 Vict., c. 3, s. 91(15).
3. *Canadian Pioneer Management Ltd. v. Saskatchewan (Labour Relations Board)*, [1979] S.C.J. No. 115, [1980] 1 S.C.R. 433 (S.C.C.).
4. (CAN) *Bank Act*, S.C. 1991, c. 46.
5. *Canadian Pioneer Management Ltd. v. Saskatchewan (Labour Relations Board)*, [1979] S.C.J. No. 115, [1980] 1 S.C.R. 433 at 465-66 (S.C.C.).
6. *Canadian Pioneer Management Ltd. v. Saskatchewan (Labour Relations Board)*, [1979] S.C.J. No. 115, [1980] 1 S.C.R. 433 at 465-66 (S.C.C.).

---

4. Bankruptcy

▼HCL-168▼ Overview. Bankruptcy and insolvency are under federal jurisdiction pursuant to the *Constitution Act, 1867*.[1] The federal jurisdiction over bankruptcy and insolvency allows Parliament to provide for a ranking of secured creditors in determining the priority of creditors during the liquidation of the assets of the insolvent. Provincial legislation in that regard is *ultra vires* the provincial legislatures because it affects the true nature of bankruptcy and would be in conflict with the *Bankruptcy and Insolvency Act*[2] and its scheme of distribution.[3] For example, even debts to the Crown or other statutory liens are not operative when a company is bankrupt. Statutory liens belonging to the Crown are not secured debts that have priority over other secured creditors. A provincially legislated statutory lien was found to be ineffective in a bankruptcy situation, even if it would be effective in other types of situations outside bankruptcy.[4]

Relationship between provincial legislations and the *Bankruptcy and Insolvency Act*. In determining the relationship between provincial legislation and the *Bankruptcy and Insolvency Act*,[5] "the form of the provincial interest created must not be allowed to triumph over its substance. The provinces are not entitled to do indirectly what they are prohibited from doing directly".[6] There need not be any provincial intention to intrude into the exclusive federal sphere of bankruptcy and to conflict with the order of priorities of the *Bankruptcy and Insolvency Act*[7] "in order to render the provincial law inapplicable. It is sufficient that the effect of provincial legislation is to do so".[8]

Notes

1. (U.K.), 30 & 31 Vict., c. 3, s. 91(21).
2. (CAN) *Bankruptcy and Insolvency Act*, R.S.C. 1985, c. B-3.
3. *Larue v. Royal Bank of Canada*, [1928] J.C.J. No. 1, [1928] A.C. 187 (P.C.), affg [1926] S.C.J. No. 4, [1926] S.C.R. 218 (S.C.C.); *Ontario (Attorney General) v. Policy Holders of Wentworth Ins. Co.*, [1969] S.C.J. No. 49, [1969] S.C.R. 779 (S.C.C.).
4. See also *Deloitte Haskins & Sells v. Alberta (Workers' Compensation Board)*, [1985] S.C.J. No. 35, [1985] 1 S.C.R. 785 (S.C.C.); *Federal Business Development Bank v. Québec (Commission de la santé et de la sécurité du travail du Québec)*, [1988] S.C.J. No. 44, [1988] 1 S.C.R. 1061 (S.C.C.); *Alberta (Treasury Branches) v. Canada (Minister of National Revenue)*, [1996] S.C.J. No. 45, [1996] 1 S.C.R. 963 (S.C.C.).
5. (CAN) *Bankruptcy and Insolvency Act*, R.S.C. 1985, c. B-3.
6. *Husky Oil Operations Ltd. v. Canada (Minister of National Revenue)*, [1995] S.C.J. No. 77, [1995] 3 S.C.R. 453 at para. 39 (S.C.C.).
7. (CAN) *Bankruptcy and Insolvency Act*, R.S.C. 1985, c. B-3.

8. *Husky Oil Operations Ltd. v. Canada (Minister of National Revenue)*, [1995] S.C.J. No. 77, [1995] 3 S.C.R. 453 at para. 39 (S.C.C.).

▼HCL-169▼ Priorities. Provincial legislation cannot determine the ranking of creditors during bankruptcy.[1] This is a federal jurisdiction pursuant to the *Constitution Act, 1867*.[2] In "a bankruptcy matter, it is the *Bankruptcy Act* which must be applied ... [and] provincial statutes cannot affect the priorities created by the federal statute".[3] In this manner, "consistency in the order of priority in bankruptcy situations is ensured" across the provinces.[4] The first goal of the *Bankruptcy and Insolvency Act*[5] "is to ensure an equitable distribution of a ... debtor's assets" to its creditors according to the federal system of bankruptcy priorities. The second objective "of the bankruptcy system is the financial rehabilitation of insolvent individuals".[6] "(1) provinces cannot create priorities between creditors or change the scheme of distribution on bankruptcy under s. 136(1) of the *Bankruptcy Act*; (2) while provincial legislation may validly affect priorities in a non-bankruptcy situation, once bankruptcy has occurred section 136(1) of the *Bankruptcy Act* determines the status and priority of the claims specifically dealt with in that section; (3) if the provinces could create their own priorities or affect priorities under the *Bankruptcy Act* this would invite a different scheme of distribution on bankruptcy from province to province, an unacceptable situation".[7]

Notes

1. *Deloitte Haskins & Sells Ltd. v. Alberta (Workers' Compensation Board)*, [1985] S.C.J. No. 35, [1985] 1 S.C.R. 785 (S.C.C.).
2. (U.K.), 30 & 31 Vict., c. 3, s. 91(21).
3. *Federal Business Development Bank v. Québec (Commission de la santé et de la sécurité du travail du Québec)*, [1988] S.C.J. No. 44, [1988] 1 S.C.R. 1061 at paras. 17 and 20 (S.C.C.).
4. *Federal Business Development Bank v. Québec (Commission de la santé et de la sécurité du travail du Quèbec)*, [1988] S.C.J. No. 44, [1988] 1 S.C.R. 1061 at para. 20 (S.C.C.). See also *Husky Oil Operations Ltd. v. Canada (Minister of National Revenue)*, [1995] S.C.J. No. 77, [1995] 3 S.C.R. 453 at paras. 21-22 (S.C.C.).
5. (CAN) *Bankruptcy and Insolvency Act*, R.S.C. 1985, c. B-3.
6. *Husky Oil Operations Ltd. v. Canada (Minister of National Revenue)*, [1995] S.C.J. No. 77, [1995] 3 S.C.R. 453 at para. 7 (S.C.C.), citing Aleck Dadson, "Comment" (1986) 64 Can. Bar Rev. 755 at 755.
7. *Husky Oil Operations Ltd. v. Canada (Minister of National Revenue)*, [1995] S.C.J. No. 77 [1995] 3 S.C.R. 453 at para. 32 (S.C.C.), citing Andrew J. Roman & M. Jasmine Sweatman, "The Conflict Between Canadian Provincial Personal Property Security Acts and the Federal Bankruptcy Act: The War is Over" (1992) 71 Can. Bar Rev. 77 at 78-79. See also Jacob S. Ziegel, "Personal Property Security and

Bankruptcy: There is no War! — A Reply to Roman and Sweatman" (1993) 72 Can. Bar Rev. 44 at 45.

▼HCL-170▼ Secured creditor. "[T]he definition of terms such as 'secured creditor', if defined under the *Bankruptcy Act*, must be interpreted in bankruptcy cases as defined by the federal Parliament, not the provincial legislatures. Provinces cannot affect how such terms are defined for purposes of the *Bankruptcy Act*".[1] While the *Bankruptcy and Insolvency Act*[2] defines "secured creditor", it defers to provincial statutes for the purpose of creating a secured claim. Provinces are entitled to define secured creditors as they wish for their own purposes, but only where a debtor has not filed for bankruptcy. However, in effective bankruptcy situations, provincial definitions which could have the effect of reordering the priorities in the *Bankruptcy and Insolvency Act*[3] will be inapplicable.[4]

Notes

1. *Husky Oil Operations Ltd. v. Canada (Minister of National Revenue)*, [1995] S.C.J. No. 77, [1995] 3 S.C.R. 453 at para. 32 (S.C.C.), citing Andrew J. Roman and M. Jasmine Sweatman, "The Conflict Between Canadian Provincial Personal Property Security Acts and the Federal Bankruptcy Act: The War is Over" (1992) 71 Can. Bar Rev. 77 at 78-79. See also Jacob S. Ziegel, "Personal Property Security and Bankruptcy: There is no War! - A Reply to Roman and Sweatman" (1993) 72 Can. Bar Rev. 44 at 45.
2. (CAN) *Bankruptcy and Insolvency Act*, R.S.C. 1985, c. B-3.
3. (CAN) *Bankruptcy and Insolvency Act*, R.S.C. 1985, c. B-3.
4. *Husky Oil Operations Ltd. v. Canada (Minister of National Revenue)*, [1995] S.C.J. No. 77, [1995] 3 S.C.R. 453 at para. 62 (S.C.C.).

---

5. Interest

▼HCL-171▼ Overview. Pursuant to of the *Constitution Act, 1867*,[1] Parliament has exclusive jurisdiction over interests.[2] The "federal jurisdiction over interest does not exclude all provincial jurisdiction over contracts involving the payment of interest so as to invalidate provincial laws authorizing the courts to grant relief from such contracts, when they are adjudged to be harsh and unconscionable".[3] The *Interest Act*[4] is valid federal legislation in respect of interest. Although "it does not deal exclusively with interest in the strict sense of a charge accruing daily, it is, insofar as it deals with other charges, a valid exercise of the ancillary power designed to make effective the intention that the effective rate of interest over arrears of principal or interest should never be greater than the rate payable on principal money not in arrears".[5]

Notes

1. (U.K.), 30 & 31 Vict., c. 3, s. 91(19).
2. *Canada v. Independent Order of Foresters*, [1940] J.C.J. No. 3, [1940] A.C. 513 at 530-31.
3. *Tomell Investments Ltd. v. East Marstock Lands Ltd.*, [1977] S.C.J. No. 91, [1978] 1 S.C.R. 974 at 985-87 (S.C.C.).
4. In this case, (CAN) *Interest Act*, R.S.C. 1970, c. I-18.
5. *Tomell Investments Ltd. v. East Marstock Lands Ltd.*, [1977] S.C.J. No. 91, [1978] 1 S.C.R. 974 at 985-87 (S.C.C.).

IX. Works and Undertakings, Communications and Transportation and Labour Relations

1. Works and Undertakings

(1) Section 92(10)(a) HCL-173
(2) Section 92(10)(c) HCL-176

2. Communication and Transportation

(1) Communication HCL-178
(2) Transportation HCL-182

3. Labour Relations HCL-185

---

1. Works and Undertakings

(1) Section 92(10)(a) HCL-173
(2) Section 92(10)(c) HCL-176

▼HCL-172▼ Overview. The interaction between ss. 92(10) and 91(29) enables Parliament to make laws over public works and undertakings. Section 92(10) vests the provinces with legislative authority over those local works and undertakings which are not specifically exempted in subsections (a) through (c). In contrast, those works and undertakings referred to in s. 92(10)(a)-(c) are within the exclusive legislative jurisdiction of Parliament, due to s. 91(29) which provides that Parliament has jurisdiction over "Such Classes of Subjects as are expressly excepted in the Enumeration of the Classes of Subjects by this Act assigned exclusively to the Legislatures of the Provinces".[1] Both the wording of s. 92(10) and the case law interpreting the section indicate that a difference exists between "works" and "undertakings". For instance, whereas s. 92(10)(a) refers to "works and undertakings", s. 92(10)(c) refers only to "works" and requires that such works be declared, either before or after their execution, to be for the general advantage of Canada.[2]

Notes

1. *Constitution Act, 1867* (U.K.), 30 & 31 Vict., c. 3, s. 91(29).
2. *Constitution Act, 1867* (U.K.), 30 & 31 Vict., c. 3, s. 92(10)(c).

---

(1) Section 92(10)(a)

▼HCL-173▼ Overview. Pursuant to s. 92(10)(a), Parliament has legislative authority over those works and undertakings connecting the province with any other of the provinces, extending beyond the limits of the province. The connection referred to in s. 92(10)(a) is an operational, not physical, connection. Even where a local railway or pipeline is physically connected to an interprovincial railway or pipeline, the local railway or pipeline is within provincial jurisdiction.[1] Moreover, a freight forwarder operating within one province was held to be an intraprovincial undertaking, despite the fact that the freight forwarder was responsible for arranging the shipment of goods by railway to another province.[2] An undertaking does not become an interprovincial undertaking simply because it has an integrated national corporate structure and contracts with third party interprovincial carriers. If neither the undertaking nor its employees are actually involved in any actual interprovincial transport, the undertaking will be under provincial jurisdiction.[3]

Notes

1. *Canada (National Energy Board) (Re)*, [1987] F.C.J. No. 1060, [1988] 2 F.C. 196 (Fed. C.A.); *Montreal (City) v. Montreal Street Railway*, [1912] J.C.J. No. 1, [1912] A.C. 333 (P.C.); *British Columbia Electric Railway Co. v. Canadian National Railway Co.*, [1931] S.C.J. No. 76, [1932] S.C.R. 161 (S.C.C.); *United Transportation Union v. Central Western Railway Corp.*, [1990] S.C.J. No. 136, [1990] 3 S.C.R. 1112 (S.C.C).
2. *Re Cannet Freight Cartage Ltd.*, [1975] F.C.J. No. 113, [1976] 1 F.C. 174 (Fed. C.A.), affd in *United Transportation Union v. Central Western Railway Corp.*, [1990] S.C.J. No. 136, [1990] 3 S.C.R. 1112 (S.C.C.).
3. *Consolidated Fastfrate Inc. v. Western Canada Council of Teamsters*, [2009] S.C.J. No. 53, [2009] 3 S.C.R. 407 (S.C.C.).

▼HCL-174▼ Single undertaking cannot be divided. Legislative jurisdiction over a single undertaking cannot be divided.[1] The test "is whether in truth and in fact there is an internal activity prolonged over the border in order to enable the owner to evade provincial jurisdiction or whether in pith and substance it is inter-provincial".[2] An undertaking whose operations include "continuous and regular" interprovincial services will be found to be an interprovincial undertaking.[3] In contrast, where the interprovincial service does not meet the "continuous and regular" standard, the undertaking will be subject to provincial jurisdiction by virtue of its local nature. For example, since Bell Telephone Company's articles "of incorporation contemplated extension beyond the limits of one province" and enabled it to carry on its business in every province of Canada,[4] the Bell Telephone Company was one single undertaking subject to federal jurisdiction.

Notes

1. *Toronto (City) v. Bell Telephone Co. of Canada*, [1904] J.C.J. No. 2, [1905] A.C. 52 at para. 10 (P.C.).
2. *Ontario (Attorney General) v. Winner*, [1954] J.C.J. No. 1, [1954] A.C. 541 at para. 54 (P.C.).
3. *Re Ottawa-Carleton Regional Transit Commission and Amalgamated Transit Union, Local 279*, [1983] O.J. No. 3281, 44 O.R. (2d) 560 (Ont. C.A.).
4. *Toronto (City) v. Bell Telephone Co. of Canada*, [1904] J.C.J. No. 2, [1905] A.C. 52 at para. 4 (P.C.); see also, *Ontario (Attorney General) v. Winner*, [1954] J.C.J. No. 1, [1954] A.C. 541 at paras. 34-35 (P.C.).

▼HCL-175▼ Multiple undertakings. Instances can arise where a company engages in two or more undertakings. In such situations, the company may be subject to both provincial and federal legislative authority.[1] Where a local undertaking and an interprovincial undertaking are managed in common as a single business, the local undertaking will be considered to be part of the interprovincial undertaking.[2] Local pipelines, processing plants and interprovincial pipelines constitute a single federal transportation undertaking "within the exclusive jurisdiction of Parliament".[3] If the local undertaking is integral to an existing federal work or undertaking, the local undertaking may fall within federal jurisdiction.[4] In contrast, a local undertaking that depends on an interprovincial undertaking will not be sufficient to bring the local undertaking within federal jurisdiction.[5] To illustrate, the employees of a private company that collected and delivered mail under contract for Canada Post Office were subject to federal jurisdiction as the work performed by the employees was essential to the function of the postal service and was carried out under the supervision and control of the Post Office authorities,[6] and thereby constituted an integral part of the effective operation of the Post Office.[7] A local undertaking that has a temporary or exceptional relationship with an interprovincial undertaking, however, will not create a relationship of dependency that is required to bring the local undertaking within federal jurisdiction.[8]

Notes

1. *Canadian Pacific Railway v. British Columbia (Attorney General)*, [1949] J.C.J. No. 1, [1950] A.C. 122 (P.C.).
2. *Luscar Collieries Ltd. v. McDonald*, [1927] J.C.J. No. 4, [1927] A.C. 925 (P.C.).
3. *Westcoast Energy v. Canada (National Energy Board)*, [1998] S.C.J. No. 27, [1998] 1 S.C.R. 322 at para. 85 (S.C.C.).
4. *United Transportation Union v. Central Western Railway Corp.*, [1990] S.C.J. No. 136, [1990] 3 S.C.R. 1112 (S.C.C.).
5. See *Canada (National Energy Board) (Re)*, [1987] F.C.J. No. 1060, [1988] 2 F.C. 196 (Fed. C.A.) (Although a local pipeline depended on an interprovincial pipeline for its gas, it was not integral to the operation of the interprovincial pipeline. As such, the local pipeline fell within provincial jurisdiction.)
6. *Letter Carriers' Union of Canada v. Canadian Union of Postal Workers*, [1973] S.C.J. No. 140, [1975] 1 S.C.R. 178 at 183 (S.C.C.).
7. *Letter Carriers' Union of Canada v. Canadian Union of Postal Workers*, [1973] S.C.J. No. 140, [1975] 1 S.C.R. 178 at 186 (S.C.C.).
8. *Re Canadian Labour Code*, [1986] F.C.J. No. 756, [1987] 2 F.C. 30 (Fed. C.A.).

---

(2) Section 92(10)(c)

▼HCL-176▼ Works for the general advantage of Canada. Subsection 92(10)(c) grants legislative power to Parliament over those works declared by Parliament to be for the general advantage of Canada. This declaratory power should be broadly construed. Courts "have never shown any disposition to so limit its operation, and a wide variety of works — railways, bridges, telephone facilities, grain elevators, feed mills, atomic energy and munition factories — have been held to have been validly declared to be for the general advantage of Canada".[1] Although Parliament's power under s. 92(10)(c) is confined to "works", a declaration may be made in respect of an "undertaking".[2] Parliament is not confined to making declarations with respect to works related to transportation or communication under s. 92(10)(c). Declarations may be made with respect to both existing and future works.[3] For example, grain elevators have been held to be works for the general advantage of Canada.[4] Although a declaration must identify the work, "s. 92(10)(c) does not prescribe any special method of identification".[5] As long as the declaration refers to a work wholly situate within a province, identification of the work by location or description is flexible.[6] A declaration incorporates a work as a functioning unit. In other words, the declaration applies to the physical shell or facility of the work, as well as the integrated activity carried on therein. Federal jurisdiction over a declared work includes the power to legislate with respect to the labour relations in the declared work.[7] For example, the power to regulate the labour relations of Ontario Hydro's employees involved in the production of nuclear energy was within federal jurisdiction.[8]

Notes

1. *Ontario Hydro v. Ontario (Labour Relations Board)*, [1993] S.C.J. No. 99, [1993] 3 S.C.R. 327 (S.C.C.).
2. *Quebec Railway, Light and Power Co. v. Beauport*, [1944] S.C.J. No. 47, [1945] S.C.R. 16 (S.C.C.).
3. *Jorgenson v. Canada (Attorney General)*, [1971] S.C.J. No. 64, [1971] S.C.R. 725 (S.C.C.).
4. *Jorgenson v. Canada (Attorney General)*, [1971] S.C.J. No. 64, [1971] S.C.R. 725 (S.C.C.); *R. v. Chamney*, [1973] S.C.J. No. 154, [1975] 2 S.C.R. 151 (S.C.C.).
5. *Jorgensen v. Canada (Attorney General)*, [1971] S.C.J. No. 64, [1971] S.C.R. 725 at 736-37 (S.C.C.).
6. *Jorgensen v. Canada (Attorney General)*, [1971] S.C.J. No. 64, [1971] S.C.R. 725 at 736-37 (S.C.C.).
7. *Ontario Hydro v. Ontario (Labour Relations Board)*, [1993] S.C.J. No. 99, [1993] 3 S.C.R. 327 (S.C.C.).
8. *Ontario Hydro v. Ontario (Labour Relations Board)*, [1993] S.C.J. No. 99, [1993] 3 S.C.R. 327 (S.C.C.).

---

2. Communication and Transportation

(1) Communication HCL-178
(2) Transportation HCL-182

▼HCL-177▼ Overview. Jurisdiction over transportation and communication is divided between the federal and provincial government. Although the terms "transportation" and "communication" are not expressly referred to in the *Constitution Act, 1867*,[1] several forms of transportation and communication are mentioned.[2] The courts have therefore used the *Constitution Act, 1867*[3] to determine legislative jurisdiction over different forms of transportation and communication.

Notes

1. (U.K.), 30 & 31 Vict., c. 3.
2. *Constitution Act, 1867* (U.K.), 30 & 31 Vict., c. 3, s. 92(10).
3. (U.K.), 30 & 31 Vict., c. 3, s. 92(10).

---

(1) Communication

▼HCL-178▼ Radio. Jurisdiction to regulate and control radio communication lies with the federal government, pursuant to the *Constitution Act, 1867*,[1] but also the peace, order and good government clause. This jurisdiction extends to both interprovincial and purely intraprovincial radio broadcasting.[2] The exclusive legislative authority of Parliament with respect to radio communication extends to the control and regulation of the intellectual content of radio communication.[3] "Programme content regulation is inseparable from regulating the undertaking through which programmes are received and sent on as part of the total enterprise."[4]

Notes

1. (U.K.), 30 & 31 Vict., c. 3, s. 92(10)(a).
2. *In Re Regulation and Control of Radio Communication in Canada*, [1932] J.C.J. No. 1, [1932] A.C. 304 at 313. See also *Halsbury's Laws of Canada – Communications*.
3. *Re C.F.R.B. and Attorney-General for Canada*, [1973] O.J. No. 2098, [1973] 3 O.R. 819 (Ont. C.A.).
4. *Capital Cities Communications Inc. v. C.R.T.C.*, [1977] S.C.J. No. 119, [1978] 2 S.C.R. 141 at 161-62 (S.C.C.).

▼HCL-179▼ Telephone. The federal government has legislative authority over telephone communication.[1] For example, in Alberta, it was held that Alberta Government Telephones, through its organizational mechanisms, "is able to provide to its local subscribers services of an interprovincial and international nature" and therefore is subject to federal authority.[2] Although Alberta Government Telephones provided telephone services only in Alberta, its physical equipment connected with other companies at the Alberta border, and it was also a member of Telecom Canada which provided a network for telecommunications services nationwide. As a result of these activities, Alberta Government Telephones was found to be an interprovincial, rather than local, undertaking. Local telephone companies also lie within federal jurisdiction.[3]

Notes

1. *Toronto (City) v. Bell Telephone Co. of Canada*, [1904] J.C.J. No. 2, [1905] A.C. 52 at para. 4 (P.C.). See also *Halsbury's Laws of Canada – Communications*.
2. *Alberta Government Telephones v. Canada (Canadian Radio-television and Telecommunications Commission)*, [1989] S.C.J. No. 84, [1989] 2 S.C.R. 225 (S.C.C.).
3. *Téléphone Guèvremont Inc. v. Quebec (Régie des télécommunications)*, [1994] S.C.J. No. 31, [1994] 1 S.C.R. 878 (S.C.C.).

▼HCL-180▼ Television. Federal legislative authority extends to the regulation of the reception of television signals emanating from a source outside of Canada and to the regulation of the transmission of such signals within Canada. "Programme content regulation is inseparable from regulating the undertaking through which programmes are received and sent on as part of the total enterprise."[1]

Note

1. *Capital Cities Communications Inc. v. C.R.T.C.*, [1977] S.C.J. No. 119, [1978] 2 S.C.R. 141 at 160-62 (S.C.C.); *Quebec (Public Service Board) v. Canada (Attorney General)*, [1977] S.C.J. No. 120, [1978] 2 S.C.R. 191 at 197-98 (S.C.C.). See also *Halsbury's Laws of Canada – Communications*.

▼HCL-181▼ Film, theatre and literature. Legislative jurisdiction over the exhibition of films is vested in the provinces.[1] The task of regulation includes the power to prevent the exhibition of films within the province. The jurisdiction of the provinces in this area is not affected by whether or not the films were imported from a foreign country. The "determination of what is and what is not acceptable for public exhibition on moral grounds may be viewed as a matter of a 'local and private nature in the Province' within the meaning of s. 92(16) ... and as it is not a matter coming within any of the classes of subject enumerated in s. 91". It is therefore "a field in which the Legislature is free to act".[2]

Notes

1. *Nova Scotia (Board of Censors) v. McNeil*, [1978] S.C.J. No. 25, [1978] 2 S.C.R. 662 at 691 (S.C.C.).
2. *Nova Scotia (Board of Censors) v. McNeil*, [1978] S.C.J. No. 25, [1978] 2 S.C.R. 662 at 699 (S.C.C.).

---

(2) Transportation

▼HCL-182▼ Water. Pursuant to the *Constitution Act, 1867*,[1] legislative authority over "navigation and shipping" lies with the federal government. "Parliament's jurisdiction over shipping and navigation under s. 91(10) has been broadly interpreted."[2] Federal power also extends to torts committed in the course of land-based activities that are sufficiently connected with navigation or shipping.[3] The "very nature of the activities of navigation and shipping ... makes a uniform maritime law which encompasses navigable inland waterways a practical necessity".[4] The broad reach of Parliament's legislative authority over navigation and shipping includes pleasure boats, tidal waters and inland navigable rivers and waterways. Federal jurisdiction over ships is also reaffirmed by the *Constitution Act, 1867*,[5] which expressly refers to "lines of steam or other ships" and "lines of steam ships". Where "the application of a provincial statute of general application would have the effect of regulating indirectly an issue of maritime negligence law, this is an intrusion upon the unassailable core of federal maritime law and as such is constitutionally impermissible".[6] The law of delict or negligence applicable on navigable waters is of exclusive federal jurisdiction.[7]

Notes

1. (U.K.), 30 & 31 Vict., c. 3, s. 91(10).
2. *Whitbread v. Walley*, [1990] S.C.J. No. 138, [1990] 3 S.C.R. 1273 (S.C.C.). See also *Halsbury's Laws of Canada – Transportation (Maritime)*. See also *Newfoundland and Labrador (Workplace Health, Safety and Compensation Commission) v. Ryan Estate*, [2011] N.J. No. 207, 2011 NLCA 42, 308 Nfld. & P.E.I.R. 1 (Nfld. C.A.).
3. *Whitbread v. Walley*, [1990] S.C.J. No. 138, [1990] 3 S.C.R. 1273 (S.C.C.).
4. *Whitbread v. Walley*, [1990] S.C.J. No. 138, [1990] 3 S.C.R. 1273 (S.C.C.).
5. (U.K.), 30 & 31 Vict., c. 3, ss. 92(10)(a), 92(10)(b).
6. *Ordon Estate v. Grail*, [1998] S.C.J. No. 84, [1998] 3 S.C.R. 437 at para. 85 (S.C.C.). See also *Newfoundland and Labrador (Workplace Health, Safety and Compensation Commission) v. Ryan Estate*, [2011] N.J. No. 207, 2011 NLCA 42, 308 Nfld. & P.E.I.R. 1 (Nfld. C.A.).
7. *Whitbread v. Walley*, [1990] S.C.J. No. 138, [1990] 3 S.C.R. 1273 (S.C.C.); *Ordon Estate v. Grail*, [1998] S.C.J. No. 84, [1998] 3 S.C.R. 437 (S.C.C.).

▼HCL-183▼ Land. The courts have considered the appropriate legislative authority for various forms of land transportation, including buses,[1] electricity transmission lines,[2] pipelines[3] and trains.[4] Parliament has jurisdiction under the *Constitution Act, 1867*[5] over land transportation where it is operated as part of an interprovincial or international undertaking. In contrast, provinces have jurisdiction under the *Constitution Act, 1867*[6] over land transportation where it is operated by an intraprovincial undertaking. Provincial jurisdiction is always subject to the declaratory power under the *Constitution Act, 1867*.[7] The right to build highways, operate highways and impose tolls on such highways fall within provincial jurisdiction.[8] The federal government also has the power to legislate with respect to traffic regulation under the *Criminal Code*.[9] Nevertheless, the suspension or removal of drivers' licences falls within provincial jurisdiction.[10]

Notes

1. See *Ontario (Attorney General) v. Winner*, [1954] J.C.J. No. 1, [1954] A.C. 541 (P.C.); *Re Ottawa-Carleton Regional Transit Commission and Amalgamated Transit Union, Local 279*, [1983] O.J. No. 328, 44 O.R. (2d) 560 (Ont. C.A.); *Ferguson Bus Lines Ltd. v. Amalgamated Transit Union, Local 1374*, [1990] F.C.J. No. 274, [1990] 2 F.C. 586 (Fed. C.A.); *Zinck's Bus Co. v. Canada*, [1998] F.C.J. No. 1093, 152 F.T.R. 279 (F.C.); *Augustine's School Bus Inc. v. Asher*, [1999] F.C.J. No. 1926, 179 F.T.R. 266 (F.C.T.D.). See also *Halsbury's Laws of Canada – Motor Vehicles*.
2. See *Fulton v. Alberta (Energy Resources Conservation Board)*, [1981] S.C.J. No. 16, [1981] 1 S.C.R. 153 (S.C.C.).
3. See *Campbell-Bennett Ltd. v. Comstock Midwestern Ltd.*, [1954] S.C.J. No. 14, [1954] S.C.R. 207 (S.C.C.); *Saskatchewan Power Corp. v. TransCanada Pipelines*, [1978] S.C.J. No. 87, [1979] 1 S.C.R. 297 (S.C.C.); *Canada (National Energy Board) (Re)*, [1987] F.C.J. No. 1060, [1988] 2 F.C. 196 (Fed. C.A.); *Westcoast Energy Inc. v. Canada (National Energy Board)*, [1998] S.C.J. No. 27, [1998] 1 S.C.R. 322 (S.C.C.); *TransCanada Pipelines Ltd. v. Ontario (Ministry of Community Safety and Correctional Services)*, [2007] O.J. No. 3014 (Ont. S.C.J.).
4. See *Montreal (City) v. Montreal Street Railway*, [1912] J.C.J. No. 1, [1912] A.C. 333 (P.C.); *Luscar Collieries v. McDonald*, [1927] J.C.J. No. 4, [1927] A.C. 925 (P.C.); *British Columbia Electric Railway Co. v. Canadian National Railway Co.*, [1931] S.C.J. No. 76, [1932] S.C.R. 161 (S.C.C.); *Ontario v. Canada (Board of Transport Commissioners)*, [1967] S.C.J. No. 82, [1968] S.C.R. 118 (S.C.C.); *United Transportation Union v. Central Western Railway Corp.*, [1990] S.C.J. No. 136, [1990] 3 S.C.R. 1112 (S.C.C.); *Winnipeg (City) v. Canadian Pacific Railway Co.*, [2003] M.J. No. 303, [2003] 11 W.W.R. 729 (Man. Prov. Ct.).
5. (U.K.), 30 & 31 Vict., c. 3, s. 92(10)(a).
6. (U.K.), 30 & 31 Vict., c. 3, s. 92(10). See *Consolidated Fastfrate Inc. v. Western Canada Council of Teamsters Consolidated Fastfrate Inc.*, [2009] S.C.J. No. 53, 2009 SCC 53 (S.C.C.).
7. (U.K.), 30 & 31 Vict., c. 3, s. 92(10)(c).
8. *O'Brien v. Allen*, [1900] S.C.J. No. 22, 30 S.C.R. 340 at 342-43 (S.C.C.).
9. (CAN) *Criminal Code*, R.S.C. 1985, c. C-46.
10. *Reference re: Vehicles Act, 1957 (Sask.), s. 92(4)*, [1958] S.C.J. No. 47, [1958] S.C.R. 608 (S.C.C.); *Prince Edward Island (Secretary) v. Egan*, [1941] S.C.J. No.

20, [1941] S.C.R. 396 (S.C.C.); *Ross v. Ontario (Registrar of Motor Vehicles)*, [1973] S.C.J. No. 130, [1975] 1 S.C.R. 5 (S.C.C.); *Bell v. Prince Edward Island (Attorney General)*, [1973] S.C.J. No. 131, [1975] 1 S.C.R. 25 (S.C.C.).

▼HCL-184▼ Air. The *Aeronautics Act*[1] and Air Regulations[2] provide "for the regulation and control in a general and comprehensive way of aerial navigation in Canada, and over the territorial waters thereof".[3] The "field of aeronautics is one which concerns the country as a whole".[4] Therefore, the field of aerial navigation is a matter of national interest and importance and is exclusively within federal jurisdiction, "by virtue of the 'peace, order and good government' clause".[5] The federal government can also assert jurisdiction over aeronautics, "because of Parliament's exclusive legislative authority to make laws in relation to a federal work or undertaking under the *Constitution Act, 1867*.[6] [7] For example, "Pearson Airport, including its air navigation system and air traffic control tower forms part of 'a work or undertaking connecting the province with any other province or extending beyond the limits of the province'" under the *Constitution Act, 1867*.[8] [9] Even though Pearson Airport was an international airport that was located entirely within one province, it was nevertheless within the exclusive legislative jurisdiction of the federal government. As a result, the Ontario *Building Code Act, 1992*[10] and Ontario Building Code[11] did "not apply to the construction of new buildings at Pearson Airport".[12] Federal jurisdiction over aeronautics includes the regulation of the operation of both aircraft and airports,[13] as well as "those things in the air and on the ground that are essential for 'aerial navigation' or 'air transportation' to take place".[14] Even purely intraprovincial airlines are within the exclusive jurisdiction of Parliament.[15] Numerous provincial and municipal laws have been declared invalid or inapplicable by virtue of their intrusion into the exclusive federal jurisdiction over aeronautics.[16] However, the courts have not always held that provincial laws that affected aviation indirectly were intruding into the exclusive jurisdiction of the federal government over aeronautics.[17]

Notes

1. (CAN) *Aeronatics Act*, R.S.C. 1985, c. A-2.
2. *Regulation and Control of Aeronautics in Canada (Re)*, [1931] J.C.J. No. 4, [1932] A.C. 54 at para. 4 (P.C.). See also *Halsbury's Laws of Canada – Aviation and Space*.
3. *Regulation and Control of Aeronautics in Canada (Re)*, [1931] J.C.J. No. 4, [1932] A.C. 54 at para. 5 (P.C.).

4. *Johannesson v. West St. Paul (Rural Mun.)*, [1951] S.C.J. No. 50, [1952] 1 S.C.R. 292 at 326-27 (S.C.C.).
5. *Johannesson v. West St. Paul (Rural Mun.)*, [1951] S.C.J. No. 50, [1952] 1 S.C.R. 292 (S.C.C.).
6. (U.K.), 30 & 31 Vict., c. 3, s. 92(10)(a).
7. *Mississauga (City) v. Greater Toronto Airports Authority*, [2000] O.J. No. 4086, 50 O.R. (3d) 641 at para. 58 (Ont. C.A.).
8. (U.K.), 30 & 31 Vict., c. 3, s. 92(10)(a).
9. *Mississauga (City) v. Greater Toronto Airports Authority*, [2000] O.J. No. 4086, 50 O.R. (3d) 641 at para. 60 (Ont. C.A.).
10. (ON) *Building Code Act, 1992*, S.O. 1992, c. 23.
11. (ON) Building Code, O. Reg. 350/06.
12. *Mississauga (City) v. Greater Toronto Airports Authority*, [2000] O.J. No. 4086, 50 O.R. (3d) 641 at para. 61 (Ont. C.A.).
13. *Air Canada v. Ontario (Liquor Control Board)*, [1997] S.C.J. No. 66, 148 D.L.R. (4th) 193 at 212 (S.C.C.).
14. *Mississauga (City) v. Greater Toronto Airports Authority*, [2000] O.J. No. 4086, 50 O.R. (3d) 641 at para. 35 (Ont. C.A.).
15. *Jorgenson v. North Vancouver Magistrate and North Vancouver (City)*, [1959] B.C.J. No. 80, 28 W.W.R. 265 (B.C.C.A.); see also *Johannesson v. West St. Paul (Rural Mun.)*, [1951] S.C.J. No. 50, [1952] 1 S.C.R. 292 at 314 (S.C.C.), where Kellock J. states: "In my opinion, just as it is impossible to separate intra-provincial flying from inter-provincial flying, the location and regulation of airports cannot be identified with either or separated from aerial navigation as a whole."
16. *Johannesson v. West St. Paul (Rural Mun.)*, [1951] S.C.J. No. 50, [1952] 1 S.C.R. 292 (S.C.C.); *Quebec (Attorney General) v. Lacombe*, [2010] S.C.J. No. 38, [2010] 2 S.C.R. 453 (S.C.C.); *Quebec (Attorney General) v. Canadian Owners and Pilots Association*, [2010] S.C.J. No. 39, [2010] 2 S.C.R. 536 (S.C.C.).
17. *Air Canada v. Ontario (Liquor Control Board)*, [1997] S.C.J. No. 66, [1997] 2 S.C.R. 581 at para. 72 (S.C.C.).

---

3. Labour Relations

▼HCL-185▼ Overview. Legislative authority over labour relations lies with the provinces for those industries that are within provincial jurisdiction, and with the federal government for those industries that are within federal jurisdiction.[1] Specifically, matters such as work hours, wages, working conditions and the right to strike and bargain collectively are a vital part of the management and operation of a commercial or industrial undertaking. The power to regulate these matters lies with Parliament where the undertaking falls within Parliament's jurisdiction. Similarly, the power to regulate these matters lies with the provincial government where the undertaking falls within the province's jurisdiction.[2] Federal jurisdiction over a declared work under the *Constitution Act, 1867*[3] includes the power to legislate with respect to the labour relations in the declared work.[4] A declaration incorporates a work as a functioning unit. In other words, the declaration applies to the physical shell or facility of the work, as well as the integrated activity carried on therein.[5]

Notes

1. *Consolidated Fastrate Inc. v. Western Canada Council of Teamsters*, [2009] S.C.J. No. 53, 2009 SCC 53 at para. 27 (S.C.C.). For further cases dealing with jurisdiction to regulate labour relations in federal undertakings, see: *Reference re: Legislative Jurisdiction over Hours of Labour*, [1925] S.C.J. No. 24, [1925] S.C.R. 505 at 510 (S.C.C.); *Reference re: Minimum Wage Act (Sask.)*, [1948] S.C.J. No. 166, [1948] S.C.R. 248 (S.C.C.); *Canadian Pacific Railway Co. v. British Columbia (Attorney General)*, [1949] J.C.J. No. 1, [1950] A.C. 122 (P.C.); *Letter Carriers' Union of Canada v. Canadian Union of Postal Workers*, [1973] S.C.J. No. 140, [1975] 1 S.C.R. 178 (S.C.C.); *Reference re: Anti-Inflation Act*, [1976] S.C.J. No. 12, [1976] 2 S.C.R. 373 (S.C.C.); *Canada (Labour Relations Board) v. Yellowknife (City)*, [1977] S.C.J. No. 25, [1977] 2 S.C.R. 729 (S.C.C.); *Quebec (Minimum Wage Commission) v. Construction Montcalm Inc.*, [1978] S.C.J. No. 110, [1979] 1 S.C.R. 754 (S.C.C.); *Four B. Manufacturing Ltd. v. United Garment Workers of America*, [1979] S.C.J. No. 138, [1980] 1 S.C.R. 1031 (S.C.C.); *Canada (Attorney General) v. St. Hubert Base Teachers' Assn.*, [1983] S.C.J. No. 36, [1983] 1 S.C.R. 498 (S.C.C.); *YMHA Jewish Community Centre of Winnipeg Inc. v. Brown*, [1989] S.C.J. No. 57, [1989] 1 S.C.R. 1532 (S.C.C.). See also *Halsbury's Laws of Canada – Labour*.
2. *Agence Maritime v. Canada (Labour Relations Board)*, [1969] A.C.S. no 105, [1969] S.C.R. 851 (S.C.C.).
3. (U.K.), 30 & 31 Vict., c. 3, s. 92(10)(c).
4. *Ontario Hydro v. Ontario (Labour Relations Board)*, [1993] S.C.J. No. 99, [1993] 3 S.C.R. 327 (S.C.C.).
5. *Ontario Hydro v. Ontario (Labour Relations Board)*, [1993] S.C.J. No. 99, [1993] 3 S.C.R. 327 (S.C.C.).

▼HCL-186▼ Going concern. "The question whether an undertaking, service or business is a federal one depends on the nature of its operation".[1] "In order to determine the nature of the operation, one must look at the normal or habitual activities of the business as those of 'a going concern', without regard for exceptional or casual factors; otherwise, the Constitution could not be applied with any degree of continuity and regularity".[2] All matters which are a vital part of the operation of an interprovincial undertaking as a going concern are matters which are subject to the exclusive legislative control of the federal Parliament within the *Constitution Act, 1867*.[3] [4] For example, a freight forwarding company that is contracted with third party trucking and railway companies to carry goods interprovincially. In that case, except for one specific instance, neither the company's employees nor equipment crossed provincial borders. The nature of the company's operations were described as entirely intraprovincial and neither the company's employees, nor its equipment, were involved in any actual interprovincial transport. Rather, the component of the company's services that involves interprovincial transport was contracted to a third party carrier. Moreover, there was no indication that contracting alone can make intraprovincial undertakings subject to federal jurisdiction. Therefore, it was held that the company's "labour relations were subject to provincial" jurisdiction.[5]

Notes

1. *Consolidated Fastrate Inc. v. Western Canada Council of Teamsters*, [2009] S.C.J. No. 53, [2009] 3 S.C.R. 407 at paras. 60-61 (S.C.C.).
2. *Northern Telecom Ltd. v. Communications Workers of Canada*, [1979] S.C.J. No. 98, [1980] 1 S.C.R. 115 at 132 (S.C.C.).
3. (U.K.), 30 & 31 Vict., c. 3, s. 91(29).
4. *Northern Telecom Ltd. v. Communications Workers of Canada*, [1979] S.C.J. No. 98, [1980] 1 S.C.R. 115 at 132 (S.C.C.).
5. *Consolidated Fastrate Inc. v. Western Canada Council of Teamsters*, [2009] S.C.J. No. 53, [2009] 3 S.C.R. 407 at paras. 69, 70, 72 (S.C.C.).

▼HCL-187▼ Facilitating interprovincial transport. "[M]erely facilitating interprovincial transport will not, without more, attract federal jurisdiction."[1] "[S]omething more than physical connection and a mutually beneficial commercial relationship with a federal work or undertaking is required for a company to fall under federal jurisdiction".[2] The "something more" that would be required is the actual transportation of goods or persons across provincial boundaries. "It is the business *performing* the interprovincial operations (*i.e.*, the interprovincial transportation) that is subject to federal jurisdiction. A shipper, whether it is a plant that ships its own rail cars or a freight forwarder that ships its own boxes or envelopes, still remains a shipper. The business that performs the interprovincial transportation — the carrier that crosses provincial boundaries — is the undertaking that attracts federal jurisdiction under s. 92(10)(a)."[3]

Notes

1. *Consolidated Fastrate Inc. v. Western Canada Council of Teamsters*, [2009] S.C.J. No. 53, [2009] 3 S.C.R. 407 at para. 78 (S.C.C.).

2. *Consolidated Fastrate Inc. v. Western Canada Council of Teamsters*, [2009] S.C.J. No. 53, [2009] 3 S.C.R. 407 at para. 79 (S.C.C.).
3. *Consolidated Fastrate Inc. v. Western Canada Council of Teamsters*, [2009] S.C.J. No. 53, [2009] 3 S.C.R. 407 at para. 80 (S.C.C.).

▼HCL-188▼ Transportation vs. communication. Whereas communications undertakings can provide international and interprovincial services from a fixed point, it is not possible for a transportation undertaking to provide services unless it performs the interprovincial carriage itself.[1] "The difference between the communications and transportation contexts ... is that communications undertakings can *operate* and *provide* international and interprovincial communication services from a fixed point. If one were to focus only or primarily on the *means* by which a communication undertaking provides interprovincial services to its customers, the result could be that two companies operating and providing identical services would be subject to different jurisdictions depending on their modes of transmission. ... In the transportation context, it is not possible for an undertaking to operate an interprovincial transportation service where it does not itself perform the interprovincial carriage. A business can, of course, act as an intermediary between interprovincial carriers and consumers who want to access those carriers at a reduced price. This does not mean that such a business becomes the operator and provider of the interprovincial carriage, however. The fact that customers may be unaware that the intermediary company is not in fact performing the interprovincial carriage is ... irrelevant to the constitutional inquiry. Section 92(10)(a) is concerned with the nature of undertakings, not how they are subjectively understood by consumers... '[T]he question whether an undertaking, service or business is a federal one depends on the nature of its operations'."[2]

Notes

1. *Consolidated Fastrate Inc. v. Western Canada Council of Teamsters*, [2009] S.C.J. No. 53, [2009] 3 S.C.R. 407 at para. 60 (S.C.C.).
2. *Consolidated Fastrate Inc. v. Western Canada Council of Teamsters*, [2009] S.C.J. No. 53, [2009] 3 S.C.R. 407 at paras. 60-61 (S.C.C.).

X. Property and Civil Rights and Provincial Authority in Relation to Local and Private Matters

1. **Provincial Power to Make Laws in Relation to Property and Civil Rights** HCL-189

2. **Provincial Power to Legislate Matters of a Local or Private Nature** HCL-191

3. **Double Aspect Doctrine in Relation to s. 92(13) and s. 92(16)** HCL-194
   - (1) Provincial Powers over Trade and Commerce HCL-195
   - (2) Provincial Powers over Public Order and Morality HCL-197

---

1. Provincial Power to Make Laws in Relation to Property and Civil Rights

▼HCL-189▼ Property and civil rights. Section 92(13) of the *Constitution Act, 1867*[1] grants to the provincial legislatures the power to make laws in relation to property and civil rights in the province. Of all the provincial heads of power enumerated under s. 92, s. 92(13) is one of the most, if not *the* most, important.[2] Section 92(13) plays an integral role in the broader division of powers tussle between ss. 91 and 92, and is often pitted against the three major heads of federal power in the jurisprudence. The general trend is for the federal government to argue that a matter concerns the peace, order and good government; trade and commerce; or criminal law power, and conversely for the provinces to argue that a matter more aptly implicates property and civil rights.

Notes

1. *Constitution Act, 1867* (U.K.), 30 & 31 Vict., c. 3, s. 92(13)
2. *R. v. Zelensky*, [1978] S.C.J. No. 48, [1978] 2 S.C.R. 940 at 979 (S.C.C.) (Pigeon J., dissenting in part).

▼HCL-190▼ Scope of Section 92(13). One of the reasons cited for the lack of experimentation and development under s. 92(16), is that the generous capacity afforded to s. 92(13) by the judiciary obviated any real necessity for it.[1] The exact scope of "property and civil rights in the province", along with the scope of any legislative power granted to a level of government, falls to the judiciary to consider. Judicial interpretation of s. 92(13) has evolved from one of wide expanse during the days of appeals to the Privy Council, to a more narrowing tendency by the Supreme Court of Canada.[2] A wide interpretation generally favours the provinces or has a decentralizing effect on the federation[3] while similarly, a narrow interpretation commonly favours the federal government and has a centralizing effect on the federation.

The regulation of a particular industry comes within property and civil rights in the province, even when the industry and particular firms extend beyond the boundaries of any one province.[4]

Notes

1. Peter W. Hogg & Wade K. Wright, "Canadian Federalism, the Privy Council and the Supreme Court: Reflections on the Debate about Canadian Federalism" (2005) 38 U.B.C. L. Rev. 329 at 338.
2. Joseph Eliot Magnet, *Constitutional Law of Canada: Cases, Notes and Materials*, 7th ed., Vol. 1 (Edmonton: Juriliber, 1998) at 297.
3. *Citizens Insurance Company of Canada v. Parsons* (1881), 7 A.C. 96 at 110 (P.C.).
4. Recently, the Supreme Court of Canada came to the same conclusion about the shipping industry; see *Consolidated Fastfrate Inc. v. Western Canada Council of Teamsters*, [2009] S.C.J. No. 53, [2009] 3 S.C.R. 407 (S.C.C.), where the majority of the Supreme Court held that labour relations in a shipping company were to be governed by provincial law, pursuant to the *Constitution Act, 1867* (U.K.), 30 & 31 Vict., c. 3, s. 92(13) .

2. Provincial Power to Legislate Matters of a Local or Private Nature

▼HCL-191▼ Overview. Section 92(16) of the *Constitution Act, 1867* grants to the provincial legislatures the power to legislate matters of a merely local or private nature in the province. "Local" may mean legislation that is either of significance to a locality in a specific part of a province, or limited to the province as a whole.[1] Despite the breadth of the phrase, s. 92(16) is rarely relied upon as a head of provincial power in its own right in practice. Instead, it is usually mentioned alongside another section, often but not limited to s. 92(13), as an alternate reason for finding provincial competence. While s. 92(16) has not featured prominently as an independent source of provincial power in the jurisprudence, the provision has nevertheless been the subject of deliberation amongst constitutional scholars for its untapped potential. It may be that the framers of the Constitution intended this section to function as a residuary source of power for the provinces, much like the "peace, order and good government" clause in the opening words of s. 91, granting all other remaining local or private matters not specifically enumerated under section 92 to the local legislatures.[2] Courts have occasionally referred to this subsection as a residuary or supplemental head of power as well.[3]

Notes

1. Joseph Eliot Magnet, *Constitutional Law of Canada: Cases, Notes and Materials*, 7th ed., Vol. 1 (Edmonton: Juriliber, 1998) at 299.
2. See, for example, Ken Lysyk, "Constitutional Reform and the Introductory Clause of Section 91: Residual and Emergency Law-Making Authority" (1979) 57 Can. Bar Rev. 531; and Albert S. Abel, "What Peace, Order and Good Government? (1968) 7 West. Ont. L. Rev. 1.
3. *Nova Scotia (Board of Censors) v. McNeil*, [1978] S.C.J. No. 25, [1978] 2 S.C.R. 662 at 700 (S.C.C.); and *Reference re: Farm Products Marketing Act (Ontario)*, [1957] S.C.J. No. 11, [1957] S.C.R. 198 at 212 (S.C.C.); and *Ontario Liquor License Case (Re)*, [1896] J.C.J. No. 1, [1896] A.C. 348 (P.C.).

▼HCL-192▼ Scope of Section 92(16). The tendency to find s. 92(16) applicable alongside another s. 92 head of power, without necessarily specifying which is most appropriate, is relatively common. Section 92(16) has been invoked along with other s. 92 heads of power to uphold the following provincial legislation matters: the construction, repair and control of highways;[1] game laws regarding the conservation of fur-bearing species;[2] and financial relief to a local benefit society.[3] Section 92(16) has been invoked along with s. 92(13) specifically to uphold the following provincial legislation matters: highway traffic;[4] the regulation of video lottery terminal gaming;[5] film censorship;[6] and even aspects of local trade.[7]

Notes

1. *Re Rogers*, [1909] 7 E.L.R. 212 (P.E.I. C.A.). Provincial legislation upheld solely under *Constitution Act, 1867* (U.K.), 30 & 31 Vict., c. 3, s. 92(16).
2. *Dion v. Hudson Bay Co.*, [1917] 51 Que. S.C. 413 (Que. S.C.). Provincial legislation upheld under *Constitution Act, 1867* (U.K.), 30 & 31 Vict., c. 3, s. 92(5) or 92(16).

3. *L'Union St-Jacques de Montréal v. Belisle* (1874), L.R. 6 P.C. 31. Provincial legislation upheld solely under s. 92(16).
4. *Prince Edward Island (Secretary) v. Egan*, [1941] S.C.J. No. 20, [1941] S.C.R. 396 (S.C.C.).
5. *Siemens v. Manitoba (Attorney General)*, [2002] S.C.J. No. 69, [2003] 1 S.C.R. 6 at para. 22 (S.C.C.).
6. *Nova Scotia (Board of Censors) v. McNeil*, [1978] S.C.J. No. 25, [1978] 2 S.C.R. 662 (S.C.C.).
7. *Rio Hotel v. New Brunswick (Liquor Licensing Board)*, [1987] S.C.J. No. 46, [1987] 2 S.C.R. 59 (S.C.C.).

▼HCL-193▼ Provincial residuary clause. While there is some judicial support of the view that s. 92(16) encompasses residuary properties[1] akin to the Peace, Order and Good Government (POGG) power,[2] it is mostly in the arena of constitutional scholarship where the question has been debated. Criticism of the argument that s. 92(16) has a residuary character tends to fall on structural considerations.[3] If s. 92(16) is a counterpart to the "peace, order and good government" clause in s. 91, the corresponding functions of the provisions are not actually reflected in the form of the text. For example, whereas the federal residuum is located in the introductory clause of s. 91, the provincial residuum takes the form of an enumerated class of subject assigned to the provinces by s. 92.[4] Despite some favourable scholarly and judicial interpretation, s. 92(16) has nevertheless not been widely regarded, nor accepted, as a "POGG for the provinces".

Notes

1. *Schneider v. British Columbia*, [1982] S.C.J. No. 64, [1982] 2 S.C.R. 112 (S.C.C.).
2. *Ontario Liquor License Case (Re)*, [1896] J.C.J. No. 1, [1896] A.C. 348 (P.C.).
3. See, for example, Gerald Peter Browne, *The Judicial Committee and the British North America Act: an analysis of the interpretative scheme for the distribution of legislative powers* (Toronto: University of Toronto Press, 1967) at 41-42.
4. Joseph Eliot Magnet, *Constitutional Law of Canada: Cases, Notes and Materials*, 7th ed., Vol. 1 (Edmonton: Juriliber, 1998) at 300.

---

3. Double Aspect Doctrine in Relation to s. 92(13) and s. 92(16)

(1) Provincial Powers over Trade and Commerce HCL-195
(2) Provincial Powers over Public Order and Morality HCL-197

▼HCL-194▼ Double aspect doctrine. Much of the case law further interpreting the scope of s. 92(13) and 92(16) involve subject areas with a double aspect. The formulation of the double aspect doctrine[1] greatly expanded the scope of provincial legislative power. Pursuant to the doctrine, provincial legislators can argue that a matter which previously had been under exclusive federal jurisdiction, could take on a second aspect when dealt with on a purely local level. Because many subject areas may have both national and local manifestations, it is the job of the courts to determine which aspect of a subject any particular law may deal with. In most cases, it is not clear whether the law in question deals with a subject that is broad and national in scope, or one that is narrow and local.

Note

1. *Reference re: Liquor License Act of 1877 (Ont.)*, [1883] J.C.J. No. 2, 9 App. Cas. 117 (P.C.).

---

(1) Provincial Powers over Trade and Commerce

▼HCL-195▼ Overview. The jurisdictional struggle to legislate over matters relating to trade and commerce stems from the need to reconcile the federal trade and commerce power under s. 91(2) on the one hand, and the property and civil rights power under s. 92(13) on the other. Trade necessarily involves the exchange of property and requires contractual relationships in order to function, and yet property and contractual rights fall squarely within provincial jurisdiction under s. 92(13). Provincial powers over economic regulation or trade and commerce matters are limited to the regulation of *intra*-provincial matters under s. 92(13).[1] Powers over *inter*-provincial or international trade, as well as "general trade and commerce" matters, fall within the federal trade and commerce power under s. 91(2).[2]

Notes

1. *Citizens Insurance Company of Canada v. Parsons* (1881), 7 App. Cas. 96 at 110 (P.C.).
2. For more, see Chapter VII ("Regulation of Trade and Commerce").

▼HCL-196▼ Tensions. A difficulty that emerges is the extent to which a province is permitted to affect inter-provincial trade while regulating *intra*-provincial trade. It is not always straightforward for courts to apply the distinction between the regulation of intra-provincial matters under s. 92(13) property and civil rights, and inter-provincial matters under s. 91(2) trade and commerce. This is particularly evident in the context of provincial marketing legislation. While provinces may not make use of their control over local undertakings to affect extra-provincial marketing, "this does not prevent the use of provincial control to complement federal regulation of interprovincial trade".[1] The determination of the validity of a provincial regulation most often hinges on a pith and substance analysis of the legislation.[2] In the case of trade transactions, "each transaction and each regulation must be examined in relation to its own facts".[3] "[A] trade transaction, completed in a province, is not necessarily, by that fact alone, subject only to provincial control, ... the fact that such a transaction incidentally has some effect upon a company engaged in interprovincial trade does not necessarily prevent its being subject to such control."[4] In most cases however, provinces may indirectly affect extra-provincial trade by decisions which affect the cost of production, or decisions which affect retail sales within a province.[5] Provincial legislation that aims to effectively control inter-provincial trade outright will typically be *ultra vires* the province.[6] Provincial regulatory schemes are invalid if they directly affect the inter-provincial movement of products by limiting production and, effectively, represent attempts to regulate interprovincial trade outright.[7] From the standpoint of provincial powers, it is noteworthy that the Court held that provincial legislation that imposed production quotas on all producers were nevertheless local undertakings subject to provincial authority, irrespective of the destination of their output.[8]

Notes

1. *Reference re: Agricultural Products Marketing Act, 1970 (Canada)*, [1978] S.C.J. No. 58, [1978] 2 S.C.R. 1198 at 1293 and 1296 (S.C.C.).
2. *Shannon v. Lower Mainland Dairy Products Board*, [1938] J.C.J. No. 2, [1938] A.C. 708 (P.C.).

3. *Carnation Co. v. Quebec (Agricultural Marketing Board)*, [1968] S.C.J. No. 11, [1968] S.C.R. 238 at 253-54 (S.C.C.).
4. *Carnation Co. v. Quebec (Agricultural Marketing Board)*, [1968] S.C.J. No. 11, [1968] S.C.R. 238 at 253-54 (S.C.C.).
5. *Carnation Co. v. Quebec (Agricultural Marketing Board)*, [1968] S.C.J. No. 11, [1968] S.C.R. 238 at 253-54 (S.C.C.).
6. *Manitoba (Attorney General) v. Manitoba Egg and Poultry Association*, [1971] S.C.J. No. 63, [1971] S.C.R. 689 (S.C.C.).
7. *Manitoba (Attorney General) v. Manitoba Egg and Poultry Association*, [1971] S.C.J. No. 63, [1971] S.C.R. 689 (S.C.C.).
8. *Reference re: Agricultural Products Marketing Act, 1970 (Canada)*, [1978] S.C.J. No. 58, [1978] 2 S.C.R. 1198 at 1296 (S.C.C.), affd in *Fédération des producteurs de volailles du Québec v. Pelland*, [2005] S.C.J. No. 19, [2005] 1 S.C.R. 292 (S.C.C.).

---

(2) Provincial Powers over Public Order and Morality

▼HCL-197▼ Overview. Whereas jurisdictional questions over trade and commerce tend to pit property and civil rights in competition with the federal trade and commerce power, jurisdictional contests over public order and/or morality tend to be played out between s. 92(13) and 92(16) on the one hand, and the federal criminal law power under s. 91(27) on the other. If a provincial offence is not clearly grounded in s. 92(13) property and civil rights or s. 92(16) matters of a local nature, but is rather in pith and substance about criminal law, it will likely be found invalid.[1] Section 92(14) of the *Constitution Act, 1867*[2] grants provinces the jurisdiction over the administration of justice within the province, including provincial policing and prosecuting of offences under the *Criminal Code*.[3] Section 92(15),[4] specifically provides that provinces have extensive powers to enact penal laws provided that they are primarily regulatory and preventative in nature, and directed clearly at property and civil rights under s. 92(13).[5] Lastly, the provinces have attempted to rely on s. 92(13) property and civil rights and s. 92(16) matters of a local nature to enact laws that are quasi-criminal in nature. Such laws are typically regulatory laws or licensing schemes that in some form protect private property interests.

Notes

1. *R. v. Westendorp*, [1983] S.C.J. No. 6, [1983] 1 S.C.R. 43 at paras 16, 21 and 22 (S.C.C.); *R. v. Morgentaler*, [1993] S.C.J. No. 95, [1993] 3 S.C.R. 463 (S.C.C.).
2. (U.K.), 30 & 31 Vict., c. 3, s. 92(14).
3. (CAN) *Criminal Code*, R.S.C. 1985, c. C-46.
4. The power under s. 92(15) is “ancillary” in nature, “authorizing the use of penal sanctions to enforce provincial regulatory schemes that are validly anchored else-

where in the s. 92 list of provincial powers"; see Joel Bakan *et al.*, *Canadian Constitutional Law*, 3d ed. (Toronto: Emond Montgomery, 2003).

5. *Nova Scotia (Board of Censors) v. McNeil*, [1978] S.C.J. No. 25, [1978] 2 S.C.R. 662 (S.C.C.).

▼HCL-198▼ Civil consequences to a crime. In addition to the provincial power or duty to prevent crime and suppress the conditions leading to crime, provinces are able to legislate civil consequences of crime already accounted for in the *Criminal Code*.[1] For example, provincial legislation that suspended the driver's licences of individuals convicted for impaired driving under the *Criminal Code*[2] was upheld as valid. The Court held that the legislation was not in pith and substance about supplementing already existing criminal provisions, but rather, about the regulation of highway traffic that was clearly within the jurisdiction of the province.[3] Civil consequences of a criminal act "are not to be considered as 'punishment' so as to bring the matter within the exclusive jurisdiction of Parliament".[4]

Notes

1. (CAN) *Criminal Code*, R.S.C. 1985, c. C-46; *Prince Edward Island (Secretary) v. Egan*, [1941] S.C.J. No. 20, [1941] S.C.R. 396 (S.C.C.); *O'Grady v. Sparling*, [1960] S.C.J. No. 48, [1960] S.C.R. 804; *Ross v. Ontario (Registrar of Motor Vehicles)*, [1973] S.C.J. No. 130, [1975] 1 S.C.R. 5 (S.C.C.).
2. (CAN) *Criminal Code*, R.S.C. 1985, c. C-46.
3. *Ross v. Ontario (Registrar of Motor Vehicles)*, [1973] S.C.J. No. 130, [1975] 1 S.C.R. 5 (S.C.C.).
4. *Ross v. Ontario (Registrar of Motor Vehicles)*, [1973] S.C.J. No. 130, [1975] 1 S.C.R. 5 at 13 (S.C.C.).

▼HCL-199▼ Double aspect doctrine and criminal law. It is well established that there is a double aspect to morality — criminal morality and local morality – and the local standards of morality are properly within provincial jurisdiction under the *Constitution Act, 1867*.[1] [2] Courts seem willing to acknowledge a double aspect regarding criminal law matters, though at times, the province is called out for intruding into the federal criminal law power.[3] A court "should favour, where possible, the ordinary operation of statutes enacted by *both* levels of government".[4] A provincial law must be firmly anchored in property or civil rights, or matters of a local nature, to be found valid. For example, the Supreme Court of Canada upheld provincial legislation which attached a condition of no nude dancing to all liquor licences issued throughout the province. A local hotel owner challenged the legislation as an intrusion into the federal criminal law power, but the Court invoked the double aspect doctrine on the basis that the legislation was "*prima facie* related to property and civil rights within the province and to matters of a purely local nature".[5]

Notes

1. (U.K.), 30 & 31 Vict., c. 3, s. 92(16).
2. *Nova Scotia (Board of Censors) v. McNeil*, [1978] S.C.J. No. 25, [1978] 2 S.C.R. 662 at 689, 691, 699 (S.C.C.).
3. *R. v. Westendorp*, [1983] S.C.J. No. 6, [1983] 1 S.C.R. 43 at paras. 16, 21, 22 (S.C.C.).
4. *Chatterjee v. Ontario (Attorney General)*, [2009] S.C.J. No. 19, [2009] 1 S.C.R. 624 at paras. 1-4 (S.C.C.).
5. *Rio Hotel Ltd. v. New Brunswick (Liquor Licensing Board)*, [1987] S.C.J. No. 46, [1987] 2 S.C.R. 59 (S.C.C.).

XI. The Environment and Natural Resources

1. The Environment

(1) Federal Regulation of Extra-Provincial Actions.......... HCL-201
(2) Peace, Order and Good Government.......... HCL-202
(3) Effect on Federal Jurisdiction.......... HCL-203
(4) Criminal Law Power.......... HCL-204

2. Natural Resources

(1) Mines and Minerals.......... HCL-206
(2) Federal Declaratory Power.......... HCL-214
(3) Forestry.......... HCL-215
(4) Fisheries.......... HCL-217

---

1. The Environment

(1) Federal Regulation of Extra-Provincial Actions.......... HCL-201
(2) Peace, Order and Good Government.......... HCL-202
(3) Effect on Federal Jurisdiction.......... HCL-203
(4) Criminal Law Power.......... HCL-204

▼HCL-200▼ Overview. The *Constitution Act, 1867*[1] does not confer authority with respect to the environment and the regulation of pollution upon a particular head of power. Accordingly, neither the federal nor the provincial government has exclusive jurisdiction to legislate and regulate in this regard.[2] Environmental issues may be relevant to Parliament in areas such as navigation and shipping,[3] sea coast and inland fisheries[4] and Indians, and lands reserved for the Indians.[5] The provinces may encounter similar environmental concerns by virtue of their individual heads of power, including the management and sale of public lands,[6] local works and undertakings[7] and property and civil rights.[8] In addition, through the *Constitution Act, 1867*,[9] both levels of government have taxation powers to influence corporate and individual behaviour with respect to pollution.

Notes

1. *Constitution Act, 1867* (U.K.), 30 & 31 Vict., c. 3.
2. *Friends of the Oldman River Society v. Canada (Minister of Transport)*, [1992] S.C.J. No. 1, [1992] 1 S.C.R. 3 at 64 (S.C.C.). See also *Halsbury's Laws of Canada – Environment.*
3. *Constitution Act, 1867* (U.K.), 30 & 31 Vict., c. 3, s. 91(10).
4. *Constitution Act, 1867* (U.K.), 30 & 31 Vict., c. 3, s. 91(12).
5. *Constitution Act, 1867* (U.K.), 30 & 31 Vict., c. 3, s. 91(24).
6. *Constitution Act, 1867* (U.K.), 30 & 31 Vict., c. 3, s. 92(5).
7. *Constitution Act, 1867* (U.K.), 30 & 31 Vict., c. 3, s. 92(10).
8. *Constitution Act, 1867* (U.K.), 30 & 31 Vict., c. 3, s. 92(13).
9. *Constitution Act, 1867* (U.K.), 30 & 31 Vict., c. 3, ss. 91(3), 92(2).

---

(1) Federal Regulation of Extra-Provincial Actions

▼HCL-201▼ Extra-provincial actions. The "environment" has not been identified as "an independent matter of legislation under the *Constitution Act, 1867*".[1] The "environment" encompasses the physical, economic and social environment and touches upon several of the heads of power assigned to each levels of government. Provinces however, can only generally legislate with respect to actions arising within their boundaries.[2] "The basic principle of the division of legislative powers in Canada is that all legislative power is federal except in matters over which provincial legislatures are given exclusive authority."[3] A province, as owner of inland fisheries in its territory, is entitled to legislate for the protection of its property. However, in respect of injury caused by acts performed outside its territory, such a matter is not "within its legislative authority when those acts are done in another province".[4] In the end, the provinces maintain jurisdiction to legislate on environmental matters, but this jurisdiction is not exclusive, as Parliament may also make laws affecting the environment within its own legislative powers.

Notes

1. *Friends of the Oldman River Society v. Canada (Minister of Transport)*, [1992] S.C.J. No. 1, [1992] 1 S.C.R. 3 at 64 (S.C.C.).
2. *Interprovincial Co-operatives Ltd. v. Dryden Chemicals Ltd.*, [1975] S.C.J. No. 42, [1976] 1 S.C.R. 477 at 507 (S.C.C.).
3. *Interprovincial Co-operatives Ltd. v. Dryden Chemicals Ltd.*, [1975] S.C.J. No. 42, [1976] 1 S.C.R. 477 at 512 (S.C.C.).

4. *Interprovincial Co-operatives Ltd. v. Dryden Chemicals Ltd.*, [1975] S.C.J. No. 42, [1976] 1 S.C.R. 477 at 516 (S.C.C.).

---

(2) Peace, Order and Good Government

▼HCL-202▼ Overview. The federal Peace, Order and Good Government power (POGG), pursuant to the *Constitution Act, 1867*,[1] may be invoked to justify Parliament's jurisdiction with respect to environmental issues.[2] The doctrine of national concern has been successfully raised to support federal authority in relation to environmental issues. Specifically, with respect to the national concern doctrine[3] and the ODCA,[4] the distinction between salt water and fresh water within the ODCA[5] had the requisite degree of singleness, distinctiveness and indivisibility to become a matter of national concern.[6] Parliament also has jurisdiction in controlling the pollution of waters within a province where it becomes a matter of national concern.[7] In essence, when provinces are incapable of legislating in environmental matters, because the effects are beyond their borders or otherwise, federal intervention will be within Parliament's powers.

Notes

1. (U.K.), 30 & 31 Vict., c. 3, s. 91.
2. See Chapter V ("Peace, Order and Good Government").
3. See Chapter V ("Peace, Order and Good Government").
4. *Ocean Dumping Control Act*, S.C. 1974-75-76, c. 55, s. 4(1).
5. *Ocean Dumping Control Act*, S.C. 1974-75-76, c. 55.
6. *R. v. Crown Zellerbach Canada Ltd.*, [1988] S.C.J. No. 23, [1988] 1 S.C.R. 401 at para. 39 (S.C.C.).
7. *R. v. Crown Zellerbach Canada Ltd.*, [1988] S.C.J. No. 23, [1988] 1 S.C.R. 401 (S.C.C.).

---

(3) Effect on Federal Jurisdiction

▼HCL-203▼ Overview. The doctrine of national concern will not automatically apply to justify federal jurisdiction over the environment. The "Constitution should be so interpreted as to afford both levels of government ample means to protect the environment while maintaining the general structure of the Constitution".[1] Given that the provincial and federal governments share jurisdiction over the environment, it is appropriate to look at the catalogue of powers in the *Constitution Act, 1867*[2] and to consider "how they may be employed to meet or avoid environmental concerns".[3] Environmental issues may be considered to varying degrees depending upon the applicable head of power.[4] Parliament has jurisdiction to evaluate the environmental impact of any project that affects any of its jurisdictions. This, however, does not preclude the provinces from doing the same. Provinces also possess the necessary jurisdiction to do the same within their jurisdictions.[5] The "federal and provincial governments can adopt mutually agreeable terms for coordinating environmental assessments"[6] and the responsible authority is "free to use any and all federal-provincial coordination tools available", even if it was nevertheless required to comply with the provisions of its enabling statute.[7]

Notes

1. *R. v. Hydro Québec*, [1997] S.C.J. No. 76, [1997] 3 S.C.R. 213 at para. 116 (S.C.C.).
2. (U.K.), 30 & 31 Vict., c. 3.
3. *Friends of the Oldman River Society v. Canada (Minister of Transport)*, [1992] S.C.J. No. 1, [1992] 1 S.C.R. 3 at 65 (S.C.C.).
4. *Friends of the Oldman River Society v. Canada (Minister of Transport)*, [1992] S.C.J. No. 1, [1992] 1 S.C.R. 3 at 67 (S.C.C.).
5. *Friends of the Oldman River Society v. Canada (Minister of Transport)*, [1992] S.C.J. No. 1, [1992] 1 S.C.R. 3 at 72-73 (S.C.C.).
6. *MiningWatch Canada v. Canada (Fisheries and Oceans)*, [2010] S.C.J. No. 2, [2010] 1 S.C.R. 6 at paras. 24-25, 41 (S.C.C.).
7. *MiningWatch Canada v. Canada (Fisheries and Oceans)*, [2010] S.C.J. No. 2, [2010] 1 S.C.R. 6 at para. 42 (S.C.C.).

---

(4) Criminal Law Power

▼HCL-204▼ Overview. Parliament may impose protective legislation relating to the environment through its criminal law power. The federal criminal law power is distinct from the doctrine of national concern on the basis that the former "seeks by discrete prohibitions to prevent evils falling within a broad purpose, such as, for example, the protection of health" while the latter operates by assigning full power to regulate an area to Parliament.[1] The "stewardship of the environment is a fundamental value of our society and ... Parliament may use its criminal law power to underline that value".[2] Criminal sanctions with respect to environmental issues need not be limited to pollution which, eventually, whether through direct or indirect action, has a serious impact upon human health.[3] The "use of the federal criminal law power in no way precludes the provinces from exercising their extensive powers" under the *Constitu-*

tion Act, 1867[4] "to regulate and control the pollution of the environment either independently or to supplement federal action".[5]

Notes

1. *R. v. Hydro-Québec*, [1997] S.C.J. No. 76, [1997] 3 S.C.R. 213, para. 128 (S.C.C.).
2. *R. v. Hydro-Québec*, [1997] S.C.J. No. 76, [1997] 3 S.C.R. 213, para. 127 (S.C.C.).
3. *R. v. Hydro-Québec*, [1997] S.C.J. No. 76, [1997] 3 S.C.R. 213, para. 127 (S.C.C.).
4. (U.K.), 30 & 31 Vict., c. 3, s. 92.
5. *R. v. Hydro-Québec*, [1997] S.C.J. No. 76, [1997] 3 S.C.R. 213, para. 131 (S.C.C.).

---

2. Natural Resources

(1) Mines and Minerals
(a) Taxation HCL-209
(b) Trade and Commerce Power........................ HCL-210
(c) Works and Undertakings under s. 92(10)(a).. HCL-211
(d) Peace, Order and Good Government HCL-212
(e) Offshore Minerals HCL-213
(2) Federal Declaratory Power................................. HCL-214
(3) Forestry.. HCL-215
(4) Fisheries... HCL-217

▼HCL-205▼ Overview. Natural resources are closely related to the environment. Unlike the environment, specific natural resources have been assigned, to an extent, to a particular head of power, and the provinces have been allocated wide jurisdiction in this respect. In particular, pursuant to the *Constitution Act, 1867*,[1] the provincial governments have authority with respect to the "Management and Sale of the Public Lands belonging to the Province and of the Timber and Wood thereon",[2] "Local Works and Undertakings"[3] and "Property and Civil Rights".[4] These powers were subsequently broadened through the introduction of the *Constitution Act, 1867*.[5] The *Constitution Act, 1867*[6] provides additional rights to the provinces with respect to lands, mines, minerals and royalties.[7] On the other hand, the federal government has a general power to legislate with respect to natural resources upon federal lands. In addition to its general power over sea coast and fisheries, Parliament may also obtain jurisdiction over certain provincial works by virtue of its declaratory power.

Notes

1. (U.K.), 30 & 31 Vict., c. 3.
2. *Constitution Act, 1867* (U.K.), 30 & 31 Vict., c. 3, s. 92(5).
3. *Constitution Act, 1867* (U.K.), 30 & 31 Vict., c. 3, s. 92(10).
4. *Constitution Act, 1867* (U.K.), 30 & 31 Vict., c. 3, s. 92(13).
5. *Constitution Act, 1867* (U.K.), 30 & 31 Vict., c. 3, s. 92A.
6. (U.K.), 30 & 31 Vict., c. 3, s. 109.
7. These rights were also transferred to the western provinces according to the *Constitution Act, 1930*, (U.K.), 20 & 21 Geo. V., c. 26. See Gérald A. Beaudoin & Pierre Thibault, *La Constitution du Canada* (Montréal: Wilson & Lafleur ltée, 2004) at 791.

---

(1) Mines and Minerals

▼HCL-206▼ Overview. The provincial and federal governments have rights with respect to the minerals located upon their public property. In that sense, both Parliament and the provincial legislature may enact laws in relation to natural resources found within their territory or on their public property.[1]

Note

1. See G.V. La Forest, *Natural Resources and Public Property under the Canadian Constitution* (Toronto: University of Toronto Press, 1969); W.D. Moull, "Natural Resources: Provincial Property Rights" (1983) 21 Alta. L. Rev. 472. See *Spooner Oils Ltd. v. Turner Valley Gas Conservation*, [1933] S.C.J. No. 54, [1933] S.C.R. 629 (S.C.C.). See also Dale Gibson, "Constitutional Jurisdiction Over Environmental Management in Canada" (1973) 23 U.T.L.J. 54; Kathryn Harrison, *Passing the Buck: Federalism and Canadian Environmental Policy* (Vancouver: UBC Press, 1996); Frank Cassidy & Norman Dale, *Native Claims? The Implications of Comprehensive Claims Settlements for Natural Resources in British Columbia* (Lantzville: The Institute for Research on Public Policy, 1988); Susan Blackman *et al.*, "The Evolution of Federal/Provincial Relations in Natural Resources Management" (1994) 32 Alta. L. Rev. 511. See also *Halsbury's Laws of Canada – Mines and Minerals*.

▼HCL-207▼ Provincial jurisdiction. Both Parliament and the provincial legislature may enact laws in relation to their natural resources when those resources are located on lands that are the property of the government. Parliament then enacts laws in relation to public property,[1] and the provinces do the same.[2] When the provinces do not have proprietary rights to privately owned natural resources, however, they may nevertheless enact legislation in this respect by virtue of their other jurisdictions, including taxation,[3] local works and undertakings,[4] property and civil rights,[5] matters of a local or private nature,[6] and natural resources.[7] Provincial legislative authority does not extend to fixing the price to be charged or received in respect of the sale of goods in the export market.[8] For example, legislation imposing taxation upon oil and gas was found to be "directly aimed at the production of oil destined for export and had the effect of regulating the export price, since the producer was effectively compelled to obtain that price on the sale of his product".[9]

Section 92A. Section 92A increases provincial jurisdiction, including taxation powers, in relation to natural resources, development, conservation and management of non-renewable natural resources and forestry resources, as well as generation and production of electrical energy in the province.[10] Furthermore, provinces are authorized "to legislate for the export of resources to other provinces subject to Parliament's paramount legislative power in the area".[11] There are limits imposed however upon provincial authority pursuant to s. 92A. Section 92A only applies to "non-renewable natural resources", and thus, it does not apply to agriculture.

Notes

1. *Constitution Act, 1867* (U.K.), 30 & 31 Vict., c. 3, s. 91(1A).
2. *Constitution Act, 1867* (U.K.), 30 & 31 Vict., c. 3, s. 92(5), 92(13).
3. *Constitution Act, 1867* (U.K.), 30 & 31 Vict., c. 3, s. 92(2), 92A(4).
4. *Constitution Act, 1867* (U.K.), 30 & 31 Vict., c. 3, s. 92(10).
5. *Constitution Act, 1867* (U.K.), 30 & 31 Vict., c. 3, s. 92(13).
6. *Constitution Act, 1867* (U.K.), 30 & 31 Vict., c. 3, s. 92(16).
7. *Constitution Act, 1867* (U.K.), 30 & 31 Vict., c. 3, s. 92A.
8. *Central Canada Potash Co. v. Saskatchewan*, [1978] S.C.J. No. 72, [1979] 1 S.C.R. 42 at 75 (S.C.C.), citing Martland J. in *Canadian Industrial Gas & Oil Ltd. v. Saskatchewan*, [1977] S.C.J. No. 124, [1978] 2 S.C.R. 545 at 568 (S.C.C.).
9. *Canadian Industrial Gas & Oil Ltd. v. Saskatchewan*, [1977] S.C.J. No. 124, [1978] 2 S.C.R. 545 at 569 (S.C.C.).
10. See commentary of Joseph Eliot Magnet, *Constitutional Law of Canada*, 9th ed., Vol. 1 (Edmonton: Juriliber Limited, 2007) at 581.
11. *Ontario Hydro v. Ontario (Labour Relations Board)*, [1993] S.C.J. No. 99, [1993] 3 S.C.R. 327 at 376-77 (S.C.C.).

▼HCL-208▼ Federal jurisdiction. Parliament has legislative authority over minerals within its own jurisdiction. Parliament may also enact laws with respect to minerals on land subject to provincial jurisdiction by virtue of powers such as trade and commerce, works and undertakings falling within the *Constitution Act, 1867*[1] and taxation, in addition to the peace, order and good government clause.[2]

Notes

1. (U.K.), 30 & 31 Vict., c. 3, s. 92(10)(a).
2. See Dale Gibson, "Constitutional Jurisdiction Over Environmental Management in Canada" (1973) 23 U.T.L.J. 54. See also Nickie Vlavianos, *The Legislative and Regulatory Framework for Oil Sands Development in Alberta: A Detailed Review and Analysis* (Canada: Canadian Institute of Resources Law, 2007) at Appendix A.

(a) Taxation

▼HCL-209▼ Overview. As a result of a constitutional amendment, the provinces may now levy indirect taxes with respect to non-renewable natural resources such as gas, oil and other minerals as long as there is no discrimination between the provinces.[1] Parliament has the power to levy taxes affecting mines and minerals within provincial jurisdiction, but its taxation power[2] is subject to the *Constitution Act, 1867*.[3]

Notes

1. See Susan Blackman *et al.*, "The Evolution of Federal/Provincial Relations in Natural Resources Management" (1994) 32 Alta. L. Rev. 511.
2. *Constitution Act, 1867* (U.K.), 30 & 31 Vict., c. 3, s. 91(3).
3. (U.K.), 30 & 31 Vict., c. 3, s. 125; *Reference re: Proposed Federal Tax on exported Natural Gas*, [1982] S.C.J. No. 52, [1982] 1 S.C.R. 1004 at 1044 (S.C.C.).

(b) Trade and Commerce Power

▼HCL-210▼ Overview. The *Constitution Act, 1867*[1] permits the provinces to legislate with respect to the inter-provincial exportation of minerals and other non-renewable natural resources. However, Parliament not only has legislative jurisdiction over the exportation of resources on an international scale, but also maintains its jurisdiction with respect to inter-provincial trade. The confirmation of provincial resource management powers[2] does not reduce any of the pre-existing powers of Parliament in relation to resources. Federal legislation would override any directly conflicting measure enacted by a province.[3] The federal government thus retains its trade and commerce jurisdiction[4] in respect of extra-provincial trade in resource production, and its authority[5] to declare unilaterally that a work wholly situated within a province — a mine or well, for instance — is a work for the general advantage of Canada, and may thus transfer that work unilaterally to exclusive federal legislative jurisdiction.[6]

Notes

1. (U.K.), 30 & 31 Vict., c. 3, s. 92A.
2. *Constitution Act, 1867* (U.K.), 30 & 31 Vict., c. 3, s. 92A(1).
3. *Constitution Act, 1867* (U.K.), 30 & 31 Vict., c. 3, s. 92A(1).
4. *Constitution Act, 1867* (U.K.), 30 & 31 Vict., c. 3, s. 91(2).
5. *Constitution Act, 1867* (U.K.), 30 & 31 Vict., c. 3, s. 92(10)(c).
6. Marsha A. Chandler, "Constitutional Change and Public Policy: The Impact of the Resource Amendment (Section 92A)" (1986) Canadian Journal of Political Science 103 at 116.

(c) Works and Undertakings under s. 92(10)(a)

▼HCL-211▼ Overview. The *Constitution Act, 1867*[1] excludes the following works and undertakings from provincial jurisdiction: "(a) Lines of Steam or other Ships, Railways, Canals, Telegraphs, and other Works and Undertakings connecting the Province with any other or others of the Provinces, or extending beyond the Limits of the Province ... ; (b) Lines of Steam Ships between the Province and any British or Foreign Country; and (c) Such Works as, although wholly situate within the Province, are before or after their Execution declared by the Parliament of Canada to be for the general Advantage of Canada or for the Advantage of Two or more of the Provinces".[2] Accordingly, Parliament may legislate with respect to mines and minerals associated with works or undertakings falling within the enumerated categories.

Notes

1. (U.K.), 30 & 31 Vict., c. 3, s. 92(10).
2. *Constitution Act, 1867* (U.K.), 30 & 31 Vict., c. 3, s. 92(10).

(d) Peace, Order and Good Government

▼HCL-212▼ National Concern and Atomic Energy. Parliament has jurisdiction over atomic energy under the national concern branch of the peace, order and good government power.[1] The production, use and application of atomic energy constitute a matter of national concern. "It is predominantly extra-provincial and international in character and implications, and possesses sufficiently distinct and separate characteristics to make it subject to Parliament's residual power."[2]

Notes

1. *Ontario Hydro v. Ontario (Labour Relations Board)*, [1993] S.C.J. No. 99, [1993] 3 S.C.R. 327 at para. 34 (S.C.C.), referring to Iacobucci J.'s dissenting reasons at para. 182.
2. *Ontario Hydro v. Ontario (Labour Relations Board)*, [1993] S.C.J. No. 99, [1993] 3 S.C.R. 327 at paras. 84-85 (S.C.C.).

(e) Offshore Minerals

▼HCL-213▼ Overview. Generally, the federal government has rights to the offshore minerals located in coastal waters. Jurisprudence in this area has focused upon whether the coastal province or the federal government owns the sea bed in question.[1] To establish whether a province owned minerals and natural resources in its waters, it must be determined whether the waters formed part of the province prior to Confederation and, if so, whether the natural resources found in those waters fall under provincial jurisdiction.[2] Even where a province such as Newfoundland entered Confederation at a much later date than, for example, British Columbia, the above reasoning may be relied upon to deny a claim to natural resources.[3]

Notes

1. *Reference Re: Ownership of Offshore Mineral Rights (British Columbia)*, [1967] S.C.J. No. 70, [1967] S.C.R. 792 (S.C.C.).
2. *Reference re: Ownership of the Bed of the Strait of Georgia and related areas*, [1984] S.C.J. No. 21, [1984] 1 S.C.R. 388 at 427 (S.C.C.).
3. *Reference re: Seabed and subsoil of the continental shelf offshore Newfoundland*, [1984] S.C.J. No. 7, [1984] 1 S.C.R. 86 (S.C.C.).

---

(2) Federal Declaratory Power

▼HCL-214▼ Overview. Certain resources which would typically fall within provincial jurisdiction can be federally regulated through Parliament's declaratory power. Pursuant to the *Constitution Act, 1867*,[1] Parliament can declare works situated in the province "to be for the general

Advantage of Canada or for the Advantage of Two or more of the Provinces".[2] An example of this was the *Atomic Energy Control Act*.[3] This statute represents an example of Parliament's declaration powers. While natural resources, including exploitation of minerals, fall within provincial jurisdiction, uranium is now an exception. The national concern dimension of the peace, order and good government clause upholds Parliament's authority to legislate with respect to atomic energy such as uranium. In contrast to atomic and nuclear energy, the provinces can regulate hydraulic energy within their provincial boundaries,[4] as long as it does not purport to interfere with an extra-provincial contract.[5]

Notes

1. (U.K.), 30 & 31 Vict., c. 3.
2. *Constitution Act, 1867* (U.K.), 30 & 31 Vict., c. 3, s. 92(10)(c).
3. (CAN) R.S.C. 1985, c. A-16, repealed by the *Nuclear Safety and Control Act*, S.C. 1997, c. 9.
4. Gérald A. Beaudoin & Pierre Thibault, *La Constitution du Canada*, (Montréal: Wilson & Lafleur ltée, 2004) at 795. See also Peter W. Hogg, *Constitutional Law of Canada*, looseleaf (Toronto: Thomson Carswell Ltd., 2007) at 30-18 in which he states that "dams, generating stations and distribution systems" fall within the *Constitution Act, 1867* (U.K.), 30 & 31 Vict., c. 3, s. 92(10) and refers to *Fulton v. Alberta (Energy Resources Conservation Board)*, [1981] S.C.J. No. 16, [1981] 1 S.C.R. 153 (S.C.C.).
5. See *Reference re: Upper Churchill Water Rights Reversion Act 1980*, [1984] S.C.J. No. 16, [1984] 1 S.C.R. 297 (S.C.C.).

---

(3) Forestry

▼HCL-215▼ Provincial authority. Several provincial heads of power authorize the provinces to legislate with respect to forests and timber falling within their territorial jurisdiction. The *Constitution Act, 1867*[1] confers provincial jurisdiction in relation to the management and sale of the public lands belonging to the provinces and of the timber and wood thereon.[2] Provinces derive further authority pursuant to the *Constitution Act, 1867*[3] which grants to the provinces jurisdiction on the development, conservation and management of non-renewable natural resources and forestry resources in the province, including laws in relation to the rate of primary production therefrom. They may also make laws in relation to the export from the province to another part of Canada of the primary production from non-renewable natural resources and forestry resources in the province except that such laws may not authorize or provide for discrimination in prices or in supplies exported to another part of Canada. In addition, the *Constitution Act, 1867*[4] also grants to the provinces the jurisdiction to enact laws affecting privately owned forests, specifically in relation to marketing and production matters.[5]

Notes

1. (U.K.), 30 & 31 Vict., c. 3, s. 92(5).
2. *Constitution Act, 1867* (U.K.), 30 & 31 Vict., c. 3, s. 92(5).
3. (U.K.), 30 & 31 Vict., c. 3, s. 92A.
4. (U.K.), 30 & 31 Vict., c. 3, s. 92(13).
5. *Paul v. British Columbia* [2003] S.C.J. No. 34, [2003] 2 S.C.R. 585 (S.C.C.).

▼HCL-216▼ Federal authority. Parliament has similar authority with respect to federally owned forests or territory, and may regulate the exploitation of forest resources through its jurisdiction over "public property".[1] In addition, historically, logging involved the practice of floating the logs down a river and to the mill. In those cases, if the waters were navigable, federal jurisdiction with respect to "navigation and shipping"[2] could be triggered and permit federal regulation of forestry in certain respects. On the other hand, if the waters were not navigable, provinces maintained jurisdiction.[3] The same type of argument could be made for federal jurisdiction over sea coast and inland fisheries,[4] where logging could interfere with fish habitat.[5] Despite federal authority in this area, it seems the provinces are not altogether restricted from legislating with respect to floating logs found on navigable waters where the intrusion upon federal jurisdiction is merely incidental.[6] The "fact that cut logs have somehow found their way into water does not mean that they have ceased to be part of the forestry resource, or that the Province should lose the right to continue managing that resource ... . Just because the logs are recovered from navigable waters does not mean that the impugned provisions must be related to navigation and shipping".[7] The court found the province salvaged the logs for economic reasons and only incidentally affected federal shipping rights when removing these hazards from the water.

Notes

1. *Constitution Act, 1867* (U.K.), 30 & 31 Vict., c. 3, s. 91(1A).
2. *Constitution Act, 1867* (U.K.), 30 & 31 Vict., c. 3, s. 91(10).
3. See G.V. La Forest, *Water Law in Canada* (Ottawa: Dept. of Regional Economic Expansion, 1973) at 30-32.
4. *Constitution Act, 1867* (U.K.), 30 & 31 Vict., c. 3, s. 91(12).

5. See *R. v. Fowler*, [1980] S.C.J. No. 58, [1980] 2 S.C.R. 213 (S.C.C.).
6. *Early Recovered Resources Inc. v. British Columbia*, [2005] F.C.J. No. 1234, 276 F.T.R. 267 (F.C.).
7. *Early Recovered Resources v. British Columbia* [2005] F.C.J. No. 1234, 276 F.T.R. 267 at para. 74 (F.C.)

(4) Fisheries

▼HCL-217▼ Legislative powers. Parliament has jurisdiction with respect to sea coast and inland fisheries under the *Constitution Act, 1867*.[1] Parliament is the owner of the exclusive right to fish in water found upon federally owned lands, and in that context can legislate in any way it wishes because, by the *Constitution Act, 1867*,[2] it has exclusive jurisdiction to legislate respecting its property.[3] The provinces may also legislate with respect to provincially owned fisheries by virtue of the *Constitution Act, 1867*,[4] but in cases of conflict federal legislation will prevail.[5] Nevertheless, federal legislative power is limited to an extent being that Parliament cannot under the guise of regulating fisheries regulate property and civil rights; it cannot, for example, grant a private fishery to one person on another person's lands, let alone provincial lands, unless, probably, a strong case is established that this is necessary to a proper regulation of the fisheries.[6] The Supreme Court of Canada has acknowledged however, that the federal power not only encompasses authority to legislate in relation to "fish" in the technical sense of the word. The judgments of the Court "have construed 'fisheries' as meaning something in the nature of a resource".[7]

Notes

1. (U.K.), 30 & 31 Vict., c. 3, s. 91(12).
2. (U.K.), 30 & 31 Vict., c. 3, s. 91(1A).
3. G.V. La Forest, *Water Law in Canada* (Ottawa: Dept. of Regional Economic Expansion, 1973) at 42. See also *Halsbury's Laws of Canada – Hunting and Fishing*.
4. (U.K.), 30 & 31 Vict., c. 3, s. 92(5).
5. G.V. La Forest, *Water Law in Canada* (Ottawa: Dept. of Regional Economic Expansion, 1973) at 69. See also *Peralta v. Ontario*, [1988] S.C.J. No. 92, [1988] 2 S.C.R. 1045 at para. 1 (S.C.C.): "At one point, however, the reasons state that the provinces are powerless to regulate fishing for commercial purposes. That is undoubtedly true of general legislation for that purpose. We would not wish, however, to be taken as accepting the proposition that the provinces lack jurisdiction to make such regulations in respect of provincially-owned fisheries as an aspect of their power to administer their public property. Any such regulations would, of course, be subject to overriding federal legislation."

6. G.V. La Forest, *Water Law in Canada* (Ottawa: Dept. of Regional Economic Expansion, 1973) at 69.
7. *R. v. Northwest Falling Contractors Ltd.*, [1980] S.C.J. No. 68, [1980] 2 S.C.R 292 at 298 (S.C.C.).

▼HCL-218▼ Proprietary rights to fish. Although power to enact fishery regulations falls exclusively within the jurisdiction of the federal government, "it does not follow that the legislation of Provincial Legislatures is incompetent merely because it may have relation to fisheries. For example, provisions prescribing the mode in which a private fishery is to be conveyed or otherwise disposed of, and the rights of succession in respect of it, would be properly treated as falling under the heading 'Property and Civil Rights'" within the *Constitution Act, 1867*,[1] and not as in the class "Fisheries".[2] [3] The "power to legislate in relation to fisheries does necessarily to a certain extent enable the Legislature so empowered to affect proprietary rights".[4]

Tidal waters. A province cannot grant exclusive rights to fish in waters where the public has the right to fish. The object and effect of the provisions of the *Constitution Act, 1867*[5] were to place the management and protection of the cognate public rights of navigation and fishing in the sea and tidal waters exclusively in the Federal Parliament, "and to leave to the Province no right of property or control in them. ... Even under the guise of their taxing powers the Government of the Province could not confer any exclusive or preferential rights of fishing on individuals or classes of individuals, because such exclusion or preference would import regulation and control of the general right of the public to fish".[6]

Notes

1. (U.K.), 30 & 31 Vict., c. 3, s. 92.
2. (U.K.), 30 & 31 Vict., c. 3, s. 92.
3. *Reference re: British North America Act, 1867, s. 108 (Can.)*, [1898] J.C.J. No. 1, [1898] A.C. 700 at para. 22 (P.C.).
4. *Reference re: British North America Act, 1867, s. 108 (Can.)*, [1898] J.C.J. No. 1, [1898] A.C. 700 at para. 11 (P.C.).
5. (U.K.), 30 & 31 Vict., c. 3, s. 91.
6. *Quebec Fisheries (Re)*, [1920] J.C.J. No. 4, [1921] 1 A.C. 413 at para. 18.

▼HCL-219▼ Federal regulation of matters affecting fisheries. Pursuant to the *Constitution Act, 1867*,[1] Parliament may enact protective legislation with respect to fisheries. Canada's fisheries are a "common property resource", belonging to all the people of Canada.[2] Under the *Fisheries Act*,[3] "it is the Minister's duty to manage, conserve and develop the fishery on behalf of Canadians in the public interest".[4] Furthermore, pursuant to the *Constitution Act, 1867*,[5] Parliament clearly has legislative authority with respect to coastal waters.[6] The courts have sought to delineate federal and provincial powers relating to various fisheries issues arising where there is a potential conflict between federal authority and provincial jurisdiction relating to trade and commerce and property and civil rights. For instance, while the provinces have authority with respect to property and civil rights,[7] the actual "catching and handling of fish" falls exclusively within federal legislative authority.[8] [9] Despite the broad scope of the federal power, Parliament cannot unduly intrude onto provincial jurisdiction.[10] The "fisheries power must be construed to respect the provinces' power over property and civil rights under s. 92(13) of the *Constitution Act, 1867*".[11]

Notes

1. (U.K.), 30 & 31 Vict., c. 3, s. 91(12).
2. *Comeau's Sea Foods Ltd. v. Canada (Minister of Fisheries and Oceans)*, [1997] S.C.J. No. 5, [1997] 1 S.C.R. 12 (S.C.C.).
3. R.S.C. 1985, c. F-14.
4. *Comeau's Sea Foods Ltd. v. Canada (Minister of Fisheries and Oceans)*, [1997] S.C.J. No. 5, [1997] 1 S.C.R. 12 at para. 37 (S.C.C.).
5. (U.K.), 30 & 31 Vict., c. 3, s. 91.
6. *R. v. Nichol*, [2007] N.J. No. 357, 270 Nfld. & P.E.I.R. 74 (Nfld. C.A.).
7. *Constitution Act, 1867* (U.K.), 30 & 31 Vict., c. 3, s. 92(13).
8. *Constitution Act, 1867* (U.K.), 30 & 31 Vict., c. 3, s. 91(12).
9. *Moore v. Johnson*, [1982] S.C.J. No. 113, [1982] 1 S.C.R. 115 at 122 (S.C.C.).
10. *R. v. Fowler*, [1980] S.C.J. No. 58, [1980] 2 S.C.R. 213 at 226 (S.C.C.); see also *R. v. Northwest Falling Contractors Ltd.*, [1980] S.C.J. No. 68, [1980] 2 S.C.R. 292 at 301 (S.C.C.).
11. *Ward v. Canada (Attorney General)*, [2002] S.C.J. No. 21, [2002] 1 S.C.R. 569 at paras. 41-42 (S.C.C.).

▼HCL-220▼ Provincial regulation. Although broad, the federal fisheries power is not unlimited, and Parliament must respect the provincial power over property and civil rights. The provincial power also is a broad, multi-faceted power, and is difficult to summarize concisely.

The regulation of fishing in relation to trade and industry within the province generally "falls within the province's jurisdiction over property and civil rights".[1] Moreover, the provinces may enact legislation which merely affects Parliament's fisheries jurisdiction. For example, certain licensing schemes which neither deny the right to fish nor determines who may fish and, therefore, have no regulatory function, may be allowable as provincial legislation as such legislation does not encroach on a federal power.[2] In addition, the provinces have the authority to regulate fish processing within the provinces.[3] In waters owned by a province, and in which the province possesses the fishing rights, legislative jurisdiction is concurrent, and in the case of conflict, the rule of federal paramountcy gives priority to federal law.[4]

Notes

1. *Ward v. Canada (Attorney General)*, [2002] S.C.J. No. 21, [2002] 1 S.C.R. 569 (S.C.C.).
2. *R. v. Breault*, [2001] N.B.J. No. 64 at paras. 64-66, 198 D.L.R. (4th) 669 (N.B.C.A.).
3. *Port Enterprises Ltd. v. Newfoundland (Minister of Fisheries and Aquaculture)*, [2006] N.J. No. 171, 269 D.L.R. (4th) 613 (N.L.C.A.), leave to appeal to S.C.C. refused [2006] S.C.C.A. No. 357 (S.C.C.).
4. *R. v. Breault*, [2001] N.B.J. No. 64 at para. 34, 198 D.L.R. (4th) 669 (N.B.C.A.).

Index — Condominiums

References are to paragraphs.

ACCESS TO INFORMATION
condominium records, HCD-37
failure to permit, HCD-39, HCD-95
restrictions on, HCD-38
status certificates, HCD-53

ACTIONS FOR DEBT
common expense arrears, HCD-98
costs and indemnification, HCD-112

ADMINISTRATORS
appointment, HCD-109

ALTERNATIVE DISPUTE RESOLUTION
mandatory, HCD-114
optional, HCD-113

AMALGAMATION
effect, HCD-117
requirements, HCD-116

ARREARS
court proceedings, HCD-98, HCD-112
loss of voting rights, HCD-66
payment by tenant, HCD-99
payment by mortgagee, HCD-100
statutory lien, HCD-97

BOARD OF DIRECTORS
see also CONDOMINIUM CORPORATIONS
annual general meeting, HCD-61
conduct of business, HCD-42
deference to, HCD-86
disclosure of interest, HCD-44
election and term, HCD-41
first board of directors, HCD-46
first-year deficits, HCD-94
general duty, HCD-40
general meetings, HCD-61
indemnification and insurance, HCD-45
number, HCD-41
offences, HCD-115
owner-developer, HCD-47
procedure for meetings, HCD-62
qualifications, HCD-41
removal, HCD-41
remuneration, HCD-45
standard of care, HCD-43
turn-over meeting, HCD-48
vacancies, HCD-42

BY-LAWS
compliance obligations, HCD-86
joint by-laws, HCD-27
noise, nuisance or harassment, HCD-103
pets, HCD-105
procedures, HCD-25
rules, provision for, HCD-26
sanctions for violations, HCD-86
special levies and fees, HCD-70
subject matter, HCD-24
tenants bound by, HCD-59

CERTIFICATES
see CONDOMINIUM CERTIFICATES; STATUS CERTIFICATES

COMMON ELEMENTS
changes to
• by corporation, HCD-83
• by owners, HCD-84, HCD-101

COMMON ELEMENTS — *cont'd*
construction, performance audit, HCD-91
dangerous activities, HCD-106
maintenance
• benefit of warranties, HCD-82
• common law, HCD-77
• statutory duty, HCD-75–HCD-76
occupier's liability, HCD-32
reasonable use, HCD-101
repair after damage
• benefit of warranties, HCD-82
• common law, HCD-77
• statutory duty, HCD-73–HCD-74
rules, HCD-26

COMMON ELEMENTS CONDOMINIUMS
see also FREEHOLD CONDOMINIUMS
declaration, requirements, HCD-17
described, HCD-7
description or plan, requirements, HCD-21
disclosure statement, HCD-50
ownership interests, HCD-10
registration requirements, HCD-15
repair and maintenance, HCD-80
statutory lien, HCD-97

COMMON EXPENSES
additions to, HCD-71
arrears, *see* ARREARS
assessments, HCD-70
contribution of owners, HCD-69
court proceedings to collect, HCD-98
definition, HCD-69
no avoidance, HCD-72
payment by tenant, HCD-99
payment by mortgagee, HCD-100
special levies, HCD-70
statutory lien, HCD-97
user fees, HCD-70
work done for owner added to, HCD-78

COMPLIANCE AND ENFORCEMENT
access to records, HCD-95
alternative dispute resolution, HCD-113–HCD-114
common elements use, HCD-101
common expense obligations, HCD-97–HCD-100
compliance orders, HCD-86
construction, failure to complete, HCD-95
costs and indemnification, HCD-112
court-appointed officers
• administrator, HCD-109
• inspectors, HCD-107
• investigators, HCD-108
dangerous activities, HCD-106
first-year deficit, HCD-94
implied covenants, HCD-95
inaccurate certificates, remedies, HCD-95
leased units, HCD-104
misleading statements, remedies, HCD-90
money held in trust, HCD-93
nuisances, HCD-103
obligations, HCD-86
offences, HCD-115
oppression remedy, HCD-110–HCD-111
performance audit, HCD-91
pets, HCD-105
phased development, HCD-96
repair and maintenance, HCD-102
sanctions, HCD-86
turn-over by developer, HCD-92

CONDOMINIUM CERTIFICATES
common expense liens, HCD-97
contents, HCD-34
effect, HCD-34
inaccurate, remedies, HCD-95
status certificates, HCD-53

CONDOMINIUM CORPORATIONS
actions by or against, HCD-32
alternative dispute resolution, HCD-113–HCD-114
amalgamation, HCD-116–HCD-117
assessment and taxation, HCD-30
board of directors, *see* BOARD OF DIRECTORS
by-laws, *see* BY-LAWS
changes to condominium, HCD-83
compliance, duty to effect, HCD-86
court-appointed officers
• administrator, HCD-109
• inspectors, HCD-107
• investigators, HCD-108
creation, HCD-14
financial matters, HCD-33
first-year deficits, HCD-94
general corporate matters, HCD-28
information, provision
• with fee, HCD-34, HCD-53
• without fee, HCD-35
leased units
• deposits, HCD-60, HCD-102
• notification, HCD-58
• termination of lease, HCD-104
members, *see* CONDOMINIUM OWNERS
money held in trust, HCD-56, HCD-93
nature of, HCD-2
objects and duties, HCD-29
occupier's liability, HCD-32
offences, HCD-115
oppression remedy, HCD-110–HCD-111
records
• access, HCD-37–HCD-39, HCD-95
• duty to maintain, HCD-36
repair and maintenance
• benefit of warranties, HCD-82
• common elements condominiums, HCD-80
• maintenance, HCD-75–HCD-76
• reasonableness standard, HCD-77
• repair after damage, HCD-73–HCD-74
• reserve fund, HCD-81
• work done for owner, HCD-78, HCD-102
right of entry, HCD-31
special levies and fees, HCD-70
termination of agreements, HCD-89
termination or winding-up, HCD-118–HCD-125
transfer of control by declarant
• enforcement, HCD-92
• procedures, HCD-46–HCD-48

CONDOMINIUM DECLARATION
amendments, HCD-23
compliance obligations, HCD-86
declarant, *see* DEVELOPERS
duty to register, HCD-54
permitted contents, HCD-20
registration, HCD-14
required contents
• freehold condominiums, HCD-17

CONDOMINIUM DECLARATION — *cont'd*
required contents— *cont'd*
• leasehold condominiums, HCD-18
• occupied rental units, HCD-19
tenants bound by, HCD-59

CONDOMINIUM DESCRIPTION OR PLAN
see DESCRIPTION OR PLAN

CONDOMINIUM DOCUMENTS
see BY-LAWS; CONDOMINIUM DECLARATION; DESCRIPTION OR PLAN; RECORDS; RULES

CONDOMINIUM OWNERS
see also CONDOMINIUM UNITS
alternative dispute resolution, HCD-113–HCD-114
arrears of financial obligations, *see* ARREARS
benefit of warranties, HCD-82, HCD-91
changes made by, HCD-84
common expenses
• contribution, HCD-69, HCD-72
• enforcement of obligation, HCD-97
compliance obligations, HCD-86
control of corporation, HCD-46–HCD-48
developer-owner, *see* DEVELOPERS
lease of units, *see* LEASE OF UNITS
maintenance obligations
• enforcement, HCD-78, HCD-102
• generally, HCD-75–HCD-76, HCD-77
• vacant land condominiums, HCD-79
meetings
• notice of matters, HCD-63
• procedure, HCD-62
• types of meetings, HCD-61
• voting, HCD-64–HCD-68
noise, nuisance and harassment, remedies, HCD-103
occupier's liability, HCD-32
repair obligations
• enforcement, HCD-78, HCD-102
• generally, HCD-73–HCD-74, HCD-77
• vacant land condominiums, HCD-79
user fees, HCD-70
work done for by corporation, HCD-78, HCD-102

CONDOMINIUM PROPERTY
assessment and taxation, HCD-30
changes to
• by corporation, HCD-83
• by owner, HCD-84
common elements, *see* COMMON ELEMENTS
construction, performance audit, HCD-91
dangerous activities, HCD-106
definition, HCD-9
easements over, *see* EASEMENTS
encumbrances against, *see* ENCUMBRANCES
expropriation, HCD-123, HCD-124
freehold property, *see* FREEHOLD CONDOMINIUMS
leasehold property, *see* LEASEHOLD CONDOMINIUMS
noise, nuisance or harassment, HCD-103

CONDOMINIUM PROPERTY — *cont'd*
repair and maintenance, *see* REPAIR AND MAINTENANCE
sale of, HCD-121
termination of agreements, HCD-89
units, *see* CONDOMINIUM UNITS
warranties, HCD-82, HCD-91

CONDOMINIUM RECORDS
access
• failure to provide, HCD-39, HCD-95
• generally, HCD-37
• restrictions on access, HCD-38
• status certificates, HCD-53
duty to maintain, HCD-36
turn-over by declarant, HCD-48

CONDOMINIUM UNITS
arrears of financial obligations, *see* ARREARS
assessment and taxation, HCD-30
changes to, HCD-101
dangerous activities, HCD-106
encumbrances, *see* ENCUMBRANCES
entry by corporation or others, HCD-31
interim occupancy, HCD-55
lease by owner, *see* LEASE OF UNITS
lien for common expenses, HCD-97
maintenance
• common law, HCD-77
• enforcement, HCD-102
• statutory duty, HCD-75–HCD-76
mortgagees, voting rights, HCD-65
owners, *see* CONDOMINIUM OWNERS
pets, HCD-105
rental units, HCD-19
repair after damage
• common law, HCD-77
• enforcement, HCD-102
statutory duty, HCD-73–HCD-74
sale of new units, *see* SALE OF NEW UNITS
warranties, HCD-82, HCD-91

CONDOMINIUMS
amalgamation, *see* AMALGAMATION
by-laws, *see* BY-LAWS
certificates, *see* CONDOMINIUM CERTIFICATES
condominium corporation, *see* CONDOMINIUM CORPORATIONS
declaration, *see* CONDOMINIUM DECLARATION
description, *see* DESCRIPTION OR PLAN
developers, *see* DEVELOPERS
fiduciary principles, HCD-5
legislative framework, *see* LEGISLATIVE FRAMEWORK
nature of, HCD-1
nomenclature, HCD-2
owners, *see* CONDOMINIUM OWNERS
plans, *see* DESCRIPTION OR PLAN
records, *see* CONDOMINIUM RECORDS
registration, *see* REGISTRATION
rules, *see* RULES
sections and sectors, HCD-10
termination, *see* TERMINATION OR WINDING-UP

CONDOMINIUMS— *cont'd*
types of condominium properties
• freehold condominiums, *see* FREEHOLD CONDOMINIUMS
• generally, HCD-6
• leasehold condominiums, *see* LEASEHOLD CONDOMINIUMS
types of property interests
• other interests, HCD-12–HCD-13
• ownership interests, HCD-9–HCD-11

CONSTRUCTION
failure to complete, HCD-95
performance audit, HCD-91
phased development, HCD-96
sale of units, *see* SALE OF NEW UNITS

CONTINGENCY RESERVE FUND
see RESERVE FUND

CORPORATIONS
see CONDOMINIUM CORPORATIONS

DAMAGE
see REPAIR AND MAINTENANCE

DANGEROUS ACTIVITIES
prohibition, HCD-106

DECLARANTS
see DEVELOPERS

DECLARATION
see CONDOMINIUM DECLARATION

DEPOSITS
leased units, HCD-60, HCD-102
purchase of new unit, interest, HCD-57

DESCRIPTION OR PLAN
amendments, HCD-23
duty to register, HCD-54
registration, HCD-14
requirements
• freehold condominiums, HCD-21
• leasehold condominiums, HCD-22

DEVELOPERS
alternative dispute resolution, HCD-113–HCD-114
control of corporation, HCD-47
court-appointed officers
• inspectors, HCD-107
• investigators, HCD-108
disclosure statement, HCD-49
duty to register, HCD-54
failure to complete construction, HCD-95
fiduciary duties, HCD-5
first-year deficits, HCD-94
implied covenants, HCD-54, HCD-95
interest on deposits, HCD-57
management agreements, termination, HCD-89
misleading information, HCD-90
money held in trust, HCD-56, HCD-93
offences, HCD-115
performance audit, HCD-91
phased development, HCD-96
sale of units, *see* SALE OF NEW UNITS
transfer of control
• enforcement, HCD-92
• procedures, HCD-46–HCD-48

DISCLOSURE STATEMENT
freehold condominiums, HCD-50
leasehold condominiums, HCD-51
material changes, HCD-52

DISCLOSURE STATEMENT — *cont'd*
misleading, damages, HCD-90
requirements, HCD-49

EASEMENTS
overview, HCD-12

ENCUMBRANCES
see also MORTGAGEES
overview, HCD-13

ENFORCEMENT
see COMPLIANCE AND ENFORCEMENT

ENTRY
see RIGHT OF ENTRY

EXPROPRIATION
condominium property, HCD-123, HCD-124

FIDUCIARY LAW
application, HCD-5

FINANCIAL MATTERS
assessment and taxation, HCD-30
board of directors, HCD-45
changes by corporation, HCD-83
corporation's money, HCD-33
first-year deficit, HCD-94
records, HCD-36
sale of new units
• deposit interest, HCD-57
• money held in trust, HCD-56, HCD-93
termination of agreements, HCD-89
unit arrears, *see* ARREARS

FREEHOLD CONDOMINIUMS
see also CONDOMINIUMS
common elements condominiums, *see* COMMON ELEMENTS CONDOMINIUMS
declaration
• amendments, HCD-23
• requirements, HCD-17
description or plan
• amendments, HCD-23
• requirements, HCD-21
disclosure statement, HCD-50
overview, HCD-7
ownership interests, HCD-10
phased condominiums, *see* PHASED CONDOMINIUMS
registration requirements, HCD-15
standard condominiums, *see* STANDARD CONDOMINIUMS
vacant land condominiums, *see* VACANT LAND CONDOMINIUMS

INSPECTORS
appointment, HCD-107

INVESTIGATORS
appointment, HCD-108

LEASE OF UNITS
common expense arrears, payment by tenant, HCD-99
dangerous activities, HCD-106
deemed covenant or condition, HCD-59
deposit to condominium corporation, HCD-60, HCD-102
notification by owner, HCD-58
short-term leases, HCD-104
tenant's compliance obligations, HCD-59, HCD-86
termination of lease, HCD-104

LEASEHOLD CONDOMINIUMS
declaration
• amendments, HCD-23
• requirements, HCD-18

LEASEHOLD CONDOMINIUMS — *cont'd*
description or plan
• amendments, HCD-23
• requirements, HCD-22
disclosure statement, HCD-51
overview, HCD-8
ownership interests, HCD-11
registration requirements, HCD-16
termination, HCD-125

LEGISLATIVE FRAMEWORK
common law role, HCD-4
compliance obligations, HCD-86
consumer protection and commercial realities, HCD-3
fiduciary law, application, HCD-5
nature of condominium legislation, HCD-2
remedial nature, HCD-85

LIENS
common expenses and other contributions, HCD-97

MANAGEMENT AGREEMENTS
termination, HCD-89

MEETINGS
overview, HCD-61
procedures, HCD-62
voting
• loss of rights, HCD-66
• matters at meeting, HCD-63
• method of voting, HCD-67
• mortgagees, HCD-65
• owners, HCD-64
• required votes, HCD-68

MORTGAGEES
see also ENCUMBRANCES
notice of lien to, HCD-97
payment of common expenses, HCD-100
voting rights, HCD-65

MORTGAGES
see ENCUMBRANCES

NEW UNITS
see SALE OF NEW UNITS

NUISANCES
remedies, HCD-103

OCCUPIER'S LIABILITY
common elements, HCD-32

OFFENCES AND PENALTIES
see also COMPLIANCE AND ENFORCEMENT
generally, HCD-115

OPPRESSION REMEDY
application of remedy, HCD-111
statutory basis, HCD-110

OWNERS
see CONDOMINIUM OWNERS

OWNERSHIP INTERESTS
see also CONDOMINIUM OWNERS
freehold condominiums, HCD-10
generally, HCD-9
leasehold condominiums, HCD-11

PERFORMANCE AUDIT
construction of condominium property, HCD-91
phased developments, HCD-96

PETS
restrictions, enforceability, HCD-105

PHASED CONDOMINIUMS
see also FREEHOLD CONDOMINIUMS
declaration, requirements, HCD-17
described, HCD-7
description or plan, requirements, HCD-21
disclosure statement, HCD-50
information disclosure, HCD-90
obligations and remedies, HCD-96
ownership interests, HCD-10
registration requirements, HCD-15
termination by developer, HCD-88
turn-over obligations, HCD-92

PLANS
see DESCRIPTION OR PLAN

RECORDS
see CONDOMINIUM RECORDS

REGISTRATION
amalgamated condominiums, HCD-117
by-laws, HCD-25
declaration and description, effect, HCD-14
freehold condominiums, HCD-15
leasehold condominiums, HCD-16
lien for common expenses, HCD-97
notice of termination, HCD-119
phased developments, HCD-96

REMEDIES
see COMPLIANCE AND ENFORCEMENT

RENTAL UNITS
declaration requirements for occupied units, HCD-19
lease by owner, *see* LEASE OF UNITS

REPAIR AND MAINTENANCE
common elements condominiums, HCD-80
enforcement, HCD-78, HCD-102
maintenance
• common law application, HCD-77
• liability for, HCD-76
• statutory duty, HCD-75
repair after damage
• common law application, HCD-77
• liability for, HCD-74
• statutory duty, HCD-73
reserve fund, HCD-81
settlement scheme, HCD-102
substantial damage, termination of condominium, HCD-120
vacant land condominiums, HCD-79
warranties, HCD-82
work done for owner, HCD-78, HCD-102

RESERVE FUND
repair and maintenance obligations, HCD-81

RIGHT OF ENTRY
condominium corporations, HCD-31
statutory rights, HCD-31

RULES
compliance obligations, HCD-86
enforceability, HCD-26
joint rules, HCD-27
tenants bound by, HCD-59

SALE OF NEW UNITS
cooling-off period, HCD-49, HCD-87
disclosure requirements
• freehold condominiums, HCD-50

SALE OF NEW UNITS — *cont'd*
disclosure requirements — *cont'd*
• generally, HCD-49
• leasehold condominiums, HCD-51
• material change, HCD-52, HCD-87
failure to complete construction, HCD-95
implied covenants, HCD-54, HCD-95
interest on deposit, HCD-57
interim occupancy, HCD-55
money held in trust, HCD-56, HCD-93
phased developments, HCD-96
rescission by purchaser, HCD-87
termination by developer, HCD-88

SALE OF PROPERTY
termination of condominium, HCD-121

SHARED FACILITIES
repair and maintenance, HCD-102
termination of cost-sharing agreements, HCD-89

SPECIAL LEVIES
powers of corporation, HCD-70

STANDARD CONDOMINIUMS
see also FREEHOLD CONDOMINIUMS
declaration, requirements, HCD-17
described, HCD-7
description or plan, requirements, HCD-21
disclosure statement, HCD-50
ownership interests, HCD-10
registration requirements, HCD-15

STATUS CERTIFICATES
see also CONDOMINIUM CERTIFICATES
inaccurate, remedies, HCD-95
requirements, HCD-53

STRATA CORPORATIONS
see CONDOMINIUM CORPORATIONS

STRATA COUNCILS
see BOARD OF DIRECTORS

STRATA PLANS
see DESCRIPTION OR PLAN

TAXATION
condominium corporations, HCD-30

TENANTS
see LEASE OF UNITS

TERMINATION OR WINDING-UP
court order, HCD-122
effect, HCD-124
expropriation, HCD-123, HCD-124
leasehold condominiums, HCD-125
overview, HCD-118
sale, by, HCD-121
substantial damage, HCD-120
with consent, HCD-119

UNITS
see CONDOMINIUM UNITS

USER FEES
powers of corporation, HCD-70

VACANT LAND CONDOMINIUMS
see also FREEHOLD CONDOMINIUMS
declaration, requirements, HCD-17

VACANT LAND CONDOMINIUMS— *cont'd*
described, HCD-7
description or plan, requirements, HCD-21
disclosure statement, HCD-50
ownership interests, HCD-10
registration requirements, HCD-15
repair and maintenance, HCD-79

WARRANTIES
construction of condominium property, HCD-91
repair and maintenance, HCD-82

WINDING-UP
see TERMINATION OR WINDING-UP

Index — Constitutional Law — Division of Powers

References are to paragraphs.

ABORIGINAL RIGHTS, HCL–42

ABUSE OF GOVERNMENT, HCL–35

ADMINISTRATION OF JUSTICE, HCL–122

ADMINISTRATIVE ACTIONS, HCL–72

ADMINISTRATIVE TRIBUNALS
administrative actions, review of, HCL–72
independence, requirement of, HCL–63

AERONAUTICS, HCL–184

AIR TRANSPORTATION, HCL–184

AMENDMENT FORMULA, HCL–4

ANALOGOUS GROUND CRITERIA, HCL–42

ANCILLARY POWERS DOCTRINE, HCL–97–HCL–98

APPREHENSION OF BIAS, HCL–64, HCL–67

ARBITRARY DECISIONS, HCL–35

ATOMIC ENERGY, HCL–212

BANKING
not included in banking, HCL–165
overview, HCL–163
provincial power, HCL–166
provincial *vs.* federal incorporation, HCL–167
security interest, HCL–164

BANKRUPTCY
overview, HCL–168
priorities, HCL–169
provincial legislation and, HCL–168
secured creditor, HCL–170

BRITISH MONARCHY
formal head of state, HCL–16
power vested in Queen, HCL–8
statutes promulgated by the King or Queen of England, HCL–6

BRITISH NORTH AMERICA ACT, 1867
see CONSTITUTION ACT, 1867

BUSINESS TAXES, HCL–148

CANADA ACT, 1982, HCL–6

CANADIAN CHARTER OF RIGHTS AND FREEDOMS
in *Constitution Act, 1982*, HCL–4
judicial independence, HCL–64–HCL–68
Parliamentary privilege and, HCL–57
unwritten principles, entrenchment of, HCL–28

CANADIAN CONSTITUTION
see also CONSTITUTION ACT, 1867; CONSTITUTION ACT, 1982; SPECIFIC POWERS
Acts referred to in, HCL–25
defined, HCL–25

CANADIAN CONSTITUTION — *cont'd*
division of powers, HCL–1, HCL–3
gaps in constitution, HCL–17, HCL–24, HCL–26
overview, HCL–1
patriation, HCL–6
preamble, HCL–26
purpose of entrenched constitution, HCL–44
supremacy of, HCL–1, HCL–32

CHARGES
see REGULATORY CHARGES

CHARTER
see CANADIAN CHARTER OF RIGHTS AND FREEDOMS

CIVIL LAW REMEDIES, HCL–124

CIVIL RIGHTS, HCL–189–HCL–190

CIVIL SERVICE. *see* PUBLIC SERVICE

COLLECTIVE INDEPENDENCE
see INSTITUTIONAL INDEPENDENCE

COLOURABILITY, HCL–92

COMMERCE. *see* TRADE AND COMMERCE POWER

COMMUNICATION
film, HCL–181
literature, HCL–181
overview, HCL–177
radio, HCL–178
telephone, HCL–179
television, HCL–180
theatre, HCL–181
vs. transportation, HCL–188

CONSOLIDATED REVENUE FUND, HCL–154, HCL–160

CONSTITUTION ACT, 1867
see also CANADIAN CONSTITUTION; SPECIFIC POWERS
House of Commons, HCL–15
judicial independence, conditions for, HCL–64
judicial review
• section 96
• • superior courts, HCL–73
• • three-step test, HCL–74–HCL–79
• • • whether a "judicial" function, HCL–78
• • • whether function "merely ancillary", HCL–79
• • • whether power conforms to required jurisdiction, HCL–75
• section 101
• • generally, HCL–80
• • test for Federal Court jurisdiction, HCL–81–HCL–85
• • • existing body of federal law, HCL–83
• • • grant of jurisdiction by federal law, HCL–83
• • • provincial superior court jurisdiction, HCL–84
• • • statutory grant of jurisdiction, HCL–82
• • • whether "Law of Canada", HCL–85
local or private matters (section 92(16)), HCL–191–HCL–193
natural resources (section 92A), HCL–207
overview, HCL–3
Parliament, HCL–13

CONSTITUTION ACT, 1867— *cont'd*
Parliamentary privileges (section 18), HCL–50
Peace, Order, and Good Government (POGG)
• as residual clause, HCL–108
• emergency context, HCL–110
• national concern doctrine
• for new matters, HCL–108
• • generally, HCL–109
• • singleness, distinctiveness and indivisibility, HCL–109
• overview, HCL–107
property and civil rights (section 92(13)), HCL–189–HCL–190
proportionate representation, HCL–15
raising revenue
• section 125, HCL–138 –HCL–139
raising revenues
• section 92A, HCL–159
Senate, HCL–14
works and undertakings
• section 92(10)(a)
• • multiple undertakings, HCL–175
• • overview, HCL–173
• • single undertaking not to be divided, HCL–174
• section 92(10)(c)
• • general advantage of Canada, HCL–176

CONSTITUTION ACT, 1982
see also CANADIAN CONSTITUTION
"Constitution of Canada", defined, HCL–25
overview, HCL–4
section 52(2), HCL–5

CONSTITUTION OF CANADA
see CANADIAN CONSTITUTION

CONSTITUTIONAL CONVENTIONS
between law and usage, HCL–18
components, HCL–21
conversion in a law, HCL–22
domestic *vs.* international conventions, HCL–23
formal legal rules contrary to, HCL–17
formation through agreement, HCL–20
gaps in constitution, HCL–17, HCL–24
general, HCL–16
the law and, HCL–22
natural formation, HCL–20
overview, HCL–16
positive rules as, HCL–21
purpose of, HCL–16
test to determine existence of, HCL–21
two heads of state, HCL–16
ultimate significance, HCL–24
vs. formal legal rules, HCL–18
vs. usage, HCL–19
violation, consequences of, HCL–19

CONSTITUTIONAL INTERPRETATION
ancillary effects
• overview, HCL–97
• seriousness of encroachment, HCL–98
determination of constitutional validity
• two-step approach
• • assignment to legislative head of power, HCL–94

CONSTITUTIONAL INTERPRETATION — *cont'd*
determination of constitutional validity — *cont'd*
• generally, HCL–88
• pith and substance, HCL–89–HCL–93
• • determination of, HCL–89
• • effect of the statute, HCL–90
• • identifying the matter of a law, HCL–89
• • interjurisdictional immunity and, HCL–104
• • purpose of the statute, HCL–91–HCL–93
• • • colourability, HCL–92
• • • efficacy of laws, HCL–93
• • • true purpose, HCL–91
division of legislative authority, HCL–86
double aspect, HCL–96
exclusivity, principle of, HCL–95
interjurisdictional immunity
• impairment test, HCL–103
• overview, HCL–102
• pith and substance and, HCL–104
• qualifications on "core" or "vital part" test, HCL–103
paramountcy
• dual compliance, HCL–101
• inconsistency, HCL–100
• onus of proof, HCL–101
• overview, HCL–99
presumption of constitutionality, HCL–87, HCL–105
reading down, HCL–105
severance, HCL–106

CONSTITUTIONAL SUPREMACY, HCL–1, HCL–32

CONSTITUTIONAL VALIDITY
see CONSTITUTIONAL INTERPRETATION

CONSTITUTIONALISM
generally, HCL–43
purpose of entrenched constitution, HCL–44

CONSTITUTIONALITY, HCL–87, HCL–105

CONVENTIONS
see CONSTITUTIONAL CONVENTIONS

"CORE" TEST, HCL–102, HCL–103

COURT OF APPEAL
see also SUPREME COURT OF CANADA
general court of appeal for Canada
• generally, HCL–80
• test for Federal Court jurisdiction, HCL–81–HCL–85
• • existing body of federal law, HCL–83
• • grant of jurisdiction by federal law, HCL–83
• • provincial superior court jurisdiction, HCL–84
• • statutory grant of jurisdiction, HCL–82
• • whether "Law of Canada", HCL–85

COURTS
see also JUDICIARY
criminal courts, establishment of, HCL–120
dichotomy between federal and provincial jurisdiction, HCL–61

COURTS — *cont'd*
establishment of, HCL–59–HCL–63
Exchequer Court, HCL–80
federal jurisdiction, HCL–60, HCL–61
general court of appeal for Canada
• generally, HCL–80
• test for Federal Court jurisdiction, HCL–81–HCL–85
• • existing body of federal law, HCL–83
• • grant of jurisdiction by federal law, HCL–83
• • provincial superior court jurisdiction, HCL–84
• • statutory grant of jurisdiction, HCL–82
• • whether "Law of Canada", HCL–85
military court
• judicial independence, HCL–70
provincial courts
• constitutional questions, HCL–84
• establishment of, HCL–59
• judicial independence, HCL–69
• remuneration, HCL–66
superior courts
• establishment of, HCL–60
• remuneration of judges, HCL–60
Supreme Court of Canada
• establishment of, HCL–80

CRIMINAL COURTS, HCL–120

CRIMINAL JUSTICE, HCL–122

CRIMINAL LAW
civil consequences, HCL–198
criminal law power
• civil law remedies, HCL–124
• components, HCL–113–HCL–114
• criminal courts, establishment of, HCL–120
• criminal justice and policing, HCL–122
• criminal law remedies, HCL–124
• criminal procedure, HCL–121
• drugs, HCL–118
• evidence, HCL–121
• gun control, HCL–119
• health, HCL–115
• introduction, HCL–111
• no necessity of harm, HCL–114
• prosecution of offences
• • federal Crown attorneys, HCL–123
• • overview, HCL–123
• the environment, HCL–116, HCL–204
• tobacco, HCL–117
double aspect doctrine and, HCL–199
introduction
• criminal law power, HCL–111
• provincial jurisdiction, HCL–112
prevention of crime, HCL–127
provincial power to enact penal laws, HCL–125
punishment, HCL–126
young offenders, HCL–128

CRIMINAL LAW REMEDIES, HCL–124

CRIMINAL PROCEDURE, HCL–121

CROWN ATTORNEYS, HCL–123

CROWN IMMUNITY, HCL–12

CROWN PREROGATIVE
Crown immunity, HCL–12
defined, HCL–8
judicial review of decisions made pursuant to
• overview, HCL–10
• scope of review, HCL–10
overview, HCL–8
power vested in Queen, HCL–8
Prime Minister
• appointment of, HCL–9
• powers, HCL–9
• responsibilities, HCL–9
• role of, HCL–9
scope of, HCL–8
specific Crown prerogatives, HCL–11
today, HCL–8

CROWN PROPERTY, HCL–139

CUSTOMS, HCL–142

DEATH DUTIES, HCL–149

DECLARATORY POWER, HCL–214

DELEGATION OF POWER
three-step test, HCL–74–HCL–79
• whether a "judicial" function, HCL–78
• whether function "merely ancillary", HCL–79
• whether power conforms to required jurisdiction, HCL–75
• • characterization of the power, HCL–76
• • preliminary questions, HCL–77

DELEGATION OF TAXES, HCL–141

DEMOCRACY
and federalism, HCL–37
as interpretive tool, HCL–40
foundations of democracy, HCL–37

DIRECT TAXES
business taxes, HCL–148
elements of, HCL–143
established types of, HCL–145–HCL–149
flat fees, HCL–145
income tax, HCL–148
inheritance tax, HCL–149
land and property taxes, HCL–146
shares, HCL–147
succession duties, HCL–149
vs. indirect taxes, HCL–142

DISALLOWANCE, HCL–20

DISTINCTIVENESS, HCL–109

DIVISION OF LEGISLATIVE AUTHORITY, HCL–86

DIVISION OF POWERS, HCL–1, HCL–3

DOUBLE ASPECT DOCTRINE
and criminal law, HCL–199
generally, HCL–96
provincial powers, HCL–194–HCL–199
• public order and morality, HCL–197–HCL–199
• trade and commerce, HCL–195–HCL–196

DRUGS, HCL–118

DUAL COMPLIANCE, HCL–101

EMERGENCY CONTEXT, HCL–110

ENVIRONMENT
criminal law power, HCL–116, HCL–204

ENVIRONMENT — *cont'd*
effect on federal jurisdiction, HCL–203
federal regulation of extra-provincial actions, HCL–201
overview, HCL–200
Peace, Order and Good Government power, HCL–202

ESTATE TAXES, HCL–149

EVIDENCE
criminal law matters, HCL–121

EXCHEQUER COURT, HCL–80

EXCISE, HCL–142

EXCLUSIVITY, HCL–95, HCL–102

EXECUTIVE BRANCH
and rule of law, HCL–35, HCL–36
depoliticized relationships, HCL–47
separation between legislative and executive, HCL–47
supremacy of Constitution, HCL–1

EXTRAORDINARY PERIL, HCL–110

FEDERAL CROWN ATTORNEYS, HCL–123

FEDERAL INCORPORATION, HCL–167

FEDERAL JURISDICTION
see also PARLIAMENT; SPECIFIC POWERS
banking, HCL–163–HCL–167
bankruptcy, HCL–168–HCL–170
courts, HCL–60, HCL–61
criminal law, HCL–111–HCL–112
fisheries, HCL–216, HCL–217, HCL–219
forestry, HCL–216
interest, HCL–171
mines and minerals, HCL–208

FEDERALISM
and democracy, HCL–37
on provincial level, HCL–39
overview, HCL–38

FEES. *see* REGULATORY CHARGES

FILM, HCL–181

FINANCIAL INDEPENDENCE, HCL–66

FINANCIAL MATTERS
banking
• not included in banking, HCL–165
• overview, HCL–163
• provincial power, HCL–166
• provincial *vs.* federal incorporation, HCL–167
• security interest, HCL–164
bankruptcy
• overview, HCL–168
• priorities, HCL–169
• provincial legislation and, HCL–168
• secured creditor, HCL–170
interest, HCL–171

FIREARMS CONTROL, HCL–119

FISHERIES
federal jurisdiction, HCL–216, HCL–217, HCL–219
proprietary rights to fish, HCL–218
provincial jurisdiction, HCL–217, HCL–218, HCL–220
regulation of matters affecting fisheries, HCL–219
tidal waters, HCL–218

FLAT FEES, HCL–145

FOREIGN JUDGMENTS, HCL–58

FORESTRY, HCL–215–HCL–216

FORMAL LEGAL RULES
see LEGAL RULES

FULL FAITH AND CREDIT DOCTRINE
foreign judgments, recognition of, HCL–58
overview, HCL–58
shared jurisdiction over recognition of judgments, HCL–58

GENERAL ADVANTAGE OF CANADA, HCL–176

GENERAL TRADE AND COMMERCE, HCL–134–HCL–135, HCL–195

GOING CONCERN, HCL–186

GOVERNMENTAL ACTIONS. *see* EXECUTIVE BRANCH

GOVERNOR GENERAL
Prime Minister, appointment of, HCL–9
role of, HCL–16
superior court judges, appointment of, HCL–60
veto power, HCL–17

GREAT BRITAIN
founding statute of the Crown and Parliament, HCL–6
statutes adopted by the Parliament of Great Britain, HCL–6
statutes promulgated by the King or Queen of England, HCL–6

GUN CONTROL, HCL–119

HARM PRINCIPLE, HCL–114

HEALTH, HCL–115

HIGHWAYS, HCL–183

HOUSE OF COMMONS
overview, HCL–15
powers, HCL–15

IMMUNITY
Crown immunity, HCL–12

IMPAIRMENT TEST, HCL–103

INCOME TAX, HCL–148

INCONSISTENCY, HCL–100

INCORPORATION, HCL–167

INDEPENDENCE. *see* JUDICIAL INDEPENDENCE

INDIRECT LICENCE FEES, HCL–158

INDIRECT TAXES
land taxes, HCL–146
vs. direct taxes, HCL–142

INDIVISIBILITY, HCL–109

INHERITANCE TAX, HCL–149

INSTITUTIONAL INDEPENDENCE, HCL–41, HCL–63, HCL–67

INTER-PROVINCIAL TRADE AND COMMERCE, HCL–131–HCL–133, HCL–195–HCL–196

INTEREST, HCL–171

INTERJURISDICTIONAL IMMUNITY
and pith and substance, HCL–104
impairment test, HCL–103
overview, HCL–102
qualifications on "core" or "vital part" test, HCL–103

INTERNATIONAL TRADE AND COMMERCE, HCL–131–HCL–133

INTERPROVINCIAL JUDGMENTS, HCL–58

INTERPROVINCIAL TRANSPORTATION, HCL–187

INTERPROVINCIAL UNDERTAKING, HCL–174–HCL–175

INTRA-PROVINCIAL TRADE, HCL–195–HCL–196

JUDGMENTS
foreign judgments, recognition of, HCL–58
interprovincial judgments, HCL–58
shared jurisdiction over recognition of judgments, HCL–58

JUDICIAL FUNCTION, HCL–78

JUDICIAL INDEPENDENCE
all courts, HCL–68
and the collective, HCL–41
collective independence, HCL–41
conditions for
• financial security, HCL–66
• institutional independence, HCL–67
• overview, HCL–64
individual and, HCL–41
inferior court judges, HCL–69
institutional independence, HCL–41
military court judges, HCL–70
origins of, HCL–41
overview, HCL–62
scope of, HCL–63
security of tenure, HCL–65

JUDICIAL REVIEW
see also CONSTITUTIONAL INTERPRETATION
administrative actions, review of, HCL–72
Constitution Act, 1867, section 96
• superior courts, HCL–73
• three-step test, HCL–74–HCL–79
• • whether a "judicial" function, HCL–78
• • whether function "merely ancillary", HCL–79
• • whether power conforms to required jurisdiction, HCL–75
• • • characterization of the power, HCL–76
• • • preliminary questions, HCL–77
Constitution Act, 1867, section 101
• generally, HCL–80
• test for Federal Court jurisdiction, HCL–81–HCL–85
• • existing body of federal law, HCL–83
• • grant of jurisdiction by federal law, HCL–83
• • provincial superior court jurisdiction, HCL–84
• • statutory grant of jurisdiction, HCL–82
• • whether "Law of Canada", HCL–85
constitutional protection, HCL–71
decisions made pursuant to Crown prerogative, HCL–10
overview, HCL–71

JUDICIARY
see also JUDICIAL INDEPENDENCE; JUDICIAL REVIEW
depoliticized relationships, HCL–47
remuneration, HCL–60, HCL–66

LABOUR RELATIONS
going concern, HCL–186
overview, HCL–185

LAND TAXES, HCL–146

LAND TRANSPORTATION, HCL–183

"LAW OF CANADA", HCL–85

LEGAL RULES
contrary to constitutional conventions, HCL–17
vs. constitutional conventions, HCL–18

LEGISLATIVE BRANCH
depoliticized relationships, HCL–47
rule of law and, HCL–36
separation between legislative and executive, HCL–47

LEGISLATURES
see PROVINCIAL LEGISLATURES

LEVIES
see REGULATORY CHARGES

LICENCES
drivers' licences, HCL–183
indirect licence fees, HCL–158
overview, HCL–136, HCL–157

LITERATURE, HCL–181

LOCAL MATTERS, HCL–191–HCL–193

"MERELY ANCILLARY", HCL–79

MILITARY COURT
judicial independence, HCL–70

MINES AND MINERALS
federal jurisdiction, HCL–208
offshore minerals, HCL–213
overview, HCL–206
Peace, Order and Good Government, HCL–212
provincial jurisdiction, HCL–207
taxation, HCL–209
trade and commerce power, HCL–210
works and undertakings under section 92(10)(a), HCL–211

MINORITIES
protection of minorities, HCL–42, HCL–44

MORALITY, HCL–197–HCL–199

MULTIPLE UNDERTAKINGS, HCL–175

NARCOTICS, HCL–118

NATIONAL CONCERN DOCTRINE
atomic energy, HCL–214
environmental issues, HCL–202, HCL–203
generally, HCL–109
mines and minerals, HCL–212
singleness, distinctiveness and indivisibility, HCL–109

NATIONAL INTEREST
see NATIONAL CONCERN DOCTRINE

NATURAL RESOURCES
federal declaratory power, HCL–214
forestry, HCL–215–HCL–216
mines and minerals
· federal jurisdiction, HCL–208
· offshore minerals, HCL–213
· overview, HCL–206

NATURAL RESOURCES — *cont'd*
mines and minerals — *cont'd*
• Peace Order and Good Government, HCL–212
• provincial jurisdiction, HCL–207
• taxation, HCL–209
• trade and commerce power, HCL–210
• works and undertakings under section 92(10)(a), HCL–211
overview, HCL–205
taxation, HCL–209

NAVIGATION, HCL–182

NEAR BANKS, HCL–166

NECESSITY
and Parliamentary privilege, HCL–56
test for necessity, HCL–56

NEUTRALITY OF PUBLIC SERVICE, HCL–45

NEW MATTERS, HCL–108

NO TAXATION WITHOUT REPRESENTATION, HCL–46

NON-RENEWABLE NATURAL RESOURCES
see MINES AND MINERALS

NON-RENEWABLE RESOURCES, HCL–159

OFFSHORE MINERALS, HCL–213

ONUS OF PROOF, HCL–101

PARAMOUNTCY
dual compliance, HCL–101
inconsistency, HCL–100
onus of proof, HCL–101
overview, HCL–99

PARLIAMENT
see also FEDERAL JURISDICTION; SPECIFIC POWERS
declaratory power, HCL–214
division of legislative authority, HCL–86
overview, HCL–13
parliamentary privileges, HCL–13
powers of, HCL–32
sovereignty of
• generally, HCL–29
• powers of legislature, HCL–32
• restrictions on, HCL–30
• *vs.* Parliamentary supremacy, HCL–31
supremacy
• *vs.* Parliamentary sovereignty, HCL–31

PARLIAMENT OF CANADA ACT, HCL–51

PARLIAMENTARY PRIVILEGE
and *Constitution Act, 1867,* section 18, HCL–50
constitutional protection, HCL–57
definition, HCL–49
determination of existence of privilege, HCL–54
inherent privileges, HCL–52
• boundaries of, HCL–53
necessity, HCL–56
• test for necessity, HCL–56
origin, HCL–49
Parliament of Canada Act, section 4 and, HCL–51
power to enact privileges, HCL–55
rationale for principle, HCL–49

PARLIAMENTARY SOVEREIGNTY
as foundation of unwritten principles, HCL–29
generally, HCL–29
powers of legislature, HCL–32
restrictions on, HCL–30
vs. Parliamentary supremacy, HCL–31

PEACE, ORDER AND GOOD GOVERNMENT (POGG)
as residual clause, HCL–108
emergency context, HCL–110
environment, HCL–202
for new matters, HCL–108
mines and minerals, HCL–212
national concern doctrine
· atomic energy, HCL–214
· environmental issues, HCL–202, HCL–203
· generally, HCL–109
· mines and minerals, HCL–212
· singleness, distinctiveness and indivisibility, HCL–109
overview, HCL–107

PITH AND SUBSTANCE
determination of, HCL–89
effect of the statute, HCL–90
identifying the matter of a law, HCL–89
indirect licence fees, HCL–158
interjurisdictional immunity and, HCL–104
purpose of the statute, HCL–91–HCL–93
· colourability, HCL–92
· efficacy of laws, HCL–93
· true purpose, HCL–91
regulatory charges, HCL–153

POGG
see PEACE, ORDER AND GOOD GOVERNMENT (POGG)

POLICING, HCL–122

POLLUTION
see ENVIRONMENT

PREROGATIVE
see CROWN PREROGATIVE

PRESUMPTION OF CONSTITUTIONALITY, HCL–87, HCL–105

PREVENTION OF CRIME, HCL–127

PRIME MINISTER
appointment of, HCL–9
political head of state, HCL–16
powers, HCL–9
responsibilities, HCL–9
role of, HCL–9

PRIORITIES, HCL–169

PRIVATE MATTERS, HCL–191–HCL–193

PRIVILEGE
Parliamentary privilege
· *Constitution Act, 1867,* section 18 and, HCL–50
· constitutional protection, HCL–57
· definition, HCL–49
· determination of existence of privilege, HCL–54
· inherent privileges, HCL–52
· · boundaries of, HCL–53
· necessity, HCL–56
· · test for necessity, HCL–56
· origin, HCL–49
· *Parliament of Canada Act,* section 4 and, HCL–51

PRIVILEGE — *cont'd*
Parliamentary privilege — *cont'd*
• power to enact privileges, HCL–55
• rationale for principle, HCL–49
solicitor-client privilege
• exceptions, HCL–48
• overview, HCL–48

PROBATE FEES, HCL–140

PROPERTY RIGHTS, HCL–189–HCL–190

PROPERTY TAX, HCL–139, HCL–146

PROSECUTION OF OFFENCES
federal Crown attorneys, HCL–123
overview, HCL–123

PROTECTION OF MINORITIES, HCL–42, HCL–44

PROVINCIAL COURTS
constitutional questions, HCL–84
establishment of, HCL–59
judicial independence, HCL–69
remuneration, HCL–66

"PROVINCIAL INABILITY" TEST, HCL–109

PROVINCIAL INCORPORATION, HCL–167

PROVINCIAL JURISDICTION. *see also* CRIMINAL LAW; SPECIFIC POWERS
administration of justice, HCL–122
banking and, HCL–166
Bankruptcy and Insolvency Act and, HCL–168
courts, HCL–59, HCL–61
criminal law, HCL–112, HCL–125
double aspect doctrine, HCL–194–HCL–199
• public order and morality, HCL–197–HCL–199
• trade and commerce, HCL–195–HCL–196
fisheries, HCL–217, HCL–218, HCL–220
forestry, HCL–215
local or private matters, HCL–191–HCL–193
mines and minerals, HCL–207
nonrenewable resources, HCL–159
property rights, HCL–189–HCL–190
regulation of trade, HCL–133, HCL–195–HCL–196

PROVINCIAL LEGISLATURES
see also PROVINCIAL JURISDICTION; SPECIFIC POWERS
division of legislative authority, HCL–86
federalism on provincial level, HCL–39
Parliamentary sovereignty, HCL–32
powers of, HCL–32
spending power, HCL–162

PROVINCIAL SPENDING POWER, HCL–162

PROVINCIAL TAXES, HCL–144

PUBLIC ORDER, HCL–197–HCL–199

PUBLIC PURPOSE, HCL–113

PUBLIC SERVICE
neutrality of public service, HCL–45

PUNISHMENT, HCL–126

QUASI-CONSTITUTIONAL NATURE, HCL–7

QUÉBEC SENATORS, HCL–14

QUEEN
see BRITISH MONARCHY

RADIO, HCL–178

RAISING REVENUE
Constitution Act, 1867
• section 125, HCL–138–HCL–139
• • Crown property, HCL–139
• • regulatory charges and, HCL–138
• • restriction on imposition of taxes, HCL–138
• section 92A, HCL–159
licences
• indirect licence fees, HCL–158
• overview, HCL–157
no taxation without representation, HCL–46, HCL–137
nonrenewable resources, HCL–159
overview, HCL–136
regulatory charges
• Consolidated Revenue Fund, HCL–154
• final destination of revenues, HCL–154
• hallmarks of a regulatory charge, HCL–151
• overview, HCL–150
• pith and substance analysis, HCL–153
• requisite nexus, HCL–152
• section 125 of *Constitution Act, 1867* and, HCL–138, HCL–155
• user fees, HCL–156
taxation
• delegation of taxes, HCL–141
• direct taxes
• • business taxes, HCL–148
• • elements of, HCL–143
• • established types of, HCL–145–HCL–149
• • flat fees, HCL–145
• • income tax, HCL–148
• • inheritance tax, HCL–149
• • land and property taxes, HCL–146
• • shares, HCL–147
• • succession duties, HCL–149
• • *vs.* indirect taxes, HCL–142
• hallmarks of a tax, HCL–140
• indirect taxes
• • *vs.* direct taxes, HCL–142
• nonrenewable resources, HCL–159
• provincial taxes, HCL–144

READING DOWN, HCL–105

REGULATION OF TRADE AND COMMERCE. *see* TRADE AND COMMERCE POWER

REGULATORY CHARGES
Consolidated Revenue Fund, HCL–154
final destination of revenues, HCL–154
hallmarks of a regulatory charge, HCL–151
overview, HCL–136, HCL–150
pith and substance analysis, HCL–153
requisite nexus, HCL–152
section 125 of *Constitution Act, 1867* and HCL–138, HCL–155
user fees, HCL–156

REMEDIES, HCL–124

REMUNERATION OF SUPERIOR COURT JUDGES, HCL–60

RESIDUAL CLAUSE, HCL–108, HCL–193

RESPONSIBLE GOVERNMENT, HCL–16

REVENUE
see RAISING REVENUE

RULE OF LAW
and abuse of government, HCL–35
application of, HCL–10
arbitrary decisions and, HCL–35
citizens and public bodies subject to, HCL–34
elements, HCL–33
normative force of, HCL–36
overview, HCL–33
superior courts, HCL–60

SECURED CREDITOR, HCL–170

SECURITY INTEREST, HCL–164

SECURITY OF TENURE, HCL–65

SENATE
appointment of additional senators, HCL–14
overview, HCL–14
powers, HCL–14
qualifications, HCL–14
Québec senators, HCL–14

SEPARATION OF POWERS
depoliticized relationships, HCL–47
not strict separation of powers, HCL–47
overview, HCL–47
separation between legislative and executive, HCL–47

SERIOUSNESS OF ENCROACHMENT, HCL–98

SEVERANCE, HCL–106

SHARES, HCL–147

SHIPPING, HCL–182

SHIPS, HCL–182

SINGLE UNDERTAKING, HCL–174

SINGLENESS, HCL–109

SOCIAL VALUES, HCL–114

SOLICITOR-CLIENT PRIVILEGE
exceptions, HCL–48
overview, HCL–48

SOURCES OF CONSTITUTIONAL LAW AND INSTITUTIONS
Crown prerogative
• Crown immunity, HCL–12
• defined, HCL–8
• judicial review of decisions made pursuant to
• • overview, HCL–10
• • scope of review, HCL–10
• overview, HCL–8
• power vested in Queen, HCL–8
• Prime Minister
• • appointment of, HCL–9
• • powers, HCL–9
• • responsibilities, HCL–9
• • role of, HCL–9
• scope of, HCL–8
• specific Crown prerogatives, HCL–11
• today, HCL–8

SOURCES OF CONSTITUTIONAL LAW AND INSTITUTIONS — *cont'd*
House of Commons, HCL–15
major sources
• *Constitution Act, 1867,* HCL–3
• *Constitution Act, 1982,* HCL–4
• • section 52(2), HCL–5
• founding statute of the Crown and Parliament of Great Britain, HCL–6
• overview, HCL–2
overview, HCL–1
Parliament, HCL–13
quasi-constitutional nature, statutes with, HCL–7
Senate, HCL–14

SPENDING POWER
limits, HCL–161
overview, HCL–160
provincial spending power, HCL–162

STATUTE OF WESTMINSTER, 1931, HCL–3, HCL–6

STEAM SHIPS, HCL–182

STERILIZATION, HCL–102

SUCCESSION DUTIES, HCL–149

SUPERIOR COURTS
establishment of, HCL–60
remuneration of judges, HCL–60
tenure, HCL–65

SUPREME COURT OF CANADA
establishment of, HCL–80

TAXATION
and Crown property, HCL–139
delegation of taxes, HCL–141
direct taxes
• business taxes, HCL–148
• elements of, HCL–143
• established types of, HCL–145–HCL–149
• flat fees, HCL–145
• income tax, HCL–148
• inheritance tax, HCL–149
• land and property taxes, HCL–146
• shares, HCL–147
• succession duties, HCL–149
• *vs.* indirect taxes, HCL–142
hallmarks of a tax, HCL–140
indirect taxes
• *vs.* direct taxes, HCL–142
mines and minerals, HCL–209
no taxation without representation, HCL–46, HCL–137
nonrenewable resources, HCL–159
overview, HCL–136
provincial taxes, HCL–144
restriction on imposition of, HCL–138
section 125 of *Constitution Act, 1867* and HCL–138

TELEPHONE, HCL–179

TELEVISION, HCL–180

TENURE
security of tenure, HCL–65

THEATRE, HCL–181

TIDAL WATERS, HCL–218

TOBACCO, HCL–117

TRADE AND COMMERCE POWER
general regulation of, HCL–134–HCL–135

TRADE AND COMMERCE POWER — *cont'd*
inter-provincial trade and commerce, HCL–131–HCL–133
international trade and commerce, HCL–131–HCL–133
matter of local concern, HCL–132
mines and minerals, HCL–210
overview, HCL–129
provincial laws, HCL–133, HCL–195–HCL–196
two branches of, HCL–130–HCL–135

TRAFFIC REGULATION, HCL–183

TRANSPORTATION
air, HCL–184
interprovincial transportation, HCL–187
land, HCL–183
overview, HCL–177
vs. communication, HCL–188
water, HCL–182

TREATIES, HCL–10

TRUE PURPOSE (OF STATUTE), HCL–91

TWO HEADS OF STATE, HCL–16

UNDERTAKINGS
see WORKS AND UNDERTAKINGS

UNWRITTEN PRINCIPLES OF THE CONSTITUTION
general, HCL–25
overview, HCL–25
preamble, HCL–26
specific unwritten principles
• constitutionalism
• • generally, HCL–43
• • purpose of entrenched constitution, HCL–44
• democracy
• • as interpretive tool, HCL–40
• • and federalism, HCL–37
• • foundations of democracy, HCL–37
• federalism
• • and democracy, HCL–37
• • overview, HCL–38
• • on provincial level, HCL–39
• full faith and credit doctrine
• • foreign judgments, recognition of, HCL–58
• • overview, HCL–58
• • shared jurisdiction over recognition of judgments, HCL–58
• generally, HCL–28
• judicial independence
• • and the collective, HCL–41
• • and the individual, HCL–41
• • collective independence, HCL–41
• • institutional independence, HCL–41
• • origins of, HCL–41
• neutrality of public service, HCL–45
• no taxation without representation, HCL–46
• Parliamentary privilege
• • and *Constitution Act, 1867,* section 18, HCL–50
• • constitutional protection, HCL–57
• • definition, HCL–49
• • determination of existence of privilege, HCL–54
• • inherent privileges, HCL–52
• • • boundaries of, HCL–53
• • necessity, HCL–56

UNWRITTEN PRINCIPLES OF THE CONSTITUTION — *cont'd*
specific unwritten principles — *cont'd*
• • • test for necessity, HCL–56
• • origin, HCL–49
• • and *Parliament of Canada Act,* section 4, HCL–51
• • power to enact privileges, HCL–55
• • rationale for principle, HCL–49
• Parliamentary sovereignty
• • as foundation of unwritten principles, HCL–29
• • generally, HCL–29
• • powers of legislature, HCL–32
• • restrictions on, HCL–30
• • *vs.* Parliamentary supremacy, HCL–31
• protection of minorities, HCL–42
• rule of law
• • and abuse of government, HCL–35
• • and arbitrary decisions, HCL–35
• • citizens and public bodies subject to, HCL–34
• • elements, HCL–33
• • normative force of, HCL–36
• • overview, HCL–33
• separation of powers
• • depoliticized relationships, HCL–47
• • not strict separation of powers, HCL–47
• • overview, HCL–47
• • separation between legislative and executive, HCL–47
• solicitor-client privilege
• • exceptions, HCL–48
• • overview, HCL–48
substantive obligations and, HCL–27

USAGE, HCL–19

USER FEES, HCL–156

VITAL PART TEST, HCL–102, HCL–103

WATER, HCL–182

WEAPONS, HCL–119

WESTMINSTER SYSTEM, HCL–49

WORKS AND UNDERTAKINGS
Constitution Act, 1867
• section 92(10)(a)
• • multiple undertakings, HCL–175
• • overview, HCL–173
• • single undertaking not to be divided, HCL–174
• section 92(10)(c)
• • general advantage of Canada, HCL–176
mines and minerals, HCL–211
overview, HCL–172

YOUNG OFFENDERS, HCL–128

Selected Secondary Sources — Condominiums

Texts

Condominium Law and Administration, 2nd Edition (looseleaf), Audrey Loeb, Carswell.

Ontario Residential Real Practice Manual (looseleaf), Gowling, Lafleur, Henderson LLP & Rosemary Bocska, LexisNexis Canada

Real Estate Practice in Ontario, 7th Edition (2011), Donald J. Donahue, Peter D. Quinn & Danny C. Grandilli, LexisNexis Canada

Ontario Real Estate Legislation, 2010-2011 Edition (2010), Howard Shuster, Canada Law Book

Title Searching and Conveyancing in Ontario, 6th Edition (2010), Marguerite E. Moore, LexisNexis Canada.

The Condominium Act, A User's Manual: *Third Edition* (2009), Audrey Loeb, Carswell.

Condominium Handbook (Ontario), 6th Edition (2008), G. Hyman, Canadian Condominium Institute.

Condos: Everything You Should Know (2008), André M. Benoît, Yves Joli-Coeur & Yves Papineau, Wilson & Lafleur.

Articles

Ontario Tarion Warranty Plan and New Condominiums, Bernard Aron, (Nov. 2010) 3 RegQuest No. 11, 1-4.

Condos are Hot, Hot, Hot, Kevin Marron, (Mar. 2010) 34 Can. Lawyer No. 3, 23-25.

Leaky Condo Class Action fails to Break New Ground, Norm Streu and Rob Ker, (Nov. 2007) 24 Construction L.L. No. 2, 4-5.

Moving Forward with Individual Suite Meters, Scott Stoll and Andrew Webste, (June 2007) CondoBus. 16-20.

Duty of Confidentiality [Ontario's Condominium Act, 1998], Patricia Elia, (Nov. 2005) Condo Bus. 26-28.

Utility Conservation: Upgrades Must Still Comply with the Condominium Act, 1998, Ron Danks, (May 2005) Condo. Bus. 22-24.

First Steps in the Theory and Practice of the Condominium Oppression Remedy in Ontario (Case Comment), Theodore B. Rotenberg, (Apr. 2004) 15 R.P.R. (4th) 201-209.

Selected Secondary Sources — Constitutional Law — Division of Powers

Texts

Constitutional Litigation in Canada, (looseleaf), Andrew K. Lokan & Christopher M. Dassios, Thomson Carswell.

Constitutional Law of Canada, 2011 Edition, (2011) Peter W. Hogg, Thomson Carswell.

Liability of the Crown, Fourth Edition, (2011), Peter W. Hogg & Patrick J. Monahan, Thomson Carswell.

Canadian Constitutional Law, Fourth Edition, (2010), The Constitutional Law Group, Emond Montgomery.

Constitutional Law: Cases, Commentary and Principles, (2008), Editor-in-chief: Leonard I. Rotman, Bruce P. Elman & Gerald L. Gall, Thomson Carswell.

Canadian Constitutional Documents Consolidated, Second Edition, (2007) Bernard W. Funston & Eugene Meehan, Thomson Carswell.

Constitutional Law of Canada, Ninth Edition, Vol. 1, (2007), Joseph E. Magnet, Juriliber Ltd.

Constitutional Law, Third Edition, (2006), Patrick J. Monahan, Irwin Law.

Public Law: Cases, Materials and Commentary, Second Edition, (2006), Craik, Forcese, Bryden, Carver, Haigh, Ratushny & Sullivan, Emond Montgomery.

Constitutionalism in the Charter Era, (2004), Grant Huscroft & Ian Brodie, LexisNexis Canada.

Modern Constitutionalism: Equality, Identity and Democracy, (2004), Joseph E. Magnet, LexisNexis Canada.

Articles

Developments in Constitutional Law: the 2009-2010 Term, Michael Plaxton & Carissima Mathen (2010) 52 Sup. Ct. L. Rev. (2d) 65-164.

Constitutional Law Update 2010, Debra McAllister & Errol P. Mendes, (July 2010) National Journal of Constitutional Law, Vol. 27.

Proportionality and the Cult of Constitutional Rights Scholarship, Grégoire C.N. Webber, (Jan. 2010) 23 Can. J.L. & Juris 179-202.

A Reply to Critics of Constitutional Goods, Alan Brudner, (July 2009) 22 Can. J.L. & Juris. 237-66.

The Constitution Act, 1982 and the Crown: Twenty-Five Years, Kenneth Munro, (2008) 17 Constit. Forum 49-57.

Public Accountability and Legal Pedagogy: Studies in Constitutional Law, Shalin M. Sugunasiri, (Oct. 2008) 2 J.P.P.L. 93-112.

Extending the Theory of the Unwritten Constitution, Cassandra Kirewskie, (2007) 37 Sup. Ct. L. Rev. (2d) 139-61.

The Federal Court's Jurisdiction to Apply the Constitution, Andrew K. Lokan & Erin Burbidge, (2006-2007) 21 N.J.C.L. 151-65.

An Analysis of the "No Hierarchy of Constitutional Rights" Doctrine, Mark Carter, (2006) 12 Rev. Constit. Studies 19-51.

Canada's "Newer Constitutional Law" and the Idea of Constitutional Rights, Eric M. Adams, (2006) 51 McGill L.J. 435-74.

In Defence of the Legal Constitution, Tom R. Hickman, (Fall, 2005) 55 Univ. of Toronto L.J. 981.

The Ancillary Powers Doctrine, Grégoire Charles N. Webber, (2002) 36 R.J.T. 121-67.

Glossary of Defined Terms in Condominium Legislation

The following Table identifies words and phrases which have been defined in the legislation set out below, and provides the text of those definitions for easy reference.

Alberta

Condominium Property Act, R.S.A. 2000, c. C-22 ("ACPA")

Condominium Property Regulation, Alta. Reg. 168/2000 ("ACPR")

British Columbia

Strata Property Act, S.B.C. 1998, c. 43 ("BCSPA")

Strata Property Regulation, B.C. Reg. 43/2000 ("BCSPR")

Manitoba

Condominium Act, C.C.S.M. c. C170 ("MCA")

New Brunswick

Condominium Property Act, S.N.B. 2009, c. C-16.05 ("NBCPA")

General Regulation, N.B. Reg. 2009-169 (*Condominium Property Act*) ("NBCPR")

Newfoundland and Labrador

Condominium Act, 2009, S.N.L. 2009, c. C-29.1 (Assented to December 22, 2009 – to be proclaimed) ("NLCA")

Condominium Regulations, 2011, N.L.R. 80/11 ("NLCR") (Filed September 13, 2011 – to come into force when NLCA is proclaimed)

Northwest Territories

Condominium Act, R.S.N.W.T. 1988, c. C-15 ("NWTCA")

Condominium Regulations, N.W.T. Reg. 098-2008 ("NWTCR")

Nova Scotia

Condominium Act, R.S.N.S. 1989, c. 85 ("NSCA")

Condominium Regulations, N.S. Reg. 60/71 ("NSCR")

Nunavut

Condominium Act, R.S.N.W.T. (Nu.) 1988, c. C-15 ("NWTCA")

Ontario

Condominium Act, 1998, S.O. 1998, c. 19 ("OCA")

General Regulation, O. Reg. 48/01 (*Condominium Act, 1998*) ("OCGR")

Prince Edward Island

Condominium Act, R.S.P.E.I. 1988, c. C-16 ("PEICA")

General Regulations, P.E.I. Reg. EC10/78 (*Condominium Act*) ("PEICGR")

Québec

Civil Code of Québec, L.R.Q. c. C-1991 ("QCC")

Saskatchewan

Condominium Property Act, 1993, S.S. 1993, c. C-26.1 ("SCPA")

Condominium Property Regulations, 2001, R.R.S. c. C-26.1 Reg. 2 ("SCPR")

Yukon

Condominium Act, R.S.Y. 2002, c. 36 ("YCA")

Term	Act	Section	Scope	Definition
"3/4 vote"	BCSPA	1(1)	means	*a vote in favour of a resolution by at least 3/4 of the votes cast by eligible voters who are present in person or by proxy at the time the vote is taken and who have not abstained from voting.*
"Act"	ACPR	1(1)	means	*the Condominium Property Act.*
	NBCPR	2		
	PEICGR	1	means	*the Condominium Act R.S.P.E.I. 1988, Cap. C-16.*
	SCPR	2	means	*The Condominium Property Act, 1993.*
"additional common facilities"	SCPA	2(1)	means	*common facilities described in a declaration.*
"additional unit"	SCPA	2(1)	means	*a unit not described in a condominium plan but described in a declaration.*
"adjacent parcel"	ACPR	46	means	*In this Part...* • *2 or more parcels that are adjoining or are separated only by* • *a highway as defined in the Traffic Safety Act or the successor to that Act,* • *a right of way for a pipeline,* • *a right of way for a public utility as defined in section 1 of the Municipal Government Act,* • *a right of way for a railway, or* • *2 or more highways and rights of way referred to in subclauses (i) to (iv).*
"affiliated body corporate"	OCGR	17(2)	means	*In subsection (1)...* *a body corporate that is deemed to be affiliated with another body corporate under subsection 1(4) of the Business Corporations Act.*
"agricultural purposes"	SCPR	2	includes	*the handling, storage, cleaning or drying of grain.*
"alienation"	QCC	1047	includes	*Each fraction constitutes a distinct entity and may be alienated in whole or in part; the...* *in each case, the share of the common portions appurtenat to the fraction, as well as the right to use the common portions for restricted use, where applicable.*
"amalgamated condominium plan"	ACPR	46	means	*In this Part...* *the condominium plan created out of the amalgamation of 2 or more condominium plans.*

Term	Act	Section	Scope	Definition
"amalgamated corporation"	ACPR	46	means	*In this Part...* *the corporation created out of the amalgamation of 2 or more corporations.*
	NLCA	65	means	*In sections 66 and 67...* *a corporation that is formed as a result of an amalgamation under sections 66 and 67.*
"amalgamated parcel"	ACPR	46	means	*In this Part...* *the parcel created out of the amalgamation of 2 or more parcels.*
"amalgamating condominium plan"	ACPR	46	means	*In this Part...* *a condominium plan that is amalgamated, or is proposed to be amalgamated, with one or more other condominium plans to create an amalgamated condominium plan.*
"amalgamating corporation"	ACPR	46	means	*In this Part...* *a corporation that is amalgamated, or is proposed to be amalgamated, with one or more other corporations to create an amalgamated corporation.*
	NLCA	65	means	*In sections 66 and 67...* *a corporation that is amalgamated with one or more other corporations under sections 66 and 67.*
	NWTCR	3(1)	means	*In this section...* *a corporation that is amalgamated, or is proposed to be amalgamated, with one or more other corporations to create an amalgamated corporation.*
"amalgamating parcel"	ACPR	46	means	*In this Part...* *a parcel that is amalgamated, or is proposed to be amalgamated, with one or more other parcels to create an amalgamated parcel.*
"amalgamation"	OCGR	1	means	*an amalgamation under Part VII of the Act and "amalgamate" has a corresponding meaning.*
"Amended Schedule of Interest on Destruction"	BCSPR	17.1	means	*For the purposes of this Part...* *an Amended Schedule of Interest on Destruction prepared in Form Z.1 for filing with the registrar.*
"annual general meetings"	OCA	1(1)	means	*a meeting of the owners of a corporation held in accordance with subsection 45(2).*
"apartment"	SCPA	13(1)	includes	*In this section...* *a flat or tenement.*

Term	Act	Section	Scope	Definition
"approval"	SCPA	2(1)	means	*respecting a condominium plan, approval or approved by the Controller of Surveys in accordance with The Land Surveys Act, 2000, this Act and the regulations, unless otherwise indicated.*
"approval authority"	OCA	1(1)	means	*the approval authority for the purposes of sections 51, 51.1 and 51.2 of the Planning Act.*
"approved"	SCPA	2(1)	means	*respecting a condominium plan, approval or approved by the Controller of Surveys in accordance with The Land Surveys Act, 2000, this Act and the regulations, unless otherwise indicated.*
"approving authority"	BCSPA	242(1)	means	*For the purposes of this section...* • *the municipal council of the municipality if the land is located in a municipality,* • *the regional board of the regional district if the land is located in a regional district but not in a municipality and is neither Nisga'a Lands nor treaty lands of a treaty first nation,* • *the Nisga'a Village Government if the land is located within Nisga'a Village Lands,* • *the Nisga'a Lisims Government if the land is Nisga'a Lands other than Nisga'a Village Lands, or* • *the governing body of the treaty first nation if the land is located within the treaty lands of that treaty first nation.*
"approving officer"	BCSPA	1(1)	means	*an appropriate approving officer appointed under the Land Title Act.*
"architect"	ACPA	1(1)	means	• *a registered architect, visiting project architect or architects corporation, or* • *a joint firm or an architects and engineers firm,* *as defined in the Architects Act.*
	MCA	1	means	*a person who under The Architects Act is authorized to practise as an architect in the province.*
	NWTCA	6(1)	means	*In this section...* *a person who is an authorized practitioner as defined in the Architects Act.*
	YCA	1	means	*a person who is authorized to practise as an architect in any province.*

Term	Act	Section	Scope	Definition
"arm's length transaction"	ACPA	1(2)	is	*A reference to an ...* *[or to a transaction being at arm's length]... a reference to a transaction that is conducted in an open market between willing parties to the transaction negotiating in their own respective self-interest where the consideration paid is competitive and not unreasonable having regard to open market conditions.*
"assessed value"	BCSPA	1(1)	means	*the value assessed under the Assessment Act.*
"assessing Act"	PEICA	27(1)	means	*In this section...* *the Real Property Assessment Act R.S.P.E.I. 1988, Cap. R-4 and any other Act pursuant to which an assessing authority is empowered to assess and levy rates, charges or taxes on land or in respect of the ownership of land.*
	SCPA	2(1)	means	*an Act pursuant to which an assessing authority is empowered to assess and levy rates, charges or taxes on land or with respect to the ownership of land, and includes any bylaws or regulations made pursuant to that Act.*
"assessing authority"	PEICA	27(1)	means	*In this section...* *the Minister charged with the administration of the Real Property Assessment Act, any municipality as defined in the Real Property Tax Act R.S.P.E.I. 1988, Cap. R-5 or any other authority having power to assess and levy any rates, charges or taxes on land or in respect of the ownership of land.*
	SCPA	2(1)	means	*a local authority or a school board or other authority that has the power to assess and levy rates, charges or taxes on land or with respect to the ownership of land.*
"association"	NSCA	2	means	*an association incorporated under this Act and an association to which this Act applies.*
"at arm's length"	ACPA	1(2)	is	*A reference to an arm's length transaction or to a ...* *a reference to a transaction that is conducted in an open market between willing parties to the transaction negotiating in their own respective self interest where the consideration paid is competitive and not unreasonable having regard to open market conditions.*

Term	Act	Section	Scope	Definition
"auditor"	OCA	1(1)	means	*a person licensed as a public accountant under the Public Accounting Act, 2004 who is appointed as an auditor of a corporation under section 60.*
"bank rate"	OCGR	19(2)	means	*In subsection (3)...* *the bank rate established by the Bank of Canada as the minimum rate at which the Bank of Canada makes short-term advances to members of the Canadian Payments Association.*
"bare land strata plan"	BCSPA	1(1)	means	• *a strata plan on which the boundaries of the strata lots are defined on a horizontal plane by reference to survey markers and not by reference to the floors, walls or ceilings of a building, or* • *any other strata plan defined by regulation to be a bare land strata plan.*
"bare land unit"	ACPA	1(1)	means	*a unit defined in clause (y)(ii).*
	MCA	1	means	*a unit defined by delineation of its horizontal boundaries without reference to any buildings on a plan referred to in subsection 6(5).*
	NWTCA YCA	1(1) 1	means	*a part of the land included in a plan and designated as a unit by horizontal boundaries only without reference to any buildings and, unless otherwise shown on the plan, comprises* • *all of the space vertically above and below those boundaries, and* • *all of the material parts of the land within the space referred to in paragraph (a) at the time the declaration and plan are registered.*
	SCPA	2(1)	means	*a unit as defined in subclause (bb)(ii).*
"beneficiary"	OCGR	1	means	*a person on whose behalf a payment described in subsection 81 (1) of the Act has been made in respect of a proposed unit or a proposed common interest in a common elements condominium corporation and includes the person's successors and assigns.*
"board"	ACPA	1(1)	means	*the board of a corporation as provided for in section 28.*
	MCA OCA PEICA YCA	1 1(1) 1(1) 1	means	*the board of directors of a corporation.*

Term	Act	Section	Scope	Definition
"board" — *cont'd*	NBCPA	1(1)	means	*the board of directors of an association.*
	NSCA	2	means	*the board of directors of a corporation.*
	NLCA	2(1)	means	*the board of directors of a corporation.*
	NWTCA	1(1)		
	SCPA	2(1)	means	*the board of directors of a corporation mentioned in section 37.*
"body corporate"	ACPR	Sch. 2, 1	includes	*In this Schedule... a company or other body corporate whenever or however incorporated but does not include a corporation incorporated under section 25 of the Act.*
	OCGR	17(2)	means	*a body corporate with or without share capital.*
"bond"	SCPR	2	means	*a bond that meets the requirements of section 16.*
"building"	ACPA	1(1)	means	*one or more buildings on the same parcel.*
	OCA	1(1)	means	*a building included in a property.*
	SCPA	1(1)	means	*one or more buildings situated on a parcel.*
"buildings"	MCA	1	means	*the buildings included in a property.*
	NBCPA	1(1)	means	*the buildings included in a condominium property.*
	NLCA	2(1)	means	*buildings and structures included in a property.*
	NWTCA	1(1)	means	*the buildings included in a property;*
	PEICA	1(1)		
	YCA	1		
"by-law"	MCA	1	means	*a by-law of a corporation.*
	NBCPA	1(1)		
	OCA	1(1)		
"bylaw"	BCSPA	1(1)	means	*a bylaw of a strata corporation.*
	NWTCA	1(1)	means	*a bylaw of a corporation.*
	PEICA	1(1)		
	YCA	1		
"bylaw instrument"	NWTCA	17(1)	means	*an instrument under subsection (2) that makes, amends or repeals a bylaw.*

Term	Act	Section	Scope	Definition
"by-laws"	NSCA	2	means	*the by-laws made by an association.*
	NLCA	2(1)	means	*the by-laws of a corporation.*
	ACPA	1(1)	means	*the bylaws of a corporation as amended from time to time and includes any bylaws passed in substitution for them.*
"candidate"	SCPA	36.11(1)	means	*In this section...* *a candidate for election as a member to the House of Commons or the Legislative Assembly or to an elected office in a municipality, school board or conseil scolaire.*
"claim"	MCA	1	includes	*a right, title, interest, encumbrance, or demand of any kind affecting land, but does not include the interest of an owner in his unit and common interest.*
	NBCPA	1(1)	includes	*a right, title, interest, encumbrance or demand of any kind affecting land, but does not include the interest of an owner in the owner's unit and common interest.*
	NLCA	2(1)	includes	*right, title, interest, encumbrance or demand affecting land but does not include the interest of an owner in the owner's unit or common interest.*
	NWTCA	1(1)	includes	*a right, title, interest, encumbrance or demand of any kind affecting land, but does not include the interest of an owner in his or her unit and common interest.*
		1(2)	includes	*In paragraphs 25(3)(f), 26(1)(b), (3)(b), 28(1)(b) and (2)...* *[does not]... a security interest as defined in the Personal Property Security Act.*
	OCA	1(1)	includes	*a right, title, interest, encumbrance or demand of any kind affecting land but does not include the interest of an owner in the owner's unit or common interest;*
	PEICA	1(1)	includes	*a right, title, interest, incumbrance or demand of any kind affecting land, but does not include the interest of an owner in his unit and common interest.*

Term	Act	Section	Scope	Definition
"claim" — *cont'd*	YCA	1	includes	*a right, title, interest, encumbrance or demand of any kind affecting land, but does not include the interest of an owner in their unit and common interest.*
"claims"	NWTCA	1(2)	includes	*In paragraphs 25(3)(f), 26(1)(b), (3)(b), 28(1)(b) and (2)...* *[does not]... a security interest as defined in the Personal Property Security Act.*
"common asset"	BCSPA	1(1)	means	• *personal property held by or on behalf of a strata corporation, and* • *land held in the name of or on behalf of a strata corporation, that is* *i. not shown on the strata plan, or* *ii. shown as a strata lot on the strata plan.*
"common elements"	MCA	1	means	*all the property except the units.*
	NWTCA	1(1)		
	OCA	1(1)		
	PEICA	1(1)		
	YCA	1		
	NBCPA	1(1)	means	*all the condominium property except the units.*
	NLCA	2(1)	means	*the whole property with the exception of the units.*
"common elements condominium corporation"	NLCA	2(1)	means	*a common elements condominium corporation to which Part VIII applies.*
	OCA	1(1)	means	*a common elements condominium corporation described in subsection 138(2).*
"common expenses"	BCSPA	1(1)	means	*expenses* • *relating to the common property and common assets of the strata corporation, or* • *required to meet any other purpose or obligation of the strata corporation.*
	MCA	1	means	*the expenses of a performance of the objects and duties of a corporation and any expenses specified as common expenses in a declaration or in section 16.*
	NBCPA	1(1)	means	*the expenses related to the performance of the objects and duties of a corporation and any expenses specified as common expenses in a declaration.*

Term	Act	Section	Scope	Definition
"common expenses" — *cont'd*	NLCA OCA	2(1) 1(1)	means	*the expenses related to the performance of the objects and duties of a corporation and all expenses specified as common expenses in this Act or in a declaration.*
	NWTCA	1(1)	means	*means expenses for the performance of the objects and duties of a corporation, including* • *expenses for maintenance of the common elements,* • *expenses for major repairs and the replacement of common elements and assets of the corporation,* • *expenses specified as common expenses in a declaration, and* • *in the case of a leasehold condominium, the rent and any other amounts owing by the corporation to the lessor under paragraph 8(6)(a).*
	PEICA	1(1)	means	*the interest in the common elements appurtenant to a unit.*
	YCA	1	means	*the expenses of a performance of the objects and duties of a corporation and any expenses specified as common expenses in a declaration or in section 5.*
"common expenses fund"	NWTCR	1	means	*one or more funds established by a corporation under sections 19.9 and 19.10 of the Act.*
	SCPA	2(1)	means	*a common expenses fund established pursuant to clause 55(1)(a).*
"common facility"	BCSPA	217	means	*In this Part...* *a major facility in a phased strata plan, including a laundry room, playground, swimming pool, recreation centre, clubhouse or tennis court, if the facility is available for the use of the owners.*
"common facilities"	SCPA	2(1)	means	*improvements on the common property and includes any laundry room, playground, swimming pool, recreation centre, clubhouse, tennis court and landscaping.*
"common interest"	MCA NBCPA PEICA	1 1(1) 1(1)	means	*the interest in the common elements appurtenant to a unit.*
	NLCA OCA	2(1) 1(1)	means	*the interest in the common elements appurtenant to*

Term	Act	Section	Scope	Definition
"common interest" — *cont'd*				• *a unit, in the case of all corporations except a common elements condominium corporation, or* • *an owner's parcel of land to which the common interest is attached and which is described in the declaration, in the case of a common elements condominium corporation.*
	NWTCA YCA	1(1) 1	means	*interest in the common elements appurtenant to a unit.*
"common property"	ACPA	1(1)	means	*so much of the parcel as is not comprised in a unit shown in a condominium plan, but does not include land shown on the condominium plan that has been provided for the purposes of roads, public utilities and reserve land under Part 17 of the Municipal Government Act.*
		14(1)	includes	*For the purposes of this section...* *facilities and property that are intended for common use by the owners notwithstanding that the facilities or property may be located in or comprise a unit or any part of a unit.*
	ACPR	21(1)	includes	*In this Part...* *common property referred to in section 14(1)(a) of the Act.*
		33(1)	means	*In this section...* *common property as defined in section 14(1)(a) of the Act.*
		63	means	*In this Part...* *common property to which section 14 of the Act applies.*
	BCSPA	1(1)	means	• *that part of the land and buildings shown on a strata plan that is not part of a strata lot, and* • *pipes, wires, cables, chutes, ducts and other facilities for the passage or provision of water, sewage, drainage, gas, oil, electricity, telephone, radio, television, garbage, heating and cooling systems, or other similar services, if they are located* i. *within a floor, wall or ceiling that forms a boundary* A) *between a strata lot and another strata lot,*

Term	Act	Section	Scope	Definition
"common property" — *cont'd*				*B) between a strata lot and the common property, or* *C) between a strata lot or common property and another parcel of land, or* *ii. wholly or partially within a strata lot, if they are capable of being and intended to be used in connection with the enjoyment of another strata lot or the common property.*
	SCPA	1(1)	means	*the part of the land and buildings included in a condominium plan that is not included in any unit shown in the condominium plan.*
"common surplus"	OCA	1(1)	means	*the excess of all receipts of the corporation over the expenses of the corporation.*
"component"	NLCR	2	means	*In these regulations... an individual item that is included in the physical analysis portion of a reserve-fund study as described in section 4, and shall include an item* • *that is the responsibility of the corporation,* • *for which major repair or replacement costs are anticipated to be incurred during its useful life; and* • *for which the costs of repair or replacement will not be covered as part of the annual operating or maintenance budget.*
	NWTCR	7(1)	means	*an individual item that is included in the physical analysis portion of a capital reserve fund study and includes items* • *that are the responsibility of the corporation;* • *for which major repair or replacement costs are anticipated to be incurred during their useful lives; and* • *for which the costs of repair or replacement will not be covered as part of the annual operating or maintenance budget of the corporation.*
	NSCR	77(1)	means	*In this Part...* *an individual item that is included in the physical analysis portion of a reserve-fund study as described in subsection 79(2), and shall include an item*

Term	Act	Section	Scope	Definition
"component" — *cont'd*				• *that is the responsibility of the corporation,* • *for which major repair or replacement costs are anticipated to be incurred during its useful life,* • *for which the costs of repair or replacement will not be covered as part of the annual operating or maintenance budget.*
	SCPR	51.1	means	*In this section and in sections 51.2 and 51.3…* *an individual item that is included in the physical analysis portion of a reserve fund study as described in section 51.3, and includes any thing:* • *that is the responsibility of the corporation;* • *for which major repair or replacement costs are anticipated to be incurred during its useful life; and* • *for which the costs of repair or replacement will not be covered as part of the annual operating or maintenance budget.*
"component inventory"	OCGR	27	means	*In this Part…* *an inventory, in a reserve fund study of a corporation, of each item of the common elements and assets of the corporation that requires, or is expected to require within at least 30 years of the date of the study, major repair or replacement where the cost of replacement is not less than $500.*
"comprehensive study"	OCGR	27	means	*In this Part…* *a comprehensive reserve fund study that meets the requirements of this Regulation.*
"condominium"	SCPA	2(1)	means	*the land included in a condominium plan together with the buildings and units and the common property and common facilities belonging to them.*
"Condominium Act"	BCSPR	17.1	means	*For the purposes of this Part…* *the Condominium Act, R.S.B.C. 1996, c. 64, or other former Act.*
"condominium appeals officer"	NSCR	1(2)	*means*	*a person appointed under subsection 82C(1) to hear an appeal of a decision of a condominium dispute officer under Section 33 of the Act and Sections 82C and 82D.*
"condominium dispute officer"	NSCR	1(2)	*means*	*a person appointed in subsection 82A(1) to hear disputes between a condominium corporation and a unit owner under Section 33 of the Act and Sections 82A and 82B*

Term	Act	Section	Scope	Definition
"Condominium Corporation Index"	OCGR	1	means	*the Condominium Corporations Index mentioned in subsection 3 (3) of the Act.*
	PEICGR	1	means	*the Condominium Corporations Index kept under subsection 5(1) of the Act.*
"condominium plan"	ACPA	1(1)	means	*a plan registered in a land titles office that complies with section 8 and includes any amendment to a condominium plan referred to in section 18 or 20, any plan or condominium plan, as the case may be, relating to development in phases referred to in section 19 or any plan or condominium plan, as the case may be, relating to redivision referred to in section 20 that is registered in the land titles office.*
	SCPA	2(1)	means	*a plan that:* • *is described in the heading of the plan as a condominium plan;* • *shows the whole or any part of the buildings and land included in the plan as being divided into two or more units; and* • *meets the requirements of section 9.*
"condominium property"	NBCPA	1(1)	means	*the freehold land and interests appurtenant to the land described in a description, and includes any freehold land and interests appurtenant to land that are added to the common elements.*
	NSCR	1(2)	means	*property as defined in Section 3(1)(s) of the Act, to which the Act applies.*
	PEICGR	1	means	*property, as defined in clause 1(1)(o) of the Act, to which the Act applies.*
"Condominium Register"	OCGR	1	means	*the Condominium Register mentioned in subsection 3 (4) of the Act.*
	PEICGR	1	means	*the Condominium Register kept under subsection 5(2) of the Act.*
"contingency reserve fund"	BCSPA	1(1)	means	*a fund for common expenses that usually occur less often than once a year or that do not usually occur, as set out in section 92 (b).*
"Controller of Surveys"	SCPA	2(1)	means	*the Controller of Surveys appointed pursuant to The Land Surveys Act, 2000.*
"convey"	BCSPA	1(1)	means	*[when referring to the conveyance of a strata lot to a purchaser] ... any of the following in respect of which an application to the land title office has been made to register:*

Term	Act	Section	Scope	Definition
"convey" — *cont'd*				• *a transfer of a freehold estate in the strata lot;* • *an agreement for sale of the strata lot;* • *an assignment of a purchaser's interest in an agreement for sale of the strata lot;* • *an assignment of a strata lot lease in a leasehold strata plan.*
"co-operative basis"	NSCA	2	means	*the carrying on of an enterprise organized, operated and administered in accordance with the following principles and methods:* • *each member or delegate has only one vote,* • *no member or delegate may vote by proxy,* • *interest or dividends on share or loan capital is limited to the percentage fixed in the articles of incorporation, or by-laws of the association,* • *the enterprise is operated as nearly as possible at cost after providing for reasonable reserves and the payment or crediting of interest or dividends on share or loan capital, and any surplus funds arising from the business of the organization, after providing for such reasonable reserves or dividends, unless used to maintain or improve services of the organization for its members or donated for community welfare or the propagation of co-operative principles, are distributed in whole or in part among the members or the members and patrons of the organization in proportion to the volume of business they have done with or through the organization, and* • *the shares in the capital stock of a co-operative association except for those referred to in Section 20, do not have attached any special preferences, rights, conditions, restrictions, limitations or prohibitions either by the articles of incorporation, amalgamation agreement, certificate of incorporation or of amalgamation, by-laws or otherwise, and shall not be redeemed at more than par value or purchased by the association at less than par value without the approval of the Inspector.*
"corporation"	ACPA	1(1)	means	*a body incorporated by section 25.*

Term	Act	Section	Scope	Definition
"corporation" — *cont'd*	MCA NBCPA YCA	1 1(1) 1	means	*a corporation incorporated under this Act.*
	NLCA OCA	2(1) 1(1)	means	*a corporation created or continued under this Act.*
	NWTCA	1(1)	means	*a corporation created by subsection 12(1).*
	SCPA	1(1)	means	*a corporation constituted or continued pursuant to section 34.*
"cost consultant"	ACPA	14(1)	means	*For the purposes of this section...* *a person who meets the requirements of the regulations to be a cost consultant or is otherwise designated as a cost consultant pursuant to the regulations.*
	ACPR	63	means	*In this Part...* *a cost consultant referred to in section 14(1)(b) of the Act.*
"Court"	ACPA ACA	1(1) 1(1)	means	*the Court of Queen's Bench.*
	NBCPA	1(1)	means	*The Court of Queen's Bench of New Brunswick.*
	NWTCA	1(1)	means	*the Supreme Court of the Northwest Territories.*
"court"	MCA	1	means	*the Court of Queen's Bench.*
	NLCA	2(1)	means	*the Trial Division of the Supreme Court of Newfoundland and Labrador.*
	SCPA	2(1)	means	*Her Majesty's Court of Queen's Bench for Saskatchewan.*
"debentures"	ACPR	Sch. 2, 1	includes	*In this Schedule...* *debenture stock.*
"declarant"	NBCPA	1(1)	means	*a person who or on whose behalf a declaration and description are submitted for approval for registration.*
	NBCPR	2	means	*the person submitting a declaration and description for registration.*
	NLCA	2(1)	means	*a person who owns the freehold estate in the land described in the description and who submits for registration under this Act a declaration and description that are registered under this Act, and includes a successor or assignee of that person, but does not include a purchaser in good faith*

Term	Act	Section	Scope	Definition
"declarant" — *cont'd*				*of a unit who pays fair market value or a successor or assignee of the purchaser.*
	OCA	1(1)	means	*a person who owns the freehold or leasehold estate in the land described in the description and who registers a declaration and description under this Act, and includes a successor or assignee of that person but does not include a purchaser in good faith of a unit who pays fair market value or a successor or assignee of the purchaser.*
	PEICA	1(1)	means	*the owner in fee simple of the land described in the description at the time of the registration of a declaration and description of the land, and includes any successor or assignee of such owner but does not include a purchaser in good faith of a unit who actually pays fair market value or any successor or assignee of such purchaser.*
"declaration"	MCA YCA	1 1	means	*a declaration to which reference is made in section 5, and includes any amendments thereto.*
	NLCA	2(1)	means	*a declaration specified in section 9 , and includes amendments to the declaration.*
	NWTCA	1(1)	means	*a declaration referred to in section 5 and includes any amendments to a declaration.*
	OCA	1(1)	means	*a declaration registered under section 2 and all amendments to the declaration.*
	PEICA	1(1)	means	*the declaration specified in section 3, and includes any amendments.*
	SCPA	2(1)	means	*a declaration mentioned in section 5.2 or subsection 16(3) as the case may be, and includes any amendments to a declaration made pursuant to section 18.*
"deed"	OCA	1(1)	includes	*a transfer under the Land Titles Act.*
"deposit receipt"	OCGR	1	means	*a deposit receipt described in paragraph 2 of subsection 20 (2).*
"depreciating property"	ACPR	21(1)	means	*In this Part...* *the property to which section 38(1) of the Act applies.*
"deputy registrar"	NLCA	2(1)	means	*the Deputy Registrar of Condominiums referred to in section 4.*

Term	Act	Section	Scope	Definition
"deputy registrar" — *cont'd*	SCPA	22(3)	means	*In subsection 2...* *Deputy Registrar as defined in The Land Titles Act, 2000.*
"description"	NLCA	2(1)	means	*a description as specified in section 11 and includes all amendments to the description that comply with section 12.*
	OCA	1(1)	means	*a description registered under section 2 and all amendments to the description.*
"developer"	ACPA	1(1)	means	*a person who, alone or in conjunction with other persons, sells or offers for sale to the public units or proposed units that have not previously been sold to the public by means of an arm's length transaction.*
		14(1)	includes	*For the purposes of this section...* *any person who, on behalf of a developer, acts in respect of the sale of a unit or a proposed unit or receives money paid by or on behalf of a purchaser of a unit or a proposed unit pursuant to a purchase agreement.*
	NWTCA	1(1)	means	*a person who is the registered owner of the land included in a condominium plan on the day on which a declaration and plan are registered under this Act, and includes a person who* • *holds himself or herself out as intending to register a declaration and plan in respect of land that he or she owns, or* • *becomes the registered owner of all parts of the land that are not sold under section 6.4.*
	SCPA	2(1)		• *a person who was the registered owner of the buildings and land included in a condominium plan on the day on which:* *i.* *the plan was presented for registration before the coming into force of this clause;* *ii.* *the plan was approved pursuant to The Land Surveys Act, 2000; or* *iii.* *titles were issued pursuant to the approved plan; and* • *includes a person who, as a result of a registration of a transfer executed by a person mentioned in subclause (i), becomes the registered owner of all parts of buildings and land included in the plan that are not sold pursuant to section 26.*

Term	Act	Section	Scope	Definition
"developer's management agreement"	ACPA	17(1)	means	*In this section...* *a management agreement that was entered into by a corporation at a time when its board was comprised of persons who were elected to the board while the majority of units were owned by a developer.*
	NWTCA	12.2(1)	means	*In this section...* *an agreement for the management of the property that was entered into before the registration of a declaration and plan, or that was entered into by a corporation at a time when the board consisted of members who were elected while the developer owned a majority of the units.*
	SCPA	29(1)	means	*In this section and in clause 114(d)...* *a management agreement that was entered into by a corporation at a time when its board consisted of members who were elected while the developer owned a majority of the units.*
"diagram"	NSCR	1(2)	means	*a compiled plan substantially depicting the extent and location of units.*
"Director"	NBCPA	1(1)	means	*the Director of Condominiums appointed under subsection 2(2).*
	SCPA	2(1)	means	*the Director of Corporations.*
"director"	MCA	1	means	*the Director of Residential Tenancies appointed under The Residential Tenancies Act.*
"Director of Surveys"	NBCPR	2	means	*the person designated by the Minister of Natural Resources pursuant to subsection 3(1) of the Surveys Act.*
"disclosure statement"	NLCA	2(1)	means	*a disclosure statement as specified in section 41.*
"district registrar"	MCA	1	means	*a district registrar appointed under The Real Property Act.*
"document"	ACPA	71(2)	includes	*For the purposes of this section...* *summons, notice, tax notice, order and other legal process.*
"doors and windows"	ACPR	72(1)	means	*In this section...* *doors and windows as referred to in section 9(3) of the Act.*
"due date"	MCA	1	means	*in relation to the completion of a phase,* • *the date specified in the declaration as the date by which the phase is to be completed,* • *if the declaration does not specify a date by which the phase is to be completed,*

Term	Act	Section	Scope	Definition
"due date" — *cont'd*				*the sixth anniversary date of the registration date of the declaration, or* • *the date to which the due date for completing the phase has been extended by an amendment registered under section 5.13.*
"easement"	OCGR	1	means	*an easement, right of way, right or licence in the nature of an easement, profit à prendre or other incorporeal hereditament, but does not include any of those that arise by operation of law.*
	PEICGR	11(1)	means	*In this section...* *an easement, right of way, right or license in the nature of an easement, profit a prendre or other incorporeal hereditament, but does not include such an easement arising by operation of law.*
"eligible security"	NBCPA	38(1)	means	*In this section...* *a bond, debenture, guaranteed investment certificate, deposit receipt, deposit note, certificate of deposit, term deposit or other similar instrument that* • *is issued or guaranteed by the Government of Canada or the government of a province of Canada, or* • *is issued by an institution located in the Province insured by either the Canada Deposit Insurance Corporation or the New Brunswick Credit Union Deposit Insurance Corporation.*
	OCA	115(5)	means	*In subsections (6) and (7)...* *a bond, debenture, guaranteed investment certificate, deposit receipt, deposit note, certificate of deposit, term deposit or other similar instrument that,* • *is issued or guaranteed by the government of Canada or the government of any province of Canada;* • *is issued by an institution located in Ontario insured by the Canada Deposit Insurance Corporation or the Deposit Insurance Corporation of Ontario, or* • *is a security of a prescribed class.*
"eligible voters"	BCSPA	1(1)	means	*persons who may vote under sections 53 to 58.*
"encumbrance"	MCA	1	means	*subject to subsection 8(8), a claim that secures the payment of money or the performance of any other obligation and includes a charge, a mortgage and a lien.*

Term	Act	Section	Scope	Definition
"encumbrance" — *cont'd*		8(8)	means	*In subsections (9) and (10)...* *an encumbrance that is, or at one time was, enforceable against all the units and common interests, but does not include a mortgage.*
	NBCPA	1(1)	means	*a claim that secures the payment of money and includes a mortgage and a lien.*
	NLCA	2(1)	means	*a claim that secures the payment of money or the performance of another obligation, and includes a mortgage and a lien.*
	NWTCA YCA	1(1) 1	means	*a claim that secures the payment of money or the performance of any other obligation and includes a charge, a mortgage, a lien or an easement.*
	NWTCA	1(2)	includes	*In paragraphs and subsections 5(1)(f), 5(4)(b), 5(7), 5(8)(c), 6(7)(b), 6(10), 6(11)(c), 6.2(3), 6.2(4), 9(1), 9(4), 17(4), 17(6), 17(7), 17(8)(c), 29(1)(c), 31(f)...* *[does not]... a security interest as defined in the Personal Property Security Act.*
	OCA	1(1)	means	*a claim that secures the payment of money or the performance of any other obligation and includes a charge under the Land Titles Act, a mortgage and a lien.*
"encumbrances"	NWTCA	1(2)	includes	*In paragraphs and subsections 5(1)(f), 5(4)(b), 5(7), 5(8)(c), 6(7)(b), 6(10), 6(11)(c), 6.2(3), 6.2(4), 9(1), 9(4), 17(4), 17(6), 17(7), 17(8)(c), 29(1)(c), 31(f)...* *[does not]... a security interest as defined in the Personal Property Security Act.*
"endorsed declaration"	SCPA	5.2(1)	means	*In this section...* *a declaration in the prescribed form that is endorsed with:* • *a certificate of acceptance granted by the minister where required by the regulations; or* • *a waiver of the requirement to obtain security where authorized by the regulations.*
"engineer"	ACPA	1(1)	means	• *a professional engineer registered or licensed under the Engineering, Geological and Geophysical Professions Act, or* • *a holder of a permit issued under the Engineering, Geological and Geophysical Professions Act, if that*

Term	Act	Section	Scope	Definition
"engineer" — *cont'd*				*holder is authorized to engage in the practice of engineering.*
	NWTCA	6(1)	means	*In this section...* *a person who is qualified to practice professional engineering under the Engineering and Geoscience Professions Act.*
"error"	BCSPR	14.12(1)	means	*In this section...* *any erroneous measurement or error, defect or omission in a registered strata plan.*
"estimated cost"	BCSPR	6.3(2)	means	*For the formula in subsection (2)...* *the estimated cost to repair or replace.*
"estoppel certificate"	NLCA	2(1)	means	*an estoppel certificate as specified in section 42.*
"existing unit"	MCA	1	means	*of a phased development, a unit, other than a phasing unit, that has been created by the registration of a declaration or a phasing amendment.*
"expected life"	BCSPR	6.2(3)	means	*For the formula in subsection (2)...* *the estimated number of years before the cost of repair or replacement is likely to be incurred.*
"extra parking stalls"	BCSPA	258(4)	means	*In this section...* *any parking stalls, on land shown on the strata plan as set aside for parking, that are in addition to the total number of parking stalls calculated by adding* • *one stall per strata lot, or any greater number of stalls required by an applicable municipal bylaw, Nisga'a Government law, treaty first nation law or other enactment, plus* • *one stall per 10 strata lots for visitor parking or any greater number of visitor parking stalls required by an applicable municipal bylaw, Nisga'a Government law, treaty first nation law or other enactment.*
"family"	BCSPA	142(1)	[has] the meaning	*For the purposes of this section...* *[and "family member"]... set out in the regulations.*
	BCSPR	8.1(1)	means	*For the purposes of section 142 of the Act...* *[and "family member"]...* • *a spouse of the owner,* • *a parent or child of the owner, or* • *a parent or child of the spouse of the owner.*

Term	Act	Section	Scope	Definition
"family member"	BCSPA	142(1)	[has] the meaning	*For the purposes of this section "family" and ...* *set out in the regulations.*
	BCSPR	8.1(1)	means	*For the purposes of section 142 of the Act...* *[and "family member"]...* • *a spouse of the owner,* • *a parent or child of the owner, or* • *a parent or child of the spouse of the owner.*
"financial institution"	ACPA	14(1)	means	*For the purposes of this section...* *a bank, treasury branch, credit union or trust corporation.*
"fixtures"	BCSPA	149(2)	has the meaning	*For the purposes of subsection (1)(d) and section 152(b)...* *set out in the regulations.*
	BCSPR	9.1(1)	means	*For the purposes of sections 149(1)(d) and 152(b) of the Act...* *items attached to a building, including floor and wall coverings and electrical and plumbing fixtures, but does not include, if they can be removed without damage to the building, refrigerators, stoves, dishwashers, microwaves, washers, dryers or other items.*
"form"	SCPR	2	means	*a form set out in Part I of the Appendix.*
"freehold condominium corporation"	OCA	1(1)	means	*a corporation in which all the units and their appurtenant common interests are held in fee simple by the owners.*
"grain"	SCPR	2	includes	*grain within the meaning of the Canada Grain Act;*
"ground lease"	BCSPA	199	means	*In this Part...* *a registered lease of land* • *granted by a leasehold landlord for the purposes of this Part, and* • *to which a model strata lot lease is attached.*
"habitable area"	BCSPA	246(4)	has the meaning	*For the purposes of subsection (3)...* *set out in the regulations.*
	BCSPR	14.2	means	*For the purposes of section 246 of the Act...* *the area of a residential strata lot which can be lived in, but does not include patios, balconies, garages, parking stalls or storage areas other than closet space.*

Term	Act	Section	Scope	Definition
"hanging line"	PEICGR	1	means	*an unclosed traverse in the form of a branch emanating from a main traverse or triangulation.*
"has been completed and installed"	OCGR	41	means	*For the purposes of subsections 40 (11) and 56 (7)...* *with respect to each building and structure that the declaration and description show are included in the common elements, constructed at least to the following state:* • *The exterior building envelope, including roofing assembly, exterior wall cladding, doors and windows, caulking and sealants, is weather resistant if required by the construction documents and has been completed in general conformity with the construction documents.* • *Floor assemblies are constructed and completed to the final covering.* • *Walls and ceilings are completed to the drywall (including taping and sanding), plaster or other final covering.* • *All underground garages, if any, have walls and floor assemblies in place.* • *All elevating devices, if any, as defined in the Elevating Devices Act, are licensed under that Act if it requires a licence.* • *All installations with respect to the provision of water and sewage services, if any, are in place and operable.* • *All installations with respect to the provision of heat and ventilation, if any, are in place and heat and ventilation can be provided.* • *All installations with respect to the provision of air conditioning, if any, are in place and operable.* • *All installations with respect to the provision of electricity, if any, are in place and operable.* • *All indoor and outdoor swimming pools, if any, are completed and operable.*
"has been constructed"	OCGR	6(1)	means	*For the purposes of subsection 5 (8)...* *[with respect to each building on the property]... constructed at least to the following state:* • *The exterior building envelope, including roofing assembly, exterior wall cladding, doors and windows, caulking and sealants, is weather resistant if required by the construction*

Term	Act	Section	Scope	Definition
"has been constructed" — *cont'd*				*documents and has been completed in general conformity with the construction documents.* • *Floor assemblies are constructed to the sub-floor.* • *Walls and ceilings of the common elements, excluding interior structural walls and columns in a unit, are completed to the drywall (including taping and sanding), plaster or other final covering.* • *All underground garages, if any, have walls and floor assemblies in place.* • *All elevating devices, if any, as defined in the Elevating Devices Act, are licensed under that Act if it requires a licence, except for elevating devices contained wholly in a unit and designed for use only within the unit.* • *All installations with respect to the provision of water and sewage services are in place.* • *All installations with respect to the provision of heat and ventilation are in place and heat and ventilation can be provided.* • *All installations with respect to the provision of air conditioning, if any, are in place.* • *All installations with respect to the provision of electricity are in place.* • *All indoor and outdoor swimming pools, if any, are roughed in to the extent that they are ready to receive finishes, equipment and accessories.* • *Subject to paragraphs 2 and 3, the boundaries of the units are completed to the drywall (not including taping and sanding), plaster or other final covering, and perimeter doors are in place.*
"has been installed and provided"	OCGR	41	means	*For the purposes of subsections 40 (11) and 56 (7)...* *[with respect to the facilities and services] that the declaration and description show are included in the common elements, installed and provided in accordance with the requirements of the municipalities in which the land is situated or the requirements of the Minister of Municipal Affairs and Housing, if the land is not situated in a municipality.*

Term	Act	Section	Scope	Definition
"hearing"	BCSPR	4.01	means	*For the purposes of section 34.1 of the Act...* *a opportunity to be heard in person at a council meeting.*
		7.2	means	*For the purposes of section 135(1)(e) of the Act...* *an opportunity to be heard in person at a council meeting.*
		8.2	means	*For the purposes of section 144 of the Act...* *an opportunity to be heard in person at a council meeting.*
"holding body corporate"	OCGR	17(2)	means	*In subsection (1)...* *a body corporate that is deemed to be the holding body of another body corporate under subsection 1 (3) of the Business Corporations Act.*
"housing association"	NSCA	2	means	*an association that has as its primary purpose the provision of housing accommodation for occupancy by its members as nearly as possible at cost or that is operated in such a manner.*
"immediate family"	NSCA	2	means	*[when used to indicate a relationship with any person]...* • *any spouse or child of the person,* • *any relative of the person, or* • *any relative of the spouse of the person,* *if that spouse, child or relative is living in the same home as the person.*
"imperial measurements"	PEICGR	1	means	*measurements in feet and decimals of a foot.*
"improper conduct"	ACPA	67(1)	means	*In this section...* • *non-compliance with this Act, the regulations or the bylaws by a developer, a corporation, an employee of a corporation, a member of a board or an owner,* • *the conduct of the business affairs of a corporation in a manner that is oppressive or unfairly prejudicial to or that unfairly disregards the interests of an interested party,* • *the exercise of the powers of the board in a manner that is oppressive or unfairly prejudicial to or that unfairly disregards the interests of an interested party,* • *the conduct of the business affairs of a developer in a manner that is oppressive or unfairly prejudicial to or that unfairly disregards the interests of an interested*

Term	Act	Section	Scope	Definition
"improper conduct" — *cont'd*				*party or a purchaser or a prospective purchaser of a unit, or* • *the exercise of the powers of the board by a developer in a manner that is oppressive or unfairly prejudicial to or that unfairly disregards the interests of an interested party or a purchaser or a prospective purchaser of a unit.*
"improved real estate"	ACPR	Sch. 2, 1	means	*In this Schedule...* *an estate in fee simple in land* • *on which there exists a building, structure or other improvement used or capable of being used for residential, commercial or industrial purposes,* • *on which there is being erected such a building, structure or other improvement,* • *which is serviced with the utilities necessary for such a building, structure or other improvement, but only when the land is being mortgaged for the purpose of erecting the building, structure or other improvement, or* • *which is being used for agricultural purposes,* *but does not include an estate in fee simple in mines or minerals held separately from the surface.*
"improvement"	MCA	1	includes	*any building or structure constructed on or added to a bare land unit after the registration of the declaration and plan.*
"incumbrance"	PEICA	1(1)	means	*a claim that secures the payment of money or the performance of any other obligation, and includes a charge, a mortgage and a lien.*
"Inspector"	NSCA	2	means	*the Inspector of co-operative associations and includes any person authorized by the Minister to perform the duties of the Inspector in his absence or incapacity or when the office of Inspector is vacant.*
"insurer"	OCGR	1	means	*the insurer under a policy.*
"insured"	PEICGR	21(1)	means	*In this section...* *a purchaser under an agreement of purchase and sale of a proposed condominium unit who has paid money to which section 32 of the Act applies to a declarant and his successors and assigns.*
"interest"	SCPA	2(1)	includes	*[that affects all owners]...* • *an interest mentioned in subsection 5.1(3) respecting a parcel;* • *an interest based on an endorsed declaration pursuant to section 5.2;*

Term	Act	Section	Scope	Definition
"interest" — *cont'd*				• *an interest based on a permanent encroachment agreement pursuant to subsection 10(6);* • *an interest based on a notice of an application pursuant to subsection 14(6);* • *an interest based on a developer's reservation pursuant to section 16;* • *an interest based on a lease pursuant to section 71.1;* • *an interest based on the exclusive use of common property pursuant to section 72.1;* • *an interest based on an easement or restrictive covenant accepted pursuant to section 73;* • *an interest based on an easement or restrictive covenant granted pursuant to section 74;* • *an interest based on a notice of termination of condominium status pursuant to clause 87(1)(b);* • *an interest based on a writ of execution pursuant to section 109;* • *a interest based on notice of a security interest pursuant to clause 110(2)(b);* • *an interest based on a claim against the condominium corporation;* • *an interest based on a right granted by the condominium corporation; and* • *any other interest not respecting a particular title or titles.*
"interested party"	ACPA	67(1)	means	*In this section...* *an owner, a corporation, a member of the board, a registered mortgagee or any other person who has a registered interest in a unit.*
"interim occupancy"	OCA	80(2)	means	*In this section...* *the occupancy of a proposed unit before the purchaser receives a deed to the unit that is in registerable form.*
"judgment"	BCSPA	1(1)	means	*a judgment of a court, and includes costs awarded in respect of the judgment.*
"land"	MCA	1	means	*land, whether leasehold or in fee simple, under The Real Property Act.*
	NBCPA	1(1)	includes	*an air space parcel as defined in the Air Space Act.*

Term	Act	Section	Scope	Definition
"land" — *cont'd*	NWTCA	1(1)	means	*land for which a certificate of title is issued under the provisions of the Land Titles Act.*
	YCA	1	means	*land, whether leasehold or in fee simple under the Land Titles Act.*
"land registrar"	OCGR	1	means	*the land registrar in whose registry or land titles division, as the case may be, the property is situated.*
"land surveyor"	ACPA	1(1)	means	*an Alberta land surveyor registered, or the holder of a permit issued, under the Land Surveyors Act.*
"land titles registry"	SCPR	2(1)	means	*the land titles registry as defined in The Land Titles Act, 2000.*
"landlord"	ACPA	1(1)	means	*an owner of a unit that is being rented and includes a person acting on behalf of the owner.*
	BCSPA	1(1)	means	*an owner who rents a strata lot to a tenant and a tenant who rents a strata lot to a subtenant, but does not include a leasehold landlord in a leasehold strata plan as defined in section 199.*
"law society"	NLCA	2(1)	means	*the Law Society of Newfoundland and Labrador referred to in the Law Society Act, 1999.*
"lawyer"	NSCA	1(2)	*means*	*a lawyer as defined in the Legal Profession Act who holds an annual certificate which is in force.*
"lease"	PEICA	33(6)	includes	*In this section...* *a license to use or occupy and any agreement in the nature of a lease.*
"leasehold condominium"	NWTCA	1(1)	means	*a condominium established by the holder of a leasehold estate described in paragraph 4(1)(c).*
"leasehold condominium corporation"	OCA	1(1)	means	*a corporation in which all the units and their appurtenant common interests are subject to leasehold interests held by the owners.*
"leasehold landlord"	BCSPA	199	means	*In this Part...* *the government of British Columbia, the government of Canada, a municipality, a regional district, a Nisga'a Village or the Nisga'a Nation, a treaty first nation or another public authority as defined by a regulation made under this Act.*
"leasehold strata plan"	BCSPA	199	means	*In this Part...* *a strata plan in which the land shown on the strata plan is subject to a ground lease.*

Term	Act	Section	Scope	Definition
"leasehold tenant"	BCSPA	199	means	*In this Part...* *a person, including an owner developer, registered in the land title office as a tenant under a strata lot lease, whether entitled to it in the person's own right, in a representative capacity or otherwise, and includes a subtenant.*
"lessor"	OCA	1(1)	means	*[in relation to a leasehold corporation]... the person who owns the freehold estate in the land described in the description.*
"letter of credit"	SCPR	2	means	*a letter of credit that meets the requirements of section 16.1.*
"Level 1"	NBCPR	2	means	*the plan delineating the surface of the ground and showing the relationship of the structures to the boundaries of the lot or lots comprising the property.*
	NSCR	1(2)	means	*the plan delineating the surface of the ground or the projection thereof and showing the relationship of the structures to the boundaries of the lot or lots comprising the property.*
	PEICGR	1	means	*the plan delineating the surface of the ground or the projection thereof and showing the relationship of the structures to parcel limits.*
"limited common property"	BCSPA	1(1)	means	*common property designated for the exclusive use of the owners of one or more strata lots.*
"loan capital"	NSCA	2	includes	*a sum contributed to an association by a member, in his capacity as a member,* • *by way of contributions to capital otherwise than by the purchase of shares or the making of loans under Section 35, or* • *by allocation or payment pursuant to Section 38 or pursuant to an enactment, of net earnings or other sums available for distribution to members.*
"loan corporation"	ACPR	Sch. 2, 1	means	*In this Schedule...* *a loan corporation registered under the Loan and Trust Corporations Act.*
"local authority"	SCPA	2(1)	means	• *a city;.* • *a municipality incorporated or continued pursuant to The Municipalities Act;* • *a town, northern village or northern hamlet within the meaning of The Northern Municipalities Act, 2010;*

Term	Act	Section	Scope	Definition
"local authority" — *cont'd*				• *the Saskatchewan portion of the City of Lloydminster; or* • *any other local authority that may be prescribed by regulation;* • *[in relation to a parcel]... the local authority governing the area in which the parcel is situated.*
"long term lease"	BCSPA	148(1)	means	*In this section...* *a lease to the same person for a set term of 3 years or more.*
"lot"	NBCPR	2	means	*any area of land delineated by a survey or described in a conveyance and includes a lot approved in accordance with the Community Planning Act or shown on a plan filed at a registry office.*
	NSCR	2	means	*any area of land delineated by a survey or described in a conveyance and includes a lot approved in accordance with the Municipal Government Act or shown on a plan filed at a land registration office.*
"major perils"	BCSPR	9.1(2)	means	*For the purposes of section 149(4)(b) of the Act...* *the perils of fire, lightning, smoke, windstorm, hail, explosion, water escape, strikes, riots or civil commotion, impact by aircraft and vehicles, vandalism and malicious acts*
	NLCA	56(2)	means	*In subsection (1)...* *the perils of fire, lightning, smoke, windstorm, hail, explosion, water escape, strikes, riots or civil disturbance, impact by aircraft or vehicles, vandalism or malicious acts.*
	OCA	99(1)	means	*In subsection (1)...* *the perils of fire, lightning, smoke, windstorm, hail, explosion, water escape, strikes, riots or civil commotion, impact by aircraft or vehicles, vandalism or malicious acts.*
	SCPR	62.1	means	*For the purposes of section 65 of the Act...* *the perils of fire, lightning, explosion or implosion, smoke, falling objects, impact by aircraft or land vehicles, riot, vandalism or malicious acts, water escape or rupture, windstorm or hail.*
"majority vote"	BCSPA	1(1)	means	*a vote in favour of a resolution by more than 1/2 of the votes cast by eligible voters who are present in person or by proxy at*

Term	Act	Section	Scope	Definition
"majority vote" — *cont'd*				*the time the vote is taken and who have not abstained from voting.*
"management agreement"	ACPA	1(1)	means	*an agreement entered into by a corporation governing the general control, management and administration of* • *the real and personal property of the corporation, and* • *the common property.*
	SCPA	2(1)	means	*an agreement entered into by a corporation with any person for the purpose of providing for the general control, management and administration of:* • *the real and personal property of the corporation that is associated with the units; and* • *the common property associated with the units.*
"master reserve fund spread sheet"	SCPR	51.1	means	*In this section and in sections 51.1 and 51.3...* *a list of the components, the cost for major repair or replacement of each component, and the normal life expectancy and remaining useful life of each component.*
"master reserve-fund spread sheet"	NSCR	77(1)	means	*In this Part...* *a spread sheet with calculations of the annual funding requirements for each component based on its remaining useful life, the basic annual contribution and the shortfall contribution options, but without an allowance for inflation or interest earned.*
"material change"	NWTCA	6.5(1)	means	*In this section...* • *a change or a series of changes that a reasonable purchaser, on an objective basis, would have regarded as sufficiently important to the decision to purchase a unit or proposed unit in the corporation that it is likely that the purchaser would not have entered into a purchase agreement for the unit or the proposed unit or would have exercised the right to rescind such a purchase agreement under section 6.4, if the information referred to in subsection 6.4(1) had included the change or series of changes;* • *does not include* *i. a change in the budget of the corporation for the current fiscal year if more than one year has passed since the registration of the declaration and plan,*

Term	Act	Section	Scope	Definition
"material change" — *cont'd*				*ii. a substantial addition, alteration or improvement that the corporation makes to the common elements after the first annual general meeting and after the developer ceases to own a majority of the units,* *iii. a change in the number of units or proposed units that the developer intends to lease, or* *iv. a change in the schedule of the proposed commencement and completion dates for the amenities of which construction had not been completed as of the date the information referred to in subsection 6.4(1) was delivered.*
	OCA	74(2)	means	*In this section…* *a change or a series of changes that a reasonable purchaser, on an objective basis, would have regarded collectively as sufficiently important to the decision to purchase a unit or proposed unit in the corporation that it is likely that the purchaser would not have entered into an agreement of purchase and sale for the unit or the proposed unit or would have exercised the right to rescind such an agreement of purchase and sale under section 73, if the disclosure statement had contained the change or series of changes, but does not include,* • *a change in the contents of the budget of the corporation for the current fiscal year if more than one year has passed since the registration of the declaration and description for the corporation;* • *a substantial addition, alteration or improvement within the meaning of subsection 97 (6) that the corporation makes to the common elements after a turn-over meeting has been held under section 43;* • *a change in the portion of units or proposed units that the declarant intends to lease;* • *a change in the schedule of the proposed commencement and completion dates for the amenities of which construction had not been completed as of the date on which the disclosure statement was made; or* • *a change in the information contained in the statement described in subsection 161(1) of the services provided by the*

Term	Act	Section	Scope	Definition
"material change" — *cont'd*				*municipality or the Minister of Municipal Affairs and Housing, as the case may be, as described in that subsection, if the unit or the proposed unit is in a vacant land condominium corporation.*
"metric measurements"	PEICGR	1	means	*measurements in metres and decimals of a metre.*
"Minister"	ACPA	1(1)	means	*the Minister determined under section 16 of the Government Organization Act as the Minister responsible for this Act.*
	NSCA	2	means	*the Minister of Service Nova Scotia and Municipal Relations or other member of the Executive Council who has the general administration of this Act.*
	OCA	1(1)	means	*the minister responsible for the administration of this Act.*
"minister"	MCA	1	means	*the member of the Executive Council charged by the Lieutenant Governor in Council with the administration of this Act.*
	NLCA	2(1)	means	*the minister appointed under the Executive Council Act to administer this Act.*
	SCPA	2(1)	means	*the member of the Executive Council to whom for the time being the administration of this Act is assigned.*
"money collected"	BCSPA	108(7)	means	*In subsections (4) and (5)...* *the money collected on a special levy and includes any interest or income earned on that money.*
"monument"	NSCR	1(2)	means	*a bar, post, stake, or any other object, thing or device used to mark or witness a boundary of surveyed lands.*
	PEICGR	1	means	*a bar, post, stake, peg, or any other object, thing or device used to mark or delineate a boundary of surveyed lands.*
"mortgage"	OCA	1(1)	includes	*a charge under the Land Titles Act, in which case "mortgagor" and "mortgagee" mean the chargor and the chargee under the charge.*
"municipal authority"	ACPA	1(1)	means	• *a municipal authority as defined in the Municipal Government Act, or* • *in the case of a national park other than a town within a national park to which subclause (i) applies, the Minister of the*

Term	Act	Section	Scope	Definition
"municipal authority" — *cont'd*				*Crown in right of Canada charged with the administration of the National Parks Act (Canada).*
"municipal corporation"	ACPR	Sch. 2, 1	means	*In this Schedule...* • *a municipal authority as defined in the Municipal Government Act, or* • *a municipality or a municipal authority created by legislation similar to the Municipal Government Act in another province or territory.*
"municipality"	ACPA	1(1)	means	*the area of a city, town, village, municipal district, improvement district, special area or national park.*
"new system"	MCA	1	means	*the system of registration provided under The Real Property Act.*
"obligation to repair"	NWTCA	23(4)	include	*[does not]... any obligation to repair improvements made to units after registration of the declaration and plan.*
	PEICA	21(1)	include	*[does not]... the repair of improvements made to units after registration of the declaration and description.*
"occupant"	BCSPA	1(1)	means	*a person, other than an owner or tenant, who occupies a strata lot;*
	NBCPA	1(1)	means	*a person, other than an owner, who is lawfully in possession of a unit under an agreement including a lease.*
"officer"	NSCA	2	includes	*a president, chairman, secretary, treasurer, member of a board of directors or other person empowered under this Act, the regulations or the by-laws to give directions relating to the business of the association.*
"operating fund"	BCSPA	1(1)	means	*a fund for common expenses that usually occur either once a year or more often than once a year, as set out in section 92(a).*
"open traverse"	NSCR	2	means	*an unclosed traverse in the form of a branch emanating from a main traverse or triangulation.*
"ordinary resolution"	ACPA	1(1)	means	*a resolution* • *passed at a properly convened meeting of a corporation by a majority of all the persons present or represented by proxy at the meeting entitled to exercise the powers of voting conferred by this Act or the bylaws, or* • *signed by a majority of all the persons who, at a properly convened meeting of*

Term	Act	Section	Scope	Definition
"ordinary resolution" — *cont'd*				*a corporation, would be entitled to exercise the powers of voting conferred by this Act or the bylaws and representing more than 50% of the total unit factors for all the units.*
"owner"	ACPA	1(1)	means	*a person who is registered as the owner of* • *the fee simple estate in a unit, or* • *the leasehold estate in a unit when the parcel on which the unit is located is held under a lease and a certificate of title has been issued under section 5(1)(b) in respect of that lease.*
	BCSPA	1(1)	means	*a person, including an owner developer, who is* • *a person shown in the register of a land title office as the owner of a freehold estate in a strata lot, whether entitled to it in the person's own right or in a representative capacity, or* • *if the strata lot is in a leasehold strata plan, as defined in section 199, a leasehold tenant as defined in that section,* *unless there is* • *a registered agreement for sale, in which case it means the registered holder of the last registered agreement for sale, or* • *a registered life estate, in which case it means the tenant for life.*
	MCA	1	means	*the owner of the freehold estate or estates or leasehold estate or estates in a unit and common interest, but does not include a mortgage unless the mortgagee is in possession.*
	NBCPA PEICA	1(1) 1(1)	means	*the owner or owners of the freehold estate in a unit and common interest, but does not include a mortgagee unless he or she is in possession.*
	NLCA	2(1)	means	*[in relation to]...* • *a corporation, other than a common elements condominium corporation, a person who owns a freehold interest in a unit and its appurtenant common interest and who is shown as the owner in the Registry of Deeds, and includes a mortgagee in possession and a declarant with respect to a unit that the declarant has not transferred to another person, or*

Term	Act	Section	Scope	Definition
"owner" — *cont'd*				• *a common elements condominium corporation, a person, including the declarant, who owns a common interest in the common elements and a freehold interest in the parcel of land to which the common interest is attached as described in the declaration and who is shown as the owner in the Registry of Deeds.*
	NWTCA	1(1)	means	*the holder of a freehold or leasehold estate in a unit and common interest.*
	OCA	1(1)	means	• *in relation to a corporation other than a leasehold condominium corporation or a common elements condominium corporation, a person who owns a freehold interest in a unit and its appurtenant common interest and who is shown as the owner in the records of the land registry office in which the description of the corporation is registered, and includes a mortgagee in possession and a declarant with respect to any unit that the declarant has not transferred to another person,* • *in relation to a leasehold condominium corporation, a person who owns a leasehold interest in a unit and its appurtenant common interest and who is shown as the owner in the records of the land registry office in which the description of the corporation is registered, and includes a mortgagee in possession and a declarant with respect to any unit in which the declarant has not transferred the leasehold interest to another person but does not include a tenant of the owner,* • *in relation to a common elements condominium corporation, a person, including the declarant, who owns a common interest in the common elements and a freehold interest in the parcel of land to which the common interest is attached as described in the declaration and who is shown as the owner in the records of the land registry office in which the description of the corporation is registered.*
	SCPA	2(1)	means	*the registered owner of a title and includes persons prescribed in the regulations for prescribed purposes.*

Term	Act	Section	Scope	Definition
"owner" — *cont'd*	YCA	1	means	*the owner of the freehold estate or leasehold estate in a unit and common interest, but does not include a mortgagee unless the mortgagee is in possession.*
"owner developer"	BCSPA	1(1)	means	• *a person* *i. who, on the date that application is made to the registrar for deposit of the strata plan, is registered in the land title office as* *A) the owner of the freehold estate in the land shown on the strata plan, or* *B) in the case of a leasehold strata plan as defined in section 199, the lessee of the ground lease of the land, or* *ii. who acquires all the strata lots in a strata plan from the person referred to in subparagraph (i), and* • *a person who acquires all of the interest of a person who is an owner developer under paragraph (a) in more than 50% of the strata lots in a strata plan.*
		219	includes	*For the purposes of this Part, an ...* *a person named as an applicant in a Phased Strata Plan Declaration.*
"owner-developer"	MCA	1	means	*the owner of a phasing unit.*
"owner-occupied unit"	OCA	51(5)	means	*In subsections (6), (7) and (8)...* *a unit of an owner who is entitled to vote in respect of the unit at a meeting to elect or to remove a director where the unit is used for residential purposes and the owner has not leased the unit within the 60 days before notice is given for the meeting, as shown by the record that the corporation is required to maintain under subsection 83(3).*
"ownership of an estate"	NBCPA	1(1)	includes	*For the purposes of this Act, the...* *[in land]... the ownership of space.*
"ownership of land"	NLCA NWTCA PEICA	2(2) 2(2) 1(1)	includes	*the ownership of space.*
"parcel"	ACPA	1(1)	means	*the land comprised in a condominium plan.*
	SCPA	2(1)	means	*all the land included in a condominium plan.*

Term	Act	Section	Scope	Definition
"parcel" — *cont'd*		93(1)	includes	*In this section...* *improvements.*
"parcel of tied land"	OCGR	1	means	*a parcel of land described in clause 139(1)(a) of the Act in the case of a common elements condominium corporation and to which a common interest of an owner in the corporation attaches under clause 139(2)(a) of the Act.*
"parking space"	SCPA	2(1)	means	*an area of the common property or services unit used for parking.*
"parking unit"	SCPA	2(1)	means	*a unit used for parking.*
"past contributions"	BCSPR	6.2(3)	means	*For the formula in subsection (2)...* *the amount already contributed to the contingency reserve fund in respect of an estimated cost.*
"phase"	MCA	1	means	*the development and creation of units or common elements, or both, that are created by the registration of* • *a declaration and plan for a phased development, or* • *an amendment to a declaration to convert a unit into additional units or common elements, or both.*
	NBCPA	1(1)	means	*the additional units and common elements in a phased-development condominium property that are created on the registration of an amendment to a declaration and description.*
	NSCR	2	means	*the additional units and common elements in a phased-development property that are created in accordance with these regulations upon the registration of an amendment to both the declaration and description.*
	OCA	145(3)	means	*In this Part ...* *the additional units and common elements in a phased condominium corporation that are created in accordance with this Part upon the registration of an amendment to both the declaration and description.*
	OCGR	1	means	*the additional units and common elements in a phased condominium corporation that are created in accordance with Part XI of the Act upon the registration of an amendment to both the declaration and description; the additional units and common elements in a phased condominium corporation that are created*

Term	Act	Section	Scope	Definition
"phase" — *cont'd*				*in accordance with Part XI of the Act upon the registration of an amendment to both the declaration and description.*
"phased condominium corporation"	OCA	1(1)	means	*a phased condominium corporation to which Part XI applies.*
"phased development"	SCPR	2	means	*a condominium developed in stages pursuant to section 16 to 20 of the Act.*
"phased-development condominium corporation"	NLCA	2(1)	means	*a phased-development condominium corporation to which Part IX applies.*
"phased strata plan"	BCSPA	1(1)	means	*a strata plan that is deposited in successive phases under Part 13.*
"phasing amendment"	MCA	1	means	*an amendment to a declaration that, upon registration of the amendment,* • *implements a proposed phase by converting a phasing unit into additional units or common elements, or both,* • *creates a proposed phase,* • *amends the description of a proposed phase described in the declaration, or* • *removes a proposed phase from the declaration.*
"phasing unit"	MCA	1	means	*a unit described in a declaration, or in an amendment or proposed amendment to a declaration, as a unit to be converted into additional units or common elements, or both.*
"plan"	MCA YCA	1 1	means	*the plan to which reference is made in section 6, and includes any amendments thereto.*
	NWTCA	1(1)	means	*the plan referred to in section 6 and includes any amendments to it.*
"policy"	OCGR	1	means	*a policy described in paragraph 1 of subsection 20 (2).*
"prescribed"	PEICA	1(1)	means	*prescribed by regulation.*
	OCA	1(1)	means	*prescribed by the regulations made under this Act.*
	SCPA	2(1)	means	*prescribed in the regulations.*
"President"	NBCPA	62(1)	means	*In this section...* *the President of Service New Brunswick appointed under the Service New Brunswick Act.*

Term	Act	Section	Scope	Definition
"previously occupied"	BCSPR	14.1	means	*For the purposes of sections 241 and 242 of the Act...* *occupied at any time in its past for any purpose, including residential, commercial, institutional, recreational or industrial use, but does not include the occupation of a proposed strata lot by the owner developer solely as a display lot for the sale of strata lots in the proposed strata plan.*
"prior provisions"	NWTCA	25(1)	means	*In this section...* *the provisions of the Condominium Act as they read immediately before the coming into force of this section.*
"program provider"	ACPR	63	means	*In this Part...* *a person who operates a purchaser's protection program.*
"projected cash flow tables"	NSCR	77(1)	means	*In this Part...* *tables that demonstrate the effect of interest earned on investments and inflation of expenses and validate that a shortfall option will not jeopardize the funding plan.*
	SCPR	51.1	means	*In this section and in sections 51.2 and 51.3...* *tables that demonstrate the effect of interest earned on investments and inflation of expenses and validate that a shortfall option will not jeopardize the funding plan.*
"property"	MCA NWTCA YCA	1 1(1) 1	means	*the land and interests appurtenant to the land described in the plan or subsequently added to the common elements.*
	NLCA OCA	2(1) 1(1)	means	*the land, including the buildings on it, and interests appurtenant to the land, as the land and interests are described in the description and includes all land and interests appurtenant to land that are added to the common elements.*
	PEICA	1(1)	means	*the land and interest appurtenant to the land described in the description, and includes any land and interests appurtenant to land that are added to the common elements.*
"proposed phase"	MCA	1	means	*a phase, other than the initial phase to be implemented by the registration of a declaration, that* • *is proposed in a declaration, or in an amendment or proposed amendment to a declaration, and*

Term	Act	Section	Scope	Definition
"proposed phase" — *cont'd*				• *has not yet been implemented by the registration of an amendment to the declaration.*
"proposed property"	OCA	1(1)	means	*the property described in the declaration and description that are required to be registered to designate a proposed unit as a unit under this Act.*
"proposed unit"	OCA	1(1)	means	*land described in an agreement of purchase and sale that provides for delivery to the purchaser of a deed in registerable form after a declaration and description have been registered in respect of the land.*
	PEICA	1(1)	means	*land described in an agreement of purchase and sale that provides for delivery to the purchaser of a deed or transfer capable of registration after a declaration and description have been registered in respect of the land.*
"proprietary lease"	SCPA	13(1)	means	*In this section...* *a lease, agreement or arrangement by which a person acquires:* • *a tenancy, or an extension of an existing tenancy, of residential premises; and* • *a direct or indirect ownership interest in residential premises through any agreement or arrangement that includes the acquisition of shares of, or a membership interest in, a corporation, other than a co-operative incorporated or continued pursuant to The Co-operatives Act, 1989.*
"public authority"	BCSPR	12.1	means	*For the purposes of the definition of "leasehold landlord" in section 199 of the Act...* *any of the following:* • *a university as defined in the University Act;* • *the Sechelt Indian Band established under section 5(1) of the Sechelt Indian Band Self-Government Act (Canada);* • *the Provincial Rental Housing Corporation;* • *a board as defined in section 1 of the School Act.*
"purchase agreement"	ACPA	1(1)	means	*an agreement with a developer whereby a person purchases a unit or proposed unit or acquires a right to purchase a unit or proposed unit.*

Term	Act	Section	Scope	Definition
"purchase agreement" — *cont'd*	SCPA	2(1)	means	*an agreement with a developer by which a person purchases a unit or proposed unit or acquires a right to purchase a unit or proposed unit.*
		13(1)	means	*In this section...* *an agreement for the sale and purchase of residential premises.*
"purchase money"	ACPR	67(1)	means	*In this section...* *all or any portion of the money paid to a developer by a purchaser for the purchase of a unit.*
"purchaser"	BCSPA	1(1)	means	*a person, other than an owner developer, who enters into an agreement to purchase a strata lot or to acquire a strata lot lease in a leasehold strata plan as defined in section 199, but to whom the strata lot or strata lot lease has not yet been conveyed or assigned.*
"purchaser of a unit"	OCA	1(1)	means	*[in relation to a leasehold condominium corporation]... the purchaser of an owner's interest in a unit and the appurtenant common interest.*
"purchaser's protection program"	ACPR	63	means	*In this Part...* *a plan, agreement, scheme or arrangement that meets the requirements referred to in section 67.*
"qualified person"	ACPR	21(1)	means	*In this Part...* *in respect of the depreciating property, an individual who, based on reasonable and objective criteria, is knowledgeable with respect to* • *the depreciating property or that type of depreciating property,* • *the operation and maintenance of the depreciating property or that type of depreciating property, and* • *the costs of replacement of or repairs to, as the case may be, the depreciating property or that type of depreciating property.*
		21(2)	includes	*For the purposes of section 23, a reference to...* *a corporate entity if the corporate entity, in carrying out the functions of a qualified person, employs or otherwise retains the services of an individual who is a qualified person to carry out those functions.*

Term	Act	Section	Scope	Definition
"qualified person" — *cont'd*	SCPR	51.1	means	*In this section and in sections 51.2 and 51....* • *an individual who, based on reasonable and objective criteria, is knowledgeable with respect to:* • *components or a particular type of component;* • *the operation and maintenance of components or a particular type of component; and* • *the costs of replacement of or repairs to components or a particular type of component;* *and includes:* • *a licensed applied science technologist within the meaning of The Saskatchewan Applied Science Technologists and Technicians Act;* • *a member of the Appraisal Institute of Canada holding the designation of Accredited Appraiser Canadian Institute;* • *a person who holds a certificate of practice within the meaning of The Architects Act, 1996;* • *a member of the Real Estate Institute of Canada holding the designation of Certified Reserve Planner; and* • *a licensed professional engineer within the meaning of The Engineering and Geoscience Professions Act.*
"records"	NLCA	23(2)	includes	*In this section...* • *financial records;* • *minutes of meetings of the members of the corporation and its board;* • *the declaration, by-laws and rules;* • *all items referred to in section 22;* • *all agreements entered into by the corporation;* • *disclosures of conflicts of interest; and* • *all other records that are specified in the by-laws of the corporation.*
"recreational agreement"	ACPA	1(1)	means	*an agreement entered into by a corporation that allows* • *persons, other than the owners, to use recreational facilities located on the common property, or* • *the owners to use recreational facilities not located on the common property.*

Term	Act	Section	Scope	Definition
"registered"	MCA	1	means	*registered under The Real Property Act.*
	NBCPA	1(1)	means	*registered under the Land Titles Act or under the Registry Act.*
	OCA	1(1)	means	*registered under the Land Titles Act or the Registry Act and "register" and "registration" have corresponding meanings.*
	PEICA	1(1)	means	*registered under the Registry Act R.S.P.E.I. 1988, Cap. R-10.*
	SCPA	2(1)	means	*respecting a condominium plan, previously registered in the Land Titles register before the coming into force of The Condominium Property Amendment Act, 2000.*
		110(1)	means	*In this section...* *registered pursuant to The Personal Property Security Act, 1993.*
	YCA	1	means	*registered under the Land Titles Act.*
"registered strata plan"	BCSPR	14.12(1)	includes	*In this section...* *any document, deposited in the land title office, that* • *is referred to in section 245 (a) or (b) of the Act,* • *forms part of a strata plan under the Condominium Act, R.S.B.C. 1996, c. 64 or a former Act, or* • *amends or replaces a document referred to in paragraph (a) or (b).*
"Registrar"	ACPR	1(1)	means	*the Registrar of Land Titles.*
	NSCA	2	means	*the Registrar of Joint Stock Companies and includes the Deputy Registrar or such person as the Governor in Council may from time to time authorize to perform the duties of the Registrar.*
	PEICGR	1	means	*the Registrar of Deeds in whose registry division the property is situate.*
"registrar"	BCSPA	1(1)	means	*a registrar of titles as defined in the Land Title Act, and includes a deputy registrar or acting registrar under that Act.*
	NBCPR	2	means	*a registrar of deeds.*

Term	Act	Section	Scope	Definition
"registrar" — *cont'd*	NLCA	2(1)	means	*the Registrar of Condominiums referred to in section 3.*
	SCPA	2(1)	means	*Registrar as defined in The Land Titles Act, 2000.*
	YCA	1	means	*a registrar or deputy registrar appointed under the Land Titles Act.*
"Registrar General"	MCA	1	means	*the registrar general under The Real Property Act.*
"registrar of land titles"	NBCPA	1(1)	means	*the registrar of land titles, District of New Brunswick, appointed under the Land Titles Act.*
"registry"	NLCA	2(1)	means	*the Registry of Condominiums referred to in section 7.*
"regulations"	BCSPA	1(1)	means	*regulations made by the Lieutenant Governor in Council under section 292.*
	NSCA	2	means	*regulations made by the Governor in Council pursuant to this Act.*
	PEICA	1(1)	means	*regulations made under this Act;*
"related common property"	ACPA	14(2)	is	*A reference in this section to...* *in relation to a unit, a reference to the following:* • *the common property or a portion of the common property that is necessarily incidental to the completion of the unit;* • *the common property or a portion of the common property that is necessarily incidental to the intended use of the unit;* • *in the case of a unit other than a bare land unit, the common property or a portion of the common property consisting of* *i. utilities required to service the unit and the common property,* *ii. a facility providing for reasonable access to or entrance into the unit,* *iii. a facility providing for reasonable access to highways, municipal roads or streets,* *iv. waste removal facilities or other facilities for handling waste, and* *v. any other improvements or areas* *A) designated by the regulations, or* *B) required under any other Act or regulations,* *that are necessarily incidental to the intended use of the unit;*

Term	Act	Section	Scope	Definition
"related common property" — *cont'd*				• *in the case of a unit other than a bare land unit, in addition to the common property referred to in clauses (a) to (c), any common property or any portion of the common property that has been represented in the purchase agreement by the developer as being or as going to be available for the use of the owner of the unit and, without limiting the generality of the foregoing, may include one or more of the following:* *i. roadways, parking areas and walkways;* *ii. fences or similar structures;* *iii. landscaped areas and site lighting;* • *in the case of a bare land unit, the common property or a portion of the common property consisting of* *i. a facility providing for reasonable access to or entrance into the unit,* *ii. a facility providing for reasonable access to highways, municipal roads or streets, and* *iii. any other improvements or areas* *A) designated by the regulations, or* *B) required under any other Act or regulations,* *that are necessarily incidental to the intended use of the unit;* • *in the case of a bare land unit, in addition to the common property referred to in clauses (a), (b) and (e), any common property or any portion of the common property that has been represented in the purchase agreement by the developer as being or as going to be available for the use of the owner of the unit and, without limiting the generality of the foregoing, may include one or more of the following:* *i. utilities required to service the unit and the common property;* *ii. roadways, parking areas and walkways;* *iii. fences or similar structures;* *iv. landscaped areas and site lighting;* *v. waste removal facilities or other facilities for handling waste.*
"remaining useful life"	NSCR	77(1)	means	*In this Part...* *the estimated time, in years, that a component can be expected to continue to serve its intended function.*

Term	Act	Section	Scope	Definition
"rentalsman"	NBCPA	53(1)	means	*In this section...* *a rentalsman appointed under The Residential Tenancies Act.*
"rental unit"	MCA	1	means	*a rental unit as defined in The Residential Tenancies Act.*
"replacement plan"	SCPA	2(1)	means	*a condominium plan that shows the parcel, buildings and units, together with any additional units and additional common facilities.*
"reserve fund"	ACPR	21(1)	means	*In this Part...* *in respect of a corporation, the capital replacement reserve fund required to be established and maintained by the corporation under section 38 of the Act.*
	MCA	1	means	*a reserve fund established under section 26.*
	NLCA	2(1)	means	*a fund established under section 49.*
	OCA	1(1)	means	*a reserve fund established under section 93.*
	SCPA	2(1)	means	*a reserve fund established pursuant to clause 55(1)(b).*
"reserve fund plan"	ACPR	21(1)	means	*In this Part...* *a plan prepared and approved in accordance with section 23(4) or 30(c).*
"reserve fund report"	ACPR	21(1)	means	*In this Part...* *a report prepared in accordance with section 23(3) or 30(b).*
"reserve fund study"	ACPR	21(1)	means	*In this Part...* *a study carried out in accordance with section 23(1) and (2) or 30(a).*
	NBCPA	1(1)	means	*a study undertaken to determine a funding plan that adequately offsets expenditures for substantial repair and replacement of common elements.*
	NLCA	2(1)	means	*a periodic study to determine whether the amount of money in the reserve fund and the amount of contributions collected by the corporation are adequate to provide for the projected costs of major repair and replacement of the common elements and assets of the corporation.*
	OCA	1(1)	means	*a reserve fund study described in section 94.*

Term	Act	Section	Scope	Definition
"reserve-fund study"	NSCR	77(1)	means	*a study undertaken to determine a funding plan that adequately offsets expenditures for major repair or replacement of components.*
"residential complex"	MCA	1	means	*a residential complex as defined in The Residential Tenancies Act.*
"residential premises"	OCCGR	2(3)	means	*In this section...* *residential premises as defined in section 1 of the Landlord and Tenant Act.*
	SCPA	13(1)	means	*In this section...* • *any premises that are intended for residential purposes, including the land on which the premises are situated; or* • *an apartment or all or part of any other place that is or may be occupied by one or more individuals as a residence; and* • *includes fixtures that, pursuant to a tenancy agreement, are to be supplied by the landlord, but does not include any other premises used for residential purposes that the Lieutenant Governor in Council may exempt by regulation from the operation of this section.*
"residential strata lot"	BCSPA	1(1)	means	*a strata lot designed or intended to be used primarily as a residence.*
"residential unit"	ACPA	1(1)	means	• *in the case of a unit that is situated within a building, a unit that is used or intended to be used for residential purposes, and* • *in the case of a bare land unit, a unit that is used or intended to be used for residential purposes or that has been represented by a developer as being intended to be used for residential purposes.*
"rule"	BCSPA	1(1)	means	*a rule of a strata corporation made under section 125 or 197.*
	OCA	1(1)	means	*a rule of a corporation.*
"schedule of interest on destruction"	BCSPR	17.1	means	*For the purposes of this Part...* *with respect to a strata plan, the schedule required by section 4(g) of the Condominium Act or an Amended Schedule of Interest on Destruction, most recently filed with the registrar.*
"section"	BCSPA	1(1)	means	*[when used in reference to a strata corporation]... a section of the strata corporation created under section 192 or 193.*

Term	Act	Section	Scope	Definition
"sector"	SCPA	2(1)	means	*a sector of a corporation established in the bylaws of that corporation made pursuant to the authority conferred in clause 47(1)(m.1).*
"securities"	ACPR	Sch. 2, 1	includes	*In this Schedule...* *stocks, debentures, bonds, shares and guaranteed investment certificates or receipts.*
"security"	SCPR	2	means	*security delivered pursuant to section 5.2, 16 or 21 of the Act and includes a bond and a letter of credit.*
"services unit"	SCPA	2(1)	means	*any unit owned by a corporation and described as a unit in a condominium plan and includes any laundry room, recreational facility, landscaping area, roadway, hallway or other area intended for the benefit and use of all owners.*
"servient lands"	OCGR	47	means	*In this Part...* *the land owned by the declarant that is not included in the property upon the registration of the declaration and description, or the most recent amendments to the declaration and description, but that will be included in the property after the declarant has created all phases that it is entitled to create in the corporation, including the buildings and structures on the land.*
"servient tenement"	OCA	151(2)	means	*In subsection (1)...* *the land owned by the declarant that is not included in the phase, including the buildings and structures on the land.*
"special resolution"	ACPA	1(1)	means	*a resolution* • *passed at a properly convened meeting of a corporation by a majority of not less than 75% of all the persons entitled to exercise the powers of voting conferred by this Act or the bylaws and representing not less than 75% of the total unit factors for all the units, or* • *agreed to in writing by not less than 75% of all the persons who, at a properly convened meeting of a corporation, would be entitled to exercise the powers of voting conferred by this Act or the bylaws and representing not less than 75% of the total unit factors for all the units.*
	NWTCA	17(1)	means	*In this section...* *a resolution that is* • *passed at a properly convened meeting of a corporation by persons who*

Term	Act	Section	Scope	Definition
"special resolution" — *cont'd*				i. *are present personally or who cast their votes by proxy,* ii. *vote with respect to that resolution, and* iii. *own 66 2/3%, or such greater percentage as may be specified in the declaration, of the portion of the common elements owned by those attending the meeting or voting by proxy; or* • *approved by the signature on the resolution of persons who own 66 2/3%, or such greater percentage as may be specified in the declaration, of the common elements.*
	NWTCR	1	means	*a special resolution as defined under subsection 17(1) of the Act.*
	NSCA	2	means	*a resolution passed, at a special or annual meeting of the association in respect of which notice specifying the intention to propose the resolution as a special resolution has been given in the manner provided by the by-laws of the association, by* • *not less than two thirds of the votes cast by such members of the association entitled to vote as are present in person at the meeting, or* • *such greater proportion of the votes cast as the by-laws require,* *and approved by the Inspector and filed with the Registrar.*
	SCPA	2(1)	means	*a resolution that is:* • *passed at a properly convened meeting of a corporation by a majority of not less than two-thirds of the votes cast by persons who:* i. *are present personally or who cast their votes by proxy;* ii. *vote with respect to that resolution; and* iii. *are entitled to exercise the powers of voting conferred by this Act or the bylaws of the corporation; or* • *approved by the signature on the resolution of not less than two-thirds of all the persons who are entitled to exercise the powers of voting conferred by this Act or the bylaws of the corporation.*

Term	Act	Section	Scope	Definition
"spouse"	OCGR	33(2)	means	*In subsection 2...* • *a spouse as defined in section 1 of the Family Law Act, or* • *either of two persons who live together in a conjugal relationship outside marriage.*
"spouse of the owner"	BCSPR	8.1(2)	includes	*In subsection (1)...* *an individual who has lived and cohabited with the owner, for a period of at least 2 years at the relevant time, in a marriage-like relationship, including a marriage-like relationship between persons of the same gender.*
"Standard Bylaws"	BCSPA	1(1)	means	*the bylaws set out in the Schedule of Standard Bylaws.*
"standard condominium corporation"	OCGR	1	means	*a freehold condominium corporation that is not a common elements condominium corporation or a vacant land condominium corporation.*
"strata corporation"	BCSPA	1(1)	means	*a strata corporation established under section 2.*
"strata lot"	BCSPA	1(1)	means	*a lot shown on a strata plan.*
"strata lot lease"	BCSPA	199	means	*In this Part...* *a lease of a strata lot arising from the conversion of a ground lease under section 203(1), and includes an assignment or transmission of a strata lot lease.*
"status certificate"	OCA	1(1)	means	*a status certificate described in section 76.*
"structural plan"	NBCPR	2	means	*a copy of the structural drawing proposed for a condominium property project.*
	NSCR	1(2)	means	*[for the purpose of clause (b) of subsection (1) of Section 12 of the Act]... a copy of the structural drawing proposed for the project, mechanically reproduced on such material as the Registrar approves.*
	PEICGR	1	means	*[for the purposes of clause 4(1)(b) of the Act]... a copy of the structural drawing prepared for the project.*
"study"	NWTCA	19.11(1)	means	*In this section...* *a capital reserve fund study referred to in subsection (2).*
	SCPA	58.1(1)	means	*In this section...* *a reserve fund study.*

Term	Act	Section	Scope	Definition
"subdivision unit"	PEICGR	1	means	*any area of land delineated by a survey and includes* • *a city lot, town lot or village lot, block, gore, reserve, common, mining location and mining lease, or* • *a lot, block, part or other surveyed unit of land shown on a plan registered or filed under the Registry Act R.S.P.E.I. 1988, Cap. R-10.*
"subsidiary body corporate"	OCGR	17(2)	means	*In subsection (1)...* *a body corporate that is deemed to be a subsidiary of another body corporate under subsection 1(2) of the Business Corporations Act.*
"substantial damage"	NBCPA	49(1)	means	*In this section...* *damage to a building for which the cost of repairs would equal at least 25% of the value of the building immediately prior to the damage occurring, or a greater percentage if specified in the declaration.*
	OCA	123(2)	means	*In this section...* *damage for which the cost of repair is estimated to equal or exceed 25 per cent of the replacement cost of all the buildings and structures located on the property.*
"substantially completed"	ACPA	14(1)	means	*For the purposes of this section...* *subject to the regulations,* • *in the case of a unit, when the unit is ready for its intended use, and* • *in the case of related common property, when the related common property is ready for its intended use.*
"sue"	BCSPA	1(1)	means	*the act of bringing any kind of court proceeding.*
"suit"	BCSPA	1(1)	means	*any kind of court proceeding.*
"superintendent"	BCSPA	1(1)	means	*the Superintendent of Real Estate.*
"Supervisor"	NWTCAA	1	means	*the Supervisor of Co-operative Associations appointed under section 2.*
"Supreme Court"	BCSPA	1(1)	means	*the Supreme Court of British Columbia.*
"surveyor"	MCA	1	means	*a person authorized to practice, and registered, as a land surveyor under The Land Surveyors Act.*
	NBCPA	1(1)	means	*a land surveyor registered under the New Brunswick Land Surveyors Act, 1986.*
	NLCA	2(1)	means	*a person registered as a surveyor under the Land Surveyors Act, 1991.*

Term	Act	Section	Scope	Definition
"surveyor" — *cont'd*	NWTCA	6(1)	means	*In this section...* *a Canada Lands Surveyor as defined in the Canada Lands Surveyors Act.*
	YCA	1	means	*a Canada land surveyor.*
"tax collection provisions"	SCPA	97(1)	means	*In this section...* *provisions of any other Act that authorize or affect the collection and recovery of rates, charges or taxes by an assessing authority by proceedings against an assessed owner and the owner's property.*
"telecommunication"	OCA	22(1)	means	*In this section...* *the emission, transmission or reception of any combination of signs, signals, writing, images, sound, data, alphanumeric characters or intelligence of any nature by wire, cable, radio or an optical, electromagnetic or any similar technical system.*
"telecommunications"	OCGR	12(1)	means	*In subsection 2...* *means the emission, transmission or reception of any combination of signs, signals, writing, images, sound, data, alphanumeric characters or intelligence of any nature by wire, cable, radio or an optical, electromagnetic or any similar technical system.*
"telecommunications agreement"	OCA	22(1)	means	*In this section...* *an agreement for the provision of services or facilities related to telecommunications to, from or within the property of a corporation and includes a grant or transfer of an easement, lease or licence through the property of a corporation for the purposes of telecommunications.*
"tenant"	BCSPA	1(1)	means	*a person who rents all or part of a strata lot, and includes a subtenant but does not include a leasehold tenant in a leasehold strata plan as defined in section 199 or a tenant for life under a registered life estate.*
"termination"	BCSPA	199	means	*In this Part...* *[in respect of a strata lot lease]...* • *the expiry of the strata lot lease without renewal, or* • *the termination of the strata lot lease under section 213(2).*
"title"	SCPA	2(1)	means	*respecting a condominium unit, the right to:* • *an ownership share in the condominium unit; and* • *a share in the common property.*

Term	Act	Section	Scope	Definition
"transfer"	ACA MCOA	158(1) 92(1)	includes	*In this Part...* *transmission by operation of law.*
"trust corporation"	ACPR	Sch. 2, 1	means	*In this Schedule...* *a trust corporation registered under the Loan and Trust Corporations Act.*
"unanimous resolution"	SCPA	2(1)	means	• *a resolution that is:* • *passed at a properly convened meeting of a corporation by all votes cast by persons who:* *i. are present personally or who cast their votes by proxy;* *ii. vote with respect to that resolution; and* *iii. are entitled to exercise the powers of voting conferred by this Act or the bylaws of the corporation; and* • *approved by the signature on the resolution of all persons who:* *i. are not present personally or who do not cast their votes by proxy at the meeting; and* *ii. are entitled to exercise the powers of voting conferred by this Act or the bylaws of the corporation; or* • *a resolution that is approved by the signature on the resolution of all the persons who are entitled to exercise the powers of voting conferred by this Act or the bylaws of the corporation.*
"unanimous vote"	BCSPA	1(1)	means	*a vote in favour of a resolution by all the votes of all the eligible voters.*
"unit"	ACPA	1(1)	means	• *in the case of a building, a space that is situated within a building and described as a unit in a condominium plan by reference to floors, walls and ceilings within the building, and* • *in the case other than that of a building, land that is situated within a parcel and described as a unit in a condominium plan by reference to boundaries governed by monuments placed pursuant to the provisions of the Surveys Act respecting subdivision surveys.*
	MCA YCA	1 1	means	*a part of the land included in the plan and designated as a unit by the plan, and comprises the space enclosed by its boundaries and all the material parts of the land within this space at the time the declaration and plan are registered.*

Term	Act	Section	Scope	Definition
"unit" — *cont'd*	NBCPA	1(1)	means	*any part of a condominium property included in the property's description and designated as a unit by the description, and includes the space enclosed by its boundaries and all the material parts of the condominium property within this space in accordance with the declaration and description.*
	NLCA OCA	2(1) 1(1)	means	*a part of the property designated as a unit by the description and includes the space enclosed by its boundaries and all of the land, structures and fixtures within this space in accordance with the declaration and description.*
	NWTCA	1(1)	means	*a part of the land included in a plan and designated as a unit by the plan, and comprises the space enclosed by its boundaries and all the material parts of the land within this space at the time the declaration and plan are registered, and includes a bare land unit.*
	PEICA	1(1)	means	*a part or parts of the land included in the description and designated as a unit by the description, and comprises the space enclosed by its boundaries and all the material parts of the land within this space at the time the declaration and description are registered.*
	SCPA	2(1)	means	• *a parking unit;* • *a services unit;* • *in the case of a building, a space that is situated within the building and described as a unit in a condominium plan by reference to floors, walls or ceilings or other monuments as defined in The Land Surveys Act, 2000 within the building; and* • *in any other case, land that is situated within a parcel and described as a unit in a condominium plan by reference to boundaries governed by monuments placed pursuant to the provisions of The Land Surveys Act, 2000 and the regulations made pursuant to that Act respecting subdivision surveys.*
		93(1)	includes	• *the owner's share of the common property; and* • *in the case of a bare land unit, the improvements to the unit.*

Term	Act	Section	Scope	Definition
"unit entitlement"	BCSPA	1(1)	means	*[of a strata lot]... the number indicated in the Schedule of Unit Entitlement established under section 246, that is used in calculations to determine the strata lot's share of* • *the common property and common assets, and* • *the common expenses and liabilities of the strata corporation.*
"unit factor"	ACPA	1(1)	means	*the unit factor for a unit as specified or apportioned in accordance with section 8(1)(j) or 20(6), as the case may be.*
	SCPA	2(1)	means	*the unit factor for a unit as specified in the unit factor schedule described in clause 9(1)(e) or apportioned in accordance with subsection 25(3), as the case may be.*
"update study based on a site inspection"	OCGR	27	means	*In this Part...* *a comprehensive study that has been revised so that it is current as of the date of the revision, where the revision is based on a site inspection of the property and where the revision has been conducted in accordance with the requirements of this Regulation.*
"updated study not based on a site inspection"	OCGR	27	means	*In this Part...* *a comprehensive study that has been revised so that it is current as of the date of the revision, where the revision is not based on a site inspection of the property and where the revision has been conducted in accordance with the requirements of this Regulation.*
"vacant land condominium corporation"	NLCA	2(1)	means	*a vacant land condominium corporation to which Part X applies.*
	OCA	1(1)	means	*a vacant land condominium corporation described in subsection 155 (2).*
"vacant land unit"	PEICGR	59	means	*In this Part...* *a unit defined by delineation of its horizontal boundaries without reference to any building, the boundaries of which shall be deemed to extend vertically upward and downward without limit.*
	PEICA	1(1)	means	*a unit defined by delineation of its horizontal boundaries without reference to any building, the boundaries of which shall be deemed to extend vertically upward and downward without limit.*
"warranty corporation"	OCGR	1	means	*the corporation designated under section 2 of the Ontario New Home Warranties Plan Act.*

Glossary of Defined Terms
Selected Legislation Relevant to Constitutional Law — Division of Powers

For words and phrases which have been defined in legislation relevant to constitutional division of powers issues, together with the text of those definitions for easy reference, please refer to the following *Halsbury's Laws of Canada* titles:

Conflict of Laws (2011 Reissue)

Criminal Offences and Defences

Criminal Procedure

Judges and Courts

Legislation

Legislatures

Police, Security and Emergencies